# THE PSYCHOTHERAPY GUIDEBOOK

**EASY TO UNDERSTAND DESCRIPTIONS OF
255 DIFFERENT THERAPIES THAT CAN ALSO BE
READ SEQUENTIALLY AS A FASCINATING STORY**

EDITED BY

# RICHIE HERINK &
PAUL R. HERINK

*SECOND EDITION*

*Fideli*
Publishing

**Library of Congress Cataloging in Publication Data**
Main entry under title:
*The Psychotherapy Guidebook.*
Includes bibliographies and index.
1. Psychotherapy—Addresses, essays, lectures.
1. Herink, Richie.
RC480.P826      1980
616.89-1      79-29716
ISBN: 978-1-60414-616-5
ISBN ebook: 978-1-60414-617-2

# Acknowledgments

We would like to thank the following people who played key roles in making The Psychotherapy Guidebook possible:

Sherida Bush, who edited the individual articles and Buddy Skydell who did the copy editing,

The people who were involved in the publication of the prior edition of this book,

The contributing authors, for without them there would be no *Psychotherapy Guidebook*,

Finally, Robin Surface who successfully turned this book into an e-book.

# Contents

# Preface

The actual number of systems and techniques of psychotherapy in existence today is unknown. Therapies such as Psychoanalysis, Transactional Analysis, Behavior Modification, Gestalt, and Client-Centered Therapy have been well publicized. Others, such as Poetry Therapy, Filial Therapy, Exaggeration Therapy, and Psychomotor Therapy, are virtually unknown except to their small circles of practitioners and patients. The reason that the latter are less well known may simply be because their originators do not have a flair for publicity, or because most therapists are interested and involved only in their own schools and forms of treatment, or because the major professional journals, in which therapeutic modalities are described, have very limited circulation. Moreover, since therapists in general have limited knowledge of the range of therapeutic systems and techniques available to them, their patients are often fitted into the treatment mode with which the particular therapist is familiar, rather than into one that is most suitable for the patient's special problem(s).

Similarly, patients are unaware of the variety of modalities that are available. Thus, they have no way of knowing how to select the right therapist for their problem(s), or how to make sure that they are receiving full value for the often expensive investment therapy demands. These facts point up the need for a comprehensive guide to the various psychotherapies. This handbook was developed in response to this need.

The working definition of the term "psychotherapy" that was used to produce this compendium is intentionally broad so that all psychotherapeutic interventions, regardless of philosophic orientation, could be considered for inclusion. In this context, "psychotherapy" is an umbrella term for all activities involving one or more patients or clients and one or more therapists, which are intended to improve a patient's or client's feelings of psychological well-being.

An extensive search of the available literature, the first step taken in preparing this book, produced a list of over 350 psychotherapeutic systems and techniques. This list is not definitive, however, since depending on how wide the net is cast, there may be said to be as many psychotherapies as there are therapists (or perhaps even as many as there are patients!). The variety of interventions reflects human diversity and illustrates that there are many approaches toward freeing man from himself—the goal of all psychotherapies.

The present format of this book was chosen because the diversity of therapies is far too great for any individual to be able to master, distill, and adequately describe all of them with any degree of success or fair-mindedness. With a few exceptions, the articles in this book were written to a uniform format and length so that each modality can readily be compared to the others. The contributing authors are all professionals in the mental health field. They were selected because they are recognized as either originators of or authorities on the therapies they describe.

The individual descriptions have not been classified because many of them do not easily fit into well-defined categories. For example, Behavioral Family Therapy can be classified as either a family or a behavioral therapy. The therapies are listed in alphabetical order by keyword. This made it possible to group related interventions together.

Alphabetical order was also the scheme favored by the contributors who did not want their therapies either to be identified with any particular philosophy or to become subordinate to some well-known therapy in a particular category. This compendium, therefore, avoids highlighting the philosophical schisms that exist between various schools of psychotherapy. It submerges the differences by focusing on the therapies themselves. It considers the modalities as being to the therapist what drugs are to the physician, i.e., tools and strategies that can alleviate human problems. Thus, this guidebook was planned as a neutral document that primarily seeks to report on the field of psychotherapy as it exists today.

RICHIE HERINK, Ed.D., Ph.D.
*Ridgewood, New Jersey*

**Note:** Psychotherapists who wish to include descriptions of additional systems and techniques in future editions of this compendium should contact the Editor, c/o *The Psychotherapy Guidebook,* Fideli Publishing.

# Foreword

This guide is based on the ground breaking book The Psychotherapy Handbook which was copyrighted and published in 1980. It has been reprinted numerous times since then. It is now out of print for various reasons including a management change at the book's publisher.

The recently awakened interest in the effectiveness of talk therapy vs. drug therapy has created a professional and public demand for information about the numerous non-drug related therapies that are available to the therapists. Since this topic was the original books primary focus, it is being reissued in the form of this guidebook to fill this need and to make it more readable in book form.

This guidebook provides an extensive overview of the psychotherapies that have been sited in major reference sources including: "Psychological Abstracts", "The American Journal of Psychotherapy, "Psychology Today", "Human Behavior", "Dissertation Abstracts", book searches in the New York Public Library and other related venues; plus recommendations from practitioners.

In all, 350 therapies are identified and documented. The total number was reduced to 255. The reasons for rejection include: same therapy but under a different name, overlaps with another therapy, nothing unique, frivolous, a non-therapy therapy, and so on.

From numerous studies over the years, we know that an "aha" moment of insight (or personal paradigm shift) can trigger a psychological change. It can occur at any time and in any place and it can be initiated by any action or event. For example, when crossing the street, while baking a cake, during free association, when listening to music, during conversation, lying on a therapist's couch, smelling a new aroma, and do on. The serendipitous nature of the insight process is what makes so many different therapies work.

While there may be many more therapies existent than the 255 described here, the intent was to provide a comprehensive but not an overwhelming overview of the variability of the different types of therapies that have been developed.

When reviewing the descriptions, remember the saying that: "what the therapist thinks makes the therapy work is different from what the patient thinks makes it work, and that they are probably both wrong." In the final analysis, there may even be as many therapies as there are therapy sessions.

How we define and attempt to treat mental illness depends on how we define a psychologically normal human being. This is a task that has yet to be accomplished to everyone's satisfaction. This is why there are so many therapies represented in this guidebook.

Dr. Dan Goleman wrote the Foreword to the original version of this guidebook. In it he stated that: "this is a document of social and historical input. It captures the current state of evolution of the therapies, their degree of maturation and individualism. It stands alone as therapy's most complete chronicle of record."

Dr. Goleman's comments are as relevant today as they were when the original version was first published.

## Other  Praise for the first edition includes:

*.... Guide through maze of psychotherapies ... the smorgasbord of available approaches to psychological problems would confuse even the most stable client. To someone who is emotionally troubled, the staggering number of choices can be staggering ... "The Psychotherapy Handbook"... describes more than 250 therapies now in use.*

— Jane Brody, *The New York Times*

*.... The argot in this volume is relatively simplistic for the laymen to comprehend and any concept that seems advanced is elucidated. I recommend "The Psychotherapy Handbook" for anyone who is indecisive about where to seek psychological help as well as for folks, like myself, who are avid readers of psychology books.*

— Anonymous, Barnes & Noble

*.... What an amazing reference for student and mental health practitioners. This book contains every therapy that you have heard of and hundreds you probably wouldn't believe ever existed.*

— Michael Cohen, Amazon.com

Finally, a suggestion to the reader, if you want an  interesting read about mental illnesses and their treatment then you should read this book as you wold normally read a novel, straight through, from cover to cover.  Surprisingly, the book reads remarkable well.

In summary, if a paradigm represents a way of thinking, then psychotherapy represents a methodology for producing a personal paradigm shift in a positive direction.

— Richie Herink, Ed.D, Ph.D.
Paul R. Herink, MA.
Ridgewood, New Jersey

# THE
# PSYCHOTHERAPY
# GUIDEBOOK

# Active Analytic Psychotherapy

*Judith Kuppersmith*

## DEFINITION

Wilhelm Stekel's Active Analytic Psychotherapy places the psychotherapist in the role of making the patient see his suppressed complexes through direct and purposeful interpretations. While Freud expected most enlightenment to come from his patients, Stekel found this stance to be passive and called for a more active role on the part of the analyst. The active role was considered essential because it would shorten treatment and require that the treating physician take greater responsibility for the "cure." According to Stekel, the analyst was to be capable of great powers of intuition, involving direct dream analysis without assistance from the patient. Stekel believed "it is not the method but the physician that cures."

The thrust of Stekel's Active Analytic Psychotherapy was to offer quickly and efficiently the findings of psychoanalysis to more and more people, so that they could indeed go on with living their lives. Stekel referred to himself as a practical man whose treatment model was an outcome of this trait: "Freud asks himself what a case offers for science. I ask myself what science can offer for the case." Stekel felt that the responsibility of the analyst was to educate the public by reaching as many people as possible. He is said to have treated over ten thousand patients in thirty-five years—as opposed to a Freudian analyst who would treat about 180 in thirty-five years. Stekel was astutely aware of the role of social forces in shaping "parapathies" (his term for neuroses). His distinction between object-sick and subject-sick patients intentionally moves away from a strict and unyielding focus on the intrapsychic conflicts of the person toward an awareness of the role that institutions, morality, religion, and the family (objects) play in shaping parapathy.

## HISTORY

Wilhelm Stekel was born on March 18, 1868, in Boyan, Bukovina (now Romania), and died in London in 1940. A neurologist by training, Stekel was one of the founding members of the Vienna Psychoanalytic Circle. He was analyzed by Freud, also a member, but left the Psychoanalytic Society in 1912 because of his disagreements with him. He felt that a "cult of orthodoxy" surrounded psychoanalysis, and that it was forbidden to doubt the master's words. The dogma and rigidity of psychoanalysis seemed to him to be limiting and dangerous. He favored a movement away from orthodoxy to what he called "independent analysis."

Stekel had a most successful career. He was a prolific writer, with a total of 369 publications (compared to Freud's 363). He helped to popularize psychoanalysis through his journalistic writing style and his desire to educate the public.

Stekel was the first to speak of the bipolarity of emotions (ambivalence); of the relationship of anxiety to the realization of the death instinct; that not all loss was castration; that mental conflicts (parapathies) were not only sexual but also moral and religious.

## TECHNIQUE

Although one of Stekel's books is entitled *Technique of Analytical Psychothera py*, he did not precisely outline his technique, and one must cull from his descriptions what one can. Many analysts have said that it was Stekel's personality that most accounted for his approach and treatment successes. He had an enormous intuitive ability that was acknowledged and admired by his colleagues. His interpretation of dream symbolism was applauded by Freud. In fact, many aspects of his approach have been likened to those of Sandor Ferenczi, who has received much greater respect and recognition.

Stekel believed in focusing on the problem presented, treating symptoms as targets for intervention, heightening emotional tension through confrontation (hence, increasing insight), and the use of reality situations involving graduated exposure until cure. (These techniques are similar to such contemporary approaches as sensate focus, systematic desensitization, progressive relaxation, and focusing.)

In order to evaluate the patient's ability to cooperate in achieving his own health, Stekel had a trial week with new patients during which time he evaluated their ability to withstand an attack on their defensive structure and to judge the degree of their resistance. He felt that not everyone was a candidate for psychoanalysis. Undoubtedly, this technique accounts for his high rate of reported successes.

Stekel preferred six sessions a week for three to four months, believing this to be the best way to combat resistances. Stekel seems to have invented short-term psychotherapy as we know it today. His main technical contributions were dream analysis with no patient associations and the use of his intuitive, direct, and suitable provocation of the patient's defenses. He claimed he would never intervene actively until he was sure of the case.

After thirty years of treating patients, Stekel came to disbelieve in the unconscious as Freud described it. Rather, he believed that patients suffered from simulated mental blindness and mental deafness that served to obscure their sense of reality, and that the analyst, working as an intuitive artist endowed with imaginative insight, would actively force the willing patient to confront his conscious mental blindspots (Stekel, 1950).

## APPLICATIONS

Stekel has been accused of superficiality in his theoretical and technical explanations. His approach and method is often referred to as illogical, imprecise, and as having insufficient elaboration. He had a reputation among his colleagues as a healer and as an artistic person—not as a scientist. In short, he was thought of as a charlatan. Many of these criticisms seem to be well founded but should not obscure Stekel's very significant contributions and insightful predictions concerning the future of psychoanalytic psychotherapies. Several of Stekel's ideas have been very popular in the 1970s and have been sufficiently elaborated upon since he first introduced them.

Stekel's case histories are prevalent throughout his works and suggest that his system is best applied to phobias, organ parapathies, sexual difficulties, homosexuality, alcoholism, drug addiction, and some obsessive-compulsive parapathies. Indeed, his confrontational approach of forcing the patient to focus directly on the problem and symptoms is exactly the kind of technique that is so popular and reportedly successful these days for sexual dysfunctions, phobias, alcoholism, and drug addiction. It would seem that Stekel finally deserves recognition for his having intuited many contemporary treatment methods.

# Acupuncture

## *Alan Shifman Charles*

### DEFINITION

Acupuncture is a treatment used to prevent disease and promote better balance of energy flow throughout the body. It may be employed to control or eliminate pain disorders. The nature of the therapy is the insertion of fine 28- to 32-gauge stainless steel needles into specific points, or *loci*, on the human body. The points are referred to as acupuncture points and they are found on specific channels or pathways called *meridians*. The meridians are fine, invisible lines that are interconnected and carry energy from the extremities to the trunk and head, and back again to the extremities. The energy coursing through these channels is referred to as *Chi* or *Prana*. These energy channels also have an internal circulation that interconnects with the various viscera or organs of the body.

### HISTORY

Acupuncture is a Chinese healing art dating back approximately 5,000 years. It is stressed that in order for there to be optimal health there must be a balance between the internal and external environments of man. The goal is to bring about harmony of mind and body. Modern Acupuncture in China reflects the interrelationship between the peripheral nerves and meridians. Textbook illustrations published for the West often show the acupuncture points printed over these large nerves. There is controversy between traditionalists and nontraditionalists as to whether Acupuncture deals directly with the nervous system or whether it deals with an entirely different energy circuit not visible to the naked eye. Regardless of which theory is correct, there is no dispute that reactions and changes (noted below) do occur with the insertion of needles into an individual.

European doctors have actively practiced Acupuncture for nearly two centuries. The French school in particular has developed a most sophisticated method of measuring the energy within the meridians through the use of highly technical electronic devices. Under the work of Dr. Nogier, interesting discoveries in ear acupuncture have been made. The entire human form is represented on the ear, and specific points have been shown to reasonably treat various conditions.

### TECHNIQUE

The goal of the Acupuncture treatment is to select an appropriate number of needles and insert them into specific acupuncture points along the meridians. The needles unblock the energy that has become obstructed along the pathway, thus correcting the imbalance and permitting an even flow of *Chi* circulation. Disease in Eastern medicine is believed due to an obstruction or blockage of energy. Ultimately, what may cause a blockage might be stress from emotions, poor posture, trauma, or inadequate nutrition. During the course of a treatment series, an individual usually experiences a change in his nervous system tone. There are subjective experiences where one reports feeling more relaxed, calmer, and at ease. Individuals usually also discover they can sleep better, have better functioning of their gastrointestinal tract, and experience a warming up of previously reported cold extremities.

## APPLICATIONS

Acupuncture functions best when treating reversible or physiological illness. Disorders of this type are consistent with an increase or decrease in the tone of smooth and skeletal muscles. Functional illnesses may be cervical and lumbar spasm (neck and low-back pain), all varieties of headaches, conditions of nausea, constipation, hypermotility of the bowel, and asthma. Arthritis of the osteo and rheumatoid varieties are also treatable. According to *The Yellow Emperor's Classic of Internal Medicine*, Acupuncture is specifically recommended for diseases of numbness and spasm.

From a neurophysiological point of view, it appears that Acupuncture is dealing with a series of both simple and very complicated nerve reflexes. The reactions often seen during a treatment are the softening of tense muscles, perspiration, lowering of blood pressure, and a state of "wakeful sleep."

From a neuroanatomical point of view, with ear acupuncture it is the vagus nerve that innervates a large portion of the ear. This powerful cranial nerve also sends branches to the heart, stomach, intestines, lungs, pancreas, and gall bladder. Thus stimulation of ear points can have profound effects on the physical body.

The goal of Acupuncture is to bring about harmony of mind and body. Acupuncture can function as that vehicle by which the practitioner can serve as a true healer.

# Adaptational Psychodynamics
## *Judith Kuppersmith*

## DEFINITION

Sandor Rado's "Adaptational Psychodynamics" is an attempt to create a comprehensive, scientific mind-body approach to human behavior. Adaptation (in the Darwinian sense) is the key concept for Rado and it is defined in his theory as a process by which the organism comes to survive in its environment through achieving a functional balance between motivation and control. Rado believes that adaptations are "improvements in the organisms' patterns of interaction with its environment that increase its chances for survival, cultural self-realization, and perpetuation of its type."

For Rado, psychotherapy involves helping the patient to plan a better adaptation to his environment. Having patients *learn to adapt* requires their developing, through treatment, cognitive capacities ("the psychodynamic cerebral system") that permit *conscious* and purposive adaptation to reality. The specifics of the treatment process appear to be of lesser concern to Rado than specifying through theory building and research method, a medical science of psychoanalysis.

In Rado's theory, evolutionary biology is the foundation for the scientific study of the physiology and psychology of human motivation (Rado was influenced by the Cannon-Bard theory of emotion) and the organism's eventual ability to gain control over its biological and psychological interaction with the environment.

## HISTORY

Sandor Rado was born in Hungary in 1890. He studied at the universities of Budapest, Berlin, and Bonn. In America he held several faculty positions, among them: Director of the New York Psychoanalytic Institute and Director of the Psychoanalytic Clinic for Training and Research of Columbia University. His two-volume work, *Psychoanalysis of Behavior*, states most comprehensively his theory of scientific psychoanalysis.

At Columbia University he was thought of as an inspirational, if somewhat eccentric, teacher. He developed a training curriculum for medical psychoanalysis and strongly felt that *all* medical doctors should be trained in scientific psychotherapy.

Rado believed that Freud's original investigative procedures of self-analysis and the analysis of *his* patients had to be subjected to the strict scientific method in order to create a systematic theory acceptable to medical science. Adaptational psychoanalysis was a result of Rado's "re-examination, re-systematization and re-wording of Freud's theories prior to 1905."

## TECHNIQUE

Treatment requires the psychotherapist to impress upon the patient the difference between his infantile and his realistic life performances. Interpretations help to achieve recognition of infantile responses as unadaptive and to teach the patient "adaptive insight," which is the development of reason and control evolving into adaptational behavior. Treatment goals include: "helping the patient toward self-reliance"; "to plan a better adaptation"; and to "instill confidence and hopeful expectation."

Rado's technique of treatment is unlike Freud's and has even been generally viewed as a conscious psychology and not a depth psychology. Because Rado's theory and technique support a concept of organismic utility, many critics view the development of adaptational responses as too focused on *purposeful control* of pleasure, pain, emotion, thought, and desire. The implication is that control can be achieved through thoughtful adaptation alone. Rado does not appear to give sufficient status to the independent power of unconscious motivation.

## APPLICATIONS

Rado's pioneering research in schizophrenia and his theory of "schizotypal organization" (schizophrenic-phenotype) paved the way toward contemporary psychiatric views of schizophrenia as a disease entity that exhibits the "interaction of genetics with environment in a specified developmental context." Rado's work seems best applied to psychiatric disorders whose correlates are more obviously mind-body related. His research in drug addiction and the addictive personality are significant observations of mind-body interaction in addictive disorders.

Critics of Rado argue strongly that his biologically based adaptational view does not hold up within the more psychodynamic disorders, i.e., characterological disturbances and schizoid orientations.

Rado's work is reflected quite clearly today in the understanding and application of biofeedback; sleep and dreams research; and in the continuing development of scientific methods to uncover mind-body relationships in psychiatric disorders that appear to have both genetic and physiological correlates.

# Adaptive Psychotherapy

*Richard T. Rada, Edgar Draper, and Robert S. Daniels*

## DEFINITION

Adaptive Psychotherapy is the term applied to the psychotherapeutic technique that: 1) fosters the adaptation, rather than the adjustment, of the patient, 2) addresses itself to the patient's specific disabling problem and maladaptation, and 3) springs ideally from ego-syntonic and adaptive features within the therapist. Adaptive Psychotherapy is a derivative of psychoanalytic therapy and its theoretical bases rest primarily on the contributions of Heinz Hartmann. Patient adaptation implies mental equilibrium, ability to enjoy life, and lack of disturbance in productivity. Adaptation differs from adjustment in that adjustment implies passive submission to the goals of society, whereas adaptation implies active collaboration with the environment and attempts to change its goals. Adaptation may be progressive or regressive. Progressive adaptation alters the environment for the better and implies intrapsychic growth. Regressive adaptation is tolerated or accepted by society but implies intrapsychic arrest or movement toward the infantile self.

## HISTORY

Adaptive Psychotherapy was developed in the setting of a general hospital psychiatric clinic and was intended to meet the needs of a large group of patients referred from other medical clinics who were poorly served by usual therapeutic intervention, particularly intensive psychotherapy (Rada, et al., 1969). These patients included those with a diagnosis of chronic schizophrenia, hypochondriasis, or borderline psychosis, as well as the elderly patient, the "doctor shopper," and the severely dependent patient.

Patients were seen in a psychiatric clinic organized along the lines of a medical clinic, but structured to provide a supportive milieu with a therapeutic waiting area experience, a receptionist-hostess, and refreshments (Rada, et al., 1964).

## TECHNIQUE

Adaptive Psychotherapy is characterized by: 1) patient contact over an extended, sometimes indefinite, period of time, 2) contacts generally less than 25 minutes and less frequent than weekly, 3) the frequent use of psychotropic drugs, 4) goals that are varied but *not* aimed primarily at insight, transference exploration (transference is when the patient shifts feelings about a significant person to the analyst), or interpretation, and 5) techniques that include support, suppression, an institutional alliance, advice, environmental manipulation, attention to life happenings, and promotion of reality testing. For some patients, frequent and intense contacts with only one therapist can lead to severe dependency and regression. In Adaptive Psychotherapy an attempt is made to foster an alliance between the patient and the institution or clinic; the institutional alliance can be more easily transferred from therapist to therapist.

Although the therapist's precise understanding of the patient's psychodynamics is essential, the therapist's intervention is judged not on the basis of the completeness or accuracy of his psychodynamic interpretations, but on the basis of the patient's subsequent adaptation (Draper, et al., 1968).

## APPLICATIONS

In Adaptive Psychotherapy attention is focused on specific maladaptations; major intrapsychic alterations of character are not a goal of treatment. With infantile and schizoid personality disorders, those aspects of the patient's behavior that defend him against overt psychosis and keep him in an acceptable role in society are strengthened and rewarded. No attempt is made to change the basic character disorder and its defenses.

In certain cases regressive adaptation is considered a goal of treatment. When progressive adaptation (ego growth and development) is considered temporarily or permanently impossible, transference cures and flights into health are encouraged. In this regard, primitive and infantile transferences are accepted and supported when they contribute in a positive way to the patient's ties to the institution or enable him to accept the therapist's interventions. Another goal of Adaptive Psychotherapy is reality education, which emphasizes sharpening objectivity, the reduction of omnipotent fears, and the correction of referential distortion when it is disabling.

Adaptive Psychotherapy emphasizes the use of the natural personality and adaptive features of the therapist as an ally to the patient's adaptive possibilities. Training in Adaptive Psychotherapy can help the psychotherapist to develop a useful repertoire of characteristics that can be valuable in assisting certain patients toward a more successful adaptation (see Daniels, et al.).

# Adlerian Psychotherapy

## Dorothy E. Peven

### DEFINITION

Adlerian theory is at once a model of personality, a theory of psychopathology, and the foundation of a treatment method. Adler's theory of Individual Psychology is based on a humanistic model of man. Among the basic principles are:

1. *Holism.* The Adlerian views man as a unit, not as a collection of drives or instincts divided against themselves.
2. *Field. Theory.* The individual can be studied only by his movement within his social field. Therefore, the Adlerian therapist is extremely sensitive to the client's interpersonal transactions. Especially examined are the "tasks" of work, sexuality, and the individual's feelings of belonging to the social group.
3. *Teleology.* (inferiority feelings and the striving for significance). While Adler's name is linked most often with the term 'Inferiority complex," toward the end of his career he became more concerned with observing the individual's struggle for significance or competence (later discussed by others as self-realization, self-actualization, etc.). He believed that, standing before the unknown, each person strives to become more perfect and is motivated by one dynamic force—the upward striving for completion—and all else (traits, drives, etc.) is subordinated to this one master motive. Thus, all behavior can be observed as purposeful movement toward a final end point of significance. Behavior is understood as goal-directed movement (the teleological point of view), though the person may not be fully aware of this motivation.
4. *The Creative Self.* It is the creative self that determines the idiosyncratic nature of behavior. Adler postulated that it is neither the individual's genetic endowment nor his social environment that determines his behavior, but that each person responds in an adaptive, creative way to the social field in which he finds himself.
   The concept of the creative self places the responsibility for the individual's personality into his own hands. It does not mean, though, that he is to be blamed for his creation, since we all believe we have chosen the best way of life under any given circumstances. But since the Adlerian therapist sees the client as responsible for himself, he attempts to show the client that he cannot blame others or uncontrollable forces for his current condition.
5. *Life-Style.* Adler believed that each individual's striving toward a guidingideal of significance and social belonging could be observed as a pattern thatmanifests itself early in life and runs as a theme throughout one's lifetime. Thislife-style pattern is seen in all aspects of a person's behavior—it is his perceptualstyle. If one understands an individual's life-style, his behavior makes sense.

## HISTORY

Alfred Adler (1870- 1937) was an Austrian physician who was invited by Freud to become a charter member of the Vienna Psychoanalytic Society. By 1911 he was president of the organization and editor of its journal, but he found himself differing from Freud in certain fundamental concepts of personality and pathology. He did not believe, for example, in Freud's idea that neuroses had a sexual origin. Their views were irreconcilable, and Adler was the first to break from Freud. In the areas in which his views differed from Freud, later developments in psychology (ego psychology, existential psychology) can be reconciled more easily with the basic assumptions of Adler than with those of Freud. The contributions of Adler have become increasingly important in modern psychology.

When Adler left the Psychoanalytic Society, he founded his own school, which he called Individual Psychology. Always interested in the practical application of psychological insights, Adler founded the first child guidance clinics in Vienna and lectured all over the world to both professionals and laymen.

## TECHNIQUE

The Individual Psychologist works with the client as an equal to uncover the values and assumptions by which the client lives. He formulates the life-style and interprets it to the client.

As the individual is not aware that he is acting according to misperceptions, it becomes the task of the therapist to not only expose the "mistakes" but also to re-orient the client toward a more socially useful mode of behavior.

The Adlerian therapist seeks to establish a climate in which learning can take place. Thus, encouragement and optimism are key concerns for the therapist. Demonstration/analysis of the person proceeds to re-orientation toward a new philosophy of life based on social interest.

Individual Psychologists work one-to-one, or in groups, hospital psychiatric units, settlement houses, schools, corrections, and everywhere else in the mental health field. Much teaching is done through demonstrations in front of an audience, especially in the child guidance centers. However, there is no one way all Adlerians practice, for Adlerian psychotherapy permits the use of a wide variety of techniques, such as psychodrama and art therapy. Essentially, Adlerian therapists use methods to help the client relieve suffering and, second, to change.

Despite the technique used, a constant factor is the stress on social interactions (including the relationship between client and therapist), and social contribution; the more social interest a client has, the less feelings of inferiority he has. The primary aim of therapy is to help the client increase feelings of belonging to the human group through contribution.

The other technique unique to Adlerians is the formulation of the life-style and the constant use of the information gathered to demonstrate the client to himself. It is the particular interpretation of the behavior and the teaching of a certain philosophy of life to prod clients into social usefulness that is uniquely Adlerian.

## APPLICATIONS

Adlerian Psychotherapy is used not only for the change desired in classical neurosis but also in the treatment of psychosis and character disorders. Especially important to many Adlerians is the education of parents and children through the use of family education centers.

Since clients are treated in every conceivable setting, every type of disorder is considered grist for the Adlerian's therapeutic mill, including those people who are without symptoms but desire a personal growth. "Sickness" and symptoms are not required if one wishes to become the client of an Adlerian therapist—only a desire for understanding and a willingness to accept the responsibility for change.

# Adlerian Group Psychotherapy

*Helene Papanek and Joan Shea*

## DEFINITION

Adlerian Group Psychotherapy endeavors to bring about a change of life-style (the pattern in a person's perceptions and behavior) by making the patient feel understood and accepted as he becomes aware of his need to relate to others socially. An increase in social feelings encourages the patient to try out new behavior, which receives social approval and reinforcement from the group.

## HISTORY

Alfred Adler's concept of the social nature of man favors the use of group treatment. This was exemplified by the Child Guidance Clinics he established in Vienna. In these clinics, a social worker or teacher described a pupil's difficulties in front of an audience of educators, psychologists, and parents. Finally, the child, the presenting professionals, and the audience joined in a discussion concerned with the child's problems and possible remedies. This approach evolved from Adler's convictions that a person's problems can be best understood and treated in a social context, and that a democratic group in a spirit of cooperation provides useful therapeutic leverage.

Adler recommended groups not only for the education of parents and teachers but also as a treatment method for the re-education of delinquents (Ansbacher and Ansbacher, 1964). His followers showed constant interest in group techniques; Walter Spiel (1950), for example, wrote a comprehensive paper on group psychotherapy. Beginning in 1928, Rudolf Dreikurs, first in Vienna and then in Chicago, practiced and wrote on the subject of group psychotherapy as have his coworkers and followers at the Alfred Adler Institute of Chicago. At the Alfred Adler Clinic and Institute in New York, under the direction of Alexandra Adler, Marvin Nelson and the late Danica Deutsch, group techniques have been taught and practiced for over twenty years. Recognizing the crucial importance of a therapeutic milieu, the Alfred Adler Clinic has for many years successfully rehabilitated psychiatric patients in its social club. Ernst Papanek, a student of Adler in Vienna, taught the technique necessary to create and maintain a therapeutic milieu in an institution for juvenile delinquents. The most notable example is the treatment approach he developed at the Wiltwyck School for Boys (1959).

## TECHNIQUE

Group psychotherapy recognizes social interest, which is also a basic proposition of Individual Psychology. In 1929, Adler wrote: "It is almost impossible to exaggerate the value of an increase in social feeling. ... The individual feels at home in life and feels his existence to be worthwhile just so far as he is useful to others and is overcoming common instead of private feelings of inferiority."

Neurotic and psychotic patients strive for security and superiority at the expense of others. To a greater or lesser degree, depending on the severity of the disturbance, they have, in the construction of their life goals, alienated themselves from their fellow man. Thus, they experience undue hardship in meeting life's tasks of work, friendship, and intimacy. In the psychotherapy group, members develop social interest and become aware of how their attitudes of fear, distrust, jealousy, oversensibility for self, and undersensibility for others do not produce the desired result—respect, acceptance, and friendship.

This therapeutic group is based on equality of all members, with the therapist as a model demonstrating respect and understanding. In this setting group members, frequently for the first time, observe social interest in an authority figure. Either through the insight obtained by the interpretations of the therapist and group members or sometimes without clear awareness of what is going on, they discover that feeling at home in the group gives them a new security. Feeling secure, they dare to relate to others with mutual empathy, and find satisfaction in productive cooperation.

To create a cooperative group out of isolated, discouraged, frequently ineffectual strangers is the task of the therapist and one in which his behavior and personality have the strongest impact. Fortunately, he is aided by the innate capacity of each human being for social interest and whatever degree of social interest already exists, no matter how distorted. In social participation, rudimentary and misdirected social feelings slowly evolve or suddenly burst forth into attitudes of mutual helpfulness, tolerance of differences, awareness of similarities through empathy, and ability for purposeful communication. All of this leads to understanding and shared feelings. It is within this context that the distortions and prejudices incorporated in the life-style during childhood are then examined.

The Adlerian therapist assumes that each individual in the group has a life-style, a cognitive framework that enables him to understand the world and select behavior that will advance him toward his goals of safety, security, self-esteem, and success, and that will protect him from insecurity, danger, and frustration. All of this is more or less erroneous, depending on whether the individual is more neurotic or more healthy. Understanding of his life-style is often facilitated by examining the individual's earliest recollections. Adlerians believe that those significant experiences the individual chooses to remember reflect his opinion of the world and himself. What he chooses to remember also reflects the path of behavior he has selected for himself to cope with a complicated world. The distortions, that is, mistakes in his life-style, are interpreted to the individual and he is encouraged within the social context of the group to correct these mistakes by substituting private meanings and behavior with socially useful ones.

Increase in security and self-esteem results not only from corrections in lifestyle, but also from the experience of being useful to the members of the human community of which the therapeutic group is a microcosm.

## APPLICATIONS

With a few exceptions, all types of patients profit from group psychotherapy. For many, it is best to add group psychotherapy to individual psychotherapy, for then individual psychotherapy becomes more supportive and group psychotherapy more interpretive. Group psychotherapy is inadvisable for very depressed patients and for psychopaths.

Depressed patients are overly sensitive to attack by other group members and the danger of suicide is always present. Psychopaths often exploit people and may damage the other members of the group. For borderline cases, personality disorders, and neurotics, the group is a valuable tool for support, self-understanding, and new modes of behavior.

# Creative Aggression Therapy
## *George R. Bach*

## DEFINITION

The Creative Aggression (CAG) approach to individual and group psychotherapy is a body of theoretic principles and practical clinical methods that minimize, by rendering harmless, the hostile, hurt-oriented component of human aggression. CAG offers new ways of maximizing the playful, assertive, "impactful," cathartic, information-rendering and affection-instigating effects of open and honest confrontations between intimates—friends, family members, spouses, lovers, and coworkers. The Fair Fight System provides angry and conflicted intimates with rules, rituals, and coping techniques that reduce the fear of aggression, avoid hurtful hostility, and facilitate basically good-willed "combatants" to fight fairly—not against each other, but for improvements in their relationship. CAG is differentiated by definition and by origin from so-called Assertion Training. CAG was developed and reported on before 1960, long before others took the assertive—I call it impact— aspect out of the context of the Creative Aggression principles. Also, Assertion Training considers anger and aggression unnecessary (as in Rational-Emotive Therapy), without providing methods of constructive utilization of this basic human energy source. The Creative Aggression approach, however, helps patients and therapists to utilize—rather than to defensively deny, displace, or overcontrol— frustration, anger, and hostile feelings.

## HISTORY

As the innovator of Creative Aggression Therapy, one of the roots of the approach was my own personality, including my way of confronting, fair fighting, and pressuring for changes. Another stimulus toward the development of CAG was my professional training. Predoctorially, I worked with both Kurt Lewin and Robert Sears, and both men influenced my interest in the psychology of aggression. My own doctoral research in 1944 impressed me with the intensity of play aggression in young children. Lewin's tension and conflict theory encouraged me to explore the role of aggression in group psychotherapy.

In the late 1940s, I sought further post-doctoral training as well as personal analysis from the late Adler student Lydia Sicher. Sicher reinforced me in my search of evolving clinical methods to put my "pro-conflict" ideas into practice, especially in group psychotherapy and couples and family therapy. During this time, my own creativity started and, then, my contribution of central significance: showing people how to utilize conflict and aggression creatively.

In my early group therapeutic practice (1945- 1953), I developed the clinical art of utilizing group processes—including my leader role—to maximize the mutual aide, the peer-therapeutic effects, in group therapy. In observing mis peer-influence factor, I was repeatedly struck by the relative failure of the nice-guy type of interaction—one might say the classical Rogerian stance of uncritical, unconditional positive regard—to move the patients through their resistances and on to new experiences. In contrast, I noticed that the more critical-aggressive confrontations, even "fights"—between patients themselves and between patients and therapists— tended to initiate new attitudes and opened people up to consider alternative ways of solving conflicts. The introduction of the time-extended "marathon group" schedule in 1963 provided longer-lasting group sessions in which the trust necessary for the open display of aggression had a chance to develop.

## TECHNIQUE

CAG exercises are designed to reduce the stress due to the basic human fear of aggression (within oneself and from others). I do not believe in tranquilizing, distracting, or numbing human aggression. It's too basic a tendency. I do not trust that aggression can be reliably held down, and even if and when it is renounced, the *price* often is detachment. I view aggression as the most effective force in shaping oneself and the behavior of others. With CAG, clients learn and practice constructive ways of utilizing a variety of "fight styles." Their aggressive behavior is shaped by the therapist to minimize hurtful hostility and enhance and maximize open, authentic, information-yielding communications.

The Fair Fight for Change is the crux of the Creative Aggression system. It provides a step-by-step procedure for two (or more) partners of an intimate, ongoing association to constructively express criticism of one another and to assertively demand and negotiate changes for the better in the quality of their emotional or material interdependence.

It is the most effective Creative Aggression technique, especially in couple therapy. The capacity to conduct a mutually productive, exciting and even joyful fight for change is proof that the student has learned all of the other procedures of the aggression control system. Every one of the Creative Aggression exercises is an essential preparatory step to ready the opponents for the Fair Fight for Change.

The preparatory exercises, such as the "H-type rituals," effectively remove hurtful hostility, punitiveness, vengeful smarting as well as irrational emotionality, such as raging anger, so that the fight for change can be not only fair but also realistic and rational. Other preparatory exercises, such as the "info-impacts," remove hostility-escalating generalities and rigid stereotyping. They also render much information about options, "beltlines," and non-negotiable territory.

The fight for change, a fifteen-step procedure, is a communication training technique aimed at establishing a process for dealing with any one specific issue. It is a zeroing-in on a *single issue*, gripe, or "beef about a specific behavior pattern with a demand for change by one partner or the other.

## APPLICATIONS

The CAG system is practiced in both individual and group psychotherapy. Its major applications are in the areas of self-improvement, pairing (where divorced adults are helped to improve their dating and mating skills), couples, and family therapy. CAG-trained therapists, as well as teachers and counselors, have effectively worked with co-workers in offices and factories, and with public-school and university students.

The CAG approach lends itself ideally to the reeducation of the "A type" abrasive personality, as well as the fight-phobic fearful personality. The CAG approach has also been found psychiatrically effective with the difficult passive-aggressive patients; CAG brings indirect hostility into the open where it can be dealt with in a rational manner.

Last but possibly of first importance is the use of CAG techniques in self-improvement and psychological self-help. Self-respect can be increased, which also facilitates decision-making.

# Aikido

## Robert Frager

### DEFINITION

*AI* means oneness, meeting, harmony. *KI* means mind, energy, spirit, the spirit of the universe. *DO* means road, path, way of life. Aikido might be translated: "the way of harmonizing with the spirit of the universe," or "a way of unifying life energy."

Aikido is derived from the Japanese martial arts, the disciplines of the samurai. In its practical application, Aikido is a combat and self-defense art, yet it is more than a physical discipline; into its techniques are woven elements of philosophy, psychology, and dynamics.

### HISTORY

Aikido is one of the most recent Japanese martial arts. Its founder, Morihei Ueshiba, or O'Sensei (great teacher), devoted more than seventy years to the study of *budo* (martial arts). He mastered many different combat arts, including various schools of *jiujitsu*, swordsmanship, and the use of the staff and spear.

O'Sensei won many matches, but he was troubled with the feeling that winning at somebody else's expense is not really winning. He came to believe that true self-defense is not winning over others, but winning over the discord within oneself. In 1925, O'Sensei had a major spiritual experience that deeply affected the development of Aikido: "I understood "*budo* is not felling the opponent by our force; nor is it a tool to lead the world into destructions with arms. True *budo* is to accept the spirit of the universe, keep the peace of the world, correctly produce, protect, and cultivate all being in Nature.'"

In 1953, Aikido was introduced to Hawaii and later to the mainland. Today there are Aikido schools and clubs in most major cities and universities of Japan and the United States.

## TECHNIQUE

There are literally hundreds of Aikido techniques. The basic principle behind all techniques is harmonizing one's movements with those of one or more partners. For the author, there are three basic aspects of Aikido training—"centering," energy flow, and harmony.

Centering practice includes focus on the lower abdomen. Beginning Aikido students learn to keep neck and shoulders relaxed and to integrate all movements from their center (lower abdomen). In the East, the abdomen is considered a major center for meditative practices, and the storehouse of vital energy in the body. It is also the area of physical balance and psychological stability. The physical and psychological aspects of centering are thought to be virtually one and the same. When we are emotionally or mentally tense, our bodies are also tense, and vice versa. And it is also true that we can become more calm and centered through physical discipline, and this will result in greater mental and emotional balance and calmness.

Energy flow is essential in Aikido practice. Conscious mind-body coordination is basic to all Aikido training. This is taught through the concept of energy and forming a mental image of energy flow. Students are taught to visualize energy extended out from the hands and fingers. Relaxed, *flowing* movement is stressed rather than jerky "muscular" movement.

Harmony is a central theme of Aikido. Stress is placed on flexibility and grace. Many of the Aikido movements are circular, with emphasis on blending with the movement of one's partner. Essential in Aikido practice is the attitude of working *with* a partner rather than fighting or competing *against* an opponent. The aim in Aikido is to go along with the partner's energy, not to fight force with force.

## APPLICATIONS

Aikido can help the therapist in relation to violent or potentially violent patients. Howard Pashenz, a psychotherapist and Aikido black belt, has given several examples of this practical use of Aikido with patients. According to Pashenz, one possible use of Aikido training combined with therapy is to begin to develop a relationship with those who ordinarily refuse to become involved with any adult authority figure; for example, acting out adolescents. Another such group is bright underachievers who have built up blocks against verbal situations. Also, Aikido can be useful along with psychotherapy, in either a supportive role or as a supplemental, nonverbal form of therapy in its own right.

Traditional Aikido practice itself stresses relaxed, supple movements, free from any form of rigidity, whether physical or mental. This training can be extremely effective in eliminating habitual physical tension as well as psychological rigidity. It can help patients deal with fears and aggressive impulses, and develop a more positive self-image.

Von Durckheim, K. *Hara*. London: Allen & Unwin, 1962.

# Ajase Complex
*Keigo Okonogi*

## DEFINITION

The Ajase Complex stems from an original theory by Dr. Heisaku Kosawa (1897—1968), considered the pioneer of psychoanalysis in Japan. As Freud found the basis for the Oedipus complex in Greek mythology, so Kosawa found the legendary background for the Ajase Complex in a parable from the ancient Buddhist scriptures— specifically, in the tale of Ajase, revolving around the Buddhist precept of reincarnation.

In the time of Buddha, so the legend goes, a childless queen (Idaike), fearing the eventual loss of her husband's (King Binbashara) love as her beauty faded, longed to have a son as a means of securing the king's love for as long as she lived. Hearing of her desire, a prophet told her that, within three years, a mountain hermit would die a natural death and start his life afresh to become her son. However, the impatient queen elected to kill the hermit before the three years had passed. Soon, as the prophet had said, she conceived and gave birth to a boy (Ajase).

Ajase reached manhood and one day, during a bout of melancholy, he was told by one of Buddha's enemies (Daibadatta) that his birth had sprung out of a fatality. Although the cause of his melancholy was ascribed by Daibadatta to "your mother's evil deed," Ajase initially reacted against his father, feeling sympathy for his mother's agony and anger against the one who had so distressed her. He helped unseat his father, then had him imprisoned and deprived of all sustenance. But Ajase soon learned that his mother was surreptitiously feeding his father honey, which saved him from starvation. The son then became so angry with his mother that he made a move to kill her, but was dissuaded from this act by a minister. At that moment, Ajase was attacked by a severe guilt feeling and became afflicted with a dreadful skin disease characterized by so offensive an odor that no one dared approach him. Only his mother stood by and lovingly nursed him back to health.

Forgiven by the mother he had intended to slay, Ajase was awakened to a real love for her and discarded his grudge against her. His mother, in turn, was able to develop a natural maternal affection for her son beyond original self-centered attachment to him.

Ajase was beset by a dual guilt feeling: the initial violent guilt manifesting itself in the skin disease, which was really a desire to inflict self-punishment for wanting to take his mother's life, and a subsequent tender sense of guilt—so prevalent among Japanese—resulting from his mother's pure act of forgiveness.

Kosawa cited the mother's female egoism as the factor causing the child's aggression against her. Thus, the Ajase Complex refers to a child's resentment against his mother's female sexual drive toward, and desire to be loved by, his father, together with the guilt feeling stemming from this matricidal impulse.

## HISTORY

This theory was first presented to Sigmund Freud in July 1932, during Kosawa's studies at the Vienna Psychoanalytic Institute in a paper entitled "Two Kinds of Guilt Feelings (Ajase Complex)."

## TECHNIQUE

In his paper, Kosawa discussed the psychological peculiarity of the Japanese, as evidenced by their acceptance of oral dependency toward the mother, and repression of the hatred and resentment of the mother that accompanies this tendency. In the case of psychoanalytical therapy for Japanese patients, the mother transference (the emotional attitude the patient has toward the therapist, who serves as a mother substitute) conflict with the therapist appears at a comparatively early stage, while therapeutic regression to an oral-ambivalent state takes place easily, particularly when compared with the process of psychoanalytic therapy for Western patients. Parallel to this psychic process, the patient experiences the feeling, peculiar to Japanese, of "being aggressive and yet being forgiven," from which develops a "guilt feeling over being forgiven and a need to make restitution for having harbored an evil intent." This Japanese type of guilt feeling is quite different, Kosawa states, from the "guilt feeling of castration anxiety, fear of punishment," which Freud embodied in his theory of the Oedipus complex.

## APPLICATIONS

On the basis of the Ajase theory, Kosawa advocated that, when treating cases of mother transference, the psychoanalytic therapist keep Ajase's mother's mental attitude continuously in mind—e.g., loving her child and forgiving his aggression against herself. The therapist should manifest to the patient the latter's negative transference in identifying his mother with the therapist. Through the patient's experience of being forgiven for his aggression—originally directed against his mother and now transferred to the therapist—he becomes free from the above conflict and develops the core of a healthy ego. In Kosawa's psychotherapy, patients, through the feeling of togetherness with the therapist—who both forgives the patient and accepts the thrust of the patient's aggression against him—experience feelings of fusion with their mothers and thus become capable of developing a basic trust in society.

---

# Alcoholics Anonymous
## *General Service Staff*

### DEFINITION

Alcoholics Anonymous is a fellowship of men and women who share their experience, strength and hope with each other that they may solve their common problem and help others to recover from alcoholism.

The only requirement for membership is a desire to stop drinking. There are no dues or fees for A. A. membership; we are self-supporting through our own contributions.

A.A. is not allied with any sect, denomination, politics, organization or institution; does not wish to engage in any controversy; neither endorses nor opposes any causes.

Our primary purpose is to stay sober and help other alcoholics to achieve sobriety.

This statement, usually read at the beginning of A. A. meetings, gives the core of the purpose of Alcoholics Anonymous, the way it works, and the role of the structure that holds it all together.

*Copyrighted © The Alcoholics Anonymous Grapevine, Inc. Reprinted with permission.*

## HISTORY

Identification with the "common problem" is what Bill W., a New York stockbroker, found was the key ingredient. After he shared his experience with Ohio surgeon Dr. Bob, he was able to get sober. Both had been considered hopeless alcoholics, yet neither man was to drink again. That was in 1935. From the initial success of one sober alcoholic's sharing his "experience, strength, and hope" with an alcoholic still drinking, an informal society of more than one million recovered alcoholics in more than ninety countries has blossomed.

A.A. has found that it cannot furnish the initial motivation for sobriety. While alcoholism has now generally become recognized as a disease, acceptance of one's own condition, in the final analysis, seems to be the result of self-diagnosis. Doctors and other informed persons may clearly see the symptoms and give helpful guidance, but the alcoholic makes the determination that brings acceptance and a desire to stop drinking. Then, these facts can be pointed out to the problem drinker: medical testimony indicates that alcoholism is a progressive illness, that it cannot be cured in the ordinary sense of the term, but that it can be arrested through total abstinence from alcohol in any form.

## TECHNIQUE

At an A.A. meeting, the alcoholic finds people who know the pain, loneliness, fear, and hopelessness that he has been living with, all the while thinking, "I'm different. Nobody really understands what I'm going through!" As other alcoholics describe their lives under the influence of alcohol, the newcomer realizes that no theories or generalities are being presented. These are people who understand because they have lived through these emotions and experiences. If they have lived through the same emotions and experiences of degradation and despair, there can be no judgment involved. Before this, the guilt, remorse, and ensuing judgment, by others and oneself, have been reinforcing the drinking pattern.

The alcoholic has now met people who truly understand. The A.A. members then say, "I found out I had a disease, and I found a way to arrest it." There is recognition of the suffering person's condition, and what is more, there is indication of a way out. At this point, the encounter with A.A. has offered the suffering alcoholic understanding, equality, and a proved solution to the problem.

Whatever deep troubles the person has, there is only one place for the alcoholic to start: he must first stop drinking. The newcomer is told that all recovery is dependent on the decision to stay away from the first drink. Total abstinence is the key. But the newcomer also is told that it is done only one day at a time. Here is the beginning of the training to bring life into perspective. By placing the decision to drink or not to drink squarely in the moment at hand, it becomes apparent—perhaps as a previously unthought-of possibility—that the alcoholic actually has a choice.

If the alcoholic is to become willing to make the choice not to drink, changes in attitude must take place. He felt relief in finding people who truly understand, but now he recognizes that this compassion does not lead to indulgence. As well as knowing the pain of the newcomer, the newfound friends also know all about the evasions, dishonesty, and manipulating techniques. Self-deception and self-pity are noted for what they are. Members explain that self-honesty is the key to recovery, and this confrontation, without judgment, lessens the need for self-deception and reinforces the basis for trust. Once trust begins to be established, recovery is on the way.

"Twelve Steps" to recovery in A. A. are suggested. Never is a person required to follow any prescribed program of therapy in order to be considered a member. But the identification and trust that develop do encourage the member to try the methods that have helped others.

Alcoholics Anonymous is not organized, in any formal sense. There are no governing officers, rules, or regulations. What structure there is has grown as A. A. has expanded, and communication and some standardization of approach have become necessary. The principle of consistent rotation of responsibility is followed in virtually all A. A. service positions.

## APPLICATIONS

A.A. does not claim to be the whole and only answer to alcoholism, though its success as a maintenance program for sobriety is uncontested. Since A.A.'s goal is to help the suffering alcoholic to recover, it is eager to cooperate with individuals or groups sharing this goal. Members of A.A. have traditionally refrained from disclosing their A. A. membership in any media, whether it be press, radio, television, or films.

---

# The Alexander Technique
## Deborah Caplan and Frieda Englard

### DEFINITION

The Alexander Technique employs conscious awareness to achieve a physical result; namely, the improved use of the body. Specifically, the Technique enables its students to move with free and well-coordinated musculature, to breathe without tension, and to use their bodies with optimum efficiency, whether walking, playing the violin, or sitting at a desk.

The Technique is both physical and mental in approach. As with most psychotherapies, it depends for its effect on what the student or patient learns to do for himself rather than on something done to him. Alexander students learn to control their bodies through the use of their minds.

# HISTORY

Frederick Matthias Alexander was born in Australia in 1869. By his early twenties he had become an actor who kept losing his voice while performing; doctors and voice coaches could provide only temporary relief. Since his voice problem occurred only while he was speaking on stage, Alexander reasoned that it was probably caused by something he did with his voice mechanism while performing. To find out what that was, he observed himself with a network of mirrors, and thus began an exhaustive ten-year process of self-exploration.

Alexander observed that tension and compression in his neck, larynx, and rib cage were causing his voice loss. He could not *feel* that he was doing anything wrong: his habitual way of speaking had come to feel "right," even though it was wrong and harmful. His efforts to speak in a less harmful way were unsuccessful until he made the discovery that the misuse of his voice was just one small part of the total pattern of misuse involving his whole body. He could not effectively improve the use of his voice until he improved his total musculo-skeletal use, a discovery that led to the development of the Alexander Technique.

The Technique has since attracted the attention and acclaim of people in diverse fields. The medical profession has shown ever-increasing interest in its therapeutic uses, as evidence mounts that many disorders are caused or aggravated by inefficient or stressful use of the body. For more than half a century many actors and musicians, who must use their bodies as vehicles for artistic expression, have considered the Alexander Technique an essential part of their training. The more philosophical aspects of Alexander's work have been explored by John Dewey, Aldous Huxley, and George Bernard Shaw, all of whom studied with him.

# TECHNIQUE

Part of the task of the Alexander teacher is to help the student accomplish in a relatively short period of time what Alexander's mirrors helped him do during his years of research: identify faulty habits. The student gives largely passive mental directions (for example, "Let the back lengthen and widen") to his own body while the teacher uses his hands to guide the student into an improved kinesthetic experience. In time, the directions become associated with improved balance and alignment, which feel and are "right," although invariably they feel "wrong" at first.

The improved use begins with the balance of the head on the neck. Alexander found that if the neck muscles are allowed to release during activity, the head will balance up off the spine instead of compressing it. The spine can then lengthen, and the whole body move in an integrated fashion. Under the teacher's guidance, the student consciously inhibits faulty use, saying no to unwanted responses and directing the body into the desired use.

# APPLICATIONS

Although the Alexander Technique has usually not been included among the psychotherapies, it constitutes a significant psychotherapeutic tool or orientation to life. Its approach is holistic, furthering positive change and self-awareness through mind-body integration. As Aldous Huxley stated, "It breaks the pattern of determinism." Frederick

S. Perls was profoundly influenced by Alexander in his development of Gestalt Therapy, since it emphasized a need for change beyond exploration of cause, catharsis, and/or body work.

As in neurosis, if a symptom is not ego dystonic or uncomfortable, the possibility for change is diminished. Avoidance and denial lead to self-stagnation even when motivation for change prevails, and the focus of the Alexander Technique on the body armoring helps break this bind. Delaying action lets memories and affects (feelings, emotions, or moods) emerge into consciousness. This may at times offer clues to the cause of the primary faulty use of the musculature. For example, a patient with a persistent squint was helped to release the tension in his eyes. Without the use of this armoring, he became nauseated. Eventually he realized that he tended to close his eyes so as not to see things as they were. As he increasingly learned to free the occipital areas, he became more open to himself.

The feeling of freedom and "lightness" produced in the body by the Alexander Technique is very helpful with depressed patients, as it provides energy for meaningful and nonhabitual behavior.

The narcissistic patient can benefit, too: his need to control others becomes slowly diminished by a feeling of mastery of the body, since the postural change also results in a more positive self-image. Thus, inhibition of superfluous activity liberates energy for new, nonstereotypic behavior. If one becomes aware of tension in the neck and shoulders, one may become aware of anger. The emotion, rather than building up into nonproductive intensity, is transformed into an awareness that something or someone is causing it. The Technique may remove the "panic from fear" (Jones, 1976) when concentration on breathing is implemented; this also reduces mind-wandering with a reinforcement of general alertness.

The Alexander Technique differs markedly from behavior modification in that the authority is not the therapist but the student, who inhibits overloading a musculature with superfluous activity and redirects it to a natural, conscious, self-integrative use. Thus, it has proved to be a very effective adjunctive tool in the enhancement of the psychotherapeutic process.

---

# Analytical Psychology
## *Yoram Kaufmann*

### DEFINITION

Analytical Psychology is the name given to the psychological-therapeutic system founded and developed by the Swiss psychiatrist Carl Gustav Jung (1875- 1961). It views the psyche as consisting of two complementary and interacting systems: consciousness and the unconscious. The two systems are motivated and guided by a powerful thrust of the psyche to become whole. This thrust finds its expression in communication between the systems via an imaginal process using symbolic language, as in dreams, fantasies, etc. Increased awareness, and thus symptomatic relief, is brought about by translation and interpretation of this language.

## HISTORY

While a young psychiatric resident, Jung read the just-published book by Freud on the interpretation of dreams. Freud's revolutionary idea of attributing unconscious motivation to human behavior resonated with similar thoughts Jung was entertaining at the time, and Jung proceeded to devise an experimental method, called the Word Association Test, that could be seen as providing an objective, scientific basis for some of Freud's ideas. The two started a warm correspondence, and struck up a friendship that lasted for many years. Jung became Freud's pupil, then colleague. The two agreed on the most basic hypothesis: in addition to the rational, conscious aspect of the personality, there is another realm of the psyche of which man is normally not aware, which they called the unconscious. But they soon disagreed as to what the contents of the unconscious is. This may have been the result of the different settings in which Freud and Jung were observing unconscious phenomena. Freud was initially dealing with middle-class women suffering from neurotic hysteria while Jung was primarily involved with mental patients in psychotic states. Jung was also, at the same time, exposed to parapsychological phenomena via a medium and her trance states. So Jung and Freud were exposed to different kinds of unconscious material. Perhaps as a result, Freud maintained that the unconscious was composed of repressed, traumatic childhood experiences that involved the clash of emerging instinctual needs and the oppressive reality of the family and society. Psychoanalysis was then developed as a technique, consisting of free associations, designed to bring the clashes ("conflicts") into awareness and thus deal with them from an adult vantage point. Jung employed this technique successfully for a while, but gradually became dissatisfied with it. Although it certainly seemed correct as far as it went, it did not go far enough. Jung found he could not, in good conscience, reduce all of a person's current life situation to repressed childhood instinctuality, especially if instinctuality primarily meant sexuality. Jung understood and acknowledged the enormous importance of sexuality in the development of the personality, but he perceived the unconscious as encompassing much more. To be sure, in his patients' material, instinctual conflicts came to the surface, but in addition he saw in their unconscious material, especially dreams and fantasies, an unfolding of a process. This process was uniquely expressed in each person, but it had nevertheless a common structure. Jung called it the "individuation process." Underlying the concept of an individuation process is the idea that a person's psyche contains a potential, is seeking its fulfillment. In other words, the unconscious is goal-oriented, it has a teleological facet. It does not just relate a person's behavior to past experiences, but, more importantly, it orients it toward the future. This differed fundamentally from Freud's point of view, and the inevitable rift occurred. Jung then established his own psychology.

## TECHNIQUE

Modern Jungian psychotherapy investigates the following four processes:

1.  *Projection and its ramifications*. The basic rule of the psyche is that what is

unconscious is projected: that is, attributed to other people or external situations. The projection may lead to an erroneous perception (as when you think your friend is sad while he himself feels quite happy), or to a correct one (your friend is very stingy and it makes you very angry). Projection is always accompanied by a strong affectivity (emotions or moods). In an analysis, the patient is made aware of the extent to which he is projecting, and how his behavior is affected by it. He is then called upon to withdraw his projections and recognize that they are aspects of his own psyche, and to take responsiblity for them.

2.  *Encounter with one's shadow*. A person's shadow is that side of his psyche to which he is unrelated. It consists of those qualities that one would rather not see in oneself, as well as unrealized potentials. Facing the shadow is mostly very painful, and theoretically endless. The analyst has to carefully guide this encounter so that the patient will assimilate only as much of his shadow as he needs to change maladaptive patterns. Care is taken that he not be thrown into more of an individuation process than he is temperamentally suited for.

3.  *Complexes*. A complex is an energy system. It is to the psyche what a mine is in a field. At its core it has an idea that acts like a vortex, draining energy from the conscious personality. Examples are: an inferiority or superiority complex, a mother or father complex, and so on. The analyst helps the patient to identify his complexes and to gradually defuse them and return the deflected energies back to the conscious ego.

4.  *Encounter with the "Collective Unconscious."* The Collective Unconscious, also called the "Objective Psyche," is the name given by Jung to the underlying structure that he found common to all people. Jung found parallels to this structure in mythologies, fairy tales, and various esoteric traditions, such as alchemy. All of them, if translated into psychological terms, were composed of similar elements. These building blocks of the underlying structure Jung called archetypes. One does not encounter the archetypes directly, but through their archetypal imagery or symbolism. Some examples of archetypes are: God, the Wise Old Man, and the Hero on a journey to find a treasure. Not everyone has experienced the Collective Unconscious directly, but most of us do so at least indirectly. The analyst guides the person in such an encounter by amplifying it with parallels in mythology, literature, and so on.

## APPLICATIONS

Analytical Psychology started as a healing technique in the medical model to relieve incapacitating symptoms, but it has become a way of viewing the world and man's place in it. It is essentially a viewpoint that endows the human condition with meaning. Toward the end of his days, Jung thought of his work more as a process of reeducation, a way of understanding psychic phenomena, than as a psychotherapeutic process per se. Although acknowledged as one of the great thinkers of our age, his work is considered controversial, and does not as yet form part of the psychological establishment. His work is most often taught in the departments of religion and literature.

# Anti-Expectation Psychotherapy Techniques

*Roger P. Greenberg*

## DEFINITION

I coined the term "Anti-Expectation Psychotherapy Techniques" in 1973 to refer to an array of procedures that have one major common element: they consistently contradict most patients' expectations of how a therapist will respond to their problems and symptoms. For example, most anti-expectation techniques involve a therapist encouraging the patient to produce or amplify symptoms, rather than a therapist emphasizing that the symptoms be suppressed, denied, or avoided. The techniques have been used mainly with patients demonstrating particular kinds of resistance to the more traditional therapy approaches and those who are unrealistically anxious about the meaning of their symptoms.

## HISTORY

My interest in these techniques grew out of a number of encounters with resistant patients who stated that they were seeking change while at the same time they clung tenaciously to the symptoms and discomforts that brought them in. Such patients tended to externalize problems and emphasize that the world was beyond their control while demonstrating the ability to control the therapy situation by fending off therapist attempts at exploration, interpretation, or direction. These patients often took the role of the help-rejecting complainer, first identified by Jerome Frank and later described by other clinicians. Thus, they continually attempted to pull advice from the therapist only to reject any suggestions that might be offered. They made their problems seem insoluble and appeared to take a special delight and pride in the insurmountability of their difficulties.

Perhaps the key to this type of patient's control of the therapy situation is his expectation that no matter what he does, the therapist will try to be therapeutic. The patient remains relatively confident that his negative view of himself will be matched by therapeutic interventions aimed at getting him to see the "causes" of his views, the alternatives he is overlooking, the positive assets he has, or the resistive nature of his communications. Typically, a static balance soon evolves in which the patient's negative statements are repeatedly counterbalanced by therapist intervention. While this kind of patient behavior may get attention and possibly preserve some inappropriate truths for the patient—such as, even the therapist can't help me solve my problems—it can prove extremely frustrating to therapists and potentially destructive of the therapeutic relationship. It eventually becomes imperative that the therapist somehow disturb the nonproductive stability of the resistant behavior. The use of Anti-Expectation Techniques allows the therapist to regain control over this impasse to therapeutic progress.

## TECHNIQUE

In dealing with resistance, the major aspect of the technique involves the therapist trying to break into the patient's closed system. This is done by aligning oneself with the patient's negative comments while echoing and greatly amplifying the views that the patient probably expects the therapist to oppose. For example, this might mean initially agreeing with the resistant neurotic housewife's complaint that she doesn't keep her house clean enough, and possibly even suggesting that she spend more than her usual ten hours a day cleaning. Or it might mean aligning oneself, at least temporarily, with a patient's statement that he must be defective since he is not perfect at everything he does. More complete case illustrations of the use of these techniques can be found in some of the references listed below.

When such techniques are employed, patients usually begin to find it extremely difficult to be resistive since there is no one to resist. From this position the therapist can begin to have the patient confront behavior and gain control over it. These techniques may be seen as "anti-expectation"—in that the therapist consistently goes against what the patient expects. It is done, however, within a framework that strongly implies that the therapist will be therapeutic. The results are: patients find themselves unable to use comfortable old defenses, since they no longer produce the expected feedback; interactions are marked by the humor of the unexpected; and patients are forced to look at their problems from a different perspective.

It should be emphasized that Anti-Expectation Techniques usually represent only one segment of the therapy. Further, they do not substitute for a theoretical understanding of case material. Thus, such techniques are probably most effectively put into play after a strong therapeutic relationship has been established, the case has been conceptualized theoretically, and there are indications that the techniques are unlikely to precipitate harmful activities—such as self-destructive behavior.

Employing such techniques is difficult and requires considerable therapist sensitivity and skill. The therapist must develop the ability to resist the pull of the patient's message and continually anticipate where an anti-expectation communication will lead. The therapist must be able to put the intervention across without sarcasm and refrain from responding, at least initially, to the humorous or almost absurd aspects of the interactions. Finally, and perhaps most important, care must be taken to insure that the techniques are being employed to further the patient's progress and not to just fulfill the therapist's needs to exert power or express hostile feelings.

## APPLICATIONS

Anti-Expectation Techniques can be used in two major ways: to directly deal with symptoms or to circumvent resistance and facilitate therapy within any theoretical framework. It may well be that the chief value of Anti-Expectation Techniques, with regard to combating symptoms, lies in their giving the patient a clear feeling that self-control can be exerted over behavior and problems.

There are a variety of other ideas expressed within the psychotherapy literature that are consistent with this approach. Behavior therapists have sometimes advocated the method of "negative practice," which involves having patients repeat again and again undesirable habits they are trying to break. A number of papers have described successful treatment of tics with this procedure. Similarly, the behavioral technique labeled "emotional flooding" involves the repeated presentation of anxiety-arousing stimuli until anxiety is extinguished. Implosive Therapy, as described by Stampfl and Levis, also involves a very similar behavioral approach based on psychoanalytic theorizing. They use the patients' own imagery to expose them to the most intense anxiety-eliciting stimuli the therapists can devise based on their theoretical understanding of the case. Again the expectation is that continuous exposure to such a stimulus without harmful consequences would cause it to lose all power to elicit anxiety.

Other examples of therapists using anti-expectation messages to undermine patient defenses and gain control over the expression of symptoms can be found in Milton Erickson's descriptions of "naturalistic" and "utilization" hypnotherapy techniques and Jay Haley's views of the psychotherapy relationship from the standpoint of communications theory.

Interestingly, Albert Ellis's Rational-Emotive Therapy suggests that disturbances can be eradicated by patients learning to tell themselves more rational and less self-defeating sentences. Anti-expectation approaches highlight the fact that certain patients can gain control over their behavior by first trying to tell themselves *more* self-defeating sentences while being made very aware of what they are doing.

# Art Therapy

### Elinor Ulman

## DEFINITION

Art Therapy includes a range of therapeutic uses of visual art materials. At one end of the spectrum art as a means of nonverbal communication is stressed. In conjunction with verbal associations and interpretations, art products serve to assist the understanding and resolution of emotional problems. At the other end of the spectrum, therapy is derived from the artistic process itself. Its usefulness depends on the age-old power of the arts to reconcile conflicting forces within the individual and between the individual and society.

Basic to the art therapist's work in all its variations is the use of expression in the visual arts as a bridge between the individual's inner and outer experience.

## HISTORY

The term "Art Therapy" was originated in 1942 by Adrian Hill, a British artist and teacher who started his therapeutic work with his fellow patients in a tuberculosis sanatorium. In the United States, Margaret Naumburg was the foremost pioneer in the field; she began to work in the early 1940s at the New York State Psychiatric Institute under the sponsorship of psychoanalyst Nolan D. C. Lewis, M.D. Other prominent American figures are Edith Kramer—outstanding both as a general theoretician and as the leading specialist in child Art Therapy—Lauretta Bender, and Paul Schilder. Schilder contributed to theory while Bender, in her work with autistic children, was among the first to put art to therapeutic use. In Europe, Lombroso, Simon, and Prinzhorn, with their early investigations into the art of mental hospital patients, were important precursors. The development of Art Therapy in the United States coincided with, and to some extent was related to, the rising influence of psychoanalysis on psychiatric thinking. Today Art Therapy is associated with many kinds of psychotherapy and ex tends, as well, into nonpsychiatric areas.

## TECHNIQUE

Where art is used mainly as a tool in psychotherapy, art materials are limited to those that produce effects quickly and without the need for a great deal of technical proficiency. Art methods aimed at spontaneity of expression are presented in the hope that unconscious material will escape censorship. Since the art works are valued mainly for their immediate communicative value, the complete development of expressive art products is not emphasized.

Therapy is primarily interpretive, with the client's own verbal associations and formulations playing a large part. Provided that the therapist has sufficient training, the development of transference (shifting feelings about significant people to the therapist) may be encouraged and its handling then becomes an important element in treatment (Naumburg, 1966).

Where therapy depends primarily on values inherent in art itself, the therapist strives to help clients make art products whose expressive quality and depth are as fully realized as the individual's capacities permit. Art materials are selected on the basis of their suitability for this purpose in the hands of people of various ages or who are in particular stages of artistic development The therapist uses his clinical background to respond to the latent as well as the manifest messages contained in the art and to help clients to be more tolerant of the less easily accepted aspects of themselves. The significance of habitual behavior and attitudes is likely to be discussed, but direct interpretations of unconscious material evident in the art work are seldom made or invited.

Art Therapy of this kind does not stand alone as an agent of profound psychological change. It complements psychotherapy by providing an area of symbolic experience, where new attitudes may be tried out, gains deepened and made an integral part of the person (Kramer, 1971).

There are many variations on these two basic technical approaches. For example, clients are sometimes asked to collaborate—in conducting a pictorial dialogue, producing a mural, or working on a single small picture. In most of these instances, emphasis is placed on the way in which the immediate experience enhances self-awareness and demonstrates or influences the relationship between group members. Both artistic development and insight gained through the interpretation of symbolic content play a relatively minor part.

## APPLICATIONS

Art therapists have found a place not only in all kinds of psychiatric institutions (ranging from mental hospitals to community mental health centers) but also in private practice. In addition, Art Therapy is used in many nonpsychiatric settings, such as geriatric centers, rehabilitation programs for the physically disabled, residential centers for children suffering from a wide range of disorders and deficiencies, special education schools and classes, prisons, and centers devoted to enriching the lives of people without any recognized psychiatric problems.

Applications to which Art Therapy has been adapted include psychological assessment, the training of members of other psychotherapeutic disciplines, intensive individual psychotherapy, formal Group Art Therapy—where art productions serve as a springboard for group discussion—assessment of family dynamics, ongoing psychotherapy with family groups, and adjunctive therapy with patients seen in informal groups.

Because the art product inevitably bears the stamp of its creator, Art Therapy cannot help impinging on the territory of psychotherapy and psychological assessment. Painting and sculpture are, in addition, susceptible to such a broad range of applications that the boundaries between Art Therapy and other uses of art materials are inevitably blurred. Recreation and rehabilitation programs use art activity to serve purposes other than those of Art Therapy, as does Occupational Therapy. Art education in residential facilities for emotionally disturbed children seldom makes the most of the therapeutic possibilities of art.

At best, all institutional uses of art materials will be coordinated by a person who understands their similarities, differences, and possible points of conflict as well as the usually untapped opportunities for collaboration among them.

# Group Art Therapy

### *Shaun A. McNiff*

## DEFINITION

Group Art Therapy is a process that combines the healing/therapeutic qualities of art with group psychotherapy.

## HISTORY

As the practice of Art Therapy has developed over the past thirty years, art has been introduced to the various modes of therapy—individual, group, milieu, and family. Although the pioneering work of art therapist Margaret Naumburg in the 1930s and 1940s was psychoanalytically oriented, philosophical approaches to Art Therapy have paralleled the multiplicity of viewpoints in the general mental health field. Psychotherapists have introduced the arts into group therapy sessions because of their interest in providing alternatives to verbal communication. The alternatives allow for the expression of feelings that cannot be completely revealed in words or the revelation of feelings that are too threatening to verbalize.

# TECHNIQUE

Virtually every manifestation of Group Art Therapy involves participants in the basic process of making art and sharing their work with others. For the most part, art is made during the group session, although therapists will often encourage clients to make art individually outside of the group session and bring in their work for discussion. The sessions tend to run from one to three hours, and group members discuss their work with each other both during and after the process of production. The discussion that follows the production of art allows for more formal and focused analysis of feelings. Art works can provide the opportunity for the sharing of the artist's motives; the analysis and sharpening of visual perception; the projection of repressed conflicts and emotions; and as a means of provoking associations to past experiences. In addition, art activity is inherently therapeutic in and of itself. Thus, group discussion often focuses on the healing power of art, with participants sharing how they are personally affected by the artistic process. This orientation to art therapy is encouraged in situations where it is important for clients to be involved in creative activity for its own sake. Practitioners of Group Art Therapy have observed that the sharing of art works and the object orientation of artistic activity take away a great deal of the fear that many clients have of discussing their feelings directly. In this respect, artistic activity helps in the early stages of a group in developing trust, mutual respect, and a sense of purpose.

Although most of the literature on Group Art Therapy describes the use of drawing materials, paint, and clay, virtually any art medium can be introduced to a therapy group, depending on the purpose of the group, its structure, and available space. There is also a growing interest in the integration of the arts (dance, drama, music, poetry, and the visual arts) in therapy. Analytically oriented group leaders will generally limit the availability of materials with the goal of developing a sense of continuity from session to session and to minimize distractions. Within this context, art is perceived as a tool in furthering the process of group therapy. Other approaches are more art oriented and make the broadest range of creative activities accessible to participants—from simple line drawings to stone and wood sculpture, to the construction of environments, to the artistic use of photography, videotapes, and so on. The art-oriented group may also place an emphasis on the artistic development of the person, because of the positive effects that this may have on the whole personality.

The structure of Group Art Therapy can again be extended along a continuum, running in this case from small, closed group sessions stressing intimacy and private sharing to the more open studio approach where individuals may work within the same space on individual projects and come together from time to time to discuss their work. It is generally agreed among group therapy leaders that a combination of both approaches is needed to maximize opportunities for creative expression. Structure in the sense of a common activity and a common artistic theme can also help a group to focus itself on personal issues. For example, if fear happens to be an important theme in a group, each individual might be asked to deal with the feeling of fear in an art work. In this way each individual is given the opportunity to intensely focus on his personal concern. When the art is shared by the group, similarities and differences in experiences are discovered. On the other hand, more nondirective approaches to art activity and group discussion can give the more independent and self-sufficient group the space needed to bring personal feelings and concerns into the group experience.

## APPLICATIONS

It is generally true that young children cannot sustain formal discussion of their art for more than a few minutes—especially if the children are afflicted by severe emotional disorders. Practitioners have discovered that behaviorally disordered children tend to function best in a structured environment where limits are clearly set. Children are also apt to show needs for accomplishment in their art and consequently, Group Art Therapy activity with children tends to be more "product" oriented than group sessions with adults. Although adults often have similar needs for pleasing "products," the literature on Group Art Therapy indicates more of a concern with the process of artistic activity and the role that art can play in furthering personal reflection, sharing, and interpersonal learning.

---

# Aversion Therapy

### *Max Mastellone*

## DEFINITION

Aversion Therapy, also known as aversive conditioning, is not in and of itself a discrete form of treatment. Rather, when properly used, it is a technique that forms but a part of a comprehensive behavior therapy.

Very simply, Aversion Therapy is an attempt to establish a durable association between an undesirable behavior and an unpleasant stimulation. Target behaviors may include overt actions as well as private events, such as thoughts or feelings. Implementation of Aversion Therapy may follow either a classical (Pavlovian) conditioning paradigm—simple association by contiguity—or an operant (Skinnerian, instrumental) conditioning paradigm wherein the unpleasant stimulation is made a consequence of the undesirable behavior. The conditioning is designed to create a learned connection between the undesirable behavior and the unpleasant stimulation, which is expected to bring about the elimination, or at the very least, a reduction of the target behavior in question. Presently, aversive conditioning is not frequently or widely used, and its application is limited to certain circumstances.

## HISTORY

Clearly it was Pavlov's extensive investigation of the phenomenon of classical conditioning that laid the basis for the therapeutic use of aversive conditioning in humans. In particular, it was his demonstration that conditioned aversion responses could be established in dogs. According to Franks (1977), work by Kantorovich in 1930 in the Soviet Union represents the first formally documented attempt to use aversive conditioning in a therapeutic situation. This investigator treated alcoholics with electrical Aversion Therapy and reported that most abstained from alcohol use for months. While other early work employed electrical stimulation with apparent success, Frank reports that through the 1930s and 1940s Aversion Therapy primarily consisted of the treatment of alcoholism by means of nausea-inducing drugs.

Due to the incorrect application of conditioning principles by ill-informed clinicians, and to the use of sedative drugs with patients of therapists who were unaware that such drugs disrupt the formation of conditioned responses, the use of Aversion Therapy as a treatment for alcoholism lost favor. With the rise of behavior therapy as a distinct field starting in the late 1950s came the resurrection of aversive conditioning. Researchers oriented toward clinical work and knowledgeable about learning theory refined and perfected aversive procedures. Behaviorally oriented clinicians undertook widespread and diverse application of Aversion Therapy. Through these experiences many behavior therapists were forcefully reminded of the complex nature of humans and found that, generally, aversive procedures had value only within the context of a multifaceted behavioral regimen. When used alone, such procedures often produced only poor or short-term results, unless the target behavior was a relatively circumscribed habit, such as smoking or hair pulling, exhibited by an otherwise well-adjusted individual.

## TECHNIQUE

As indicated earlier, Aversion Therapy can be practiced through either classical or instrumental conditioning. Under each of these conditions the technique would vary somewhat, as it would between overt, physical aversion procedures and covert, cognitive aversion procedures. The basic technique involves pairing the undesirable behavior with a noxious stimulation or having the latter occur very shortly after the former. For example, a smoker may be treated by delivering a brief, high voltage, low amperage, harmless shock to the hand holding the cigarette as he begins taking a puff. Treatment might consist of a number of sessions on different days, each comprised of a series of smoking-shock trials. An instrumental conditioning paradigm is illustrated in a study by Meyer and Crisp (1964). They administered electric shocks to two obese patients at some stage during their approach to, or eating of, favorite foods. The shocks were stopped as soon as the patients pushed the food away or stopped eating it. As avoidance behavior became established, the patient was exposed to the tempting food for progressively longer periods while the frequency of shocks was diminished. This design is an example of instrumental escape learning.

In recent years Aversion Therapy procedures have been adapted and developed for self-administration. Using a pocket-size, battery-operated shock box, an individual can deliver shocks to himself whenever he intends to commit or does commit an unwanted behavior. Such a device gives an individual the freedom to administer noxious stimulation on potentially 100 percent of the occurrences of the behavior in question. In the same vein, the application of a rubber band worn on the wrist can be an aversive procedure (Mastellone, 1974). In one case, a fifteen-year-old girl had the habit of pulling strands of hair from her scalp, one after the other. She was instructed to wear a rubber band, stretch it and snap it on the underside of her wrist immediately after each instance of hair pulling, or whenever she had the urge to pull out her hair if she became aware of this first.

The recent emphasis in behavior therapy on the development of procedures to enhance self-control has coincided with (if not been encouraged by) the reemergence of the view that cognition is an important determinant of behavior. A significant contribution to these events was Cautela's (1966) introduction of the covert sensitization technique.

This is a self-administered, cognitive aversion therapy procedure. It involves having the individual imagine a scenario wherein he experiences a highly aversive stimulation, such as severe nausea and vomiting, in connection with committing the unwanted target behavior. The technique may be extended to apply to covert behavior, such as obsessive ideation, as well.

In addition to chemical and electrical noxious stimulation and the others mentioned above, such things as noxious odors, smoke inhalation, high-intensity auditory signals, and traumatic respiratory drug-induced paralysis have also been used.

## APPLICATIONS

In regard to the application of aversive conditioning procedures we need to distinguish between those of the physical, other-administered sort and those that are cognitive and/or self-administered. For many behavior therapists, use of the former type—mainly electrical stimulation—has become limited to those behaviors for which a more desirable alternative does not exist. For example, in cases of head banging or other forms of self-mutilating behavior, sometimes observed in severely retarded or autistic individuals, Aversion Therapy is the treatment of choice. In such instances the potential consequences of the behavior are so dire that they overshadow the ethical and humanistic concerns over the use of electric shock to modify human behavior. Despite the controversy surrounding it, some workers in the field continue to use electrical aversion therapy in the treatment of homosexuality, transvestitism, and fetishism. Controversy also exists in connection with the abuse of aversive conditioning in certain federal correctional institutions. Punitive measures have been employed under the legitimizing guise of "behavior modification." In some state institutions inmates have been involuntarily subjected to Aversion Therapy for the treatment of sexual deviations. In my opinion, any such use of therapeutic technology must be opposed and eliminated.

Ethical questions are essentially avoided by the use of self-administered aversive procedures. There is a qualitative difference between these and externally controlled electrical stimulation that permits a much wider range of application. These techniques may not be as powerful, but deficiencies in power are made up by combining such techniques with other behavioral techniques in a well-rounded therapeutic program.

In general, just about any unwanted behavior is fare for techniques such as covert sensitization or the wrist-worn rubber band. Target behaviors may include more serious symptoms, such as obsessions and compulsions as well as less serious nervous habits, such as nail biting or hair pulling. Hayes, et al. (1978) used covert sensitization in the treatment of exhibitionism and sadism. I used the rubber band technique to discourage sexual arousal to the sight of men, in a male homosexual. I used other behavioral techniques in conjunction with that one in order to establish sexual arousal in response to women.

Covert and other self-administered techniques have been used with behaviors such as smoking, overeating, substance abuse and tics, as well as numerous unwanted idiosyncratic behaviors. Because these techniques are not amenable to the same rigorous control as is possible with electrical stimulation, some would say that they are really not scientific conditioning procedures. Clinical experience suggests that self-administered aversion procedures enhance the client's view of his ability to control his own behavior.

Sometimes just the knowledge that he can invoke the procedure is sufficient to enable the client to inhibit the target behavior. Rather than simply representing an escape or avoidance response, it would appear that the inhibitory behavior is being mediated by changes in attitudes and/or beliefs. More research is needed to elucidate the bases of self-administered aversion procedures.

# Selective Awareness Therapy
*Wendy Helms*

## DEFINITION
Selective Awareness Therapy (S.A.T.) is a short-term, holistic approach to the treatment of physical and psychological symptoms through integration of body and mind. The underlying assumption of S.A.T. is that both physical and mental symptoms are the product of unresolved thought/emotion complexes that upset the natural homeostatic balance of the individual through misallocation of energy. Through a combination of deep relaxation, breathing, and imagery, clients learn how to achieve insight into the connection between the symptom and the thought/ emotion process of which it is a manifestation. Once insight is achieved, clients are taught to get in touch with their own self-healing potential to release blocked energy and regain and maintain natural health and vitality.

## HISTORY
Dr. Peter Mutke became aware of the need for a new approach to medical and psychological problems during his career as a physician and surgeon. He was fascinated by the variety of different ways in which people react to illness or injury, and he noticed that patients' belief systems and mental attitudes seemed to be powerful factors influencing survival and speed of recovery. In his search for a tool that could utilize these powerful factors, Dr. Mutke turned to Hypnotherapy, which he used, for a time, with great success. However, he was troubled by the numerous misconceptions and expectations associated with hypnosis, especially the client's expectation of being passively controlled. So, Dr. Mutke began to develop a new approach that would have the advantage of neutral expectations. Based on sound principles of psychophysiology, S.A.T. combined positive aspects of hypnosis—such as deep relaxation, access to amnestic material, and use of creative imagery—with techniques for teaching clients to adjust their own physical and psychological functioning to normal and to take responsibility for their own well-being. S.A.T. differs from Hypnotherapy in several important ways. The S.A.T. relaxation induction purposely avoids any connotation of "trance" or "sleep," and is regarded rather as a state of "super-consciousness" that facilitates increased insight and receptivity to

change. The client's consent is sought at all stages of therapy, giving reassurance that the client is in control and can return to social awareness at any time.

S.A.T. has elements in common with a number of other therapeutic approaches. Autogenic training, for example, also employs deep relaxation and positive imagery, which are effective in temporary relief of symptoms. However, Autogenic training is a lengthy procedure that fails to provide techniques for dealing with emotional abreactions (reexperiencing a previous emotional event) and amnestic material that may spontaneously appear during relaxation. Thus, clients cannot achieve the insight essential to lasting change.

The structure of S.A.T. is unique and it is one of the few therapeutic approaches that effectively bridges the gap between psychology and medicine, giving clients an awareness of their power to influence their own physical and mental health.

## TECHNIQUE

S.A.T. is a short-term therapy; a series of from three to five one-hour sessions at weekly intervals are expected to lead to significant change in a client's illness pattern. After identifying and breaking the perpetuating thought/emotion/physical symptom chain, the client is helped to adjust attitudes and self-image accordingly so that the changes will become permanent. When a client has a number of unrelated symptoms, it is necessary to explore the dynamics of each symptom in turn, allowing two or three sessions for each disease. An initial S.A.T. session begins with a short inquiry into the client's social and medical history and current complaint. Evidence of a recent medical work-up is essential when treating physical symptoms outside of a medical setting. After discussion of the S.A.T. approach, the client is introduced to the state of selective awareness through a process of deep relaxation. An eight- to ten-minute tape of the relaxation induction is made during the session and the client is asked to listen to the tape twice a day. Finger signals are established to facilitate communication on a subconscious level and especially to check for the client's consent at all stages of therapy.

A typical second session begins with a brief relaxation induction into a state of selective awareness. Then the client is asked to orient himself back to the most recent time when he experienced the symptom (for example, stomach pain, insomnia, depression), to describe the situation, and to reexperience the thoughts and emotions that were dominant at that time. Examination of a succession of such "symptom-producing events" leads back to an original "sensitizing event" and reveals a clear pattern of relationship between the symptom and a triggering thought/ emotion complex. When the client gains insight into the origin of the symptom and begins to take responsibility for ill health, then healing and change begin to take place.

A third session would make use of "bio-automation" or creative image rehearsal" to sever the connection between symptom and thought/emotion complex. Bio-automation involves using mental imagery to gain positive influence over autonomic functions of the body, such as circulation, digestion, and healing. Negative patterns of behavior and communication can similarly be influenced through creative image rehearsal, a process of mentally visualizing and rehearsing desired changes in behavior. A tape is made of this therapeutic process, which includes positive feedback to reinforce the client's new symptom-free self-image. Positive feedback is important at all stages of therapy to ensure that the client takes credit for the fact that he is using his own natural healing potential to create change in himself. After the third session, therapist and client review progress and decide on the number of additional sessions needed. At the conclusion of therapy, a single review session is scheduled in four to six weeks to reinforce progress and change. The structure of S.A.T. is of great importance, but within the basic framework there is great scope for creativity in catering to the needs of each particular client. S.A.T. combines well with other approaches such as Gestalt, Transactional Analysis, and Psychodrama, and it can also be used effectively as a tool for self-help.

## APPLICATIONS

Theoretically, there are few physical and emotional symptoms that cannot be alleviated with S.A.T. However, the success of S.A.T. is directly proportional to the client's motivation and ability to concentrate and use mental imagery.

S.A.T. is particularly well suited for use in a medical setting where holistic counseling can take place in cooperation with a team of medical personnel. However, therapists and counselors with training in psychology must be cautious about treating physical symptoms without first obtaining evidence that the client has had a complete medical checkup.

Psychosomatic complaints that respond particularly well to short-term treatment with S.A.T. include migraine headaches, muscular pains, digestive and circulatory disorders, skin allergies, and asthma. S.A.T. has also been used effectively with before surgery patients, helping to promote rapid healing, and postoperative recovery.

Habit disorders, such as smoking, obesity, and nail biting, respond well to the S.A.T. approach, which facilitates direct insight into the negative thought/emotion complexes that underlie such symptoms.

# Bates Method of Vision Training
## Janet M. Goodrich

### DEFINITION
The Bates Method of Vision Training utilizes relaxation, movement, light, and visualization to gain clear eyesight without the use of glasses or artificial lenses.

### HISTORY
In the preface to his revolutionary book. *Perfect Sight Without Glasses,* Dr. William H. Bates expressed regret that ophthalmic science had at that point already become so rigid that creative searching for preventive and truly curative measures had ground to a halt. Faulty vision, we are still told, is annoying, but nothing can be done for it beyond the prescribing of refractive lenses or, in more severe cases, treatment by drugs and sur-

gery. Unconvinced, Bates performed many experiments with nearsighted, farsighted, and astigmatic people, both adults and children. He discovered that visual distortions are directly linked to states of tension and emotional stress. Upon this basis, Bates devised educational techniques for relieving eyestrain and staring brought on by the effort to perform visually and by mental-emotional imbalances.

The effectiveness of the Bates method was evidenced by innumerable case histories. Students of both Bates and Margaret D. Corbett, who trained teachers at her School of Eye Education in Los Angeles during the middle of this century, learned to direct their own seeing-healing process, and dispensed with eyeglasses. Because this therapy was never accepted by the orthodox professionals, objective research of this method is rarely found. More recently, a handful of optometrists have expressed interest as the trend toward holistic measures moves into professional circles. The Bates practice is currently enjoying a great resurgence of activity among the many people who are seeking alternatives in all areas of their life.

## TECHNIQUE

A teacher of the Bates method sits with the students for one to one and a half hours patiently leading their bodies, minds, and eyes into a state of relaxed functioning. A typical lesson may begin with "sunning" the closed eyes: while absorbing the light, warmth, and energy of the sun, a slow, easy movement of the head is employed to stimulate the retinal cells and to induce deep relaxation of facial and eye muscles. Following sunning, swinging of the head or the whole body may be taught. This slow, rhythmic motion, which can be done to music, reverses the rigid staring process and helps restore the natural mobility of the eye. The students can sit in chairs easily and turn their heads from side to side, sometimes imagining a fluffy feather or paintbrush extending from the ends of their noses. This gives a feeling of smoothness that creates many fine movements of the eyes. The standing body swing is done by standing easily, turning from side to side in a half circle by swinging the heels outwardly one at a time.

The students are advised not to look outward from themselves at objects, to peer, or fix their gaze. The suggestion is given that they allow all the wonderful colors and details of the world to come into their minds softly, realizing that *all* vision, whether eyes are open or closed, is in the imagination.

Cupped hands are then placed gently over the eye, shutting out all light, and the visualization of pleasant scenes is described by the teacher and sometimes by the students as their powers of imagery grow. Emphasis is placed upon images that are conducive to general body and sensory enjoyment, such as vacationing on a tropical isle or scanning a panoramic mountain view. When students open their eyes once more, they are encouraged to blink easily and retain the sensation of ease and well-being as they swing their attention gently about the room. The idea of centralizing may be introduced as the students "edge" or outline one object at a time, using a make-believe pencil on the ends of their noses.

Massage of the shoulders, neck, head, and face may be brought in to relieve accumulated tension in these related areas. All through the process, expansiveness of breathing is encouraged and much yawning ensues.

## APPLICATIONS

The foregoing procedures have application to people of all ages and types of visual problems. In general, the students who seek out the method are those interested in activating their own native capacity for vision. Motivation, persistence, and understanding are the deciding factors in the outcome of any individual's practice of the Bates Method. Its relationship to all other psychosomatic therapy procedures is being revealed in the light of present-day holistic endeavors. For example, the teachers of Reichian-oriented or Bioenergetic therapies often refer to the relationship between refractive problems and emotional repressions. The near-sighted person may carry subsurface feelings of apprehension, anxiety, and fear. The farsighted person may be expressing a blockage of anger. This person stares intensely at the world and can suffer from fierce eye pain and headaches. Corbett-trained vision teachers often spoke of cross-eyed children throwing temper tantrums as they released the pent-up energy held in their eyes and heads.

Emotional flexibility, release of body tension, and visual functioning are closely tied together. Students of the Bates Method react with pleasure when experiencing a "flash" or natural clearing of vision. When asked how they felt when first taking off their glasses, typical replies were: "insecure," "unbalanced," "my jaw was tight all the time," "mistrustful of what I see." When asked later how they felt upon their first experience of a "flash," these replies came through: "I enjoyed letting the world into me," "It was exciting and expansive," "I felt lightheaded and transparent," "I was relaxed, thrilled, and balanced."

# Behavior Modification

## Carl V. Binder

## DEFINITION

The term "Behavior Modification" was originally coined by practitioners to emphasize the treatment of behavioral deficits and excesses per se, rather than the hypothetical psychological states or processes claimed by others to cause human behavior (Ullmann and Krasner, 1965). Behavior change—the implicit or explicit goal of all psychotherapy—is conceived of as a learning process; Behavior Modification, from the practitioner's point of view, is thus an "educational" endeavor (Binder, 1977). Because Behavior Modification refers to outcome rather than method, it does not distinguish between various means of changing behavior (for example, reinforcement techniques versus chemotherapy or psychosurgery). This ambiguity has led to a good deal of public confusion in recent years. And among professional practitioners, terms such as "behavior therapy," "contingency management," "learning therapy," "applied behavior analysis," "applied behaviorism," "programmed instruction," and "precision teaching" (which refer to more clearly defined subcategories of behavioral treatment) are often used instead of the term Behavior Modification.

# HISTORY

The roots of Behavior Modification can be traced to early experimental studies of human and animal learning, most notably in the traditions of Ivan Pavlov and B. F. Skinner (Barrett, 1977; Rachlin, 1970; Skinner, 1953; Wolpe, 1973). A vast literature of more than sixty years' accumulation (Britt, 1975) attests to the power of the quantitative experimental method that forms the basis of the applied behaviorist's practice (Hersen and Barlow, 1976).

# TECHNIQUE

The conceptual and methodological foundations of behavioral treatment are to be found in what is known as the functional analysis of behavior (Skinner, 1953, 1969), according to which the measured interactions between behaviors and environmental events specify their functions for the behaver. That is, *in a functional analysis, behavioral and environmental events are defined in terms of their causal relationships with one another.*

In application, functional behavior analysis seeks to discover, through the experimental method, events preceding behavior (antecedents) and those following behavior (consequences) that have demonstrable effects on such measurable behavioral dimensions as frequency, duration, intensity, and location of the behavior in space and time (Lindsley). Functional behavior analysis applies to both manipulation of already existing behaviors and the development (i.e., teaching) of new forms of responding (cf. Barrett, 1977). For example, the term "reinforcement" is applied to an event that follows a behavior if—and only if—it can be demonstrated that the subsequent event actually increases the frequency (that is, *functions* as a reinforcer) of that behavior exhibited by the individual in question.

The applied behaviorist seeks to alter behavior by manipulating antecedent and consequent events in such a way as to achieve an explicit behavioral objective—a specific, measurable behavior change. Thus, clinical assessment, in the framework of behavior analysis, always involves measurement of past and current behaviors and the conditions under which they occur, either through direct observation or through the client's verbal report.

# APPLICATIONS

All human behavior falls within the domain of the behavior therapist, and practitioners of behavioral treatment are to be found among educators and special educators, psychologists, social workers, medical professionals, and paraprofessionals in every area of human service.

The frequent criticism that applied behaviorism ignores subjective (i.e., mental) events has been blunted in recent years by an increasing interest in the manipulation and treatment of "covert processes" (Cautela, 1973). Thoughts, sensations, and other private experiences now appear to be as open to functional analysis and modification as overt behavioral events. A serious problem is that of measurement reliability insofar as private events are directly observable only by the person within whose body they occur. Nonetheless, behavior therapists have found that systematic arrangement of covert events (for example, practiced imaginary sequences) can alter the frequency of both covert and overt behaviors, and that overt events may have reliable effects on covert behaviors (Kazdin, 1977).

Self-management is another major focus of behavior therapy in recent years (Thoresen and Coates, 1976). Clients are taught to make changes in their environments and to practice procedures that lead to modification of their own behavior. Relaxation training, or systematic desensitization (Wolpe, 1973), for example, involves procedures clients are encouraged to practice between therapy sessions in order to acquire the ability to relax "at will." Self-reinforcement, thought stopping, behavioral contracting, and other related procedures also involve attempts on the part of the therapist or educator to teach clients a set of skills leading to self-control and to the eventual obsolescence of the therapist, except perhaps in an infrequent consulting role.

The literature of Behavior Modification contains examples of application to nearly every form of human activity. Psychotic and neurotic behavior, all kinds of educational objectives, social and sexual behavior, physiological functioning and pain control, organizational behavior, overeating, and addictive behaviors have all been addressed by the practice of behavior therapy. A more thorough perspective on the practice of behavior therapy and applied behavior analysis can be gained through study of the works listed in the bibliography.

# Assertive Behavior Therapy
## Robert E. Alberti

## DEFINITION

Assertive Behavior Therapy (also known as Assertiveness Training, Assertion Training, or Social Skills Training) is a procedure which trains the client in socially appropriate behaviors for self-expression of feelings, attitudes, wishes, opinions, and rights. Included in the procedure are:

*Skills training*, in which specific verbal and nonverbal behaviors are taught, practiced, and integrated into the client's behavioral repertoire.

*Anxiety reduction*, which may be achieved directly (for example, through desensitization or other counter-conditioning procedures), or indirectly, as a by-product of skills training.

*Cognitive restructuring*, in which values, beliefs, cognitions, and/or attitudes that limit the client's self-expression may be changed by insight, exhortation, or behavioral achievements.

## HISTORY

Assertive Behavior Training procedures are rooted in behavior therapy. However, a considerable humanistic-gestalt influence is evident. Foundation for the process lies in Andrew Salter's Conditioned Reflex Therapy, which centered on making assertive (or "excitatory") behavior more spontaneous; and Joseph Wolpe's "psychotherapy by reciprocal inhibition," a counter-conditioning technique which attempts to inhibit neurotic anxiety or fear by evoking other emotions. More recently, my work with Michael Emmons and the work of a number of others (Alberti, 1977) have popularized the technique, integrated concepts and procedures from the humanistic-gestalt framework, and extended its application to a wide range of nonclinical "training" settings.

## TECHNIQUE

Techniques utilized in Assertive Behavior Therapy follow the three general forms noted above.

Skills training techniques include modeling, behavior rehearsal, systematic feedback and coaching, homework assignments, games and exercises, journals, and systematic assessment. Treatment of choice is often in a therapy or training group in order to provide an adequate social environment, except for highly anxious and inhibited clients. The emphasis is usually on rehearsal and coaching of behavioral skills required in interpersonal situations. In simulated situations, the client is called upon to express positive or negative feeling toward another person, or to stand up for his/her rights. In addition, clients are urged to extend their new skills into life situations outside of therapy/training, and to report their progress.

Anxiety reduction techniques include the traditional desensitization procedures, as well as desensitization resulting from skill building and successful approaches to the actual feared situation.

Cognitive restructuring procedures include didactic presentations regarding individual human rights, social conditioning, values clarification, decision making. Barriers to individual expression—that is, society, culture, age, sex, socio-economic status, family—are examined and challenged against the standard of individual rights.

It should be noted that a variety of "games," "techniques," and "manipulation procedures" have, unfortunately, evolved in the wake of the popular interest in Assertive Behavior Training/Therapy. Responsible practitioners avoid any procedure which does not both enhance the client and respect the rights of others.

## APPLICATIONS

From its beginnings as a therapeutic procedure for pathologically inhibited individuals, Assertive Behavior Therapy has found application far beyond its considerable value as a clinical tool.

In therapy, the procedure is useful with clients who suffer from moderate to severe social inhibition due to anxiety, skill deficits, or faulty belief/attitude systems. It is, as any therapeutic tool, best applied after careful assessment, and in conjunction with other techniques appropriate to meeting the client's needs.

As a training procedure, assertive skills training has been effectively utilized in women's organizations, management training, children's programs, and minority rights groups. Other applications have included health-care personnel, delinquent youth, alcoholics, couples, divorced people, job seekers, employees, phobics, overweight persons, the handicapped, senior citizens, prisoners, and correctional institution staff, among others.

# Broad Spectrum Behavior Therapy

*James P. McGee, II*

## DEFINITION

Behavior therapy is defined by Ullmann and Krasner as "treatment ... that aims to alter a person's behavior directly through the application of general psychological principles." More specifically, Wolpe relates behavior therapy to psychological learning theory by describing it as ... the use of experimentally established principles of learning for the purpose of changing unadaptive habits."

Until recently the rather narrow definitions of behavior therapy provided by Krasner and Wolpe, which stressed the alleged sociopsychological and learning theory foundations of behavioral approaches, dominated the field. Broad Spectrum Behavior Therapy, a concept invented by Arnold Lazarus, was developed to extend the scope of behavioral intervention to include not only external, observable, and measurable behavioral deficits and excesses but also to alter internal private events such as maladaptive thoughts and feelings, attitudes and beliefs (Lazarus, 1971). "Narrow band" behavior therapy stresses the notion that behavior is acquired and maintained and thus also changed through processes of "conditioning" or learning. In contrast, the Broad Spectrum approach is essentially atheoretical in that it proposes the use of techniques that derive from various, and at times competing, theoretical frameworks. Broad Spectrum Behavior Therapy is a form of "technical eclecticism" wherein the practitioner relies on not only strictly behavioral techniques, such as desensitization or assertive training, but also on more traditional strategies, such as interpretation, reflection, cognitive restructuring, as well as the relationship aspects of therapy. The selection of treatment approaches by the Broad Spectrum Behavior therapist is more determined by his perception of the needs of the patient and the patient's individual responses than to any specific set of theoretical assumptions.

## HISTORY

The origins of behavior therapy, or the more generic term Behavior Modification, can be traced back to the philosophical tradition of empiricism as characterized by the British philosophers Locke, Hume and Hartley. Here emphasis was placed on the mind as a *tabula rasa*, or blank slate, upon which knowledge and behavioral tendencies were impressed by experience.

In the United States, the Behavioral School of Psychology was founded by John B. Watson, regarded by many as the "father of modern behaviorism." Some of Watson's early work in the 1920s, in which he applied learning principles to alter behavior patterns in children, can be seen retrospectively as behavior therapy. Watson's work was influenced by the research of Ivan Pavlov on the conditioned reflex and the pioneer learning theorist E. L. Thorndike. Thorndike's "law of effect," which articulated the influence of reinforcing consequences on behavior, provided the foundation for B. F. Skinner's Behavioral Psychology of Operant Conditioning. Krasner (1971) regards the work of

Skinner as the most important of fifteen various "streams of influence" that converged in the early 1960s to give birth to the field of behavior therapy. Perhaps the two other most important trends affecting the evolution of Behavior Therapy were the development of a social learning theory of psychopathology as a viable alternative to the disease or medical model, and a growing dissatisfaction with psychoanalysis and psychodynamic therapies because of their alleged inefficiency.

Current developments on the level of broad conceptualizations, as opposed to specific techniques, are directly linked to the work of Arnold Lazarus and his Broad Spectrum Behavior Therapy. This approach goes well beyond the strict Skinnerian and Pavlovian conditioning formulations that characterized the early history of behavior therapy. Even more recently, Lazarus has proposed a scheme he calls Multimodal Behavior Therapy (Lazarus, 1976) as the legitimate successor of Broad Spectrum Behavior Therapy. The mulitmodal approach to assessment and treatment stresses that the clinician attends to what Lazarus regards as the seven successful domains or "modes" of human functioning: behavior, affect (moods, emotions), sensation, imagery, cognition, interpersonal, and drugs (neurological, biochemical functioning). The first letters of these seven modes spell out the acronym "basic id." According to Lazarus, failure to adequately deal with a patient's functioning in the areas of the basic id accounts for a large portion of relapse in patients treated by other therapies—including other behavior therapies.

## TECHNIQUE

Subsumed under the heading of Broad Spectrum Behavior Therapy are all the standard behavioral strategies that are based largely on principles of Skinnerian and Pavlovian conditioning and imitation learning, plus the techniques of cognitive therapy, such as those developed by Albert Ellis and Aaron Beck. The more purely behavioral techniques include the following: systematic desensitization, implosion, flooding or response prevention, emotive imagery, assertive training, massed practice, modeling based procedures, operant conditioning based procedures, techniques of aversive control, behavioral methods of self-control, covert conditioning and covert reinforcement, and biofeedback.

(For a definition and description of these various techniques, consult either of the texts by O'Leary and Wilson or Rimm and Masters cited in the Bibliography.)

## APPLICATIONS

Broad Spectrum Behavior therapists utilize any of the behavioral and cognitive techniques listed above either alone or, more frequently, in combination to treat all varieties of human deviance and psychopathology. For example, with the patient who shows neurotic anxiety and depression, assessment might reveal that this includes both "free-floating" and situation-specific anxiety. This patient may also suffer significant social-interpersonal anxiety that results in his acting withdrawn, passive, and submissive in social situations. Such a patient frequently experiences sexual difficulties, such as periodic impotence. The patient may also experience episodic depressive states characterized by feelings of low self-esteem, which are the result of the person's having very critical thoughts about himself. For this type of patient a combination of relaxation training and systematic desensitization for his free-floating anxiety and specific phobias is indicated. Secondary to that, the patient could receive a program of assertive training designed to reduce social anxiety while simultaneously increasing his repertoire of appropriate assertive responses. For the sexual difficulties some variation of the Masters and Johnson treatment for impotence might be utilized. For the patient's depression, a cognitive therapy strategy might be taken where the patient is encouraged to examine his irrational thoughts and self-condemnation, and to replace these with rational beliefs that include notions of self-acceptance.

# Bereavement Counseling

## Roberta Temes

### DEFINITION

Bereavement Counseling is the therapy that takes place when a professionally trained bereavement counselor meets regularly with a person or group of persons who have experienced the death of a loved one. Unresolved grief can remain for many years after the death of a significant person in one's life. Thus, recipients of Bereavement Counseling are not necessarily recently bereaved. The trained bereavement counselor may or may not be a professional therapist. Often those who elect to be trained are members of the clergy, widows who have successfully completed their own mourning, or funeral directors.

The focus of Bereavement Counseling is on health and normalcy. Bereavement is a psychologically healthy and appropriate response to the death of a relative or friend.

### HISTORY

When extended families, religious rituals, and ethnic traditions were the norm, mourners received ample support from their culture. As assimilation and alienation pervaded American society, people became removed from necessary support systems, from a caring community. With no secular mourning rituals to serve as guides through grief, and no known formalized way to complete the emotional relationship with the deceased, mental health professionals saw symptoms of depression in the bereaved population.

Various services for the bereaved were initiated in the mid-sixties. Telephone "hot lines" were established by hospitals and community agencies. Phyllis Silverman, at Harvard Medical Laboratories, established a Widowed-to-Widowed program, where a professionally trained widow reaches out to a newly widowed member of her community on a one-to-one basis. In the early seventies, groups of parents who lost children to leukemia formed a national support network, as did parents whose babies succumbed to Sudden Infant Death Syndrome. By the midseventies most major cities had one or more programs for Bereavement Counseling services.

Bereavement Counseling is now a clearly defined subcategory within the mental health professions. The symptoms of depression experienced by a mourner are no longer judged pathological but rather as legitimate, time-limited responses to a profound loss.

## TECHNIQUE

Most Bereavement Counseling services are modeled after Grief Groups, established in New York City in the mid-seventies. Groups of bereaved people meet for three months, one and a half hours each week, under the direction of a professionally trained counselor. Each group is composed of members who have experienced a similar loss, such as the loss of a parent, or loss of a spouse. The groups provide members with role models; those who have endured the same trauma.

Each meeting has a different agenda. During the first month, emphasis is placed on educating members about the bereavement process and the stages of grief. The second month meetings are particularly concerned with permitting the ventilation of feelings in a safe environment. Alliances within the group develop at this time. Meetings during the last month focus on future-oriented issues, such as values clarification and goals.

Occasionally, the leader will suggest specific assignments at strategic points for particular individuals. An example of such a homework assignment during the second month may be to write a letter to the deceased, and during the third month the homework may be to send for catalogues from all continuing education programs within a fifty-mile radius. The groups are neither encounters, sensitivity groups, nor psychoanalytic experiences. Leaders do not attempt to deal with pre-existing emotional disorders.

## APPLICATIONS

Bereavement Counseling workshops are equally effective for children or adults. Anyone who has experienced the loss of a signficant person—parent or spouse, child or lover, friend or relative—needs to complete the mourning process in order to get on with the tasks of life. A Bereavement Counseling workshop provides help for those who need support in passing through the stages of grief.

---

# Bibliotherapy

### Sharon Henderson Sclabassi

## DEFINITION

Bibliotherapy is a technique that utilizes the reading of literature. The belief that reading can affect an individual's attitudes, feelings, and behavior is as old as reading itself. Bibliotherapy involves the reading of selected literature, planned and conducted as a treatment procedure with therapeutic objectives. It is not an esoteric technique, but is founded upon an acknowledgment of the dynamic process that takes place within the reader.

In the professional literature, Bibliotherapy is usually defined in terms of its objectives. The objectives of the technique and the values attributed to it are numerous, thus creating many definitions. For example, it has been defined as a "technique for the development of wholesome principles of conduct and the prevention of delinquency ..." (Kircher, 1966), or "the prescription of reading materials which will help to develop emotional maturity and nourish and sustain mental health" (Bryan, 1939). Despite the many objectives, all definitions include the reading of literature to achieve specific desired results.

## HISTORY

Throughout history, dating back to ancient times, the concept of growth through reading is evident from various writings. Although the value of books had long been recognized, the underlying concept of Bibliotherapy was not formally identified until the twentieth century.

Among the first professional people in America to set the tone for Bibliotherapy were two physicians, Benjamin Rush in 1815 and John Minson Gait II in 1853. They recommended reading as part of a patient's treatment plan. In 1904, it became recognized as an aspect of librarian ship, and the first partnership between librarian-ship and psychiatry began at the McLean Hospital in Waverly, Massachusetts. Other professionals, such as educators and psychologists, became interested in the subject.

During the next several decades numerous articles were published on Bibliotherapy. Although much of the writing indicated uncertainty and speculation about the new concept, a definite trend toward expansion was obvious. The exploration of new approaches was investigated, with practical applications outrunning theoretical projections. It was not until 1949 that a comprehensive attempt was made to formulate a theoretical base for Bibliotherapy (Shrodes, 1949).

Several decades have passed since Bibliotherapy became recognized as a therapeutic technique, and it continues to be applied for various purposes. However, it still remains largely unexplored, and not all is known about its application and effects.

## TECHNIQUE

Depending upon objectives and level of intervention, either diagnostic or imaginative literature is employed. If didactic literature is utilized, the objective is generally to facilitate a change within the individual through a more cognitive understanding of self. The literature is instructional and educational, such as handbooks, documents or how-to books. Subjects that may be included are child rearing, marriage and sex, coping with stress, relaxation and meditation.

Imaginative literature refers to the presentation of human behavior in a dramatic manner. This category includes novels, short stories, and plays. The theoretical base postulates a relationship between personality and vicarious experience. The reader is simultaneously involved and detached from the story, as is true in the vicarious situation. In psychoanalytic terms, the process may be explained as paralleling the primary phases of psychotherapy: identification, catharsis, and insight.

There is no one particular manner of applying Bibliotherapy in the treatment situation. For example, specific literature can be recommended or "prescribed" by the therapist for reading between sessions and discussed subsequently, or the actual reading may take place in a group session and serve as a springboard for personal disclosure, or the therapist may read a story as an adjunct to a play therapy session. Bibliotherapy has been viewed both as a major technique as well as an adjunct to various other therapeutic means.

No explicit methodology exists for the selection of appropriate reading materials. There are bibliographies that list suggested literature for use in therapy; however, it is most important that the therapist know not only the patient but also be familiar with and appreciate literature.

## APPLICATIONS

Bibliotherapy has been utilized in a variety of settings for a number of specific problems. People in various parallel professions have been involved in its application. It has been utilized extensively in neuropsychiatric hospitals as well as in outpatient psychiatric treatment. It has been applied to children, adolescents, and adults, in short-term or long-term treatment plans, and for a variety of psycho-pathologies .

The objectives of the application of Bibliotherapy are numerous. Using both didactic and imaginative literature, the levels of intervention may be divided into four broad areas: intellectual, social, behavioral, and emotional (Sclabassi, 1973). On the intellectual level, Bibliotherapy is used to stimulate the individual to think and analyze attitudes and behavior between sessions and allow the person to realize that there are choices in the way problems are handled. The individual may obtain facts needed for solution of problems, and acquire knowledge about human behavior to help understand one's own self and gain intellectual insight. It may also widen the individual's sphere of interests.

On the social level, Bibliotherapy can be used to expand an individual's awareness beyond his own frame of reference and to increase social sensitivity by being, in the imagination, in the place of others. It may be used to reinforce social and cultural patterns, absorb human values, and give a feeling of belonging. It may also help channel socially unapproved expressions of emotion and impulse, and facilitate the reader to form satisfactory life goals and thus live more effectively.

Behaviorally, Bibliotherapy can contribute to competence in activities. It can also give the individual an opportunity to experiment imaginatively with various modes of behavior and envision the probable effects. It may help to inhibit infantile behavior, promote growth in reaction patterns, and develop wholesome principles of conduct.

Emotionally, Bibliotherapy may provide a vicarious experience without initially exposing the person to the risks of actual experience. The reader may gain confidence in talking about problems ordinarily difficult to discuss, due to such feelings as fear, shame, or guilt, and it may encourage discussion without the initial embarrassment of explicit self-revelation. It may enable the reader to bring submerged feelings and experiences to consciousness, effect controlled release of unconscious processes, and develop emotional insight. It may provide successful solution of similar problems in others, thus stimulating eagerness to solve one's own problems. It can also help the individual to understand the motivations of self and others in a particular situation.

# Biocentric Therapy
## Nathaniel Branden

### DEFINITION

Biocentric Therapy is a cognitive-experiential approach to problems of development, personal growth, and self-actualization. It developed around a perspective that sees human beings, first and foremost, as living organisms whose primary task is to exercise their capacities effectively to satisfy their needs and thereby preserve and enhance their well-being. The way in which an individual deals with this task is seen as the key to his psychology.

If a person is to act effectively, if he is to maintain and further his life, he requires a knowledge of his environment, of his own state of external and internal reality, of the world, and of self. Thus, Biocentric Therapy sees a person's mental functioning as being psychologically maladaptive to the extent that the functioning of his consciousness is unimpeded by blocks; his psychology is biologically maladaptive to the extent that blocks obstruct the functioning of consciousness.

Thus, a central goal of therapy is to remove obstructions to awareness and restore the integrated power of the mind.

### HISTORY

The biocentric approach, developed by this author, was first presented systematically in my book *The Psychology of Self-Esteem*. The primary background of this approach is in philosophy, specifically in the Aristotelian orientation and, more recently, in the Objectivist philosophy originated by Ayn Rand. My approach does have important differences, however, with both of these schools.

The most significant aspect, perhaps, of the evolution of Biocentric Therapy is an increasingly experiential orientation, a greater focus on an emotional self-awareness and self-acceptance, and the unblocking of feelings as a pathway to the integration of mind and emotion.

### TECHNIQUE

Biocentric Therapy tends to see "symptoms" as representing undesirable "solutions" to real problems arising in the course of the individual's development. The blocking or disowning of feelings, for example, can have obvious short-term functional utility for a child struggling to survive in a terrifying and painful environment—even though there are very real long-term dangers in learning this strategy.

The goal-directed character of "neurotic symptoms" cannot be adequately understood without an appreciation of a human being's need of self-esteem and the profound role this plays in his development. Self-esteem is defined in Biocentric Therapy as the experience that one is competent to live and worthy of living.

As a being with the ability to seek awareness or to avoid it, to exercise his mind or to suspend it, he carries the responsibility of knowing that his method of functioning is appropriate to reality, to the requirements of survival and well-being, to the need of self-esteem. Self-esteem is seen as varying inversely with reality-avoidance strategies.

Virtually all techniques aim at making the client conscious of reality-avoidance strategies, conscious of the goal such avoidance strategies are intended to fulfill; they aim further at opening awareness to alternative pathways to well-being.

Methods to achieve this vary from a variety of emotional-release processes, to psychodrama, to fantasy exercises, to breathing exercises, to homework assignments, to designed experiments with new types of behavior, to what is perhaps the most distinctive technique used in Biocentric Therapy: sentence-completion work. In this technique, the client is given a sentence stem and asked to keep repeating the stem with new endings. Then a new stem is provided, building on clues suggested by the earlier responses, and so on, taking the client deeper and deeper into his feelings. This results in an explosion of awareness that is simultaneously cognitive and experiential.

The primary values transmitted in Biocentric Therapy are those of self-awareness, self-acceptance, self-responsibility, self-assertion, and personal integrity, all of which are seen as being indispensable to self-esteem.

Biocentric Therapy differs from cognitive-oriented therapies in its heavy emphasis upon emotional-release work and emotional self-awareness. It differs from the emotion-oriented therapies in its heavy emphasis on the cognitive component of learning and growth.

It is easy enough to pay lip service to the ideal of integrating thought and feeling, mind and body in the course of doing therapy. It is unlikely that any psychotherapist would dispute the desirability of this ideal. However, psychologists who emphasize the intellect, cognition, reason, often tend to take a disparaging attitude toward emotions. On the other hand, psychologists who emphasize emotions and specialize in emotional-release types of therapy tend to be hostile to reason and the intellect, though there are exceptions. Biocentric Therapy does not sharply dichotomize conscious and subconscious, but thinks instead in levels of awareness or unawareness and holds that the making conscious of material viewed as profoundly subconscious is not nearly as difficult as certain schools, notably psychoanalysis, seem to believe.

## APPLICATIONS

Biocentric Therapy has been used successfully with a wide variety of problems, ranging from sexual disorders, anxiety, and depression to alcoholism and a host of other such behavior disorders. However, its primary focus is less on the treatment of symptoms than on the process of personal growth and self-actualization—the opening up of the individual's positive personality potentials. A great many problems are seen to fall of their own weight, without requiring separate and specific treatment, with the removal of blocks to self-actualization and with a greater utilization by the individual of his powers and abilities.

# Bioenergetic Analysis

## Elaine Waldman

### DEFINITION

The core of Bioenergetic Analysis brings us back to the energetic and functional unity of mind and body. We do not simply *have* bodies; we *are* our bodies. Our living bodies are expressions of our total selves—our past and present, our personal and interpersonal experience, our conscious and our unconscious attitudes, our motion and our emotions. We are embodied beings.

In this functional unity of human experience, Bioenergetic Analysis recognizes antithesis. Energetically, in every aspect of the individual, the presence of the opposite is implicit. When this oppositional dimension is energized, it can make contact with its polar counterpart and move into a new integration of life force at a higher energy level. One-sided individuals tend to exhaust themselves in struggle and become run down energetically.

At the same time, the unitary process is an organismic phenomenon. No matter how complicated individuals are, we function on an organismic level, as a single cell. The essence of the organismic function is pulsation—continuous expansion and contraction, charge and discharge, reaching out and pulling back, giving, and taking. In this way, we are always moving and our movement is regulated by the goal of pleasure and "grounding."

The principle of charge and discharge and their relationship to each other account for the energy level in the personality. The living organism can function only if there is a balance between energy charge and discharge. Breathing charges up the energy level, while self-expression discharges the energy. Since the two go on simultaneously, the amount of energy taken in will influence how much is given out and vice versa.

The difference between health and illness is our grounding of both pleasure and-reality functions in the pulsatory process of our biological life force. A person's balance and grace are based in this pulsatory process that couples the excitatory and the inhibitory in a functional unity. The complete loss of such rhythmic excitation is death.

The energetic movement within the organism is manifested by movement in the body fluids—the blood, lymph, interstitial fluids (between the cellular components of an organ), and intracellular fluids. The body's motility depends upon this involuntary flow of excitation. Experiencing this flow of excitation can take us beyond our anatomical boundaries into interaction with the world. We can thus become aware of the functional identity of ourselves and the world at the same time.

What disturbs the flow is muscular armor, based on chronic tensions and rigidities. Muscular armor is not a static phenomenon, but rather a dynamic contraction that has functioned chronically over a long period of time to block excitation or defend against a hostile environment. Since muscular armor has usually persisted for many years, release requires consistent work over an extended period if a significant difference in behavior and personality is to occur.

All the tension patterns of an individual add up to character structure, which is the way the self has chosen to survive in the world. As Dr. Alexander Lowen said in 1971, "Energy, tension, and character are interrelated since the total tension pattern controls the amount and use of the body energy. Therefore, bioenergetic analysis is basically a character analytic method of seeing people." Character armor both blocks and asserts our way of being in the world. It is a way of saying no to the self in order to say yes to existence. To survive in childhood, a system of defense is often necessary and functional. In Bioenergetic Therapy, a person begins to experience both the blocks and their origins. As the character armor begins to soften, pulsations fill deadened areas of the body with a new consciousness of life.

Grounding ourselves in our body and in our relationship to the earth is the main contribution of Bioenergetic Analysis to character analytic work. When we can identify with our flesh and blood, our needs and desires, our participation in reality we are grounded. The functions of grounding, as Dr. John Bellis has pointed out, are related to the development of the ego and its contact with reality: 1) its motor functions—standing, rising, walking, 2) its perceptual functions, including the integration of what is heard and seen with its motor functions and its intellectual functions, 3) its vocal functions, including the individual's attainment of his own voice and an extended somatic character typology, the harmony of heart with ego functions.

## HISTORY

Bioenergetic Analysis was developed by Dr. Alexander Lowen out of Wilhelm Reich's theory of muscular armor and life energy. As a student of Reich in the 1940s, Lowen absorbed Reich's innovative energetic concepts: the muscular basis of character armor and the physical basis of the libido in the energy economy of the body. Reich called this energy "orgone energy," derived from the term "organ-ismic," and used such therapeutic techniques as touch to loosen bodily rigidities, deepen the breathing, increase the pulsations, and release the life force, with the goal of full orgasmic potency. In the process of modifying Reich's work, Lowen dropped the term "orgone," and added the concept of grounding, and techniques that include structured exercises and stress positions.

In 1956 Lowen, with his colleague Dr. John Peirrakos, founded the Institute for Bioenergetic Analysis in New York. Other centers and institutes have developed around the country, including, most notably, Stanley Keleman's in California and John Bellis's in Connecticut.

## TECHNIQUE

The basic bioenergetic technique integrates direct body process and experience with an understanding of the character and grounding patterns in the body. Character patterns can be recognized in the body's form and motility. For example, masochistic bodies are dense and highly muscled; rigid bodies are unyielding and stiff; schizoid bodies are fragmented; psychopathic bodies are often top-heavy.

By getting in touch with the language of the body the individual becomes aware of the layers of his armor. The experience of their defensive function invokes new sensory patterns. New pathways to the brain are thereby generated with excitement, form, and imagery.

When, in the first instance, we find ourselves maintaining social position with a determined jaw, a stiff neck, and fixed eyes, we discover that our face to the world is masking our inner feelings and blocking energy input from the environment. There are two techniques of enlivening the energy underneath the mask: first, by pressure over certain parts of the face (such as the labial levator muscle), which releases the ability to smile; second, by making a face as children do and connecting it to an appropriate sound, such as a lion's roar. The eyes and voice will often tell us what the person really feels behind the mask.

When, in the second instance, we find ourselves tightening our abdomens, inflating our chests, and locking our legs, we discover that we are utilizing our long skeletal muscles to hold back anger and sexual feelings and, at the same time, stopping the unexpressed energy from flooding us. Stretching seems to diminish the ability of the muscle to hold energy. The technique of lying down and kicking the bed helps to unbind the energy by increasing breathing and triggering pulsatory sensations. The technique of hitting the bed from a standing position will get the energy moving toward the ground and mobilize the individual's aggression against his own character blocks.

When, in the third instance, we find ourselves gritting our teeth, constricting our breathing, and tightening our throat, we discover that we are utilizing the muscles of the joints and sphincters to take up stress that had been released elsewhere. For example, if we sense our jaws clenching and our voice choking up, we may discover that we are trying to block an unwanted response to the sexual feelings in our pelvis. The technique of accompanying every release phenomenon with vocal sound—such as crying, sighing, singing, laughing, shouting, and screaming—will inhibit this segmental armoring by stabilizing the energetic release and the individual capacity to flow.

When, in the fourth instance, we find ourselves barely breathing and clutching our solar plexus, we discover that we are utilizing the diaphragm and the semi-voluntary muscles of digestion, respiration, and the voice to deaden ourselves against anxiety and alienate the horror in a threatening environment. Techniques to restore natural breathing patterns include the use of a bioenergetic stool, which is an adaptation of the old wooden kitchen step stool. One or two tightly rolled blankets are strapped to the stool. If you lie with your back over the stool and relax, your breathing deepens spontaneously. The pelvis, abdomen, thorax, and throat will expand in turn as each of them is filled by the waves of inspiration moving upward and will, in turn, let go as the expiratory wave starts at the mouth and flows downward to the pelvis that moves slightly forward. Such total body action may contact suppressed feelings of sadness and sexuality in your stomach and fear of reaching out in the chest. Crying and other vocal sounds, like singing and laughing, not only release the feelings but also connect the ego functions with the heart.

As the person's energy level is increased through deepened breathing, the pathways of self-expression through the eyes, voice, and movement need to be opened up for the release of increased energy. Since life is an energetic process, breathing, pulsation, and expression are not simply devices to liberate some feeling, but rather a life system to generate, expand, and focus organismic growth, and thus achieve, in a word, grounding.

Grounding techniques enable us to possess our energies as well as express them. The technique of pitting the individual against the field of gravity helps to bring out negative feelings about giving in or collapsing. The field of gravity represents the social stress of our success-oriented culture, which has been introjected (via the family) into the ego at the expense of our pleasure functions. Our fear of falling or failing prevents us generally from falling asleep, falling in love, and giving in or letting go. Ultimately, terror of collapse results in a physical collapse of the body. After giving in to the force of gravity, the individual is able to give in to the natural functions of the self. Combined with direct work with the body armor, including massage, controlled pressure, and gentle touching, the bioenergetic parts come together and find roots in the human ground.

## APPLICATIONS

Bioenergetic Analysis applies not only to our way of being in this world—how much coordination and grace we have, where there is weakness and where rigidity, which parts are overdeveloped and which deprived, and where there are habitual constrictions—but also to our way of becoming—how we face the unknown, our sense of helplessness in the midst of the new, what happens to us when old boundaries break down, our incompleteness, anxieties, our hunger for the embodiment of more wholeness, contact, feelings, sexuality, and tenderness. Both expansion and containment are involved: on one hand are the people whose hearts long for love, whose feelings insist on expression, whose bodies want to be free; on the other are those whose defenses choke off impulses, whose anxiety may lead to retreat and closing off, whose depression may keep the energy level low, desires at a minimum, and life immobilized.

Bioenergetic Analysis applies to those who are willing not only to *know* themselves but also to *be* themselves, and to those who want to go beyond the known. It applies to those who want to develop a sense of identification with their biological processes and to those who feel alienated. It applies to those who wish to awaken their emotions and to those who wish to care for and nurture their felt excitation. It applies to those who seek a capacity for deep feeling and to those who feel inhibited in sexual expression. It applies to those who want to affirm themselves as individuals and to those who feel themselves bound up in the stress syndrome.

Self-confidence comes from restoring our natural life rhythm, vibration, and pulsation. The pulsatory process enables us to go out into the world and back to the self in a continuous exchange of sensations and information. As we recognize the self talking to the self, our innate responsiveness becomes clear: we are engaged in generating an internal body that hears our voice, expresses our knowing, and gives us a wholeness of being in this world. This, the enhancement of our life process is the ultimate application of Bioenergetic Analysis.

# Bioplasmic Therapy

## Earl J. Ogletiee

### DEFINITION

Bioplasmic Therapy is based on the concept that all living matter contains energy forces and a material or physical body. This energy (called etheric or bioplasmic forces) works in a formative way on physical, emotional, and intellectual development in the human being. This invisible energy keeps the body chemistry and organs functioning properly, is responsible for regeneration, growth, and reproduction, and is the builder and molder of the physical body and energy force for speech and cognition. These are the forces others have claimed to have photographed using the Kirlian photographic process.

### HISTORY

Through the ages the bioplasmic or etheric body of energy forces has been known as "subtle body," "etheric body," "fluidic body," "beta body," "counter body," "prephysical body," to name a few.

Rudolf Steiner (1861–1925), philosopher, scientist, and educator, rediscovered the etheric forces in 1900 and applied them to the areas of education, therapy, medicine, and pharmacology. The etheric forces are the basis of homeopathic and acupuncture medicine.

Research by Russian and American scientists and Steiner found that not only are the organs and the physical body maintained in their form and development by the flow of the etheric forces throughout the body, but each organ has an independent, yet intradependent etheric body. Underlying the physical brain is an etheric brain, the physical liver, an etheric liver and so on. Kirlian Photography has shown that the physical body and organs appear to mirror what happens.in the energy bodies.

The physical cells and organs of the body are in reality temporal deposits of these dynamic, metamorphosing etheric current flows, moving at various rates throughout the body. Fingernails and hair grow rapidly; it takes ten days for the substance of the liver to be replaced; seven years to replace all the skin cells; and six months for new molecules to appear in the bones. Every cell and organ is the effect; the etheric current flow is the cause.

The existence of the etheric or bioplasmic forces are evidenced when a limb falls asleep. When normal circulation returns, there is a "needles-and-pins" sensation, indicating a return of the bioplasmic body to the physical limb. Additional evidence is the phantom limb phenomenon. A person with a missing limb often continues to sense the physical limb as if it were still there.

Another factor is the phenomenon of regeneration. Human beings do not have the power of cell and organ regeneration as lower animals do. For example, a flat-worm can completely regenerate itself when cut in half longitudinally or transversely; a rain worm can regrow a tail; a lungfish, a severed fin; and an amphibian can regrow an amputated limb. In the human being, who lacks the ability of organ and limb regeneration, these etheric forces are transmuted into the higher functions of personality and cognitive development.

Good health is the free and unimpeded circulation of energy, flowing from organ to organ, along an invisible network of intercommunication channels affecting the flow of blood and fluids to cells and tissues; Illness is the result of a blockage and imbalance of the natural flow of these etheric currents.

## TECHNIQUE

The various methods of stimulating the etheric energy flow include: acupuncture with needles, massage, chemical stimulation, electrical and laser beam stimulation of the acupoints on the skin surface, or by eurythmic therapy. In medicine the two techniques of revitalizing the etheric forces are homeopathic medicine and acupuncture .

Homeopathy is based on the concept that the basic mineral and plant medicinal elements were created by etheric forces. The patient is given a medicinal element (lead, copper, carbon, etc.) in a micro-dose form that is similar to, and duplicates, the symptoms of the illness. The micro-dose (one part of the element to one or ten thousand parts sugar water) creates simulated symptoms of the illness in the patient, causing the etheric to overreact to the diseased portion of the body, restoring normal etheric current flow, cell regeneration, and finally, health.

Acupuncture works similarly except it is accomplished by stimulation of one or more of the eight hundred acupoints on the skin surface using a needle, massage, or heat. This brings about a rebalancing and normal flow of energy along one or more of the fourteen meridians, affecting rehabilitation of the afflicted part of the body.

Eurythmy (created by Rudolf Steiner in 1912) is another method of etheric energy stimulation. Eurythmy (not to be confused with Dalcroze's "eurythmics," a form of dance to melody) is a disciplined movement of the arms and body that visibly expresses the vowels and consonants of speech and the tones and intervals of music. The eurythmic gestures relate to speech, the definite forms produced in the air when a word is spoken. The eurythmic gestures emulate these air formations (speech and song) by the movement of the arms and body.

Steiner studied the movement of the organs of speech as they produced the sounds and found them to be akin to the etheric current movements in the body. He discovered that the air formations created by the spoken word and song are an image of the etheric forces that created them. The etheric forces, the basis of growth, regeneration, health, and personality, and cognitive development, also produce speech and singing.

As indicated, illness, disease, and depression can result from misdistributed, unbalanced, or weak etheric energy flow. In order to prevent pathological conditions, or to improve a condition if something has already gone wrong, these misdirected etheric current movements have to be removed, rebalanced, arid strengthened. This is how eurythmy is used as a therapeutic art of movement. That is, the formative movements of speech, which are the creation of the etheric forces, are transformed into the movements of the body through eurythmy. The integral relationship of speech and psychology develops by means of the etheric forces making eurythmy a natural media to stimulate etheric current flow in a wholesome way.

## APPLICATIONS

In eurythmy the formative laws underlying speech and music are carried over into the larger expressive movements of the arms and body. There are three types of eurythmy: speech, tone, and therapeutic. Speech and tone eurythmy are performed on stage as an art form, as a teaching media, and as a therapy. Therapeutic eurythmy differs from its artistic counterpart in that the movements are emphasized more dynamically and with more intensity for particular maladies. Unlike the other forms of eurythmy, therapeutic eurythmy exercises are prescribed by a physician.

Some exercises have psychological benefits while others are for physical disorders. For example, the "a" exercise (crossing of arms) gives strength and self-confidence to a shy or depressed person. The "e" exercise (stretching movement) corrects poor posture and curvatures of the spine. The "u" exercise (parallel movement of arms) improves blood circulation and improves coordination. Some eurythmy exercises wake up the person physically and mentally while others build physical substance and stamina in the body.

In summary, eurythmy can have a healing effect on the respiratory, nervous, and metabolic system and other organs of the body by rebalancing the etheric or bioplasmic forces of growth and development. It takes four to five years of intensive training to become a eurythmist.

# Bio Scream Psychotherapy
## Nolan Saltzman

### DEFINITION

Bio Scream Psychotherapy, also known as Bio Psychotherapy, is a direct, responsible way to help a patient learn to feel safe with his deepest emotions.

### HISTORY

Two schools of psychotherapy that elicit screaming, associated with the names Casriel (New Identity Group Process) and Janov (Primal Therapy), originated independently in the early 1960s. A few years later, Bio Scream Psychotherapy evolved from the New Identity Group Process at a time when Casriel groups, still strongly influenced by the Encounter Therapy for drug addicts at Synanon, were often filled with hostility and the threat of humiliation.

My purposes in creating Bio Psychotherapy were to provide greater emotional support to my individual patients and to structure my groups to encourage warm, empathetic exchanges among group members. What was therapeutic, I came to believe, was that the patient experiences his climactic screams, which can be uttered only at a moment of abandonment of defenses, thus bringing about rapport with others.

# TECHNIQUE

The principal process of Bio Scream Psychotherapy involves eliciting emotional cries in a setting where they meet with a validating response. I call this process "Scream/ Love" or "S/L." The "Scream" referred to is one of several kinds human beings can produce: it is a biological expression of emotional pain, the intense form of the need for love. "Love," or good feelings toward the patient, is abundantly available (from the therapist in one-on-one Bio Psychotherapy and from fellow patients in the group form) when the patient's expression is the open scream of emotional pain. Similarly, in response to the scream of fear, comfort and reassurance; to the roar of anger, at least an acknowledgment of the anger, and often much more, an empathetic sense of a common triumph; to the cry of joy, a sharing of the joy.

Here are three techniques of Bio Psychotherapy, briefly sketched. (At the end of this section I list a number of others.)

1. *Helping the patient achieve climactic emotional expression.* A patient isenabled to identify his emotion, perhaps using one of the modal phrases—"I'mscared," "I hurt," "I'm angry," or "I feel good." He is asked to repeat the phraselouder and more rapidly, that is, with less time for recovery between phrases.

The therapist knows what a biological expression of emotion looks and sounds like. He guides the patient toward the movement and vocal resonances that allow a complete release. For example, when a woman with a lot of suppressed anger beat at her thighs in frustration at not being able to sound angry, I said, "You don't have to punish yourself anymore. Hit out with your fists!" I urged her to scream louder, more angrily, and to "blast out" with her voice. My own voice, crackling with anger, suggested the staccato quality she was striving toward.

When the therapist hears the naked resonances of the scream emerge in the modal phrase, he says "Just say, 'Ahhh,' " and urges the patient on to the climactic release.

The goal is for the patient to learn (or relearn) to feel safe with his emotions so that they are no longer fearful and painful to him. Thus, the therapist may say, "It's safe to express all that fear," or "It's safe now to let out all that pain." When the patient works through the complete expression of one or more of the emotions, he generally feels very good, even exhilarated. The therapist shows his own pleasure in the patient's work, embracing him if appropriate and, in the group setting, inviting him to go around to receive the love (embraces) of his fellow group members.

What has this to do with real life? Everything. One who has learned (for example) to feel safe roaring out his anger can say, when necessary, "I'm not going to stand for that—cut it out!" and his voice will have an assertive edge to it. One who has screamed out his pain, and felt safe with it, can say to a friend or lover, "I need you," and his voice will have a quality that draws others to him.

2. *Paracatastasis, or projecting a significant figure in order to deal with him asthough he were present.* To elicit feelings toward a spouse or lover, or a parent,who may even be dead and so unavailable for a confrontation, the therapist maysay, for example, "See your mother in that chair." (The therapist looks to the emptychair as though seeing her there.) "What would you like to say to her?" Thetherapist helps the patient identify his emotion and urges him through the completeexpression as in technique #1, above. Afterward, the

therapist may say "Look ather again. What's she doing now?" It is a remarkable aspect of the mind that thepatient will often be able to see his mother as though she were present, and makinga characteristic response. "She's turning away"; or "She's saying 'How dare youopen up your mouth to me.'" "And how do you feel about her saying that?"Thus, a long, overdue emotional dialogue may be initiated.

3. *Abreaction of early trauma and deprivation.* Some patients come to the first session ready to deal with a lifetime of pain and emotional deprivation. Others swiftly reach that level in the course of attempting to organize an emotional expression, or in projecting a parent into a chair. The therapist asks the patient to lie down on a mat. The therapist often takes his hands. I sometimes cradle my patient's head against my side or chest when he is screaming out (abreacting) early pain.

The heart of Bio Scream Psychotherapy is this: the therapist gives love to the patient. The love evokes the patient's pain, fear, and rage at never having gotten what he needed in infancy and childhood. He is able to scream out his early emotions and learn once more to feel safe with his own needs.

Paying too much emotionally for love, or playing Don Juan, or drug, alcohol, or junk-food addiction, or impotence in men or lack of orgasm in women—these and other self-defeating patterns serve to avoid situations in which some feeling must be expressed. Often the feeling is so fundamental that it would scarcely be said in so many words, such as, "I have the right to be loved." Bio Scream Psychotherapy, in allowing the patient to learn once again to feel safe with his emotions, prepares him to engage in rewarding love relationships.

(In the cassette set referred to in the Bibliography, I discuss the above techniques in much more detail, and also treat many others. Space limitations permit me only to list a few here: *eliciting emotions from dreams and memory fragments; changing dysfunctional attitudes and expectations in love relations with scream/love methods; confrontations.*)

## APPLICATIONS

Bio Scream Psychotherapy works for a wide range of neurotic and character/disordered patients. It does not work well for psychotic patients outside of a residential setting. It has not been adequately tested for psychotics in a residential setting.

It is not a miracle cure. It may be considered a miracle that it exists at all, that with hard work and love a therapist can help a truly committed patient effect great changes, even a new integration of his character in a briefer time than a conventional therapist could have imagined. One reason for the very high rate of success of Bio Psychotherapy is that we skim off the cream of the patient population. We do not attract patients who merely want to mark time. Those who want a "miracle cure" bounce out in a session or two. Those who throw themselves into the work make the miracle happen.

# Body Energy Therapy

## Hector A. Prestera

### DEFINITION

Body Energy Therapy is a somato-psychic approach to evolutionary blocks in any given personality structure. It is based on the premise that during growth, not only are psychological adaptations made to various stressing forces but also physical compensations are produced. It is on these physical compensations that Body Energy Therapy focuses attention. In short, the body is a physical template reflecting the interactions of our whole self in its entire historical perspective. Certain generalizations in terms of body structure allow for a typology to be produced that may be exemplified as that of a needy person, an overburdened person, a rigid person, or an overblown person. It would be simplistic to consider that only the above four adaptations suffice to describe every human personality. In fact, the physical modes of adaptation are far more complex and have been summarized elsewhere (Kurtz and Prestera, 1977). The central notion of Body Energy Therapy is that a person's physical stance in the world is a direct statement of his emotional stance.

### HISTORY

The concepts included in Body Energy Therapy are a product of some ten years of personal work by the author in private practice as well as at the Esalen Institute in Big Sur, California. This work summarizes the antecedent and pioneering conceptualizations elaborated by Wilhelm Reich, Ida P. Rolf, and Fritz Perls. These pioneering geniuses established the unquestionable validity of the theoretical framework that sees the mind-body as a functional whole. In their work they make repeated references to organismic functioning. The duality that Western culture has produced, separating consciousness into functions of the mind or head from that of the instincts or body, was refuted by their work, which integrates the two. The principle to be underscored is that our life at any given moment is a function of all our awarenesses, be they mental or physical.

### TECHNIQUE

Knowing that our expression at any given moment reflects the posture of our entire being, it becomes possible—through observation, looking without attachment, and listening for what surfaces—to contact those areas in the total body and mind that are obstructed from free flow. The therapist may then intervene in several ways. In any case the therapist aids in the resolution of an energy impasse by the addition of his energy. This may take the form of energy directed at the site of a block, for example, at the jaw, if it is clenched and held in anger (remembering that this is in reference to a fixed posture of anger, not simply a transient expression). To release this holding, the therapist may directly manipulate the held musculature or, on the other hand, the therapist may encourage verbalizations or energetic sound releases on the part of the subject. Both of these approaches have been incorporated from the aforementioned therapies of Reich, Rolf, and

Perls. More unique to Body Energy Therapy is the addition of the therapist's energy in still another direction. In this latter case, the therapist recognizes that within the total being there exists a force that is expansive and directed toward self-healing equal to that which is obstructing life growth. It is apparent that if a block exists, then it exists in opposition to a flow. Behind the anger of a clenched jaw, which expresses striking out and hence separation, there exists an equal force that reaches out toward inclusion rather than separation. The therapist is then in a position to feed energy into the force that wants to be included. For example, in group therapy an individual may sit rigid and unyielding outside the circle, only to become pliable, flexible, and joyous when openly invited within.

## APPLICATIONS

The applications of this technique include both those directed at diagnosis through body analysis and those directed at therapy for resolutions of intrabeing conflicts. Often, simply bringing awareness—this being the therapist's only energetic contribution—will allow the subject to heal himself from within. This was alluded to above as the inner life self-healing force, which is always present.

# Breathing Therapy

*Magda Proskauer*

## DEFINITION

Breathing Therapy uses the breathing function, at times combined with small movements, as a tool for the achievement of greater awareness. One learns to experiment with one's breath in order to become conscious of hindering influences, so that the realization of certain obstacles can introduce the desired change. The breathing function proves valuable for allowing subliminal feelings and sense perceptions to come to the surface because of its intimate connection with the emotions as well as with the two kinds of nervous systems: the voluntary consciously directed one and the autonomous or vegetative one, which works without the mind. Normally, we breathe automatically from the moment of birth, but we can also take a breath or hold it for a certain time. In this respect respiration differs from other autonomous functions, such as digestion. The stomach and intestines cannot be contracted by will. The breath thus forms a bridge between the conscious and unconscious systems. By watching it one can observe a normally unconscious function at work, one can learn to exclude interferences, and thus help self-regulating processes to set in, such as yawning before becoming overtired, sighing before feeling overly restricted.

## HISTORY

Movement has fascinated me from early childhood, and through calesthenics, athletics, and sports, I learned the sense of joy and release that any genuine movement can bring about. In my case the release from too rigid a pattern of behavior and social adaptation. At the age of twelve the Mensendieck system of gymnastics was my first introduction to the new direction movement and dance were to take. This led me to a degree in physiotherapy from Munich University Medical School, hospital work in Germany, Yugoslavia, New York Presbyterian Medical Center, and private practice. During these years I had ample opportunity to explore the traditional ways of treatment with the application of breathing exercises to asthma, polio, cerebral paralysis, and related diseases. Already during my early studies the growing development of psychoanalysis had shed new light on the psychosomatic character of many disturbances. Orthodox therapy was confronted with challenging questions and new schools of thought arose.

Practical work with some of these schools shaped my technique to a considerable degree. The strongest influence on my work was the analytical psychology of C. G. Jung.

## TECHNIQUE

Instead of correcting faulty habits we take the individual breathing pattern, disturbed as it may be, as the point of departure. One concentrates on the act of breathing, observing its inner movement until the breath left to itself finds its way back to its genuine rhythm. One learns to experiment with one's own nature and harmoniously train the body for its own purpose We try, for instance, to locate the place where we can feel the movement of the breath within. Or lying on one's back with the knees bent we focus on the phase of exhalation by slowly and gently expelling the air while we allow the abdominal wall to sink toward the back. We then wait until after a slight pause, and the inhalation occurs by itself, as if a balloon were blown up within the abdominal cave. This is diaphragmatic breath. Or one learns to visualize an inner body space while simultaneously concentrating on one's exhalation, as if the breath were sent into that particular space. We may choose to experiment with a small movement of a joint, like the hip, by slightly bending it with the incoming breath and releasing it with the outgoing breath as if the breath were opening up a tight joint. After a few repetitions one is asked to compare the other hip to find the possible difference. Or one experiments with the weight of one's body or its parts by trying to give it over to gravity while exhaling, which leads to release of tensions and the experience of one's inner weight.

## APPLICATIONS

Just as we behave, move, and act according to our specific makeup and express ourselves uniquely through gestures, so does our breathing pattern express our inner situation. The usual arhythmic breath goes with our normal diffusion of attention and changes with emotional states: agitated in anger, stopping in fear, choking with sadness, sighing with relief, etc. Normally, when at jest and at peace, one breathes more with the diaphragm. Complete chest breathing occurs only at times of maximum stress or maximum effort. To express it simply: where the abdominal breath is disturbed, the inner life is disturbed, one is driven, unreceptive, and may live too intentionally.

On the other hand, those who cannot open their chest cage are often anxious, inhibited, self-conscious, with a sense of inferiority. With neurotics we frequently find a reversed breathing pattern. During inhalation the abdomen gets pulled in tightly and there is almost no exhalation. The bottle is filled with consumed air. In our work with the breath we allow these faulty patterns to reverse themselves.

# Dynamically Oriented Brief Psychotherapy

*D. H. Malan*

## DEFINITION

Dynamically Oriented Brief Psychotherapy is a form of psychotherapy conducted within an arbitrary limit of about forty sessions, in which the therapeutic aim is to give the patient insight about unconscious conflict.

## HISTORY

Psychoanalytic treatment is generally regarded as a very lengthy process, in which the patient is seen several times a week over a period of years. Throughout its history, however, sporadic cases have been observed in which marked improvements follow after only a few sessions. It has generally been supposed that such patients can only be those with mild illnesses of recent onset, that the technique should be superficial, and that this leads to an essentially superficial therapeutic result. In 1946, Alexander and French published a series of case histories that strongly contradicted this view, but their work was never generally accepted. In the 1950s and 1960s, however, attempts were made to investigate the subject systematically at three main centers in the English-speaking world: the Tavistock Clinic in London (Malan); the Massachusetts General Hospital in Boston (Sifneos); and the Montreal General Hospital (Davanloo). Although these three schools differ in their approach, all agree on the same fundamental observation: patients exist who can be selected according to known principles, who do not necessarily suffer from mild illnesses of recent onset, with whom a far from superficial technique can be used, and who show permanent and apparently deep-seated improvements.

The present article will concentrate on these three schools, but it is to be noted that many non-English-speaking centers also exist, notably in Lausanne under Gillieron, in Basel under Beck, and in Buenos Aires under Kesselman.

## TECHNIQUE

The three main schools agree on certain fundamental principles of patient selection:

1. Patients who are obviously unsuitable must be eliminated from the beginning: those showing strong suicidal tendencies, serious danger of depressive or psychotic breakdown, poor impulse control, chronic alcoholism or drug addiction, or extreme dependence.
2. Correspondingly, the patient must be judged to have the basic strength to face his anxieties without breaking down, and to carry on life independently after termination.
3. The patient must: view his problem as psychological; be able to interact with the

interviewer in an emotionally meaningful way; have the motivation not merely for symptom relief, but for achieving emotional growth through acquiring insight about himself.

4.   The initial evaluator must be able to formulate a feasible therapeutic plan or focus in terms of some aspect of the patient's pathology that needs to be worked through.

The three schools agree on the following main aspects of therapy technique:

1.   The therapist must plan a limited aim or focus from the beginning and follow this single-mindedly. This may involve selective neglect of other aspects of pathology, but if the patient is correctly selected and the focus is appropriate, most of the material will be relevant to the chosen focus.

2.   The main therapeutic tool is *interpretation:* that is, explaining to the patient aspects of his feelings of which he is as yet unaware.

3.   One of the major therapeutic techniques is to show the patient that feelings that he has toward the therapist—for which the word "transference" was coined by Freud—are derived or transferred from similar feelings directed toward important people in the patient's past, especially parents. This is identical with one of the basic principles of psychoanalysis.

There are also certain clear differences among the schools: for example, I tend to set a time limit from the beginning whereas the other two do not; Sifneos tries to *bypass* resistance, while I interpret it; and with certain types of patients, Davanloo employs a highly active technique, forcefully confronting the patient with his avoidance of painful feeling.

Correspondingly, the range of patients treated differs among the three schools:

1.   Sifneos concentrates on patients suffering from conflicts involving an over-intense, guilt-laden, sexualized relation with the parent of the opposite sex ("Oedi-pal" problems). With such patients, treatment lasts about fifteen sessions.

2.   I accept patients of this kind but also accept many others, particularly those suffering from intense mixed feelings (ambivalence) about important people in their lives, and those suffering from unresolved dependence and deprivation, provided this is not too severe. Grief and anger about the loss of the therapist at termination may figure prominently in therapies of this school, which also tend to be longer than those of Sifneos—up to thirty sessions.

3.   Davanloo, by his confronting technique, is able to extend the range to include certain types of passive, obsessional patients who would not be considered by the other two schools. He has demonstrated dramatic results with such patients, with therapy lasting up to forty sessions.

Ali three schools have demonstrated that the results of their forms of therapy can consist not only of symptomatic recovery, but also of extensive reorganization of the patient's personality, lasting for a follow-up period of up to ten years after termination.

## APPLICATIONS

This kind of therapy can be applied in any psychiatric setting, though it of course requires well-trained therapists or at least experienced supervision. It has been applied in the psychiatric departments of general hospitals (including in-patient departments), in psychiatric emergency services, student health services, psychotherapeutic clinics, and private practice. It depends on the careful selection of suitable patients, but when correctly used it results in a marked increase of efficiency. Straker has descrive the beneficial impact of Brief Psychotherapy on a psychiatric department burdened with long waiting lists and poor staff morale. The methods are particularly important at the present time in the United States, in view of schemes for financing a limited number of psychotherapeutic sessions through health insurance.

# Burn-Out Prevention

*Gurushabd Singh Josephs and Gurucharan Singh Khalsa*

## DEFINITION

Burn-Out Prevention addresses a major problem among staff members of psychiatric clinics, drug abuse clinics, and crisis intervention centers: "burn-out." Burn-out is a chronic low-level fatigue that is the result of Constant encounters with difficult clients. Burn-out causes therapists to protect themselves by contacting their patients less fully or by treating their patients automatically and impersonally. It is not uncommon for those affected by burn-out to choose to leave their profession entirely.

Burn-out can be prevented. Through techniques that raise the counselor's energy level and improve clinical work, the Burn-Out Prevention workshop offers a viable alternative to a problem faced by ali those in parallel professions.

## HISTORY

Burn-Out Prevention was developed in 1976 by the authors. Since then, the Burn-Out Prevention workshop has been given at six regional conferences of the Association for Humanistic Psychology, at the AHP Eastern Education Conference, and at the AHP National Conference. This workshop has been taught throughout the country as part of in-staff training at counseling centers, hospitals, mental health, and alcohol clinics, and as an accredited course at graduate schools.

## APPLICATIONS

This kind of therapy can be applied in any psychiatric setting, though it of course requires well-trained therapists or at least experienced supervision. It has been applied in the psychiatric departments of general hospitals (including in-patient departments), in psychiatric emergency services, student health services, psychb-therapeutic clinics. and private practice. It depends on the care ful selection of suitable patients, but when cor-rectly used it results in a marked increase of efficien-cy. Straker has described the ben-eficial impact of Brief Psychotherapy on a psychiatric department burdened with long waiting lists and poor staff morale. The methods are particularly important at the present time in the United States, in view of schemes for financing a limited number of psycho-therapeutic sessions through health insurance.

## TECHNIQUE

The Burn-Out Prevention workshop applies the ancient teachings of Kindalini Yoga to the specialized needs of the therapist. In each of the following areas, yogic and meditative techniques are used to build the therapist's resilience and to increase his effectiveness.

1. *The human aura.* It is currently becoming recognized and accepted that human beings have around them an electromagnetic field, the visual manifestation of which is called the aura. Kirlian Photography, a photographic process that produces an auralike image on film, demonstrates that happiness can increase the radiance of an aura while depression, even the mere presence of a depressed person, can reduce the aura's radiance. Participants in the Burn-Out Prevention workshop learn to experience their own magnetic field and that of others, to change the quality and quantity of their aura, and to ensure that contacts with their patients are positive and nurturant.

2. *Intuition and creative therapy.* Often the therapist will contact a client through empathetic techniques that reduce his own equanimity, consequently reducing his effectiveness. The Burn-Out Prevention workshop teaches yoga and meditation techniques that open the therapist to working within an intuitive mode. At such a time the therapist's reactions and interventions are perfectly tuned to the patient's needs, and the truly creative breakthroughs occur. This is not an accident. The Burn-Out Prevention workshop teaches the therapist to increase the frequency and effectiveness of the intuitive mode.

3. *Defense mechanism relaxation and healing.* When a therapist has identified a client's problem and has created a nurturant environment, he is then ready to effect a positive change in the client. This involves relaxing defense mechanisms and preparing the client to receive the therapist's healing energy. The Burn-Out Prevention workship teaches the art and science of using the power of the voice to work through defense mechanisms and contact clients. Relaxation techniques, special meditations, yoga therapy, and massage are used in various combinations to help a client develop his own healing inner rhythm.

4. *Becoming more effective.* The difference between an average therapist and a truly effective therapist can lie as much in their own personal lives as in their behavior in their clinical work. Participants are shown techniques to make their own lives more consistently free of depression and anxiety, thereby making them stronger and more effective in their personal relationships, as well as their relationships with clients and colleagues.

## APPLICATIONS

Originally designed for psychotherapists and drug rehabilitators, Burn-Out Prevention has been found to be effective for psychiatrists, psychiatric social workers, "hot-line" counselors, nurses, educators, the clergy, and all those who work in professions of close human contact.

# C1C2 Project Psychotherapy
### *Dorothy Tennov*

## DEFINITION

C1C2 projects aim to provide peer support and "counseling" on a one-to-one basis. They are based on the premise that many women go to psychiatrists and psychotherapists because it is helpful at times to talk about one's self, one's decisions, and one's troubles to a person who is committed to focusing attention on *you*, but who is not a close friend or member of your family. Respectful attention without interpretation or analysis, without fear of challenge or interruption is helpful when trouble strikes or when decisions must be made.

No distinction is made between those who provide assistance and those who receive it (in fact, we tossed a coin). "C1" is the person focused on (counselee) and "C2" is the listener in a given session (counselor). A person could be a C2 one day and in need of a C2 another day.

## HISTORY

In recent years women have found their experiences in small group sessions to effect profound and positive changes in their lives. For many, it may have been the first time that they were listened to both respectfully and attentively. In the nonjudg-mental and unhurried atmosphere of the consciousness-raising session, women discovered again and again that what they had perceived as personal, even neurotic, problems were, in fact, the inevitable result of living in a sexist society. As the society was understood through the testimonies of group participants, a commonality of oppressions emerged. Thus, individual guilt and social isolation were replaced by concepts of political solution and the experience of sisterhood.

The focus in consciousness-raising, therefore, is primarily on individual problems as they relate to the comprehension of a society in which women are regarded as second-class citizens. Careful detailing of individual situations is an essential aspect of this process. However, when an individual demands and elicits response in the form of advice and evaluation, there may develop negative consequences both to the consciousness-raising experience and to interpersonal relationships within the group.

The guidelines for consciousness-raising and C1C2 are very similar. In both, respectful attention and freedom from challenge, criticism, and interpretation are fundamental. C1C2 is a one-to-one relationship in which C1 has the opportunity to dwell at length on the minute details of her situation.

## TECHNIQUE

The following guidelines constitute basic training for the role of C2:

1. Listen attentively and respectfully. Try to understand the situation from C1's point of view. Your goal is to help her decide what she really wants to do.

2. Do not give advice.

3. Do not be dishonest, but also do not feel obliged to express all your reactions and feelings. Your opinions are best left unsaid, especially if they are negative or critical. You do not use the methods of encounter groups.

4. Respecting C1 means accepting her at face value. It means hearing what she said, not what you think she meant. Assume that she makes sense and that if you do not understand, you are the one with the problem. Listen harder.

5. Exert no pressure on C1—not even subtle pressure. Be careful that questions of clarification never sound like criticisms or attacks.

6. Do not feel obliged to do anything. A sympathetic ear has great value in itself.

7. Freely give any information that you happen to have that may be useful to C1, or try to help her secure that information. You might want to collect a file containing information about available community services, but be careful that giving information is not done in such a way that it sounds like giving advice.

Self-management procedures may also be taught (Tennov, 1977) if C1 is interested in them.

## APPLICATIONS

Although designed as a self-help service for women, C1C2 procedures are applicable over a wide range of situations. The crucial concept is the acceptance of C1 at face value, as opposed to interpretation, especially psychoanalytic interpretation. The procedures are designed for use by parents, educators, and members of the clergy, as well as by those employed by an organized C1C2 group.

In the years since the C1C2 procedures were first presented, various groups have come into existence across the country. The major problem encountered was at the structural/financial level. It is recommended that the C2 be provided with compensation at a skilled clerical level. The purpose and value of a C1C2 project is to make the service available at low cost. It is based on the findings of outcome research which suggest that training for psychotherapists is unrelated to effectiveness (Tennov, 1976).

# Catalyst Therapy
## Nelita Ano

### DEFINITION

Catalyst Therapy is a method of psychotherapy that originated out of a need to communicate with children who were not readily accessible to the traditional approaches to therapy. In this method of therapy two modalities of communications are used: drawing and language. These two methods of communication act as catalysts to stimulate patient-therapist interaction.

Catalyst Therapy is a brief method of psychotherapy that can be used as a communication bridge between the child and the therapist. It is used with children who are overwhelmed by guilt feelings, who have a tremendous sense of aloneness, or have had catastrophic experiences that immobilize them. Catalyst Therapy focuses on the child as a communicator of change and as a communicator of past history. The boundaries of the child are vulnerable to intrusion and so the therapist offers two ways of communicating to protect the child and to help him to relate at a pace that is less threatening than usual communication methods.

### HISTORY

Catalyst Therapy evolved as the author recognized the need for broader communication modalities when working with children who were not readily accessible to traditional therapeutic approaches.

Winnicott's (1971) use of the squiggle game suggested the effectiveness of graphic communication with children. In personal communication, Robertson and Barford (1970) suggested the long-range significance of graphic communication. Singer (1973) and others have indicated the significance of images as they relate to the inner world of childhood. It was out of this background that I evolved Catalyst Therapy, which uses a graphic/language therapeutic approach.

### TECHNIQUE

Catalyst Therapy is a three-stage method of therapy. In the initial communication the child and therapist draw one or more pictures together. Verbal communication is minimal.

The therapist says, "We are going to draw a picture. Watch." The therapist then draws a tree, a path, or some other environmental feature. The therapist then says, "Now you draw."

This dual graphic communication continues until the session terminates. As the therapeutic process develops, the verbal communication changes and becomes more diversified. However, children in Catalyst Therapy are reluctant communicators, so it is important to proceed slowly to prevent the child from becoming inaccessible again.

If the child is responding with some autonomy, the therapist then moves on to the second stage by introducing an animal with humanlike characteristics. Animals such as a mouse or a rabbit are usually unthreatening and can become easy vehicles for such exploration as anger, sexuality, etc. The child may then be ready to focus on a more aggressive type of animal, such as a tiger. The graphic communication thus offers a broader channel to express aggression safely, which is frequently necessary for reluctant communicators. When communicating through animals appears to be developing without too much anxiety, the therapist then initiates the third stage by introducing the use of communication through thoughts and through words. Balloon-shaped drawings are placed above the animals, in a manner similar to the balloon shapes used in cartoons. However, there are broken-line balloons for thoughts and dreams and solid-lined balloon shapes for words. This is both a recognition of the thought process of children and an expanded way for the child to respond. Usually the child will initiate more direct communication in this stage of graphic/language communication by saying, "I want to talk," or expressing in different words a wish to be a more direct communicator.

### APPLICATIONS

Catalyst Therapy is a short-term therapy that offers entrance into more traditional psychotherapy. It is effective with pediatric populations who are usually in the hospital only briefly. It has proved useful with selected anorexia nervosa patients. It has also been helpful with children who have poor self-concepts and feel threatened by a predominantly verbal or acting-out therapeutic approach.

# Cathartic-Meditative Therapy

*Bernard J. Somers*

### DEFINITION

Cathartic-Meditative (CM) Therapy represents a model of human beings capable of moving from distress and rigidity to liberation from the cumulative effects of pain, oppression, and rigid cultural patterns. All humans are moving naturally toward greater lovingness, responsibility for self and others, creative intelligence, and discovery. The CM therapist knows that the cumulative effects of stress, distress, conflict, oppression, and family and cultural patterns can obscure this naturally expanding state of human beings. The therapist joins with the natural healing and synergistic (cooperative) forces in the person, among which we can include, as a minimum, the urge to discharge painful emotion (such as anger, fear, embarrassment, hurt, boredom) by talking, crying, raging, shaking and trembling, yawning and laughing; the individual's agency (will); the creative, imaginative, problem-solving intelligence of the person; the human's emancipatory drive to overcome all forms of oppression, internal as well as external; our desire for loving and cooperative relationships with all other humans.

Strategies are devised for compassionately and effectively opposing the client's illusions, rigidities, and repetitiousness, distractability, hatred of self and others, addictions, and other forms of human irrationality. Healing-synergistic actions occur best in those human relationships marked by safety, trust, transcendental love, compassionate understanding, inventiveness, and playfulness. The CM therapist identifies with the spiritual essence, the vital center of awareness in all human beings.

## HISTORY

My present synthesis of psychotherapy reflects the dialectic of helping relationships that I have experienced and processed over a twenty-five-year span of clinical work and thinking. The years are much less important than these experiences and my synthesis. My commitments have included: Client-Centered Therapy; Psychoanalysis and Analytic Psychology; Reevaluation Counseling (developed by Harvey Jackins of Seattle; the supporting theory for cocounseling); communicational pragmatics; meditational systems and Psychosynthesis; and body therapies. My relationship to cocounseling (the helping modality in which two persons alternate as client and counselor, exchanging effective help with each other) continues to be of great benefit to me personally as well as in my therapeutic work and thinking.

## TECHNIQUE

CM therapy emphasizes emotional release, the meditative attitude towards one's experience, validation and support for the client, and rational thinking and actions.

The most basic technique is the nontechnical, holistic, flexible use of my awareness from moment to moment with my client—how he is experiencing and viewing himself, his world. This free attention of mine works best in the framework of a positive, evolution-oriented model of the person. It is my capacity to see this person in a nonjudgmental way, accurately noting how he is similar and different at this moment from himself and all other persons I have known in the past. The less emotional distress and negative attitudes I have, the more clearly and flexibly I convey my awareness to this person, the client. I think about how my client might feel, think, and act if he didn't have his pain, rigidity, and feelings of powerlessness. His visions of such a utopian future are encouraged.

I am interested in and focused upon my client's painful feelings; his rigid, repetitive thoughts and actions; the person's difficulty in attending to these feelings, thoughts, and actions with nonjudgmental attention; my client's loving, creative, and imaginative strivings; validating and supporting my client as the essence of will, energy, love, and responsibility in his perceptual "sea" of distress and demoralization; this person's mastery, accomplishments, and success.

I am especially active in helping the client experience and release painful emotions with such methods as: focusing; body movements; self-appreciation; role playing; guided imagery; meditation; repetition of phrases and postures that allow for discharge of feelings. Where possible, I train the client in specific meditation work, taking account of his cognitive style, style of emotional control, degree of free attention, and interests. Meditation and other forms of homework are drawn up by a contract method. Homework can include affirmations and other forms of self-appreciation that support positive thought and energy.

The emphasis is on getting the client to *do* something different in the therapy session and then out in the real world. This something different is new or further discharge of painful feelings, thinking different thoughts and taking different actions, including those with the body. I place less emphasis on reporting interpretations to the client. I do name rigidities in thought and action that I have observed and for which I have created, or inspired the client to create, some useful interruption.

I support my client at all times. I do not support his negative evaluations of himself. I support his essence, his rationality, his creative imagination, and respect his experience of painful emotions. I do not consider his feelings to be a definition of him as a person or a reliable guide for his thoughts and actions.

The dumping of my painful feelings, such as anger, disappointment, fear and embarrassment, on my client seems ridiculous, unimaginative, unfair, and downright inefficient. I take these feelings to an appropriate setting where I can work on them. The therapist can never afford to neglect working on his own case, hopefully using the very methods that he finds helpful when doing therapy with others.

### APPLICATIONS

CM Therapy is useful in one-to-one psychotherapeutic work, and with couples, families, and groups. Each member of the group is helped in those communicational patterns that block the effective use of the therapeutic model that has been described here. The goal is to facilitate the use of each member as a helper for the other members of the group. This is the essence of what is done in a cocounseling class.

In addition to the above applications, this model has practical use in other helping relationships, such as health-care worker/patient relationships, supervision, classroom teaching, child rearing and child care work, and in all of our personal relationships. Finally, therapeutic work on the effects of oppression can be facilitated greatly with the use of this model.

---

# Chiropractic
## *Julius Dintenfass*

### DEFINITION

Chiropractic is the health profession that concerns itself with the communication and control systems of the body, particularly the nervous system, and their relationships to health and disease.

### HISTORY

Although widely separated in location, there are interesting parallels in the origin and development of the therapeutic approaches of Freud and the American, D. D. Palmer. Both have links to the brilliant eighteenth-century physician Anton Mesmer, who ripped esoteric healing from the supernatural. To Mesmer, all health or sickness had to be explained in terms of natural laws or physical forces. His investigation of bodily and mental disorders led him to demonstrate that many people could be made well by using subtle energies and forces of the body, which he called "magnetic" healing. It was his theory that "magnetic" forces acted through the body, accounting for both disorders and the process of healing. These forces could be influenced by manual contacts to the body of a static or stroking nature. He also investigated the state of trance and determined that he could devise a basic procedure to place people in this condition for therapeutic purposes. This, of course, is now known as hypnosis.

Freud first resorted to hypnosis in his search for a better treatment of mental diseases. He learned this method, originally called mesmerism, from the famous French physician Charcot. Later, he collaborated with Josef Breuer in employing hypnosis in the treatment of cases of hysteria. In 1895, he discarded this practice for one he found to be more effective—free association. This was the kernel from which the new analytical psychiatry, psychoanalysis, was developed.

At the same time, in America, a frontier doctor, Daniel David Palmer, was practicing magnetic healing. Paul Carter, an internationally known practitioner of magnetic healing, taught him this art, which was much in vogue at that time. Palmer practiced this method with success for a period of ten years. He utilized various local body contacts, and the stroking of the body in different directions, to affect the flow of body forces or energies.

In 1895, searching for better methods to help his patients, Palmer made an extraordinary discovery. He found that the manual corrective structural adjustment, applied specifically to subluxations (minor displacements) of the vertebral column, had a more positive therapeutic potential than could be accomplished by magnetic healing methods alone. It was this discovery that evolved into the chiropractic profession.

Palmer's revolutionary concept was that, in order to survive and function effectively, the human body must transfer information between tissue cells and organ structures in widely referable parts of the body. In 1910, Palmer frankly admitted in his book, *The Chiropractic Adjuster*, that although he was not the first person to replace a displaced vertebra manually (spinal manipulation can be traced to the ancient Greeks and Chinese), he was the first to determine the effect of the spinal adjustment upon the functions of the nervous system.

Today the chiropractor is recognized as a doctor and a primary physician by all fifty states as well as in many countries abroad. He is thoroughly trained in the healing arts at chiropractic colleges accredited by the United States Office of Education.

## TECHNIQUE

Contemporary chiropractic practice emphasizes a holistic approach to health and disease, utilizing modern methods of diagnosis and emphasizing nondrug therapies designed to restore and maintain the homeostatic balance of the body. These procedures include structural correction of the body by manual and mechanical means; nutritional and dietary guidance; various instruments of physiotherapy for rehabilitation to stabilize and maintain maximum function; and guidance to help the patient obtain a proper balance between the emotional, nutritional, and mechanical aspects of health.

The unorthodoxy of the chiropractic approach has allowed it to advance into a number of new areas of knowledge relating to health and disease. This includes body-oriented procedures using specialized manual and mechanical methods of restructuring nerve pathways in order to restore normal communication. The profession has developed techniques employing light manual skin contacts to activate the neurotransmitters and receptors located in abundance in the outer coverings of our bodies. A more recent contribution is the development of applied kinesiology, which performs both diagnostic and corrective functions.

A most unique part of the chiropractic examination is known as structural analysis. This is a diagnosis of the body's compensations to the force of gravity, known as basic and compensatory compensations. It considers the fact that when a weight-bearing structure is distorted, the body automatically attempts to restore body balance by developing compensatory counter distortions. Included in this chiropractic analysis is the evaluation of the ratio of the curves of the spinal column, body posture, chronic contraction and tension of muscles, spinal fixations, joint mobility, and the kinesiological testing of muscles. These factors are of great significance in determining the differential diagnosis of a problem and in setting up a treatment program for the patient.

## APPLICATIONS

Psychopathological reactions may be the cause of or may occur as a result of structural stress. Disturbance of psychic energy may cause muscle spasm, visceral dysfunction, distorted posture, and imbalance in muscle action and body mechanics. With these physical defects the pattern of total input and output of the nerve tracts of the musculoskeletal system is disturbed and distorted, forcing the spinal cord to deal with conflicting reports from the periphery of the body, and affecting basic vital functions. Chiropractic care, by correcting these disturbances in the neuromusculoskeletal system, reduces abnormal input to the spinal cord and the cerebrum, lowering cortical activity, allowing a return to homeostasis not only of the body but also of the mind.

This author's case history files, gathered over a period of forty years, and those of his colleagues, contain many recoveries from different phases of mental illness. These patients go to chiropractors because they are troubled by acute or chronic pain. Some patients may have old neurotic problems, whereas others may react neurotically to their present painful condition. In many instances the development of pain may trigger patterns of anxiety, compulsion, depression, or hostility, as well as phobias complicating their condition.

The manual techniques used bring the chiropractor in close physical contact with the patient. At the same time, these manipulative procedures set in motion physiological and psychological changes. For example, when a spinal fixation is released, there are changes first in the vertebral complex: relaxation of muscle and ligament contractures and an increased flow of blood to the part with decreased irritation of local receptors. Breathing and pulse rate become more regular. Simultaneously, there is relief from pain, a feeling of ease and well-being, and a marked change in the attitude and posture of the patient. Our clinical experience shows that after completion of a period of progressive rehabilitative chiropractic care, dissipation of anxiety, hostility, depression, and other problems of mental health usually occurs.

In conjunction with chiropractic treatments, patients are taught that they must assume some responsibility for their physical state. They are involved in helping themselves to stabilize and maintain their physical improvement. They are given guidance on how to use their bodies more efficiently in their daily activities of sleep, work, and play.

I do not contend that all psychophysiologic problems are responsive to chiropractic care. When the chiropractic physician recognizes that the patient has a deep neurotic or psychotic problem, a referral is made to a psychologist or psychiatrist. There is often a successful team effort between practitioners with psychotherapy and chiropractic care proceeding simultaneously.

# Christian *Psychotherapy*
## William P. Wilson

### DEFINITION

A recent condensation and summarization of the three basic forms of psychotherapy—the dynamic, the behavioral, and the experiential—has been published by Karasu (1977). He has provided a framework within which we can evaluate a technique with standardized dimensions, which I shall use to present my concept of Christian Psychotherapy. Christian Psychotherapy is defined here as a therapy that uses as its base the concept of the nature of man and the teachings about conflict resolution and behavioral control that are found in the Bible. This framework is completed by incorporating compatible theory and techniques found in the disciplines of psychiatry and psychology.

### HISTORY

Although pastoral counseling has been performed since the beginning of the Christian church, it has been a real concern of the church only during the last few decades. Because there was no historical precedent for the development of a discipline that began with a distinctive Christian base, secular concepts have been seen as sufficient to meet the needs of persons who counseled Christians. Only a few writers have begun with a Christian base and have attempted to elaborate a truly Christian psychotherapy. (The reader is referred to Tweedie's excellent historical review found in his book, *The Christian and the Couch*.)

### TECHNIQUE

The starting point of all psychotherapies is the concept of the nature of man. The Bible teaches that man's nature has three parts: flesh, soul, and spirit (1 Thess. 5:23). The flesh is made up of more than the body, for it also incorporates the biological drives such as sex, sleep, and appetite. These give rise to certain behaviors that serve to satiate the appetites. The soul has within its functions the things that psychology places in the intellect. The spirit is an animating force that resides in man and operates through the flesh and soul.

In the Christian psychotherapeutic scheme, the spiritual aspect of man's existence is of great importance, for it is in this area of functioning that God operates. Christians believe that there is a prime mover in the universe, and that he is God (Rom. 1:19, 20), a person who manifested himself in the form of man, Jesus Christ. This Jesus died, was resurrected, and, after returning to the Father, sent His spirit (the Holy Spirit) to live in believers in order to reveal truth, to give power and to fill them with love for their fellow man. God is experienced transcendentally by man through His spirit (1 Cor. 2:12) and His word (2 Tim. 3:16), the Bible. One of the most useful ideas in the Christian belief system is that God gives his followers the power to live according to the values he has given them in the Bible.

In his discussion of psychotherapy, Karasu used eleven dimensions. The reader is referred to his work for details. We will use his conceptual framework here.

Christians believe that at birth man has an inherited force called sin and that this force causes him to want to control and guide his own destiny. He cannot obey God's rules. Because he disobeys, he remains alienated from God and is not whole. When he is incomplete, he suffers. When he rebels, his behavior brings him pain, which causes him to suffer.

The prime concern of the Christian psychotherapist is, therefore, man's alienation from God and his lack of wholeness. His concept of pathology is that incompleteness gives rise to emptiness and meaninglessness, and his rebellion gives rise to suffering because of the consequences of sin.

The concept of health usually considered to be characteristic of Christian Psychotherapy is that of holiness or wholeness. Wholeness or sanctification begins with a transcendental experience (salvation), but at the outset man remains incomplete. After salvation, the Christian life is one of constant self-inspection and therapy. Confession, reproof, instruction, and the performance of good works in love are all part of the process through which behavior is modified and men are made whole. It is necessary to emphasize the point that the body also be whole, for our view of the nature of man includes the body.

The mode of change in Christian Psychotherapy involves a synthesis of the various mechanisms used by the proponents of three kinds of psychotherapy—depth insight, direct learning, and immediate experiencing. Christian Psychotherapy adds as its primary goal reconciliation with God. With the completion of the man, the use of the three modes of therapy described by Karasu is enhanced.

In Christian Psychotherapy, we have to recognize that the "present is viewed through the past in anticipation of the future." (Marias, 1971) Therefore, an understanding of the past is necessary to determine what changes must take place in order that the new patterns of behavior can be established. The objective reality of the patient's present situation must, therefore, be examined in order to determine the significance of the subjectively remembered past. The intellectual and emotional knowledge gained can be used to help the patient understand his current behavior. After the therapist and patient have examined their findings in the light of the biblical ideas, it is then easier to change behavior.

The Christian therapist begins by establishing an atmosphere of mutual acceptance in order to encourage the patient's self-expression. He has to determine his relationship to God, and to make this right, if it is wrong. He then has to uncover conflicts and assist in their resolution. If behavioral patterns need changing, he must program, reward, and shape responses. The therapist must further determine the order in which he will undertake these tasks.

The Christian psychotherapist should use all of the tools and methods commonly used in psychotherapy. He uses such techniques as free association, structured interviewing, persuasion, dream interpretation, hypnosis, psychodrama, visualization, role playing, and others to help the patient get in touch with his long-repressed feelings, so that he can take definitive action to deal with them. He will then use forgiveness and surrender as a method of ridding the patient of the undesirable emotions that have so influenced his behavior.

Conversion, as mentioned before, is an essential condition of Christian therapy, especially if this has not occurred. The fact that it is a useful and desirable change is documented in the secular literature (Wilson, 1972). Prayer and the understanding of biblical ideas concerning conflict resolution and behavioral control are part of the therapy. Prayer, Bible study, and worship outside of the therapeutic sessions also help the patient continue to focus on a problem until he can effect a change. Finally, the promise of love, joy, and peace (Gal. 5:22, 23), to say nothing of abundant life and eternal life (John 10:10; Mark 10:30), are powerful incentives for working toward healing.

The treatment model utilized by Christians will be varied. Carlson presented Jesus as relating in roles that were priestly, pastoral, and prophetic. These are the same roles that are assumed by therapists in Karasu's system. Jesus was critic, preacher, teacher, interpreter, mediator, confronter, admonisher, advocate, sustainer, supporter, lecturer, advisor, burden bearer, listener, reprover, warner, helper, consoler, and pardoner. Christian therapists cannot, therefore, commit themselves to a single role model. Their treatment model must be all-inclusive.

If Christian therapy is to be effective, there must be something unique about the nature of the therapist-patient relationship. The relationship must be a loving and accepting one. The therapist assumes the role of a knowledgeable fellow struggler in a harsh world. It is an accepted fact that both draw on the same source of strength and wisdom. The therapist is a disciplined guide.

Earlier, we discussed the role and stance of the therapist as varied. His stand should, therefore, be varied. There are times when he will be loving, accepting, permissive, gratifying, direct, problem solving, and practical. At other times, he will need to be indirect, dispassionate, or frustrating. Each stance, however, will be taken in love.

## APPLICATIONS

Christian psychotherapeutic techniques are applicable to all illnesses where wholeness is a desirable therapeutic outcome. It must be recognized that psychotherapy, whether secular or Christian, is not considered to be a primary treatment for biologically determined diseases such as manic depression and schizophrenia. If used in either, it must be recognized that Christian Psychotherapy is applied with caution. We have found it to be inadvisable in manic-depressive illness of the manic type. It has not proved useful in schizophrenia. The technique is particularly useful in alcoholism, drug addiction, chaotic personalities (the adult who was a maltreated child), and neurosis. The Christian dimension of therapy should be applied only in those patients who do not object to its inclusion in the therapeutic effort.

# Client-*Centered Therapy*
## Douglas D. Blocksma

### DEFINITION

Client-Centered Therapy is a method of counseling devised by Carl Rogers that stresses empathic listening and dependence on the client's perception of himself, his problems, and his resources. The counselor limits himself to reflecting stated thoughts and feelings, whether done in a one-to-one or group setting. The counselor controls the client only with regard to length and time of sessions. The client is free to vent his feelings in any way he sees fit without benefit of intervention, interpretation, or imposition of counselor values. No diagnosis, no case history, and no evaluative judgments are made. However, there is a tacit encouragement for the client to be expressive, to deal with the present or past, and to prescribe goals or action for himself as he sees fit. Meanwhile, the counselor practices participative listening.

### HISTORY

Carl Rogers is a psychologist who recognized early in his career that children as well as adults could do a lot of independent altering of their lives if given understanding and love. He turned away from the moralisms of religion, from the testing methods of psychology, and from the diagnostic and interpretive methods of psychiatry. He utilized his intuition, experience, and research methods to develop a nondirective or client-centered system of reacting to counselees.

He made his first observations of the effect of counselor behavior on clients during the 1930s at the Rochester (New York) Guidance Center. During the early 1940s, he researched Client-Centered Therapy at Ohio State University and wrote *Counseling and Psychotherapy*. This book contained one of the first of a long series of presentations of what was actually said by client and therapist in therapy sessions. From 1945 to 1957 he continued his therapy, research, and teaching at the University of Chicago. He published *Client-Centered Therapy* in 1951, which included some theory as well as applications of his viewpoint to settings other than individual therapy.

From 1957 to 1964, he worked with psychotics at the University of Wisconsin and then moved to La Jolla, California, where he developed a training center for therapists and leaders of organizations. Today he is active in applying client-centered principles to leadership education.

## TECHNIQUE

The client-centered therapist gives the patient the time and attention he needs to explore his situation in his own way and at his own pace. The therapist shows interest, patience, understanding, and humor; further, he reflects the emotional quality of the client's comments as he restates or rephrases what the client said. Rogers's research indicates that the therapist's sensitivity to the client's feelings and comments, and his nonjudgmental acceptance of them, helps the client to absorb anger or whatever feelings have created tensions, organ reactions, or relationship problems for him. If the client wants to deal with the past, he can do so. If he chooses to sit in silence, he may do so. If he wants to transfer his feelings to the therapist, the therapist will reflect this but not interpret it. Thus, a unique atmosphere is created in which the client can be himself and not be judged, rejected, or advised, which he probably has been in his everyday life.

Learning Client-Centered Therapy as a *therapy* takes years of disciplined training under supervision and observation via tapes and audio-visual aids. Learning reflections of feelings as a *technique* has been helpful to thousands of educators, ministers, business managers, policemen, and parents.

## APPLICATIONS

During the 1950s, at the University of Chicago, Carl Rogers recognized that client-centered principles could be effectively utilized in groups as well as individual relationships. He noted that his graduate classes, which were based on participation, free expression, and self-initiated learning activities, and were taught without prescribed curricula or grades, resulted in the same outcomes as in individual therapy. Throughout the 1970s, he has used groups almost exclusively in educating therapists and organization leaders. It is a rewarding experience to enter one of Rogers's groups and find that there is no one telling you what to do; nor is anyone competing with you for grades. Group members cooperate to help one another with whatever problems surface in the group. Members become co-therapists with Rogers. Learning activities are self-generated.

Thus, Client-Centered Therapy methods and attitudes can be applied in any setting where people interact with people. Client-Centered Therapy may not completely answer the problems of individuals and groups, but it can open up many normal and neurotic people who are well enough to communicate and to relate within normal limits.

During his fifty years in psychology, there has seldom been a workday in which Carl Rogers did not do individual or group therapy. Client-centered therapists have done research on therapy sessions that can be examined by any scientist in the field. Experience and research characterize Rogers's contribution which may be somewhat simplistic in its method but is profound in its effect.

Client-centered reflection of situational feelings is a technique that any therapist can use effectively in communicating. As a complete therapy, the client-centered approach can be used mainly with well-motivated, communicative clients. It does not work as a complete therapy with psychotics, clients with health problems, silent or resistive clients, or those who need diagnosis and evaluation for placement. Client-Centered Therapy is an excellent technique but is limited as a total therapy approach.

# Cognitive *Therapy*
## John Rush

### DEFINITION

Cognitive Therapy is an active, directive, time-limited, structured approach used to treat a variety of psychiatric disorders (for example, depression, anxiety, pain problems, phobias, etc.). It is based on an underlying theoretical rationale that an individual's affect (moods, emotions) and behavior are largely determined by the way in which he construes the world; that is, how a person thinks determines how he feels and reacts (Beck, 1967, 1976). His thoughts (cognitions) are verbal or pictorial mental events in his stream of consciousness. These cognitions are based on attitudes or assumptions (schemas) developed from early experience. For example, if a person is concerned about whether or not he is competent and adequate, he may be operating on the schema, "Unless I do everything perfectly, I'm a failure." Consequently, he may think about a situation in terms of adequacy even when the situation is unrelated to whether or not he is personally competent.

The symptoms of a disorder are related to the content of the patient's thinking. For example, people who develop depression have schemas concerned with self-dep-recation; those developing anxiety states have schemas concerned with the anticipation of personal harm; paranoid patients are controlled by thinking patterns relevant to unjustified abuse or persecution.

Cognitive Therapy techniques are designed to identify, reality-test, and correct maladaptive, distorted cognitions and the dysfunctional beliefs (schemas) underlying these cognitions. The patient learns to master problems and situations that he previously considered insuperable by reevaluating and correcting his thinking. The cognitive therapist teaches the patient to think more realistically and adaptively, thus reducing symptoms.

### HISTORY

Freud, Adler, George Kelly, Albert Ellis, and others have emphasized the importance of cognitions in psychopathology. Aaron Beck specified the critical role of cognitions in neurotic disorders (cognitive theory of emotional disorders). He has enumerated techniques to change cognitions in treating anxiety, depression, and other outpatient disorders. The most well-refined and researched cognitive therapy methods are those used with depressed persons. A number of psychotherapy outcome studies have shown the effectiveness of cognitive therapy in treating depressed outpatients (Rush, et al., 1977).

### TECHNIQUE

Cognitive techniques are aimed at delineating and testing the validity and reasonableness of the patient's specific misconceptions and maladaptive assumptions. Therapy involves highly specific learning experiences aimed to teach the patient how to do the following: a) monitor his negative, automatic thoughts (cognitions); b) recognize the connections between cognition, affect, and behavior; c) examine the evidence for and against his distorted negative cognitions; d) substitute more reality-oriented interpretations for his distorted negative cognitions; and e) learn to identify and alter the dysfunctional beliefs that predispose him to distort and negatively evaluate his experiences.

Behavioral assignments are used with more severely depressed patients not only to change behavior but also to elicit cognitions associated with specific behaviors. A sampling of these behavioral strategies include a Daily Activity Log, in which the patient logs his hourly activities; a Mastery and Pleasure Schedule, in which the patient rates the activities listed in his log; a Graded Task Assignment, in which the patient sequentially attempts various steps to accomplish a task that the patient believes is impossible. Furthermore, behavioral assignments are created to help the patient test out certain maladaptive cognitions.

Various verbal techniques are used to explore the logic behind, and basis for, specific cognitions and assumptions. The patient is given an initial didactic explanation of the rationale for Cognitive Therapy. Next, he learns to recognize, monitor, and record the negative thoughts associated with incidents in which he felt particularly upset (sad, anxious, etc.). The cognitions and underlying assumptions are discussed and examined for logic, validity, adaptiveness, and enhancement of positive behavior versus maintenance of pathology. For example, the depressed person's tendency to feel responsible for negative outcomes while consistently failing to take credit for his own success is identified and discussed as a specific verbal technique. Therapy focuses at times on specific target symptoms (such as, suicidal impulses). The cognitions supporting these symptoms are identified (for example, "Life is worthless and I can't change it.") and then examined with logic and empirical methods.

## APPLICATIONS

The therapist and patient work collaboratively to identify unrealistic cognitions and to test them out (by having the patient undertake, for example, certain homework assignments designed to check the validity of the thoughts and schemas). When unrealistic thoughts and beliefs are found, new, more realistic ones are substituted for the old ones. The patient is then asked to practice acting on these new thoughts and beliefs to see if they are realistic. Such use of homework assignments between treatment sessions not only maintains the patient's active participation but also provides an opportunity in his daily life to use the techniques learned in treatment.

# Cognitive-Behavioral Therapies

## Michael J. Mahoney

### DEFINITION

Cognitive-Behavioral perspectives represent an amalgam of biomedical, intrapsychic, and environmental approaches to human behavior. Generally speaking, the Cognitive-Behavioral therapist assumes that both adaptive and maladaptive behavior are determined by: a) biological factors (genetic as well as transient biochemical variables), b) psychological factors (e.g., the phenomenologically *perceived* stressor, irrational thought patterns, misperceived contingencies, and learned coping skills), and c) environmental factors (e.g., the density, clarity, nature, and compatibility of current stimulation). The relative contribution of each of these elements may vary from one case to another and one individual to another. Likewise, Cognitive-Behavioral therapists vary in their attention to these respective variables. This perspective defends both intrapersonal (psychological and biochemical) determinants as well as environmental influence. It likewise recognizes that the two arbitrary classes are interdependent and continuously interactive, suggesting that arguments about the primacy of person or environment are misdirected. Inter-actionism, or "reciprocal determinism," is suggested as a more appropriate conceptualization.

### HISTORY

Although its historical roots can probably be traced well beyond twentieth-century figures, the cognitive-behavioral hybrid owes much of its current visibility to a handful of relatively contemporary workers (Mahoney, 1977). The writings of George A. Kelly were particularly influential, as were the works of two of his early collaborators—Julian B. Rotter and Walter Mischel. In addition, Aaron T. Beck and Albert Ellis helped to emphasize the potential importance of irrational thought patterns in human distress and dysfunction. Finally, Albert Bandura was influential in developing a theoretical framework ("social learning theory") that offered an integrative structure to these diverse approaches. Bandura's book, *Principles of Behavior Modification* (1969), was instrumental in encouraging an interface between cognitive and traditional behavioristic traditions. This was accomplished via both conceptual and data-based arguments supporting the notion that human learning is basically a *cognitive*—rather than *conditioning*—process. Bandura was quick to point out, however, that these cognitive *processes* seem to be most efficiently activated by *procedures* similar to those employed by traditional behavior therapists. The opportunity for cognitive-behavioral interface was thus apparent, and an extensive literature was soon developed (cf. Mahoney, 1974; Mahoney and Arnkoff, 1978).

### TECHNIQUE

In Bandura's (1977) formulation, four primary forms of learning are recognized: direct associative experience, vicarious learning, symbolic instruction, and symbolic logic. Since therapy is viewed as a learning experience, these four forms are often integrated into Cognitive-Behavioral Therapy. Directed skills training (behavior rehearsal), for example, represents an application of associative experience. Symbolic, live, and imaginal models are often used to demonstrate skills and communicate realistic contingencies. Verbal techniques ranging from didactive instruction to logical self-scrutiny are relied upon in instances where irrational thought patterns or inadequate coping skills are believed to be operative (cf. Ellis, 1962; Beck, 1976; Meichenbaum, 1977). In many instances the techniques (or procedures) employed by the Cognitive-Behavioral therapist are not dramatically different from those used by more traditional behavior therapists (although it is also easy to find procedural differences). This may reflect the fact that the primary source of ideological divergence between these two groups lies more within the realm of presumed *process* (cognition versus conditioning) rather than *procedure*. Since the Cognitive-Behavioral therapist places greater emphasis on the potential importance of intrapersonal factors, however, it should be no surprise that his assessment and selected method of treatment often reflect this cognitive-affective concern.

At the molecular level of techniques, the Cognitive-Behavioral therapist employs many of the standard behavior modification procedures: self-observation, behavior rehearsal, contracting, relaxation training, desensitization, and so on. At the more molar level, however, these techniques are woven into a more broad spectrum approach that aspires to teaching coping skills that will serve the client in future stress situations. Generalization and maintenance are strongly emphasized, along with responsible client participation in the selection of therapy goals and procedures. Three somewhat overlapping categories of Cognitive-Behavioral Therapy are distinguishable: the cognitive-restructuring therapies, the coping-skills therapies, and the problem-solving therapies (Mahoney and Arnkoff, 1978). All share a varying emphasis on the use of direct, vicarious, and symbolic instruction such that the person's general adaptation skills are enhanced. These skills include accurate perception and evaluation of a stressor, the ability to identify and evaluate perceived contingencies, and the ability to participate actively in one's own coping through acquired cognitive skills.

## APPLICATIONS

Despite their relative recency, Cognitive-Behavioral therapies have been applied to a wide range of adult outpatient problems. To date, the most extensive documentation of their efficacy rests in the areas of anxiety disorders and depression, although considerable work is now underway in such areas as obesity, creativity, impulsivity, gerontological problems, and psychotic patterns. Overall, this research suggests that the cognitive-behavioral interface may well represent a promising and progressive problem shift in clinical science. There are, of course, the enthusiastic claims that usually accompany new arrivals in the arena of psychotherapy, but a more cautious optimism would seem preferable. Whether these clinical hybrids will survive the test of critical empirical scrutiny remains to be seen, but it seems clear at this point that they have at least demonstrated the need and potential promise of that scrutiny.

# Dynamic Cognitive Therapy
## Melvin L. Weiner

### DEFINITION

The fundamental tenet of Dynamic Cognitive Therapy is that the growth of cognitive processes—the ways in which we perceive, remember, reason, judge, solve problems, and learn—cannot be separated from the growth of personal and interpersonal processes—that is, how we develop self-esteem and a sense of identity, express and control impulses, and relate to other people. The aftereffect of a traumatic, disorganized, or deprived childhood is the partial or complete impairment of both these psychological processes. The goal of psychotherapy is to replace these faulty structures with more adaptive ones. The inherent limitation of our usual therapeutic methods is that the typical therapist-patient interaction is *verbal-idea-tional*, while the patient's impaired psychic structures have their origins in and remain on the *nonverbal-cognitive* level. The Dynamic Cognitive approach developed by the author (1975) succeeds in communicating on the cognitive level, making core conflicts and structures more accessible. As a result, it proves more effective in promoting growth.

### HISTORY

The Dynamic Cognitive approach reasserts emphases Freud gave early in his career to consciousness and reality relations, and to cognitive-affective structures (affect refers to moods and emotions). By systematically explicating the individual's cognitive style and its relation to his affective structures, we provide a link between the thinking of cognitive developmentalists—such as Piaget (1974), and Witkin and Goodenough (1977)—and psychoanalytic theorists, such as Kohut (1976), and Mahler, Pine, and Bergman (1976). Hence, our therapeutic approach is compatible with psychoanalytic ego psychology, and offers practical implementation for many of its theoretical and clinical insights.

### TECHNIQUE

When a patient's cognitive style gets him into difficulties in his daily life, instead of simply asking him to talk about it, the Dynamic Cognitive therapist says:

> I think it is important to find out how you actually see (or think, remember, or solve problems). I have some perceptual tasks that I would like you to do, but I am not only interested in what you see, but how you go about seeing the tasks and *what feelings* are associated with them. So when you are attempting to solve the various puzzles I am going to give you, try to tell me how you are going about it. Also tell me all the things that go through your mind, even the tiny details you might not ordinarily think

important. Let me know when you encounter any difficulty; and when there are any fleeting impressions or feelings or memories flicking through your mind, even those which you think aren't related to the task, tell me those because everything may be important.

Thus, instead of taking off only from dreams or emotional conflicts, the patient also proceeds from his current cognitive activities. We find that associations to a cognitive task typically lead back to critical developmental events that played an important role in the formation of the patient's present difficulties. Feelings, images, and events that he may have completely forgotten and that, up to that moment, seemed totally irrelevant return in full vividness and coherence. The most immediate gain is the breaking of tenacious resistance; the long-term gain is the opening up of new dimensions of both cognitive and affective processes that have been impairing the individual's current adaptation.

Eighty-five cognitive tasks in the visual, auditory, tactile, olfactory, and kinesthetic modalities have been developed. Each one is specifically designed and utilized in the course of a normal therapeutic session to help the patient become aware of the nature of his cognitive style and how it interferes with the attainment of gratifications and ability to cope with life's problems. Further, explication of cognitive processes allows the patient to bypass stubborn defenses and to permit new understanding of personal and interpersonal processes, but on a new, more meaningful level—the level of his impaired psychic structures. These new insights into the individual's cognitive structure may outweigh even a high-level treatment alliance between therapist and patient on the verbal-ideational level.

Let me illustrate with a clinical case. Jeanne, a nineteen-year-old college student, was referred to me by a psychoanalyst who had been working with her for eight months. He could not break through her defenses, in spite of his diligent attempts to understand her problems. I found Jeanne a bright and engaging person who could not communicate her feelings, had no insight into her problems, and was perplexed over the sudden change in her ability to cope with them. During our first session, I began to see how easily we might get bogged down, for her associations were not productive and my questions and comments did not seem to penetrate her defenses. However, in the course of our discussion of her difficulties with a college course, I presented her with a simple cognitive task, and from the results obtained, selected succeeding tasks that I thought most relevant to her particular problems. Little by little, as I picked up clues to the detailed cognitive processes underlying her behavior as well as the affective context from which they developed, I closed in on those facets of her cognitive functioning originally hidden from view. During the second session, I carefully adapted a task for Jeanne where the solution involved those particular cognitive characteristics that I had learned were closely related to her problems.

This task—the "horse-and-rider puzzle" (see below)—involves fitting the three pieces together (without bending, folding, or tearing) in such a way that the riders sit on top of the horses.

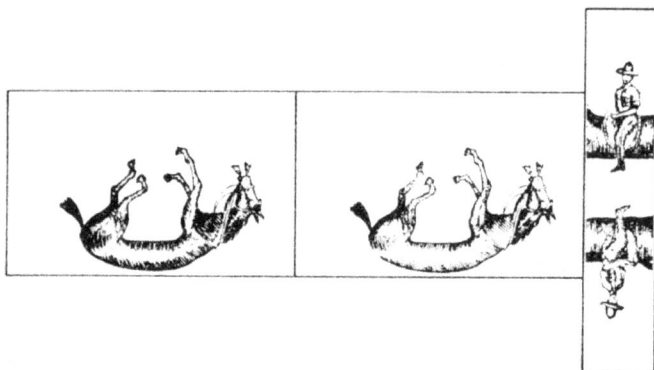

After several minutes of unsuccessful attempts to place the pieces together, Jeanne grimaced and said, "Oh, I'm getting that awful feeling." After a few questions, Jeanne revealed she had this nauseous feeling often:

"I've been waking up every morning this past week and it really hurts, my stomach. I wasn't sick—I didn't have a fever or something wrong. I don't know if it's related, but my boyfriend has this girl, this girlfriend that he goes down to see, and this particular weekend I didn't want him to go down—I hadn't seen him for a long time because of the vacation. What's really disgusting is that next weekend she's coming up here! That about kicked me over the edge. Could it be that the pains in my stomach come from that, that I'm more afraid of losing him than I think?"

Jeanne's feeling of nausea set her off on a successful exploration of a whole new emotional dimension. She began to recall and examine related feelings and events that she had forgotten, denied, or avoided mentioning in her therapy sessions. For example, she was able to recognize the significant part that fear of abandonment had played in her development. For the first time, she could talk about her feelings of loneliness and her severe panic over separation and loss of love. Speaking about her distant and strained relationship with her parents, she remembered how different it was when, as a small child, she was close to her father. As Jeanne continued to examine critical events and feelings in her past, her nausea abated. Soon after, while playing around with the puzzle, much to her surprise, the pieces of the puzzle fell into place—almost without trying, she had found the correct solution (see next page.

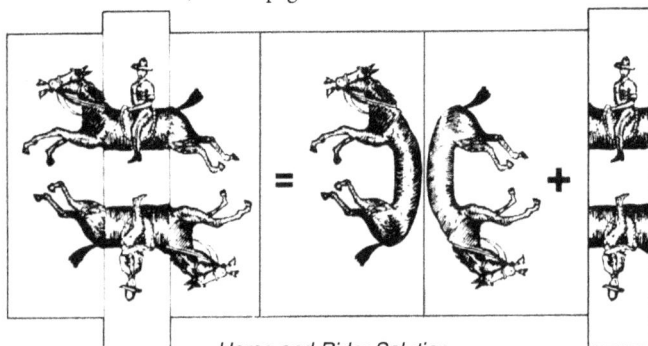

Horse-and-Rider Solution.

Exploring other cognitive tasks gave Jeanne new insight into the nature of her cognitive processes and their source in affective traumas, and, equally important, into the way they contributed to her current life difficulties, particularly to her academic failures. She discovered how her unresolved emotional problems played a role in producing cognitive difficulties, and previously elusive aspects of her emotional life came into focus. Jeanne's therapeutic endeavor consequently took on a new and broader scope, as a coherent picture of her emotional problems, their interrelationship with her cognitive problems, and their roots in unresolved affective and cognitive disorganization began to emerge.

## APPLICATIONS

Anna Freud wrote, "... much of the history of psychoanalysis is dominated by two efforts: 1) to deny, even in face of evidence to the contrary, that analytic understanding reaches further than analytic therapy; 2) to restore by whatever means the former unity between exploration and cure."

Dynamic Cognitive Therapy, with its ability to reach new and deeper levels of core psychic structures, has proven effective in its attempt to restore the harmony between exploration and cure. It does not, however, intend to set out to conquer new territories, such as drug addiction, but to maximize the "optimum scope" for psychoanalytic therapy: the treatment of anxiety neuroses, hysteria, the phobias, the obsessional neuroses, and particularly those disturbances where extensive and severe use of defense mechanisms, such as repression or denial, makes it difficult or unlikely that therapy can progress successfully. Furthermore, its emphasis on nonverbal cognitive communication has led to the pioneering attempts that are presently being made in the treatment of those disorders where verbal communication becomes a stumbling block to progress: adolescent abnormalities and borderline psychotic states. Current clinical research will determine the feasibility of these latter applications.

# Emotional Common Sense

## Rolland S. Parker

## DEFINITION

Emotional Common Sense is a technique for educating the public to improve the balance in their emotional life between constructive action and self-destructiveness. I conceptualize it as follows: "Try to give the same good advice to yourself as you are capable of giving to your friends." Self-destructiveness is defined as disregarding the predictable consequences of our actions.

This approach balances self-awareness, understanding of how people behave, and increased personal control or spontaneity as required. Many people benefit directly. Others find themselves prepared for psychotherapeutic consultation.

# HISTORY

Looking at the world around us reveals tens of millions of people who are avoidably self-destructive, that is, they have life-styles that lead to suicide, jail, ruined marriage and other relationships, unnecessary failures in school and on the job, etc.

Some of the concepts evolved from personal experiences, when I became aware of some of my own self-destructive goals and values. Personal psychotherapy and experiences in performing psychotherapy for others also clarified my understanding. Important theoretical concepts include: the Freudian unconscious and transference of feelings; Adler's ideas about style of life and fictitious goals; the effect of early fantasies and experience with our parents in forming images and self-concepts that subsequently affect us (Harry Stack Sullivan and Melanie Klein); the concept of role playing developed by Jacob Moreno; and my own study of evolution and human physiology.

Finally, leadership of many human relations workshops and larger goal-directed participation-discussion groups have been useful in helping me to understand the problems that people have in today's society, and to learn successful self-help techniques for overcoming them.

# TECHNIQUE

Emotional Common Sense has been applied through: large participation-discussion groups focused upon a particular topic; smaller human relations workshops in which people are invited to exchange their thoughts and feelings on common problems; reading the basic text (Parker, 1973); a teaching component in group and individual psychotherapy.

The participant is invited to learn and accept these *assumptions*:

1. Degradation and manipulation of others poison the emotional atmosphere in intimate and business relationships, and are thereby self-destructive.
2. There is rarely any excuse to permit ourselves to be degraded by family, friends, employers, colleagues, etc.
3. By not erasing destructive experiences and images of the past, we retain out-of-date values, feelings, and memories that affect our self-esteem, perception of authority, etc.
4. People may not express their emotions appropriately. They hold back anger and pain, or exaggerate them to manipulate others through abuse.
5. Our own feelings are not always trustworthy. Displaced anger, low self-esteem, over-sensitivity, and the like are examples.
6. Substantial differences exist between people which derive from persistent constitutional (bodily) and temperamental (mood) qualities between people. These have their origin in the body's biological structure and functioning.

Achieving Emotional Common Sense involves:

1. *Improving self-understanding.* People are encouraged to be sensitive to their dark moods (anxiety, depression, anger, loneliness) and to the social situations that arouse them. The question, "What sort of a person am I?" helps us to improve the balance of constructive to self-destructive actions.
2. *Recognizing out-of-date values.* It is important to live life according to the values

taught by our own experience, not those of yesterday's world taught by parents and teachers, or the media, etc. We must be particularly alert to values that are unsuitable for a person with our history and personal qualities.

3  *Resist the temptation to act according to "unfinished business" from earlier experiences.* The pain, humiliation, anger, and frustration of earlier life are compensated for at that time through fantasies, goals, and expectations about the future. We develop ideas while growing up as to how we want to be, what kind of a partner we want, how we ought to behave, fantasies of love and revenge, and so on. These scripts are played out by themselves toward our children, employers, lovers, and friends. Since the other party is not aware of the role we project on him, there is resistance and we may try to manipulate him to fulfill our needs. This is particularly true when people don't take no for an answer in love affairs. Emotional Common Sense is designed to help people evaluate their needs and take action according to today's world.

4.  *Not knowing how to express feelings appropriately.* Most of us have been trained to hold back our feelings of pain and anger. Consequently, we are pushed around since we can't defend ourselves. "Keeping a stiff upper lip" when we should object is an example of a false value.

5.  *Trusting our feelings excessively.* Many people believe that their feelings offer completely accurate information. In contradiction to many encounter group leaders and others who state that "we should always trust our feelings," Emotional Common Sense teaches that many feelings have their origin in early experiences, misunderstandings, incomplete information, propaganda, and the like. It is self-destructive to act immediately in significant circumstances without some cognitive evaluation of the situation.

6  *Relying upon momentary gratification.* Small triumphs and momentary pleasure do not create a fulfilling life-style. Many people exercise little self-discipline, then enter into trivial relationships, do not prepare their work properly, or do not invest time in education. Quick sexual adventures, time frittered away with acquaintances, and so on can interfere with achieving significant goals.

Some active principles of Emotional Common Sense:

1.  *The "ouch principle."* This is advised when people do not defend themselves properly. They are told, "If somebody steps on your toes, say 'Ouch.' This will give them a chance to explain why they have done something painful. It may be a misunderstanding, or it may have been inadvertent. If they apologize, it's one thing. If they insist on their right to mistreat you, leave."

2.  *Eliminating degrading relationships from our lives.* These relationships include those with parents, children, and employers. Most people feel that this cannot be done, but exploration sometimes reveals that the emotional difficulties are so great that there is little choice. In the area of work, for example, it is useful to have a "parachute" in the form of some savings, so that one may quit a job without undergoing exploitation and abuse.

3.  *Developing the capacity for autonomy, as well as good relationships.* Many individuals have not learned to feed themselves emotionally. Therefore, they have excessive need for continuous close contact with other people. They participate in very

unsatisfactory relationships from fear of being alone. When we develop our resources—emotional, spiritual, and vocational—we are better companions since we are less demanding, as well as more interesting.

4.  *Developing self-assertion and self-acceptance.* This evolves from a knowledge of who we are, so that we do not end up meeting the needs of others who have a clearer idea of what they want out of life than we do. Increasing our self-esteem is part of this process, so that we feel entitled to getting good things out of life. By developing self-esteem, we do not require excessive support from others.

5.  *Working on good relationships.* It is important to develop a less critical attitude towards others, as well as to be understanding and know how to meet others' needs. Emotional Common Sense emphasizes techniques of reaching out to others, accepting their good will, and increasing capacity for intimacy.

6.  *Developing a suitable life-style.* An emotionally fulfilling life includes productivity (offering something of use to the community), relatedness (enjoying and being able to reciprocate with people), and autonomy (enjoying our own personality and functioning comfortably by ourselves).

### APPLICATIONS

Emotional Common Sense techniques are designed to alleviate stress, emotional pain, guilt, anxiety, worthlessness, overcoming loneliness, deprivation, and depression. They also deal with improving self-assertion and emotional problems of employment, creativity, productivity, and decision-making.

---

# Communication *Therapy*[1]

## Elaine Yudkovitz

### DEFINITION

Communication Therapy in childhood psychosis involves treatment of speech, language, and interactional behavior as well as attention to the cognitive substrate that underlies communication performance. As such, Communication Therapy with the psychotic child is concerned with the child's difficulties with the structure, the meaning, and the function of a speech act.

The particular approach to be described here is based on the hypothesis that self-awareness and other awareness deficits that characterize childhood psychosis have consequences for speech, language, and concept acquisition and maintenance. A child who is psychotic is not adequately aware of his own internal states and action, and not

---

[1]Development of this program was supported by NIHM Grant Nos. MH 05753-13, 14, The Ittleson Family Foundation, and The Grant Foundation. The contributions of Nancy Lewison and Judy Rottersman to its development are gratefully acknowledged.

adequately open to receiving information from the environment. The development of language and concepts seems to be dependent on: 1) the ability to adequately monitor one's own actions and thoughts, 2) the ability to monitor actions and events outside the self (including language), and 3) the ability to assess and make comparisons between the two. It is the continual ability to make such comparisons and, consequently, to make any necessary adjustments in language and thought (concepts) that characterize a developing and active child in Piaget's developmental psychology (equilibration theory) and in the auditory feedback model of language acquisition and maintenance. From the viewpoint of communication, then, psychotic children exhibit deficits in auditory monitoring, both as it relates to attending to salient and relevant language and associated nonlanguage experiences outside themselves (external monitoring), and as it relates to attending to information about language and the world that they have already taken in and stored in their memories (internal monitoring). This auditory monitoring disturbance, crucial to their communication failure, exists as part of their total disturbance in self-awareness and self-regulation.

## HISTORY

From the earliest reports of childhood psychosis, deficits in language expression and comprehension have been seen as a prominent symptom (see Baltaxe and Simmons, 1975). In recent years, the communication deficits have been focused on even more specifically, often with the underlying assumption that the disorders of childhood psychosis encompass a central language and/or central cognitive deficit (see Rutter, et al., 1971; Cohen, et al., 1976).

Much of the reported work in specific language therapy with psychotic children has focused on those children who are nonverbal or who have very limited verbal behavior, with training occurring primarily through operant techniques (see Lovaas, 1966) and, more recently, through the use of signed speech, gestures, and manipulation of visual symbols (see Fulwiler and Fouts, 1976). Some other reported treatments of communication include Rutusnik and Rutusnik's (1976) use of Lee's Interactive Teaching Approach and Shopler and Reichler's (1971) use of teachers and parents. Yudkovitz, Lewison, and Rottersman (1975, 1977); Yudkovitz and Rottersman (1973) developed a rationale and treatment approach based upon auditory monitoring and feedback principles and Piaget's equilibration theory for use with psychotic children. Their pilot study (1975) indicated changes in the selective attention abilities of four speaking psychotic children, as well as modification of such specific communication errors as tangentiality, run-on language, interruption behavior, and grammatical errors. An ongoing two-year experimental study has thus far indicated similar results for selective attentional behavior and communication failures, such as lack of referential clarity, overuse of specific statements when a more abstract one would be expected, and a lack of attention to contextual shifts in deriving meanings.

## TECHNIQUE

The program consists of three therapy stages: 1) creation of a listening attitude, 2) general error sensitivity, and 3) modification of a particular language, speech, or interactional communication behavior.

*Creation of a listening attitude.* Through tasks of auditory focusing and sensitivity, the child learns to scan for, and focus on, auditory stimuli for features the clinician defines as salient and relevant, and to make comparisons between various aspects of auditory inputs. In this phase of therapy, the clinician pays no attention to specific communication deficits, beyond that of paying attention, and during the therapy tasks of this stage there is only limited verbalization demanded of the child. For example, in one type of task, a nonverbal child might be asked to indicate when a sound occurs that matches the drum sound he has just heard; a verbal child might be asked to indicate if a particular word occurred in a sentence. Many kinds of selective attending and comparing activities are used at this stage.

Sounds and language are slightly amplified, or highlighted, by the child's wearing earphones during all stages of the program. Because we believe it is important the child be aware of errors, the child's discovery of any errors he makes while carrying out a task is rewarded. Thus, a self-validation procedure is incorporated into all parts of the program, with the child being asked to respond a second time to task materials and to judge whether his first response was adequate.

*General error sensitivity.* This is a transitional stage that is designed to highlight error detection. Again, the focus is not on the child's production but rather on his attending to and comparing two language stimuli produced by the clinician. One is identified as "correct" and a second, which varies from the first, is identified as containing an "error" that the child must detect. For example: 1) The boy has four new toys. 2) The boy has four new *feet*.

In both Stage 1 and Stage 2, 95 percent accuracy is required for each activity before a new task, or the next stage, can begin.

*Modification of a particular language, speech, or interactional communication behavior.* One error specific to the child is chosen. Several techniques are employed: 1) interpersonal scanning (including recognition of the correct form when necessary), 2) intrapersonal scanning, 3) comparing, and 4) modeling for change. While the techniques may generally be used in any order as the needs of the child indicate, this stage always begins with interpersonal scanning.

1. *Interpersonal scanning.* The objective is to create an awareness in the child of his particular error as it is deliberately produced by the clinician. The child is required to identify the error from within a larger verbal stimulus. The error must be contrasted with the correct form. In addition, before the child can scan the clinician's output for instances of the error, he must be able to recognize the correct linguistic form as well as understand the underlying concept.

   Once the child can consistently recognize the correct form, he is required to identify the error the clinician produces in increasingly complex linguistic environments—for example, sentences, paragraphs, interactions. Moreover, the child may experience the clinician making the error: speaking on tape, speaking to him directly, or conversing with another speaker on tape. We find the latter mode particularly beneficial because it displays a microcosm of the consequences of the behavior, it validates his judgment of the effects of a particular communication, and it offers some limited experience in role-playing—something that is difficult for psychotic children.

2. *Intrapersonal scanning.* The focus is still on the child's active awareness of error rather than on correction of it. While this active awareness may be important for any language-impaired child, the psychotic child's deficiency in self-awareness makes this an even more critical procedure for him. The child begins by identifying errors of previously taped samples, thus removing the scanning task from the need to communicate. Later, a child may be asked to identify errors as he is speaking, using a kind of simultaneous feedback. While correction is not the objective here, frequently proficiency in error detection leads to anticipation of error, elimination of error, or even introduction of the new or correct communication behavior.

3. *Comparing.* The clinician may produce the content of the child's utterance but use the correct language behavior in immediate juxtaposition. Placing the correct and incorrect side by side in this way increases the possibilities of perceiv-ing differences.

4. *Modeling for change.* The focus of modeling is on the child's *production* of the correct speech, language, or conceptual behavior. Within a meaningful language context, the child follows the clinician's correct behaviors with his own production, but codes a different set of stimuli, although they are of the same type as the clinician's. The child is, at some level, abstracting the rule that governs that particular communication behavior since he is not purely imitating the clinician's utterances. Comparison is always operative and leads to searching as the child attempts to produce a behavior that is like the clinician's.

In the recognition and modeling techniques, in particular, the clinician attempts to bring the model stimuli near enough to the child's present level of cognitive-linguistic functioning to allow him to assimilate the new behavior. In accomplishing this, the clinician not only considers developmental characteristics of the linguistic or conceptual form itself but also the effects of the situational context in which it occurs or the linguistic context in which it is embedded.

## APPLICATIONS

Because the label "childhood psychosis" appears to encompass a multitude of subgroups, it seems necessary to state that the therapy program as presented has been designed specifically for a group of children who, although they have serious commu-nication problems, are rather verbal already, generally function intellectually in the bor-derline dull-normal to bright-normal range, and for two-thirds of whom a positive, if equivocal, diagnosis of organicity has been applied. However, it seems that the process considerations and their therapeutic implications are applicable, with some modification, to other subgroups of psychotic children as well.

In addition, while this therapy model is designed particularly for communication behavior, the issues that it builds on to effect behavioral change in childhood psycho-sis are more far-reaching. Other remedial approaches, for example, those in the motor sphere, might consider these issues as well. Psychotherapy with these children has fre-quently been concerned with the lack of, and thus the development of, self and other awareness.

# The Companionship Therapy Model

## *Gerald Goodman and Chris Barker*

### DEFINITION

There is no unique "Companionship Therapy." It is not a therapeutic orientation in the sense of being a set of techniques; rather the term denotes that process resulting from a specific combination of interpersonal ingredients. The recipe can be stated roughly as: take a nonprofessional or paraprofessional counselor chosen for his interpersonal competence, orient him toward *not* giving advice, pair him with a client, structure frequent contact into the relationship that evolves, and have a professional oversee its progress.

The companionship model combines elements of friendship with elements of therapy. Its theoretical basis stresses the value of empathic, nonjudgmental, playful contact for the resolution of emotional difficulties. Therapy is removed from the therapist's office to the client's natural surroundings: his home or place of recreation. Client-counselor contact may cover the full gamut of activities that come under the rubric of companionship, as well as those more traditionally associated with therapy. Thus activities may range from attending sports events or sharing hobbies, on the one hand, to engaging in intimate discussions on the other.

Companionship Therapy places little stress on therapist strategy or technique. It gives counselors and clients freedom to choose the activity for each session, although counselors are selected for qualities that will foster intimate conversation. The companionship model minimizes the need for extensive training that characterizes the traditional "expert helper" model, and it discourages its counselors from taking a "professional" stance toward their clients. In other words, the therapy emphasizes selection rather than training, and two-way intimacy rather than patient management.

Of course, all is not as simple as the "recipe" given above implies. The choosing, orienting, pairing, structuring, and overseeing all take considerable planning by a given companionship program's administrators, and, as with traditional therapy, the precise impact of Companionship Therapy for different combinations of clients/counselors/circumstances is still partly an open question. However, one of the strengths of this approach has been its willingness to evaluate itself, and a substantial body of knowledge about its effects is now beginning to accumulate. The brief description to follow will attempt to introduce those concerned with the problems of running a companionship program to what is known about their solutions.

### HISTORY

Historically, companionship programs reach back at least to the 1930s, an early example being the Cambridge-Sommerville Youth Study (Powers and Winter, 1951). Geographically, they spread as wide as the ubiquitous Big Brother and Big Sister programs. Guerney (1969) gives an idea of current activity in the area. For our purposes, the approach will be illustrated by focusing on a single program, author Gerald Goodman's Berkeley project (see Goodman, *Companionship Therapy*, 1972). This project is similar to others in that it employed the companionship dyad as the unit of therapy, but different in that it developed systematic selection methods for both clients and counselors, and that it incorporated a complex research design to both evaluate the overall effect of the program and determine specific predictors of outcome.

## TECHNIQUE

Goodman's project took place in Berkeley in the mid-sixties. The "clients" were 5th-grade and 6th-grade boys, selected by a systematic city-wide screening of the public schools. The counselors were male Berkeley undergraduates, recruited through advertisements in the newspaper. The "companionships" were structured to meet from one to four hours per visit, with two visits per week, and to last for the duration of the academic year. The typical pair met approximately fifty times over a span of eight months, and their average meeting lasted almost three hours.

The techniques of Companionship Therapy do not exist so much at the level of the response—such as interpretation in psychoanalysis, or confrontation in encounter—but more at the level of the relationship as a whole. They consist of the methods used to compose and structure the individual companionships.

The program was influenced by the client-centered tradition. Following Carl Rogers, the hypothesis was that people can change through other people's openness, understanding, and acceptance. Thus, counselors were selected for their capacity to self-disclose, empathize, and show positive regard for the feelings of others in actual performance situations. They were given a brief orientation about the value of being more honest with themselves and their clients, and of avoiding giving advice or trying to "treat" their boy. As one of the variables in the study, half of the counselors also participated in weekly sensitivity training groups led by experienced clinicians.

Counselor interpersonal skills were measured by an instrument developed within the project, the Group Assessment of Interpersonal Traits (GAIT). The GAIT is a method that uses brief performance samples to rate participants on a number of interpersonal skills. The primary scales are "understanding," "open," and "accepting-warm," which together form a therapeutic talent composite.

The "companionships" were designed to generate processes occurring in two forms of human relationships: psychotherapy and companionship. The dyads in the project engaged in the sustained pursuit of collaborative activities and the sharing of personal interests, which are the essential characteristics of social companionships.

In contrast, psychotherapy is usually based on the expectation that patients will frequently disclose private feelings. While the participating boys did not expect to discuss private topics, it was hypothesized that the counselor's interpersonal style would draw forth much personal disclosure. Thus, the policy for structuring relationships was intended to foster the collaboration common to social companionship, while the selection and orientation of counselors was intended to foster the exploration of intimate topics common to therapy.

In terms of final outcome, the project had mixed results. Overall, while the participating group of 88 boys showed positive change on several of the variables, so did a matched control group. To assess the results, the study used observations from parents, counselors, teachers, the boys and their peers. The correlations between the various measures of change were complex and defied simple explanation. As a result, the predictor variables did not yield clear-cut findings. However, it did seem that the counselors' GAIT empathy scores were positively related to outcome, and some dyad characteristics also emerged as possible predictors. For example, black boys with white counselors especially seemed to benefit. Also quiet boys with quiet counselors seemed to benefit significantly less: a quiet/outgoing variable emerged as one of the strongest predictors in the study. A replication of Goodman's work showed a substantially similar pattern of results (see Dicken, et al., 1977). Thus, despite the lack of global outcome, the research implies that judicious selection and pairing will yield companionships that have positive therapeutic impact.

## APPLICATIONS

For the practicing psychotherapist, Companionship Therapy suggests ways in which the therapist's role may be expanded. Traditional practitioners seem excessively role-bound by a number of now arbitrary anachronisms: the fifty-minute hour, the formal office setting, professional distance, and circumscribed notions of what client activities are therapeutic. Hopefully, the companionship model will provide an impetus towards a therapeutic repertoire of greater breadth and flexibility From a broader perspective, Companionship Therapy is an example of the trend toward de-professionalizing mental health delivery, which Sobey (1970) has aptly labeled "the non-professional revolution." Companionship and similar programs are proliferating. Various formats have been used: interracial pairs, elderly pairs, college students with chronic mental patients, and such cross-age pairings as high school students with younger children, and parent-child dyads. A current direction is to train preexisting pairings—couples, friendships, and working relationships—in interpersonal skills. This capitalizes on an already existing companionship, adding a training ingredient to further the therapy component (although the intention here may be prevention rather than repair).

Companionship therapies appear to provide a workable format for the future. Their compatibility with rigorous research has become clear as selection, pairing assignments, relationship duration, training format, and so on can be systematically arranged. The easy interplay between such a widely appealing, economical, low stigma therapy and modern research design indicates the potential of Companionship Therapy in the future development of both community mental health and psychotherapy.

# Computer Therapy

## John H. Greist

### DEFINITION

Simply put, Computer Therapy in psychiatry involves the use of computers to treat persons with psychiatric problems. Behind this simplistic definition lies an extremely complex field that seeks to integrate the rapid and continuing progress in computer hardware (computing machines) and software (computer languages and programs) with the still poorly understood art of psychotherapy.

## HISTORY

Development of the first computers made it possible to process mathematical symbols at a rapid rate. Programming languages to deal with linguistic symbols soon followed and, with steady refinement, have allowed easy programming to process language strings that can express quite complex meanings. With the advent of on-line computing, in which each user interacts directly with the computer through a computer terminal rather than indirectly, immediate computer responses to user inputs became possible. Time-sharing techniques permit a single computer to interact simultaneously with many users, dramatically reducing computing costs (now less than $1 per hour on some machines). Harnessing the interactive computer medium to psychotherapeutic tasks seemed a natural step in the rapidly growing use of computers, and proponents prophesied widespread availability of expert and inexpensive computer therapies.

By 1965, a program that crudely simulated Rogerian psychotherapy had been developed (see Weizenbaum, 1966). Colby, who has been a seminal and steadily productive worker in this field, had begun his studies, Slack had conducted medical interviews that had apparent psychotherapeutic effects, and other workers were beginning to apply computers to studies and treatments of psychophysiologic problems (see Lang, 1969). Despite this early promise, there has been neither the widespread interest nor extensive development of Computer Therapy that many people expected.

Interviews can be carefully written to display warmth and humor and to be nonjudgmental or confrontational, as appropriate. In these interviews, therapeutic education, reassurance, suggestion, modeling, support, and authorization to express emotion are all possible.

Colby's work has gone far beyond the simple and directly linked question-answer branching of most computer medical interviews to develop more complex models of human thought with a capacity to evolve in different directions based on the continuing patient-computer interaction. His program for autistic children who had no socially useful speech was helpful in initiating speech in thirteen of seventeen patients with whom it was tried (see Colby, 1973). Another Colby program simulates a paranoid patient so successfully that it is virtually impossible to determine that one is interacting with a computer rather than a person.

## TECHNIQUE AND APPLICATIONS

There are several different techniques of Computer Therapy in psychiatry based on different patient problems and different conceptualizations of etiology and therapy. The hallmark of most computer therapies has been a direct interaction between the patient and the computer. It is this immediacy and anthropomorphization of a machine that some find so threatening, regardless of any associated benefits.

Reactions of most psychiatric patients to computer interviews that collect past history and present symptom descriptions are strongly positive, and some patients in a variety of settings have found the interview experience itself helpful and, in their own words, "therapeutic."

The biofeedback field has blossomed with the availability of small computers that can convert the patient's physiologic functions into electronic signals that then guide the patient in modifying those very functions. Though this field has pulled back from its overly optimistic and simplistic beginnings to a more reasoned and focused position, the on-line computer will clearly play an important role in defining the ultimate applications of biofeedback to medical problems.

Computers have also been used to a limited degree in the development of hierarchies for systematic desensitization as well as controlling tape recorders that conduct actual systematic desensitization therapy. Though the necessity for relaxation as a part of this behavior therapy has been seriously challenged, the use of computers in providing behavior therapies clearly offers the possibility of widely available, standardized treatment at low cost.

One of the major problems in psychotherapy practice and research has been to systematically define the treatment technique, so that it may be taught to other therapists and applied in a standardized fashion to patients whose disorders may respond to that particular kind of psychotherapy. Even in the face of widely variable individual drug metabolism and incomplete compliance with psychopharmacologic treatments, standardization of psychoactive drugs has permitted substantial progress in this area. As with the rest of medicine, the task for computer therapists is to develop specific computer therapies and test them with specific psychiatric disorders. Unlike psychotherapy administered by human therapists, which tends to vary greatly between different therapists and even in a single therapist's treatment of different patients with the same disorder, computer psychotherapy will have the possible advantage of holding constant the computer statements across a whole series of similar patients.

Work is now underway to develop a psychiatric interview administered directly by computer to psychiatric patients that will provide research-quality diagnoses. Diagnoses with specific implications for treatment assignment may lead the computer into a therapy-broker role where the computer recommends the most appropriate initial treatment for a patient based on a comprehensive evaluation. Treatment recommendations might include psychotherapy of a specific kind (administered by a computer or a human with demonstrated effectiveness in treating patients with a particular disorder), medications, or electroconvulsive therapy, alone or in combination.

There has been occasional criticism of the use of computers in psychiatry in general and for data collection from patients in particular. Computer psychotherapy seems even more threatening to some individuals, yet clearly, the use of nonhuman devices in medicine is far from inhumane since technological advances in many fields have brought substantial health benefits to patients. Critics often speak on behalf of a patient constituency without consulting them. Whenever patient-computer interactions have been evaluated by patients, the reaction has been strongly positive, often to the point of preferring the computer as an interviewer over the doctor. This seems to be especially true when sensitive subject matter is being discussed as is often the case in psychotherapy. Too often, there is an immodest overestimation of the benefits of human psychotherapy based on an absence of comparisons with other treatments and occasionally on simple self-interest. Compounding these deficiencies is a large public health problem poorly met by present-day techniques. There is clearly a need for computer therapies in psychiatry, though their proper development will require careful work and will be limited more by the problems inherent in psychotherapy than by practical computing considerations.

# Conditioned Reflex Therapy
## Andrew Salter

### DEFINITION

Conditioned Reflex Therapy is the application of the concepts of Ivan Pavlov and V. M. Bechterev to the practice of psychotherapy. Particularly important are the concepts of inhibition, excitation, and disinhibition.

### HISTORY

Andrew Salter's book, *Conditioned Reflex Therapy*, appeared in 1949. In Joseph Wolpe's words, "*Conditioned Reflex Therapy* ... contains the first detailed account ever to be published of the application of the principles of conditioning to the treatment of human neuroses. The therapeutic methods it describes were originated by Salter

### TECHNIQUE

Conditioned Reflex Therapy declares that fundamentally everybody has the same problem and the same cure.

Dr. A is a dentist, and is afraid of blood.

Mr. B has claustrophobia, and is afraid of elevators.

Miss C is an actress, and finds it difficult to face an audience.

Mrs. D is a writer who cannot concentrate on her work. Mr. E says that life isn't worth living.

Some of these people were brought up In the country, and some in the city. Some had kind fathers, some had stern ones. Some were indulged by their mothers, and some were frequently punished. Some were jealous of an older brother, and some were not. Some were only children, some were the youngest, and some were the oldest. In short, these people had entirely different histories and, presumably, entirely different problems.

After taking a phenobarbital pill or a stiff drink:

Dr. A, the dentist, does not mind blood at all.

Mr. B rides comfortably in the elevator.

Miss C finds it easy to appear before an audience.

Mrs. D sits down at the typewriter and works for two hours.

Mr. E decides that the world is a fairly interesting place after all.

To be sure, the problems return when the phenobarbital or alcohol wears off, but five different persons, with five different problems, stemming from five different pasts, have been temporarily "cured" by one and the same thing. What other conclusion seems possible, save that all five suffer from the *same* disturbance: excessive inhibition in social relations.

Although each person represents a different problem, the purpose of therapy with every individual is identical—to produce a free, outward-flowing personality in which true emotions are represented in speech and action.

The neurotic feelings and behavior of the patient were caused by earlier inhibitory *social* experiences. Therapy consists of teaching the patient how to overcome his excessive inhibition. With this in mind, the current social relations of the patient are discussed. The target of therapy is the excessively inhibitory behavior of the patient with wife (husband), girlfriend (boyfriend), friends, acquaintances, employer (or employees) and even with superficial social contacts.

The "expressive" behavior advocated by Salter in *Conditioned Reflex Therapy* was renamed "assertion" by Joseph Wolpe (1958), and the term assertion has stuck. "The word *assertive*," wrote Wolpe, "has rather a wide meaning here. It refers not only to more or less aggressive behavior, but also to the outward expression of friendly, affectionate, and other nonanxious feelings. It covers exactly the same ground as Salter's word expressive."

So-called assertive techniques play a very important role in Conditioned Reflex Therapy. Nevertheless, desensitization techniques, relaxation techniques, self-control techniques, and the constructive use of imagery are also used.

## APPLICATIONS

Conditioned Reflex Therapy has been used successfully in the treatment of a wide spectrum of personality disturbances—anxiety, shyness, alcoholism, stuttering, psychosomatic disorders, work block problems of the creative, phobias, masochism and its manifestations, and sexual disorders.

In Alan Kazdin's words, in his authoritative *History of Behavior Modification*, "Fuller versions of techniques initiated by Salter are still being employed by contemporary practitioners of behavior modification."

# Confrontation in Psychotherapy
## Lester A. Gelb

## DEFINITION

The Oxford English Dictionary defines the verb "confront" as "to bring a person face to face with." Exactly how psychotherapists bring their patients "face to face with" their problems in a way that will lead to change is what differentiates the various psychotherapies that have developed since the classical psychoanalytic approach of Freud. The dictionary's alternative definition of "confront," "to face in hostility or defiance ... to oppose," has lead many people to view "confront" as an aggressive means to express opposition. This is not the sense in which the term is used in psychotherapy.

## HISTORY

The psychoanalytic use of confrontation was, of course, originated by Sigmund Freud. Freud believed that the pathological factor in neurosis was not the patient's ignorance of his mental mechanisms but his "inner resistance," which brought the ignorance into being in the first place. Therefore, Freud generally remained passive and limited confrontation to interpretation of transference and resistance, and to occasional reality testing. Freudian psychoanalysts have in general continued to follow this practice.

Many analysts who followed Freud used confrontation in a less limited way. Karen Horney, who broke with Freud over the importance of the influence of cultural factors, rejected the role of the analyst as merely an "interpreting voice" rather than a reactive human being. If she believed the patient was "running into a blind alley" she would not hesitate to actively intervene and suggest alternatives.

Alfred Adler was the first of these analysts who actively confronted his patients with their self-deception. He encouraged them to relinquish negative "life-styles" and to adopt "positive roles." Sandor Rado, who also began as a classical analyst, originated the "adaptational" school of analysis. He confronted patients with the need for change and emphasized that insight occurs only through practice in daily living as the patient "automatizes" new, more healthy behavior. Bernard Robbins was originally identified with Horney, but later went on to develop confrontation to its ultimate therapeutic advantage. He believed that it is necessary for therapists to actively intervene in getting patients to change their actual practice: "Inner growth does not come from within, but through man's practice on the outside world (Robbins, 1952).

Many family therapists use even more active confrontation techniques. For example, Salvator Minuchin uses confrontation in a process he calls "restructuring operations" which are "the therapeutic interventions that confront and challenge a family in the attempt to force a therapeutic change."

## TECHNIQUE AND APPLICATIONS

The techniques of confrontation described here are used by many present-day practitioners, especially those who employ short-term therapy, family therapy, group therapy, and crisis intervention. From the foregoing history it is clear that *what* the patient is confronted with and *how* the therapist makes the confrontation have changed through the years. Today, practitioners of the various schools of therapy generally continue the original techniques.

The theory and technique of confrontation that follows is based on the proposition that neurosis is a disturbance or distortion of our view of ourselves and of others, and Can be changed ultimately only through new, correct, and undistorting experience. Of course, as in all scientific processes, the therapist must wait until a significant block of information is gathered to point to the modes of thinking and functioning that most likely are producing the patient's problems. The therapist's views must be communicated at the appropriate time, and in a manner that can be clearly understood and accepted by the patient. This is the essence of what is called "timing" and "interpretation." New ideas in the form of the resulting "insight" do not in themselves produce change. The confrontation of interpretation is only the beginning of the process of an active interchange between the patient and therapist. Since we are interested in useful change for the patient, and not merely insight, further confrontation is required to insure a change in the actual interpersonal and social activities of the patient. The requirement of confrontation is absolute in therapy when a change in behavior is crucial to avert a crisis. This confrontation must take place in a friendly and supportive manner, and in the spirit of collaboration, so that the patient understands that it is the therapist's wish to help him or her live in a new way that is more effective, productive, and gratifying. This is the type of confrontation that has made short-term therapy possible and can increase the efficiency of other therapies.

How can the therapist, through such confrontation, help the patient to overcome resistance to change, which in routine psychoanalysis takes years to "work through"? It is the acute suffering of most of the patients who seek our help that is the main source of motivation to change. Resistance to change is often overcome by suffering. Moreover, once relief from immediate pressure occurs, the patient is willing to examine other areas of disturbed functioning with diminished resistance. In assessing sources of difficulty, it is essential to confront the patient not only with the effects of his own behavior and thinking but also with the effects of confusing, limiting, and exploiting behavior of others. This includes the basic limitations embedded in the patient's specific social and economic reality. In this way we can help patients deal with destructive life situations that are not exclusively of their own making. When we help patients to realize what they are *not* responsible for, they are more able and willing to accept their actual contributions to existing problems.

Since all dysfunction takes place within a disturbed *system* of human interaction, it is additionally essential that wherever possible we bring family, peers, and even appropriate community members into the therapeutic situation. In this way, not only can confrontation be appropriately directed, but needed change in whole social units can be effected. Individuals in these units can learn to be therapeutically confronting with one another.

Pointing out sources of the patient's difficulty should be only a prelude for the confrontation of needed change. When the therapist sees that change is required to avoid a crisis he, using appropriate timing and supportive manner, will confront the patient with the needed changed activity. Changed activity will produce a new, healthier consciousness and existence. This is the only source of inner growth and useful insight. We know a person's consciousness only by its practice. Confrontation leading to changed human practice will produce the therapeutic "cure"—a changed person with a changed consciousness.

---

# Contextual Therapy of Phobic Behavior
## *Manuel D. Zane*

### DEFINITION

The psychotherapeutic technique called "Contextual Therapy" is based upon the observation and functional analysis of a person's disturbed behavior in the natural contexts where it occurs and changes. This approach allows identification of factors and relationships inside and outside the person, and conceptualization of processes that make behavior get better or worse.

# HISTORY

Such a contextual approach was originally developed to observe, comprehend, and deal with disturbed motor behavior and learning occurring in the physically handicapped during their rehabilitation programs (Zane, 1962, 1966). In the past eighteen years this approach has been intensively applied to the study and treatment of phobic behavior both privately and in clinics.

# TECHNIQUE

People who are phobic automatically develop, in commonplace situations, fear and distress that can intensify uncontrollably to cause unbearable feelings and overwhelming panic. Contextual Therapy finds that in all phobias these terrifying developments are the result of an automatic, fear-generating process. This "phobogenic process" is activated and accelerates as the person involuntarily reacts more and more to growing numbers of imagined dangers and less and less to comforting realities in the phobic situation.

If a trusted person is present or available in reality or in imagination, the phobic person can then react more to comforting realities and less to imagined dangers in the phobic situation. The level of fear then drops or remains controlled and panic is averted.

Recognizing the central role of the phobogenic process in disorganizing body and mental functioning, it is hypothesized that Contextual Therapy slows or inhibits the phobogenic process, and so stops the panic. It does this by creating conditions that reduce the person's disturbing reaction to unmanageable, imagined dangers and builds up his comforting responses to manageable, existing realities. Mainly, this is achieved by creating a trusted, familiar therapeutic presence for the patient to respond to realistically in the phobic situation. Sometimes this is the therapist, or a recollection of him or of his theory, or of ideas built with his concurrence. The operations of the phobogenic process are then impeded and the rising panic stops. New, constructive experiences and learning can then take place in the phobic situation from which more realistic beliefs, expectations, and behavior can come.

An example might best illustrate the technique. A thirty-five-year-old woman was afraid of and avoided closed-in places, elevators, high floors, tunnels, and airplanes. Traditional office psychotherapy had helped her in many ways but not with her phobias of ten years' standing. At our first meeting I obtained the history of her phobia and its surrounding circumstances. Then I explained my belief that she could help herself best if she could encounter, deal with, and study her phobic reaction in my presence. She then agreed to step into my windowless, unlocked, walk-in closet alone and tell me, when she could, what she felt and thought. Almost as soon as I closed the door she swung it open. She said she became panicky when she thought I might be trying to trick her. Immediately she felt trapped, felt increasing difficulty in breathing, experienced waves of heat and heart palpitations, pictured herself smothering if she continued, and abruptly opened the door. I assured her I was opposed to any tricks and that it was for her to decide if she wanted to undertake the task. She then returned to the dark closet and soon consented to my walking away and leaving her alone. Quickly she felt great fear and strong impulses to bolt. But this time she was able to stay as she reminded herself that she was safe, that it was a closet in my office with sufficient air, that she could open the door if she so chose, that it was for her good that she was doing this, and that I was a doctor and would help her if she fainted or had any trouble.

Afterward we went over the experience and identified the factors—mostly thoughts, feelings, and imagery—that had made her fear and behavior get better or worse. Alluding to our shared, concrete experience, I pointed out how staying with the realities despite her feelings of fear had helped and getting lost in imagined dangers had created disturbances and panic, compelling her to run out. What had just happened, I said, was a model combining what had always made her problem worse in other phobic situations and what she must now try to do over and over again to help herself.

In steps, she began to practice going into her phobic situations—with me, with a non-professional helper, with her husband, and eventually alone. We kept examining her successes and failures to help her learn how her phobic behavior was affected by many identifiable factors, particularly by her thinking. Gradually, she became less afraid of becoming afraid in the phobic situation. This happened as she learned to keep her fear under satisfactory control in the phobic situation by reacting increasingly to manageable things in the present and less to unmanageable anticipated dangers. After ten visits over a three-month period, she was able to ride elevators to high floors many times by herself, drove through a tunnel, first with me and then alone, and took an airplane with her husband to Europe. Often, when her fear and distress arose, she could halt or slow the phobogenic process by remembering the successful closet experience, by recognizing that her increasing feelings of fear were coming from her imagined dangers, and by staying connected and responding to comforting realities. She returned to her referring psychotherapist considerably improved and in possession of a method that enabled her to continue to work on her remaining phobic problems.

## APPLICATIONS

The same technique is used for all kinds of phobias. Some people will respond more quickly and many will take much more time, requiring the slow buildup of new realistic beliefs that can stand up to the impact of long-standing fear and patterns of distorted thinking. Very similar techniques and methods of treatment have been developed by others, particularly by Claire Weekes of Australia.

Like animal ethnology, Contextual Therapy observes and studies behavior as it changes in its natural contexts. And like the emerging cognitive therapies, this method recognizes the powerful role in human behavior of changing thought and imagery. While the contextual approach also explores hidden mental processes, it differs greatly from contemporary psychoanalysis, which directly observes behavior only in the office. And despite sporadic similarities in technique, Contextual Therapy differs very much from those behavior therapies whose theories are derived from laboratory studies of animals.

# Therapeutic Contracts

## Klaus Kuch

### DEFINITION

Contracts form a centerpiece of psychotherapy. They detail methods and specify goals. The agreement must make sense or the patient may not follow it. It evolves during a course of therapy and reflects the changing views patient and therapist hold of the problem as well as of each other.

Both parties bring a basic philosophy and a set of expectations into their relationship; they observe, select as relevant, and interpret events accordingly. A behaviorist would monitor chains of stimuli and responses, whereas an existentialist would relate to their meaning. An analyst would interpret a disturbed relationship as a result of childhood memories. Meanwhile, a frightened patient might see signs of mental illness and ask for reassurance. Reality is obviously multidimensional. Cognitively oriented therapists consider the patient's conceptions and explain to him the effects of his own interpretative style and how it colors his views. They do not intervene right away with a prescribed procedure. An emphasis on subjective experiences at the expense of matter-of-fact observation is first confronted and shifted toward a more balanced view before an otherwise alien technique is suggested. Cognitively oriented contracts are designed to be compatible with the patient's concept of reality.

### HISTORY

The philosopher Nietzsche distinguished between three contrasting purposes in his essay on the "Use and Disadvantage of History to Life": it may stimulate a collector's curiosity, serve as a tool of intellectual critique, or be chosen as a heroic monument. Psychotherapeutic systems differ equally in their approach to time, space, and individuality. Psychoanalysts attend to highly personal "free associations" and relate them to past experiences. Gestalt therapists cultivate "here and now experience." Behaviorists prefer standardized techniques to modify observable habits. Many neurotic patients seem to get better in spite of all this controversy once they find a therapist who believes in the same things, regardless of the method used. Therapy should make deliberate use of such nonspecific effects and proceed in accordance with beliefs about help, as long as this would seem reasonable. Counterproductive beliefs are then confronted through cognitive reappraisal.

### TECHNIQUE

The patient is allowed to develop his style freely, be it storytelling, demanding, pleading, planning, inquiring, ventilating, explaining or complaining, as long as the relationship gains momentum. His responses to suggestions indicate if he wants an active therapist. Will he feel unique, understand himself in biographical terms, display feelings, or adopt a detached scientific stance? Descriptive style and transactions with the interviewer reveal preferences in problem-solving. These insights are applied to strengthen the budding therapeutic alliance. The initial interview style is then approximated successively to the most desirable one by first exploring, later challenging, counterproductive beliefs and unrealistic priorities. To a client complaining of severe shyness, ambiguous social cues—such as someone not paying attention—are presented as allowing a variety of interpretations. The inattentive person might be, for example, preoccupied with something else, not necessarily rejecting. The client's tendency to always expect rejection has perhaps evolved as a result of past experiences and a lack of social skills, and the explanation introduces a touch of intellectual detachment into the client's perception. Assumptions about the importance of being liked are examined in regard to their usefulness. A sense of being "special" may be dealt with by pointing out the operant effects of such a belief. Complaining and demands for compassion gradually give way to ventilating, recording neglected data, trying out new explanations, testing assumptions, and finally, to formulating a rationale for an intervention—such as refining social skills.

A substantial proportion of patients are not conversant in the terms of scientific psychology and cannot be expected to cooperate on this basis alone. Instead, a compromise is negotiated. An understanding cannot be taken for granted even when a client actively seeks out a particular therapeutic bias. He may look for a behaviorist to have physiological responses recorded rather than having to discuss a personal embarrassment or consult with an analyst because he hopes to avoid demands for behavior change. Therapists may justly examine their preferences along similar lines.

## APPLICATIONS

Correct perception does not provide all the necessary skills for an appropriate response. They have to be taught separately. The cognitive strategies outlined here are therefore not understood as therapy per se. They are employed to introduce specific treatment techniques. These techniques in turn should be selected according to the results of comparative research.

# Cooking as Therapy

*Louis Parrish*

## DEFINITION

Cooking is a practical mode of therapy through which the patient can channel anxieties, tensions, and aggressions via physical tasks such as cutting, chopping and beating into positive (and socially acceptable) outlets. Through cooking, the depressed patient can begin to reorient himself toward a simple goal-fulfilling task; the sense of accomplishment can be of great value in treating mild depression.

## HISTORY

The kitchen, since the beginning of time, has been the central room or gathering place for the family. In this era of depersonalization, cooking together is a constructive activity that can better communication between couples as well as parents and children. Cooking as a psychotherapy is probably a product of modern times. Prior to that, cooking was a necessary means of providing an adequate diet. Today, when people can eat out or bring in their meals, cooking is not all that essential for physiologic survival. However, the more one knows about cooking and the more one prepares his own meals, the more likely he is to have a healthy diet.

And there is little doubt that cooking for the sake of cooking has helped stabilize the psyches of many people. The number who naturally take to the kitchen to soothe or release their emotions is amazing. It is such a common activity that we too often overlook it as a therapeutic modality.

## TECHNIQUE

While cooking does not provide treatment for severe mental or emotional problems, it does afford the basically well-adjusted, functioning patient suffering from the anxiety/depressive syndrome so common today a means of working on his emotions and putting his problems into perspective. The technique is essentially Occupational Therapy. It is not only constructive but it utilizes a wide variety of basic activities that can express basic emotions. Cooking necessitates an involvement that can become a diversion. All the fundamentals of cooking, from the mechanics of slicing vegetables to the art of seasoning, can be used to good advantage.

## APPLICATIONS

In prescribing cooking as therapy it is important to emphasize that part of the preparation of the meal—whether it is shopping, preparing the ingredients, creating a dish, or serving—best suited to the individual patient's problems and needs. In the process of his utilizing the prescribed techniques to get a better perspective on his mental attitudes, the patient also gets a better understanding of nutrition. The overweight individual, for example, can be instructed as to how to prepare slimming but flavorful meals. In doing so, he feels a sense of accomplishment rather than the deprivation so often associated with dieting.

The person who needs a physical outlet for the pressures of daily life may find that beating a tough piece of meat until tender is a safe way of "taking it out" on something. If an individual is feeling emotionally shaky, or less than stable, "no fault" meals and menus—dishes he has prepared so often that he cannot make a mistake—in all likelihood are a useful kitchen prescription for a sense of security.

# Correctional Counseling

*Robert A. Shearer*

## DEFINITION

Correctional Counseling is the application of counseling techniques to the development, treatment, and rehabilitation of public offenders. Correctional Counseling is a major part of the services delivered to public offenders in the broader area of correctional treatment and the term best describes the setting of counseling rather than describing a particular counseling technique or theory.

## HISTORY

The employment of counselors in correctional facilities began just after World War II, but until 1965 most counselors in corrections were isolated, untrained, and unrecognized. In 1965, the Office of Law Enforcement Assistance was created and was later expanded in 1968. Corrections became of more interest, therefore large amounts of money were made available for rehabilitating the public offender. Many counseling and treatment programs were initiated with the goal of changing the public offender. Many correctional treatment programs were effective, but others were ill-conceived and not implemented according to sound counseling theories and techniques. Recent efforts have been concentrated in the area of evaluating which of these programs are effective and which are not.

## TECHNIQUE

A variety of theoretical counseling models have been applied to counseling public offenders. Most of these have been applied in two different areas of counseling:

1. *Corrective counseling and therapy.*
   The thrust of this counseling is a change in behavior or in the causes that led to the offender's involvement in crime; this counseling is done because the individual has committed a criminal act. The goal of this counseling is to help the offender integrate himself back into society by treating the specific area of the individual's personality or behavior that caused him to come in contact with the criminal justice system.

2. *Developmental counseling and therapy.*
   The thrust of this counseling is to facilitate growth and positive functioning on the part of the offender; this treatment concentrates on the offender as a person, apart from his crime. The goal of this counseling is to help the offender understand the negative aspects of imprisonment or institutionalization. Consequently, the goals of this counseling are growth and development in general as opposed to being crime-specific.

Correctional Counseling is encompassed in the broader "correctional treatment point of view," which serves as a philosophical base for the implementation of more specific theoretical approaches:

*Assumption I.* Most public offenders need help in constructive behavior changes.

Assumption II. Most public offenders can benefit from correctional treatment services offering information on constructive behavior changes.

*Assumption III.* Many public offenders would prefer to follow a more positive, socially constructive life-style.

*Assumption IV.* Correctional treatment should not make offenders more dependent on institutions or community services.

*Assumption V.* Correctional treatment of offenders should meet both the individual needs and social needs for help.

*Assumption VI.* The only real and effective correctional treatment is voluntary and uncoerced.

*Assumption VII.* Participation in correctional treatment services in no way substitutes for, or detracts from, legal disposition for crimes committed by offenders.

*Assumption VIII.* Participation in correctional treatment in no way detracts from or minimizes the seriousness of the crime committed by offenders.

*Assumption IX.* Participation in correctional treatment services in no way minimizes the necessity of protecting society from public offenders while the offender is involved in treatment.

*Assumption X.* Correctional treatment is designed to return to society a more socially useful citizen and worker who does not recidivate in crime.

In addition to training in traditional counseling techniques, effective correctional counselors have additional training in the following areas:

a) An understanding of the criminal justice system.
b) A knowledge of deviancy theory.
c) Skills in counseling the highly manipulative, "con artist" personality.
d) Skills in functioning in a highly untherapeutic environment.

The techniques employed in counseling in correction vary according to the theoretical models that have been applied, and no one theory of counseling prevails in corrections.

## APPLICATIONS

Correctional Counseling is applied to a specific group of clients defined by law as offenders. The function of Correctional Counseling may be carried out by workers with a variety of titles, such as caseworker, social worker, offender counselor, correctional treatment specialist, or counselor. In any case, it will be the person charged with helping the offender at various points in the criminal justice system. Counseling occurs with individuals who are in juvenile or adult institutions, who are on probation or parole. Counseling occurs at pre-release centers, work-release centers, halfway houses, or community corrections programs. Correctional Counseling may occur within the court system or law enforcement agencies. The present criminal and juvenile justice systems are a myriad of agencies and programs, so the applications of Correctional Counseling are quite diverse.

# Correspondence Therapy

## George M. Burnell

### DEFINITION

Correspondence Therapy is a technique of individual psychotherapy using written communication. In addition to letters it includes diaries, suicidal notes, poetry, manuscripts, magazine clippings. It is often used as an adjunctive technique when a therapist-patient relationship already exists, and when certain conditions dictate its use or when some clinical considerations would aid the progress of psychotherapy.

### HISTORY

Freud used correspondence in his self-analysis and in one case he exchanged letters with the father of a boy in his "Analysis of a Phobia in a Five-Year-Old Boy." Farrow also recommended this approach for self-analysis (1948). At the invitation of a patient, Grotjahn continued therapy during a period of absence after which he resumed regular sessions (1955). Alston carried on a detailed psychoanalytical relationship with a patient hospitalized for tuberculosis and showed that "familiar phenomena of psychoanalytic therapy" manifested themselves through this type of communication (1957).

In a brief monograph consisting of papers presented at a meeting of the American Psychological Association in 1965, the attitudes and ideas of three psychologists were expressed followed by a critique by Raimy (see Pearsons, 1965). Burton, in the first paper, stated the opinion that written communications in psychotherapy should be an adjunctive process, implementing other methods, and viewed as an expressive and creative act that might provide additional material for analysis. Ellis described his use of varying techniques, including diaries, journals, and correspondence, primarily for diagnostic purposes. He indicated that these were not likely to replace more direct therapies and that the preferred usage should be for those patients already having a relationship with the therapist. In the third paper, Harrower reported the use of letters, notebooks, and record transcriptions under special circumstances and conditions that provided the only way, or the most appropriate way, to achieve the therapeutic results desired. She also pointed out specifically the potential disadvantage of losing the patient's trust and confidentiality when the material was published. In his critique of these three papers, Raimy stated that he looked on the use of written communication as a modification of technique, but he observed that in using the written word all three therapists seem to follow the same principles and conception which they used in their typical office procedure.

### TECHNIQUE

There are three major sets of conditions which lead to the use of written communication between therapist and patient:

## Conditions based on physical circumstances.

1. When the patient or therapist is away for a prolonged absence.
2. When the patient or therapist transfers to another area, and the patient needssupport to follow through with a new therapist.
3. If the patient lives in a distant area and visits are infrequent.
4. Therapy is indirect, using the help of a relative or friend who has access to the patient in a distant place.
5. The patient is considered dangerous to himself or others and knowledge of his whereabouts would be useful in coordinating further care.
6. The patient is institutionalized for a chronic illness (e.g., tuberculosis, leprosy).

## Conditions based on transference or countertransference.

1. When the patient wishes to avoid expressing strong positive or negative feelings toward the therapist in the course of therapy.
2. The patient wishes to gain the therapist's approval and admiration by producing creative writings to express deeply felt and intimate experiences.
3. When the patient has difficulty facing termination of therapy and chooses the written word to avoid an intense emotional experience.
4. The patient wishes to give the therapist a follow-up report about his condition after moving away. This may help the patient cope with separation anxiety and decreases the intensity of the affective experience by maintaining contact with the therapist.
5. The therapist wishes to clarify the current status of the therapy contract with a patient who has been unable or unwilling to keep his appointments or follow through with treatment recommendations.
6. The patient's obsessiveness compels him to structure or resist the therapy sessions by bringing in written material.

## Conditions based on special ability or limitation in verbal communication.

1. The patient has particular talent, inclination, or ability to express feelings creatively through prose or poetry.
2. The patient is deaf or physically unable to speak (aphasic, weak, voiceless, or mute).
3. The therapist is deaf.

## APPLICATIONS

Through the content of the written material, the therapist can isolate the similarities and differences from psychotherapy in the office. In most communication the phenomena of transference (an emotional attitude the patient has toward the therapist), countertransference, and resistances are evident as they are during therapy sessions.

The differences are evident in two areas. First, the therapist cannot assess the intensity of the patient's emotional response associated with the written productions. Second, the delay of feedback from patient to therapist and from therapist to patient dilutes the impact of the communication. This is especially true if there was a fear of losing control (on the part of the patient). The therapist's countertransference, experienced as very high amounts of anxiety, could also be diffused in this way. Both patient and therapist have more time to prepare for a response. The therapist can review his reply and even obtain consultation from a colleague, thus permitting a review of the case in the same way as by examining a taped session. The therapist can also assess the level of ego disintegration present. Some patients might find an opportunity to describe their thoughts and feelings more thoroughly while others might become more inhibited. Occasional vagueness can represent another distancing response to the termination of therapy. Some patients, who become quite dependent on their therapists, might emphasize details, sharing time and place when the material was written, as if to include the therapist in the experience itself. In either case this information (or lack of it) might shed further light on the current status of the therapist-patient relationship. Sometimes a referral to a therapist, in a distant town or city where the patient has moved, might be facilitated by a letter to the patient.

There are, however, some definite problems and limitations in using written communication in therapy. Correspondence Therapy must be considered an adjunct to psychotherapy. It lacks the important ingredient of spontaneity of patient-therapist exchanges. It also lacks the observation of nonverbal clues. Furthermore, it is likely to make the therapist more cautious and less apt to write down interpretations that might be quoted later in situations outside of his control (such as a legal setting). The possibility of distortion, misunderstanding, or quoting out of context remains a reality. And the matter of confidentiality—not knowing who might come to read the material—presents special problems with this technique.

Despite these constraints, corresponding with a patient may offer definite advantages. First, whenever office visits become impossible or very difficult because the patient has a severe physical disability limiting ambulation, a chronic illness (tuberculosis), or a handicap (deafness), this approach may be useful. Other reasons might include: distant and isolated living situations and transportation problems. Second, some patients are particularly gifted in expressing themselves in writing, and in some cases this talent can be maximized in the therapeutic relationship. For some of these patients, additional insights, cathartic experiences, and increase in self-esteem can result through a sense of creativity in their writings. For others, it may diminish separation anxiety in the termination of therapy. Sometimes, the written communication represents a symbolic gift to the therapist, or it may be another form of resistance by avoiding confrontation in the therapy session.

In summary, written communications have a definite therapeutic impact and serve as an effective adjunctive technique where a therapist-patient relationship already exists, and the therapist uses them with the same degree of care as other interventions in psychotherapy.

---

# Co-therapy
## *Karen Hellwig*

### DEFINITION

The development of Co-therapy as a valid mode of treating patients in a group setting has accompanied the proliferation of psychotherapeutic techniques since World War II. The word "Co-therapy" itself encompasses a variety of definitions that reflect its process of evolving as a unique form of therapy. An increasing number of articles describing, refining, criticizing, and extending the uses of Co-therapy point to its expanding popularity as a therapeutic technique.

Although Co-therapy has been associated with other names, such as "multiple therapy," "joint interview," "cooperative psychotherapy," "three-cornered therapy," and "dual-leadership" (Treppa, 1971), it is a process with its own definable qualities. Co-therapy involves the use of two or more psychotherapists who work to develop a therapeutic relationship with an individual or members of a group in order to assist the individual(s) to function better interpersonally and intrapersonally. Co-therapists may be of the same or opposite sex; they may belong to the same or different disciplines (e.g., psychology, psychiatry, psychiatric nursing, and social work); one may be a senior, more actively involved partner and the other a junior, observer partner; or the relationship between co-therapists may be egalitarian. Co-therapy provides an excellent situation in which to teach trainee therapists how to apply their therapeutic skills.

## HISTORY

The Vienna Child Guidance Clinic was the scene of the first documented use of Co-therapy by Adler in the 1920s. Reeve attested to the therapeutic as well as educational values of pairing a social worker and psychiatrist to work with patients in the mid-1930s. And Whitaker et al. confirmed in the 1950s that Co-therapy facilitates the therapeutic process; they were the first to report the intensive use of multiple therapy for treating patients.

## TECHNIQUE

Before any therapy commences, and as the therapeutic process proceeds, the co-therapists must be able to freely and openly communicate their feelings to each other. Otherwise, the incidence of hostility, jealousy, and anger that can occur between therapists could have a devastating effect on the individual(s) undergoing treatment. The basis of Co-therapy lies in the ability of the therapists to be able to relate to each other in an open and trusting manner, develop a sense of peership, accept each other's opinions, identify each other's strengths and weaknesses, and deal with criticism in a constructive manner. In addition the therapists should feel approval from each other, feel compatible with each other, and be able to collaborate and settle differences in opinion outside of the therapy sessions. As long as both therapists are using the same therapeutic model, whether it be psychoanalytical, Rogerian, or eclectic, the type of psychotherapy that is practiced with the group or individual is less important.

The co-therapy process generally proceeds through four phases: the therapists must first develop a relationship between themselves and with the patient(s); then each patient's dynamics must be analyzed through consultation between the therapists and open discussion with the patient; the co-therapists assist the patient to understand himself; and finally, the patient is helped to reorient himself to his new self-concept and patterns of behavior (Dreikurs).

Co-therapy allows for a variety of techniques to be employed in the therapeutic process. For example, one therapist can provide support for a patient while the other can zero in on deeply imbedded feelings. Or, if a co-therapy team consists of both sexes, a patient may be able to use the same-sex therapist as a role model while dealing with parental conflicts with the therapist of the opposite sex.

Co-therapy also provides the background for the successful identification and utilization of transference feelings (an emotional attachment) toward one or both therapists. For example, if a patient develops strong transference feelings toward Therapist A, and Therapist A develops countertransference feelings or is unable to identify the occurring transference phenomenon, Therapist B can act as observer and, by identifying the transference, can prevent an impasse and aid both Therapist A and the patient to visualize and deal with the transference.

As with any group, members of a co-therapy group may develop resistance by comparing co-therapists unfavorably, scapegoating one therapist, assuming the role of therapist, using the therapist to perpetrate symptoms, or avoiding relationships with patients of the "other" therapist (Pine). These resistive patterns must be identified by the therapists and can then be used to initiate changes in patient behavior.

Limit-setting is another important aspect of both group and individual psychotherapy and is more easily accomplished through the joint efforts of co-therapists than by a single therapist. This has been demonstrated repeatedly in therapy sessions with adolescents and psychotics.

## APPLICATIONS

Co-therapy is applicable in a variety of settings and has been used successfully with schizophrenics, psychotics, and neurotics; with adolescents and college students; with married couples, and increasingly with families. It is used in private practice, in community mental health centers, in psychiatric facilities, and in teaching hospitals for the benefit of student psychiatric practitioners.

# Crisis Intervention

## *Donna C. Aguilera*

## DEFINITION

The Chinese characters that represent the word "crisis" mean, appropriately, both danger and opportunity. Crisis is a danger because it threatens to overwhelm the individual or his family, and it may result in suicide or a psychotic break. It is also an opportunity because during times of crisis individuals are more receptive to the therapeutic influence. Prompt and skillful intervention may not only prevent the development of a serious long-term disability, but may also allow new coping patterns to emerge that can help the individual function at a higher level of equilibrium than before the crisis.

The outcome of a psychological crisis can be either growth or deterioration; it is a decisive moment. A person in crisis faces a problem that he cannot readily solve by using the coping mechanisms that have worked for him before. As a result, his tension and anxiety increase, and he becomes less able to find a solution. A person in this situation feels helpless; he is caught in a state of great emotional upset, and feels unable to take action on his own to solve his problem. Crisis Intervention can offer the immediate help that a person in a crisis needs in order to reestablish equilibrium. This is an inexpensive, short-term therapy that focuses on solving the immediate problem.

## HISTORY

The crisis approach to therapeutic intervention has developed only within the past few decades, and is based on a broad range of theories of human behavior, including those of Sigmund Freud, Heinz Hartmann, Sandor Rado, Erik Erikson, Lindemann, and Gerald Caplan. Its current acceptance as a recognized form of treatment cannot be directly related to any single theory of behavior; all have contributed to some degree. The following is a brief summary of some of the knowledge incorporated in the present practice of Crisis Intervention.

Sigmund Freud was the first to demonstrate and apply the principle of causality as it relates to psychic determinism. Simply put, this principle states that every act of human behavior has its cause, or source, in the history and experience of the individual. It follows that causality is operative, whether or not the individual is aware of the reason for his behavior.

An important outcome of Freud's deterministic position was his construction of a developmental, or "genetic," psychology. An individual's present behavior is understandable in terms of his life history or experience, and the crucial foundations for all future behavior are laid down in infancy and early childhood.

Since the end of the nineteenth century the concept of determinism has undergone many changes. Although the ego-analytic theorists have tended to go along with much of the Freudian position, there are several respects in which they differ. As a group, they conclude that Freud had neglected the direct study of normal, or healthy, behavior.

Heinz Hartmann, an early ego-analyst, postulated that the psychoanalytic theories of Freud could prove valid for normal as well as abnormal behavior. He emphasized that man's adaptation in early childhood, as well as his ability to maintain his adaptation to his environment in later life, must be considered. Hartman also believed that although the behavior of the individual is strongly influenced by his culture, there is a part of the personality that remains relatively free.

Sandor Rado saw human behavior as based upon the principle of motivation and adaptation. He viewed behavior in terms of its effect upon the welfare of the individual, not just in terms of cause and effect. Rado's Adaptational Psychotherapy emphasizes the immediate present without neglecting the influence of the developmental past. The primary concern is with failures in adaptation today—what caused them and what the patient must do to learn to overcome them.

Erik Erikson further developed the theories of ego-psychology, which complement those of Freud, Hartmann, and Rado, by focusing on the stages of development of the ego, and on the theory of reality. His theory of development is characterized by an orderly sequence of development at particular stages, each depending upon the other for successful completion. Erikson's theory is important in that it offers an explanation of the individual's social development as a result of his encounters with his social environment. His theories have provided a basis for the work of others who further developed the concept of maturational crisis, and began serious consideration of situational crisis and man's adaptation to this current environmental dilemma.

Lindemann's initial concern was in developing approaches that might contribute to the maintenance of good mental health and the prevention of emotional disorganization on a community-wide level. In his study of bereavement reactions among the survivors of those killed in a nightclub fire, he described both brief and abnormally prolonged reactions occurring in different individuals as a result of the loss of a significant person in their lives.

In his experiences in working with grief reactions, Lindemann concluded that it would be profitable to develop a frame of reference constructed around the concept of an emotional crisis, as shown by the bereavement reactions. Lindemann's theoretical frame of reference led to the development of crisis-intervention techniques. In 1946, he and Gerald Caplan established a community-wide program of mental health in the Harvard area.

According to Caplan (1961) the most important aspects of mental health are: 1) the state of the ego, 2) the stage of its maturity, and 3) the quality of its structure. As a result of his work in Israel, and in Massachusetts with Lindemann, he evolved the concept of the importance of crisis periods in individual and group development.

## TECHNIQUE

Why do some people go into a state of crisis and others do not? What factors decide whether an individual will regain a state of equilibrium or enter a state of crisis? There are three factors that seem to make the difference.

The first factor is the "perception of the event." The therapist asks the individual what the event means to him. How is it going to affect his future? Can he look at the event realistically, or does he distort its meaning? The second factor is termed "situational supports." In other words, what person in the environment can the client depend upon to help him? Who is available for him to talk to about this stressful event, and give him support? The third factor is called "available coping mechanisms." What does he usually do when he has a problem? Does he sit down and try to think it out? Does he cry it out? Does he get angry and try to get rid of his feelings of anger and hostility by swearing, kicking a chair, or the cat? Does he get into a verbal battle with a friend? Does he try to sit down and talk it out with someone? Does he need to temporarily withdraw from the situation in order to reassess the problem? These are just a few of the many coping skills people use to relieve their tension and anxiety when faced with a problem.

Some of the questions that should be asked for assessment are directed toward finding out the precipitating event—in other words, what happened— and the balancing factors. One of the first questions asked is: "Why did you come for help today?" Sometimes the client will try to avoid answering this question by saying: "I've been planning to come for some time." This reluctance may be countered with, "Yes, but what happened that made you come in today?" Other questions the therapist should ask are: "What happened in your life that is different? When did it happen?"

In crisis, the precipitating event usually has occurred within ten days to two weeks before the individual seeks help. More often it is something that happened the day before, or the night before. It could be almost anything: the threat of divorce, discovery of a spouse's extramarital relations, finding out a son or daughter is on drugs, loss of a boyfriend or girlfriend, loss of job or status, an unwanted pregnancy, and so forth.

The therapist next focuses on the first factor, or how the individual perceives the event, by asking the questions noted above. Then the therapist can go into available situational supports. Who or what person in the environment can the therapist depend on to help the person? Who does he live with? Who is his best friend? Whom does he trust? Is there a member of the family that he feels particularly close to?

Because Crisis Intervention is limited to only six weeks or less, the more friends and relatives that are involved in helping the person the better. Also, if those involved are familiar with the problem, they can continue to give support when the Crisis Intervention therapy is terminated.

The third factor is finding out what the person usually does when he has a problem he can't solve. What are his coping skills? Questions asked would be: Has anything like this ever happened to him before? How does he usually get rid of tension, anxiety, or depression? Has he tried the same method this time? If not, why, since it usually works for him? If the individual has tried his usual method and it doesn't work, he may be asked why he thinks it doesn't work. What does the person feel he could do to reduce his symptoms of stress? Clients can usually come up with something the therapist hasn't thought of, and some will recall methods they haven't used in years.

One of the most important parts of the assessment is to find out if the individual is suicidal or homicidal. The questions must be very direct and specific: Is he planning to kill himself... or someone else? How? When? The therapist must find out and assess the lethality of the threat. Is he merely thinking about it, or, does he have a method picked out? Is it a lethal method, such as a loaded gun? Does he have a tall building or bridge picked out, but won't reveal where? Will he say when he plans to do it?—for example, a housewife may choose a time after the children leave for school. Usually, if the threat doesn't sound too immediate, the therapist can arrange for medication. If the suicidal intent is carefully planned and the details specific, the person is sent for psychiatric evaluation and hospitalization, in order to protect him or others in the community.

Experiences have verified that Crisis Intervention can be an effective therapy modality with chronic psychiatric patients. If a psychiatric patient with a history of repeated hospitalizations returns to the community and his family, his reentry creates many stresses. While much has been accomplished to remove the stigma of mental illness, people are still wary and hypervigilant when they learn that a "former mental patient" has returned home to his community.

In his absence the family and community have, consciously or unconsciously, eliminated him from their usual life patterns and activities. They then have to readjust to his presence and include him in activities and decision making. If for any reason he does not conform to their expectations, they want him removed so that they can continue their lives without his possible disruptive behavior.

The first area to explore is to determine who is in crisis: the patient or his family. In many cases the family is overreacting because of its anxiety and are seeking some means of getting the "identified" patient back into the hospital. The patient is usually brought to the center by a family member because his original maladaptive symptoms have begun to reemerge. Questioning the patient or his family about medication he received from the hospital and determining if he is taking it as prescribed are essential. If the patient is unable to communicate with the therapist about what has happened or what has changed in his life, the family is questioned as to what might have precipitated his return to his former psychotic behavior.

There is usually a cause-and-effect relationship between a change, or anticipated change, in the routine patterns of life-style or family constellation and the beginnings of abnormal overt behavior in the identified patient. Often, families forget or ignore telling a former psychiatric patient when they are contemplating a change because "he wouldn't understand." Such changes could include moving or changing jobs. This is perceived by the patient as exclusion or rejection by the family and creates stress that he is unable to cope with; thus, he retreats to his previous psychotic behavior. Such cases are frequent and can be dealt with through the theoretical framework of Crisis Intervention methodology.

Rubenstein (1972) stated that family-focused Crisis Intervention usually brings about the resolution of the patient's crisis without resorting to hospitalization. In a later article in 1974, he advocated that family Crisis Intervention can also be a viable alternative to rehospitalization. Here the emphasis is placed on the period immediately after the patient's release from the hospital. He suggested that conjoint family therapy begin in the hospital before the patient's release and then continue in an out-patient clinic after his release. His approach has also served to develop the concept that a family can and should share responsibility for the patient's treatment.

In Decker and Stubblebine's study (1972), two groups of young adults were followed for two and one-half years after their first psychiatric hospitalization. The first group was immediately hospitalized and received traditional modes of treatment, and the second group was hospitalized after the institution of a Crisis Intervention program. The results of the study indicated that Crisis Intervention reduced long-term hospital dependency without producing alternate forms of psychological or social dependency, and also reduced the number of rehospitalizations.

The following brief case study illustrates how one can work with a chronic psychiatric patient in a community mental health center using the crisis model.

## Case Study: Chronic Patient in the Community

Jim, a man in his late thirties, was brought to a crisis center by his sister because, as she stated, "He was beginning to act crazy again." Jim had many prior hospitalizations, with a diagnosis of paranoid schizophrenia. The only thing Jim would say was, "I don't want to go back to the hospital." He was told that our role was to help him stay out of the hospital if we possibly could. A medical consultation was arranged to determine if he needed to have his medication increased or possibly changed.

Information was then obtained from his sister to determine what had happened (the precipitating event) when his symptoms had started and, specifically, what she meant by his "acting crazy again." His sister stated that he was "talking to the television set ... muttering things that made no sense ... staring into space ... prowling around the apartment at night," and that "this behavior started about three days ago." When questioned about anything that was different in their lives before the start of his disruptive behavior, she denied any change. When asked about any changes that were contemplated in the near future, she replied that she was planning to be married in two months but that Jim did not know about it because she had not told him yet. When asked why she had not told him, she reluctantly answered that she wanted to wait until all of the arrangements had been made. She was asked if there was any way Jim could have found out about her plans. She remembered that she had discussed them on the telephone with a girl friend the week before.

She was asked what her plans for Jim were after she married. She said that her boyfriend had agreed, rather reluctantly, to let Jim live with them.

Since her boyfriend was reluctant about having Jim live with them, other alternatives were explored. She said that they had cousins living in a nearby suburb but that she did not know if they would want Jim to live with them.

It was suggested that Jim's sister call her cousins, tell them of her plans to get married and her concerns about Jim, and, in general, find out their feelings about him living with them. The call was placed, and she told them her plans and concerns. Fortunately, their response was a positive one. They had recently bought a fairly large apartment building and were having difficulty getting reliable help to take care of the yard work and minor repairs. They felt that Jim would be able to manage this, and they would let him live in a small apartment above the garage.

Jim was asked to come back into the office so that his sister could tell him of her plans to marry and the arrangements she had made for him with their cousins. He listened but had difficulty comprehending the information. He just kept saying, "I don't want to go back to the hospital."

He was asked if he had heard his sister talking about her wedding plans. He admitted that he had and that he knew her boyfriend would not want him around— "They would probably put me back in the hospital." As the session ended, he still had not internalized the information he had heard. He was asked to continue therapy for five more weeks and to take his medication as prescribed. He agreed to do so.

By the end of the sixth week he had visited his cousins, seen the apartment where he would be living, and had discussed his new "job." His disruptive behavior had ceased, and he was again functioning at his pre-crisis level.

Since Jim had had many previous hospitalizations and did not want to be rehospitalized, time was spent in discussing how this could be avoided in the future. He was given the name, address, and telephone number of a crisis center in his new community and told to visit it when he moved. He was assured that the center could supervise his medication and be available if he needed someone to talk to if he felt he again needed help.

Jim's sister neglected to tell him about her impending marriage, which he perceived as rejection. Because of his numerous hospitalizations, he feared that his sister would have him rehospitalized "to get rid of him." He was unable to verbalize his fears, retreated from reality, and experienced an exacerbation of his psychotic symptoms.

The therapist adhered to the crisis model by focusing the therapy sessions on the patient's immediate problems, not on his chronic psychopathology. It is important to remember that the therapist's role is to focus on the immediate problem. Both client and therapist must actively participate to solve the problem on a short-term basis. There is not enough time, nor is it necessary, to go into the patient's past history in depth.

Crisis Intervention may seem easier and simpler than it is. It requires a knowledge of psychodynamics, and a lot of experience on the part of the therapist. Crisis Intervention requires the therapist's total involvement, a commitment, and a keen sense of responsibility for the individual's well-being.

# Culturalist Therapy

### Lester A. Gelb

## DEFINITION

The culturalist sees personality as emerging from social experience. The culturalist practitioner rejects the Freudian concepts of the id, ego, and super-ego, and the view that human behavior is basically derived from instinctual (mostly sexual) drives; that man is a prisoner of his own biology; that the unconscious is a separate division of the mind and operates independent of the external world. In culturalist psychoanalytic therapy, the therapist recognizes the impact of the cultural milieu as a major force in shaping the personality of the individual, and the need for the disturbed patient to be able to cope in his culture in a new, constructive, and contributing way.

## HISTORY

Alfred Adler was a forerunner of culturalist thinking. He emphasized the equal importance of the individual and the social milieu in the development of the "life-style" of each person. He saw social feeling as a measure of mental health. Although Karen Horney accepted Freud's concepts of psychic determinism and unconscious motivation, she did not accept the concept of libidinal drives. In its place, cultural and interpersonal factors were considered the cause of neurosis. Harry Stack Sullivan insisted on formulating his views on the data obtained by observing interactions of an individual with others, with the therapist as a participant-observer. His "interpersonal" methodology put emphasis on the social and cultural context in which personality develops. Abram Kardiner and Erich Fromm, each in his own way, focused on the relationship of man and society; they considered the character of a person as being both developed and measured by how a person relates to the world and its social institutions.

Although the above-noted pioneers laid the foundations for the cultural school of psychoanalysis, each one also postulated "basic strivings," "inner drives" or "urges" to explain at least part of motivation. Bernard Robbins was possibly the first analyst who did not accept the concept of innate drives. He believed that man is not the blind product of forces either within or around him, but that relationships are established between the person and the outside world and are reciprocal in nature.

## THEORY AND TECHNIQUE

The theory of Culturalist Therapy begins with a consideration of the origins of the human being—with a study of evolution and cultural anthropology. Anthropologist Hallowell noted that what anthropologists call "culture" is not instinctual but learned. It includes the transmission of learned behavior through the symbolic means of language. A system of social interaction was necessary for human evolution. This development could not have taken place without the evolution of the human brain; with advancing cortical development came the ability to use words as symbols for percepts and concepts that are passed on from generation to generation. This ever-accelerating ability to transmit knowledge produced a psychosocial evolution that was thousands of times faster than anything that could have occurred through ordinary biological evolution.

This would indicate that social existence is not only created by man but also continually creates and develops man. This concept is the key to Culturalist Therapy. What is required in therapy is to change the social existence of patients so that they will experience more productive and creative lives. Through new life experiences made possible by therapy, they can be, as it were, "newly created." The friend, the spouse, the family, the community and the society form a continuum that must be considered for possible change. Thus, the culturalist therapist, although working with individuals, will emphasize family therapy, group therapy, and community mental health programs.

The degree to which therapy can help an individual is limited by the extent to which he can be helped to find a healthy social field for adequate functioning. The health of the social field, in turn, depends on the extent to which healthy individuals are acting to bring about needed changes. The relationship between social environment and the individual is truly reciprocal.

## APPLICATIONS

An example of a socio-cultural approach to therapy will best illustrate its clinical application. A twenty-two-year-old woman was brought in by her husband because of depression and anxiety. She complained that she was depressed because of frequent episodes of panic during which she was convinced she would die. She was a thin, taut, attractive young woman in obvious panic, with a pulse rate of 144 and rapid breathing. She spoke in a meek, thin, and whining voice and looked away from her husband. She was the only daughter of religious European-born parents who, when she was eighteen, arranged a marriage to a highly religious man. They had two children.

The husband complained that his wife, previously a scrupulously clean, orderly, and attentive housewife, had begun to sulk and to neglect the home and the children. She gradually became more depressed and periodically panic-stricken.

The patient was given a short-acting tranquilizer for a few days to reduce her panic, hyperventilation, and rapid heart rate. The therapeutic encounter was a difficult one because of her reluctance to reveal her feelings about her personal situation. After some period of confronting her with evidence of her rage and the need to deal with it, she was able to confide her sense of entrapment in a marriage to a man she doubted she loved, her sense of having been placed in servitude, and a bitter resentment about being deprived of an education and a career. The therapist proposed that she continue to clarify the sources of her anger, and that she make moves to correct her situation rather than "go on strike." Her panic seemed due to her feeling that she was losing everything. Her physical symptoms soon abated but her depression persisted.

As the couple was seen together, she gained the courage to demand an opportunity for education and for fewer religious strictures. The therapist tried to help them come to some agreement on these issues and to develop a more loving relationship. Both the husband's and the wife's parents (who were also seen) did not believe that the wife needed a college education or that she should take the time from her home responsibilities. Psychological testing, done to assess her career potentials, revealed a passive, angry person with an intelligence so superior that it almost reached the limits of the test. Her husband finally agreed to her finishing high school and beginning college. However, he soon felt threatened by her rapid progress and began to disparage her. She gradually realized that she really didn't love him and couldn't continue to live with him. When she confronted him with this, he became abusive and she had to flee to her parents' home.

The patient required several years of weekly or intermittent therapy to help her deal with her real frustrations and privations and to arrive at partial and gradual solutions. She also required help from community support systems and from her family. Therapy later focused on assertiveness training so that she could deal with people in a full-voiced and firm manner without being competitive or controlling.

The patient is now divorced, has finished college, and is a part-time instructor in college while attending a graduate Ph.D. program. She is now functioning constructively in a changed cultural milieu. She has been caring for her children while she works and studies, and has been able to be compassionate and helpful with her parents. It is interesting that they, because of their specialized cultural values, mournfully view their daughter's present status as a failure. After her divorce her father became depressed and also required therapy.

The therapeutic attempts for this family required close attention to and manipulation of the socio-cultural institutions that had helped shape and limit the lives of the family members. These include, to mention only a few, the limited mobility of women in our culture and other conflicts intrinsic to the transcultural situation of this particular family.

# Dance Therapy

*Penny Lewis Bernstein*

## DEFINITION

Dance Therapy is defined as the psychotherapeutic use of movement toward the physical and psychic integration of the individual. It is viewed as a holistic healing process that assumes there is a natural flow of energy existent in all living entities. Disruptions of this flow, manifested by maladaptive movement, posture, and breathing patterns, are seen as an indication of conflict. Movement, a fundamental source of communication, is the primary medium used for the understanding of somatopsychic dysfunction and the facilitation of change.

## HISTORY

Movement ritual has allowed man since the beginnings of civilization to bridge the gap between himself and his universe. It has afforded a vehicle for his expression and transmission of fear, sadness, anger, and ecstasy in his quest for survival and the meaning of life. Dance was used for allaying feelings of powerlessness and transmitting any potential anxiety into a creative release that permitted man to feel that he did, in fact, have some control over his existence.

Twelfth-century Europe turned its back on this form of therapeutic dance—a trend that continued until the beginnings of the twentieth century, when Isadora Duncan emerged barefoot and emotive on the stages of the West, and modern dance was born.

Therapy evolved gradually, with a firm foundation in the worlds of ritual, modern dance, and psychology. Roots in the latter have stemmed more directly from the concepts of Jung, Wilhelm Reich, and the ego psychologists than from Freud. It was Mary Whitehouse, a California creative dance teacher, who, after Jungian analysis, began to draw connections between the authentic movement expressions of her students and the flow of symbolic unconscious material being shared at the end of her classes. Her shift into the, at the time, undelineated role of dance therapist was a gradual evolution.

In the East, private patients of some leading psychiatrists in a large federal hospital, St. Elizabeth's, were among those attending Marian Chace's dance classes. As the psychiatrists observed the effects of these classes on their clients, they decided in 1942 to invite Chace to work with them, in the drugless wards of St. Elizabeth's. With highly honed creative and intuitive processes, she engaged the most severely disturbed nonverbal individuals in movement.

Two other prime contributors to the development of Dance Therapy are Trudi Schoop, who, with an improvisational developmental approach, paralleled much of Chace's work on the West Coast, and the followers of Rudolf Laban. Laban devised a system of observation and notation of movement entitled "effort-shape," which focuses on how an individual moves. The Dance Notation Bureau, founded in New York City by Irmgard Bartenieff, provided a center where emerging dance therapists could learn a movement language for evaluative, communicational, and testing purposes.

By 1964, a small number of dance therapists were ready to become a professional body. With Chace as their president, seventy-three people formed The American Dance Therapy Association the following year. The association's goals are to denote and promulgate professional standards and to afford a vehicle for communication for isolated dance therapists. In 1972, a registry was instituted to further delineate professionalism.

## TECHNIQUE

The techniques vary with the frame of reference utilized. They will therefore be discussed in relation to the most widely employed theoretical approaches to the movement therapeutic process.

1.  *Chace Dance Therapy.* An empathetic, synchronistic, being-with-the-patient at his energy level characterizes the relationship of the Chace dance therapist. Music that reflects this energy level is played, and a group approach is employed. With reinforcement given through careful mirroring of movement by the therapist, the repetitive rhythmic music, and the other participants, the individual begins to trust the others and risk expression through dance-movement. The therapist picks up on and develops potential expressive gestures and patterns into total body releases of the blocked emotions of the group. Member interaction, breathing in service to the developing emotion, as well as verbal associations are encouraged. Expressive peeks of anger, sadness, fear, and joy ebb and flow; times of sense awareness focus,

nurturance and verbal communications connect the experience to the overall existence of the individual and group.

2. *Jungian Dance Therapy.* Here the dance therapist, with as few suggestions as possible, creates an environment for the client to enter into his unconscious through active imagination. A bridge for primary-process authentic movement is formed and seemingly simple gestural patterns emerge. Repetition of these patterns are encouraged. These movements frequently enlarge and encompass more of the body. Breathing and sounds originate from the emotive impetus. Often images imbued in mythological themes develop as the client experiences in symbolic bodily form what they mean to him. The dance therapist acts as witness and guide, and facilitates a verbal discussion of the experience in the light of analytic intuitive processes.

3. *Developmental Dance-Movement Therapy.* With a physiologic ego-psychology orientation, the dance therapist first ascertains, through observation and interpretation of his movement repertoire, the developmental level at which the individual is functioning. Effort-shape as well as other systems are utilized in this evaluatory process. The therapist then creates an environment through the therapeutic relationship and developmentally related movements. This environment attempts to facilitate the organization and integration of the conflictual areas.

4. *Gestalt Movement Therapy.* Body awareness and movement as an experiment are the prime tools of the movement therapist here. An understanding of the somatized conflicts as viewed by Reich form the basis of conceptualizing the bodily manifestation of unresolved Gestalts. Experiencing the figures through dramatic bodily movement serves to draw polarized conflictual patterns into contact and resolution.

## APPLICATIONS

Emphasis is placed on the specific choice of Dance Therapy for those individuals who have not had success with other modes of psychotherapy. Individuals who have benefited from Dance Therapy are: those who are on, or have regressed to, a nonverbal level of functioning, such as with certain autistic and psychotic patients; those who tend to somatize their conflicts, such as clients with ulcers, migraines, low-back pain, tension, obesity, vaginismus, etc.; those who utilize intellectualization as a primary defense in lieu of experiencing their existence and growth process; and those who have both a functional and organic dysfunction such as a stroke, Parkinson's disease, or cerebral palsy, or a learning disabled individual with emotional difficulties.

# Depth Therapy

## Benzion J. Rapoport

### DEFINITION

Depth Therapy is a new phenomenon (developed in the sixties and seventies) which is based heavily on Otto Rank's theory and technique. In the initial stages of the psychoanalytic approach, the Freudian model (dating from the 1890s to the present day) endeavored to keep the psychoanalyst as neutral as possible so that the psychotherapeutic process of "making the unconscious conscious" would not be interfered with by the contamination of an outside personality. This, as is well-known, lends itself to a prolonged process of intellectual discovery of the unconscious, leading to many years of consistent therapeutic involvement, often on a daily basis.

### HISTORY

Rank, in the 1920s and 1930s, became dissatisfied with this approach, attacking not only the technique itself but some of the very basic Freudian theoretical formulations (Oedipal complex, libido theory, etc.). He was in essence the first to break through the length of the process and accelerate the reaching of the unconscious. He claimed that he could help a person transform from a highly blocked, disturbed existence to a highly creative and artistic way of life within a nine-month period (the time period being equal to the time involved in the process of pregnancy), at which point the birth of the self would take place.

With the introduction of this concept into psychoanalytic thought came many new approaches and techniques. Among the more well-known are Psychodrama, Gestalt theory (Fritz Perls), and many more psychoanalytically based systems that deal more directly with the intrusion of the therapist's personality into the therapeutic process. As with Freudian theory, most of the modern therapeutic systems have also been influenced by Rankian theory. This is basically the case with Depth Therapy.

Otto Rank's theories were largely disseminated in the United States at the University of Pennsylvania's School of Social Work. Depth Therapy extends that theory somewhat by including more fully the idea that to be totally alive one must be creatively involved in daily living, just as an artist is involved in creating art. This includes freedom of choice, freedom of will, and constant creativity. In Depth Therapy, which includes some aspects of Will Therapy (Rank), the therapist's personality, creative ability, and skill are more fully integrated into the process of psychotherapy. Further, Depth Therapy extends Rank's "positive will" theory by including in it a method to stimulate motivation through the positive will.

Depth Therapy, or more accurately an intensive experiential interacting with a therapist, is dynamically grounded in the overall psychoanalytic framework, with a strong leaning toward a Rankian theoretical and technical base. It accepts the premise that there is an intra-uterine psychobiological influence that culminates in its impact in the birth process. The birth process is probably the essence of a future ability to change (Rank, 1952). The combination of the following factors seems to set the blueprint for a future ability to grow and change: the sensitivity of the nervous system and the impact of the intra-uterine existence suddenly erupting into a totally different physical, emotional, and sensuous experience by exposure to a drastically new environment. The severity of the change at birth, correlated with the physiological sensitivity of the nervous system, could well be the basic determinant of future adjustment to change, growth, and use of the "force of life."

As the infant develops, the other factors of parental (especially maternal) influence, their sensitivity, reactive behavior, care, and, above all, acceptance of the child as a separate being that is continuously developing, create the all-important environment in which the newly forming self becomes a uniquely creative, separate entity.

The end product of this growing child is an accomplished individual who is creative in life, relationships, job, and society. This is the ultimate goal in achieving a full life. If the self is a uniquely creative entity, the taking in of stimuli from the environment goes through a process of creativity within the unique self. The result is constant vibrance, freshness, and consistent growth into new horizons and experiences.

Within the spectrum of Rankian and psychoanalytic theories, we see that in the vast majority of homes parents, in their reaching out for eternity by remaining parents, fear the individuation of their child. When their child becomes a unique being different from themselves, their job is done and they are ready to be discarded by nature and die (this, of course, is their unconscious conviction based, in part, on their own lack of a unique self). In view of this death fear, the parents hold onto the child as an extension of themselves and do not allow for individual expression. This causes the child to grow into a shadow of the parent with severe guilt about his or her uniqueness and drive toward unique creativity (Rank, 1935).

Yet the child cannot help but try, throughout childhood, to reach out toward expression of the self. Guilt is increased, and being unique and creative becomes a dangerous phenomenon. This, in turn, encourages the child to be submissive, noninventive, guilt-ridden, and helpless. The child, and later the adult, becomes filled with anger, depression, feelings of inadequacy, and so on.

Why don't children take more of a risk and tear themselves away at an early age to grow on their own? To an extent, some do: the artists, the inventors, etc. Yet there is always the threat of death. If mother and father do not approve, they will withdraw care, love, protection, food, and the child will die. Therefore, the child, battling all the way, finally gives in as an adult, enters into the "family of man," and becomes a creature of dependence and a conformist.

## TECHNIQUE

The goal of Depth Therapy is to help the individual coming for help diminish the conditioning of the self from all the defense mechanisms and conditioned responses that are based on the concept of "right," "wrong," "good," and "bad." The process helps expose the buried self to stimuli and utilize the feeling aspects of our system rather than the intellectual aspects as the basis for survival and creativity.

In attempting rediscovery of the feeling self, the environment in the therapeutic milieu becomes one of womblike security and safety, later to become a source of environmental acceptance. Finally, the therapeutic relationship provides encouragement to the newfound self to separate the real in the relationship from the distorted (transference) part. To accomplish this final goal of separation, the process of therapy becomes the process of growth into a creative, separate self. All this, of course, cannot be totally accomplished since contamination of conditioning is great by the time the person seeking help comes into the office. Yet one can succeed in helping individuals reach a level of functioning that is much more creative, satisfying, and even exciting.

The therapeutic process is as follows:

The first stage is that of establishing an intense relationship with the therapist. It is vital that, above all, the therapist must be talented beyond the average in the ability to *accept and even enjoy* individual differences. In this first stage, this acceptance of differences must only be hinted at. The goal of the first stage is to help the individual enter into a symbolic, womblike existence with the therapist (on an emotional level). This helps to motivate the individual to enter, in future work, into the "dangerous" territory of feelings that were never allowed before.

The second stage helps the individual to begin to get in touch with his or her feelings. Within the safety of the newfound intensive relationship and the therapist's acceptance of the individual's unique feelings, the person in treatment becomes more accepting of his or her own feelings.

The third stage is the working through of the new experiences caused by the new feelings, i.e., what to do with one's feelings of rage, anger, frustration, love, hate, fear, sexuality, tenderness, and so on. In this stage, the individual works through these feelings, with the therapist acting as a representative of reality.

The final stage is one of separation, and it is extremely difficult both for the individual seeking help and for the helper. Despite his or her professional background, the separation is difficult for the therapist in this particular approach, due to the intensity of the relationship that has existed for several years. The pain and anxiety of separation are part of the process that engages both the helper and helpee. Yet it is ultimately the helper who must involve the individual coming for help in a process of separation and let go of the newly alive person.

Due to the brevity of this paper, the more complex, intricate, and complete explanation of the psychoanalytic and Rankian basis for this therapeutic approach cannot be dealt with. Yet the reader surely notes the relationship of the theory and process to the above-mentioned approaches. One of the most significant differences between Depth Therapy and similar approaches is that it emphasizes more fully the use of the therapist's own talent, capacity for intensity, appreciation of difference, and love of the uniqueness of life.

## APPLICATIONS

Depth Therapy can be applied to most of the emotional and mental disturbances that are listed in the psychiatric nomenclature. This is due to the emphasis in this theory on the qualities of the therapist necessary to help the patient grow (skill, talent, capacity for intensity, etc.) rather than the diagnosis of the patient. The selection of the proper therapist for a particular individual seeking help is vital, and this is where diagnosis of the patient is important in order to match the individual with the personality of the therapist.

As Depth Therapy has as its goal the effecting of major change in the personality and life of the individual seeking help, it is more applicable to ongoing individual psychotherapy of long duration rather than to crisis intervention work. More recently, however, Depth Therapy techniques have been applied with some success to short-term psychotherapy.

# Dialogue Psychotherapy

*Maurice Friedman*

## DEFINITION

Dialogue Psychotherapy is that form of "meeting psychotherapy" in which genuine dialogue—meaningful speech, experiencing the other side of the relationship, confirmation of the other in his uniqueness and otherness—is particularly stressed.

## HISTORY

The most important historical base of Dialogue Psychotherapy is the philosophy of dialogue expounded by Martin Buber, but it has been developed further both theoretically and practically by: Swiss psychoanalyst Hans Trüb, American psychologist Carl R. Rogers, German psychiatrist Viktor von Weizsäcker, English family psychiatrist Ronald D. Laing, American psychoanalyst Leslie H. Farber, Hungarian-American family psychiatrist Ivan Boszormenyi-Nagy, and American philosopher Maurice Friedman—all of whom, to one extent or another, were influenced by Buber.

Paradigmatic for the history of Dialogue Psychotherapy is Hans Trub, who went through a decade-long crisis in which he broke away from his personal and doctrinal dependence on Jung in favor of the insights that arose from his face-to-face meeting with Buber. In such unreserved interchange Trüb found it impossible to bring any concealed motive into the dialogue and let it affect it. In his work with his patients, Trüb became aware that his consciousness invariably tended to become monological so that he allowed his patient to be there for him only as a content of his own experience. But he also found that he was forced out of this closed circle into genuine dialogue with the patient when, despite his own will, he found himself confronting his patient as human being to human being. These experiences taught him the true role of the analyst as one who becomes responsible for those things that have been lost to the consciousness of the patient and helps bring these forgotten things into the light of relationship. It was not consciousness, as Freud thought, but the *outgoing to the other* which revealed the secret meaning of these "repressed contents of the unconscious."

Viktor von Weizsäcker's "medical anthropology" points the way toward a dialogue of question-and-answer between doctor and patient, without which all information about function, drives, properties, and capacities is falsified. This comradeship takes place through, not despite, technique and rationalization just as long as there is a self-understood relation between doctor and patient—an "inclusive," or "comprehensive," therapy in which the therapist allows himself to be changed by the patient. Even the physical and psychic needs that cut the patient off are facts of relationship that can be used to attain another level. The self-deification and self-degradation of the psychotic arise from the fact that he has no Thou for his I; it is this that produces cleavage of the self and the inner double.

# TECHNIQUE

Guilt means a rupture of the dialogical relationship, an injury of the common existential order, and as such must be repaired by again entering into dialogue with that person or with the world. It is in the real guilt of the person who has not responded to the legitimate claim and address of the world that the possibility of transformation and healing lies; for the repression of guilt and the neuroses that result from this repression are not merely psychological phenomena but real events between men. The therapist helps the patient become aware of himself in general, and of his responsibility in particular, through playing the part both of confidant and big brother. He gives the neurotic the understanding that the world has denied him and makes it more and more possible for him to step out of his self-imprisonment into a genuine relation with the analyst. To do this he must avoid both the temptation of dealing with the patient as an object *and* the intimacy of a private I-Thou relationship with him. The roots of the neurosis lie both in the society's rejection and non-confirmation of the patient and in the patient's closing himself off from the world.

Consequently, the analyst must change at some point from the consoler to the person who puts before the patient the claim of the world. He must help him resume that real dialogue with the community that can only take place in the community itself. The patient becomes whole in order that he may concern himself with the world and be at once responsible for himself and in responsible relationship with his community. The therapist embodies for the patient a loving inclination of the world that seeks to restore the latter's dispirited and mistrustful self to a new dialogical meeting with the forces of nature and history. Equality of respect is attained not by the insistence on a complete mutuality of situation, as Rogers maintains, but by the recognition of the *betweenness* itself as the common concern that each of them share and on which each of them work. Only this attitude enables the therapist to answer both for the patient and for the world, to risk personal commitment, even to the neurotic self-entanglement of the patient, and to face with the patient the cure's often unexpected completion.

In *The Knowledge of Man* (1965), Martin Buber sees the overcoming of existential guilt as taking place through the three stages of illuminating that guilt, persevering in that illumination, and repairing the injured order of being by reentering the dialogue with the world. In exact parallel, Ivan Nagy sees knowledge of the self and increased assertiveness as finding their places in the context of the accounts of fairness and justice in close relationships. One of the great opportunities of Nagy's three-generational approach lies in the possibility of rehabilitating the member's painful and shameful image of his parents through helping the member understand the burdens laid on his parents by their families of origin.

Nagy's three-generational family therapy culminates in that reciprocal justicing that rebalances the "merit ledger" between the generations. This can be done only through listening to each member's subjective construction of his accountability to the rest of the family. Nagy's touchstone of reality is not functional efficiency but the intrinsic balances between hidden loyalty ties and exploitations. This leads, in turn, to that "dialogue of touchstones" (Friedman) in which each person's point of view is confirmed precisely through coming into dialogue with the opposing views of others. The goal of Nagy's family therapy is not the community of affinity, or like-mindedness, but the "community of otherness" (Friedman).

In *Touchstones of Reality* (1972), I set forth the beginnings of a psychotherapy based on a "dialogue of touchstones." When two people really touch each other as persons, this touching is not merely a sum of impacts: it is a mutual revelation of lifestances. The real "dialogue of touchstones" means that the therapist responds from where he is, including opposing the client, if necessary, in order that the latter may experience the confirmation of coming up against a person with a touchstone of his own. At the same time the therapist can help the client escape the hopeless either/or of choosing between suppressing his own touchstones in favor of the language of others or attempting a communication that will lead only to rejection and nonconfirmation.

## APPLICATIONS

The concept of reality-testing in Freudian psychology is a comparatively mono-logical one in which the patient is either reality-bound or subject to distortion. This means, as Ronald Laing has pointed out, that the psychiatrist determines what is "normal" and invalidates the experience of the patient. Buber's and Nagy's concept of the "just order of the human world," in contrast, is a dialogical one. However pathological it may be, the unique experience of each of the persons in the family is itself of value: it enters into the balance of merit and into that dialogical reality-testing that I call the "dialogue of touchstones." The scapegoater in the family can be looked upon as needing help and the scapegoat as a potential helper; for the former is taking an ever-heavier load of guilt on himself and the latter is accumulating merit through being loaded on by others.

Leslie H. Farber has made an important application of Dialogue Psychotherapy to the psychopathology of the will. Farber sees the origin of willfulness as the desperate need for wholeness. When dialogue, which is the proper setting for wholeness, eludes us, "we turn wildly to will, ready to grasp at any illusion of wholeness the will conjures up for our reassurance." The more dependent a person becomes on the illusion of wholeness, the less he is able to experience true wholeness in dialogue. Willfulness is that addiction to will in which the person attempts to make up for the absence of dialogue by handling both sides of the no longer mutual situation.

Nagy's dialogical intergenerational family therapy also has wide-ranging applications. If the partners in marriage do not intuitively perceive that two quite different family systems of merit are joined, each mate will struggle to coerce the other to be accountable for those of one's felt injustices and accrued merit that come from his or her family of origin. By improving their reciprocal loyalty with their families of origin, Nagy's family therapy helps the married couple relate to each other and their children. Only constructive repayment of indebtedness to the parents' family of origin can redress the injustice of the parentification of children. Only when the adults' unmet dependency needs and unresolved negative loyalty ties are recognized and worked through—wherever possible with the families of origin themselves—can the family therapist help the children give up their assumed adultlike roles.

In my concept of a "dialogue of touchstones," I point to the real possibility of a "community of otherness," arising out of the context of Dialogue Psychotherapy. Through the therapist's genuine respect for the value of the client's touchstones of reality, through his own greater experience in struggling through to genuine dialogue, and through sharing his own confusions and complexities, the therapist can help the client find his way out of his isolation into that dialogue in which he can share what is uniquely his own and bring it into a common reality.

# Direct Decision Therapy

## Harold Greenwald

### DEFINITION

Direct Decision Therapy is based on a synthesis of a number of previously existing therapies, including Psychoanalysis, Individual Psychology, Rational-Emotive Therapy, Behavior Modification—all within an existential framework. It rests firmly on a philosophic foundation that is not just a means of therapy but also a philosophy of life.

### HISTORY

Direct Decision Therapy was first enunciated by myself, while teaching at the University of Bergen in Norway and is therefore sometimes referred to as the Bergen School. It was first established in 1970, and the first publication was at the Spanish National Congress of Psychology, held at the University of Madrid in 1970, followed by articles in *Voices* and *The Journal of Contemporary Psychotherapy*. In 1974 it was published as a book, *Direct Decision Therapy*. I have given courses in this therapy not only in the United States but also in other parts of the world; it made considerable headway in Scandinavia. At the present time it is employed by a number of practitioners throughout the United States and has shown interesting growth in the brief period that it has been in existence.

### TECHNIQUE

The technique of Direct Decision Therapy is very clear-cut and can be reduced to the following steps:

1. The patient or client is asked to state his problem as completely as possible. In encouraging the statement of the problem the patient is sometimes asked, "What goal do you have?" because many decision therapists have found it more useful to speak in terms of goal rather than problem. Here the humanist bent of this approach is very clear.

2. An important and original part of Direct Decision Therapy is in this step. The patient and therapist together examine the past decisions that helped create the problems that prevent the patient from reaching his goal. In discussing past decisions, it is clear that the patient may not be aware of it. Therefore, the therapist will help the patient become aware of his decisions as they express themselves—in his activity, attitudes, and philosophy of life.

3. Another innovative step in Direct Decision Therapy is the examination of the payoffs for the decisions that are behind the problem. These payoffs may be positive—such as gaining attention or experiencing feelings of superiority—or they may be the negative payoff of avoiding anxiety.

4. The question is then asked, "What is the context within which this decision was originally made?" Direct Decision therapists believe that all decisions, when first made, had validity to the person making them; even though they

may no longer be functional, they were once very important to the psychic economy of the individual.

5.  The patient is then invited to examine what options or alternatives he has, in order that he may function in a way other than that based on his past decision. For example, many clients suffer from a decision of perfectionism in which they try to do everything as well as they possibly can. This may have been important for them in their early functioning because this was the only way they felt they could survive within their own family. When they are asked to examine the options, some will see that they no longer need such perfectionist demands. They can accept their human limitations and, while still trying to do well, will not attack themselves for not doing as well as they might like to do. Their new option or new decision may then be that they will try to do as well as they can, but will still accept the possibility of not fulfilling their own exalted demands on themselves.

6.  A new decision is made and the client is helped to carry through this new decision. A great deal of the emphasis in therapy frequently requires help in carrying through this new decision. Take the example of someone who had decided to withdraw from the world because he found it too anxiety provoking, but now makes a decision to be more assertive, to enter into both social and intellectual relationships. The therapist may help him develop, through practice and homework, a series of aids, and self-administered rewards in carrying through this new decision. It is also made clear that many of these decisions have to be made over and over again. If, for example, the individual who makes a decision to lose weight does not put it into practice, it is considered only a wish. It becomes a decision only when it is put into practice, and the client is helped to see that the decision must be made over and over again every time the individual sits down to eat. He also is helped to see that just because he fails once in not carrying out this decision to limit his weight, it does not mean that he has to give up the entire procedure of dieting; he can return and try to carry out the decision in the future.

## APPLICATIONS

The applications of Direct Decision Therapy are many and varied. In addition to its use in individual therapy, it is also widely applied in group therapy and especially in family therapy, where family decisions are examined. Families often have decided, for example, that one member of the family is the disturbed one. The family is helped to understand the payoffs for this kind of decision—what it arose from and what alternative decisions may be made by the family as a whole. The practice of making family decisions has been found to be a very useful way of increasing family cohesiveness. But in addition to the field of therapy, the approach has also found acceptance in educational organizations. I am invited to speak to educational organizations as frequently as to psychotherapy organizations, since it is quite clear that a major problem many young people have is that they haven't made the decision to learn—or they have made the decision not to learn. Other applications are to industry, because industrial management and government workers find that the art of decision-making is crucial to their role in management.

# Direct Psychoanalysis

## *John N. Rosen*

### DEFINITION

Direct Psychoanalysis is a method of treatment for the emotionally disturbed. It utilizes the insights and dynamics established by Freud and his co-workers, but modifies them in an effort to enhance their therapeutic value with a greater emphasis on treatment rather than investigation. It proffers that the manifest content of the illness is analogous to the cry of a baby, which indicates that something is wrong. With a baby, if the disturbance is corrected, the cry stops and the baby regains peace of mind. With the sick patient, if the disturbance is corrected, the symptoms stop. If the mother simply observes the crying baby—for instance, the loudness of the cry, the redness of the baby's face, the writhings of the baby's body, etc.—it might be excellent research, but would hardly stop the baby's crying. On the other hand, if the mother discovers the reason for the crying and does what has to be done about it, the crying will stop. In order to listen in a meaningful way, a special kind of knowledge is required. A direct psychoanalyst can discover the reasons for the disturbance.

### HISTORY

Direct Psychoanalysis began in 1939 with my personal analysis. From my world of internal medicine and pathology my attention was increasingly directed toward psychosomatic medicine, and finally to full-time work in a state hospital and the world of deep psychosis. There I was taught shock treatment and drugs, which were ineffectual and cruel. I heard about a patient with acute catatonic excitement who died and was about to be autopsied. I went to the morgue where the autopsy was performed and was astonished to discover that there was no anatomic cause of death. Death came about from the agonies in the patient's mind. It was said there were other such patients in the hospital, that it was just a question of time before they died, and that nothing could be done about it. I went to the wards where these patients were kept and I was surprised to find that they were not out of contact in the sense that I could understand what they said. I treated these patients and they did not die, but recovered. From this initial discovery, that what a patient said made a certain kind of sense, I began to listen over the decades to hundreds of patients and almost invariably I was able to understand the peculiar language of the neurotic and the psychotic. To this body of knowledge, both theoretic and clinical, Paul Federn gave the name Direct Psychoanalysis in order to distinguish it from orthodox and indirect psychoanalysis. Freud said that since the psychosis is like a dream and since we awaken in the morning from a dream, it was his hope that one day a method would be discovered that would awaken the psychotic from his relentless nightmare. Many colleagues report that Direct Psychoanalysis offers the possibility of doing just that.

# TECHNIQUE

There are many different techniques involved in treatment by Direct Psychoanalysis, in large measure they depend on the nature of the case and the varying skills and personalities of different therapists. Since no teaching institution has been able to give us a consistent model for physicians or patients, the Direct Psychoanalytic Institute has abandoned this effort and devotes its attention to those areas where we can standardize and categorize the areas of similarity.

First and foremost, we agree that a hospital is the least desirable place to treat a patient. In this situation, the number of patients, the inexperience of the personnel, and the jealousies and frustrations that are aroused by the attention any given individual gets make therapy exceedingly complicated. Ideally, the place for treatment should be arranged in the best interest of the individual patient. The way my colleagues and I did it during research on Direct Psychoanalysis at Temple University Medical School in the late 1960s was to obtain three row houses, which were then staffed with psychologically trained personnel. There should be three such helpers: one, a woman who acts as the foster mother; the other two should be males, because protection is required both for the patient and the community at large.

There are daily sessions with the therapist in the presence of those responsible for the operation of the treatment unit. This consists of what we call the therapeutic dialogue, where the therapist listens, observes, and uncovers the meaning of what is said and done—usually a crumb at a time, until as much of the whole as possible becomes visible. Over the balance of the twenty-four-hour day, the assistant therapists continue along the lines that the therapist has established so that treatment becomes a continuous process. Here, like the baby we referred to in the beginning, we find that the psychotic has regressed to the earliest infantile levels. This might include such behavior as soiling, wetting, or the inability to feed or clothe himself. Like a baby, the patient must be cared for day and night.

The therapeutic dialogue uncovers the fact that transference (where the client shifts feelings about a significant person to the therapist) and intense resistance will dominate the scene. This, as in conventional analysis, follows the understanding of repetition compulsion. If these are successfully managed, the patient develops a childlike dependence on the therapist and at this positive phase of therapy, education and discipline can begin to be achieved.

Termination takes place automatically when and if the patient regains normal judgment. The family, the patient, and the therapist agree that the patient can be returned to society at large. Since one cannot be sure that the end point has really been achieved, it is understood that if the patient exhibits unusual behavior, he should either visit the therapist on an outpatient basis or, if necessary, return to the treatment unit.

# APPLICATIONS

We have found this method of therapy most useful with people classified as psychotic. It is especially useful in depressives who have already made a suicidal attempt or where the possibility of suicide is present. Obviously, as a precaution, the patient must be guarded twenty-four hours a day or he may very well be lost. The treatment unit is best suited for this protection.

Direct Psychoanalysis can do nothing for a patient who has been lobotomized. The more a patient has been subjected to shock therapy or, to a lesser degree, drug therapy and hospitalization, the more guarded the prognosis becomes. Neurotic patients, particularly those with anxiety hysteria, are the easiest to treat. We have found that hysterics, agoraphobics, claustrophobics, and various forms of psychosomatic fixations are sometimes quickly resolved.

# Directive Psychotherapy
## Frederick C. Thome

### DEFINITION

The terms "direct" and "directive" have meanings that have not always been differentiated. Direct Psychotherapy involves dealing directly with the client without any intervening variables. It implies using the simplest, most straightforward approach in dealing with problems. Directive Psychotherapy involves directing, guiding, influencing, or establishing requirements of the client along lines authoritatively set by the therapist. The therapist may introduce ideas, attitudes, or contents not previously expressed by the client.

Operationally, the therapist *manages* the process of psychological case handling according to a therapist-directed plan. Therapist-centered and client-centered methods lie at opposite ends of a continuum represented by maximum versus minimum therapist management of case handling.

### HISTORY

Prior to the introduction of client-centered methods of counseling and psychotherapy in 1942 by Carl Rogers, little attention had been directed to the degree of authoritarian control, directiveness, regulation, and manipulation exerted by the therapist in the case-handling process. Coming at a time during World War II, when public demands for the treatment of mental disorders and psychological problems were greatly expanded, Rogerian nondirective methods received widespread acceptance, particularly among psychologists, because they had an appealing underlying theoretical rationale; they emphasized the client's feelings and emotions, dealt with immediate problems, and were easy to learn and apply. During the emergency of World War II, Rogers proposed training courses in nondirective methods lasting only three weeks.

In 1944 I had become critical of the expansive claims being made for nondirective therapy, which many at that time seemed to regard as a universal panacea for all problems and ills. Accordingly, I published a series of papers in the *Journal of Clinical Psychology* (1945–1950) under the title "Directive Psychotherapy," which presented operational analysis of the methodology of the principal methods of psychological case handling. In 1948, I outlined the principles and theory of directive methods, but indicated that the differentiation between directive and nondirective was only an arbitrary classification along one dimension. I renounced any implication that directive methods constituted a school of psychotherapy or that I regarded myself as a directive therapist in *Principles of Personality Counseling* (1950), which advocated an eclectic approach. I applied the "law of parsimony" in *Psychological Case Handling* (1968), which insisted that clinicians were more aptly designated as case handlers until positive therapeutic results actually could be objectively demonstrated. All case handling is regarded as directive management since even the decision to be nondirective involves minimal management.

Most general textbooks of psychotherapy consist largely of descriptions of direct(ive) methods. Jurjevich (1973) edited a two-volume handbook of case handling methods describing variations of direct therapy. This book may be regarded as a source book of direct and directive principles.

## TECHNIQUE

Since every positive clinical decision and case-handling action dealing direct or directively with the client involves *management*, it follows that all methods involve some degree of therapist-centered activity. All the methods described in Jurjevich's handbook may be classified on a continuum according to the level of authoritarian case handling. Only an operational analysis of specific case-handling methods can reveal what the therapist is actually doing, as opposed to what he claims to be doing.

The general rule appears to be that the case handler should operate nondirectively during early phases of treatment and should continue as long as the client is making progress in expressing himself, in recognizing problem areas, in developing curative insights, and in learning to cope better with life. Directiveness tends to be indicated when the client has no insight into problems, is unable to communicate with the case handler, has insufficient information to solve problems, or is blocked and inhibited in relation to conflict resolution. In general, the case handler does for the client what the client is unable to do alone.

The case handler needs to be aware of when directiveness is indicated and when it is not, as well as the dangers of over- or under-directiveness. If the case handler is too therapist-centered, there may be complete failure to understand and influence the client. If the case handler is too nondirective, the therapeutic process may never uncover or deal with the client's real problems.

## APPLICATIONS

In general, nondirectiveness works best with highly intelligent and motivated clients who have the resources to solve problems with minimal case-handler management. Directiveness is most clearly indicated where the client does not have the resources to solve problems or is unmotivated or blocked.

# Drama Therapy

## David R. Johnson

### DEFINITION

Drama Therapy can be defined as the intentional use of creative drama toward the psychotherapeutic goals of symptom relief, emotional and physical integration, and personal growth. Drama Therapy, like the other creative arts therapies (art, music, and dance therapies), is the application of a creative medium to psychotherapy. Specifically, Drama Therapy refers to those activities in which there is an established, therapeutic understanding or contract between client and therapist, and where the therapeutic goals are primary, not incidental, to the ongoing activity. Thus, creative drama in a strictly educational setting, for example, though probably helpful to the participants, should be differentiated from Drama Therapy.

Broadly defined, Drama Therapy includes any psychotherapeutic use of role playing, such as J. L. Moreno's psychodrama. In its more narrow usage, however, the term Drama Therapy refers to those approaches that stress the appreciation of creative drama as a medium for self-expression and playful group interaction, and which base their techniques on improvisation and theater games.

### HISTORY

For centuries, creative drama and role playing have been used in both primitive and advanced cultures as a cathartic and psychotherapeutic tool. In this century, role-playing techniques have been developed by J. L. Moreno (psychodrama), Fritz Perls (Gestalt), Albert Pesso (psychomotor), encounter group leaders, and several behavior therapists.

Drama Therapy, as the specific use of creative drama in psychotherapy, has more recently been developed by practitioners initially trained in the dramatic arts who have applied improvisational techniques to clinical populations in hospital settings. Foremost among these are John Hudson (England), Gertrud Schattner (New York), Susan Jennings (England), and Eleanor Irwin (Pittsburgh). Many of these were greatly influenced by the work of Peter Slade and Brian Way in child drama, and Viola Spolin in improvisational techniques.

At the present time, a national association is in the formative stage, which will lead to the establishment of standards for the training and practice of drama therapists, a critical step in the development of Drama Therapy as an independent profession.

### TECHNIQUE

At the heart of the drama therapist's technique is the use of improvisation and spontaneous role playing as a means of encouraging self-expression in the individual. The therapist aims to create a supportive "free play" environment in which the individual's feelings and thoughts become reflected in the improvised roles. The therapist usually participates with the group members in the activities, and serves as a relatively nondirective facilitator of the group "play." His interventions (either verbal or nonverbal) are always focused on the *processes* within the group or individual that are inhibiting free expression, and not on the quality of the individual's performance in the role playing. Drama therapists strive for a flexible and multifaceted use of their medium, devising specific structures appropriate to the situation as it emerges in the therapeutic process. Depending upon the type of population involved and the specific goals of the therapy, a wide variety of techniques are used to encourage the individual's growth and insight.

One set of techniques in Drama Therapy is oriented toward the goal of developing interpersonal relationships and group values. For most people, and especially for severely disturbed patients, forming a group is an exceptionally difficult and threatening task. The utilization of creative drama and movement has been found both to engage people who are hesitant to join groups and to encourage group formation in general. The focus of Drama Therapy is not usually on the relationships that members have had in the past or with people outside of the group, but rather on the development of interpersonal relationships within the group itself. The group's activities, being relatively unstructured, encourage each individual's interpersonal style to emerge and his problems with others or the group to be expressed. The therapist's goal is to help the group develop methods of examining these problems as they arise. While this may take the form of group discussion, problems usually are explored further in the role playing itself.

A second major focus is on stimulating the individual's creativity and spontaneity. Here, the therapist's interventions are directed at the disruptions in the spontaneous play of the group. Anxieties within individuals and conflicts between members inevitably arise and interfere with the ongoing flow of the session and with the spontaneity of the members. For example, the play may become blocked and repetitive (known as an "impasse"), may break down entirely, or may actually become confused with reality. These inhibitions in the role playing are quite vivid to both patient and therapist, and can serve as diagnostic indicators of the individual's specific difficulties.

Another basic technique in Drama Therapy might be described as "role analysis." In improvisational role playing, one's role is intimately connected to one's real self, as there is no script to give it any other content. Over the course of a Drama Therapy experience, recurring patterns of behavior emerge in the role playing of each individual, which are, as it were, crystallized versions of his basic interpersonal stances. The person often feels powerless to change them, even though they dissatisfy him. The therapist can help the individual become aware of these patterns, and then to examine the reasons why he continues to choose them. Drama Therapy attempts to increase the individual's self-control by providing him with the opportunity and group support to experiment with other, more satisfying roles.

Drama therapists may use a variety of props or costumes, and may emphasize movement, mime, or art work. Many also use scripts and even produce plays with their clients, though in these cases, too, their goal is to examine the process that develops between the individual and his assigned roles.

## APPLICATIONS

Drama Therapy is currently used in the treatment of both groups and individuals, children and adults, in hospitals, mental-health clinics, prisons, and schools. It has been found to be effective with psychiatric patients of all diagnoses, alcohol and drug abusers, the handicapped, and the elderly. Drama Therapy shares the advantages of art and dance therapies in being able to reach more severely disturbed or handicapped populations, which are less available to insight-oriented verbal psychotherapy. Creative drama is a symbolic medium that allows people who have difficulty with verbalization to express themselves. Yet the verbal and complex role-playing aspects of Drama Therapy have also been utilized to engage highly intellectual and verbal patients who are more fearful of nonverbal means of self-expression.

Drama Therapy is also being increasingly appreciated for its diagnostic applications, both as a powerful projective device and as an indicator of the individual's cognitive style and personality organization.

# The Use of Dreams in Couples' Group Therapy

*Renee Nell*

## DEFINITION

Dreams deal with the unconscious dynamics underlying the manifest problem the patient brings to the group. While confrontations based on conscious material are often met with denial and aggression, confrontations involving one's own dreams are much easier to accept.

## HISTORY

The use of dreams in individual psychotherapy has become a standard procedure of many therapists, but only a few use dreams in couple counseling. And the number of therapists taking advantage of dreams in group therapy for couples is even smaller.

## TECHNIQUE

Jung's technique of interpreting dreams on the subjective level is of great advantage in couple counseling. For example, Margaret, a married woman who had been in group therapy for several months with her husband, recounted a dream: "I am in the living room with my husband. He is painting something black. I tell him not to paint furniture in the living room, but stubbornly he continues. I am beside myself and scream that he never wants to listen to me and that he is always stubborn." Margaret gave the obvious interpretation: "Dennis never listens to me." Dennis, of course, denied this.

Every person not acquainted with dream interpretation has a tendency, just like this dreamer, to interpret the dream on the objective level only. By objective level, Jung means that we find out if the real Dennis is as stubborn as he is in the dream. On the objective level, the black paint is simply taken as black paint. More helpful, though much more confronting, is the interpretation of the dream on the subjective level. It means that every part of the dream, be it a person or just paint, is symbolic of a part of the dreamer's personality.

## APPLICATIONS

For Margaret it is, of course, much more important, though more unpleasant, to find out that the stubborn Dennis is a symbol of her own stubbornness; that she is, so to speak, "married" to this stubbornness. The group reminded her how often they had accused her of "painting things too black." Then she admitted that the night preceding the dream she had been arguing with Dennis about his wish to accept a job in another town; she had painted life in that town in the blackest colors. This was irritating to Dennis and one of the causes of marital strife.

The dream always brings hidden and often negative material to the surface. Therefore, the dreamer at first resists understanding the meaning of the dream. He needs the help of one or several people to interpret it and help him accept it. Often, people are embarrassed to admit, even to themselves, what their fears are. Here, too, the dream can help.

George had a dream reflecting his reaction to an upcoming party: "I was in a lovely, sunny meadow. I was afraid of wild beasts that might be lurking in the high grass and, therefore, took refuge in a stone tower." When it came to meeting people, George often felt as he did in the dream He had often been reproached by his wife for "withdrawing into an ivory tower" at such times. Once George had brought his anxieties to his peers, he felt closer to them, especially since he found out that they were not "wild beasts lurking in the grass."

Dreams are also helpful in the discussion of sexual problems. For example, Tom was such a hard-working young scientist that his zeal had gotten him into trouble with his young wife, who complained about his working too much. Tom reported this dream: "A vital young nature girl led me to a romantic old European town. We were very much in love and were hiding out in a castle. We made love and were very happy. When the time came to leave, the girl stepped from the window and flew around, beckoning me to follow. I did, and both of us now flew together over a charmed landscape. I woke up in an elated, happy mood."

As usual, the group at first got involved with the manifest content of the dream, guessing whether the dream suggested an affair with his lab assistant, Beth, an attractive young nature girl. But this was not what the dream meant.

In further group interaction, Tom explained that Beth, in spite of her heavy work, did all the outdoor things he had done in his youth with girls of her type. "I don't want to marry such a girl. I just wish I hadn't stopped mountain climbing myself. If I could now climb for even just a couple of hours, I would really feel as if I could fly." The therapist suggested a contract between him, the group, and his wife, in which he obliged himself to get back into nature at least every second weekend. His wife was very happy that the group had achieved for Tom what she hadn't been able to. The group members realized that it would really have been a fatal mistake for Tom to have asked for a divorce in order to marry an outdoor girl, or to go to bed with Beth. In each case, it became obvious to the group that dreams of love or hate were not meant for acting out. The goal was working out the inner problem the dreams point to.

In summary, there are many advantages to using dreams in couples' group therapy. Unconscious material comes quickly to the surface, providing additional guideposts in diagnosis and prognosis, and reflecting the developmental stages in the group process. Dreams allow for a rapid comprehension of the dynamics underlying the particular conscious problem and they help to clarify the characteristic behavior and anxieties of particular psychological types, such as the introvert, George. Last, they provide a valid appraisal of readiness to terminate.

I want to avoid the impression that interpretation of dreams is used exclusively in couples' groups. The methods of group interaction used are those most group therapists would apply: staying in the here and now, replacing accusations by working through and invoking feeling responses. Dreams should not be looked upon as a cure-all but should be respected as an additional tool for the profession.

# Senoi Dream Group Therapy
## *Eric Greenleaf*

### DEFINITION

Senoi Dream Group Therapy organizes the experience and telling of dreams within natural and therapeutic social groups according to several simple rules of conduct. The rules emphasize conduct within dreams and between dreamers in waking life to achieve the integration of dreamed private experience with waking interpersonal actions. Adequate action toward oneself and others is held more important than is adequate understanding of dream imagery.

### HISTORY

Senoi Dream Group Therapy was initially based on Stewart's (1951, 1953) discovery of systems of dream use among the Senoi people of Malaya. In 1969, I began utilizing the principles of the Senoi dream work, first in classes on dreaming, then as leader and member of dream groups (Greenleaf, 1973). Several students of mine and psychologists have since initiated dream therapies based on Senoi or other ancient approaches to dreaming and to life. Many techniques in psychotherapy have long been in the public domain in one form or another, but they are "rediscovered" from time to time and put to use in modern life.

### TECHNIQUE

First and most important: tell your dreams. Tell them to your mate; tell them to your children; tell them to the people who appear in your dreams. This can be done at home, at work, at school. Second, listen to the dreams of the people you live and work with. Third, continue unfinished dreams, either the next night, or in waking daydreams, or active imagination (dreams continued in the presence of a sympathetic guide or friend).

Dreams are most often interrupted by fear. It's crucial to continue the dream to a successful conclusion. So, if you dream of falling, continue the dream to see where you fall. If you dream of a contest or battle, carry the fight through with the aid of friends summoned in the dream. If you dream of love, carry the lovemaking through in the dream until the partners are satisfied.

The Senoi suggest ways of dealing with the most common emotions in dreams. *Fear:* call on your allies and friends to help you. Continue to fly, or travel in the dream. *Anger:* fight monsters until you subdue them, then they will become allies in your later dreams. Also, give a gift in waking life to those you've injured in your dreams. Request a gift in waking life of those who've injured you in dreams. *Lust:* within the dream, make love with whomever you choose. In waking life, if the dream lover is available to you, court him or her. *Curiosity:* explore, investigate, pursue the dream. In waking life, test the discoveries and plans made in dreams to see if they work out.

Besides these principles, the Senoi suggest ways of dealing with important figures encountered in dreams, those majestic, or frightening or helpful images that visit us: the "archetypes," or common figures of human emotion and thought, which C. G. Jung has described (1952). In daydreams, or in nightly dreaming, we're advised to talk and to strike a bargain with these figures. Inquire what they wish of us, and then, if we agree whole-heartedly to give to them (love, attention, activity of some kind), we find that they will guide us in future dreams and in our waking lives. Often, the shadowy side or monstrous aspect of our own selves appears to us in dreams as frightening. By incorporating this side of ourselves, we grow less afraid and more whole (Greenleaf, 1975). An example:

GUIDE: What did you dream?
DREAMER: The image of a grotesque face: jowls, fat lips, a stubbly beard. His mouth
    always moving, angry, hostile.
GUIDE: Wrestle him to the ground and see how he can help you.
DREAMER: He says, "Death" to me, defiantly. Then I wrestle him. He says, "Live, or
    I'll spit in your eye."
GUIDE: Ask him how you can be of help to him.
DREAMER: He says, "Cuddle me and love me." He's awful, but I do it. He's not so
    grotesque anymore.

## APPLICATIONS

Methods of dealing with dream imagery during dreaming, or in waking imagination, are practiced in all forms of psychotherapy (Greenleaf, 1977). Indeed, all forms of human interaction use the sort of methods we think of as therapeutic, from calming a child after a nightmare to rousing the passions of athletes before a contest. Mental rehearsal and mental problem solving utilize these techniques. The Senoi sense that we may share our fearful and curious dreams, gain strength from our families, friends, and communities, and pit human love against the fearsome demons of the night. This makes all the difference between using the wonders of the private images of life and hiding from them in fear and bitterness. Senoi Dream Group Therapy is an attempt to use the communal sense to relieve this fearful isolation.

Some of the application of dream principles comes from the spontaneous good sense of peole confronted with challenge. The therapeutic application of dream principles is necessary only when fear or violence overcome the heart. The first two dreams of my three-year-old son show the deep-sources of the Senoi principles:

"I dreamed me and my friend are outside and we hit the monsters with baseball bats and knock them down dead."

Then, several nights later: "I dreamed of the deer jumping through each other's horns and I riding one. And I swimming with the ducks in the water."

# Eclectic Psychotherapy
## Frederick C. Thorne

### DEFINITION

An eclectic, in psychotherapeutic terms, is one who selects what is valid or useful from all available theories, methods, and practices. The eclectic approach rejects adherence to any one school or system and instead utilizes what is most valid or relevant from the whole therapeutic spectrum. It is composed of contributions from many different sources, used according to whether they are valid, applicable, and indicated.

### HISTORY

Prior to the advent of basic science, there were countless schools and systems of theory and practice based on the teachings of some authority. For example, in clinical medicine, before the advent of scientifically oriented medical centers such as the Mayo Clinic (1880) and standardized medical school curricula such as that developed by Sir William Osler at Johns Hopkins (1894), there were about four hundred proprietary medical schools in the United States. These medical schools had no standardized curricula, few validated methods, and were operated by self-anointed medical "authorities." In 1912, the American Medical Association authorized the Flexner Report, which investigated the qualifications of the four hundred medical schools. As a result, three hundred and twenty were disbanded and the remaining eighty schools adhered to standardized basic science curricula. An eclectic approach was introduced for training and practice that has remained in operation to the present.

In scientific psychology, Robert S. Woodworth of Columbia University was the first to introduce the eclectic viewpoint during the 1930s—a time when there were literally as many schools and systems of psychology as there were psychologists. In academic psychology, large textbooks were written on systematic psychology, presenting theoretical discussions of everything from Adlerian Individual Psychology to Zen Buddhism. Modern theoretical psychology is still a morass of competing systems, models, vocabularies, jargons, interpretations, and personal idiosyncrasies.

I (1950) was among the first clinicians to adopt a thoroughgoing eclectic approach by analyzing all available methods of psychotherapy operationally, listing what was known about the advisability of their use (indications and contraindications) with different conditions and selecting what was most valid and useful from all available methods. From 1950 to date, I have advocated eclecticism at every possible opportunity. A trend toward eclecticism seems to be indicated by the fact that in 1950 none of the members of Division 12 of the American Psychological Association classified themselves as eclectics, while by 1975 over 50 percent of the members were identifying themselves as such.

The trends in clinical psychiatry are less clear. Grinker (1970) for some years has been a leading proponent of eclecticism in psychiatry. However, theoretical psychiatry since World War II has been very heavily influenced by psychoanalysis and a variety of social psychiatries, such as Eric Berne's *Games People Play*, encounter and transaction analysis therapies, and Adlerian Individual Psychology. Also, the validity of current professional psychiatry has been questioned by the contentions of Thomas Szasz, which state that mental illness is a myth or is, at least, often caused by traditional psychiatric methods. The application of eclectic methods to clinical psychology and clinical psychiatry is long overdue, if methods are to be standardized and validated objectively.

## TECHNIQUE

In summary, eclecticism is an approach rather than any one single system or method. Operationally, the eclectic studies all available methods, familiarizes himself with their nature, learns their indications and contraindications in relation to specific problems or pathologies, and then attempts to apply them using the best clinical judgment possible. Eclecticism places a huge responsibility on the clinician to keep up with current scientific knowledge in order to know everything possible about all available methods.

Eclecticism is based on the postulate that individual cases require individually prescribed treatment methods. There is no one therapeutic system that is effective for all clinical conditions. Each method of counseling and psychotherapy has its own specific nature, its own specific methods, and its own specific applications.

Eclecticism has been attacked on the grounds that it has no logical theoretical rationale, that it is only a hodgepodge of methods idiosyncratically applied, and that it is too difficult to learn and apply validly. I (1973) have rebutted these criticisms at length, arguing that the medical profession has been utilizing the eclectic approach for over seventy-five years, until it is now an unquestioned standard practice. Psychotherapy has suffered because neither basic-science clinical psychology nor clinical psychiatry has adopted eclecticism systematically.

The eclectic approach in the United States has been gaining acceptance quietly but steadily. Eclecticism has never stimulated the enthusiasm attached to many schools or therapy systems, since it is more difficult to master. However, I believe that if a novice wishes to ever become a master clinician, he must adopt eclecticism, since no psychotherapy has a universal application.

The most important overall influence of eclecticism on the theory and practice of psychotherapy has been to enlarge the spectrum of clinical therapies, encouraging the clinician to become familiar and competent with all available methods, and discouraging cultism, involving undue reliance on any one method. As clinical knowledge accumulates on new methods, clinicians in general will become better balanced and more competent. One of the best examples of how a once-popular method was whittled down to size is psychoanalysis, which was once the method of choice but is now indicated only with limited clinical conditions.

# Eidetic Therapy
## Akhter Ahsen

### DEFINITION

Eidetic Therapy is a system of mental growth and treatment through the eidetic image, which is an inner psychical visual image of unusual vividness, with therapeutic potential. When surfaced, the eidetic is seen clearly in the mind as a movie image, and this inner "seeing" is accompanied by a profound transformation of consciousness. Since the eidetic has the special qualities of conducting healthful orientation and of remaining sensuous and constant, concentration on this transforming mental image brings fast results. Through conscious access to the healthful image, the individual learns a new experiential basis for change of emotional perspectives. The eidetic is a universal capacity for new experience but remains latent unless activated through special eidetic awareness techniques.

### HISTORY

Rooted historically in the German school of the twenties and developed clinically in the fifties by myself, Akhter Ahsen, Eidetic Therapy was first described in 1965 in my book *Eidetic Psychotherapy: A Short Introduction*. This was followed by three more books, the last to appear being *Psycheye: Self-Analytic Consciousness* in 1977.

### TECHNIQUE

Eidetic Therapy aims at personal involvement in the demonstration and analysis of experience. The technique demands that each aspect of the eidetic picture selected from a level of experience be looked at repeatedly through a centered projection—a process different from hurried thinking, which usually superimposes a false movement on the original structures. Through repeated focal attention on eidetics, the natural order of experience slowly surfaces and reinstates, resulting in transformation of consciousness. The demonstrative eidetic maneuvers remove confusion, apprehensions, misconceptions, and false notions from the mental process. A broad spectrum of eidetic analyses has revealed that initially many individuals view their developmental history in reverse, and their views, active recall, and even imagination are infected with a superficial, upside-down view of reality. One-dimensional memory, which is a partial, biased, and distant envisioning of the original experience, is ordinarily used due to the immediate pressures of day-to-day living, and the individual's view of reality becomes narrow and corrupted. Total suspension of one-dimensional memory and in its place enactment of natural experiential structures secures a break from the negative pressures, helplessness, and obstruction of life functions. Demonstration of the difference between eidetic evocation and ordinary experience and recollection is thus important for removal of conflict and regeneration of healthful consciousness. The systematic experience of the original and uncorrupted psyche is the essence of eidetic cure.

## APPLICATIONS

The eidetic approach is especially effective for mental growth and treatment of complex emotional problems, such as chronic neuroses and schizophrenia. By developing the ability for new experience, fresh expression and awareness of central issues through the eidetic, the individual can restructure his processes of adjustment and stop the splitting process. Because the eidetic images operate in a highly specific manner, demonstrating the link between various experiential states, levels, and their related body processes, Eidetic Therapy can also bring about dramatic results in a variety of psychosomatic problems.

The eidetic experience is a piece of life process itself. Until the mental process has established itself from many angles, the meaning of life is only partially known. As the person intimately experiences the eidetic, remaining open to its various dimensions, he reaches an original, fundamental contact with his nature. Through the eidetic, the mind is able to see experience from the surface to the deepest structures, and the creative aspects of the process spread at many levels. Since each person responds at a truly deep level to the standard eidetic imagery, here lies a glimpse into the truly creative side of Eidetic Therapy. The synthesizing direction of Eidetic Therapy has been examined in many scientific journals, receiving a positive response. *The American Journal of Psychiatry* (Vol. 132, 1975, 314), for example, termed it "a methodological advance."

# Electroconvulsive Therapy
### Thomas D. Hurwitz

## DEFINITION

Electroconvulsive Therapy (ECT), though not a system of psychotherapy based on psychological variables, is one of the oldest somatic treatments still in use for emotional illness. As currently used, ECT constitutes the electrical induction of a grand mal convulsion, or epileptic-like seizure in an individual generally anesthetized with an intravenous agent, as in a simple oral surgical procedure. This seizure without the use of muscle relaxant medication would be indistinguishable from that of a pathological seizure disorder, or epilepsy, manifested by an initial constant contraction of body musculature followed by rhythmic jerking movements of the extremities and a subsequent period of sleep and lethargy. Every human being is capable of experiencing a convulsion, although most individuals (i.e., nonepileptics) require a stimulus such as an exogenous electrical current to raise their central nervous system activity above a critical "seizure threshold" level. This does not, however, predispose the individual to the development of epilepsy. There are drugs that are capable of inducing seizures, but these have generally been abandoned for the use of electricity in contemporary practice. It is critical to note that although the individual experiences preanesthetic and anesthetic drugs, electrical stimulation to the head, a convulsive seizure, and a period of somnolent recovery, the seizure is the only variable that has a positive therapeutic effect. Although the mechanism mediating therapeutic change is not thoroughly understood in terms of neurophysiology and biochemistry, there is an ever-increasing body of knowledge relating the physiologic effects of ECT to the biochemical abnormalities seen in certain psychiatric illnesses.

The efficacy of ECT is very well documented, primarily in affective illness (disorders of mood), especially depression. There are numerous studies demonstrating that ECT produces results that are equal to, if not better than, those produced by the antidepressant medications that are commonly used. Here we are referring to disorders with disturbances apparent in psychological and biological functions; that is, in addition to disordered mood, these individuals experience difficulty concentrating, disturbed sleep with frequent nocturnal awakenings and early morning insomnia, appetite and weight loss, constipation, decreased libidinous interest, psychomotor changes, and a characteristic daily variation of mood with increased depression early in the day. In illness such as this, an individual is markedly impaired and indeed at risk of death from not eating, and/or suicide. There is general agreement that such illness with very tangible biological dysfunction must be treated with somatic intervention and ECT has been so effective in the treatment of depressive illness that it has provided the standard against which the antidepressant medications have been compared.

In many states, the use of ECT is felt to represent dramatic intervention and is relatively more strictly regulated than other somatic therapies. A careful review of the literature permits the conclusion that when properly performed in rationally selected cases, ECT is safe, effective, and at times lifesaving. Its widespread use in large institutions prior to the era of antipsychotic and antidepressant medication has contributed to some of the contemporary fears and concerns. As I will note, ECT is currently the beneficiary of increasingly rigorous research and careful modification.

## HISTORY

ECT was first introduced in Italy in 1938 after prior work with injectible agents elsewhere in Europe. The original theoretical basis for this means of treatment was the mutual exclusivity of schizophrenia and naturally occurring epilepsy. Hence, it was believed that seizures held some prophylactic value against mental illness and could also represent a curative factor when introduced artificially. Electrically induced convulsive therapy was brought to the United States shortly after its European inception and became widely employed for varied types of psychiatric illness, particularly psychotic processes. Ironically, the originally noted negative relationship between schizophrenia and epilepsy has proven over time to be erroneous.

In more recent years, the use of ECT has been dramatically refined. When originally introduced, seizures were produced in awake patients by relatively crude apparatus. The patients would then convulse, often restrained by attendants. This rather dramatic and elementary form of treatment has left successive generations of patients, physicians, and public with a negative bias toward what is felt to be a harsh, if not brutal, form of therapy. This is unfortunate, for ECT in its modern form is no more traumatic than a minor surgical procedure under general anesthesia, as will be described below.

## TECHNIQUE

After a thorough physical examination, laboratory examinations of the blood and urine, and X-rays of the spine to assess the patient's condition and ability to tolerate the procedure, he is taken to a facility with full medical equipment. Here the psychiatrist, often with the aid of an anesthesiologist, delivers a dose of short-acting intravenous anesthetic and a muscle relaxant that prevents the muscular contractions of the seizure. This does not interfere with the physiologic seizure activity in the brain so essential to effective treatment. Through electrodes held or attached to one or both temples, a pulse of 70 to 130 volts over an interval of 0.1 to 0.5 seconds is applied. Only a small amount of current actually passes the resistance of skin, muscle, and skull, but this is sufficient to produce a convulsion lasting approximately one to one-and-one-half minutes during which oxygen can be applied through a face mask. The only external signs of the seizure are the twitching of eyelids or toes that reveal a successful induction. Nevertheless, the teeth are protected by a rubber or gauze bite block. The anesthesia wears off quickly, the patient recovers as from a nap, and is often on his feet within an hour of treatment. This can be repeated at varying intervals, usually three sessions per week for a total of six to twelve treatments. Multiple seizures in one session have been studied but are not widely used. This is in marked contrast to the often high number of treatments given in the past to chronically institutionalized patients and thus, side effects such as transient memory loss are less severe. In fact, some workers stimulate only the nondominant side of the brain and find even less memory impairment in some cases.

The risk of death with ECT is from 0.01 to 0.5 percent, increasing with age. This is of particularly low order when dealing with life-threatening illness, and it is minimized by proper medical and electronic monitoring of physiological functions. Complications can include all those of any general anesthesia, such as respiratory or cardiac difficulties, allergic reactions, and additional problems of dental injury, muscle strains, rupture of viscera, and post-convulsive confusion. These are particularly infrequent with modern application of treatment. The amount of current actually passing through brain tissue is small and there is no recorded incidence of structural brain damage. Memory disturbance and some degree of confusion occur frequently and are almost always transient, generally clearing over a two- to four-week period. Cases of long-term memory dysfunction are extremely rare, and have never been definitively ascribed as resulting directly from ECT. The musculoskeletal complications, such as sprains, tears, and fractures, seen in the early days of unmodified ECT, are practically nonexistent with the use of muscle relaxants.

One risk, like that in the use of antidepressant medication, is that patients beginning to recover from a severe depression may become energized just enough to act on suicidal impulses. Though selected patients may be treated on an ambulatory basis, the severely ill are always treated during hospitalization. Particularly in the latter group but essentially with all use of ECT, the treatment is adjunctive and complementary to all other aspects of treatment, such as milieu therapy, individual and group psychotherapy, and pharmacotherapy. To the extent that a patient treated with ECT may be confused, other treatments are often strictly supportive until the confusion clears and additional therapy can be used to enhance adaptational coping, interpersonal relationships, and/or psychodynamic change.

## APPLICATIONS

In contemporary usage, ECT is most widely indicated for the treatment of depressive illness described above. It is particularly useful when the severity of nutritional debility or suicidal potential warrants a quick response to avoid the lag period found with the use of antidepressant medications. ECT is also effective in the immediate symptomatic treatment of manic excitement that is unresponsive to treatment with drugs. Schizophrenia is less dependably responsive but cases of catatonic excitement or withdrawal do respond dramatically. Schizophrenic illness that is resistant to treatment with drugs frequently responds, though it often requires a larger number of treatments.

# Dynamic Empathy Training

*Robert F. Ostermann*

## DEFINITION

Dynamic Empathy Training uses group simulation exercises to stimulate participants to experience emotions similar to those experienced by others. This enlarges that resource of personal experience in which one can find and reflect feelings and meanings similar to what another person feels and means.

The various definitions of empathy include two dimensions: cognitive and emotional. Empathy denotes not only understanding but also acceptance—acceptance without identification. However, there is a third element: what makes progress possible for the client is not that he is understood and accepted, but that he perceives himself to be understood and accepted.

To influence the empathic process it is necessary to know not just what it is but also how it occurs. Gordon, in his text, *Interviewing*, points out that the extent to which one can understand the feelings of another depends on: 1) the completeness and accuracy of one's knowledge of the other, 2) the extent to which one has experienced the same or similar situations as the other, and 3) the degree to which one has accurately observed, remembered, or imagined his own past experiences. To this must be added 4) the clarity of response that conveys understanding and acceptance to the other person. The difficulty, as Gordon points out, lies in the likelihood of similarity—from the universal aspects of biological behavior to the individual aspects of personal behavior. Therefore improving one's ability to empathize requires at least an increase in the likelihood of similarity of experience— especially with respect to negative and unpleasant aspects of the personal behavior of the other person, for which that person needs to feel understood and accepted.

While one may increase the ability to know what someone means, by reading and by other vicarious experiences, it is unlikely that an appreciation of what someone feels, certainly at the level of advanced accurate empathy, comes about without directly experiencing those emotions. Therefore a comprehensive training process to improve empathic responding must include expanding emotional experiences, and emotional experiences can be expanded through experiential training.

Succinctly then, Dynamic Empathy Training attempts to:

1. Train accurate perceiving of what another person feels and means in his personal experiences.
2. Train accurate observing and recalling of one's own feeling experiences.
3. Expand one's emotional experience repertoire.
4. Broaden one's "acceptance threshold" with respect to the experiences of others.
5. Train effective reflecting of one's understanding and acceptance toward another.
6. Help block identification with another's feelings and experiences.

## HISTORY

Group training processes that predated group psychotherapy emphasized intellectual content and processes. Later group psychotherapy also incorporated psychological principles of personal adjustment and growth. Many early group processes, as in psychodrama, gestalt, and encounter groups, involved empathic responding among participants. However, empathy training is not the primary function of these processes.

Recently, specific attention has been given to empathy training in counselor and therapist training. However, the focus has been piecemeal, largely emphasizing cognitive and communicative aspects. In 1952, Carl Rogers suggested an exercise in which an individual would repeat his understanding of the other person's statement before responding to it. Carkhuff (1969) identified and systematized the components of the helping interaction, including specific empathic responding. In typical workbook exercises by Gazda (1973), Danish and Hauer (1975), Jerome Kagan (1969), and Egan (1975), trainees select or compose the most appropriate empathic response, or role play a counseling dialogue emphasizing specific empathic techniques. Ivey's approach in micro-counseling is a live approach of the same type. The emphasis in these training forms is clearly on communication skills; there is no attempt to expand one's repertoire of emotional experience, to broaden one's range of acceptance, or to inhibit identification.

It is apparent that empathy is generally considered an observable characteristic of interpersonal behavior that is measurable (at least as a cognitive and communicative process) and modifiable through training. In contrast, Dynamic Empathy Training draws heavily on modern dynamic group processes because they are experiential, growth oriented, and primarily affective (dealing with moods and emotions) process-learning situations that focus on changes *within* the learner.

## TECHNIQUE

*Step 1: Needs and strength assessment.* The trainees write responses to the phrase "Someone could help me with ..." After the trainer reads them aloud, the trainees individually respond to the phrase "I could help someone with ..." The trainees then discuss their reactions to receiving or not receiving help, selecting or rejecting areas for helping. Throughout this exercise the trainer notes evidenced needs and strengths.

*Step 2:* The group is presented with someone's personal experience that has a single, emotional theme—rejection, for example. The presentation, which lasts only a minute or two, can be staged, in person, written, or with video or audio recordings. Then each trainee responds to the phrase "This person feels ..." The inadequacy and confusion of naming an emotion becomes obvious. A typical problem solving exercise then follows to describe the emotion in terms of its operational processes and its correlate concrete behavior.

*Step 3: Discovering one's own similar emotions.* The trainees sit in a circle and each responds to "I feel rejected when ..." The responses are continued until exhausted. Other phrases are introduced in turn and pursued in the same manner to broaden the awareness of the feeling. Dialogue between trainees provides an opportunity for practice of those reflective probes that are helpful at clarifying and understanding the feelings of another person.

*Step 4: Intensifying and expanding one's feeling repertoire.* Personal emotional awareness is intensified and new emotional experiences are created by various experiential interaction exercises. An example is a guided fantasy reinforced by popular music on the same emotional theme or by the projection of a slide, during which the trainees are asked to imagine in turn the other person with these feelings, oneself with these feelings, being together with the other person during the feeling experience, and finally, leaving the other person alone with these feelings. Emphasis is placed on both imaginative and physical experience.

Many standard interaction exercises can simulate unpleasant emotions; others, designed to simulate positive experience, can be varied to simulate just the opposite. A group can also devise original interaction exercises that simulate the emotions in one another.

*Step 5: Skill in reflecting emotional awareness.* The exercises of heightened emotional experience are extended into reflecting responses by having each trainee extend an appropriate nonverbal response to one another. (This response will also allay the unpleasant emotional experiences of the exercise.) The trainees then in turn address one other trainee by completing the phrase "You are feeling . . ." These responses should progress from inclusion of those aspects of the emotion previously mentioned in the presentation (primary accurate empathy) to expressions that include aspects not previously mentioned (advanced accurate empathy).

*Step 6: Evaluation.* Before conclusion the trainees process what has transpired. Individual reactions will be one source of evaluation. The other source lies in the observed comparison of earlier responses with concluding responses for the accuracy and depth of those responses, the number of responses, and the number of trainees responding.

Trainees should enter into these emotional experiences with sufficient bodily involvement to indicate acceptance of the feeling as their own. In accepting the feeling as a legitimate feeling for oneself is found the beginning of accepting that feeling in another person. By abruptly ending the self-perception phase of each exercise and returning to a perception of that feeling in the other person there is a tendency to block identification. In observing reflecting responses, the trainer should discourage indications of identification (use of "I" or "we") and emphasize the use of the word "you."

## APPLICATIONS

Dynamic Empathy Training has its most extensive application—as part of a comprehensive training program—in helping skills or human-relations training for therapists, counselors, and social workers. Variations of Dynamic Empathy Training can be useful 1) in such areas as cross-cultural training, role conflict, and consciousness raising, 2) in individual and group therapy, where clients are having difficulty in appreciating, accepting, or reflecting the feelings of others—as in marital conflict and sexual dysfunction, and 3) in assisting patients who present problems of low or inappropriate emotional reactions.

Because of the intensity of the group experience, especially with regard to painful and unpleasant emotions, this is not a training technique that can be used without serious consideration given to the readiness of the trainees and the expertise of the trainer.

# Encounter Therapy
## Will Schutz

### DEFINITION

Encounter is a method of relating based on openness and honesty, self-awareness, self-responsibility, awareness of the body, attention to feelings, and an emphasis on the here-and-now. It usually occurs in a group setting. Encounter is therapy insofar as it focuses on removing blocks to better functioning. Encounter is education, recreation, and religion in that it attempts to create conditions leading to the most satisfying use of personal capacities.

### HISTORY

The Delphic precept, "Know thyself," is a succinct statement of a fundamental tenet of encounter. Socrates used group stimulation in his dialogues, although they emphasized intellectual material rather than feelings, a preference not found in Encounter.

Perhaps the ancient Greek city of Epidaurus is most closely approximated by a modern growth center such as Esalen in California, a location where, among other activities, Encounter group workshops take place. Epidaurus also had its variety of methods concentrating on the body, the unconscious, dreams and mystical elements.

Recently Max Lerner, a student of American civilization, has traced the history of Encounter through the American culture, beginning with Thomas Jefferson and encompassing the Oneida Community, various liberation movements, and several other phenomena. Lerner sees Encounter as the culmination of a variety of indigenous movements that have sprung up in America from its inception to the present.

Thus, the modern Encounter group is an integration of a wide variety of influences, ancient and recent. Many modern influences have made their mark on the present form of Encounter, including: group psychotherapy, T-Groups, group dynamics, psychodrama, Gestalt therapy, and theater and dance.

# TECHNIQUE

Encounter usually takes place in a group of eight to fifteen persons in a room that has a rug and is devoid of furniture, with all participants sitting on the floor or on pillows. An Encounter workshop usually consists of several meetings, each typically two hours long, spread over a weekend or five days. Ages vary from fifteen to seventy-five, with most participants between twenty and fifty. The workshop is held in a residential setting where all participants live. There is no formal agenda. The group members focus on becoming aware of their feelings, on expressing them honestly, and on taking responsibility for them.

Following are the principles of Encounter:

1. *Unity of the organism.* You are a unified organism. You are at the same time physical, psychological, and spiritual. These levels are all manifestations of the same essence. You function best when these aspects are integrated and when you are self-aware.

2. *Honesty.* Honesty and openness are the keys to your evolutionary growth. You must expend great amounts of energy to hide your feelings, thoughts, or wishes from other people, and even more energy to keep them from yourself. To withhold secrets requires a tightened body; it requires curtailment of spontaneity lest the secrets be revealed; it requires vigilance, shallow breathing, physical exertion, and a preoccupation with your own safety.

3. *Awareness.* A main purpose of Encounter is to help you become more aware of yourself: to break through self-deception, to know and like yourself, to feel your own importance, to respect what you are and can do, and to learn to be responsible for yourself. You achieve these best through self-awareness.

4. *Choice and self-responsibility.* Coming to an Encounter group is always a voluntary act. Presence in the group assumes that you have chosen to be there. There is no need for concepts such as sick or well, psychotic or normal, neurotic or happy. Choosing to go to an Encounter group in no way implies sickness; it implies only a desire for more joy, honesty, self-acceptance, and awareness.

If you, as a potential group member, do not feel ready to go to a group, or if you have a dread of being brainwashed, denuded, robbed of all privacy, or made dependent, your path is clear: don't go. As the group leader, I routinely announce that you are responsible for making the choice of entering the Encounter group, and that you are responsible for everything that happens to you during the life of the group. All choices about yourself are yours. You may choose to have your brain washed or to use your judgment, to go crazy or to be sane, to learn something or to be inert, to be bored or to be interested, to enjoy or to be miserable, to resist or welcome efforts at opening yourself up, to reveal your sexual intimacies or to keep them secret, to be physically injured or remain intact. I regard you as capable of being responsible for yourself.

By assuming that you are responsible, I feel I elicit your stronger qualities. If I assume that you are not capable of being responsible, I tend to infantilize you and elicit your weaker qualities.

My assertion that you are self-responsible does not mean that I cannot choose to be responsible for you. I decide how responsible for you I want to make myself.

5. *Naturalness and simplicity.* I trust natural processes. My reliance on natural unfolding extends to virtually every facet of human functioning. All profound truths are simple.

6. *Way of life.* Encounter is a way of life, not just a therapeutic technique. It concerns itself with relations among people and offers an alternative to the present structure of society, a structure that is based on deception (diplomacy), masking feelings (tact), disowning the body (as primitive, irrational, obscene), and similar duplicities.

7. *The rules of Encounter.* From the philosophy and theory underlying Encounter emerge very specific ways of leading a group; these ways can be expressed as a set of rules for group interaction. The rules implement the principles stated above.

The first set of rules establishes open and honest communication:

- Be honest with everyone, including yourself.
- Start with the here-and-now.
- Pay close attention to your body.
- Concentrate on feelings.

The next set of rules focuses on the body, integrating it into the group activity:

- Meet in rooms and in clothes that allow maximum freedom of movement.
- Sit or stand in a position that allows you to move toward any other person easily.
- Don't drink coffee or eat during a meeting.
- Fight when it feels right.
- Take off your clothes when it feels useful.
- Whenever there is an opportunity to express something physically, rather than verbally, do it physically.
- Don't take drugs.
- Don't smoke.
- Don't wear glasses or contact lenses.

To establish your identity and to encourage you to take responsibility for yourself, several other rules are helpful:

- Take responsibility for yourself.
- Make statements, not questions.
- Speak for yourself.
- Don't use globalisms.
- Take responsibility for your choices.
- Speak directly to the person addressed.
- Avoid noncommittal words.
- If something is happening that you don't like, take responsibility for doing something about it.

The use of body energy to help expand the limits of the self-concept gives rise to two important rules:

- If you are saying something about yourself that you have said before, stop, and say something else.

- Do whatever you are most afraid of doing.

## APPLICATIONS

Encounter as a style of life, rather than merely as a group technique, has been adopted widely. The Encounter movement is part of the larger social phenomenon embodying the various liberation movements, the renaissance of religion, and the call to honesty. The Encounter culture encompasses not only the use of the techniques associated with encounter and the human potential movement in general but also those social trends that express the basic tenets of Encounter: honesty, self-responsibility, awareness, understanding and acceptance of the body and of the self, and an appreciation of the unity of the organism.

Applications have been made to psychotherapy, industry, theater, education, childbirth, parent-child relations, religion, society, and daily life.

---

# Eriksonian Therapy

## Paul Roazen

### DEFINITION

Eriksonian Therapy is an approach that can be found in the ego psychology of Erik H. Erikson that, in contrast to the negativism of earlier Freudian thought, concentrates on the ego strengths appropriate to specific stages of the life cycle.

### HISTORY

Erikson trained to become a child analyst at the Vienna Psychoanalytic Institute between 1927 and 1933. Unlike most of his colleagues at the time, who described the ego's functions in terms of warding off quantities of drives, Erikson wanted to go further and extend his reach beyond neurotic defensiveness to adaptation. Early on, Erikson was interested in the problem of what enriches and strengthens a child's ego, and not just in what may be constricting and endangering.

After emigrating to the United States, Erikson was willing to expand his clinical awareness through anthropological field work. He studied two American Indian tribes, gaining a new appreciation of social forces. He compared how two so-called primitive cultures could differently synthesize configurations of ideals for living. Different cultural values, for instance, infused and gave meaning to particular elements in child training. Erikson concluded that any clinical concept of human nature demands historical self-awareness. Erikson's field work also gave him insight into the ways an observer necessarily participates in the lives of his subjects; what a field worker finds out is determined by the limitations of his personality as well as his methodology. Erikson believes that a clinician necessarily interacts with his evidence, thereby affecting it. The psychoanalyst influences what he observes, and therefore becomes a part of what he is studying. For Erikson, how data gets collected is a key component in evaluating the results of any research.

## TECHNIQUE

Erikson has wanted to expand the scope of psychoanalysis to include an understanding of successful means of coping, in addition to the early Freudian emphasis on symptomatological failure. Clinically, Erikson is apt to perceive as fluidity what might once have been deemed pathology. In his interest in the recuperative capacities of the ego, Erikson has cited instances of individuals who recovered from psychic distress. To Erikson, the therapist's task is not just that of clarifying the patient's early history, or the patterns of past drives. The present and future exert significant pulls in addition to any tendency toward regression. In behalf of the patient's need for ego identity, the therapist should support present developmental strengths. A symptom may represent a defense in behalf of identity formation. Erikson believes that nowadays even a periodic emphasis on dream life can be wasteful if not dangerous. Earlier psychoanalysts were too concerned with promoting rational, intellectual insight, and not sufficiently aware of the extent to which apparent regressions can be constructive. The psychoanalytic method can make people worse off than before, and Erikson has been wary of the psychoanalyst's illusory objectivity leading to a license for interpretive sadism.

As a child psychoanalyst Erikson used drawings with children, and relied on play constructions, as well as disruptions, in order to understand emotional conflicts. He believes the therapist should share a meal with the family before accepting a child as a patient. Adolescents in particular (who may be suffering from "identity crises") need ego bolstering; and Erikson proposes that therapy strengthen the resynthe-sis of the constitutents of the ego identity of such patients. Young people in trouble are not, Erikson thinks, in need of the couch, but require a degree of support, sanction, and confirmation from the therapist. Therapy can in itself provide patients with a key period of delay in commitment, a "moratorium" for youth. Alongside his own positive therapeutic suggestions, Erikson has repeatedly warned against the dangers implicit in the biases of the only apparently neutral, old-fashioned psychoanalytic situation. He has likened the use of a couch to a method of sensory deprivation.

## APPLICATIONS

An affirmative mood pervades Erikson's writing, as he takes a more hopeful and less tragic stance than that of Sigmund Freud. The therapeutic model has limited uses for a general theory of human nature, since in the context of treatment the therapist confronts a disabled ego. Erikson may be best known as an early advocate of psychohistory; he sees a focus on historical greatness as a way of examining and emphasizing ego strength. He has insisted on the differences between a clinical case history and a life history. For patients are undermined by their neurotic conflicts, whereas in history such human problems add an essential ingredient to all extraordinary effort.

In his tolerance for the human need for legend, as in his respect for the idealizations of heroes, Erikson is at odds with Freud's own negative view of the function of illusions and, in particular, of religion. Erikson is undoubtedly right in believing that myths can be a means of mastering anxieties, and of finding external support for our aspirations. But it would have been better to have distinguished between myth and deception, for had Erikson acknowledged the moral shock of a lie, he would have appreciated the limitations of fable. Unlike Freud's ideal of a relentless quest for scientific truth, Erikson has been content with a more elusive sort of artistic insight.

Erikson has also sought to spell out the moral implications implicit within psychoanalysis. He has tried to get away from the excessive egoism of the early Freudian concept of the mind. He has stressed a religious dimension to human experience, and his concept of "mutuality" serves to replace the older goal of genitality. In general, Erikson has tried to humanize the "biologism" of earlier psychoanalysis, yet his views on female psychology have largely restated Freud's theories on femininity within Eriksonian categories. But Erikson has been unwilling to define adulthood negatively as the absence of infantile conflict. He wants to measure normality not by the original psychoanalytic standard of what in a personality is denied or cut off, but rather define if by all the extremes an individual's ego is capable of unifying.

# Exaggeration Therapy

## *Gerard van den Aardweg*

### DEFINITION

Exaggeration Therapy (synonymous with "anti-complaining therapy") borrowed its name from the fundamental technique used in this therapy: the exaggeration technique, which is a verbal technique consisting of the humoristic aggravation of neurotic feelings of self-pity, and of neurotic complaining behavior, by the invention of increasingly dramatic stories until the client starts smiling or laughing.

Exaggeration Therapy as a whole comprises two central elements: 1) self-observation by the client of his neurotic, infantile complaining behavior and of the self-pity in his neurotic, displeasurable feelings and thoughts and 2) application of the exaggeration technique, telling and imagining lamentable scenes about these perceived complaints in order to destroy them by the humor response. It is an interplay between recognition of infantile complaining and combating it with humor techniques: the latter constitutes the principal therapeutic factor. Exaggeration mobilizes the curative power of humor responses.

To understand why and when exaggeration techniques are used, it is necessary to become familiar with the basic principle of anti-complaining therapy, namely that of *compulsive infantile complaining* as the propelling force of neurotic disturbances. Neurotics appear to harbor the feelings of a chronically "complaining or self-pitying child" who creates symptoms (negative feelings or thoughts, worries, fears, inferiority feelings, depressions, physical pains, as well as frustrating situations, etc.) in order to lament about them. In Exaggeration Therapy, this pathogenous force of compulsive complaining is thoroughly analyzed and then attacked by its emotional antipode, the laughing response.

## HISTORY

The mechanisms of compulsive infantile complaining and their treatment with exaggeration techniques were described by Dutch psychoanalyst Johan Leonard Arndt (1892–1965) in a series of publications since 1950. At present, it is practiced and elaborated on by Dutch and Brazilian psychologists, in private practice and in penitentiary institutions. Much experience has been acquired, notably with the treatment of homosexuals and neurotic delinquents.

## TECHNIQUE

Exaggeration Therapy proceeds through the following phases:

1. A theoretical study by the client of the autonomous "inner self-pitying child" and of the laws and ways of its functioning. The idea is that self-pity or self-dramatization is an instinctive reaction in childhood or adolescence to feelings and perceptions of being rejected, inferior, or not loved. It has a healing effect, since tears of self-pity and lamentations are recuperative reactions that bring relief. However, when present during a longer period of time, self-pity easily creates a dependency, so that the infantile mind will come to seek it for its own sake, gradually becoming obsessed by a need for drama in order to indulge in narcissistic feelings of "poor me."

2. Analysis of the specific "complaining child" within the client, of the "child's" principal theme of complaining. For example, "I am a poor, ugly one," "I am a poor, neglected one," "a poor weakling," "a poor failure," "a lonely one without a home," or "a poor, unjustly treated one."

3. Daily self-observation. The client screens his thoughts and emotions in all kinds of situations, trying to detect infantile complaints. In principle, any unpleasurable feeling may contain infantile self-pity. Self-observation leads to formulations of the contents of complaints, such as, "I am so lonely—poor me," "I feel so tired—poor me," "I shall be the victim of something—poor me," and so on.

4. These verbalized complaints are the objects of the exaggeration technique. The client imagines his "self-pitying child of the past" as if this were standing before him, bearing the complaint just formulated. Then he talks to this child, exaggerating his suffering, making such an absurd tragedy of it that he stirs some humor reaction. For instance, to the child who complains "Nobody loves me," he may say: "Poor little one, half crippled, blind, clothed in rags, everybody spits at you when you are walking down the street. The dogs bark at you, groups of boys taunt you and throw rotten eggs. When you knock on the door of your house, your cruel father (friend, wife...) beats you with an enormous stick ..."

Exaggeration of the concrete complaint has to be continued until it provokes a liberating smile. It has to be applied many times a day, immediately upon the perception of some impulse of complaining. The therapist guides and encourages the process, but the work itself has to be done by the client. He will build his repertory of exaggerations, dependent on his stereotype complaints and his particular sense of humor. He has to overcome often strong resistances to recognition of his complaining and self-pity as well as to subjecting these feelings to this form of humor. However, if he comes to apply the method, he will gradually free himself from his "complaining sickness" and experience feelings of increasing happiness and emotional satisfaction. A drastic personality change may be achieved when the emotional immaturity inherent to the "complaining child" dies away, which indicates how infantile complaining pervades most sectors of the neurotic's mental life and behavior.

There are common elements with other therapies. As in Transactional Analysis, the client in Exaggeration Therapy is taught to analyze his "inner child," the difference being that he has to recognize—and exaggerate—the complaining behavior at the root of his infantile impulses. Alfred Adler's "inferiority complex" is incorporated in the concept of compulsive complaining; "I am only ..." is a way of complaining, "poor me." Exaggeration resembles implosion (Thomas G. Stampfl) and paradoxical intention (Victor Frankl), but with some important differences: a) it is not so much the neurotic symptoms in themselves that are exaggerated (anxieties, worries, etc.) as the complaining behavior underlying them. Because of this, "exaggeration" is also called "hyperdramatization" b) *all* negative emotions and thoughts are exaggerated, and not just fears and anxieties c) the client applies the technique himself in his daily life, and d) exaggeration is humorous, its purpose being to provoke laughing.

## APPLICATIONS

Exaggeration Therapy is used with those neurotics who suffer from the infantile complaining compulsion: obsessive compulsive neurotics, anxiety neurotics, depressive neurotics, persons with inferiority complexes, hypochondriacs, homosexuals and delinquents. These neurotics are characterized by specific "principal complaints."

---

# Existential-Humanistic Psychotherapy
## *James F. T. Bugental*

## DEFINITION

Existential-Humanistic Psychotherapy is an approach aiding persons to live more fully and (if they choose) to explore some of the transpersonal possibilities that are latent in being human. It involves a very intense relationship, great commitment to the work and purposes of the therapy, and a readiness to make major life changes. Its primary functions are: a) to identify and reduce or eliminate the constrictions that limit the client's realization of his deeper potential and b) to aid the client in rediscovering and increasing the power of the inward searching capacity that is native to each of us.

## HISTORY

This approach is rooted in the work of the existentialists (e.g., Heidigger, Boss, May, Koestenbaum) and the humanistic psychologists (James, Kelly, Rogers, Buhler, Jourard, and so on). Its existentialism consists in a continual grounding of theory, postulations, and method in the simplest givens of being as these are apparent to an unsophisticated (but aware) observer: human beings are conscious, finite, able to act or not to act, confronted with inexorable choice, at once part of all other beings and apart from them, and embodied. We all learn a way of seeing the world and of identifying ourselves that we are told is "reality." This purported reality is often conflict-filled and limits vitality. It overemphasizes (at least in our culture) the objective and the environmental at the expense of the subjective and the creative potential of the individual. Psychotherapy that is to be truly liberating must call into question the life of the individual and the constraints on that life.

Existential-Humanistic Psychotherapy is human-centered in values, holding that the fullest possible realization of human potential is a primary good, that each human being is ultimately worthy of trust when released from destructive interpretations of his own nature and of the world, that the route to such release is that of a mutually respecting and caring relationship in which one learns to use the potential that is native to us all but frequently submerged.

## TECHNIQUE

Technique, in the Existential-Humanistic view, is regarded as distinctly secondary to the accomplishment of three main purposes:

1. Development of client commitment to thorough, life-changing inner exploration in a setting characterized by authentic mutual respect, caring and honesty.
2. Attainment by the client of discipline and skill in the process of inward searching—a process that can revitalize life during and after psychotherapy.
3. Perseverance by the client through the anxiety and anguish of relinquishing the structures of personal and world identity with which life formerly was organized, and confronting and incorporating the essential openness of being (the existential crisis).

There is, as with all matured perspectives, an important body of implementing methodology. This has some roots in psychoanalytic procedure, as it recognizes the importance of dealing with the resistances to authentic being, but it calls for much more mutual engagement between therapist and client than is characteristic of much psychoanalytic work. The core of the methodology centers around aiding the client in coming to appreciate the naturalness, power, scope, and incredible productivity of the process of inward searching.

Inward searching, in very simple terms, is the process we all use when pondering a life issue, trying to come up with a fresh idea, or weighing choice alternatives. But most of us use this inherent capacity with very little awareness and scarcely more development. Truly effective inner searching involves:

1. Drawing on the tremendous power of the human sense of concern by getting deeply in touch with what matters in one's life right at this moment.

2. Getting and keeping as subjectively centered as possible while opening awareness to whatever emerges under the impetus of the feeling of concern.

3. Maintaining an expectancy of inward discovery (in contrast to the tendency of many clients primarily to report to the therapist what is already known about oneself).

4. Recognizing and relinquishing the blocks to full and freely ranging awareness. These blocks arise from faulty and constricting conceptions about oneself and the world (such as, "I'm too awkward to be in charge of other people" or "There's no use really hoping for someone to love me; everybody's just out for what they can get for themselves").

5. Opening the newly freed inner awareness to the kind of inner vision that permits actualization of enlarged being with greater congruence of feeling and action.

The psychotherapist aids this powerful process by maintaining and making evident his belief in the client's capacity to deal with his own life concerns, by calling on the client to use that potential rather than seeking to depend on other resources, by providing support during the inevitable times of despair and anguish, by identifying the resistances to full inner awareness as those resistances are disclosed, by insisting at all times on the client's truly being involved and present, and by taking the client very seriously.

As client courage, perseverance, and determination join with therapist skill, empathy, and courage, clients find a sense of greater personal power and durability, feelings of meaningfulness and choice, changes in how and with whom they want to live their lives, and some experiences that transcend the ordinary life boundaries. These transpersonal openings may include such subjective phenomena as: discovery of greater depth, richness, and meaningfulness of the stream of subjective awareness: a changed experience of time, causality, or relationship; synesthesia and other alterations in perception; conjunction in subjectivity (e.g., telepathy, markedly increased empathy); recognition of the ultimate unity of all being; discovery of the healing powers of consciousness; and recognition of death as an event, rather than an ending. Walsh (1976) has described in rich detail his own experience in this therapy and some of the products it yielded.

It seems likely that the basic searching process is a tool of the liberated consciousness that can be employed in infinite exploration and with unending discovery and continually renewed emancipation of being.

## APPLICATIONS

Existential-Humanistic Psychotherapy has had its greatest area of application with that segment of the population possessing more than average advantages of education, socioeconomic support, and incentives toward self-exploration and self-development. However, reports are becoming more frequent—if still informal—of the extension of the basic concepts and methodology to other population segments with varying but encouraging degrees of success.

To date, this approach has gone on under the general rubric of intensive individual and group psychotherapy. Clients are usually seen several times a week for several years. Now, work is progressing in developing group and other methods for increasing the availability of this approach.

# Existential Group Psychotherapy: The Meta-group

*Ted Smith and Nina Smith*

## DEFINITION

The Meta-group is a spiritually oriented (value-centered) form of existential group therapy that is radically different from the usual modes of most group therapies. It is not personal, interpersonal, psychoanalytic, or psychodynamic, and avoids group dynamics, interaction, and encounter, thus eliminating competition among members. It is nonpersonal, encouraging joint participation in a harmonious, hermeneutic process of discovering, clarifying, and elucidating the truth as it sheds light on the basic issues of existence.

A spiritual perspective is a center of consciousness from which one sees purely without subjective or objective considerations. An individual's mode of being in the world is determined by his perspective or belief systems. As spiritual beings we participate in absolute reality, which can be realized only in consciousness. Consciousness is the agency by which God (absolute reality) becomes known to man.

The concern of the Meta-group is with the quality and content of consciousness. Every group session is a vehicle, enabling members to focus on learning to see reality ever more clearly as a context within which life becomes meaningful, intelligent, spontaneous, and harmonious.

## HISTORY

In a general sense, Meta-groups have existed whenever people have gathered to explore and understand some task, project, or issue, grounded in a spirit of love and mutual respect. Wherever people participate together in a spirit that transcends them individually, such a group becomes a Meta-group, a manifestation of that higher spirit. An example would be a symphony orchestra or a string quartet gathering to play Mozart. In a more specific therapeutic sense, the Meta-group is a phenomenon arising from Metapsychiatry.[2*] Metapsychiatry is a dimension of existential analysis that is the healing application

---

[2*] The term "metapsychiatry" originated in the United States with Professor Stanley Dean of Miami, Florida, but has been used extensively by Dr. Thomas Hora of New York City to describe his system of psychotherapy.

in the realm of the psyche of theistic existentialism, which presupposes the existence of God as the center of reality, and man as a spiritual consciousness. Its philosophical background is the existential philosophy of Martin Heidegger. By contrast, most existential analysis leans toward the atheistic existentialism of Jean-Paul Sartre. Metapsychiatry developed out of the practice of existential analysis of Thomas Hora, M.D., a New York psychiatrist, and is taught through the New York Institute of Metapsychiatry.

## TECHNIQUE

The presence of God (reality as ultimately good) is the core of the Meta-group process. The process is a practical exploration of "the good that already is" and clarifies the meaning of the obstacles or errors in perception that prevent people from seeing that good. Existentially valid spiritual principles are the guidelines of the Meta-group and are of key importance in distinguishing the truth from erroneous thinking.

The Meta-group becomes a workshop where problems or questions related to life situations are presented and examined within the context of a higher vision of absolute truth—absolute reality—absolute love, the cornerstone of existence. Each issue raised affords the opportunity to focus on the path to the realization of that absolute reality through the maze of infinite possibilities along the path.

Although life may take many forms, there is only one *authentic* direction in life's journey toward the truth. In this light, spiritual principles guide the members to a perspective designed to heal and bring them into conscious alignment with the harmonizing principle of the Universe (God).

A Meta-group leader clearly needs to be a facilitator, inspired by these principles. The quality of his or her presence will be reflected in the quality of the group process. The leader helps to channel the members' thinking about the issues raised, in an existentially valid direction. The first step is understanding the meaning of any experience or phenomenon. All experiences and phenomena are "what seems to be," and reflect the thinking of the experiencer: "We think in secret, and it comes to pass/The world is but our looking-glass" (Anon.). The second step is transcending appearances ("what seems to be") and elucidating the truth of what really is, represented by the basic existentially valid spiritual principles. Entering a higher authentic level of perception enables group members (often suddenly) to see their everyday problems and errors in living in a radically new light. Thus, the Meta-group is punctuated repeatedly by outbursts of spontaneous laughter. The sharing in this communal vision creates a loving fellowship. The quality of the members' participation is a reflection of their interest and commitment to the process of learning, which is limited only by false ideas or errors in perception. In a loving context, no one is blamed for or identified with any expressed ignorance and is repeatedly invited to participate harmoniously and authentically in the group task. As each individual member is unconfirmed at an inauthentic level, enormous healing takes place.

Each meeting is a preview of the Kingdom of Heaven (a metaphor for harmonious existence centered on the good of God, revealed in the attributes of love and intelligence). The ability to see clearly is cultivated from week to week and transforms the quality of an individual's mode-of-being in the world.

## APPLICATIONS

The Meta-group is a viable and workable process wherever and whenever individuals seek to grow in the light of inspired truth. A typical example of the application of the Meta-group process is as follows:

A man in the group began the session with the statement of a problem he faced. "When I relate to someone I admire and by whom I want to be well thought of, it seems that I fall all over myself and act foolishly. I want to be respectful and appreciative, but give the opposite impression, and seem insulting and unfriendly. How can I understand this better?"

The leader then asked the group about the best way to approach the problem, and it was correctly suggested that the meaning of what seemed to be would have to be explored. (The meaning of any phenomenon is its mental equivalent, i.e., the idea or ideas of the individual reflected in the phenomenon.) From this beginning, the group members identified the following ideas in the mind of the presenter: 1) a desire to impress and 2) a "wanting." Wanting was identified as personal desire. The leader concurred and asked the group what the difficulty was in intending or wanting to be respectful, since it seemed innocent and innocuous enough. Exploration of the theme of personal desire led to the insight that such intention implied a personal mind, i.e., a mind of one's own. This is clearly a false assumption in the light of the Metapsychiatric understanding that there is only one mind, the divine love-intelligence which is called God. It was seen that since there is only one mind, there can be only one intention, one will. When an individual realizes that there is only one reality, one will, he will seek to come into harmony with that one will, and thus become a vehicle for love-intelligence to work through. In such a condition, willing only that the will of God be manifest in every situation, the quality of one's responsiveness is loving, intelligent, and spontaneous—harmoniously in accord with the only will that is free. It became clear to the member who raised the question that by personally willing to be "respectful," he lost his connection with the will of God, and was in fact being calculative and manipulative. Calculative thinking is obviously destructive to the spontaneity that comes from being joyously in harmony with the truth. Therefore the man saw his difficulty as that of calculating how to accomplish his personal will, rather than trusting the truth to make him free.

At this point another insight occurred in the group. A woman thought of her difficulty with her two young children who were "unmanageable." It occurred to her that she began virtually everything she said to them with "I want." "I want you to eat your cereal," "I want you to go to bed now." "I want some peace and quiet." It became clear that the children copied their mother and responded to her "I want" with a rebellious "I don't want what you want, and I want what you don't want." The mother's assertion of personal will was leading to a continual power struggle with the children. She began to see the necessity of seeking first "the kingdom of God," i.e., a mind centered on love-intelligence, which would become a harmonizing principle in the household. Indeed, at a later session the woman reported that there had been much improvement as she sought to do the will of God rather than her own.

# Experiential Analysis

## Donald W. Tiffany

### DEFINITION

Experiential Analysis belongs to the third force movement in psychology that concerns itself with the manner in which we experience our inner and outer worlds and focuses upon understanding psychological adjustment and growth in the normal person rather than being limited to the psychopathology of maladjustment (Tiffany, 1967). Experiential Analysis portrays experience as a gestalt of person-environment relationships. It provides a model for understanding man in society and for identifying both the sources of control and the contexts that act as primary determinants in psychological growth and adjustment.

### HISTORY AND TECHNIQUE

*Theory of experienced control.* The theory of Experienced Control pertains to the psychological forces that actuate, regulate, facilitate, or inhibit a person's psychological functioning in its broadest aspects (Tiffany, et al., 1969; Tiffany, et al., 1970; Tiffany and Tiffany, 1973). The experienced control model shown below is a schematic representation of the individual's experiential space. Inside the small circle, the space denoted FI (internal states within the organism) represents controlling forces experienced *within oneself.* OI is the symbol used to indicate control experienced *over* the self. During the process of socialization, the locus of control shifts from the condition of being controlled by organismic forces to control *over* these impulses.

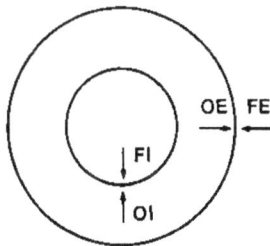

*Figure 1. A conceptual model of four kinds of control.*

Forces from the environment, shown as FE in the outer zone of the model, may be exerted by other individuals or groups, or by situations or physical factors. OE factors represent perceived control *over* the environment. They arise from within the individual and the manner in which the individual responds depends on his or her technical, physical, or interpersonal skills. While FI and OI have an internal reference, i.e., the experience of internal forces and the ability to control these forces, OE and FE have an external reference and consist both of experiencing forces *over* and *from* the environment.

*Structural properties of experienced control.* Two major structural properties of experienced control are 1) that FI and FE are significant experiences in life that the individual does not initiate and as such are non-self-determining factors and 2) OE and OI represent the self-determining activities that characterize the cognitive aspects of man and constitute response patterns. Thus, a dynamic interplay exists between FE and OE and between FI and OI as well as between the specific processes, internal and external. The ratio OI/FI and OE/FE for the two loci averages around 1.30 to 1.80 for different groups and for different situations. For psychiatric patients it is always less than 1.0. However, for individuals with adjustment problems that do not reach psychiatric proportions, the ratios may be low only in certain situations.

*Dynamic properties of experienced control.* The basic dynamic property of experienced control is that forces *from* internal FI and *over* external OE act in concert against the environment. Impulses of FI, for example, the raw unreasoned quality of rage, joy, sexual excitement, or whatever FI is present, may be channeled through a selected OE to act on the environment. Both forces act outward from the individual and are the means by which the person can have maximal impact on the environment. The individual is capable of manipulating circumstances to bring about a desired FI, which, in collaboration with the proper OE, may result in a powerful environmental impact. If these collaborative efforts are carried out in a particular social system, such as the government, military, or other large social structure, they can represent an enormous amount of focused power.

The reverse of the above is also possible. Forces from the environment FE and over internal OI act toward or upon the person to such a degree that he becomes almost totally inhibited. It is then almost impossible to employ the spontaneous or creative processes at FI or the skills at OE to produce the cognitive effects necessary. Not infrequently one must escape to a "safe" environment to realize one's creative potential.

*Veridicality of experience.* Experienced control theory is based on subjective events of experience at any moment in time rather than upon "reality" as it can be described in physical or objective terms. Allport refers to *veridicality*, when there is "agreement between a percept description and the related physicalistic experience of the object" (Allport, 1955). This phenomenal interpretation of experience is used in experienced control.

*Balance between self-direction and non-self-direction at both loci.* As experiential data is being used, a change of balance at either loci can take place without affecting the environment. Each person develops styles for particular situations and when any of the four components is changed for that situation there will be adjustments within the remaining components to achieve a state of dynamic equilibrium.

*Focal and contextual characteristics of components.* For each of the four components there are focal and contextual experiences that interact to provide the total experience. We are daily involved in delineating focal from contextual determinants. The contextual experiences exist at many different levels. At the first level is the focal determinant itself, then a primary contextual level, a secondary contextual level, and so on. The control experienced at any of the levels depends upon the perceived meaning of the focal determinant. What lends a determinant meaning is largely its interaction with its context. The interaction of focal to contextual determinants parallels the concept of figure-ground in Gestalt psychology.

## APPLICATIONS

The greater the consciousness of self, the greater the number of OEs and OIs that are available to the person for problem solving and coping behavior. Thus, as one increases his consciousness, he simultaneously has greater control over life. Sometimes it becomes necessary that a particular focal determinant be altered. This is done by fractioning the determinant in such a way that awareness includes only those aspects that are positive (e.g., "look at his good side"). In this condition of consciousness, part of the experience becomes nonveridical. The more conscious we are of ourselves and our environment, the more decisions we can make to fractionate determinants (components). Greater awareness also enables us to juxtapose components properly. Where improper alignment of the components takes place, it does so because one of the components may be in a nonconscious zone. This misalignment is observed frequently in psychiatric patients in that they are unable to evoke the appropriate OE to cope with a particularly stressful FE. For example, a profile of maladjustment would include degrees of the following: an absence of focalizing, focal/contextual reversals, extreme nonveridical perception, and improper juxtapositioning of components.

# Experiential Focusing and Psychotherapy

*Eugene T. Gendlin*

## DEFINITION

Experiential Focusing is a method of attending inwardly to let a "felt sense" form. This is a holistic sense of a problem or unresolved situation. It forms if one attends to how the body feels from inside. At first there may be a blank or some vague tension of ease, but in less than a minute one can feel a whole sense of the problem forming there. This felt sense is not just physical as with muscle sensations, not just psychological, nor just cognitive. It is bodily, affectively (emotionally) and cognitively meaningful before these three are split apart. Once a felt sense forms, it is found to lead to steps. New feelings, perceptions, and courses of action emerge. Focusing usually involves many steps before a problem is resolved. Therefore one is willing to receive and welcome what emerges at a given step. One knows it will soon change further. Whatever emerges is checked against the felt sense to see if it produces an immediately felt effect that signals the Tightness, for that moment, of what is said or done. When one changes one can feel this concretely, in a bodily way. Whatever words or procedures fail to attain to this "felt shift" are immediately discarded so that words or actions that do have this effect can form.

## HISTORY

Experiential Focusing comes from a series of research studies (Gendlin, et al., 1967) that found that those patients who were successful later were those who, during tape-recorded therapy, often attended to what was felt but not yet cognitively clear. This led to procedures to teach people exactly how to do what the research had found. My (Gendlin, 1962, 1973) logic of relationships between felt meaning and symbols led to specific definitions, especially the difference between felt sense and feelings of the usual type.

## TECHNIQUE

Experiential Focusing gets into direct touch with the concrete level, in us, where our troubles really are. Most of psychotherapy consists of talking *about*, which doesn't reach down and touch, let alone change, that in us that needs changing. So we get wiser *about* what's wrong, without actually working with it.

The level, in us, where this concreteness is, is below thinking and emotions. Even feeling familiar emotions intensely often does not put us in touch with what they come *from*. There is a level below them. To reach it one has to be willing to be a little confused, unclear, for a minute or two. It works this way:

One asks for a felt sense of the whole problem to form. This isn't something most people usually have. Most people go right into their problem to their usual bad place, and they feel bad and stuck. Focusing begins by asking you not to go to your usual place, inside the problem, just yet. Instead, let a whole sense of it come. "What is it like, having that whole problem, just now?" (It takes less than a minute for such a holistic sense of the entire problem to form. But it must form. It isn't just there.)

Getting such a holistic sense, one next asks: "What is that whole feeling?" And the answer will be one word or a phrase, such as "scary" or "heavy" or perhaps a private word like "funny." Or it might be a gesture, like clutching oneself. The move here is to get a handle on this whole felt sense of the whole problem, by finding one word that gets it just right.

The hardest part of focusing is to let a felt sense form, as just described. It takes a little patience. At first, most people get a lot of words: explanations, arguments at themselves, or a lot of heavy emotions. A felt sense is none of these. It is a direct bodily sense, but it isn't conceptually clear. It's a feel for the whole problem, not the emotions in the problem.

As an example of a felt sense, think of two people you know. Got them? Pick them now, then the example will work for you. Now, take the first one. You get a distinct feel quality for that person, the whole feel of them, their texture or taste, or quality, so to speak. It includes everything you have ever experienced with them, everything they ever did that you know about, how you have ever seen them. Yet it is none of these things one by one. It is a feel of them, a felt sense.

Now switch to the other person; notice that you get a very different felt sense. It would take a lot of words, and some time, to *say* what these two felt senses are like, but you can feel them directly.

Once you have a hold of the felt sense of a problem, then stay with that for a minute or two. Don't do anything, just see what *it* does. If it changes or moves, let it. Just say something like: "What's so scary?" (or whatever one-word handle you have on it). But it's important not to answer that question; just ask it and let the felt sense be there and expect the felt sense, after a while, to do the answering.

When a felt sense "answers," it also shifts. One can feel a concrete release or movement, bodily. Perhaps also an involuntary breath "Whew ... yes, *that's* what's so scary." Words that come with a felt shift, are usually right. One checks such words back: "Is that right? ... whew, yeah " The individual feels the release over again.

Sometimes there are small steps before there's a bigger shift. Words come to say something that's clearly right, but there is no big body release. Let's say what comes is "What's scary is he'll leave me." Then the next step would be, "OK, what's so scary about him leaving me?" Again it is important to let the felt sense answer the question. It takes a few moments, repeating the question, not answering it.

Of course the person in my example knows many reasons why she'd be scared of his leaving. But those known arguments get in the way, and one can lose hold of the feeling. To get it back, she asks "Can I still feel that scared" and wait. After a few moments, there it is again. She waits to see what comes from the feeling. She lets the words come from the feeling, ignoring all other words. "What's so scary about his leaving?" Can I still feel it? ... yeah ... *there* it is, again. What's that?" (One shouldn't answer; let it answer, wait with it.) Whatever comes, she takes it and goes another step. Why again is *that*, now? And don't answer, let it. There should be one big step, a felt shift, a big release, a big "Whew ..." There are exact steps for focusing, but the above will give some idea.

Such a big felt shift is a sign of real change, and after it, it's time to stop focusing for a while. Everything is now a little different. It takes the body a time to let that change filter through everything else. It may not solve the problem but there is a distinct unquestionable sense of being in a somewhat different place, and not just verbally, not just conceptually, but in a concrete, living, bodily sense.

The method of focusing cuts across all methods of therapy. All can work if used with focusing, and none work well without it. Without focusing most therapy is just talking about, or it is painful potshots that can hit something, that doesn't add up to a continuing self-propelled change process. Also, with focusing one knows when one is changing; it is a concrete, body experience. Many people in therapy or working on themselves wonder if it's getting them any further. But if one can't sense oneself changing, one probably isn't.

Focusing lets one use whatever anyone (including therapists) says. There is no need either to believe or to disbelieve someone's interpretation of you. You can go straight down to where it's at, and be in touch—and then, if you try the interpretation *there*, it either produces a felt shift or it does not. If not, then it isn't right, at least not now.

The experience of focusing, once you have it, lets you sense your own inward concreteness. The body senses inwardly, and is wiser than the mind. The body totals up the millions of details you can't think of, except one by one. Focusing is between the ordinary level of thoughts and emotions, and the deep level of meditation, where there is no content at all.

## APPLICATIONS

Experiential Focusing has been used in psychotherapy and taught to schizophrenics (Prouty, 1977), "borderline" patients, and people generally (van den Bos, 1973).

Focusing is also being applied in a spiritual context, in creative writing, in business (Iberg, 1978), in problem solving (Zimring, 1974; Kantor, 1976), with EEG correlates of felt shift, in dance, in healing (Olsen, 1978), with imagery (Gendlin, 1970), and in relation to dreams.

# Guided Fantasy in Psychotherapy
## *Gary F. Kelly*

### DEFINITION
The past twenty-five years have seen a renewal of interest in conscious inner human experience and its implications for therapy. Counselors and psychotherapists have begun to tap the potentials of fantasy for facilitating personal growth and therapeutic change. Through outside suggestion, a person's fantasizing may be channeled and directed toward positive ends. In most of the fantasy therapies, the therapist structures the situation by describing some imaginary situation for the client. Then the client is encouraged to let his own imagination develop the theme and create a rich fantasy experience, as the therapist gently guides by comments and suggestions.

### HISTORY
The historical foundations of Guided Fantasy are found in psychoanalysis. In the famous case of Anna O. (Breuer and Freud, 1895), a directed mental imagery technique was employed, but Freud later discarded the use of guided imagery, and developed methods involving free association and dream analysis. Growing out of this analytic tradition, Kretschmer (1922) and Happich (1938) developed meditative approaches to psychotherapy, and Schultz (1956) used a systematic method for using the mind's images called the "autogenic training technique." Especially significant to the more recent publicizing and legitimizing of fantasy psychotherapy were the methods of French psychotherapist Robert Desoille and German psychiatrist Hanscarl Leuner. Desoille's (1966) work with the waking dream (*rêve éveillé*) demonstrated that therapist-directed daydreaming could lead patients to increased self-understanding and emotional maturity. Leuner's (1969) "guided affective imagery" technique involves the guiding of the subject through a series of structured fantasy situations, each with a specific theoretical purpose in analysis and therapy.

Contemporary approaches to Guided Fantasy have moved away from emphasis of the analytic value of imagery and more toward the inherent therapeutic value of the fantasy experience, along with action-oriented approaches for integrating the fantasy experience into positive growth (Kelly, 1974). Shaffer (1972), for example, has used "induced guided fantasy" as a primary mode of treatment with several clients in therapy. "Psychosynthesis" makes use of a variety of Guided Fantasy methods (Crampton, 1969).

Behavior therapists have often modified and structured Guided Fantasy for use in Systematic Desensitization. The real history of Guided Fantasy is being written now, as more therapists make use of these techniques and as journals and societies focusing on mental imagery begin to appear. For a more definitive discussion of the history of fantasy therapies, see Margaret Crampton's (1974) historical survey.

## TECHNIQUE

One of the advantages of Guided Fantasy techniques is their flexibility and adaptability to diverse settings. I shall describe my general approach to fantasy in counseling situations; see my paper (Kelly, 1972) for further detail. The effectiveness of Guided Fantasy seems to depend on several factors: the characteristics of the client, how well the counselor has introduced and structured the situation, and the effectiveness of the counselor's guiding during the actual situation.

*Client characteristics.* There are several client characteristics that seem to be especially reliable in predicting a positive outcome from a fantasy experience in counseling or therapy:

1. Deep commitment to the counseling process and its goals.
2. Willingness to share the responsibility for the counseling relationship and towork toward growth and change.
3. Trust in the counselor, whose accepting manner is firmly established.
4. Lack of intense anxiety or undue concern over increasing insight, fantasies, or dreams.
5. Some comprehension of the existence of unconscious needs, motivations, and repressions.
6. Willingness to participate in a Guided Fantasy without viewing the experience as unduly threatening, mystical, or unorthodox.

Some clients simply indicate they are afraid of such methods or would prefer not to participate in them. Some therapists would interpret this as resistance to be broken down; I prefer to respect the client's wishes.

*Preliminary structuring.* There are several ways in which the counselor may prepare the client for a Guided Fantasy, facilitating a positive, nonthreatening atmosphere and protecting against fearfulness generated by the unexpected. Several steps should be followed:

1. Introducing the technique to the client, emphasizing that it may give some new insights into thoughts and feelings.
2. The therapist should explain the client's role in the fantasy, and indicate that the imagination should be given freedom to develop the experience without much censoring. I tell clients not to try to make the images go where they think they ought to, but to visualize and fully sense whatever images come along. I also explain that as they keep me fully informed of their fantasy, I shall be making suggestions from time to time, but that they are free to reject any of these suggestions.
3. The client should be prepared to feel emotion during the fantasy and

encouraged to fully *experience* whatever emotions are evoked.

4. It should be emphasized that the client has full autonomy and control in the fantasy, and that the fantasy is simply taking the directions the client allows it to take.

5. The client should be in a relaxed, quiet atmosphere, as free from extraneous stimuli as possible. A reclining position, with the eyes closed, seems best for most clients.

6. The opening situation given by the counselor to initiate the fantasy should be thoroughly detailed and, whenever appropriate, tailored to a particular client's needs. Often, the opening themes I suggest are quite general and suggest venturing into some uncharted territory (such as, going into a cave; getting to the other side of a large stone wall; drifting in a rowboat in fog). Other times they are more specific, and designed to work on a particular client concern (for example, entering one's own body; confronting a room full of people known to the client).

*Guiding and termination.* An essential part of effective Guided Fantasy is the skillful guiding on the part of the counselor. There must be an adequate amount of empathic, verbal participation without becoming over-involved to the extent of pulling the client away from the fantasy. The counselor should encourage description of detail to develop the richness of the experience, and at times may wish to restructure the fantasy toward more productive directions. When predicaments or frightening obstacles are encountered, the counselor may be important in guiding the client through the fantasized problem. It is wise for the counselor to attempt to terminate the fantasy at as positive a point as possible, leaving the client with relaxed and contented feelings. It is important that the client experience a sense of success and accomplishment regarding the fantasy.

*Outcome and processing.* Guided Fantasy experiences are more powerful and productive for some clients than for others. On one end of the spectrum are those who find fantasy to be a mildly pleasant and relaxing, or neutral, experience. On the other end are the clients who are profoundly moved by the fantasy, and come away with a real sense of having changed and grown. For some, the therapeutic nature of fantasy is increased by participation in a series of guided fantasies over a period of several sessions.

Some counselors and therapists feel that fantasies should be "processed" in detail with clients, including retrospective analysis of content, discussion of emotional reactions, and looking at possible symbolism. Gestalt therapy approaches may be used to further integrate symbols or upsetting images that occur in the fantasy. I find that the Guided Fantasy usually is able to stand by itself as a significant and understood part of the counseling process. Some clients actually work through conflicts on a symbolic level during fantasy. Following the experience, they are able to transfer this resolution into real situations.

## APPLICATIONS

Guided Fantasy represents one of many specialized approaches that may be used to help clients achieve healthier and more satisfying levels of personality functioning through increased insight and self-acceptance. It may also help clients deal with conflict and situations to which they experience phobic reactions. In addition to the use of fantasy in the systematic desensitization and aversive counter-conditioning of behavioral therapy, it has been made a part of some approaches to Implosion Therapy or emotional "flooding" as a way of extinguishing fear.

Shaffer has described the therapeutic value of Guided Fantasy in dealing with nightmares and dream fragments, and as a way to help clients experience fantasized age regression. Another popular use of the technique may be in helping clients focus on bodily concerns and their causes (Alexander, 1971). Guided Fantasy has been useful in the treatment of children, adolescents, and youth. Hartman and Fithian (1974) employ Guided Fantasy to explore body imagery in clients with sexual dysfunctions. There are also reports of success in sex therapy to resolve psychological conflicts that are playing a part in generating dysfunctions (Kelly, 1976).

Some counselors and therapists have begun employing Guided Fantasy in group settings, and these approaches represent an exciting new trend in the therapeutic use of mental imagery. Adaptability and flexibility are the characteristics that render Guided Fantasy a valuable tool for a variety of psychotherapeutic models.

# Behavioral Family Therapy
## William J. Di Scipio

### DEFINITION

Behavioral Family Therapy (BFT) denotes the application of scientific methodology in order to modify faulty or maladaptive patterns of social interactions among the symptomatic members of a family. While "behavior modification" has been the most popularized term applied to this approach, there are, in fact, at least three distinct contemporary approaches to the scientific understanding of human social learning: behavioral consequences, mediational or anxiety cues and social learning, or vicarious learning. While varying therapeutic technologies have been developed within each of these approaches, they are all broadly defined as behavioral because of their basic adherence to the hypothesis-testing, experimental analysis of human behavior. For a behavioral family therapist, a family may be defined as two or more people who mutually influence the reward and punishment contingencies of each other.

### HISTORY

Early discoveries in the study of environmental influences on behavior patterns or responses are attributed, in part, to the well-known works of Pavlov, Thorndike, Clark Hull, and J. B. Watson. At least two experimental paradigms, currently labeled "classical" and "operant" conditioning, were to emerge and survive in the field of human and animal learning. The recent proliferation of operant conditioning (behavior modification) has been widely influenced by B. F. Skinner and his associates, and has been most systematically applied to families by G. R. Patterson (1975). Elements of the classical-conditioning model are more readily apparent in the work of Joseph Wolpe, which is concerned with the deconditioning of mal-adaptive anxiety neurosis in individuals. Direct application of Wolpe's approach has not been fully explored in relation to family interaction. Adherents of the approach, which emphasizes vicarious or observational learning, are best represented by the currently popular social psychology of Albert Bandura. While the influence of modeling (learning by observation) on a child's behavior are obvious to both therapists and families, the systematic use of such principles in modifying or guiding adaptive social patterns has only begun to be explored in the psychotherapeutic setting.

## TECHNIQUE

Methods based upon changing the consequences of the observable and measurable Behavior of a symptomatic family member predominate the current Behavioral Family literature. The symptomatic individual, usually a child, is viewed by the family as the problem. A coalition is formed between parents and therapist and the therapist proceeds to "target" the misbehavior. The frequency of occurrence of the target behavior is recorded for a period of time, usually taken in the natural setting without further direct therapeutic interventions. This period is known as a "baseline" and is used to establish consensus on the degree of severity of the problem, as well as serve as a comparison with which to assess the effects of later programmed interventions. If the problem is one of excess behavior (for example, temper tantrums), techniques including differential reinforcement of other more acceptable behaviors (DRO) might be used, as well as systematically diminishing the inadvertent reinforcement parents often give by excessive attention to the child during a tantrum (extinction procedure). If the problem is a deficit behavior, positive reinforcement of gradual steps toward achieving the final desired behavior might be the preferred conditioning technique (shaping). Altering the consequences of behavior through manipulation of the contingencies of reinforcement extends beyond the few examples mentioned above and may also be monitored by the therapist in the form of a verbal or written contract. The "contingency contract" specifies the treatment plan in a precise and operational manner and has become the most popular tool of the operant conditioning family therapist.

When the therapist views the family problem from a cognitive-behavioral model, he is most likely to apply techniques derived from classical conditioning. Problems of interpersonal relationships thought to be mediated by anxiety, faulty beliefs, or lack of self-assertion are usually treated individually, but changes in all family members will invariably result if the behavior of one member is radically altered in a short period of time. The changes in maladaptive anxiety states or cognitions are altered by techniques such as progressive desensitization, covert conditioning, cognitive restructuring, and assertive training (Craighead, et al., 1976).

Focusing on the vicarious processes of social learning presents another behavioral perspective from which the family-oriented therapist might proceed. The use of modeling, behavioral rehearsal, and guided participation for increasing adaptive social skills has recently begun to occupy a more standard and systematic set of techniques for applying to one or a number of family members. They are applied alone or in addition to the operant conditioning and cognitive-behavioral techniques.

## APPLICATIONS

While the behavioral therapies may be applied to any broadly defined maladaptive overt or covert behavior that has its origins in environmental contingencies, the following areas are representative of several readily modifiable problems:

1. Child management problems in which either or both parents are willing to participate in behavioral training programs as cotherapists (for example, temper tantrums, negativism, antisocial behavior).

2. Marital difficulties involving the absence or deficit of negotiation skills and inappropriate mutual reinforcement exchanges.

3. Maladaptive behavior of one member of the family that results in exclusion of that member or undue stress or breakdown of other family members (as in anorexia, school or other phobic behavior, asthma, etc.).

4. Maladaptive behaviors resulting from inappropriate or incorrect attitudes and beliefs that are not a function of an acute psychotic state of any member.

---

# Comprehensive Family Therapy

*Arthur Stein*

## DEFINITION

Comprehensive Family Therapy (CFT) aims at optimizing family function by remediating immaturity, correcting psychosocial pathology, and developing latent behavioral potential through integrated educational, reparental, and psychoanalytic procedures.

CFT grew in stages. First concerns were with symptoms in child patients. Initially, family contact focused on correcting the parents' rearing of the child. But parental ineptness with one child often meant difficulties with other offspring. Consequently, professional aims were to potentiate the *rearing* transaction—the entire network of relations among parents and children—plus the children's *independent* transactions. However, marital disharmony seriously impaired parental effectiveness and therapeutic contact was necessarily extended to engage rearing and marital transactions concomitantly. Furthermore, the couple's extrafamilial functioning was found related to both parental and marital process, requiring inclusion of the spouses' *independent* transactions in the professional work. Thus, CFT contacted all family members and the empirical breadth of family process, realizing the necessity of dealing with the entire membership and all difficulties within terms of one professional relationship.

CFT was introduced in 1964 and taught at the Bleuler Psychotherapy Center of New York City, and since under various sponsorship.

# TECHNIQUE

CFT is not distinguished by specific techniques but rather by its emphasis on understanding the family dynamics, the need to establish family goals and to concentrate on approaching "target" behavior by means of an integrated therapeutic interplay. Defining ideal family process is critical for professional purpose, direction, and efficiency. The ideal model for CFT is derived from empirical observation and clinical experience and it purports to reflect the common structures of well-functioning families.

The marriage is at the hub of the family dynamism. The positive involvement of the spouses helps maintain proper emotional balance with children and promotes growth in the couple. In the "progressive marital trend," the mates assist each other through supportive teamwork and intramarital parenting to learn and improve ego functioning within terms of their complementary parental and coping roles. This enhances family organization, adjustment to reality, and security. A counterpart "regressive marital trend" emanates out of the mutual elicitation and outplay of impulses and desires that occur when a couple maintains investment and psychological contact with one another. The provocation of repressed material ("repetition compulsion"), notably love and hate, within an affirmative interpersonal context of disclosure and understanding allows for the integration of the underlying contents into the ego. Gradually, successively deeper psychological expression, self-contact, and intimacy ensue. Continuing over a lifetime, the progressive and regressive marital trends incur ego growth or "progressive abreactive regression" (PAR).

The practitioner may begin CFT with the entire family or any part, devolving or escalating contact with members. The frequency, length, attendance, and overall pattern of meetings are therapeutically determined and variable. Initial procedures are affected by membership attitudes toward professional intervention, family power relations, nature of surface psychopathology, and requirements of starting and developing the treatment program. The family's subsystems (all combinations of members) and extensive behavior are influenced through the couple.

The practitioner potentiates the family's rearing transaction by dealing with the spouses as parents, with the pair as husband and wife, and with the couple's independent transactions by his involvement with their extrafamilial selfhoods and careers. Generally, offspring are professionally affected through the parents and not directly. However, the practitioner sees children adjunctly, alone or otherwise, for evaluation, building parental capacity or the child's positive response, and also for assisting with psychopathology beyond parental reach. Older offspring may be approached individually to increase healthy privacy and independence.

Contact is maintained with total family process, which is worked with coherently to avoid imbalance or disorganization and to maximize progress. Family events denote the spousal leadership and members' functioning and guide the practitioner's effort. Therapeutic leverage is significantly amplified by using family repercussion tactically. There are many ways of doing this, such as by swaying family plans, assigning tasks, encouraging closeness or distance, or settling or stirring conflict. Also, family members in therapeutic alliance with the practitioner are employed to interpret, confront, assist, reward, or punish another's behavior. Selfhood in one party may be particularly developed, not only for that person's benefit, but for growth influence on someone else.

The roots of family malfunction are traceable to parents' immaturity and/or neurotic process, which are tackled respectively by the "progressive" and "regressive therapeutic impingement." In the progressive impingement, the practitioner educates and parents (feeds, inspires, goal sets, models, rewards, disciplines, role plays, etc.) to compensate for the deficient parenting that the couple received as children. In this mode he is aggressively forward looking, utilizing available potentials to overcome ineptness and fill in ego gaps. He develops esteem, goals, functional knowledge, ability, and teamwork for mastery of interdependent parental, marital, and extrafamilial roles.

In the regressive, or analytic, therapeutic impingement, the practitioner is backward looking, encouraging expression and ventilating suppressed feelings. Under assistance of introspection and insight, latent psychological contents abreact; that is, the individual relives early experiences, with the practitioner being given emotional meaning as an image of childhood figures. Properly instigated and managed, regressive abreaction makes repressed mental contents accessible, with freeing and widespread benefit.

By establishing fresh standards and mobilizing new action, the practitioner's progressive impingement suppresses preexisting nonproductive behavior and causes the damming of impulses and psychophysical tension. On the other hand, regressive relations free structures and build potential for the progressive development of ego and transactive functioning. Thus, the regressive impingement supports the progressive and vice versa, and the practitioner shifts between those two modalities.

In consequence of professional intervention, the couple is simultaneously developing in competence and positive ambition. At the same time, the pair's deepening commitment and better communication make them willing and able to intramaritally parent and help the partner overcome personal immaturities that undercut teamwork and stifle self-assertion and achievement. Consequently, we find improving marriage to be associated with heightened reciprocal growth pressure and ego building, which adds significantly to the professional's progressive impingement.

As the CFT building of relating and coping proceeds, the mates become able lovers. Increasingly, they take over the professional function. The couple understands the forceful determinancy of unconscious process and they value and give each other experiential room, mutually supporting and assisting regression. But at the same time, growing in consensual direction and respect, they set new standards and goals for themselves and their children. Consequently, they have less need for the professional relationship; the practitioner becomes a consultant to the couple, then terminates his relationship.

Ideally, the PAR dynamics will continue over the lifetime of the couple. Succinctly, the pair's behavior simplifies and focuses as the "repetition compulsion" plays itself out and conscious process pervades. Movement is toward androgenous development of "masculine" and "feminine" power, of work and love. Regressive dissolution of repressed process energizes behavior and frees structures for creative work and coping economy. It activates symbiotic potentials that increasingly bond the couple for the care of each other through advancing age, meanwhile causing positive emotional detachment and encouragement of offspring's independent growth.

## APPLICATIONS

CFT does not distinguish family, marital, and individual psychotherapy, since rearing, marital, and independent transactions are engaged and all combinations of members affected. Categorization of families by clinical symptoms (for example, culturally deprived, drug abuse, psychosomatic, schizophrenic, neurotic) gives some indication of system properties and level of organization, but is not useful for deciding applicability. Professional intervention is adapted to the organizational character and failure of the particular family. Ability to maintain professional contact, to cooperate, and a capacity for psychosocial growth are required. The goal is uniform—optimal family process.

Dealings with unmarried pairs, unwed parents and children, childless couples, families split by divorce or death, recombined families and older spouses with grown offspring are variations or aspects of model CFT procedures. Likewise, individual work with adolescents and adult singles utilizes part of the more extensive process.

# Conjoint Family Counseling
## Sharon Wegscheidei

### DEFINITION

Conjoint Family Counseling is an experience in which an outsider, the counselor, is invited into a group of individuals related to each other for the sake of stimulating healthy relationships. Often the group or family invite the counselor into the system because of their painful concern about one member they identify as the focus of the problem. The challenge presented to the counselor is to use his eyes, ears, and sensibilities to give new insights or added reaffirmation to the family's view of itself. Even though the family's goal is the solution of their problems, the therapeutic hope of the counselor is that the family will discover a process for growth, namely, the nurturance of the self-worth of the individual members.

### HISTORY

Theoretically, family counseling grew out of clinical experience. Over the last twenty years family counseling done conjointly was first an experiment used when individual therapy became stuck or ineffectual. The conjoint counseling was used when the myriad of problems defied solution and the clients remained helpless. Now the use of family counseling is becoming accepted. It is based on the premise that we become very similar to those people with whom we surround ourselves.

Virginia Satir, Don Jackson, Jay Hayley, and others from the Palo Alto area of California are among those who have worked with families to help them become people who know they count, who risk saying what they feel, who make their choices with their own growth as a priority.

### TECHNIQUE

Family Counseling (or process counseling) can be looked at clinically and theoretically. The clinical styles of counselors are as different as the makeup of the counselors themselves. Yet, there are enough similarities in clinical experiences to furnish some basic observations. This clinical description will address the family intake form, the seating patterns of clients, and the story of the clients.

*The intake form.* An agency requires statistical information for its planning, evaluation, and research and it is important that some information be gathered about each member of the family system. This sounds very routine. Yet, many times the family member who fills out the intake form forgets to put information about himself down. Also, sometimes all the children are not listed, and there may be some significance to this. The youngest ones may be left off "because they are too young for all this." Or the older children who have moved out are no longer listed. The process of their departure could be very enlightening in understanding present fears and pains. The general rule to follow is that those bearing meaningful influence should be noted on the intake form. For example, the family concerned about their pregnant teen-ager may find it helpful to include the father-to-be.

The ages of the family members may be important. Children born close in age may have some implications on both the marriage relationship and the sibling relationship. Spouses who are of greatly divergent ages may have some things to work through that may not occur to contemporaries. Who came after whom in the family may indicate alliances or rivalries. Birth order does not give any conclusions; however, it may give some educated guesses.

Questions about current stress points are helpful. Such changes as a new home, a different school, new jobs, people going back to school, transfer from night work to day work, sudden illness, deaths among relatives carry much meaning. Changes are neutral, but the choices they prompt are either constructive or destructive to a family's balance. Past and present use of alcohol or mood-altering medicines can also furnish valuable pieces to the puzzle. In summary, the intake form contains something about each member of the family system, and for a family who comes to the agency with a specific problem this is the first step.

*Seating.* The surroundings most conducive to family work is an area large enough to move about, light enough to be cheerful, pleasant enough to be comfortable. One asset in seating in a family session is having cushions or chairs as movable as possible. Ideally, when a family is ushered into the room the chairs or cushions could be either stacked in the corners or arranged in a chaotic state. The first invitation of the counselor to family members is to choose where they will sit. Often, the identified patient is readily apparent, since he takes a position far away from any member of the family. The children with high energy often pile the cushions high in the corner. Children who are family favorites often sit close to their protector. The very reasonable ones attempt to sit just outside of the circle, where they can observe the rest of the family in an objective fashion.

Such a simple thing as asking them to sit down can speak volumes of how a family sees itself. When there is nervousness or conflict, the stress of the artificial situation exaggerates the family's defenses. Once the family has sat down, the counselor has a spontaneous sociogram. He has at least one picture of the relationships within the family. If the children are noisy, moving around a lot, bored, or daydreaming, the counselor may see who disciplines the children. Different meanings can be studied if the disciplinarian is the mother, the father, or the older child. If no one gives direction, this says much about the family, too. The counselor looks at the choices the family makes to take care of itself.

*The story.* Most clients find it hard to share their private family business with an outsider. They are not only asking for help, but also admitting failure. Admitting failure takes self-worth. If their self-worth is low, as many times it is, their admission of failure involves a great deal of pain. In family counseling the family gets a chance to tell its story. Usually the person who made the appointment speaks first—most often one of the parents. He or she is nervous and has mentally rehearsed what to say. The parent has a story to tell that is both a description of the problem and a justification for coming.

When someone is talking in the family the others naturally react. For example, when a mother shares her background, her hopes, and her worries, it is important that the therapist is aware of all the other people in the room. Sometimes it takes two counselors to do this. The identified patient reacts to his mother talking about him. He is quiet, holding his breath and hoping that this experience will pass. The spouse may react strongly if he suspects that he is being blamed or torn down. The other kids in the background sometimes feel that their mother exaggerates everything.

Some kids very enthusiastically share data as proof that this identified person is really the troublemaker everyone says that he is. Then the identified person will withdraw totally within himself or become angry. He might try to use anger to start a debate, picking up on words here and there in order to show that what they are saying is not true. Or he may discount what everybody is saying with "How do you know?" or "You weren't there."

The work of a family counselor is similar to the work of an orchestra conductor. He needs to maintain a certain amount of order so that he can hear the music. He notices certain instruments yearning to play and gives them permission to be heard. Clinically, the counselor needs to hear stories, especially in the first session. Yet the stories are important only to get at the process. When a family uses the story as a sales pitch to justify their coming, the counselor helps them change the use of the story to getting in touch with new ways of processing, new ways of communicating, and new ways of validating self-worth. That jump is a monumental step toward growth.

Some of the theoretical concepts central to Satir's work are self-worth, rules, and systems. Self-worth is a person's self-affirmation that he is important, has limitations, has talent, and has a right to be here. A person with a high self-worth can afford to say what he means. He can allow open communication, can follow and give flexible rules, can even tolerate error. When a person owns himself, he takes responsibility for self. He is capable of building and maintaining relationships.

The power that rules have over us is illustrated in the names that people have given them. They are called programs, life-styles, tapes, scripts. All rules come to us from outside of ourselves. As we become more and more aware of our own energy, they help us be ourselves. We choose to make them our own. The rules that are valuable to us become our value system. The rules with which we comply out of fear of being rejected or hurt always remain separate from ourselves. They are the things we do to get something else. We follow some rules to get approval from someone. They are the "shoulds," the expectations of others. Outward compliance and inner resentment at being manipulated cause stress, conflict, and anger. How we cope with the stress depends on how much we really believe in our own worth. How we cope will affect others in our system.

The idea of systems working efficiently and effectively is dependent on two factors. One is the developing into what we call a whole person. The second factor is how whole persons or the opposite—fragmented persons—affect the functioning systems.

## APPLICATIONS

The idea behind system therapy is that persons develop communication patterns that tend to protect their personal self-worth. The person finds whichever communication pattern best protects him in his system, and that is the personality he begins to develop. It seems that people tend to learn their survival patterns from the family they grew up in and take it with them in choosing mates; they then continue their dysfunction into their own families.

To summarize, Family Counseling can be a time of clear communication and maintaining relationships. Family Counseling can be a time when the family members begin to learn from each other. The occasion of Family Counseling can be the beginning of an appreciation of their differences and their similarities.

# Family Context Therapy

*John Elderkin Bell*

## DEFINITION

Family Context Therapy is based on the operational principle that families are modifiable through changing the environments within which they live. Families have many environments and are also involved in creating environments for themselves. The environmental forces provide a complex dynamic for the functions of individuals and the total family. Creating changes in these forces to reduce pressures toward destructive functioning and to accentuate pressures toward family adjustment and accomplishment is the adopted task of the family context therapist.

Therapists plan and carry out selective efforts to modify the families' contexts whenever family functions are being limited or destroyed by aspects of the environment, and new environmental resources and opportunities are needed for developing beneficial family processes. Targeted changes are sought in the social, functional, and physical aspects of the community at large, the basic and helping institutions within it, and the families' immediate environments. Though the therapist's primary and direct interventions are in the environment, the higher goals of family problem solving and family development are reached through the impacts of environmental modifications on the family.

## HISTORY

In 1963, I was assigned by the National Institute of Mental Health to a long-term program to reduce the isolation of hospitalized mental patients from their families. This assignment was a response to the growing experience that family group therapy was proving ineffective with the majority of hospitalized patients. Since that time much of my professional work has been turned toward the goals of understanding the problems that create patient isolation, developing and testing methods to reduce isolation, and constructing a theoretical framework to lead to specific techniques for intervention.

In 1964–65, in relation to this program, I was sent by NIMH to study about 150 African and Asian hospitals and other medical facilities, including some for psychiatric patients. In most of the observed settings, families accompany patients and stay with them full-time during the period in hospital. The insights developed during this study (Bell, 1970a) provided the experiential base on which Family Context Therapy was conceptualized, developed, and applied in a range of projects (Bell, 1976, 1977a, 1977b). These projects, and others, extend far beyond families that include mental patients. Projects have been focused especially on families where one member is institutionalized, as in all types of hospitals, nursing homes, prisons, and shelters.

I presented the rudiments of a formulation of Family Context Therapy in 1969 at the Memorial Conference for Don D. Jackson. An opportunity in 1973 to become free from many years of administrative responsibilities and to turn attention to program development in a hospital gave me a fresh chance for experience and thought, for defining the nature and scope of Family Context Therapy, and for testing methods. The timeliness of this development has been accentuated by the growing acknowledgment of the need to accomplish family-oriented improvements in our community and national life.

## TECHNIQUE

Techniques have been and are being developed. Typically, they involve supporting and expanding outside resources for families, facilitating their use, and improving the settings from which resources, energy, and time for improved family relations may be drawn. Inevitably, the methods used to induce environmental changes are multiform and specific to target families. The most common locales for the development and application of change methods are within community institutions. As an illustration, analysis is being made to discover ways to improve family access to various community institutions. For instance, on the assumption that intensified family involvement in schools will improve the morale of parents, their investment in the work of the school, the performance and success of their children, and the internal functioning of the family, the context therapist takes on the task of devising changes in the school to improve family access. The therapy is accomplished when and if improvements are made in access with positive results for families, which is not always the case.

Most of my work has been and continues within hospitals, changing contexts for all manner of patients. A few interventions, made by colleagues and me, can serve as examples: changing policies, for instance, in regard to visiting; removing physical and other barriers to family access—opening locked doors, easing parking problems, arranging for family meals; educating staff to allow families to do tasks for patients, especially those carried over from home, such as feeding the patient, or serving as monitor; assuring that patients, according to their condition, have the opportunities and privacy for continuing to participate in family life and affairs; and ordering the patient's program and opportunities for family involvement according to anticipated placement, such as return to home, transfer to an extended care facility, or life in the hospital until death.

Such interventions are not random. They are based on many sources, such as direct experiences with families; identification of features of the hospital or patient programs that have actual or potential impact on families, and the quality of that impact; projections in fantasy of an ideal hospital for patients *and* families; study of family relations of nonmedical institutions, for models to apply; application of theories and investigations of organizations, their interrelations, and process of modification, from the fields of sociology, ecology, anthropology, and political science, to understand and change the hospital.

Staff are directly involved in the planning of interventions; comprehensive or modest programs for change are set forth; evaluations of timing and of needed supports for change are conducted; complex education efforts and negotiations are commonly undertaken before determining that a change can be instituted; and, when an intervention is made, studies of the extent and frequency of family involvement follow. Through such approaches, hospital culture changes are accomplished for the sake of families.

## APPLICATIONS

The first application is in extending the theory of family change. As dramatic as the step from individual psychotherapy to family therapy, Context Therapy provides a corrective to the constriction of family-centered thought.

Second, family context processes suggest therapy methods for many institutions— prisons, courts, business and industry, recreation, commerce, churches, synagogues, and other religious organizations, to mention a few. Within each institution, the interventions must become specific, however, to its program and staff, and to the families who are associated.

Finally, Family Context Therapy provides a bridge for family therapists to many programs and persons concerned with family welfare, though they are not engaged in family therapy. Collaboration may be eased with family education, planned parenthood services, public health services, family social work, community planning, recreation services, institution adminstration and development, family law and justice, personnel services, religious communities and services, and many others. The efforts will concern such issues as: the relative priorities given to the family as a whole in relation to those directed elsewhere; the family implications of centering resources on individuals, programs, and institutions; and the interactive effects of various programs for family welfare—do they complement, compete, or cancel out each other. All these issues are being raised, but typically in relation to recipients of program resources and services. If the recipient is other than the family, redirection of efforts and resources through Family Context Therapy may accomplish both stated and family objectives.

# Family Crisis Therapy

## Donald G. Langsley

### DEFINITION

Family Crisis Therapy is an active intervention technique to help a family (conjointly) resolve a crisis. The crisis is a state of increased tension, a suspension of long-term goals, and a revival of past conflicts. It is usually precipitated by stress and occurs in an individual or family that is especially susceptible. Very often the consequence of the crisis is regression, the development of psychiatric symptoms in one or more members of the family, and there may be a request for admission to a mental hospital. The crisis state may be resolved by efforts to master or remove the stresses that precipitated it.

Stresses may have sudden causes, such as an accidental death or the loss of a job. Other stresses occur around adolescence, a change in the composition of a family, or retirement. Stresses also occur when there is a change in role, the revelation of an old secret, or some other type of change requiring adaptation. The crisis can be resolved (and in most families usually is mastered) by taking some action to remove or master the stress, a change in role assignment, a change in rules, a change in goals, or even a change in the way the family understands the past. The degree of maladaptive response is less related to the stress or the amount of change required than to the adaptive capacities of individual family members. Certain families avoid change, scapegoat individuals, or threaten dissolution. Tension increases and pressure may be placed on one member of the family to make impossible alterations. At this point a susceptible member of the family may become symptomatic or may seek escape through suicide, psychosis, and/or psychiatric hospitalization. The treatment is basically an effort to clarify the process to the family, to establish an atmosphere in which the member of the family identified as a patient may help the family reduce tension to the point where the immediate crisis is resolved. The family may learn to resolve similar problems more effectively in the future.

### HISTORY

This crisis intervention technique was developed at the Colorado Psychiatric Hospital when I, along with Kaplan, postulated that those in need of immediate admission to a mental hospital could be treated by conjoint family interviews on an out-patient basis in order to avoid hospitalization. A full-time team was recruited in a five-year demonstration project carried on from 1964 to 1969. The results of Family Crisis Therapy in 150 families were compared with the results of mental hospital treatment for a similar size group of families. In all cases the families included an identified patient judged in need of immediate admission. A variety of psychiatric illnesses was included, among them actively suicidal individuals, grossly psychotic persons, and the usual types of psychopathology seen in the population of an acute mental hospital population. The follow-up studies demonstrated that those treated by Family Crisis Therapy instead of hospitalization were far less likely to be admitted to a mental hospital in the future, were more effective at managing crises, and were functioning as well in terms of socialization, work, and absence of symptoms of mental illness as those hospitalized. The techniques are applicable to seriously disturbed individuals seen in mental health emergency services and also useful in somewhat modified fashion for predictable kinds of family crises seen by mental health professionals and other human services personnel. The principles of family crisis intervention are somewhat similar to those used in crisis intervention for individuals, though the more seriously disturbed are best treated in a conjoint family mode.

## TECHNIQUE

This type of treatment is short-term and crisis-oriented. In the Denver experience the treatment consisted of an average of five office visits and one home visit over a three-week period. It can be described in a series of six steps, which may be simultaneous instead of consecutive:

1. *Immediate aid.* The family should be seen at once whenever the crisis occurs and help is requested. This may be at any hour of the day or night and the promise of immediate availability around the clock should be made from that time on.

2. *Define the problem as a family crisis.* The absent members of the household should be called in. Attempts to avoid defining the problem as a *family* crisis by considering the difficulty to be limited to one member should be blocked. The most convincing way of defining the problem as belonging within the family is to insist on conjoint meetings only and to refuse to see any member of the family individually. Hospitalizing any single member of the family gives the group a clear message about the locus of the problem.

3. *Focus on the present.* The history of events leading up to the crisis should be obtained. The past may be used to understand the present and past strengths are stressed. The history of the current problem serves to define the nature of the crisis and the problems that precipitated it.

4. *Reduce tension.* Block excessive regression by reassurance and support. Medication is used as needed for symptom relief in any member of the family, not just the identified patient.

5. *Resolution of the current crisis.* Tasks are assigned for resumption of functioning and for resolution of the crisis state. The therapist takes an active role in managing as a substitute executive until the family can take over necessary functions themselves. The conflicts in role assignment and role performance as well as overt and covert family rules are negotiated with the family as a whole.

6. *Management of future crises.* The availability of crisis intervention for future problems is stressed. For long-term maladaptive behavioral problems referral may be made, but this should include direct contact with the agency to whom the referral is directed.

This type of treatment is one that requires an active type of intervention by the therapist. It is also different from long-term family therapy in which interactional conflicts of long-standing are the focus of attention. A great deal of flexibility is required. Meetings vary in length from a few minutes to two or three hours, but the average length of a session seems to be from one to one and a half hours. It could be carried on by one therapist, but there are often advantages to having co-therapists. The number of family members seen together ranges from two to as many as nine or ten. It is often useful to insist on all family members, including young children, being present while reserving the right to eliminate young children from the group at the time of later visits. The family, for purposes of this type of treatment, is defined as all of those who live under one roof, though extended family members who live nearby may also be included.

A home visit is highly useful in doing family crisis work because this gives the family opportunity to reveal strengths and to maintain freedom of movement while yielding a great deal of information about family composition and current interaction. The telephone is used freely. After an initial contact in which therapist and patients view one another face to face, the telephone is a useful adjunct. Once a relationship is established there is little that can be done in the office that cannot be done by telephone, except perhaps giving medications or evaluating new symptoms.

It is sometimes helpful to focus immediately on the least involved member of the family while ignoring the identified patient. It is equally useful to avoid acknowledging psychopathology. The negotiations with the family must avoid blame and support must be constantly available. The ideal attitude toward the identified patient is one of ignoring or avoiding symptoms while maintaining sympathetic respect for the message that these symptoms transmit. Symptoms are translated as a comment on the problems in the current situation rather than evidence of sickness.

## APPLICATIONS

The technique was developed for acute situations, particularly recent onset of dysfunction and symptom development. Acute schizophrenic reactions, depressions, or crisis situations in those who have been labeled as having personality disorders are often relieved in this type of therapy. The termination should include instructions about future crises as well as an attitude of expecting them to occur. Telephone contact is often all that is necessary when the prior crisis intervention has resulted in rapid relief of symptoms and return to functioning.

# Multiple Conjoint Psychotherapy

## *Herbert Potash*

## DEFINITION

Multiple Conjoint Psychotherapy can be best described as a treatment strategy rather than as a separate system of psychotherapy. It is used to alter a disturbed relationship between family members (husband and wife, or siblings) by focusing on the interaction between the participants. Typically, two therapists (multiple or co-therapists) meet with the family members in group sessions (conjointly). This therapy therefore involves four or more people (two therapists and two clients) and can be either the exclusive means of treatment or it can be used as an adjunct to the individual therapy of separate family members (with occasional multiple conjoint sessions). Usually the two therapists will be of both sexes, and the most common group of people treated by this method are married couples.

## HISTORY

Conjoint therapy has been used as a parsimonious means of resolving communication difficulties within a family (Satir, 1967). Systematic attention to family interaction enabled the family therapist to propose healthier means of communication, and to assist various family members in accommodating themselves to each others' needs and growth patterns. Conjoint treatment lends itself to different theoretical approaches as revealed by the varied literature on family therapy.

Multiple or co-therapists were initially used in group therapy as a means of heightening transference reactions in group members. (Transference occurs when a client shifts feelings about a significant person to the therapist.) Warkentin (1951) found that using two therapists with one client offered the therapists a greater range of responses to their clients as they could share control of the sessions. Kell and Burow (1970) introduced a second therapist into sessions as a means of breaking the impasse that was blocking progress. They also began to meet with husbands and wives (as a group of four) to help their clients deal with unresolved difficulties, particularly their transference reactions to opposite sex parents. This use of Multiple Conjoint Therapy offered the additional advantage of providing a healthy model of male-female communication to their clients.

## TECHNIQUE

Communication among four people increases the range of responses and points of view that require attention and resolution than is offered by individual, multiple, or conjoint therapy. Clients gain a broader perspective in which to view their therapists, and can learn better means of dealing with each other by observing the therapists, who provide an implicit model of communication. A comfortable and trusting relationship between the two therapists is a necessity for the therapy to work well. Furthermore, Multiple Conjoint Therapy will be indicated when the major problem to be dealt with is the relationship between the clients. Two therapists, rather than one, will be used if the initial assessment reveals a high degree of resistance to change or much sexual stereotyping by the clients. Occasional multiple conjoint sessions will be added to individual sessions when heightened communication difficulties necessitate therapeutic intervention in order to sustain the relationship and the growth of both individuals. Since Multiple Conjoint Psychotherapy is more of a treatment strategy than it is a separate therapeutic system, it can be used with a variety of theoretical orientations.

## APPLICATIONS

The most common population to be given Multiple Conjoint Psychotherapy are couples experiencing marital difficulties. However, it is useful in treating many long-standing relationships and especially cases of hysteria and *folie a deux*. Where the clients have a symbiotic relationship, they will necessarily show a high resistance to change. Two therapists are better able to resolve such resistance than is one therapist alone. This is true because the communication network between clients often will operate to exclude the therapist, and a second therapist can support in an intervention strategy. A common means of resistance that is most readily overcome is the distorted interpretation of a therapist's comments between sessions. The second therapist can point out the discrepancy and act as impartial arbitrator, thus defusing this issue.

When sessions include therapists of both sexes, it is easier for clients to introduce a wider range of topics earlier in the therapy and also to find ongoing support from at least one individual during therapy. The presence of a second therapist can compensate for, or overcome, deficiencies in a single therapist. For these reasons, Multiple Conjoint Therapy has been found to provide an excellent means of training new psychotherapists, and is a vehicle for adding to the repertoire of responses of experienced psychotherapists.

---

# Multiple Family Therapy

## H. Peter Laqueur

### DEFINITION

Families are considered as systems made up of individuals and internal alliances— such as parents vs. children, or male vs. female family members—as subsystems. These may sometimes function poorly as a whole integrated family unit.

In Multiple Family Therapy, several family systems are brought together for a series of twenty, forty, sixty, and more therapeutic sessions, as the need arises. In these sessions, under the guidance of trained therapy teams, the families learn from each others' problems by analogy, modeling (learning by observing others' behavior), and indirect interpretation. They improve their internal structures as well as their mutual communication and understanding.

### HISTORY

Since 1951 I have worked with hundreds of families in a variety of groups, first in a state hospital in New York where it was unusual and unexpected to let patients, families, and staff work together in joint meetings. Later, I also worked in private psychiatric offices and clinics in New York, and at present at the Vermont State Hospital and at the University of Vermont.

## TECHNIQUE

Four or five families are combined randomly in an open-ended group. The open-endedness of the group allows us to use more advanced, improved families to help the beginning family in the process and also avoids the occurrence of too many similar problems in the same group. Too many similar problems would lead to focusing on these problems and symptoms rather than on the family structures that caused poor communications and cooperation.

We treat families with the most diverse problems in one group together. To mention some examples: extremely pathological families in which no one can relate to anyone else; families with a simple generation gap, that is, problem parents or problem children; "sex gap" families in which the father and sons stick together, leaving mother and daughters disgruntled at home; families in which the mother is "in the control tower" so that everyone has to check out first with her before they can talk to each other or do things together; families in which scapegoating of one member is the problem; families in which a pathological symbiosis between mother and a son, or father and a daughter, leaves the other family members hanging; families with in-law problems; families in which an unfaithful father or mother leaves the spouse and children to their fate. Differences in value systems—economic, religious, racial, cultural—between the families of origin of husband and wife can be at the root of severe differences and problems in their own present family.

As a rule, the four or five families meet in the following way. We explain the purpose of our treatment: "better mutual understanding and cooperation." We then begin by letting all the fathers stand together and explain their families' problem to the group by answering the very specific question, "What kind of a father and husband do you believe you are?" By analogy all fathers immediately begin to compare notes. Then we do the same thing with the mothers, and subsequently with the "problem" children about whom complaints have been voiced, and finally with the so-called good children who usually are associated with father, mother, or both.

In this way, everyone in the group gains quickly by analogy and identification quite a bit of essential information about the other families. In subsequent introductory sessions, we apply various exercises. For example, people who have difficulty expressing themselves can bodily show what happens to them if they are asked to join hands, or to stand back to back, or to rest their hands on their opponent's shoulders, pushing and shouting yes to one and no to the other. We also have patients build "family sculptures," showing us the past and present interaction mode in their family and how they wish to change this. Not only the verbal but also the nonverbal relationships become much clearer through such exercises. The therapeutic team and video playbacks may be used to model and explain to patients how they relate; patients actually see how they deal with each other in a way they never do when they just talk in the group.

Further sessions: most families show interest and curiosity in the beginning phase; increasing resistance and even depression and despair in a second phase; and only when they stop saying, "You have to change to make me change," and arrive at "I guess I have to risk changing my behavior so that in the long run you may do the same," do they enter the most therapeutic 'working through" phase. Then the changing family begins to serve as a model for the beginning and intermediary families in the group.

There are successes and relapses, but eventually 70 to 80 percent of the family systems show marked change and improvement with this technique. Sometimes one family member improves and another gets worse for a while (consistent with Don Jackson's family homeostasis theory), but eventually all show change, adaptations, and improvement in their relations and functions.

These weekly evening sessions of 75 to 90 minutes each show the following effects on family systems:

a)  increased adaptability and elasticity
b)  better sensitivity to changes in the external milieu and internal constellation
c)  better ability to process overloads of events, demands, and information in an efficient and effective manner
d)  family systems learn to make realistic selections, with good judgment, between correct and incorrect impressions and information
e)  families learn to focus on essential reality tasks and to avoid procrastination and drifting off into fruitless repetitive battles
f)  family systems learn to make logical plans, to perceive and execute necessary tasks correctly while checking for results with a refine feedback control.

## APPLICATIONS

This form of Multiple Family Therapy can be used in mental hospitals, community mental health clinics, physicians' and psychologists' offices, even in schools with educators, parents, and youngsters, in correctional institutions with probation officers and clients.

I have helped to start, and subsequently seen in operation, Multiple Family Therapy groups not only in the United States but also in the Netherlands and Belgium. I also found interest in the therapy in Germany, Spain, and at international meetings.

Because of the efficient use of trained help, this therapy can be useful for areas where individual therapy would be too expensive, reaches too few people, and actually never repairs the internal and social difficulties of the total family systems.

---

# Feeling Therapy

## Joseph Hart and Richard Corriere

### DEFINITION

The aim of Feeling Therapy is to help each patient feel better and live more effectively. Most psychological disorders are literally emotional disorders—that is, the emotionally disturbed person mixes up meanings, feelings, and expressions and fails to complete feeling impulses. In Feeling Therapy, patients are helped to shift from incomplete, disordered feelings to complete and realistic feelings.

Tension is caused by unexpressed or incompletely expressed feelings, and tension is sustained by the substitution of thoughts for expressions. When therapy is effective there will be measurable physiological signs of decreased tension and measurable psychological signs of direct responding instead of substitute responding. Enhanced functioning—social, psychological, and physiological—must be demonstrated before therapeutic effectiveness can be claimed.

## HISTORY

The Center for Feeling Therapy was founded in Los Angeles in 1971 by seven professionals (five psychologists, one psychiatrist, and one marriage and family counselor). The founding therapists were: Jerry Binder, Ph.D., Dominic Cirincione, M.A., Richard Corriere, Ph.D., Steve Gold, Ph.D., Joseph Hart, Ph.D., Werner Karle, Ph.D., and Lee Woldenberg, M.D. Six years later the Center had become one of the largest private psychotherapy clinics on the West Coast. In the beginning the therapy was strictly a long-term, community-based, intensive psychotherapy. The basic emphases were: 1) all therapists should continue to receive weekly individual and group therapy sessions for themselves and 2) all patients should be trained within one year to do co-therapy sessions with one another. These dual practical emphases on therapy for therapists and patients as co-therapists have continued and have led to important discoveries in theory and method.

Much of the research related to Feeling Therapy was conducted under the sponsorship of The Center Foundation (a nonprofit research, educational, and service organization), which was established in 1973.

The first widely published reports about the techniques and theory of Feeling Therapy were published in a book entitled *Going Sane: An Introduction to Feeling Therapy*. The first major research reports that showed important physiological and psychological changes in patients were reported in 1976 (Woldenberg, et al., 1976; Karle, et al., 1976). In 1977 the reports of highly significant dream changes in Feeling Therapy patients were first reported (Corriere, et al., 1977).

Since 1975, the theory of Feeling Therapy has been broadened to connect it to the general functional approach to psychotherapy, which can be traced historically to Pierre Janet, Trigant Burrow, and William James. The Clinic for Functional Counseling and Psychotherapy was established in 1977 to provide short-term help for clients who could not afford or who did not need the long-term intensive program offered at the Center for Feeling Therapy. In 1977, The Training Center for Functional Counseling and Psychotherapy was established in Los Angeles to train professionals in the functional approach.

## TECHNIQUE

The functional approach to psychotherapy emphasizes the pragmatic: what works. But it is not an eclectic school. In Feeling Therapy the therapist systematically examines both how a person feels and the personality dynamics that influence how he feels. There is a threefold emphasis on: 1) feelings as basic mediators of behavior, 2) practical programs for inducing change, and 3) the need for sustained group support to maintain therapeutic changes.

The functional approach contains both behavior therapy's practical concern with results and the psychoanalytic concern with insight. Therapists work with the patient's positive and negative images, his defenses, the sources of his defenses in the past, and the programs of change required to replace those defenses in the present. At all times, the therapist focuses on the following feeling dynamics: feeling level, activity level, level of expression, and level of clarity. *Expression* is always stressed as a requisite of therapeutic change; neither insight nor behavioral compliance are considered sufficient.

Two key technical concepts are the "feeling moment" and the "feeling cycle." The concept of the feeling moment is that a patient can always sense *when* he is moving toward or away from expressing a feeling. The feeling cycle concept specifies an orderliness to the undoing of emotional disorders: first a defense is felt, then the source of the defense is felt, then an alternative functional expression is tried out, and, finally, the new level of feeling is integrated into the person's life.

## APPLICATIONS

Both long-term Feeling Therapy and short-term functional counseling have been successfully applied to a variety of psychological disorders, including psychosomatic complaints, marital problems, sexual problems, anxiety disorders, phobias, and compulsions. Because the therapy is conducted in an out-patient clinic, it has not been widely applied to psychotic disorders.

One special application of Feeling Therapy is the Community Training Program for Professionals. In this program *groups* of professionals who are working together (or intend to work together) in clinical settings come to the Center for Feeling Therapy in Los Angeles for two months. During the two-month period they participate in the therapy program both as patients and as trainee therapists. They then return to their home base and follow a very carefully planned program of community training and business cooperation. Every six months, for two years, trainers from the Center in Los Angeles visit the C.T.P. professionals to help them develop their therapeutic community.

A second special application consists of psychological fitness programs (Corriere and Hart, 1978). These are educational programs offered to the general public that teach the psychological fitness model vs. the disease, adaptation and psychopathology models of personality change. The psychological fitness model emphasizes: 1) the need for personality exercise, 2) the experience of psychological "exercise effects," and 3) the maintenance of "fitness effects."

# Feminist Therapy

## Jean Ferson

## DEFINITION

Feminist Therapy, or sisterhood therapy, had its beginnings in the Consciousness-Raising (C-R) groups of the women's movement. It should be added that to some feminists, *any* practice of therapy is demeaning. "No sister should commit therapy on another sister," wrote Tennov, one of psychotherapy's most radical critics.

## HISTORY

C-R groups often succeeded in helping women surmount their difficulties after years of conventional therapy had failed. This phenomenon was so striking and widespread that women involved in both feminism and the mental health professions could not fail to analyze it and make use of it. There already existed in the professional literature several thoughtful and articulate criticisms of psychotherapy in general. Its political uses were being exposed. Women intellectuals were therefore ready to combine a general skepticism about the value of psychotherapy with a growing awareness of sexism. In this context the blossoming of C-R groups came as a rebirth of hope. "The heart and soul of the women's movement," Gornick called them, and many politically active feminists agreed, especially when their action groups bogged down in what seemed irrelevant, personal talk. But that need to talk had to be taken seriously. C-R groups turned out to be the primary education of the women's movement. Once a woman had learned in a group how sexism infected her everyday behavior and how she could combat it with the group's guidance and support, then she might be ready for political action.

## TECHNIQUE

Brodsky (1973) has published a clear and comprehensive analysis of how and why C-R groups served as effective therapy. Her article serves as an excellent single reference, or beginning to a more detailed study. Many other women have also written well on the topic, and *Ms.* magazine published and sold reprints of a guideline for the formation of C-R groups. Maslin (1971) compared C-R groups with what various textbook authorities said about the operation of successful counseling groups and found many similarities. To summarize most of the agreed-upon elements:

1.  The group must be relatively small—no less than five nor more than fifteen. Many participants reported that eight to ten worked well.

2.  The group must meet often enough and long enough to satisfy the needs of each member for self-expression and response from other members. Once a week for two to three hours was usually successful.

3.  Participation by each member has to be encouraged and protected. Leadership or domination by one member or a small clique of members has to be avoided. To this end no formal leader is appointed. The members typically meet in each others' homes on a rotating basis, or in some neutral place. Hostessing tasks are minimized.

4.  Each member when speaking has to receive the respectful attention of all other members. What she says has to be accepted without criticism, although expressing disagreement and skepticism will be expected and allowed. Rules of communication, whether spoken or unspoken, have to foster full and free disclosure. No member is under pressure to say or do anything, but all have to have a chance. Under these circumstances many women discovered for the first time that they had almost *never* been allowed to speak freely and confidently before a respectful audience. It was a joyous and heady experience, transforming many shy women.

5. Once members of a group begin to know and care about one another, regular attendance is expected. Opinion varies on whether open or closed groups serve C-R purposes better; in practice, groups tended to close and expect a high level of commitment.

6. Members are expected to keep confidential what is said in group. To this endit is convenient not to know each other on the outside, but outside friendships are not forbidden.

7. Usually a topic of discussion is introduced to organize and clarify the overall topic of the group; namely, how being raised female has restricted and distorted the personal experience of the various members. A sampling of popular topics: earliest memories of sex differences, school experiences, childhood fantasies of what adulthood would mean, courtship, marriage, childbearing and rearing, prostitution, feelings about one's body, menstruation, aging and sexuality, fashions and cosmetics, women's magazines.

Maslin points out that the attractiveness of a group, its perceived power and prestige, is believed to be a vital therapeutic element. She notes how often C-R participants reported themselves as previously hostile to all-female groups. In their complete antipathy to the "ladies' auxiliary" concept, C-R groups offered relief, security, and acceptance to women who had formerly felt alienated from other women and inevitably, themselves. Love and admiration for one's own sex grew along with self-love. Women found themselves talking and caring less about male opinion. They sought out female counselors of all sorts: physicians, lawyers, accountants. They wanted to read novels by women and see paintings by women. In a rush of belated appreciation they reappraised mothers, aunts, teachers. They paid homage to all the neglected heroines in both their personal and collective histories.

## APPLICATIONS

Having learned in a powerful way that the personal is political, women asked themselves: what place remains for "therapy"? Professional feminist counselors must now struggle with this important question. The relevance of C-R for political action is clear enough. But what has it to do with changing one's own behavior? Some women have turned to assertiveness training, an old technique borrowed from the behaviorist tradition. Others look to body awareness exercises, biofeedback training, Gestalt groups. Whether or not there is a Feminist Therapy is hotly debated. Graduate schools and practicing therapists have in some instances tried to purge themselves of sexist prejudice. But, as we C-R veterans discovered, that is not such an easy thing to do.

A possible way out of the professional therapist's dilemma may be found in the contributions of Grinder and Bandler. They analyze and teach only the process of communication and change, and they advocate a "content-less" therapy. They claim they can teach a person ways of solving her own problems without her even telling another person what they are. In so doing she exploits her own resources, her own past experiences of mastery and success. The strategy is to *access* (find) the positive feelings, *stabilize them*, and *transfer* them to the problem situation. They advocate learning skill in moving from one state of consciousness to another, and their techniques have much in common with hypnosis and the use of eidetic images. If therapists succeed with these techniques, then the ideal of an apolitical, nonsexist therapy may be realized.

# Filial Therapy

## Louise F. Guerney

### DEFINITION

Filial Therapy is a behavioral method of intervening in the psycho-social development of children under eleven years of age, using the parents as agents of change. Individually or in groups of six to eight, parents are taught to conduct nondirective play therapy sessions with the instruction and supervision of professionals.

### HISTORY

Bernard Guerney, Jr., then Director of the Rutgers University Psychological Clinic, conceived of the approach in an effort to develop a more efficient, effective, and longer-lasting therapy for children and to extend the ability of professionals to help a greater number of families (Guerney, 1964). Filial Therapy was the first systematic, programmatic effort to utilize parents as therapists. Because of its innovative nature, the therapy was slowly and carefully developed by Guerney and his colleagues, Dr. Lillian Stover, Dr. Michael Andronico, and Dr. Louise Guerney. The first pilot groups were composed of parents unrelated to each other, each individual representing a separate family, and were conducted by one of the above clinical psychologists. By 1970, successful experience with the method allowed the training of graduate students to utilize the method, and the parent groups to be composed of couples, singles, foster parents, etc., in any combination of convenience.

The most comprehensive study conducted on Filial Therapy was limited to mothers, since they are the most common participants. Findings on a study funded by the National Institute of Mental Health (Guerney and Stover, 1971) demonstrated that mothers successfully employ the skills of play therapists and that their children show significant gains on measures of psycho-social adjustment. More recent studies at The Pennsylvania State University indicate that the same kinds of gains are demonstrated in mixed-sex parent groups with student group leaders (Horner, 1974).

Again, because of the desire to exercise great caution with the method, children with the slightest hint of organic disorder were originally excluded. Currently, exclusions are made of only autistic and severely schizophrenic children. No parents are excluded except those who are actively suicidal or homicidal.

### TECHNIQUE

Nondirective play sessions require the therapist to employ the commonly accepted core-helping skills of empathy, genuineness, warmth, and unconditional positive regard (Axline, 1969). Generally, children are free to direct the activities of the session in any way they wish. However, limits are structured into the play sessions for a variety of therapeutic reasons. Thus, the play sessions provide both an unparalleled opportunity for self-expression and at the same time structure for the acceptance of responsibility for one's overt behavior.

Parents are taught the behavior of the play therapist by a group leader, or leaders, via demonstrations, role playing, and practice with feedback. Parents observe all sessions with all children of the group, including children of the families other than the target children, who are also offered play sessions if they are within the approximate age range.

After attaining minimal proficiency as play therapists at the treatment site, parents begin conducting play sessions at home with each of their children, individually, once a week for one-half to three-quarters of an hour. Written reports are reviewed at the group meetings and feedback is provided. Demonstration sessions are scheduled at the treatment site approximately once a month in order to monitor the status of the children and possible "drift" in parent conduct in the sessions.

After six to twelve home sessions, depending on progress made, leaders begin to direct attention to behavior of the children *outside* of the play sessions, and attempt to help parents relate differences in their behavior in play sessions to observed differences in child behavior. Finally, at the last stage, though play sessions continue, attention is turned almost entirely to adaptations of parental play therapy behavior for application in the real world. The skills of reinforcement and parent expression to children (all but eliminated from the play session) are added. While earlier groups typically lasted twelve to eighteen months, current groups cover the four phases outlined above in six to nine months. Most recently, a carefully controlled study has shown that there are highly significant gains in parental attitudes of acceptance and children's psychological adjustment within two months of treatment (Sywulak, 1977).

The play sessions then serve a dual function: the more traditional one of a therapeutic method for the children, but also as a laboratory for parents to acquire new behavioral skills, which can gradually be adapted for use in situations outside the playroom.

## APPLICATIONS

Filial Therapy is of value in treating psycho-social adjustment problems, mild or severe, whether these are manifested as phobic, aggressive, withdrawn, anxious, or mixed behavioral problems.

Anticipated outcomes are the following: 1) reduction of symptoms in the children, 2) increased self-esteem and psycho-social competence of the children, 3) improved parent-child communication and cooperation, and 4) increased ability of the parents to be successful in their parental roles.

Any child-parent dyad or larger family grouping, for whom one or more of the above outcomes would be desirable, could be considered for Filial Therapy. Its major use so far has been for child therapy, but the method has been adapted successfully to serve a variety of other purposes: 1) a modified version, shortened with only home "special times" has been offered for preventive purposes. This has been used most extensively with foster and other substitute parents, 2) in smoothing over problems resulting from situational loss or acquisition of parents through divorce and remarriage, 3) teachers and other school staff, such as aides, have been employed for working with children requiring special attention in the school setting, and 4) child welfare workers have utilized it with low-functioning families.

For children beyond ten years of age, a special time, instead of the standard play session, is suggested; the parent preserves the same atmosphere as in the play session, but offers a greater range of activity choices to the child.

---

# Fischer-Hoffman Process

## Joan Ellen Zweben

### DEFINITION

Fischer-Hoffman Process is a highly structured, time-limited, intensive psychotherapy designed to alter the early childhood identifications on which the client's current psychological distress is based. Its core assumption is that the client's stated problems are a result of character traits and behaviors adopted in childhood (before the age of thirteen) in an attempt to win parental love, and that any lasting therapeutic intervention must modify this conditioning to allow for genuine choices. It is a psychoanalytically based model that utilizes contemporary techniques to mobilize the relevant feelings and produce behavior change. There is a strong emphasis on the development of the spiritual aspect of the self, both as a resource during the therapy and for future problem solving.

### HISTORY

Robert Hoffman, founder and director of the Quadrinity Center in San Francisco where the process is now based, reports that he received the process psychically from his dead friend Sigfried Fischer in 1967. Fischer was an orthodox psychoanalyst and neurologist who had died six months earlier. Hoffman, at the time a businessman in Oakland, California, had a long-standing interest in psychic phenomena. He began teaching the process to his psychic development groups, and by 1969 began to receive serious attention from local psychiatrists and psychologists for whom he increasingly served as a consultant. Many of them were sufficiently impressed with their own experiences in going through the process that they sought training as teachers.

The staff of teachers at the Quadrinity Center has been and continues to be composed of both professionals and clinically experienced but non-credentialed personnel. Because of its high training standards, which include many hours of individual supervision even for highly experienced professional clinicians, the process is not easily mass produced. Hence its visibility is less than that of other contemporary approaches. The Quadrinity Center staff is identified with both spiritual and educational traditions, and views its work as an alternative to psychotherapy.

### TECHNIQUE

The process is currently taught in groups of about thirty, using a combination of weekly group meetings of three to five hours, sessions with the client's individual teacher, and extensive writing assignments. Teachers make lengthy taped responses to the client's written homework, and these tapes are listened to by the client at the beginning of each weekly group session. Individual sessions occur around specific tasks, or when blocks arise. The client may easily spend twenty hours a week for the thirteen weeks required to complete the process. Most of this work can be done on weekends, as the structure is designed to be as compatible as possible with the conventional work schedule. Motivation is the most crucial selection factor; even highly disturbed clients have successfully completed the process if they are capable of doing the assignments (see Smith, 1975).

In all its aspects, the design of the process includes the most powerful existing techniques for mobilizing relevant emotional experiences, in combination with a focus on cognitive integration of these experiences. In this it differs from several contemporary approaches in which expression of mood or emotion, body work, or powerful spiritual experiences are felt to be enough in themselves. At each stage, written responses on an emotional, intellectual, and spiritual level are elicited from the client, thus allowing the teacher to continuously monitor what the client is experiencing. This also provides a permanent record for the client, termed the "book of life."

One can describe the process in four stages:

1. *The groundwork stage.* In this crucial orientation stage, two events occur simultaneously. The first is a grounding in certain spiritual concepts and experiences designed to mobilize positive internal resources, not only for completing the process but also for use when it is over. Many clients have had experiences with institutionalized religion that have alienated them from their own spirituality. The teachers are highly skilled at working with these resistances and enabling each person to connect with the spiritual part of himself. Contact with the "spiritual guide" (external to the self) and the "spiritual self" (an aspect of the self) is begun immediately, as they must be developed in sufficient strength to replace the teacher. This is usually accomplished by the time the client completes the process.

   The second task can be referred to as character analysis, or an identification of the negative traits and behavior that are creating difficulties for the client. Often the behavior and traits are something the client takes for granted. It is the teacher's job to call them into question by continuous confrontation, either in person or in the weekly taped responses. For the client, this usually creates an experience of frustration and confusion about his current identity, as previously automatic patterns are repeatedly challenged. The client is encouraged to utilize the spiritual resources as an anchor at this stage.

2. *The repudiation stage* (prosecution of mother/father). In this stage, the negative traits of the client are then redefined as not being truly the client's, but rather as traits adopted to please the parents and buy their love. At this point, the client focuses exclusively on his mother, and after completing stage three, repeats the sequence with the focus on his father. With the aid of specific techniques to facilitate recall, the client describes those scenes from early childhood that led to the development of traits or coping patterns that proved later to be dysfunctional, and which were essentially an imitation of, or rebellion from, parental traits and behavior. Repeatedly, the client is required to connect these patterns with current difficulties. In the group sessions, experiential techniques are used to help the

client reexperience the pain of not receiving the love he so deeply needed and vent the rage at the parents for fostering the adoption of the destructive traits. This stage culminates in the "bitch session" in which the client repudiates the traits and expresses fury at the parents, from the standpoint of the unloved child who failed to receive the love that was both needed and deserved.

3. *Forgiveness and compassion* (defense of mother/father). After a major catharsis of the rage and pain is effected, the group moves on. Clients are not permitted to hang onto the rage, even though this is the point at which major improvements begin to occur in the client's self-image. During this stage, the client re-creates each parent's childhood experiences, from the standpoint of the parent as an unloved child. The client thus comes to a genuine understanding, and forgiveness, of the parental behavior. Fischer-Hoffman Process differs from other therapies in that this aspect of the process is systematically approached and carefully monitored by the teacher. Reaching true compassion is not viewed as possible until after the pain and rage have been expressed.

4. *Consolidation and relearning.* One of the features that distinguishes Fischer-Hoffman Process from many of its predecessors is the degree of conscious and explicit attention given to relearning new patterns once the deprogramming has been accomplished. A primary tool for this task is called "recycling," in which the client transforms the negative behavior pattern into its positive opposite by a conscious, symbolic act. Clients are instructed to continue recycling after finishing the process, to promote assimilation and also as a tool for future problem solving. Most clients are highly enthusiastic about its usefulness, both during and after the process.

Other facets of the consolidation process include restructuring the relationship between the emotions and the intellect so that neither is sacrificed or overvalued. In the final stages, attention is also given to the client's capacity to tolerate *positive* experiences, to offset the exclusive problem focus that can itself become a source of difficulty for clients who may already be inclined to selectively attend to negative experiences.

The process ends with a final "closure ritual" in which the highlights of the process are summarized prior to a ceremony that affirms the changes the client has experienced. Clients are strongly urged to continue to use the tools for problem solving, and there are reunions and social events periodically. However, the center deliberately avoids promoting post-process workshops, seminars, or activities that would perpetuate the therapeutic dependency.

## APPLICATIONS

As currently taught, Fischer-Hoffman Process provides an intensive therapeutic experience for those whose difficulties do not yield to interventions that approach problems mainly in their here-and-now manifestations. A high level of motivation and the capacity to complete the rigorous assignments are the major selection factors.

There is currently a need for trained teachers to begin exploring how much the process can be simplified and still be effective. This would permit its application in a wider variety of settings. There is also a need for additional systematic research on the process itself, and particularly follow-up studies.

# Flooding
### Edna B. Foa

## DEFINITION

The term Flooding is applied to a range of treatment procedures that involve confronting the patient with situations, objects, or thoughts that provoke a high level of anxiety or distress. In contrast to Systematic Desensitization, Flooding denotes a rapid and prolonged exposure, usually accompanied by substantial emotional arousal. Such exposure may occur in imagination or in real life *(in vivo)*.

## HISTORY

The use of exposure *in vivo* has been noted by several scholars of divergent theoretical orientations (for example, Freud, 1919). Guthrie (1935) described how an adolescent girl with a phobia of riding in cars was kept in the back of a car, continuously driven for hours. Her anxiety reached a panic level, but gradually diminished. At the end of the four-hour session, she was quite comfortable and was rid of her phobia. More recently, Malleson (1959) reported the use of Flooding in imagination. The patient was an Indian student who was terrified of failing his examinations. He was asked to imagine all the "disastrous" consequences of failing in school—being derogated by colleagues in India, disappointing his family, losing money, etc. After two days, during which he was treated twice a day and practiced several times a day by inducing those images on his own, he reported no fear of examinations.

The recent mounting interest in the study of Flooding and its application to a variety of disorders was influenced by Thomas G. Stampfl's writing (Stampfl, 1967; Stampfl and Levis, 1967). Labeling the technique 'implosion' Stampfl stressed the importance of obtaining an intense reaction by presenting the patient with "horror" fantasies. The content of these fantasies include fears reported by the patient and material hypothesized by the therapist to be present but repressed (such as hostility, aggression, and sexual feelings). The psychodynamic part of the treatment is unique to Stampfl and Levis and their followers. Most other behaviorists elicit fantasies based solely on fears expressed directly by the patient.

## TECHNIQUE

During the past decade numerous studies have been conducted with animals, volunteers, and patients. While these studies have not thrown much light on what mechanisms make Flooding work, they have provided valuable information about how to use it effectively.

Stampfl and Levis's theoretical formulation of Flooding suggested the use of scenes that are highly fearful. And, indeed, early reports indicate that patients were confronted with horrific images. Since then the role of anxiety in exposure has been questioned. Hussain found that Flooding in combination with the drug Thiopental was more effective than Flooding with no relaxing drugs. Similarly, my colleagues and I have reported that presentations of pleasant scenes associated with the feared object were as effective as presenting horrifying ones. It seems, therefore, that it is not necessary to include cues that maximize the distress.

The optimal point for terminating a Flooding session is not known. However, it is advisable to keep the patient exposed to the fearful situation until substantial diminution in anxiety or distress is reported. For such diminution to occur, a longer exposure (one or two hours) is required. It was indeed found that both agoraphobics and obsessive-compulsives benefited more from Flooding *in vivo* when sessions were of longer duration (two hours vs. a half hour).

Most clinicians conduct therapy sessions in their office. Such practice often forces the therapist who employs this technique to rely on exposure in fantasy. Yet most studies established the superiority of Flooding *in vivo*. When exposure *in vivo* is not feasible, the therapist should stress the importance of exposure to real-life situations, hitherto avoided, through self-practice between sessions.

To minimize stress experienced by the patient during Flooding, some gradation may be employed. Although sudden and gradual exposure were found to be equally effective in one study, patients felt more comfortable when a hierarchy of about five situations was constructed. Using a scale that rates anxiety, patients would be asked to rate several situations according to the amount of subjective anxiety each evoked. Treatment involves exposure to a moderate anxiety-evoking situation, and progresses as rapidly as possible toward the more fearful ones.

In summary, a gradual and prolonged exposure *in vivo*, rapidly proceeding towards the most fearful situation seems to constitute the most effective treatment program. Self-exposure exercises between sessions are important. Flooding in fantasy may be applied when the feared situation cannot be produced in reality (for example, the fear that a dear person will die if certain rituals are not performed); it may also be used to facilitate later exposure *in vivo*.

## APPLICATIONS

Flooding in fantasy, notably implosion, has been applied to a wide range of problems including depression, schizophrenia, phobias, and obsessive-compulsive disorders. Yet the measurements used in these studies do not permit definite conclusions regarding the efficacy of implosion with some of these disorders.

Flooding in fantasy was found to be effective in specific phobias (for example, animal phobias) and in agoraphobia. However, Systematic Desensitization seems to produce greater improvement in specific phobias than in agoraphobia while the reverse is true for Flooding. Numerous studies summarized by Marks (1975) have demonstrated the efficacy of Flooding *in vivo* with agoraphobics, in individual as well as in group setting. Several studies have also shown Flooding *in vivo* to be effective in the treatment of obsessive-compulsives. In both agoraphobics and obsessive-compulsives, marked improvement has been achieved by this technique in a relatively short period (one to four weeks). Reports on the effectiveness of densensitization as well as Flooding *in fantasy* with these disorders are inconclusive.

# Folk Healing

## Robert C. Ness and Ronald M. Wintrob

### DEFINITION

All societies have evolved organized responses to cope with the medical and psychosocial consequences of illness and injury. We will refer to the interrelated beliefs, behavior, and medical material comprising these responses, which have evolved indigenously within specific cultural settings, as systems of Folk Healing.

The rich cross-cultural variation within folk-healing systems can be categorized into four major systems of belief or "theory" about the causes of illness (Murdock 1978):

1. *Natural causation.* Any theory that accounts for an ailment as the natural (e.g., physiological) consequences of some act or experience of the victim in any manner that would appear reasonable to modern medical science (including notions of germs, physical or emotional stress, physical deterioration, and accident).

2. *Mystical causation.* Any theory that accounts for an ailment as a direct (and often automatic) consequence of some act or experience of the victim that is mediated by a putative impersonal causal relationship (e.g., fate, destiny, soul loss, violation of a taboo).

3. *Supernatural intervention.* Any theory that ascribes an ailment to the arbitrary, hostile, or punitive intervention of some malevolent or affronted supernatural being (e.g., ghosts, ancestral spirits, gods).

4. *Magical causation.* Any theory that ascribes an ailment to the aggressive intervention of an envious, affronted, or malevolent human being (witch, sorcerer) who employs magical means to injure a victim.

Within any specific cultural setting, of course, cultural groups may recognize (and attach varying degrees of importance to) more than one of these causal theories.

While natural causation is the theoretical cornerstone of "scientific" medicine, cross-cultural research by anthropologists and psychiatrists continues to document the salience of beliefs about supernatural and magical causation not only in non-Western societies but also within many religious and ethnic subpopulations in urban North America. Among black Americans, for example, the role of "rootwork" and associated beliefs in magical causation have been described in a number of clinical cases by Wintrob (1973). Similar magical beliefs within the United States related to the onset and treatment of illness have been reviewed by Snow (1974) and an increasing number of case reports have substantiated the prevalence of such beliefs. In the Hispanic population, Garrison (1977) and Harwood (1977) have documented the crucial role of *espiritismo* (spiritism) among Puerto Rican groups. The significance of *curanderismo* among the largest Spanish-speaking group in the United States, the Mexican-Americans, has been demonstrated by Alegria and his colleagues (1977), Martinez (1977), and Kiev (1968). Many people who utilize folk-healing systems also seek assistance from health professionals, either simultaneously or in sequence. Consequently, an understanding of these systems can significantly improve the professional's clinical effectiveness.

## ROOTWORK: HISTORY AND TECHNIQUE

Rootwork refers to beliefs and practices used to cope with the physical and psychological effects of malign magic. The belief in malign magic derives from the assumption that any person, envious and resentful of the attributes or achievements of another, may be able to invoke an evil spell on that person; consequently, the victim may experience grave misfortune, illness, or death. It is believed that the individual is most likely to be victimized by people with whom he interacts closely—friends, co-workers, extended family. Rootwork beliefs incorporate elements of European witchcraft, West African sorcery, and West Indian voodoo, and are encountered mainly in the southeastern states among both whites and blacks. It is generally believed that "working roots" on someone—also called mojo, hoodoo, hexing, and many other terms—can cause the victim to succumb to crippling physical and psychiatric illness. Symptoms almost always include abdominal pain, nausea, vomiting; psychiatric symptoms often include delusions and hallucinations of a persecutory type, marked anxiety, agitation, and fear of death. People who feel they may be victims of rootwork can be expected to seek treatment from a rootworker or spirit doctor, often combining this with treatment by physicians and hospital medicines. Rootworkers are individuals whose innate healing abilities are believed to include particular spiritual strength.

Treatment by rootworkers begins with an evaluation of the subject's social situation, and whether the symptoms may have been caused by a hex. From the beginning, consultation and intervention usually involve family and/or friends, as well as the "rooted" person. Having determined malign magic is indeed a cause, the root worker usually prescribes and administers an infusion of herbal medicine. The rootworker may identify the antagonist or advise the victim to avoid contact with certain people. A prayer session often follows the administration of herbal medicines. The process is repeated at regular intervals until recovery; the subject's family administers herbal preparations at home and ensures that the patient precisely follows instructions about diet, medicines, social activities, and prayer.

It should be emphasized that the intensity of peoples' beliefs in rootwork varies considerably. Some consult rootworkers only at the urging of their family and with marked skepticism or ambivalence. Others are firmly convinced that their illnesses can have no other cause but malign magic. But whatever their degree of conviction, nearly all studies have pointed out that rootwork believers frequently make use of physicians and hospital medicines to relieve physical discomfort. The two systems of healing are usually viewed as complementary rather than competitive.

## CURANDERISMO: HISTORY AND TECHNIQUE

*Curanderismo* is a system of beliefs commonly encountered among Mexican-Americans concerning the causes and management of personal and social misfortune, including illness. *Curanderismo* is prevalent among Mexican-Americans throughout the Southwest and West and extends as far north as Chicago. The complex of beliefs includes: 1) the ancient humoral theory of illness, 2) characterological strengths and weaknesses that relate to individual susceptibility to illness, 3) "naturalistic" folk conditions such as *empacho* (Intestinal distress), 4) mystical causes such as fate, destiny, *susto* (soul loss), and *mal ojo* (evil eye), and 5) magical causes such as *embrujo* (witchcraft) and *mal puesto* (hexing). In summary, these diverse beliefs and healing practices represent an interweaving of Iberian Catholic and indigenous Mexican traditions. Reports from Chicago as well as San Antonio indicate that the folk healers, called *curanderos*, conduct flourishing practices.

Studies of these healers have demonstrated that their clients show a wide range of symptoms. Physical symptoms such as headache, gastrointestinal distress, back pain, and fever are particularly common, as are psychological complaints such as anxiety, irritability, fatigue, depression. Less commonly seen, especially in urban settings, are the particular folk conditions of *susto, empacho, mal ojo*, and *mal puesto*. More uncommon still are cases of overt psychosis, a condition healers recognize but may be reluctant to treat.

As with *espiritistas* and rootworkers, the healing techniques of *curanderos* usually involve a combination of herbal infusions, dramatic healing rituals, and prayer. There is considerable variation in the relative emphasis accorded each of the three elements of healing, as well as the involvement of others in the healing ceremonies— family, community members, and apprentice healers. Much of the variation is related to the social status and reputation of the particular healer and the development of his "calling." For all healers, the religious nature of their calling and of their healing rituals is a fundamental theme. The religious faith of the patient and his family is assumed to be an important reason for recovery. Persistence or intensification of symptoms may be attributed to lapses of faith or to the complications of witchcraft or hex.

In the case of *mal puesto*, Martinez (1977) reports that it is quite common for Mexican-Americans who seek the help of mental health personnel to suspect or be convinced that they are victims of malign magic. Furthermore, the victim is almost always convinced that the hex has been perpetrated by jealous in-laws or other close relatives. As with other healing practices, the serial or simultaneous use of physicians and hospital medicines is to be expected.

## ESPIRITISMO: HISTORY AND TECHNIQUE

*Espiritismo*, or spiritism, is a system of Spanish, African, and Indian folk-healing practices based on the belief that the visible and invisible worlds are inhabited by spirits that are temporarily encased in a human body in the material world. These beliefs and related healing techniques are widely encountered among the nearly two million Puerto Ricans living in the northeast states.

It is believed that spirits, who are neither inherently good nor bad, have a mission, through which they may acquire increasing understanding or perfection. Several incarnations and reincarnations may be necessary in order for a spirit to accomplish its mission, which culminates in unity with God. Some disincarnate spirits (*causas*) have trouble achieving their mission and attempt to intrude on people during their dreams or to enter someone's body in order to satisfy unmet desires from an earlier incarnation. Spirits are thus considered a primary source of trouble for the living, generating stress, nervousness, physical and psychiatric illness. Faced with these symptoms, many Puerto Ricans consult an *espiritista* (medium or spiritist) if: 1) they have obtained no relief from a physician for the somatic symptoms, 2) disturbances of mood persist such as "bad nerves" or depression, or 3) interpersonal relationships continue to deteriorate.

There are no specific or typical somatic complaints that lead people invariably to consult an *espiritista*, although it has been found that *espiritistas* urge clients to use doctors and hospital medicines to relieve physical symptoms while they (the mediums or spiritists) focus on disturbances of feelings and interpersonal relationships attending the illness. A substantial proportion of spiritists' clients could be shown to have personality disorders or neurotic reactions; a small number have been considered to be schizophrenic. Clients displaying bizarre behavior and clearly impaired judgment may be referred to a mental health clinic or psychiatrist. Others may be urged to develop their innate, God-given abilities as an apprentice spiritist.

*Espiritistas* may be consulted in a private session or at regularly announced meetings called a *reunione*. Diagnosis and treatment is a complex form of psycho-drama during which the practitioner communicates with the spirit world.

A *reunione* usually begins with a reading from Kardec's *The Scriptures According to Spiritism*. Then there is a call to the mediums to receive spirits. After a period of silence one or more mediums may begin to writhe in possession by a spirit. The president will demand that the spirit identify itself and describe or name the petitioner (ill person) with whom it is involved. The spirit, acting and speaking through a medium, then identifies an individual in the audience and may pose a series of questions that essentially describe the problem bothering the petitioner. This individual is expected to humbly confirm the problem as described. During this time the meeting's president is expected to: 1) question the spirit in order to clarify the petitioner's problem, 2) protect the possessed medium, other mediums, and the petitioner from other malevolent spirits, and 3) assist other mediums not possessed in the "education of the spirit" by arguing with and criticizing the spirit for the anguish it has caused the client.

The goal of this activity, which may require repeated visits, is to convince the spirit of its wrongdoing and reorient it toward its proper mission. Clients may be advised to purchase herbal medicines or ritual objects, engage in prayer at home, and perhaps consult a physician. Clients currently seeing physicians are usually urged to continue complying with the treatment regimen prescribed.

## APPLICATIONS

The holistic conception of health implicit in religio-magical healing systems is summarized by Frank (1977): "Health is a harmonious integration of forces within the person coupled with a corresponding harmony in his relations with other persons and the spirit world." The implications of this world view for understanding the therapeutic effectiveness of indigenous healing ritual, as well as individuals' health-seeking behavior, are considerable.

A primary factor in the apparent effectiveness of folk healers is their ability to arouse hope by capitalizing on the ill person's feelings of dependency, anxiety, and decreased self-esteem. The healer's personality as well as the powerful symbolic value of his healing instruments and materials encourage hope and trust, which together promote the expectation of help and ultimate recovery. The healer is viewed as a powerful mediator between the ill person and particular magical or supernatural forces of the spirit world. The therapeutic ritual provides a specific plan of action for the ill person to execute, and gives him a sense of purpose and mastery. Since the ritual generally involves active participation by the healer and group, the individual's hope is strengthened by this demonstration that the healer and audience are his allies.

Another central feature of folk-healing systems involves elements that increase the participants' self-esteem. First, involvement in religious activities may be seen as a virtue in itself. Second, concerted group activity, viewed as evidence of community support, heightens a client's self-esteem. Third, the healer may call upon supernatural forces on behalf of a specific individual, indicating that he is worthy of that ultimate form of help.

Taken as a whole, the intense concern of healer and audience, in conjunction with emotionally stirring music, prayers, offerings, and dramatic performances by the healer serve to make explicit and visible abstract cultural beliefs about the ultimate causes of misfortune in general and illness in particular.

Our discussion of the generic features of Folk Healing leads us to a consideration of the practical application of understanding folk-healing systems: How can we improve our treatment of people who share such beliefs? First, we need to be continually sensitive to the possibility that people who consult mental health professionals may not share our assumptions, our world view about the causes of illness. People who believe in folk healing may be very reluctant to discuss anything but physical complaints or vague feelings of nervousness because of the fear of being misunderstood, not being taken seriously, or ridiculed. Therefore, we need to demonstrate a nonjudgmental interest in, and knowledge about, folk healing so that we can obtain an accurate description of the problems as conceptualized by the patient and his relatives. Second, we need to make a more realistic assessment of our treatment objectives. In this respect, we should be prepared to accept as a given that many patients who subscribe actively or passively to folk-healing beliefs have limited confidence in the effectiveness of medical treatment. They accept the utility of this treatment in providing relief of somatic symptoms such as headache, dizziness, abdominal distress, or nervous tension, but they will seek Folk Healing for relief of psychosocial and spiritual distress.

Medical interventions deal mainly (or only) with the proximal causes and manifest symptoms of a problem that the patient may regard as a complex physical-social-spiritual problem involving not only himself but also his family, social network, and his relations with the spirit world. Viewed from this perspective, we should expect that many patients will undertake treatment from health professionals and from folk healers simultaneously or in sequence. Accordingly, we need to accept in many cases the more limited therapeutic objective of symptom reduction rather than psychodynamic insight. We should recommend a plan of treatment that will be consistent with the patient's expectations, thus ensuring a high probability of patient compliance.

A considerable body of evidence from cross-cultural research in Folk Healing suggests that folk-healing techniques can be strikingly effective. However, debate continues to rage on the question of "legitimizing" Folk Healing by co-opting folk healers to provide treatment within the hospital or clinic setting, or even whether referrals should be encouraged between health professionals and folk healers. These issues will not be easily resolved.

# Frommian Influence

## Erwin Singer

(Some Implications of Erich Fromm's Thoughts for the Practice of Psychoanalysis)

To discuss Erich Fromm's thinking on psychoanalysis as a therapeutic process is a difficult task. He has written little directly related to this topic except for some passages here and there, most prominently in his book *The Forgotten Language*. However, he has contributed extensively in areas bearing significantly on the work of the practicing analyst, notably in delineating his conceptions on personality and its development. Therefore, the following paragraphs will deal mainly with his thoughts in these areas and their implications for psychotherapy.

### DEFINITION

Basically, Fromm maintains that neurological givens, i.e., the capacity for reason and consciousness, place man in a difficult position. Consciousness and reason acquaint us with several potentially very unpleasant realities: the time-limited nature of our existence, the fact that death is inevitable; our relative insignificance in the larger scheme of things, our being but drops of water in the sea, grains of sand on the beach; and finally, our lack of what Fromm calls "rootedness," that is, knowing and being known from core to core. Rootedness is almost an impossibility to attain. Man, Fromm insists, is unavoidably and always alone, though not necessarily lonely.

Given these "dichotomies" in living, Fromm proposes that we are constantly in search of ways to regain rootedness, constantly trying to find a road to overcome separateness in order to regain connection with the world and others. Fromm states that there are a variety of solutions in this quest to transcend the boundaries of one's separate being, a variety of social answers to this biologically determined reality of separateness.

He schematizes these answers into two categories: the development of nonproductive orientations and the possibility of the growth of a productive stance. By nonproductive orientations Fromm means the attempt to join others, or the development of the illusion of joining others, via a multitude of nonproductive relationships. This, he proposes, is accomplished by forging positions of exploitation and manipulation; by hoarding to achieve power over one's fellows; or, as he thinks rather prevalent today, by attempts to "market" oneself and make oneself marketable as a desirable commodity. All these and similar orientations are seen as nonproductive means of bringing about the illusion of reaching another person. They are in Fromm's thinking essentially pathological character orientations. Juxtaposed to these nonproductive orientations, he posits a productive one characterized by efforts to bring to others something of genuine value rather than the illusion thereof. The productive orientation is characterized by concern with, devotion to, and respect for others. Fromm believes that such an orientation of love in the widest sense of the term blossoms only when self-respect and concern for oneself, one's time of life and its limits, is paramount. We encounter in these formulations Fromm's concept that man *against* himself will be against others while man *for* himself will also be man for others. To some, this seems a paradox but really is not: Only the acceptance of one's own aloneness and separateness makes reaching others in their separateness possible, and carries with it the hope of alleviating loneliness.

It is well to remember Fromm's insistence on a single dominant drive in man: the drive to break the narrow confines of one's being and to gain contact with others. This can be done by creating, or if circumstances block this avenue, by destroying; thus, to Fromm, creating and destroying are simply opposite sides of the same basic impulse. Both positions bring about contact with others *and* the development of something new. It is as if Fromm maintained that man feels compelled to create even if by destroying, that the only thing the human being cannot tolerate is the maintenance of the status quo, whatever its nature. And he proposes that the avenues taken in this quest will parallel the basic socioeconomic lines and forces dominating a given culture and a given era.

In recent years Fromm has written prominently about what he refers to as "biophilia"—the love of life and creating—and "necrophilia"—the love of death and destruction. These concepts must be seen as subtle refinements of productive and nonproductive character orientations, brought about both by forces already outlined and by temperamental and/or biological tendencies. It would represent a gross misunderstanding of Fromm's theoretical stance to imply, as is occasionally done, that biophilia and necrophilia are conceptually analagous to Freud's biologically given life drive and death drive.

Finally, Fromm believes that an individual may find himself in a situation that makes the burden of his separateness, and/or the particular method he took to relieve this unbearable state, so repugnant that he will more or less abandon awareness of himself. A personal dilemma is thus seemingly solved by psychological suicide. Fromm proposes that by giving up consciousness, the person has rather perniciously staged an "escape from freedom." What is deeply pathological in this state is that the sense of self, of being a free and therefore responsible being, is abandoned. This giving up of self for the sake of gaining connection represents to Fromm the deeper meaning of Oedipal strivings. No wonder that he sees in blind nationalism an expression of the Oedipus complex in our age.

## HISTORY

Thoughts expressed by Fromm have ancient and contemporary roots found in Eastern and Western thinking, and are refined by his clinical observations and acumen. Strains of existential thought from antiquity to the present-day are recognizable. Fromm has acknowledged Spinoza's significant influence, as well as that of Marx's writings. Strains of biblical thought and Zen insight in his comments are also noticeable.

Freud's monumental work moved Fromm to try to go beyond where Freud had to stop. As Tauber and Landis point out, Fromm is neither anti-Freudian nor simply a cultural relativist. His was primarily the effort to take psychoanalysis out of its predominantly biological orientation and to reformulate in sociological terms the gigantic human drama Freud had posited, without denying the biological strivings of the organism. It may be appropriate to suggest that these biological forces were made more relevant by Fromm's exposition of the human situation in which they occur, and by his proposing sociological and economic forces as *additional* dimensions in human character development, not the basis for it (Tauber and Landis, 1971).

It follows that early revisionists of Freudian thought, such as Adler, Jung, and a host of others, have made comments that seemed significant to Fromm, though obviously he differs from them markedly in his system and in his emphasis.

## TECHNIQUE

Similar to Freud, who wrote little on technique, Fromm has stayed away from the discussion of technical issues. He is more concerned with the nature of the analyst's stance, with his willingness to make an effort to enter the patient's experience, to meet him "from core to core." He deems this essential even if it implies that the patient is likely to learn a good deal about the psychological makeup of the analyst, and even though this may mean that the analyst is likely to learn a good deal that is new about himself. In *Zen Buddhism and Psychoanalysis*, Fromm makes this point succinctly when he says: "Hence, the analyst not only cures the patient but is also cured by him." Whatever furthers this process of deep engagement with essentials rather than with trivia, whatever furthers genuine introspection and examination of motivation, seems technically admissable; whatever detracts from this process, whatever interferes with the true learning of both participants, whatever smacks of the patient being given directions, and whatever furthers sham and superficiality is frowned upon. And all this in the hope that the patient may regain the freedom to choose; perhaps he will choose a productive orientation over a nonproductive one.

In summary, it must be recalled that Fromm is essentially a psychoanalyst committed to helping the patient achieve consciousness of what is dissociated. It is clear that he eschews libido theory and substitutes sociological vantage points. Furthermore, much of supposedly psychoanalytic technique is avoided because the "original" traumas dissociated by the patient are not to be found in regressive, instinctual impulses that must be recalled; rather, they are found in the orientations the person chooses and develops vis-a-vis his dilemma of unrootedness.

## APPLICATIONS

Implicit in Fromm's writings is an ingrained conviction that "the truth shall make you free." Nowhere is there the suggestion that this is limited to some people or is not true for some of the dramatic emotional disorders of living. We may therefore assume that Fromm sees little limitation in the applicability of psychoanalytic therapy. If analyst and patient meet in seriousness to explore the motivations of a life and to achieve clarity about them, that will be curative in itself by helping the person shoulder the enormous burden that freedom entails. No wonder that many of his students and close collaborators have worked with, and continue to work with, people exhibiting manifestations of all kinds of difficulties in living.

Beyond this, Fromm seems firmly convinced that psychoanalytic insights can make significant contributions to our understanding of political, social, and economic problems. The very titles of his books, such as *The Sane Society, Marx's Concept of Man, May Man Prevail?, and The Anatomy of Human Destructiveness*, readily suggest his beliefs concerning the applicability of psychoanalytic concepts. But perhaps above all he sees the utility of these understandings for the process of education toward creative freedom.

# Future Oriented Psychotherapy

*Frederick Towne Melges and Patricia Blevins Webster*

## DEFINITION

Future Oriented Psychotherapy focuses on the future rather than on the past or present. It is designed for: 1) helping patients choose and clarify realistic personal goals and 2) inducing them to develop and rehearse plans of action that will achieve their chosen goals. Future Oriented Psychotherapy is a short-term cognitive therapy that can be a useful adjunct to past and present oriented therapies, since it helps patients to crystallize what to do next and how to go about it.

## HISTORY

Future Oriented Psychotherapy was first explicitly described by Frederick Melges (1972), although it stems from diverse theoretical and experimental backgrounds. Considerable experimental evidence indicated that behavior is controlled by consequences. With the human capacity for foresight and planning, human behavior appeared to be controlled largely by extensive anticipated consequences (Kelly, 1955; Miller, et al., 1960). These considerations prompted the central question for the genesis of Future Oriented Psychotherapy: if a psychotherapist can help a patient to modify his expectations and the structure of his anticipated reinforcements, will this change the patient's behavior, including his self-image and his interpersonal relationships?

Also, research dealing with human psychopathology had indicated that disturbances in psychological time and misconstructions of the personal future were involved in various psychiatric symptoms and syndromes—such as depersonalization, inner-outer confusion, paranoia, depression, low self-esteem, suicidal thoughts, and impulsive behavior (for review, see Melges and Bowlby, 1969; Melges and Freeman, 1977). In contrast, adaptive behavior and high self-esteem could be predicted from evaluating a person's degree of detailed future planning in which the person viewed himself, rather than luck or other people, as the agent of change (Ezekiel, 1968). Thus, from the standpoint of research findings, it appeared that clarifications and extension of future outlook might be therapeutic in a variety of syndromes.

## TECHNIQUE

There are essentially two basic therapeutic methods for Future Oriented Psychotherapy: 1) "image therapy" for clarifying personal goals and 2) "future autobiography" for rehearsing plans of action to meet the chosen goals. Image therapy precedes future autobiography, and thereafter the two procedures are interrelated. These procedures are carried out after the therapist has established rapport with the patient and gathered sufficient historical material to discover the key elements of what Eric Berne (1972) has termed the patient's "script"—that is, the life-plan that the patient has adopted unwittingly from those who reared him. Knowledge of how the patient is scripted helps the therapist identify habitual self-defeating behavior the patient may choose to change.

Image therapy helps the patient to get a clear image of the kind of person he wants to become. To do this, the patient is projected into the future to a specific day about three months ahead. The day chosen should be one that entails involvement with people important to the patient, such as a holiday, and has the potential of the patient changing his own behavior and attitudes so that the experience becomes positive and rewarding. The patient is asked to visualize as concretely as possible all the sequences and interactions of this day. He is prompted to talk out loud about his visualizations using the present tense, as though the future day were occurring in the here-and-now. He is prompted to see himself interacting with others according to the kind of person he chooses to become. He is then prompted to visualize how others will react to him and how he feels about himself. Once a positive yet realistic future self becomes vivified, the therapist then introduces people that the patient's history reveals are troublesome, such as a guilt-provoking mother, in order to get the patient to modify his inner and outer reactions according to his chosen self-image.

After the projection into the future, it is often helpful to have the patient fill out a semantic differential scale of the self-image. This helps codify the projected images into words that later can be used as reminders of his projected self-image. On the scale, the patient rates contrary adjectives. Some of the key dimensions are: trusting vs. distrusting, self-assured vs. self-conscious, assertive vs. defensive, competent vs. inadequate, real vs. unreal, warm vs. distant, caring for others vs. self-absorbed, sincere vs. phony, strong vs. weak, active vs. passive, good vs. bad, feminine vs. masculine. Also, the patient is encouraged to generate adjectives that are more fitting to his future self-image by, for example, having him fit adjectives to the first letters of his or her name, such as Joan = joyous, organized, assertive, no-nonsense. The images can be further ingrained, if appropriate, through the use of hypnosis. The basic idea behind crystallizing such personal goals is that the person has to structure his ego-ideal specifically enough so that he will know when his behavior matches or mismatches his chosen self-image. Only then can he become self-reinforcing.

After the patient has crystallized a satisfying yet realistic future self-image, the next step is future autobiography. This also involves guided imagery into the future, but the focus is on specific plans of action and behavior that meet the patient's chosen goals of his future self-image. One technique is for the patient and therapist to pretend that it is actually one week ahead in time, and then the therapist takes a "history" of what the patient did in this time span, now viewed as past, in order to meet his chosen self-image goals. It is important to prompt the patient to talk in the past tense, as though the events had already taken place. This helps the patient avoid the host of "ifs" and "if only such would happen" that are likely to occur when the future is viewed as open and unpredictable, compared to past events that are fixed. Such a future autobiography often reveals the patient's self-defeating pattern or script. When this happens, it is pointed out to the patient and he is asked to start again, revising his future autobiography so that his actions meet his chosen goals. When the patient shows such self-reinforcement, or matching, the therapist prompts the patient to register the self-rewarding behavior and associated good feelings. Although the image therapy can be therapeutic in itself, it is given considerable impetus by the future autobiographical methods.

## APPLICATIONS

Jerome Frank (1974) points out that the central task underlying all forms of psychotherapy is to combat demoralization and to instill hope. Since the aim of Future Oriented Psychotherapy is to provide specific ways of restructuring the ego-ideal and for enhancing self-reinforcement in the future, it is designed to instill hope and self-direction. As such, it has wide applications to patients who are demoralized. Future Oriented Psychotherapy is particularly useful for patients with low self-esteem, identity diffusion, and impulsive characters, especially those who believe that the future is beyond their control.

# Gestalt Therapy[3*]

## *John O. Stevens*

## DEFINITION

Gestalt Therapy is phenomenological and existential: it explores the changing phenomena of awareness as they unfold in the individual's perceived existence, here and now. The therapist's job is to be a guide in this exploration, and this function can be divided into four broad areas: 1) feeding back the verbal and nonverbal experience and behavior of the patient—particularly those areas that the person is less aware, or unaware, of—to intensify and clarify the ongoing process, 2) suggesting experiential here-and-now experiments for the person to try out as a means to self-discovery, 3) expressing his own awareness of his responding to the patient (in this, the therapist is providing information about the person's impact, as well as providing a model for the open communication of experiencing), and 4) acting as teacher by providing principles and strategies that are useful guides to deepening awareness. Thus, Gestalt is also experiential, behavioral, experimental, and educational.

Gestalt makes a crucial and fundamental distinction between perceptual reality and mental fantasy. My reality, the solid ground of my existence, always results from perceptual contact with ongoing events: what I see, hear, smell, taste, or feel in the present moment. Fantasy is any mental representation of events that are not perceived in the moment: images, memories, assumptions, planning, thinking, guessing, imagining, hoping, fearing, etc. Much of my living is based on uncertain fantasy rather than perceptual reality. My ideas often blind me to my actual feel ings, keep me from expressing myself as I would like to, or sometimes keep me behaving in ways that are self-destructive or not productive. Simply making clear what is reality and what is fantasy can point out how little of my living is based on fact and how much is conjecture, and it can lead to a softening and questioning of my rigid ideas and beliefs.

---

3* From *Legacy from Fritz* © 1975 Science and Behavior Books, Palo Alto, California.

The word "gestalt" means (roughly) the configuration of the whole; all the different parts relate to each other in a functional structure/process. Every aspect of a person's functioning is part of his gestalt, and has meaning only in relation to the whole. Each and every thing or process that he becomes aware of exists as a distinct, differentiated, interesting figure against a more or less indistinct, undifferentiated, uninteresting background. As my interest shifts from this writing to the sounds in the room, for example, the writing process recedes into the background of my awareness. After a short rest, this writing again becomes foreground. If I simply pay attention to my awareness and follow it, I can discover what my authentic interests and concerns are. Often the roots of my troubles are in the relatively unaware background of my living, and it is useful to reverse the figure-ground relationship. If my disappointment is in the foreground, the background is my unfulfilled expectations. With the expectations in the foreground, I can recognize that they are unreasonable and give them up if I want to avoid future disappointment.

Most of us are fragmented, with at least some perceptions, feelings, behavior, or thoughts that are puzzling, unrelated, troubling, because they are not integrated with the background, the rest of our functioning. The task of therapy is to discover the relatedness of these alienated aspects through awareness. A symptom is not just an annoyance to be eliminated, but an important message whose meaning can be explored and understood. Alienation, saying, "That's not me" can be countered by identification, saying, "This is me." The process of identification is an essential and ubiquitous tool in gestalt work. If I am ill and I identify with my illness, I find myself saying, "I'm going to give you a chance to be still and rest from doing 'useful' things." With sufficient experiential understanding, healthful change will occur of itself, without planning or outside direction, through the natural tendency of the organism to create a more functional gestalt. Once I discover that my frequent illness expresses a need to rest, I can accept that need and learn to take time to rest before getting exhausted and sick.

The only barrier to awareness is my avoidance of unpleasantness and difficulty. Often I would rather blame someone else for my unreasonable expectations; I may rather whine in the hope that someone else will rescue me than stand on my own feet and take responsibility for my successes and failures in a difficult world. I can become aware of this too, and at least take responsibility for *not* taking responsibility. Awareness, in and of itself, is curative, and every bit of awareness strengthens and promotes growth.

## HISTORY

Gestalt Therapy took shape in the 1940s with the publication of *Ego, Hunger and Aggression*, as Frederick (Fritz) Perls broke away from his orthodox psychoanalytic training of the 1920s and 1930s. Other early influences were Perls's work with gestalt psychologists, his experiences in theater and psychodrama, and the thinking of Wilhelm Reich. Later Perls made considerable use of ideas from Zen Buddhism, Taoism, Existential Phenomenology, and general semantics. A second book, *Gestalt Therapy*, coauthored by Goodman and Hefferline, was published in 1951. Perls continued to develop and modify his work by invention, and by adapting techniques—such as the "empty chair" and group format—from other therapies until his death in early 1970. Gestalt Therapy gained widespread recognition only in the late 1960s, and it was during this time that

Perls produced two more books, and a great number of films and audiotapes demonstrating his work.

## TECHNIQUE

The fundamental technique is for the client to pay attention to the continuum of his awareness in the here and now, to see what he can discover about his ongoing experiencing. In principle, he doesn't need a therapist. However, in practice, a perceptive guide can be very useful in pointing out aspects of his experiencing that he's not aware of, and in suggesting procedures or experiments that can be short cuts to greater awareness.

The following is taken from a filmed session with Fritz Perls, "The Case of Marykay." This fifteen-minute first session with a young woman, in which she asks to work on resentment toward her mother, shows most of the essentials of gestalt practice.

Rather than abstractly discuss her resentments, the session begins with Perls asking her to bring them into the here and now, by imagining her mother in the "empty chair" and expressing her resentments directly to her. She smiles while expressing resentment, an inconsistency Perls brings to her attention. She is asked to talk in the imperative and to make her demands explicit, instead of dependently whining. When she again retreats into whining a minute later, this is brought to her attention by mimicking.

The second purpose of the "empty chair" is to enable her to identify with an alienated part of herself—her "mother." Actually this is her memory/image/fantasy of her mother, since her actual mother is absent. The relationship between herself and "mother" is defined by *both*. By playing her "mother's" alienated side, she can achieve more definition of the conflict and re-own the power that she has invested in the fantasy of her mother. When she again plays herself, she responds with much more expression and much less manipulation (wailing,), and this is pointed out. The following is a transcript of how the session continues:

1.  MARYKAY: I feel—a—just a deadness inside. Sort of an "Ah, what's the use?" And yet, behind that deadness there's—there is resentment.
2.  FRITZ: Now can you say the same paragraph to your mother?
3.  MARYKAY: (Sighs) You make me feel dead. You make me feel like I'm just not even anything. And I *know* you don't mean it. I know that it's because *you're* afraid, and I know that if—and I know you love me. And I know that you're afraid. But why did I have to be the victim of your fear? Why did it have to turn out that *I* am the victim of *your* great needs?
4.  FRITZ: Change seats again. You notice the fighting is beginning to change to a little bit of mutual understanding.
5.  MARYKAY: (*as mother*) I never meant it to be that way. All—I never meant it to be that way at all. I guess I just couldn't admit my own fears. I wanted—I *am* proud of you. I'm *really* proud of you, Marykay (*her voice breaks*).
6.  FRITZ: Say this again.
7.  MARYKAY: I'm really proud of you, you know. I show your picture (*She is crying despite trying to hold back tears*) to all the people at work. And I (*as Marykay, to Fritz*) I feel so sorry for her. (*still crying, hands in front of face*).
8.  FRITZ: Can you imagine going to her and embracing her?

9. MARYKAY: *(with great vehemence)* No! No, I can't! I can't! I can't imagine—I can't imagine embracing—anybody—I couldn't even—I couldn't even embrace my Dad when I left *(still crying)*. You just can't—you just can't show feelings 'cause they're not right.

10. FRITZ: *(softly)* You're showing feelings now. *(She is still sobbing.)* Come here, Marykay. *(He embraces her.)*

11. MARYKAY: *(breaking into fuller crying)* Oh, please—Oh, please—Oh, I just love you ... *(then she pulls away and holds her hands in front of her face).*

12. FRITZ: Is it so bad?

13. MARYKAY: I have to stop. *(Fritz takes her hands and holds them.)* I have to stop because you always have to stop to take care of yourself. *(She puts her head down, then straightens up and pulls her hands away again.)* Yeah, you really do have to take care of yourself, *(hands to face again, wiping away tears).* Do you have a handkerchief?

14. FRITZ: You know, I miss something. I know the psychiatrist's tools are skill and Kleenex. *(laughing)* I'm missing the Kleenex. *(They both smile. Someone hands Fritz a Kleenex, which he gives to Marykay.)*

There is a crucial turning point when she shows some understanding of her mother (3) and this is pointed out to her (4). (The numbers correspond to those at the left of the transcript.) When she plays her mother again (5) she changes from game playing to authentic expression of sorrow and appreciation. Marykay responds with deep feelings of sorrow for her mother that break through (5) (7) as she is playing her mother. When she is asked (8) to contact her mother more fully, she expresses an important assumption of hers, "You can't show feelings," (9) that keeps her isolated and that she previously blamed her mother for. Perls points out (10) that she is showing feelings in contrast to the injunction not to, and then embraces her. His embrace is both an authentic response to her and an offer for her to try embracing. She gives in fully to the embrace (11) and to more expression of feeling for a short time, and then pulls away. Fritz tries to get her to stay with the experience of embracing (12) (13), and when she pulls away again, he breaks off the session with a joke (14).

Of course there is still much to be done. She is still mostly uncomfortable with expression of feeling and closeness, and she probably has more work to do with her "mother." She has discovered a lot in this fifteen minutes; more often gestalt work takes somewhat longer.

The techniques of Gestalt Therapy in themselves often produce striking results, and have often been adopted into other therapeutic frameworks without full understanding. When this occurs, the techniques usually yield much less than they could, and sometimes the results are anti-therapeutic. For a much more comprehensive, yet short, description of Gestalt, see the excellent chapter by John Shaffer and David Galinsky.

## APPLICATIONS

Gestalt Therapy is much more than a specific treatment or therapy. The gestalt philosophy underlying it claims to be a valid description of human functioning and problems that any person or group can use as a guide to fuller living and experiencing. Gestalt principles are as valid in everyday living as in the therapy situation, as valid with a gifted child as a disturbed one, as valid in the hospital as in the home. Besides the wide range of psychotherapeutic settings and populations, gestalt principles have also been applied to education, to the treatment of eyesight problems, and other physical illnesses.

# Gestalt Synergy
## *Iiana Rubenfeld*

### DEFINITION

Up until the last decade, psychotherapy focused on a person's verbal behavior. Body work was separate. We are now beginning to see, however, therapeutic forms that treat the whole person, using both verbal and nonverbal (body/mind) approaches. Gestalt Synergy addresses each person as an inseparable combination of body, mind, and spirit. It recognizes that all sensory channels of the human organism provide entry to the whole in different ways at different times.

Gestalt Synergy, founded and developed by myself, is a means for contacting, expressing, and working through emotions and body tensions with touch, gentle body movements, and Gestalt Therapy. Combining the theoretical and practical elements from the work of F. M. Alexander, Moshe Feldenkrais, and Fritz and Laura Perls, this unique client-centered therapy is guided by the following concepts:

1. The responsibility for change rests with the client. The synergist is there to guide and facilitate that change.

2. Respect is given to the client's "boundaries." The client does only what he is ready to risk doing.

3. The synergist gives special attention to the client's nonverbal experience—breathing patterns, body image, body position (alignment and posture), gestures, facial expression, and tone of voice—bridging what the client *thinks* he is doing with what he is *actually* doing.

4. The focus is on the present—the here-and-now. The client reviews the past in present time resolving "unfinished business."

5. Life attitudes are reflected through our posture, movement patterns, and energy release.

6. Every act involves the whole psychophysical person. The use of one part of the body affects the whole body.

7. Without awareness, we cannot change.

8. The minute you "think," muscles receive the message to move.

9. You may be unknowingly hurting yourself by habitually maintaining a posture which "seems" right.

10. In general, habit patterns are not reflexes; they are learned.

11. Conscious control can be exerted over habit patterns. You have the ability to"inhibit" habitual patterns and choose an alternate route.

12. Conscious bodily control increases a person's life choices.

## HISTORY

I can best describe the history of Gestalt Synergy by relating my own experience. Formally trained at the Juilliard School of Music, I played the viola and piano and conducted choirs and orchestras for over twenty years. This strenuous activity finally took its toll; and I began to suffer severe backaches and physical tension. Friends recommended the Alexander Technique—a system designed to teach proper use of the body—to help relieve the physical pressure (see the Alexander Technique). I soon began taking lessons with Judith Liebowitz.

As the lessons progressed, I was often confused by the emotional and physical changes I underwent. My try-harder-goal orientation was being questioned. I once asked my teacher during a session, "How am I doing? Getting better?" To which she replied, "You're doing. When you notice and accept your body as it is, change will be possible." Although I didn't understand what was happening, intellectually, I continued with the lessons because I felt better. The teacher's touch often facilitated emotional release—I felt sad, angry, happy, etc. She, untrained as a therapist, suggested I seek professional psychotherapeutic help to understand the intense feelings released during the body work. For several years, I saw a psychotherapist every week while continuing with my Alexander lessons.

Some years later, I trained with Fritz and Laura Perls, the founders of Gestalt Therapy, who encouraged me to integrate therapy with my familiar body/mind work. Like my previous psychoanalysis, Gestalt Therapy had provided the skills to process the stored emotions often released during an Alexander lesson.

Another component of Gestalt Synergy emerged in 1971 when I met Moshe Feldenkrais, whose work in body awareness and movement is recognized as a unique advance in the field of body-mind-environment integration. I studied and trained with Feldenkrais learning his two-part technique: functional integration—one-to-one guidance through touch—and awareness-thru-movement, a system of exercises, gentle body movements, both designed to reorganize the body's muscular, skeletal, and nervous system.

My training in body/mind work and touch and psychotherapy helped me to produce my new therapeutic form, Gestalt Synergy. This synergy does not treat the individual in terms of a series of structural and postural changes. Rather, it includes the realms of emotions, thinking, body structure, spatial concepts, and movement. It treats the individual as a whole, working with both body and emotions, integrating the physical, intellectual and emotional aspects of the person. In 1977 I inaugurated Gestalt Synergy's first intensive training programs, running concurrently in New York City and California.

# TECHNIQUE

The "listening and open hand," a skill that takes two to three years to develop, provides the Gestalt synergist with feedback. Through touch, the synergist feels what is occurring in the client's body—identifying blocks and tensions. Nonverbally, the synergist "listens" to the client. A client may claim to be relaxed; by touching, the synergist recognizes whether or not this is true and can share this with the client.

Soft and strong touch establishes the relationship between synergist and client, and through its gentleness and responsiveness builds trust between them. The synergist responds through touch to the client's consent to change, and guides the client through bodily/emotional resistances—opening locked joints, releasing tense muscles, lengthening a compressed and shortened spine. Although it may appear that the synergist is doing something *to* the client, it is the client who initiates and allows the release. The touch guides and teaches the client to master his own body.

Communicating with the "listening and open hand" makes special demands on the synergist. In addition to being intellectually and emotionally aware (as in verbal therapy), the synergist must also be sensitive to and aware of physical processes. The synergist pays close attention to breathing patterns, while maintaining a dynamic, well-balanced body. Much of the training in Gestalt Synergy is devoted to developing this body/mind awareness.

The Gestalt synergist guides the client in developing body/mind awareness. For this purpose, the Feldenkrais exercises—a sequence of gentle body movements— are used. With body awareness, the client can develop the ability to "inhibit" destructive movement and consciously choose a new movement pattern. This technique, says Feldenkrais, "leads to the creation of new habits, redirecting the brain's habitual patterns of response to movement in the gravitational field, using more natural and efficient paths for mobility and deployment of body energy."

Following is an example of a Feldenkrais sequence: The synergist may begin a group or one-to-one session by having the clients lie on their backs. This position allows the person to experience the maximum degree of tension release in relationship to gravity. Next, the clients are asked to notice where and how various parts of the body touch the floor (or surface area). After this initial inventory, the synergist leads the clients through a sequence of movements. Throughout the sequence, the synergist asks them to pay attention to what they are experiencing in their bodies as they move, to notice what is happening to their backs, spine, head and neck muscles, ribs, pelvis, etc., and to the way they breathe. One feature of this technique is the absence of drill. Students are instructed to go only as far as is comfortable, not to make the extra try to reach a given position. Each movement sequence includes before-and-after comparisons of the body's position. By consciously making this comparison, the brain registers the change, informing the student whether or not change has occurred. The student may discover he can now maintain and move in a position that formerly he thought was impossible.

Students also learn dynamic postural balance and structural body alignment in relationship to gravity. For structural change to occur, however, students must first become kinesthetically aware. Through touch and movement, one develops a kinesthetic awareness so that eventually, a student can think and imagine a part of the body without moving or touching it. By becoming kinesthetically aware, students develop the ability to consciously control their movements. This, in turn, leads to structural and postural change. By first becoming aware of what you are doing, and then leaving yourself alone, suspending judgment, you can imagine other possibilities. This ability is very useful not only for learning new ways of moving, but for changing other habit patterns.

The Gestalt synergist uses Gestalt and other therapeutic techniques to work through the emotional material often released during the body work. Several of the techniques used are: dramatization and role playing; fantasy and imagination; classical "open chair" work: negative and positive accommodation (Albert and Diane Pesso's Psychomotor technique); exaggerating movement, posture, and sound; and rewriting one's life script confirming it both during therapy and in daily life. In addition to private one-to-one sessions, the synergist often uses a group setting to help process emotional material.

A Gestalt synergist may begin an intensive workshop "warming up" the group by leading them through a sequence of body/mind experiments. Then the group may begin a Feldenkrais movement sequence that often leaves the workshop participants feeling more alert, "softer," breathing more deeply and fully, and more conscious of their bodies and feelings in the here-and-now. The Gestalt synergist may invite an individual to work. This one-to-one session may begin verbally and lead into body work, or begin with touch and lead into verbal processing. The synergist asks the group to participate in the one-to-one session by paying close attention. Not only does the presence of the other group members facilitate the one-to-one work, but the individual working, in turn, may encourage self-reflection on the part of the group members. The individual sessions often touch on such universal themes as death, grief, loss, separation, joy, and these can awaken sympathetic and constructive responses in the workshop participants.

## APPLICATIONS

Gestalt Synergy is appropriate for those interested in coordinating their physical and emotional development. Clients may approach the Gestalt synergist with either physical or emotional concern. As a result of their Gestalt Synergy experience, psychiatrists and psychologists have indicated an increased sensitivity to their patients, and athletes have enhanced their performance. Physical and emotional needs are addressed through a variety of intra- and interpersonal processes.

In essence, the Gestalt Synergy experience is an intimate dialogue. Both synergist and client bring their total selves to the therapeutic encounter, transforming it into a collaborative effort that fosters acceptance, caring, humor, and mutual growth.

# Goal-Directed Psychotherapy

*Stanley E. Slivkin*

## DEFINITION

Goal-Directed Psychotherapy is a coordinated effort to effect limited changes in specific behavioral responses. This effort utilizes those cognitive, conative (the faculty of striving, making an effort), or affective (dealing with moods or emotions) components of mental functioning that are available in any individual or group of individuals. Goals are highly variable because of the differing potentials brought into the therapeutic relationship by the recipients of our best treatment efforts. Carl Rogers has postulated that the goals for therapy itself may be somewhat more limited than the goals for an effective life, in that therapy is not expected to produce an optimally adjusted person but only to start the development of a new pattern of adjustment. The concept of a limited goal and limited success as the building blocks for enhancing self-esteem is very valuable in moving toward a healthier psychological functioning.

## HISTORY

Goal-Directed Therapy had its beginnings in the description of the psychotherapeutic process by Rogers (1961). He describes the process as a series of small steps (limited goals) by which the patient progresses toward major personality changes; he also describes the sequence in which such steps are taken. The acceptance of limited goals as part of the foundation for stable progression was a major step toward increasing therapeutic options.

The neurotic patient generally brings with him a high degree of cognitive, conative, and affective functioning so that he responds well to Goal-Directed Psychotherapy. Sifneos has developed an anxiety-provoking, goal-oriented brief psychotherapy with neurotic individuals that leads to successful self-actualization in a relatively short period of time. A major preexisting requirement for patient selection is the fact that the patient has had at least one meaningful relationship with another person during his lifetime.

Balint and his colleagues described brief, insightful treatment oriented toward removal of a specific symptom (1972). He called this essentially goal-directed approach by another name—Focal Psychotherapy. Focal Psychotherapy directed therapeutic efforts toward removing a disruptive symptom that both patient and therapist accepted as a root cause of emotional distress. Balint selectively focused on material that related to the disturbing symptom, so that insight helped the patient reach the agreed-upon goal of symptom relief. Ornstein and Ornstein, who were collaborators of Balint, participated in the pioneering development of Focal Psychotherapy as a goal-directed, dynamic approach.

Detre and Jarecki have pointed out that the multiplicity of criteria used to define a successful outcome adds to the problems inherent in comparing treatment plans (1971). The goals of treatment must, of necessity, vary with the severity of the syndrome presented. Goal-Directed Therapy will have as many goals as there are differing symptom complexes. The goals for the mentally retarded, organically brain-damaged, or chronic schizophrenic are hardly consonant with those for the neurotic patient. Slivkin and Bernstein have pointed out the effectiveness of Goal-Directed group psychotherapy in improving social functioning and work capacity in moderately retarded adolescents (1968).

Goal-Directed Psychotherapy encourages the development of channels for addressing those cognitive, conative, or affective components of personality structure existing in patients that are available to effect behavioral change and emotional growth. Achievement of a limited focal goal can initiate the successful return to a more integrated behavior pattern. Focal success often inspires additional personal growth, and higher levels of responsiveness and improved coping responses in other areas of social functioning.

## TECHNIQUE

A first requirement is the assessment of the presenting complaint and its antecedents. The most distressing problem in the patient's view is discussed, so that some mutually acceptable limited goal may be set. It is important to make a realistic and objective assessment of what coping skills are present and how they can be supported most effectively. Once a goal has been set and there is an alliance between patient and therapist, all available coping skills are utilized to effect changes and achieve the designated goal. In the case of the neurotic patient, the goal may be insight, but in the schizophrenic, it may be control of hallucinations by psychopharmacological means. The importance of choosing an attainable goal cannot be overemphasized, since failure to achieve success means reinforcement of preexisting maladaptive functioning.

In my experience with retarded adolescents, permission to choose the special type of doughnut they liked in warmup sessions prior to group therapy was ego building. It was novel to these retarded adolescents that anyone could tolerate freedom of choice for them. It represented moving away from primitive narcissism towards reality, as well as taking part in simple decision-making.

In the case of terminally ill patients, the goal may be the encouragement by the therapist to control some small portion of their environment. This behavior often makes the dying process more tolerable. With the organically handicapped, a goal may be the utilization of a mechanical aid to reduce helplessness. Goal-Directed Therapy is limited only by lack of enthusiasm and imagination in patient or therapist. There are a limitless number of goals that inspire renewed hope and improved coping mechanisms.

### APPLICATIONS

Goal-Directed Therapy has a wide range of applications. It can be used to develop insight in the neurotic patient. At the same time it offers aid, comfort, and renewed coping skills to as diversified a group as the mentally retarded, chronic schizophrenic, organically impaired, and even the terminally ill. Since it requires the setting of a limited, attainable goal by patient and therapist together, it is applicable in all cases where there exists some potential for employing cognitive, conative, or affective patient skills. The results of Goal-Directed Therapy can be wide-ranging, since the pyramiding of limited goals can lead to extensive personality and functioning changes.

# Activity Group Therapy

*Alvin I. Gerstein*

## DEFINITION

Activity Group Therapy is a specific form of group therapy devised for latency age children. It is basically an experiential form of treatment in which the process of change and working out of problems derive primarily from the interaction among the various members, the therapist, the therapeutic environment, and the wide variety of materials (crafts, toys), in the context of age-appropriate activities. Intrapsychic exploration and interpretation are of minimal importance. This therapy helps the individual to deal with problems of self-esteem, authority, ego control, sibling rivalry, and the issues of overcoming fear in social situations, learning how to accept both success and defeat, taking turns, and having needs gratified. This approach relies most heavily on the desire of a human organism for acceptance by, and association with, others. The presence of an adult, the therapist, symbolically adds elements of family life.

The therapist is relatively permissive and responsive to the needs of the children, and thereby establishes an environment that, by its nonjudgmental nature, enhances the expression of aggression and repressed hostility. This atmosphere offers a healing, corrective, maturing process that results eventually in intrapsychic change.

## HISTORY

The term "activity group therapy" was first coined by Samuel Slavson in 1944 to describe a treatment technique that was based on psychoanalytic principles and developed at the Jewish Board of Guardians in New York City. Prior to Slavson, periodic articles cropped up in the 1930s on group play and group activities as related to psychotherapy. Slavson continued as the "father" and major proponent of Activity Group Therapy through the early 1950s. His pupils, S. Scheidlinger and M. Schiffer in particular, while still adhering to psychoanalytic theory, shifted their focus somewhat to deal with the use of activity groups with children in the public school system and with children experiencing pronounced cultural and emotional deprivation. Other authors expanded the use of group techniques to include preschool age children and psychotic youngsters. Until the 1960s, information regarding this form of therapy could be obtained only through research articles or occasional chapters in books on group therapy. The 1960s saw three major books devoted solely to group therapy with children. Other than H. Ginott, who relied on nondirec-tive principles, the other two authors still relied heavily on psychoanalytic principles.

Since the late 1960s, a gradual dissatisfaction with permissiveness as well as with the psychoanalytic orientation has crept in, culminating in 1972 and 1973 in two books on behavior modification in small groups of children. However, such techniques are quite different from what would be classically considered Activity Group Therapy.

## TECHNIQUE

Under ideal conditions the therapeutic environment is developed through the selective use of physical space, symbolic toys, craft materials, actual gratification of needs, and the promotion of mastery and skill acquisition through educationally oriented activities. Which of these elements will be emphasized depends on the areas of the child's ego functioning that are being treated, and these in turn are determined by an awareness of the child's underlying personality dynamics. It is apparent that many of the "abortive" groups reported in the literature failed to take these factors into consideration.

In light of the variables mentioned above, it is difficult to describe a specific set of techniques that would hold for all groups of children. The major technique is actually the interaction of children with each other in activities appropriate to their typical interests; for example, older boys setting up organized games, older girls involved in cooking projects, six- to eight-year-olds involved in arts and crafts. Feedback from peers, in conjunction with acceptance by a benign authority, may often have a stronger impact on self-perception and perception of others than a relationship with an individual. Self-esteem can be enhanced as the result of playing games as well as by the therapist pointing out behavior that may or may not be conducive to the child having his needs met.

The typical group consists of five to seven children meeting one hour weekly with one therapist. The initial phase of caution dissipates rapidly and an active testing of the extent of the therapist's apparent passivity and acceptance takes place. The fact that the therapist does not appear to be an assertive leader may raise the child's anxiety level, but does provide the basis for his becoming more independent and responsible for his own actions. Within the boundary of safety, the codes and rules for behavior as well as the choice of activities come from the group. Such groups may be time limited to the clinic year, but many run for several years.

Of greater importance than the above techniques is the initial selection of the children for the group. More than two impulsive and aggressive members of a group could produce a chaotic rather than a therapeutic climate, while a group primarily of fearful, withdrawn youngsters would be oppressive. In essence, under ideal conditions, selection should be such as to bring out the more shy members and place some constraints on the more impulsive, action-oriented participants.

## APPLICATION

In its classical form, Activity Group Therapy is not the treatment of choice for children whose impulse controls break down under minimal stress, whose reality testing is significantly defective, who become panicked regarding social contact, who are retarded, or who are psychopathic. It is most suitable for children who are defiant, dependent, socially fearful, compulsive, withdrawn, and aggressive, but with adequate impulse controls. However, modification of the materials, the therapist's interventions, and size of the group can allow for the effective use of activity groups with many of the children with the limitations specified above.

# Group-Analytic Psychotherapy
### Elizabeth T. Foulkes

## DEFINITION

Group-Analytic Psychotherapy is an intensive form of treatment in small groups. The synonymous term "group analysis" also covers applications in and beyond the therapeutic field. It fully incorporates psychoanalytic knowledge, but it is not merely a method of applying psychoanalysis to larger numbers; "group-specific factors" are considered to modify the psychodynamics. It is therapy *in* the group, *of* the group, and *by* the group, the group being an active agent of treatment. The individual person is seen and treated in the context of the group. The aim is radical and lasting change and emotional growth. It is indicated for patients with good motivation for an analytic approach, suffering from various neurotic, psychosomatic, and non-acute psychotic conditions.

## HISTORY

Group-Analytic Psychotherapy was developed and has been practiced since 1940 by S. H. Foulkes (1898- 1976), first in private practice. Later, during World War II, it was introduced into British army psychiatry at Northfield Military Neurosis Centre, where it was eventually expanded into the first "therapeutic community," with group methods being used throughout the hospital at all levels.

Since 1946, it has been increasingly practiced at many hospitals and in private practice. Between 1950 and 1964, Foulkes trained many psychiatrists, including overseas doctors, in this approach to group therapy during their postgraduate training at the Maudsley Hospital. The Group-Analytic Society (London) was founded in 1952 to further group-analytic theory and practice. In 1971 the Society set up the Institute of Group Analysis, which is now responsible for training and qualification.

## TECHNIQUE

Many of the conditions for group meetings and concepts first formulated in group analysis have become commonplace in group work generally.

In the strict group-analytic situation with out-patients of mixed symptomatology, the "standard group" consists of the therapist (termed "conductor") and seven or eight patients, (usually four men and four women), having no contact or relationship with each other in ordinary life (stranger or "proxy" groups). They meet at a regular time and place, once or twice a week, for one and a half hours, sitting in a circle with the conductor on identical chairs.

The group-analytic situation is largely unstructured. There is no program, no directions are given. The importance of regular attendance, punctuality, and abstaining from contact outside the sessions are explained to members at an initial interview, and will again be pointed out as necessary in the course of therapy—not as rules laid down by the conductor, but as conduct required in the interest of therapy.

Groups are encouraged to communicate spontaneously, voicing their concerns and difficulties in "free-floating" discussion. The resulting "group association" is the equivalent of free association in psychoanalysis. The conductor, receptive at all times, usually remains in the background but may be quite active on occasion. The emphasis is on communication, all observable behavior, including symptoms being gradually analyzed and decoded, working through to insight, and the "translation" of problems into verbal expression.

The main focus is on the here and now, on current conflict situations in life as well as in the group. Recollections and repetitions from the past are accepted as they come up spontaneously, but the persistent bringing up of material from early childhood is considered defensive. The conductor pays special attention to unconscious communication and to the analysis of resistances and defenses against change. He also watches the interaction and possible interference of the patients' own networks of intimate relationships with the therapeutic process ("boundary incidents").

Diagnostically heterogenous groups are preferable, though members should share a compatible background. Groups may sometimes be formed to deal with special problems, such as couples with marital difficulties (a hybrid group, partly "proxy" partly family). Patients are not usually prepared beforehand in individual treatment, beyond one or two interviews; nor is simultaneous individual and group therapy advocated (unless for specific groups), as these procedures complicate the transference situation. Co-therapy is used chiefly for training purposes.

In private practice, and at some hospitals and clinics with out-patient psychotherapy departments, most groups are open-ended ("slow-open"), each member joining and leaving according to individual needs. This is a very intensive treatment, allowing for slow movement. "Closed," time-limited groups are useful particularly in institutional settings, e.g., conducted by therapists in training, and for research. "Open" groups are often for larger numbers and faster changeover, for instance, for patients waiting to be assigned to psychotherapy.

### APPLICATIONS

Apart from the strict proxy group, group analysis is applied for diagnosis and therapy to groups in their natural setting, such as families and networks of closely interdependent persons; to groups treated for their own better functioning and efficiency, in education, industry, and sport; in large group settings, such as therapeutic communities, hospitals, and schools. Method and depth of approach will vary with circumstances. It is valuable in training programs, particularly for psychotherapists, workers in the mental health field, and hospital personnel; it is also valuable for educators, managers, and others. A personal group analysis is required as part of the training of future group analysts. It is also a useful diagnostic and research tool in many varied group situations.

# Guided Group Interaction

## Richard M. Stephenson

### DEFINITION

Guided Group Interaction is a group-centered treatment program aimed at altering or modifying certain established behavior patterns of its members. The group is both the target and medium of change, since the development and processes of the group are thought to produce the change in the individual. The program is based on the assumption that the same group processes that inducted a person into a course of action and gave support to it can be used to free him from it and develop alternative modes of adaptation.

## HISTORY

Although Guided Group Interaction is rooted in earlier forms of group treatment, its origins may be traced to a specialized method used among military personnel at Fort Knox Rehabilitation Center during World War II. Lloyd W. McCorkle, who had worked in this program, was brought to New Jersey by F. Lovell Bixby, Director of Correction and Parole, to organize group therapy in the state correctional system. Subsequently, he was appointed director of Highfields, a facility for sixteen-and seventeen-year-old male delinquents, where the first full and integrated program of Guided Group Interaction was instituted at the former estate of Col. Charles Lindbergh near the town of Hopewell. A residential program, accommodating approximately twenty youths sent to Highfields as a condition of probation, was designed to include: a workday at a nearby state facility; two group interaction sessions each evening involving ten boys in each; visits to Hopewell for movies, haircuts, and small purchases; minor kitchen and housekeeping duties; periodic home furloughs; and release to regular probation after a period of four months or less, depending on progress made. Boys with prior institutional commitment, obvious psychiatric difficulties, or mental deficiencies were excluded as unsuitable for the program.

This program proved feasible and subsequently two other facilities for males and one for females were developed in the state and are still in operation. In addition, two experimental, nonresidential centers, now terminated, were conducted: one for sixteen-and seventeen-year-old males in urban Newark and the other for fourteen-and fifteen-year-old males, who received special education at a state teacher's college in lieu of a work program. In the late 1950s a facility called Pinehills, patterned after Highfields, was developed in Provo, Utah; in 1961, a similar program called Southfields was opened near Louisville, Kentucky; and in 1964 Silverlake began operation in Los Angeles, California. In addition to these residential centers, elements of the Guided Group Interaction technique have been incorporated into a variety of correctional programs in some ten states in the United States, and in Sweden and Australia.

## TECHNIQUE

Guided Group Interaction combines and extends elements of both group-centered and total milieu therapy. Traditional group therapy involving periodic group discussions is extended to include all activities of the group members. The milieu therapy model is extended to include the community by linking it to the program in order to avoid the structure of a "total institution." Guided Group Interaction differs from group psychotherapy in that the group rather than the individual is the focus of treatment. Although some informal, individual psychotherapy may take place as a by-product, the program is not organized to treat presumed psychopathologies or explore in depth the psychodynamics of individuals.

By examination and discussion in evening meetings of events prior to, as well as during, the program, each individual is expected to locate his "problem." Problems are anything that brought the person to the group and continue to inhibit playing an effective and satisfying role in it. Through daily interaction with and help from others in all phases of the program, each person is charged with making progress in handling his problem and helping others with theirs. All the activities of each person are involved in the treatment process. What happens on the job, during meals, in leisure activity, while in the community, or during the course of informal interaction at any time are subjects for open discussion in the evening meetings. At the meetings, conceptions and attitudes that give rise to problems are challenged and analyzed. Alternatives and reasons for them are discussed and debated in sometimes heated exchange, where often for the first time, inner thoughts and feelings are expressed in a situation that links them to overt action. At the same time, the daily round of activities provides opportunity to test and practice insights and understandings acquired during the meetings.

Since each person is involved in seeking solutions to his own problems while helping others to solve theirs, all are involved in a collective therapeutic effort, and the group as a whole has responsibility for designing and carrying out its course of action. In the process, it is possible for the individual to be freed from group domination as he learns the dynamics of group interaction, as he is forced to recognize responsibility for his own behavior and its consequences for others, and as he is encouraged to develop confidence in self and respect for others. Each group develops a culture of its own, reflecting the characteristics of its members, the situation at the time, and the larger design of the program, which encourages innovation and flexibility in the absence of fixed, formal rules or regulations. The role of the staff is largely nondirective and consists of guiding the group toward self-sufficiency, through interpreting and questioning events and discussion in the meetings, assuring that the group confronts individual and collective difficulties, and maintaining a focus on striving for realistic solutions that involve respect for self and others.

Evaluative research involving comparison with alternative correctional programs was part of the original design of the group programs in New Jersey, Utah, Kentucky, and California. The results of this research generally have not indicated marked superiority of this technique with respect to recidivism. However, they have demonstrated that: youths will participate in a community-centered, noncustodial setting without danger to themselves or others; those who complete the program are more successful than those who do not; completers are more successful after release than comparable releasees from reformatories; the volume of prior offenses diminishes after release; and the program seems to be particularly adaptable to boys with longer histories of delinquency, black youths, and those from lower socioeconomic strata who are often considered to be poor risks in delinquency treatment.

# Multidisciplinary Group Therapy

## *I. H. Hart*

### DEFINITION

Multidisciplinary Group Therapy is a group therapy for acutely distressed "revolving-door" patients, conducted by a team of multidisciplinary facilitators under the guidance of a staff therapist. The multidisciplinary group was devised to meet the problem of revolving-door, in-hospital patients. The objective is to maximize stimulation, interest, and rapport by providing a wide variety of roles, models, and experiences with which patients might be induced to identify and interact.

## HISTORY

Multidisciplinary Group Therapy is an amalgam of crisis intervention group work, multi-therapist intervention, and interdisciplinary treatment team concepts. Emphasis on brief hospitalization has brought with it the phenomenon of the revolving-door patient, which presents a human tragedy demoralizing patients and staff. The typical revolving-door patient is a chronic psychotic who repeatedly returns to the hospital in a severe state of personality fragmentation. These patients have responded to repeated experiences of interpersonal upheaval and lack of success in community living with apathy, hallucinations, and overwhelming feelings of helplessness. Some patients are so frustrated by repeated experiences of failure that they are on the verge of exploding into some form of violent action.

## TECHNIQUE

The group contains patients of both sexes. Age and sex differences in the patient group have their equivalents in the therapist group, helping to mediate generation-gap and life-style differences. As patients and facilitators compare viewpoints and life experiences, there is opportunity for reality affirmation and correction of distortions. The facilitators primarily apply crisis-oriented problem-solving techniques. They try to get the patients to recapture the sequence of events that led to hospitalization, and get them to come to grips with what they are saying and doing and its influence on others. With help the patients are frequently able to reconstruct the behavior that culminated in their current hospitalization, and even gain some awareness of the roles they played in their predicament. A basic assumption is that for patients to recognize the relationship between their bizarre acts, between the neglect of their children, their household and themselves, and hospitalization, is an important step in breaking the cycle of rehospitalization. The multidisciplinary group also tries to have the patients gain awareness of their maladaptive attitudes and feelings, how these affected themselves and their relationships, and how they earned rejection. The major emphasis is on helping the patients to become more adaptive and to recognize the possibility and desirability of alternative and more effective problem solutions.

During the sessions, seating is arranged so that a member of the facilitator group is seated between every two patients. The interspersing of patients and facilitators makes it possible for the nearby facilitator to easily reach out to a highly anxious patient or to place a comforting arm around a sobbing patient. The regular staff therapist tends to become involved in pulling the various interactions together, in finding the common thread or theme, in keeping the discussion relevant to the group, and in preventing the fragmentation that results in patients' dissatisfaction and disgust. The staff leader may point out dynamics while keeping the focus on feelings and attempting to minimize the intellectualizations related to the cognitive aspects of problem solving. At the end of each session, the group leader summarizes the essence and meaning of what took place to reinforce the patients' attempts at understanding their interpersonal relationships. Immediately after each session, the leader and facilitators analyze what went on to gain consensus and understanding concerning the nature of the interactions, and to plan approaches for the next session.

## APPLICATIONS

It might be feared that a group of ten patients would tend to be overwhelmed by the presence of four facilitators and a leader. However, stimulation, not intimidation, appears to be the principal effect. Young male patients become responsive to the interest shown in them by the young female facilitators. The young female patients are piqued by the attentiveness of the young male facilitators. Patient mothers and facilitator mothers tend to compare experiences and viewpoints regarding the handling of difficult husbands, child-rearing problems, and family crises.

For the most part, patients are initially either confused or evasive about their difficulties, or defend themselves against fear of blame for their actions by denial. Typically they are preoccupied in the beginning with recollections of harsh and exploitative treatment by board-and-care home operators, the harassment of malicious neighbors, and unprovoked beatings by husbands.

The physical proximity of the members of the facilitator group to the members of the patient group encourages social relatedness. Private comments are readily picked up and brought out for general group discussion. The interspersing of the facilitators among the patients tends to control highly agitated and potentially assaultive patients. Frightening and destructive verbal fights can be quickly dampened by the facilitators' presence or intervention. In groups led by solitary therapists, there have been occasions when physical clashes have erupted, leaving both patients and therapists extremely upset, and sometimes irreparably damaging group morale. In the multidisciplinary group the several therapists can readily intervene and relieve an explosive situation and, if necessary, intercede to forestall a physical clash. Some of the revolving-door patients get into such a high state of tension and anxiety that they cannot tolerate remaining in the group. In such an instance, the solitary therapist is left to decide between allowing both the remaining group and the fleeing patient to remain disturbed, or going after the patient with the group feeling abandoned. In the multidisciplinary situation, one therapist brings the patient back to work through the anxiety or remains with the patient outside the group if necessary. The therapy group is freed enough from concern about the precipitous departure to permit it to carry on therapeutic work. Thus in the multidisciplinary group, disrupting upsets are reduced, group security enhanced, and feelings of mutual protectiveness are developed.

# Halfway House

*Harold L. Raush*

## DEFINITION

The psychiatric Halfway House is a residential facility specially designed to enable those persons who are or have been severely psychologically impaired to develop and maintain a life within a nonhospital community. As the term "halfway" suggests, emphasis is most often on the transitional functions of the Halfway House, on its "bridging the gap" between mental hospital and community.

## HISTORY

Although there were precursors to Halfway Houses and one currently active facility was founded as early as 1913, a formal definition of the Halfway House as a transitional facility between hospital and community did not appear before 1953. An American survey reported in 1960 found ten psychiatric Halfway Houses, seven of which had been founded since 1954. By 1963 some forty facilities in the United States were identified as Halfway Houses. A British report noted approximately the same number of Halfway Houses in England and Wales for that same year. By 1969 the number of houses in the United States had increased to about 130, and by 1973 there were over 200 psychiatric Halfway Houses. There have been parallel expansions in the development of Halfway Houses to serve other populations—alcoholics, mentally retarded, drug addicts, and ex-prisoners.

## TECHNIQUE

The Halfway House is *not* a form of therapy. It is a living arrangement designed to enhance living in and relating to the ordinary social community. The emphases are primarily rehabilitative—helping residents develop and maintain social relationships, manage tasks of daily living, get and hold jobs, and move toward independent living. Staffs are generally nonmedical, institutional-type rules are minimal, men and women usually are not segregated by group, the median population is small (estimates range from medians of fifteen to twenty), and architecture and atmosphere are homelike. Unlike the hospital, the Halfway House is *within* the community, most often a large house in an anonymous section of an urban community, close to public transportation and shopping. A few Halfway Houses have made use of large urban apartment houses that may include families and a few offer a rural farm setting with emphasis on communal living and communal self-support. Typically, residents participate in the care and maintenance of the house and in establishing house rules; very often, with some supervision, they manage house decorating, menu planning, shopping, and cooking. Costs, unlike that of hospitals, are comparable to the living costs of persons living independently.

Like work and recreational activities, therapy in most halfway-house settings takes place outside the house. Houses often have psychiatric or other professional consultants who serve as advisory resources for day-to-day live-in staff on problems such as medication, psychiatric emergencies, or simply daily management. There may or may not be arrangements for regular consultation between individual psychotherapists and house managers about the client-resident they share. Moreover, almost all Halfway Houses require attendance at weekly group meetings where issues of house functions and interpersonal problems within the house are discussed. Some houses view such meetings as therapy, but most are content to confine such "therapy" to the immediate problems of daily communal living.

Although the Halfway House is not a type of therapy, its aim toward enhancing residents' entry into the social community demands special sensitivities and skills on the part of operational managing staff. Staff must develop techniques for motivating residents toward developing and sustaining vocational and social relations with the outside world. The administrative structure of the house and its routines must be designed to further residents' socialization. Engagement in ordinary household tasks must be recognized as providing opportunities not only for learning task skills but for developing interpersonal exchange and social intimacy. Staff-resident interactions can serve to enhance residents' capabilities to manage critical events and to promote a capacity for reality-oriented self-determination and growth. Unlike the hospital situation, opportunities to engage in and test multiple roles are fostered. However, when staff members lack the aims, sensitivities, or skills required to enrich the living experiences of residents and to further integration into the community, the Halfway House degenerates to a boardinghouse offering low-quality custodial care.

## APPLICATIONS

As noted, the most common conception of the Halfway House is as a transitional bridge between hospital and community. Close to 90 percent of residents have been hospitalized previously and about 75 percent come to the Halfway House directly from a mental hospital. Most residents are in the Halfway House for less than a year (summary data on median length of stay range from five to twelve months), and most residents re-enter the community on leaving the Halfway House. Some 15 to 20 percent return to a hospital from a Halfway House, a rate that compares very favorably with reported results on hospital readmittance for ex-patients.

The fact that as many as 10 percent of residents have no prior history of hospitalization suggests that for some the Halfway House may serve a preventive function and as an alternative to hospitalization. At the opposite pole from the resident for whom the Halfway House can serve as a temporary protective "moratorium" setting is the resident—most often a long-term hospital patient—for whom the Halfway House tends to become a permanent home. Although most houses avoid such "hard-core," chronic clientele, there is increasing awareness of a need for residential settings that can serve an "in-between" rather than transitional function. Current programs to eliminate mental hospitals or to reduce hospital populations by discharging patients into the community accent the need for "quarter-way" houses or community care facilities. Ideally, such institutions can provide relatively permanent care in a protective setting, with richer personal and social life than is possible in a hospital. Ideally, too, hospitals can then serve their more legitimate functions of emergency care and treatment and avoid the debilitating problems of the large-scale custodial institution. The dangers are that financial, personnel, and social support resources for such community-care residences are apt to be underestimated, with a resulting proliferation of so-called Halfway Houses that are nothing more than small-scale custodial institutions.

Whether or not Halfway Houses succeed wholly in effecting the entry of their residents into full-scale independence in the community, what they have to offer may be valued for itself. A comfortable setting, a supportive social community, work that contributes to social and personal life are in themselves worthwhile. To the extent that the Halfway House provides these, whether for a few days or for the remainder of a lifetime, it meets human needs and succeeds in its humane functions.

# Holistic Counseling

*William B. Woodson*

### DEFINITION

Holistic Counseling, a comprehensive approach to mental health, allows the total person to develop—mind, body, and spirit. It is based on the fundamental understanding that any effort to achieve mental health must include attention to physical well-being. A sound mind in a healthy body is the optimal human condition.

Holistic Counseling is directly concerned with "wellness," not with sickness. Unlike psychotherapy, which is designed to remove symptoms of mental illness, Holistic Counseling, using practical techniques, provides a way that people can obtain and integrate physical, mental, emotional, and spiritual health. The objective of Holistic Counseling is total "wellness."

The role of the holistic counselor is to clarify and educate the total person. In the "clarification" process, the counselor helps clients obtain perspective about their behavior, particularly as it relates to their immediate dilemmas. When clients comprehend that their activities are manifestations of the universal laws of human behavior, confusion and uncertainty disappear, courses of action become apparent, and, in the long run, consciousness becomes clarified.

The counselor teaches clients how to cleanse their bodies and minds, balance their emotions, and gain more energy. Toxins reside in the body as a result of improper or incomplete food processing. Mental "toxins" (unhealthy emotions or behaviors) result from improper or incomplete emotional processing. The holistic counselor teaches effective ways of eliminating both.

Preoccupation or obsession with a single problem limits our effectiveness and ability to function. Often, the individual's behavior becomes limited to painfully few emotional responses. He feels "out of control," uncomfortable in life, or just plain "unwell." With the holistic counselor, clients learn how to gain more control over their emotions and attain a healthier balance.

When we can simultaneously release previously restricted energy, experience inner calm, and remain alert, we have made significant strides toward self-realization. The holistic counselor assists clients make such gains.

Clients facilitate their own progress by taking responsibility (not blame) for their health. To ensure success, they practice exercises and carry out agreed-upon routines between sessions. The new techniques become an integral part of their lives.

### HISTORY

Holistic Counseling began evolving in 1975 when, after three years of full-time study at Arica Institute, I (Bill Woodson) began to introduce Arica practices into the more traditional approach to counseling and psychotherapy I had been using. At first I added relaxation techniques, physical conditioning, and Chua K'a (a system of muscle tension release) to a form of counseling that emphasized clarification and cleansing of both mind and emotions. Later the sessions were expanded to include meditation, visualization, nutrition, and techniques drawn from disciplines other than Arica. From its inception in 1975, however, the underpinnings of Holistic Counseling have been firmly rooted in the theory of human development set forth by Oscar Ichazo (1976).

One important aspect of the theory is that the healthy or "natural-ego" emerges when our instinct for self-preservation, social relations, and harmony with the world are in balance and are satisfied. When this natural ego is the principal actor, the whole self knows (understands and intuits) that: 1) there are natural laws that determine our behavior, 2) there is an equilibrium for the psyche that must be sustained if we are to maintain optimal health, 3) in the normal course of living, we experience psychic pain that we compensate for in specific ways, and 4) there are discrete levels of consciousness that human beings experience and move through. As Ichazo states, everyone has an internal drive to achieve the natural-ego, and the process can be accelerated. Introducing expanded consciousness techniques into the counseling process is one way of accomplishing this.

In 1977, I began working at the Center for the Healing Arts in New York City in collaboration with other mental health and health professionals familiar with the Arica system and have continued to develop the concept of Holistic Counseling.

## TECHNIQUES

Currently, there are six groups of techniques used in Holistic Counseling: 1) clarification processes, 2) Chua K'a, 3) exercise, 4) relaxation, 5) meditation, and 6) nutrition. The six work together to help clients cleanse, energize, and balance themselves.

1. *Clarification processes.* These help clients understand the effects of their assumptions (or mental structures), unresolved emotional conflicts, and their expectations. Interventions are based on Ichazo's theory of human development. By clearly isolating and examining their belief systems, clients begin to see patterns of behavior and the effects these patterns have on their lives.

Psychic cleansing, one of the dimensions of the clarification process, is accomplished by showing clients how to release distress associated with past traumatic events. In many cases, the trauma has been so intense that the client retains only a vague, murky recollection of the incident and has a strong aversion to recalling any of the details. The cleansing process helps the client trigger clearer memories. It is similar to reviewing a movie rerun of an incident that was uncomfortable and confusing when first experienced but became comprehensible and even amusing when viewed with detachment and objectivity. The "rerun" is introduced verbally by the client with the counselor giving technical advice on ways of getting clarity. The catharsis occurs when the client locates the point of impact where distress was first experienced and is able to identify the fears and belief structures crystallized in that moment.

The client, guided by the counselor, learns to defuse the highly charged emotions associated with the original trauma. The result is the ability to recall the incident with detachment and objectivity.

Another aspect of the clarification process is providing clients with information about the "maps of consciousness" set forth by Ichazo. A number of charts or templates for measuring the territory of the psyche are communicated when relevant. The ones most commonly used are: the "levels of subjectivity," the systems of the body, the "domains of consciousness," the personality types or "fixations," and the "doors Of compensation"—ways we attempt to alleviate pain. With this additional information, clients become able to begin seeing their behavior in greater perspective, increasing their understanding of their behavior and allowing change to occur.

2. *Chua K'a, muscle tension release.* Many therapies either implicitly or explicitly accept a mind-body dualism. In Holistic Counseling, the mind and the body are viewed as one. If the physical body is constricted, inelastic, or imbalanced, so is the mind. "When we liberate the tensions in our body, we also liberate psychic tensions, because every group of muscular cells is connected to our brain." (Ichazo, 1976b) Chua K'a is the basic form of muscle-tension release used in Holistic Counseling. Its function is to release tension stored in the body, to cleanse the body of toxins, and to restore maximum flexibility of thought as well as of action. After pressure is applied along the bones, more vitality is experienced within the body, muscles and tendons return to their proper positions, and the body/mind becomes an effective, healthy instrument for perceiving and responding to the world.

3. *Exercise.* This is important because the body must be kept in good physical condition if it is to be psychologically healthy. Holistic Counseling emphasizes use of such activities as Psychocalisthenics, Hatha Yoga and T'ai Chi Chuan. All of these exercise forms increase the flexibility and elasticity of the body, restore and maintain the balance of body and psyche, increase the flow of vital energy, and elicit a sense of inner calm.

4.*Relaxation.* Even though the above exercises condition and relax the body, there are others that are taught because their primary benefit is relaxation. Included in this group are breathing and deep relaxation exercises. Many Americans, unfamiliar with these simple, effective methods of relaxing and regenerating, benefit greatly from this instruction.

5. *Meditation.* Three different types of meditation are used to activate the healing energies within the body: a) meditations with repeated words or phrases (mantra) are used to quiet the constant useless chatter in the head; b) meditations with precise body positions are used to make the body receptive to positive emotions; and c) meditations with visualization and visual symbols awaken the body's natural healing energies. These meditations are selectively taught and assigned to complement the work in the sessions.

6. *Nutrition.* The idea that the food we eat is a primary source of energy upon which our physical and mental wellness depends is gaining wide acceptance. However, most people know little about the real benefits of certain foods and the dangers of the chemical/commercial food production and preparation processes. The holistic counselor devotes attention to such areas as the significance of food selection, preparation and combining, as well as to food additives, preservatives, supplements, and to the importance of the periodic cleansing diets or fasts.

## APPLICATIONS

Holistic Counseling has application in individual and group work with adults and adolescents who are facing difficult and stressful life situations. It may be used with equal effectiveness for couples, families, and groups of adults or adolescents who have similar conflicts or concerns.

It has also been beneficial for persons suffering from psychophysiological disorders, such as hypertension, arthritis, and colitis as well as with post- and pre-heart attack patients who have been prepared to adopt a definitive program of stress reduction. Business and professional persons experiencing situational depressions, those experiencing tension headaches or extreme body tensions have also found relief and obtained insights for more satisfying living. Businessmen and women experiencing anxiety or indecision about career choices, as well as those in the throes of mid-life crises, have gained assistance from Holistic Counseling. Couples who have found their relationship in difficulty or on the verge of failure have found ways of resolving their situations.

Up to the present, this nontraditional approach has been used only in private practice. With the appropriate facilities and supportive environment, however, the approach can be equally effective in corporate and educational settings.

# Horneyian Therapy
## *Morton B. Cantor*

### DEFINITION
Karen Horney saw her technique and theory of psychoanalysis as falling within the framework of Freudian psychoanalysis, not as constituting an entirely new system. She wanted psychoanalysis to outgrow the limitations she felt were originally based on mechanistic, reductionistic, and genetic thinking.

Horney's approach was holistic, looking at man in all aspects of his being—how he behaved in sickness and in health, his physical and psychological processes as a social and spiritual being (interpersonal and intrapsychic), in work and in leisure, as an individual and with others as part of the cosmos. She saw individual and environment mutually influenced by and influencing, extending into each other and only arbitrarily separable. Curative forces being as inherent in the mind as they are in the body, the therapist's task was to give a helping hand toward removing the harmful forces and supporting the healing ones (Horney, 1950).

This process involves the therapist becoming an active and aware participant in a cooperative venture that is also a learning process. The ultimate objective is to aid the patient to more effectively utilize living experiences without professional help, but it is questionable whether this is possible without the therapist growing in the process as well.

### HISTORY
Horney's primary interest was not in formulating a theory of personality functioning and organization but in therapy. Her theory was derived out of delineating the neurotic process through therapy. Horney's dissatisfaction with her therapeutic results as a

classical Freudian led to a series of papers and books beginning in 1917, which enlarged on concepts of resistance, and challenged orthodox views of feminine psychology and the death instinct. By 1924 she was focusing on neurotic trends and character structure. In 1937 this culminated in her first book that also emphasized the role of cultural factors, basic anxiety, and the importance of the actual life situation of the patient. Her next book in 1939 was a critique of Freudian theory following her twenty-five years of experience with it. While separating out what she felt was debatable (libido theory, primacy of pleasure principle, fixation and repetition compulsion, penis envy, the goal of gaining mastery over instincts), she delineated what she felt were the most fundamental contributions to psychoanalysis.

These included psychic determinism, the role of the unconscious and free association, repression, the meaningfulness of dreams, that neuroses are the result of conflict in which anxiety plays a central role, and that childhood experiences play a crucial role in neurotic development. Of all Freud's discoveries, Horney valued most highly that one can utilize for therapy the patient's emotional reactions to the analyst, which include his symbolic experiences of early childhood figures; but she went beyond orthodox concepts of transference to also include all the patient's more recent interpersonal and intrapsychic experiences. In similarly extending the original concepts of counter-transference, she emphasized the personal equation of the analyst as a real as well as a symbolic person.

This was extended by her foremost colleague, Harold Kelman, who wrote extensively on the analyst as instrument, communing and relating, psychoanalysis as process, and the symbolizing process. (Kelman, 1971). He and his colleagues extended Horney's budding interest in phenomenology, existentialism, Zen Buddhism, Krishnamurti, and general systems theory to add further dimensions for exploration in working with patients.

## TECHNIQUE

Horney emphasized, as did many others, that there can be no one special technique since each patient and therapist is unique in what they start with, in their interacting and constant evolving. Because therapy was seen as a uniquely human cooperative venture, anything that suggested dogma or rules—rigid techniques that could lead to dehumanization—was contrary to the spirit of her theory, philosophy, and goals in therapy.

One might begin helping the patient with a particular problem regarding his work or social relationships, or the specific symptoms that brought him into therapy, or to allay his overwhelming anxiety, or to focus on helping him feel more integrated when he feels he is falling apart. Or the analyst may focus on building a trusting, mutually respectful relationship. Although the latter is not only humanly required but also an essential precondition for all psychotherapeutic work; with some patients (e.g., borderline patients) this may be the *only* initial objective for quite some time.

The therapist begins with the patient's present emotional state, with more specific objectives shifting in a process of constant diagnosing and prognosing, measuring and sensing the patient's motivation and ability to move forward. This means helping the patient identify on an experiential level his neurotic character structure, the complexities of his defensive mechanisms and underlying psychodynamic conflicts as well as his talents, capacities, and assets, including his dreams, which have evidenced themselves in his past and present life. How much a therapist can accomplish depends on the patient's ability to "let go" of some of his externalizing, his rigid self-idealizing, and his self-hate.

Horney was most emphatic in seeing the initial interview as pregnant with therapeutic possibilities beyond what is conveyed between two strangers who are becoming acquainted for the purpose of working together. The therapist indicates a hopeful attitude, which encourages more opening up, by conveying that he is interested in the patient nonjudgmentally and is not shocked or frightened by his pathology. In suggesting possible connections between the past and various aspects in his present life, the therapist is aiding the patient to dispel an attitude of mystery and helplessness about his condition by implying that these things have meanings, can be understood, and therefore changed. Practical arrangements include the number and times of sessions, the fee and how it is to be paid, cancelled and missed hours and instructions regarding free associations, dreams and the use of the couch. The central issue here is that the session be considered as supplying analytic as well as "practical" material, to be freely discussed at a time when it can be used most productively to maintain the forward momentum of the analytic process with an attitude of flexibility and mutual respect for the life practicalities, thinking and feelings of both patient and analyst (see Cantor, 1957).

"Working through" includes questioning, underlining, clarifying, eliciting, and encouraging extended or new communication, as well as general help by the analyst. The analyst tries to help the patient to become more aware of all the manifestations of his attempted solutions and conflicts and how they evolved from early childhood, to recognize the compulsive nature of all these elements, to appreciate the subjective value of his defense mechanisms, and to feel the adverse consequences of his situation. Only then can he experience what has been involved in his self-idealization, how trapped he has been in vicious circles, and how detrimental all this has been to his growth and happiness. His incentive for changing must be powerful enough to overcome the drive to maintain the status quo and outweigh the retarding forces of the neurotic process (see Cantor, 1967).

The notion of total "cure" is impossible in holistic process terms since self-realization can never be complete. Indications suggesting interruption of therapy, which is a mutual recognition and decision, include seeing how much progress the patient has made in terms of his experiencing himself as a more authentic person: that is, one who is more capable of taking responsibility for his own actions, becoming more genuine with other people, and respecting them as people apart from his own needs, which also includes the analyst ("resolving the transference"). The patient also begins to recognize how much analytic work he has been able to do without his analyst's help and will welcome the opportunity to continue on his own, aided with the knowledge that should he need help in the future, his analyst will still be available.

## APPLICATIONS

Horney used the term "neurotic" in a general sense, not distinguishing in theory between neurosis, character disorder, borderline states, and schizophrenia. Her technique has been applied to all these diagnostic entities because the underlying psychodynamics have been felt to be similar. Different emphases are based on individual personality configurations, and according to which stage of development and life experience the onset and depth of pathology occurred. Variations in technique follow from the above variations; the patient's degree of self-hate, the intensity of his need, and ability to relate and trust determine the tempo, rhythm, and length of therapy, and the order of focus and goals. Horney's theory and technique have proved valuable as bases for understanding and communication in crisis intervention, group and family therapy, and counseling.

# Horticultural Therapy
## Paula Diane Relf

### DEFINITION
Horticultural Therapy is the utilization of a more or less structured series of contacts between a trained therapist and a client; the therapist, employing the media of horticulture, tries to produce certain beneficial changes in the client's emotional state, attitudes, and behavior. The therapeutic influence is primarily exerted by words, acts, and rituals within the horticultural milieu, in which the client and therapist and group (if there is one) participate jointly.

### HISTORY
Gardening has long been advocated for its beneficial effects on mentally ill individuals. Dr. Benjamin Rush noted in 1812 that "digging in the garden" was one of the activities that often led to recovery of patients in the mental hospitals. From the time Friends Asylum for the Insane opened in Philadelphia in 1817, patients have been involved in vegetable gardens and fruit production. Pontiac State Hospital, opened in 1878, made extensive use of agriculture. However, in the early stages of the program, as with many others, the goal was production and any therapy was a fortunate by-product.

The idea of gardening as a kind of labor beneficial to patients was given support by Dr. Thomas Kirkbride, founder of the American Psychiatric Association. He wrote in *Hospitals for the Insane*, published in Philadelphia in 1880, that vegetable gardens "will be found [to be] the very best dependence for outdoor labor for the patients."

During the latter part of the 1800s, horticulture gained recognition as being of value to ease the stressful lives of the urban poor and as an aid in teaching retarded individuals.

The early 1900s brought significant changes in the utilization of horticulture in patient treatment. In 1919, Dr. C. F. Menninger and his son, Karl, established the Menninger Foundation in Topeka, Kansas. From the start, plants, gardening, and nature study were integral parts of the patients' activities. Between 1920 and 1940 almost all Occupational Therapy books mentioned gardening as an adjunctive program.

After World War II, the use of horticulture as a therapeutic tool had a significant increase in veterans' hospitals as part of the treatment of returning GI's. Professional occupational therapists were joined by thousands of volunteer garden club members to bring flowers and horticultural activities to the hospitals. This wide use of horticulture as an adjunctive therapy set the stage for the development of Horticultural Therapy as a profession.

In the late 1940s and early 1950s, perceptive proponents working individually throughout the country acted as the catalyst to create the profession. Rhea McCandless at the Menninger Foundation and Alice Burlingame in Michigan were two of the prime forces in this early development. In 1959, the New York Institute of Rehabilitation Medicine Center, under the direction of Dr. Howard Rusk, added a Horticultural Therapy greenhouse.

An important step in the evolution of the idea of Horticultural Therapy—from that of simple outdoor work to a fairly well-defined concept of the behavioral benefits of gardening and related activities—was made with the establishment of a cooperative program between the Menninger Foundation and Kansas State University to train students for degrees in Horticultural Therapy. In 1973 Clemson University offered a graduate degree in Horticultural Therapy. In that same year a national professional organization was formed under the auspices of Melwood Horticultural Training Center, a vocational school for the mentally retarded in Upper Marlboro, Maryland. Today the National Council for Therapy and Rehabilitation Through Horticulture has approximately eight hundred members throughout the United States and several foreign countries.

At a conference by the Department of Health, Education and Welfare on new and emerging careers, held in Washington, D.C., in the spring of 1976, Horticultural Therapy was recognized as one of the top ten most significant new careers in the United States today.

## TECHNIQUE

A Horticultural Therapy program may use a variety of activities and settings to accomplish its aims. Many of the programs are conducted out-of-doors, but outdoor space is not a prerequisite for a successful Horticultural Therapy program.

The types of horticultural activities that have been used successfully in therapy and rehabilitation programs include: vegetable gardens, greenhouse projects, lawn and ornamental plant care, commercial production of various crops, indoor gardening with or without lights, flower arranging, nature crafts, as well as many other plant-related projects.

Depending on the goals of a specific program, the plants, garden services, or other horticultural products may be sold for a fee, given to worthy causes, or utilized by the participants in the program. Through sales of services and products, some programs are able to generate sufficient income to be partially self-supporting.

The specific goals of a Horticultural Therapy program may differ distinctly from one institution to another and from one population of handicapped individuals to another. However, the ultimate goal of these programs is the improved physical and mental health of the individual. The benefits may be seen in four areas: intellectual, social, emotional, and physical development.

The projects or activities may be conducted on an individual, one-to-one basis or with groups. However, a small group of approximately five individuals seems to predominate in most programs. The activities may be so geared as to bring about interaction between client and therapist, between members of the group, or between clients and nonclients, as in programs where mentally retarded patients sell plants they have grown to the general public.

## APPLICATIONS

Horticulture has been used effectively as a part of the therapeutic program with a diverse population of individuals. Among the facilities utilizing Horticultural Therapy are: old-age and nursing homes, schools and homes for the retarded, institutions for the mentally ill and emotionally disturbed, correctional and rehabilitative institutions for youthful and adult offenders, schools and homes for the physically handicapped and sensory impaired, private and public hospitals for the chronically and acutely ill, Veterans Administration hospitals, community centers for inner city residents, centers for alcohol and drug abusers, halfway houses, and schools for the blind and the hearing impaired.

Programs now exist in each type of institution, both public and private, large and small. Most of them are supported in varying degrees by state and federal funds. Some programs are considered primarily vocational rehabilitation, and their ultimate goal is placement of the client in a job. However, the majority have as their primary goal the change in attitudes and behavior of the client.

---

# Hotline

*Gail Bleach*

## DEFINITION

Since their inception in 1968, Hotlines have continued to grow in number and in the conceptual clarity of their functions and goals. Hotlines are emergency telephone services for individuals in crisis that provide a listening ear and, when necessary, referral to agencies and professional back-up. Their purpose is to aid the caller with his immediate crisis and with future crises as well by mobilizing his problem-solving skills. Listening, understanding, and providing support are important parts of this process. Established by hospitals, mental health associations, colleges, and others, Hotline services typically share the following characteristics: 1) they operate during weekend and evening hours when traditional helping agencies are closed, 2) they are staffed by nonprofessional or paraprofessional workers, 3) they accept calls from anyone in the community and on any topic the caller presents, and 4) they offer advice, information, and referral services.

## HISTORY

The history of Hotlines is brief, as the oldest Hotlines are barely a decade old. One of the first Hotlines grew out of the Los Angeles Suicide Prevention Center. In response to troubled individuals who called with a wide range of social and emotional problems, the center broadened its concept to include dealing with any concerns—from loneliness to pregnancy to drug use—the caller presented. Hotlines sprang up rapidly all over the United States. Some were funded through governmental and private agencies; others developed on shoestring budgets, considering themselves part of the counterculture and refusing both dollars and intervention from mental health professionals. Presently, Hotlines seem destined to continue to exist in the community and to become more integrated into the traditional mental health picture.

## TECHNIQUE

Hotline services are best understood within the crisis intervention model advocated by Gerald Caplan (1961). According to Caplan, a crisis occurs when a person faces an obstacle to important life goals that appears insurmountable through the utilization of his customary problem-solving methods. A period of disorganization ensues during which the individual makes many abortive attempts at solution until eventually some kind of adaptation is achieved. Crisis intervention is the set of activities designed to influence the course of crisis so that the more adaptive outcome, the one in the best interests of the troubled person, is chosen. Favorable resolution of the current crisis should strengthen coping mechanisms so that the person will be better able to deal with future crisis as well.

Using crisis intervention theory as a general basis, Hotlines attempt to provide or guide an individual to the amount and kind of support necessary for successful resolution of his crisis. Specific intervention techniques have been outlined by Rapoport (1962). The crisis worker should: 1) clarify the problem that led to the call for help, 2) indicate explicit acceptance of the disordered affect (emotions, mood), irrational attitudes, and negative responses, 3) use interpersonal and institutional resources to provide support and mobilize energy for reaching out to others, and 4) recognize that the worker is not the sole available resource. Rapoport also lists four broad principles that a worker can employ after he understands and indicates acceptance of a problem: 1) keep an explicit focus on the crisis, 2) help with cognitive mastery, 3) offer basic information and education, and 4) create a bridge to other community resources. Rapoport's first list speaks generally to giving emotional support and counseling to an individual while her second list deals with acquainting him with information. These two functions (counseling and information giving) are the core of the Hotline services offered to those in crisis.

In comparison to other therapies, which are traditionally conducted face-to-face, Hotlines are uniquely suited to reach individuals in crisis. Hotlines can be contacted over the telephone and without a wait for an appointment; they can also be reached on weekends and evenings, periods when most helping agencies are unavailable. Besides ease of accessibility, Hotlines differ from other therapeutic techniques in that they preserve the anonymity of their clients, which is especially attractive to the adolescent population, and they provide the client with a large amount of control over the process—he can hang up whenever he chooses.

## APPLICATIONS

The primary function of Hotlines is to provide services to those individuals who would not otherwise come to the attention of mental health workers. Hotlines are not a substitute for traditional face-to-face therapy but hopefully an entry point into the mental health delivery network. A typical Hotline caller is an adolescent who is lonely or depressed or who is having difficulty getting along with family or friends and who would not walk into an unfamiliar community agency for counseling.

Questions have been raised about the effectiveness of Hotline services and attempts have been made to evaluate Hotline workers (Tanley, 1972; Belanger, 1973). Studies have not been done, however, because of difficulties in obtaining caller samples, Hotline cooperation, and sensitive measuring instruments.

The rapid proliferation of Hotlines and the large volume of calls received suggest that Hotlines are meeting community needs. In addition, the relatively low cost of operation and the benefits to the Hotline workers themselves appear to justify continued research and development of crisis intervention telephone services.

# Hypnointrospection

*Seymour Halpern*

## DEFINITION

Hypnointrospection is a quasi-hypnotic method of psychotherapy which is based on Freudian psychology. It comprises a twofold approach to healing: 1) the reduction of stress and 2) the resolution of psychic conflict. It is organized around the notion of the dialogue. The patient is encouraged to explore his subjective states (intentions or wishes, thoughts, images and feelings or sensations) in terms of body image and self-concept, which are bio-cultural categories of thought referring to the way in which a person experiences and interprets himself. These experiences constitute the raw material of the dialogue.

Subjective states are psychic correlates of physiological events and processes. These states are decoded and regulated during disciplined attention involving the selective inhibition of movement. Such activities reveal an autonomous consciousness that we designate as self.

Hypnointrospection seeks to correct or mitigate the disturbances or disorders in the information-processing (metabolic) activities of the organism, which are construed as essentially semiotic. Healing is deemed inseparable from knowing, which itself is a bio-semiotic process in which physiological events are progressively revealed to the knower in various psychic forms. The negation of knowing in its multifarious actions tends to obstruct growth and health.

Hypnointrospection comprises both a verbal and perceptual means of healing: analytic in terms of therapeutic conversation and meditative in terms of disciplined attention during the selective inhibition of movement. As a distinctive therapeutic modality,

Hypnointrospection inaugurates the completion of self-control through the extension of volition mediated through visceral-somatic structures.

## HISTORY

In the 1950s, there was a renewal of interest in the problems of consciousness. This climate fostered the revival of hypnosis and introspection. My interest in hypnosis as a tool for the investigation of subjective states led me to explore its therapeutic potential for the treatment of schizophrenic patients. These patients are generally resistant to hypnotic induction. An analysis of this resistance culminated in the method of Hypnointrospection.

I discovered that the repetitive practice of voluntary immobilization lowered repressive barriers and released psychic energies in even severely regressed patients. These observations made it plain that repressions are manifested in postural states and neuromuscular functions, i.e., "attitude"; action and thought are.revealed in predispositions or habitual response patterns. Conflicts as emotions are expressed as attitudes. Conflicts (knowing vs. unknowing) are sustained through their visceral-somatic connections.

These investigations persuaded me that the theorem of regulation of visceral functions through an "autonomic nervous system" was fallacious. Visceral functions are inextricably involved with somatic activities, a point of view that is now thoroughly established. The freedom of locomotion, thinking, and feeling are indivisible. We think, act, and feel with the totality of our being. What began as an interview technique evolved into a therapeutic dialogue.

## TECHNIQUE

Upon entering the consultation room, the patient is invited to sit down and encouraged to express his thoughts and feelings. This allows for the release of information that may be reformulated as questions whose answers will lead to a sense of ease. The therapist, while listening to these complaints, seeks to find the implicit theme, the question that the patient is trying to pose. Patients characteristically are incapable of acting effectively because they are incapable of putting the proper questions to themselves. One cannot make a decision on the basis of ambiguous thoughts and misperceptions. The inability to decide paralyzes action and renders the patient restless and anxious. So, initially, contact with the patient is to put him at ease and to assist in the formulation of meaningful questions.

The second phase begins when the patient is asked to lie down and assume a comfortable recumbent posture. This posture, which calls for a fully extended supine attitude with arms at the side and neck extended, permits the patient to become aware of his bodily tensions. He is asked to close his eyes, to relax, not to move, and to monitor the totality of subjective events that constitute his stream of consciousness. In effect, he is assuming an attitude of critical reflection and reports the sequence of events intermittently. He is asked not to interpret. In this phase of therapy, designated inner dialogue, the patient is afforded the opportunity of extending his conscious self through the reduction of residual tensions. He is relaxing his muscles and sustaining the flow of information through the corrective action of selective inhibition.

Voluntary immobilization as practiced in the inner dialogue must not be confused with a self-imposed rigidity, progressive relaxation, or auto-hypnosis. The patient as observer seeks to maintain an attitude of vigilance. In this attitude of vigilance, attention is an essential precondition for the integration of memories. It is through the neurophysiological channel of attention that the information derived from the operation of nerve and muscle is amenable to integration by the higher centers of the brain. The posture of hypnointrospection thus contributes to psychophysical harmony.

Selective inhibition serves to release information ordinarily held in abeyance by bodily tensions and therefore restrained from entering consciousness; repressions are attenuated during the inner dialogue. Attention to the release of repressed information mitigates its impact on the observer, thus permitting him to bring under control and maintain in check tendencies that have formerly been or are fearsome, troublesome, and provocative of guilt. When the flow of information has subsided or the effects of immobilization have made the patient uncomfortable, he is asked to sit up and the verbal phase of therapy, the outer dialogue, begins.

In the outer dialogue the material elicited during the Hypnointrospection is further analyzed. Having taken the first step in the enlargement of his own awareness through selective attention to the contents of consciousness, the patient's second step in the expansion of self-understanding is taken conjointly with the therapist. The role of the therapist in the outer dialogue is to assist in the clarification of the material. The social experience in the outer dialogue serves to provide the patient with a meaningful exchange in which feelings of fear and loneliness may be overcome through trust and mutuality. A further consequence of the outer dialogue is the reduction of apprehension engendered in the procedure of immobilization. By interpreting these bodily experiences the patient is prevented from terminating the interview in a state of excessive excitation or confusion. The evaluation of experiences during the outer dialogue further serves to clarify his understanding of the nature of the interrelations among conflict, emotion, and attitude. The patient leaves with something significant to ponder—an issue that seems to characterize the direction of his growth at that point.

## APPLICATIONS

The release of inhibitions or repressions, allowing for a rehabilitation of personality, renders this approach eminently suitable for children whose growth allows the ready incorporation of cognitive and perceptual-motor changes. With the severely disturbed child it becomes necessary to involve the parent, as required by the therapeutic regime. For the normal child, Hypnointrospection as part of physical education serves to enhance normal cognition and promote mental hygiene. The perceptual (nonverbal) aspect of Hypnointrospection is beneficial across a broad range of disorders characterized by meager language facility.

In research and training, it lends itself to correlations of a psychophysiological nature in which the symbolic is connected to the somatic, thus rendering it suitable for psychosomatic studies and treatment.

By virtue of the radical modifications of the excitation-inhibition mechanisms of the nervous system, Hypnointrospection must be used with caution and discretion. It is generally inapplicable in all those conditions that are characterized by stubborn resistance to interpersonal relationships.

# Hypnosymbolic Psychotherapy

## C. Scott Moss

### DEFINITION

Hypnosymbolic Psychotherapy is a method that uses hypnosis to guide the client to interpret his own highly charged affective symbolic materials (his own fantasies and nocturnal dreams) as an aid and facilitant to effective treatment.

### HISTORY

When Freud published the *Interpretation of Dreams* (1900), he regarded dreams as being "the royal road to the unconscious." In a later foreword he wrote, "Insight such as this falls to one's lot but once in a lifetime." At the same time he lamented that the only experimental evidence produced thus far was by a physician, Schroetter (1911), who used hypnosis as a technique in the investigation of dreams. Schroetter was later joined by two other Viennese physicians, Roffenstein (1924) and Nachmansohn (1925), using the same technique to explore the function of dream distortions to preserve sleep. These first imaginative studies were not actively pursued until the later works by Erickson and Kubie, Farber and Fisher, and still later by Wolberg, Watkins, Schneck, Saradote and others.

Hypnosymbolic Therapy grew out of my effort to integrate all such studies into a concise, intensive, time-limited psychotherapy that makes use of hypnosis as a means of at first reducing and then eventually eliminating the therapist's projections from dream interpretation. The second contribution was the attempt to further objectify dreams (and their analysis) through relating them to Charles E. Osgood's Mediation Theory of Learning and using his semantic differential technique to measure dream symbolism. (My orientation throughout was fundamentally that of a researcher into the quantitative measurements of unconscious meaning; only secondarily as a direct intervention to clients. Fortunately both goals seemed obtainable.)

### TECHNIQUE

The therapist is *directive* in structuring the situation initially and training the person in hypnosis; he must then become *highly nondirective* in either attempting to produce the content or in the interpretation of the dreams themselves; and he becomes once more *fairly directive* in the final effort to integrate the translation of the symbols back into the client's conflicted life pattern.

The therapist can make use of this method either when resistances display themselves in the conduct of regular psychotherapy or, better yet, if the client seems disposed to utilize symbolic material to speak of things he is not yet ready to commit to conventional language or even to think of in the usual waking manner.

A cardinal point in Hypnosymbolic treatment is that in dealing with a person's dreams, the therapist is dealing with content that contains a very high degree of emotional imagery. There is no such thing as a neutral symbol—they are highly charged with affective (emotional) meaning. Dealing with dreams under hypnosis brings these feelings alive again and, if handled correctly, Hypnosymbolism provides a corrective emotional experience.

Whereas psychoanalysts value dreams as providing access to infantile sources of conflict, the Hypnosymbolic technique instead deals primarily with the immediate meaning of each dream element; that is, how it relates to the here-and-now of current problem situations.

Finally, once the therapist knows what the symptoms represent, he is then in a position to employ in fantasy or real life what behavior therapists call "reinforcement principles" to remedy the underlying pathology.

## APPLICATIONS

As stated, this method is an intensive, time-limited, crisis-oriented type of psychotherapy. The total involvement is, typically, a dozen sessions or so. If the client does not possess the ability to produce and to translate his dreams under hypnosis, then some other method of dealing with his primary problems should be used, such as Gestalt dream analysis or various behavioral interventions such as desensitization.

On the basis of twenty-five years of experience, it is estimated that one out of four clients would benefit from this time-saving method.

The basic premise underlying this crisis intervention approach is that successful resolution of even one major immediate problem can lead to an enhancement of the client's psychological equilibrium. This is a method used on typical neurotics; it has not been used extensively with psychotics, although exploration recently began with character disorders, i.e., adult male inmates.

# Hypnotherapy

*Lee* G. *Wilkins*

## DEFINITION

There are as many definitions of hypnosis as there are practitioners, yet no adequate theory of hypnosis is available today. Nonetheless, most would agree at this time that it is a mechanism that effectively lifts repressions, uncovers memories, encourages abreactions (the reexperiencing of a previous emotional event) and dreaming (in terms of affective experiencing), and enhances both motivation and a working alliance. It is also effective in activating a rapid transference reaction.

For the purposes of this article hypnosis will be defined as a normal psychophysiological phenomenon we all experience in varying degrees every day of our lives. This phenomenon can be deepened by an intense focusing of attention upon a specific inner or outer stimulus with a consequent blurring or blotting out of peripheral stimuli. It can be likened to tunnel vision with hypnotic psychophysiological concomitants.

The term Hypnotherapy covers the entire range of hypnotic techniques currently in use. Hypnoanalysis involves the use of both hypnosis and the dynamic understandings of psychoanalytic theory. Robert Lindner (1958) reminds us that it was psychoanalysis that finally gave hypnosis an air of respectability.

Dynamic psychotherapists tend to use hypnosis more frequently than do behavior therapists. However, there is a growing impetus in integrating various therapeutic modalities and hypnosis appears to be a technique that will be increasingly utilized by all therapists.

## HISTORY

Hypnosis is as old as civilization itself. Primitive man was mesmerized not only by the burning eyes and incantations of the medicine man but by the rhythmic beating of the drums and the laying on of hands, as well. The priests used it in the temples.

Interest in hypnosis has waxed and waned over the years since Mesmer, Charcot, Breuer, and Freud first experimented with its potential as a therapeutic instrument. After Freud's disillusionment with the technique it was ignored until the advent of World War II, when it proved useful in treating traumatic war neuroses. Since then it has become an accepted practice in medicine, dentistry, and psychology.

## TECHNIQUE

There are an infinite number of induction techniques available. In Hypnotherapy I employ the following one after the patient is trained in trance induction, deepening techniques, and verbalizing comfortably in the trance state.

> Make yourself comfortable. When you are ready, close your eyes. Your body is feeling increasingly heavy /light [as suits the patient]. You are finding yourself becoming acutely aware of two important things about yourself.
>
> First, look for and find—deep within yourself—a solid inner core of strength that is uniquely your own. It consists of your considerable ability, all your capacities and understandings—your experiences—everything that makes you the unique person that you are.
>
> You can call upon this resource whenever you wish to help you function at a very high level. It is your hidden source of power and strength.
>
> Again—look for it and find it.
>
> Second, you also have within you an inner clock that you can slow down or speed up as you wish. I would like to suggest that you slow it down to the point where all tension and inner pressures disappear. Take all the time you need—so much time that a minute feels like an hour and an hour stretches out for as long as you desire. This can be accomplished in the waking state so that a tremendous amount of productive work can occur, with no feeling of stress in what is actually a limited time span.
>
> You have the ability to do this. Note how your breathing, your pulse, your blood pressure have all slowed down to within normal limits. So pleasant—so comfortable—so serene and safe.

And now, imagine yourself unlocking a heavy, iron door; as it creaks open, you will become aware of feelings, thoughts, images slowly coming to mind. You are curious about these sensations and making connections that encourage understanding.

As you talk to me about these experiences, you will find yourself relaxing more completely, feeling the solid/light outline of your body on the mattress /chair, as though you are talking to me in your sleep while you are dreaming. It will all seem so real—no need to awaken—very much in control ... You know you can open your eyes if you wish but you will not want to do so.

So push that heavy door open and let that part of you that is beyond your awareness come through at its own rate of speed. You can ignore your body completely because your unconscious will allow images and thoughts to come through at a rate you will handle well.

[The therapist guides, suggests, questions, asks that a dream be completed, etc. When it is time to awaken the patient he reviews in his mind whether there are suggestions that should be removed, and what post-hypnotic suggestions he may additionally wish to give.]

You can remember or not as you see fit. [Sometimes it is important to suggest amnesia.] At the count of five you will be fully awake—feeling rested, alert, confident—as though you have been resting for a long time.

Each time you try this you will go deeper—responding only to a professional to whom you have given your verbal consent. Awakening slowly—one—two —three—four—five. Wide awake!

## APPLICATIONS

The altered condition of awareness is conducive to accepting suggestions relative to tension relief, altering pain states, revealing unconscious resistances, encouraging fantasy exposure to phobic material, teaching diaphragmatic breathing to emphysema patients (Wilkins, 1970), treating psychosomatic conditions, addictions, obesity, cigarette smoking; the list is extensive.

It is the magical expectation of the patient that creates the desired state. However, only a skilled therapist can guide and direct the experience in order to attain a therapeutic goal. When used appropriately, Hypnotherapy becomes a delicate, sophisticated psychotherapeutic instrument. It should be practiced only by a trained professional.

# Indirect Hypnotic Therapy
### Florence A. Sharp

## DEFINITION

In Indirect Hypnotic Therapy the therapist, by his verbal and nonverbal behavior, "guides" the patient into an impasse of behavior and/or thinking. To escape feelings of confusion and frustration, the patient spontaneously and unknowingly goes into a hypnotic trance. The unconscious mind then takes responsibility for the patient's behavior and begins to search for a way out to solve the dilemma. Paradoxically, the seemingly reasonable approach of the therapist compels the patient to make a "free spontaneous choice" of behavior and to act upon it in the right way without knowing that he has done so.

## HISTORY

In 1954 Milton H. Erickson, M.D., published the first paper on the use of Indirect Hypnotic Therapy (Erickson, 1967b). His second article on the subject appeared in 1963 (Erikson, 1967a). Other papers by Dr. Erickson demonstrate the use and effectiveness of this therapy without labeling the technique where it is employed (Erickson 1967b).

In 1964 I (Florence A. Sharp), presented a paper demonstrating the use of this therapy in a residential treatment of a child (Sharp, 1966).

In books dealing with the treatment of behavior problems in children one will find other examples. The occurrence of the spontaneous trance may well have gone unnoticed, and therefore unmentioned, by the therapist (Beecher, 1955).

## TECHNIQUE

Some of the tactics used in Indirect Hypnotic Therapy are tactics that have a long history of use, but not necessarily for therapeutic purposes. The "surrender tactic" may not have been used first by Jesus, but he certainly codified it and stated it most explicitly (Haley, 1969):

But I-say unto you, That ye resist not evil: but whosoever shall smite thee on thy right cheek, turn to him the other also. And if any man will sue thee at the law, and take away thy coat, let them have thy cloak also. And whosoever shall compel thee to go a mile, go with him twain. (Matt. 5:36-41)

Such a tactic also has been called "fighting fire with fire."

In treatment this tactic is used for the benefit of the patient. The "stupid child" is confronted with an equally "stupid" therapist. Requests are graciously granted but "misunderstood"; that is, the word water, in a glass, is given on a request for water by a child capable of getting her own water. The patient's false reality is accepted at face value and acted upon, to the dismay of the patient.

The patient may be asked to perform consciously what he has claimed to be unconscious behavior. A bedwetter may be required to deliberately wet the bed on retiring.

The patient's symptoms may be reflected to him by the therapist. The patient who speaks "word-salad" may be spoken to in the same manner (Erickson, 1967d).

In Indirect Hypnotic Therapy the therapist does not analyze and interpret the patient's remarks and dreams or behavior. The therapist is not concerned with finding and bringing to consciousness the origin of the neurosis. Transference is not encouraged or discussed. No attempt is made to educate the patient by logical discussion of his difficulties. These methods are useful with the cooperative and somewhat flexible patient.

## APPLICATIONS

Indirect Hypnotic Therapy is the therapy of choice with the passive resistant patient, since behind this passivity lies an intense aggression and power struggle on the part of the patient. This was the choice of treatment that was planned for Lee, the child impostor (see Sharp, 1966). This type of treatment is described briefly in the following paragraphs.

The therapist, by consciously inhibiting her own normal responses and by confronting Lee's maneuvers of "stupidity" and "passivity" with the same, thus thwarting her unhealthy and antisocial expectations, would create the need for Lee to broaden both the scope and range of her behavior and of her thinking. The fighting "fire with fire" would also serve to mirror Lee's own behavior. Her "helplessness," since it was inappropriate for her age and intelligence, was ignored. No meals (except fruit juice for health reasons) were supplied for several days, and then on her direct request.

Indirect Hypnotic Therapy is also the therapy of choice where the patient's verbalization is lacking or severely limited and where there is evidence of intelligence and a well-developed pattern of frustration (and often despair) that may be employed therapeutically as a motivational force. This was the situation of Dr. Erickson's patient with organic brain damage. This highly intelligent woman of thirty-eight had suddenly developed a headache and had gone into a coma. She later developed what was diagnosed as a thalmic syndrome, right-sided muscular and sensory dysfunctions, as well as aphasia and alexia. By the time she came to Dr. Erickson, the patient was in a profoundly vegetative state from which she could be aroused only by unusual stimuli.

The treatment plan devised was complex and it varied not only from day to day, but within the day itself, so that outside of certain items the patient never knew what to expect; and even what was done often did not make much sense to her. As a result the patient was kept in a striving, seeking, frustrated, struggling, and emotional state in which anger, bewilderment, disgust, impatience, and an intense, almost burning desire to take charge and do things in an orderly and sensible manner became overwhelming.

Dr. Erickson gives a brief but representative example of the indirect method of fixating the patient's attention, regressing her in her thinking and remembering to earlier times and situations, and literally inducing, through attention and fixation, a trance state by drawing from her husband many facts about her life history.

This patient's food was deliberately served in unsuitable combinations, such as mustard on ice cream. Frustration compelled her to take action. It left no opportunity for passive withdrawal (Erickson, 1967).

A tactic especially applicable to certain child patients is to confront the child with a secure reality. In one such case Dr. Erickson reports how he had a mother sit calmly for an extended time on her destructive son, while he had time to think how he could change his behavior. This treatment surprised the boy, filling him with anger and frustration. Finding his temper outburst ineffectual, he turned his thoughts inward, developed a spontaneous trance state, and devised a change of behavior for himself, including making amends for past destruction (Erickson, 1967b).

Indirect Hypnotic Therapy is particularly applicable to the type of patient who does not respond to verbal therapy.

# Multiple Impact Therapy

## Robert MacGregor

### DEFINITION

Multiple Impact Therapy is a team-family method for diagnosis, treatment planning, and for freeing natural growth processes in families to deal with mental health problems. Scheduled in half-day segments, the multiple interactions include: a brief team conference; a team-family conference; separate conferences concurrently between parts of the team with segments of the family (for example, by generation); overlapping sessions; and a reconvened team-family conference. The convener, such as a pastor, psychiatric nurse or a probation officer, enlists the expertise of others. The team in the public or private sector includes people already "on the case" (such as school counselor), others who may be disciplined in needed aspects of the health endeavor, and an advocate for the family.

### HISTORY

The team-family method was originally developed in the Youth Development Project of The University of Texas Medical Branch in Galveston and reported in the 1964 book *Multiple Impact Therapy with Families*. The team was multidisciplinary and the staff, accompanied by trainees, was expert in group and individual therapy. The hospital chaplain sometimes functioned as the family advocate. The converging and reinforcing viewpoints developed in separate sessions lent strength to understanding the problem and led my colleagues and me to speak of it as "Multiple Impact Therapy."

### TECHNIQUE

Recruitment of the team is as much a part of the method as are the ways of intervention. In cases of considerable interagency complexity it may be well to have a meeting, a day or so beforehand, of those involved outside the family to select the team, reduce problems of bureaucracy, and to review devisive manipulation by family members that can set one agency against another. Where the convener is a therapist on a clinic staff he might enlist, for example, the family's welfare worker, the youth's probation officer, and the family pastor that referred the case to the clinic.

The family, on the defensive, is prone to function as a relatively closed living system that shuts out needed information and nurture. This retreat, caused by the complaint behavior, yields an arrest in development, usually manifested by the disturbed behavior of a member. Our method brings a relatively open system, a team to help the family resume growth. In addition to opening the closed system or lending strength to a weakened system, there are specific strategies to diagnose the level of developmental arrest.

1. *Opening team conference.* This meeting takes about twenty minutes. The convener briefs those new to the method as to their part of the work. The respect shown the referring person strengthens his relationship with the client. While he might want to give an extensive briefing to the team out of earshot of the family, he is informed that his task is to entrust the family to the team by the way he briefs the team in the presence of the family. The team members observe each other for excesses of involvement and plan which team members will go with the segments of the family into separate sessions.

2. *Opening team-family conference.* Because the family has its system as well as the defensiveness of individual members, it is possible for the team to quickly address itself to the most serious matters. As a team, members do this rapidly because they do not have to remain neutral or "outside the system." Other team members defend the family against criticism so that each person feels his defenses are respected and useful. The first sessions are delivered as a consulation to the referral agent. Provocative material is often addressed to him or other team members so that the defensive one can listen without being under attack. Issues are developed clearly enough so that after about forty-five minutes, separate conferences can be negotiated in which one segment of the family and team may critique the discussion so far while another pursues an aspect agreed upon by the group.

3. *Separate conferences.* When children are seen separately, it is more productive to have all the siblings together. Because they may expect to be exploited for the family secrets, it is important to treat them with dignity by consulting them about the opening conference. One team member, typically the convener, seeks instruction from the group as to what issues he should, as their representative, take back to the conference with parents. He is called the overlapping member.

4. *Overlapping conference.* This team member then enters a concurrent separate conference. When convenient, a team member gives the overlapping person an interpretation of what has been going on. This gives the clients a chance to hear what they may have resisted and a chance to find out that they were heard. Then the entering therapist can relate what he has observed elsewhere to what is happening here.

5. *Closing team-family conference.* Now team-family members become increasingly aware that there was unintentional collusion in the family to protect members only presumed to be inferior. The half day concludes as those from separate conferences hear about the effectiveness of the overlap from their representative. The next conference is planned in terms of other available resources. For example, team-family conferences may be suspended while a particular family member or the marital pair engages in training or psychotherapy. It is important that the team member conducting or arranging the interim work be empowered to arrange the next conference and to communicate to the team reactions to the session not evident during it.

## APPLICATIONS

Team-family methods are developed to deal with family issues that contribute to personal problems. Team members seek to make sense out of difficulties often called mental illness or delinquent behavior, and by their interaction with the family achieve an understanding of the way the difficulty came about. Once identified as a family problem, the behavior can be seen as an aspect of arrest in development of part of the family system due to collusion that was thought to protect. Distrust of collusion is the reason the team does not consult apart from the family after the opening team conference. The goal is to have behavior that was a part of such unwitting collusion become a matter of choice.

Multiple Impact Therapy makes family therapy available to the many because it utilizes together those already on the case or who will be. It does not require of any one person the level of expertise that is increasingly demanded of family therapists who work alone or with a co-therapist.

# Implosive Therapy

*Lowell H. Storms*

## DEFINITION

Implosive Therapy is a form of desensitization, which means that it involves repeated exposure to anxiety-provoking stimuli. These stimuli are usually presented in the form of visual imagery guided by the therapist's vivid descriptions. A continuous series of such images lasting fifty minutes or more is presented, with the imagery becoming more and more frightening and more catastrophic. The subject is encouraged to feel as much anxiety and fear as possible. This contrasts with Systematic Desensitization, which involves short presentations of mild images that are terminated when the subject reports anxiety. A very similar approach called "Flooding" was developed independently in England. Flooding involves not only imagery, but sometimes exposure to real life or *in vivo* fear-producing stimuli. Occasionally Implosive Therapy may also involve *in vivo* exposure to stimuli.

Implosive Therapy is more likely (than Flooding) to include material inferred from the patient's "dynamic" conflicts.

## HISTORY

Pioneered in the 1950s by Thomas Stampfl. the first published description of Implosive Therapy appeared in 1964. In 1966 a series of promising published reports of empirical studies on the effectiveness of Implosive Therapy began appearing. A few years later reports from England on the successful use of flooding began to be published. Active investigation of the technique is still under way.

## TECHNIQUE

The rationale for Implosive Therapy involves extinction of conditioned fear and anxiety. Fear is learned by the pairing of previously neutral stimuli with painful events. Neurotic symptoms develop as ways of avoiding the conditioned fear-producing stimuli or related stimuli. In order to extinguish the fear, it is necessary to circumvent the avoidance behavior and persuade the person to face the fear-inspiring stimuli repeatedly. This is where Implosive Therapy comes in.

Implosive Therapy begins with two, and perhaps more, evaluative interviews with the patient. The first interview includes history taking and general exploration of the patient's fears and other major complaints. What the patient is afraid of, the situations that elicit the fears, when they began, and how they have affected his life are discussed. I find it helpful to give a fear survey schedule, an MMPI (Minnesota Multiphasic Personality Inventory), and perhaps a life-history questionnaire before the second interview. In the second interview there is further investigation to obtain as much detailed information about the patient's fears as is possible. Inferences are made about these fears from what the therapist knows about the patient's history and his modes of adapting to life situations.

A story is then developed using the data at hand and the therapist's imagination. The story consists of a series of scenes to be described by the therapist in vivid imagery as the patient visualizes the sequence of events. The story generally begins with imagery related to the relatively mild and more peripheral fears and then becomes progressively more disastrous, catastrophic, and gruesome. In contrast to Systematic Desensitization, Implosive Therapy builds up to the most frightening material as rapidly as the patient can tolerate it.

To accustom the patient to visualization, a pleasant or neutral scene is described and the patient is asked to visualize it with his eyes closed. During this practice and from time to time during the story itself it is important to check how well the patient is visualizing. The patient is asked whether he is seeing it clearly and also how he is feeling. Rather than relaxing, the patient is encouraged to experience as much fear and anxiety as possible, including suggestions of rapid heartbeat, sweating palms, etc.

The story—which may contain such gruesome elements such as the patient being brutally beaten and murdered, being immersed in feces, or being condemned by the eye of God—must continue for forty-five minutes to an hour. Research evidence suggests that shorter stories are less effective. Although it is not standard procedure, I add a relaxation exercise taking about ten minutes at the end of the story. This reduces the residual tension and helps heighten the contrast between the frightening fantasies and the safety of the office.

The same story is visualized repeatedly until the patient is bored with it and reports no more fear. Sometimes the most gruesome scenes are not included in the first presentations of the story but are added later. Early portions of the story that no longer elicit anxiety may also be dropped.

An audio tape of the story can be made to be listened to by the patient once or twice a day at home. While there is some evidence that audio tapes are not as effective as implosion in the office, playing a tape at home may speed up treatment for cooperative patients who visualize the scenes clearly.

Sometimes a patient will experience increased fear after the first session of Implosive Therapy. For this reason it is helpful to schedule the first two sessions in quick succession, preferably on successive days. Research suggests that five sessions or more are necessary to get results; Stampfl suggests ten to fifteen sessions for most cases.

## APPLICATIONS

There is no evidence to support the opinion of some writers that Implosive Therapy is unsafe. In a few cases, patients have had an increase in their fears after their first session of implosion, but the patients returned for further treatment and showed notable improvement. It appears that if a patient does the extensive and vivid visualization repeatedly for at least forty minutes per session and at least five sessions, he is likely to improve.

While more research is needed on the indications for appropriate use of Implosive Therapy, some kinds of patients appear to be especially likely to benefit from it. People with agoraphobia (fear of leaving home) apparently benefit more from Implosive Therapy than from Systematic Desensitization. Such patients characteristically have multiple fears, and other patients with multiple fears also seem to benefit. Obsessive patients, who do poorly in insight-oriented psychotherapy, are frequently helped by implosion. Hospitalized depressed, anxious patients showed greater improvement with Implosive Therapy than standard hospital treatment or a free association desensitization technique. A five-year follow-up showed this improvement was also maintained better. Another indication for the use of Implosive Therapy appears to be when fears are attached to a person's impulses or fantasies. For example, many patients are afraid of their own anger, and implosive imagery involving expressions of anger can be helpful.

In general, I believe that *in vivo* desensitization, especially with modeling, is the treatment of choice where it is possible. For simple, specific phobias, systematic desensitization may be more reliably effective than implosion. However, neither *in vivo* desensitization nor systematic desensitization have much to offer for the kinds of cases we have described above.

---

# Information Feedback
## Jaques Kaswan and Leonore R. Love

## DEFINITION

Information Feedback is a set of procedures developed to facilitate people's ability to scan, actively and objectively, their own perceptions and behavior, and to trace the impact of these on their interpersonal interactions. The approach is based on the assumption that much behavior that is ineffective for the self, or noxious for others, results from habituated attitudes of nonattention to the interpersonal arena; learning to attend, in new ways, produces new information that opens up opportunities for new behavioral choices.

An important emphasis in this approach is that people identify for themselves any changes they consider appropriate or desirable. The role of the professional is that of a relatively impersonal consultant who provides opportunities for viewing and attending in novel ways to characteristics of self and others. His techniques help to explicate, in specific, active and objective ways, personal and interpersonal patterns in the people with whom he works; but the motivation for and choice of behavioral change is left to the clients involved.

Information Feedback, therefore, is neither a therapy process nor a treatment intervention in the usual sense. It is a set of experiences designed to improve interpersonal interactions within people's existing motivational and response repertoires.

## HISTORY

The Information Feedback procedures were developed and evaluated in the Psychology Department Clinic at the University of California, Los Angeles, between 1960 and 1970, as a demonstration program entitled "Consultation for Psychological Problems of Children." The goal was to enable parents and teachers to identify perceptions and behavior on their part that served to provoke or maintain ineffective, uncontrolled, or undesirable behavior in elementary school children. If adults could identify and improve such disturbing behaviors on their own parts, it was hypothesized that the quality of the interpersonal environment in which the children were living would be bettered, and the children's behavioral difficulties would in turn be ameliorated.

The effectiveness of Information Feedback was compared with two standard interventions for children's behavior problems: counseling for the parents and psychotherapy for the child. Using the children's behavior and grades in school as outcome criteria, it was found that the two interventions that focused on the adults' role in the children's difficulties (Information Feedback and parent counseling) resulted in significant improvement for the children over a two-year period. Differences in the families of children in these two groups were clearly related to socioeconomic factors, with more highly educated and economically successful parents responding more favorably to Information Feedback, and lower socioeconomic parents improving more when offered the suggestions and advice characteristic of the parent counseling approach. Psychotherapy provided for the child did not result in significant improvement in the child's effectiveness at school.

## TECHNIQUES

Techniques are of two types. In one, videotapes of interactions provide complete, objective data against which individual expectations and assumptions about appearance, voice, interactional style, and the like can be tested. Or more generally, parallel sets of verbal instruments (adjective ratings and inventories of behaviors) are administered to participants. These elicit perceptions, judgments, and reports about frequency, range, and contexts of interpersonal behavior. Responses to these are translated by the consultant into visual displays (usually superimposed graphs) that highlight similarities and differences between respondents. This feedback is the stimulus for the participants' consideration and decision making about their interactions.

## APPLICATIONS

In the original project, the main focus of feedback was on the parents and teachers of troubled children. In later work at UCLA, the techniques have been adopted as a format for a Family Check-up Service for families who wish to improve their functioning, even though they do not seek clinical services for any specific problems.

Additionally, the formats have been adapted to facilitate group discussion of interpersonal relationships in some Los Angeles junior and senior high schools.

In Ohio, Dr. Kaswan has used this conceptual approach as a framework for consulting with various types of community groups and agencies.

# Insight Psychotherapy

## Michael T. McGuire

### DEFINITION

Insight Psychotherapy explains behavior, affects (moods and emotions), and thoughts with interpretations.

### HISTORY

The history of Insight Psychotherapy can be traced to Freud. Early in his studies and treatment of psychopathology, Freud found that the interpretation of forgotten memories (the attribution of psychoanalytic meaning to such memories) did not uniformly lead to psychological improvement in his patients. With additional experience he recognized resistance (the instinctive opposition to laying bare the unconscious), the intrapsychic mechanisms of defense, and transference (the projection of feelings, thoughts, and wishes onto the analyst who has come to represent someone from the patient's past). He found these forces compromising the effectiveness of interpretations. Thus, he shifted his therapeutic emphasis from his original focus on past events to explaining patients' resistances, defenses, and transferences vis-a-vis treatment and the analyst. Today, the term "insight psychotherapy" can refer to either of the above approaches: using interpretations to explain forgotten memories or to explain psychological events that occur within treatment.

It is unfortunate that the term "insight psychotherapy" has perhaps led to unnecessary confusion. In the broad sense of the word, all verbal therapies condone insight. Moreover, most humans interpret their behavior and find it useful to do so. What is at issue is the kinds of interpretations one uses. Freud and other psychoanalysts stressed interpretations dealing with their patients' unconscious desires, fears, and psychic mechanisms. Insight, then, is a well-established way of knowing; by convention, it applies to situations where psychoanalytic and like interpretations are used, but this need not be so.

Current theoretical discussions are concerned primarily with the depth, focus, and timing of the interpretation. Questions relating to the depth of the interpretation deal with whether or not early life and fundmental psychic conflicts and desires should be interpreted when patients are seen for brief periods of therapy (less than twenty weeks), or infrequently (once per week or less); questions relating to the focus of the interpretation deal with whether past or present conflicts should be explained in order to maximize the effects of interpretation; and questions relating to the time of the interpretation deal with the question of *when* is the most efficacious time to explain the event. The generally accepted rule is: the shorter and/or the more infrequent the therapy, the less focus on early fundamental conflicts and the greater emphasis on current conflicts.

## TECHNIQUE

The fundamental premises of this kind of therapy are: 1) that unrecognized intrapsychic conflicts result in symptoms and behavior that are displeasing to the patient and 2) that identification of these conflicts and their appropriate interpretation result in an alteration of the displeasing symptoms and behavior.

Successful Insight Psychotherapy involves a critical interpretation/timing feature: the therapist must wait until the patient has discussed significant internal conflictual material several times and failed to make sense of it. In addition, he must wait for a moment when a patient is emotionally distressed, shows evidence of desiring change, and is responsive to the therapist's views. An interpretation will then have the effect of refocusing the patient's approach to the conflictual material and restructuring intrapsychic relationships. For example, a young man who is disappointed in his relationships with women might be unaware of his childlike pleading to his therapist to magically make certain fears and distress disappear. The therapist, interpreting this behavior as emanating from the young man's wish to have the therapist act as a mother toward him, has a reasonable probability of refocusing the patient's view of his distress. Thus, the patient sees that he brings desires appropriate only to childhood to an adult situation where such desires are inappropriate, therefore adversely affecting his relationships with women.

## APPLICATIONS

It is traditionally argued that Insight Psychotherapy works best with patients who have above-average intelligence, who lack psychotic symptoms, who are motivated to change themselves, and who see themselves and *not* the world about them as the principal cause of their distress. They usually have values similar to those of their therapist and a desire to improve their place in life. These are preconditions.

A fundamentally more important issue concerns the kind of psychopathological disorder from which patients suffer: those who suffer from conflicts that can be verbalized (e.g., conflicts relating to desires, fears, misunderstandings, etc.) often benefit from Insight Psychotherapy while patients who cannot verbalize their problems benefit less, although they will often learn the language of insight.

The preceding point about verbalization is particularly critical in the selection of patients. While prospective patients are increasingly sophisticated in psychoanalytic ideas, initial impressions are frequently misleading. Patients who are confused, who suspect that there is something wrong within themselves, and who find their distress troublesome are most likely to benefit from Insight Psychotherapy. On the other hand, patients who have a highly schematized view of themselves and a strong commitment to certain causes of their disorder seem to benefit less.

When Insight Psychotherapy works, it seldom does so dramatically. Time is required for the interpretation to take effect. Behavior can change rapidly, but fears change slowly because new experiences and trials at being less fearful are needed; and deep-seated desires change very slowly. But change does occur and with such change goes a revised view of one's self as well as one's place in the world.

# Instigation Therapy
## John L. Shelton

### DEFINITION

Instigation Therapy is closely allied to behavior therapy. It refers to the systematic use of homework assignments that the client completes outside the therapy hour. Planned jointly by the therapist and client, Instigation Therapy puts the client to work outside the consulting room in an effort to increase efficiency, enhance self-regulatory skills, and to promote transfer of training.

In addition to the increased efficiency that comes from putting the client to work using the hours of the week he is not in therapy, Instigation Therapy results in a number of benefits often not achieved by other forms of therapy. For example, Second and Bachman (1964) noted the increase in self-control skills acquired by clients who perceive themselves as the principal agent of change during therapy. Additional reports by Phillips (1966) and Davidson (1968) have shown that instigation procedures result in a greater motivation and maintenance of changes resulting from therapy.

### HISTORY

Although in this writer's opinion, few traditional psychotherapists make adequate use of homework, the basic notions surrounding Instigation Therapy are not new. Even before the arrival of behavior therapy, writers such as Dunlap (1932), Herzberg (1941), and Karpman (1949) pointed out the advantages that come from putting clients to work outside the therapy hour.

Three modern developments have helped make Instigation Therapy an important therapeutic endeavor. The first of these three developments was the work of Kanfer and Phillips (1966, 1969), who coined the term "instigation therapy" and provided the vital theoretical concept for this approach.

The second development was the work of professionals like Masters and Johnson (1970), who make systematic homework assignments an important part of their therapy with men and women with sex problems. However, the most important work to date has been done by Shelton and Ackerman (1974) and Shelton (in press). They took the abstract notion of Instigation Therapy and translated it into more than 150 examples of homework assignments useful with a wide variety of client ailments. Their study was a landmark in as much as they were the first to discuss homework as *the* focus of therapy rather than as a seldom-used adjunct.

## TECHNIQUES

Instigation therapists believe counseling and psychotherapy to be primarily an educational, skill-building endeavor. The more clients participate in the endeavor, the greater their chances of making desired changes. Ideally, the client and therapist co-participate in treatment; they work together to clarify, select, and attain the goals of therapy. A cooperative rapport is best established between a client and therapist who share a bond of empathy, warmth, and genuine caring. Besides conveying empathy, warmth, and genuineness, the effective therapist is an active, directive teacher, expert in skill training. A friend to his client, the professional also guides the client toward attitudes and behavior that will increase the client's ability to live a more satisfying life. Under the direction of the therapist, the client practices new behavior and develops new attitudes. Homework provides an ideal vehicle for clients to extend practice of new skills from the therapy hour to the world in which they live.

The above beliefs about psychotherapy leads this writer to follow a particular sequence, consisting of six steps, in conducting therapy:

1. The careful identification of client problems.
2. A precise definition of therapy objectives in behavioral terms.
3. A contractual agreement between the client and therapist to work toward these objectives.
4. A rank ordering of the therapeutic intervention so that the first objective pursued will make the most difference to the client and is, in the judgment of the therapist, technically the most feasible to pursue.
5. Selection of skills and methods of skill training acceptable to the client and effective for working toward the first behavioral objective.
6. Systematic skill training using homework assignments as integral parts of behavioral skill building.

When client and therapist agree upon the behavioral objectives of the therapy contract, work toward attaining these begins. The therapist directs the latter portion of most therapy hours so that a precise set of homework instructions is written before the sessions end. At that time, the reason for and nature of the homework is carefully explained to the client by the therapist. Summarized homework instructions usually are written on NCR (no carbon required) paper so both therapist and client have a copy. The homework provides continued practice for the client in acquiring the knowledge, attitudes, or skills upon which the therapy session was focused.

The format for homework includes one or more of the following instructions:

1. A *do* statement. "Read, practice, observe, say, count ... some kind of homework/'

2. A *quantity* statement. "Talk three times about...; spend thirty minutes *three* times...; give *four* compliments per day...; write a list of at least *ten* ..."

3. A *record* statement. "Count and *record* the number of compliments; each time he hits, *mark* a on the chart; whenever that thought comes to you, *write* a on the..."

4. A *bring* statement. "*Bring* ... your list; the chart; the Cards; your spouse ... to your next appointment."

5. A *contingency* statement. "Call for your next appointment after you have done...; for each activity you attend, one dollar will be deducted...; each minute spent doing _____ will earn you_____; one-tenth of your penalty deposit will be forfeited for each assignment not completed."

An example of this format, as written out for the client, is the following:

1. Both read two marital papers.
2. Discuss 3 times for fifteen to thirty minutes each time.
3. Write separate lists of at least three behaviors you want more of from spouse. (These are positive behaviors, not negative ones.)
4. Make next appointment after above is done.
5. Bring lists with you to next appointment.

The therapist should give manageable amounts of homework. Early in therapy, especially following the first session, a single item of homework may be enough. As the professional becomes more acquainted with the client's attitudes, expectations, and habits, the amount and complexity of homework may be increased. Excessive amounts of homework require too much planning time, may frustrate the client, and simply may not get done.

---

# Integrated Psychiatric Treatment
## *Julian Lieb*

### DEFINITION

Integrated Psychiatric Treatment is an approach to patient management that includes psychodynamic, neurobiological, pharmacological, social, and learning dimensions.

### HISTORY

Disparate treatment ideologies have not allowed for the smooth incorporation of basic and clinical science research advances into the practitioner's mode of patient care. The introduction of Chlorpromazine into American psychiatry, for example, was viewed with intense skepticism by many psychiatrists who could not believe that a drug could alter the course of a mental illness (Swazey, 1974). To this day, proponents of psycho-chemotherapy (the major drug houses, psychopharmacologists, and pharmacologically oriented practitioners) have, on occasion, to apologize for using drugs. In some instances elaborate etiological and treatment models are constructed in an effort to persuade non-pharmacologically oriented practitioners to incorporate drugs into their clinical practice (Ostow, 1962). Obviously an integrated approach to psychiatric care that includes clinically effective approaches arising from any ideology is justified.

## TECHNIQUE

The technique of Integrated Psychiatric Treatment simply embraces the principles of good patient care. Patients are given the benefit of a complete psycho-bio-social history and mental status examination. Old charts are systematically reviewed and contact is made with clinicians with whom the patient had prior contact. Based on the history and initial clinical findings, further investigations are arranged as required (e.g., psychological testing, neurologic examination, electroencephalogram). Patients who have not had a physical examination within the prior twelve months are referred for a complete physical work-up. The completion of the first stage of the work-up includes a tentative diagnosis and formulation and documentation of any physical illness that might be contributing to the clinical picture or might impact on psychiatric management.

The next stage in the evaluation is a determination of whether a psychoactive medication should be administered. This decision may be relatively easy to arrive at, especially when based on obvious clinical criteria, such as the presence of hypomanic symptomatology or distinct symptoms of depression accompanied by profound neurovegetative disturbances, e.g. such as with insomnia or anorexia. In other instances a decision for medication and the type of medication to be used may be more equivocal and may rely more on the practitioner's ability to synthesize data and his clinical imagination. When a strong argument cannot be made for definitive pharmacochemotherapy it may be advantageous to discuss a medication trial with the patient. A positive trial is of obvious benefit, whereas a negative trial may be of use in removing from the practitioner concern as to whether a specific medication might be helpful.

The third step is to decide whether psychotherapy, sociotherapy, behavior therapy, or an admixture is indicated, with or without the adjuvant use of medication. Decisions are made as to whether a patient should be treated in individual time-limited psychotherapy, long-term psychotherapy, couples therapy, family therapy, sexual dysfunction therapy, and so on. While every practitioner should be equipped with the widest range of skills, it cannot be expected that any one individual can be an expert in all fields. Thus, one should be willing to call on experts in specific fields for consultation, or to take over management. Another option is conjoint management, where clinicians with diverse skills orchestrate a comprehensive treatment effort.

Circumstances and the complexities of human behavior militate against an orderly progression between phases. Psychotherapy may be under way for a considerable time span before a medication decision can be made. Similarly, psychotherapy may be well advanced before sufficient data are available to compile a complete history.

## APPLICATIONS

Integrated Psychiatric Treatment represents a philosophy of patient care that can be applied to all psychiatric patients.

# Integrative Psychotherapy
## Philip H. Friedman

### DEFINITION

Integrative Psychotherapy is an approach to psychotherapy that integrates and synthesizes systems—humanistic, behavioral, psychodynamic, and spiritual approaches—to psychotherapy. The goal of Integrative Psychotherapy is to facilitate an individual's growth toward becoming a balanced, holistic, integrated individual responsible for his life experiences or a family's and couple's movement toward becoming a functioning, growth-producing, harmoniously balanced group of intimately interconnected and related individuals. Theoretically, Integrative Psychotherapy relies heavily upon an integrated, three-dimensional meta-model. The three dimensions of the *meta-model* are: 1) focus (intrapersonal, interpersonal, transpersonal), 2) structure (concepts, techniques, roles), and 3) category (humanities, economic, political-legal-judicial, social, philosophical-ethical, spiritual-religious, pure science, applied science, recreation). The three-dimensional meta-model can be considered a three-dimensional *matrix of metaphors*. The integrative psychotherapist draws upon this meta-model or matrix of concepts, techniques, and roles to guide him in his transactions with individuals, couples, and families. The matrix allows him to organize his therapeutic experiences in a way that permits him unusual clarity and flexibility of style and approach.

The meta-model or matrix allows the therapist to see the whole terrain from which conceptual, technical, and role metaphors can be selected and not just isolated plots, i.e., models. Consequently the meta-model requires a number of basic assumptions: 1) The map—i.e., the matrix of metaphors—is not the territory of the therapist's experience; 2) The matrix is a way of organizing the experience of a therapist so that he can choose wisely from a wide variety of conceptual, technical, and role metaphors; 3) The matrix permits the therapist to see the individual, couple, or family through many different lenses without being overly attached to any one lens; 4) The matrix not only contributes to clear thinking but also helps the therapist take increased responsibility for the conceptual, technical, and role metaphors he employs.

### HISTORY

Integrative Psychotherapy has its roots in an earlier system of psychotherapy that I (Philip H. Friedman) developed and labeled in 1972. At that time I defined my approach as 44 Personalistic Family and Marital Therapy" (Friedman, 1972) and saw it as an outgrowth of a broad spectrum *behavioral* approach to therapeutic interventions, a *system-oriented*, three-generational approach to conceptualizing family problems and a *humanistic* concern for the uniqueness and worth of each family member. Even then the emphasis of that article was on *integrating* a systems, behavioral, and humanistic approach toward psychotherapy. I originally used the term "personalistic" to emphasize the personhood of the therapist, his compassion, humor, playfulness, wisdom, dedication, caring, perseverance, etc., and by that I meant that the personhood of the therapist is always the determining force behind the selection of concepts, techniques, and roles. I also emphasized in that article and in a 1974 technique article (Friedman, 1974b) the need for a personal fitting of techniques to the therapist's style and the family's needs. My 1972 article in addition to my more theoretically oriented 1974 article (Friedman, 1974a) also emphasized an *ecological* approach to therapeutic interventions. Essentially then these three articles focused on *interpersonally* oriented concepts, techniques, and roles.

In a brief 1970 paper on cognitive-behavior therapy (Friedman, 1970) I had previously spelled out an *intrapersonally* oriented approach to working with individuals as well as a marital and family perspective. In the 1970 paper I stressed the necessity of conceptualizing intrapersonal problems along a number of dimensions, i.e., cognitive, behavioral, affective, imaginal, sensory-somatic, and physiological. At that time I referred to a group of techniques that could be utilized to intervene along these *intrapersonal* dimensions. Since 19741 further developed my orientation to psychotherapy to include not only an *intrapersonal* and *interpersonal* approach but also a *transpersonal* one (Friedman, 1976). The transpersonal approach focuses on the *spiritual* dimensions of life with an emphasis on the role of forgiveness of others in interpersonal relations and forgiveness of self intrapsychi-cally. Thus, a professional cycle that began in 1970 expanded into a very integrative orientation to psychotherapy, a creative synthesis of many different concepts, techniques, and roles. Consequently, I presently refer to this approach as Integrative Psychotherapy.

## TECHNIQUE

Techniques of Integrative Psychotherapy are found in the second column of the "structure" dimension of the meta-model. They are classified according to the nine subdivisions of "category" dimension. The "category" dimension is extremely useful in organizing the matrix. It appears that all or almost all of the concepts, techniques, and roles in the field of psychotherapy can be meaningfully classified along the nine "category" subdivisions. For example, when couples and families are seen in therapy the interpersonal techniques (action metaphors) that are employed (Friedman, 1974b) include: 1) role playing, modeling, 2) contracting, negotiating, mediating, side taking, reinforcing, 3) confronting, go-between process, rebalancing, 4) persuading, re-structuring, joining, rule-setting, 5) instructing paradoxically, 6) storytelling, 7) de-triangling, transforming, catalyzing, energizing, facilitating, nurturing, 8) feeding back, programming, teaching, 9) assigning tasks, counter-attacking, and parrying. These action metaphors (techniques) are organized according to their respective categories in Table 1 and the corresponding role played by the therapist is listed to the right of each technique.

Table 1 is also helpful in clarifying for the therapist different ways in which a family or couple can be viewed. For example, a troubled family or couple can be conceptualized as 1) a malfunctioning, power-laden, hierarchical organization with a specific set of structures, territories, generational boundaries, rules, coalitions, tasks, and feedback systems, 2) a loyalty-based set of dialectical, intergenerational, reciprocal balances invisibly connected by a subjective expectational system of justice based on merits, accounts, and ledgers, 3) an undifferentiated system of interlocking triangles with dyadic pairs alternately over- and underfunctioning in a complementary way and triangulating third parties, 4) a triadic-based system of coalitions, alliances, go-betweens, scapegoats, and silencers, 5) a coercive sequence of behavioral interactions with an excess of negative reinforcements and a deficit of positive reinforcements.

When the integrative psychotherapist works with individuals in addition to relying upon interpersonal metaphoric lenses for viewing a client, he may use intraper-sonal metaphoric lenses such as the intrapersonal family, intrapersonal conflicts, defenses, oppositions, resistances, and incongruities, subpersonalities, ego states, and states and levels of consciousness. He might utilize techniques such as: role playing (1), modeling (1), guided imagery (1), contracting (2), negotiating (2), directing (4), confronting (3), cognitive-restructuring (4), persuading (4), instructing paradoxically (5), sermonizing (5), philosophizing (5), hypnotizing (6), storytelling (6), desensitizing (7), relaxing (7), eliciting catharsis (7), educating (8), biofeedback (8), coaching (9), bioenergetic exercises (9), and assigning tasks (9). The category which each of these techniques belongs to is listed in parentheses after the technique.

Finally, when the integrative psychotherapist uses transpersonal techniques for spiritual growth, he usually does so in conjunction with intrapersonally and interper-sonally oriented techniques. Various techniques that can be utilized include: guided imagery (1), dream induction (1), inner dialoguing (1), journal keeping (1), contracting (2), service (4), paradoxical instructing (5), storytelling (5), self-hypnosis (6), meditation (6), prayer (6), energy stimulation or polarization (7), deep relaxation (7), catalyzing (7), educating (8), reading assignments (8), Yoga postures (9), psychocalisthenics (9), Aikido (9), or Tai Chi exercises (9). These techniques are also classified according to the nine "category" subdivisions.

Of central importance in the use of transpersonal or spiritual techniques are exercises having to do with *forgiveness*. Utilized in conjunction with meditation, deep relaxation, self-hypnosis, prayer, and reading assignments, individuals, couples, and family members are asked to review their lives and to see which resentments, bitter feelings, hurts, and condemnations toward themselves and significant others they are willing to let go of and whom they are willing to forgive. The healing power of forgiveness to themselves and others is emphasized and they are encouraged to incorporate forgiveness as an ongoing spiritual force in their lives.

## APPLICATIONS

Integrative Psychotherapy has been and can be used with a wide variety of individuals, couples, families, or groups. To date, it has been used primarily with nonpsychotic populations, although there is certainly no a priori reasons why it cannot be used, frequently in conjunction with psychotropic medication, with psychotic populations as well.

1. Humanities
2. Economic
3. Pol., Legal Judicial
4. Social
5. Phil. Ethical
6. Spiritual Religious
7. Pure Science
8. Applied Science
9. Recreation

Intrapersonal

Interpersonal

FOCUS

Transpersonal

Role

Technique

Concept

STRUCTURE

*Three-Dimensional Meta-Model*

---

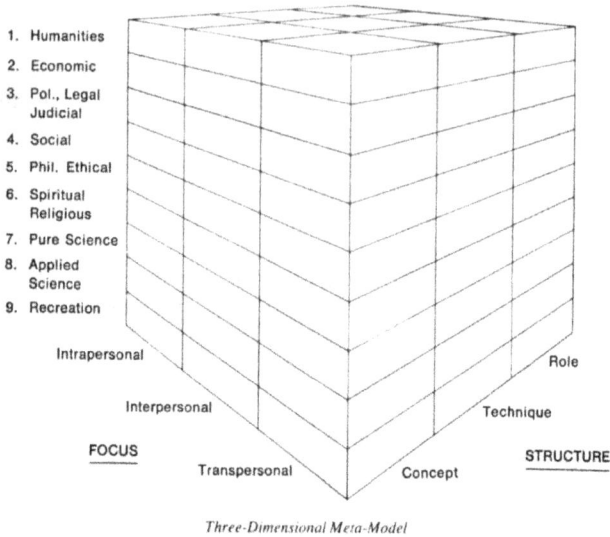

**Table 1.** Interpersonal Dimension of the Meta-Model
(Matrix of Metaphors for Marital and Family Therapy)

| | CATEGORY | CONCEPT | TECHNIQUE | ROLE |
|---|---|---|---|---|
| 1. | Humanities | Dramatic Action | Role Playing Modeling | Director Actor |
| 2. | Economic | Contracts Negotiation Mediation Coalitions Reinforcements | Contracting Negotiating Mediating Side-taking Reinforcing | Contractor Negotiator Mediator Side-taker Reinforcer |
| 3. | Political Legal Judicial | Power Go-between Loyalty, merit justice balance | Confronting Go-between process Rebalancing the ledger | Confronter Go-between Judge or lawyer |
| 4. | Social (Sociology, Anthropology, Ecology) | Organizational Hierarchies, Structures, Boundaries Territories, Rules Attitude, roles | Directing Restructuring Joining Rule setting Persuading | Director Tribal leader or chief Rule setter Persuader |
| 5. | Philosophical Ethical | Paradox Dialectic | Instructing paradoxically | Zen master |
| 6. | Spiritual Religious | Parables Forgiveness | Storytelling Meditation | Priest-Rabbi Guru-Healer |
| 7. | Pure Science (Math, Chemistry, Physics, Biology, etc.) | Triangles (Triads) Transformation Chemical Catalyst Energy Cycles Seeds | De-triangling Transforming Catalyzing Energizing Facilitating Nuturing | Mathematician Transformer Catalyst Energizer Facilitator Nurturer |

**Table 1.** (continued)

| | CATEGORY | CONCEPT | TECHNIQUE | ROLE |
|---|---|---|---|---|
| 8. | Applied science (Cybernetics, Computers, Education) | Feedback, systems Programs Education | Feeding Back Programming Teaching | Systems analyst Programmer Teacher |
| 9. | Recreation (Athletics, etc.) | Football, team Karate Aikido | Assigning task Counter-attacking Parrying | Coach Master Master |

# Integrity Groups

## O. Hobart Mowrer

### DEFINITION

Many factors influence how human beings feel emotionally, mentally, and physically, including environmental stresses, constitutional predispositions, and nutritional problems. Integrity Groups deal with the additional factors of personal integrity and guilt. Secrecy and duplicity in one's interpersonal relations constitutes a breach of integrity (discrepancy between what one has agreed, or "contracted," to do and what one actually does); and when this incongruency becomes sufficiently serious (in persons of good character, as opposed to psychopaths), an *identity crisis*, to use Erik Erikson's apt term (rather than "neurosis"), is likely to ensue. By improving one's integrity, clarity of identity (personal integration, wholeness, authenticity) also tends to return.

### Integrity Groups HISTORY

Originally called "integrity therapy," what is now known as Integrity Groups, or the I. G. Process, came into existence in the late 1950s in response to the failure of both traditional religions and secular psychotherapies (including psychoanalysis) to take personal guilt seriously and to provide a realistic and effective means of resolving it. Clergymen attempted to deal with guilt primarily by invoking divine forgiveness and leaving the human, interpersonal aspects of the problem largely untouched. Psychotherapists tended to deny the objectivity of guilt and to interact with patients only in terms of guilt *feelings*. From its inception, the I. G. Process has taken guilt seriously, particularly when kept hidden from "significant others" (persons playing important roles in one's life), and has sought to deal with it in terms of *honesty* (self-disclosure, confession), *responsibility* (making amends, restitution), and *involvement* (concern for and aid to others). In short, my colleagues and I were, and still are, primarily concerned with what Henri Ellenberger has called the "pathogenic secret" and its constructive management.

### TECHNIQUE

The precursor of Integrity Groups was a form of treatment that involved the usual one-to-one relationship but was distinctive in that, from the outset, the therapist exhibited (modeled) what it was he wished the patient to learn; namely, personal openness. This modeling of personal openness greatly increased the rapidity with which self-disclosure occurred and facilitated the recovery of integrity and clarity of identity, provided the patient was willing to extend this type of relationship to other meaningful interpersonal situations.

But then it was found that this process could be still further expedited by two or more patients meeting simultaneously with the therapist and talking to each other as well as to the therapist. From this it was but a short step to the emergence of groups, ranging from six to ten participants. Thus, the phenomenon of mutual aid and interaction increased so that today Integrity Groups are self-operated and function without professional intervention, except insofar as the expertise developed by experienced group members constitutes a professionalism of sort. No fees are charged, although modest contributions are accepted to help with minor expenses.

## APPLICATIONS

Integrity Groups have therefore emerged as a natural resource for the Community Mental Health movement. Although for a number of years my colleagues and I remained unfamiliar with the details of the twelve-step recovery program of Alcoholics Anonymous, we were pleased and gratified to learn eventually that there are striking parallels between Integrity Groups and this older organization. The latter is generally recognized as the largest and most successful lay venture in Community Mental Health.

The pertinence of Integrity Groups is further highlighted by the growing literature on the "iatrogenic" (treatment-produced) negative effects of much traditional psychotherapy, which has encouraged its clients to emancipate themselves from interpersonal commitments. Currently there is a growing realization that such "treatment" tends to be not only ineffective, but in some instances personally and socially harmful. Today there is growing recognition that "rugged individualism" is not the cure, and that everyone needs social support systems, membership in which involves not only privileges but also commitments, contributions, and cooperation. Recovery and personal change involve the willingness and capacity to give as well as receive, to be interdependent instead of independent.

# Intense Feeling Therapy

*Sidney Rose*

## DEFINITION

Intense Feeling Therapy is a therapeutic approach that puts emphasis on the breaking down of personality defenses and inducing a regressed state in which the most primitive feelings are expressed.

# HISTORY

Intense Feeling Therapy goes back to early Freud. Freud encouraged his patients to express themselves freely. And as these early patients did so, he discovered that each of them found unexpected feelings coming to the surface. These were deep, intense feelings, no longer appropriate for the patients currently living, but connected with emotionally painful experiences in childhood.

Before coming to Freud for treatment, each of these patients had developed defenses against these feelings—methods of controlling, disguising, and repressing them that varied from patient to patient. As by-products, however, the defenses produced a bewildering array of symptoms, uncomfortable and sometimes incapacitating—tics, tremors, phobias of all sorts, sexual difficulties ranging from impotence to indiscriminate promiscuity, and many others.

Freud focused on getting each patient to understand both his feelings and his defenses, on the assumption, which later therapists shared with Freud, that this understanding would undermine the defenses and heal the patient. In practice, however, the undermining and the healing were successful only in part. The problem was apparently that the therapy was kept on a verbal level, and the very process of trying to put the feelings into words tended to hamper their free expression.

The aim of Intense Feeling Therapy is to go far beyond verbalization in aiding the patient to express his innermost feelings with great depth and intensity. Using the techniques of Wilhelm Reich, Fritz Perls, J. L. Moreno, and Arthur Janov, this form of therapy puts emphasis on the participation of the whole person, body as well as mind.

# TECHNIQUE

There are three stages to the therapeutic process. The *first phase* is the three-week intensive in which the patient is seen daily in open-ended sessions lasting as much as three hours. Some patients need only one or two weeks, and a few need no intensive. In this period, the patient is isolated in a hotel, forbidden to see anyone, and not allowed to smoke, watch TV, or indulge in any other of his usual anxiety-relieving tactics. In the sessions with the therapist, he is encouraged to regress and allow his deepest feelings to take over his whole being. Mentally and emotionally he becomes again the child he once was, reliving his past and expressing the feelings he had to suppress in childhood.

In this regressed state, he uses the language of childhood. He cries out for help, or vents in cries and screams the rage he could never before allow to reach consciousness. Now, however, he has with him a part of his adult self that can inject new elements into these recordings of old memories.

He is able to digest and complete the unfinished business of the past, freeing his potential for growth. In time, he becomes capable of achieving voluntary regression, and from that point on he is, in a large part, his own therapist. Intense Feeling Therapy is not the kind of treatment you can begin in June and leave in July. Once the defenses are down, they must be kept down, and this is only possible if there is someone to take your place while you're away.

At the end of the crash program, the patient enters a group for three sessions a week. This is the *second phase* of treatment. He has learned to "primal." These groups, however, are vastly different from those of traditional group therapy. As the patients enter the room, they have little to say. Each goes to a different part of the room, lies down, and goes into the voluntary regressed state he has learned to enter in the intensive program. If he has difficulty, as often happens, the therapist helps him. After about two hours the patient may leave without saying a word to the other patients, or he may remain and join a discussion group to talk about new insights and childhood memories he may have come upon. Interaction, however, is not encouraged. Occasionally a patient, listening to the others, may find pain stirred up, and instead of reacting to the other patients, he may leave the group to go into his regressed state again to see whether the feeling will lead him to old memories and the source of the pain.

It is very difficult for patients to relate to each other in the group just after completing the two- or three-week intensive. In this stage, some group cohesion exists based on sharing what they experienced in the regressed state.

This regressed state, the "primalling," is an altered state of consciousness in which the individual is "acting in" instead of "acting out." retreating from the present world, in the regressed state he goes back to earlier periods, before behavior patterns were developed to contain, control, or channel conflicting feelings. In this regressed state, all kinds of primitive, raw feelings emerge and then what is projected on the screen in his imagination are the scenes in his childhood that led to the need to hide and disguise feelings. What emerges are feelings he was not aware of, directed to figures of the past. Raw feelings come first, followed by scenes depicting their origin, followed by insight. This leads to an awareness that he is not reacting to present events as they are but in terms of past conditioning, and he learns about this in vivid visual, dramatic details.

Gradually, the nature of the group participation changes. Whereas before acting out was permitted to allow regressed feelings to surface, now an attempt is made to tap other group cohesive elements. This is the *third phase* in which group games, encounter techniques, psychodrama, and transactional analysis tactics are invaluable to enable patients to develop new behavior patterns.

One outstanding feature of the intense feeling approach is for the patient to welcome pain and, if the everyday situation permits, to allow it to take over. If this happens, it leads to very intense feelings connected with childhood, and sometimes to actual memories of the original source of the pain. The patient does not need explanations or interpretations from the therapist; he learns from his own innermost feelings.

Patients, after a year, are able to be on their own and stop coming regularly, but will come occasionally when needed. They have developed the capacity not to run away from pain, to remain with it, and when necessary, go into the regressed state to discharge tensions and to connect with early sources.

Most insight therapies deal with the neurotic superstructure. This approach by its attack on the neurotic defenses, goes all at once to the core of the neurosis—the pain, the leftover, unfinished feelings from the past that had to be suppressed and repressed in order for the child to survive.

Janov's approach has proved of enormous value, but his view is a limited one. He looks upon character structure as involving only one feeling axis—the strength-weakness axis. This is an outgrowth of our times, because it is necessary to have strength to be alone and not feel the loneliness which is inevitable today. In today's world there is no tribe, there is little family, there is almost nothing to belong to as there always has been in the past. In addition, the scene changes from day to day, so that rootedness is impossible. It is more and more difficult for an individual to feel any responsibility for the welfare of others. Each person has to resort to the strength in himself.

Janov describes the post-primal patients as being free of tension, with much less sex drive or social drive. They do not sound like life-loving people with a feeling of responsibility to others or to society. Further, they seem contemptuous of others who have not been through this therapy.

Janov is disappointed because he discovers that his patients become apolitical. In a sense he overcures them, so that the healthy dependency and need for others disappear with the resolution of the neurotic dependency. The individual is still left with a void, even though he is free of tension. It is because of this void that the third stage of therapy is important.

Another difficulty is that there are some individuals who make the new therapy a way of life. They keep talking about how they are getting there, but they tend to stay at the same level. The "primalling" for them has become a ritual. They have developed a malignant transference, a morbid dependency that is the bane of all therapies.

## APPLICATIONS

The therapy is not a cure for neuroses, as Janov claims. However, for many patients it is the most effective approach. It is not a therapy for patients who have not made any adjustment to adult life (which is why Janov will not take patients under age twenty-six). There should be some ego strength manifested by some ability to relate to others, to hold a job, etc. It is not a suitable form of therapy where the genetic factor is pronounced as in schizophrenia or in some depressions. Furthermore, those who feel they are already "primalling" before they begin therapy have weak defenses and it is a mistake to encourage them to enter this therapy. There are others who cannot regress. Some are locked into a possessive love need and will seek this treatment when they lose their love objects.

They use the therapy briefly for catharsis and quickly return to the neurotic solution of seeking a partner as soon as they get temporary relief.

Still others who are locked into a vindictive solution to their conflicts cannot really regress but instead of "primalling," remain on an adult level as they give expression to their inner rage in an adult manner. They want to smash things now, hurt people in their present environment instead of acting-in and regressing to childhood.

In time, the effectiveness of the intense feeling approach, with its crash program, will prove itself and be used more widely.

It was Arthur Janov who first put emphasis on the importance of breaking down the defenses in a crash program as described in his book *The Primal Scream*. Intense Feeling Therapy adopts the same approach but in addition, recognizes the need for a relationship between therapist and patient so that other influences can be brought to bear to help the patient resolve inner conflicts and integrate himself into society.

# The Intensive Journal[4*]

## Felix Morrow

### DEFINITION

The Intensive Journal process is a method of personal and spiritual growth in which the individual primarily works by himself in his Intensive Journal workbook. The person learns the principles and techniques involved by attending a basic Intensive Journal workshop conducted by Dr. Ira Progoff or a Journal Consultant authorized by Dialogue House; or one can begin by reading Progoff's *At a Journal Workshop* (1975), which contains a complete Intensive Journal experience. Those who sustain work in this method are likely to attend a workshop from time to time as they feel the need, read and reread the key books dealing with the process, and perhaps occasionally see a Journal Consultant in a one-to-one meeting. Their main effort, however, is working by themselves in the Intensive Journal workbook.

### HISTORY

Progoff's work began with his doctoral thesis, *Jung's Psychology and Its Social Meaning* (1953). In *The Death and Rebirth of Psychology* (1956), *Depth Psychology and Modern Man* (1959), and *The Symbolic and the Real* (1963), Progoff set forth his ideas on depth psychology, which is a synthesis of the later work of Freud, Jung, Adler, and Rank. In it depth psychology leaves behind its medical and analytic origins and, indeed, goes beyond psychotherapy to a conception of man as a growing and spiritual being. In 1957 Progoff began to use a journal as an adjunct to psychotherapy in his private practice. He asked people to keep notebooks in which they recorded the events of their inner life. A great deal that was therapeutic was achieved by working with this psychological journal. Progoff observed, however, that the affirmative effects of using this unstructured workbook were too closely connected with the questions he raised or the way he raised them. The results for the individual were at that point, then, very closely linked to Progoff's personal style in conducting the therapeutic consultations and the way he led the group sessions.

The next and most decisive step, therefore, was to structure a journal capable of mirroring the inner process of the psyche of each individual without falsification of any kind and without the intrusion of special doctrines or authorities. This next step was the creation of the Intensive Journal workbook, which, after a series of provisional attempts, took its present form in 1966. Progoff was able to create the Intensive Journal workbook by applying to it what he had learned from a decade of study of the lives of creative persons. He had done this work as director of the Institute for Research in Depth Psychology at the Graduate School of Drew University (1959- 1971), where he and his students had systematically collected the life histories of persons for a comparative study.

---

4* Intensive Journal is a trademark of Dialogue House.

## TECHNIQUE

In the workshop, in an initiation into the varied techniques for using the Intensive Journal workbook, the beginner learns a nonjudgmental, nonanalytic, nondiagnostic means of working out a broad answer to the question: Where am I now in the movement of my life? There are twenty sections to the workbook. Sixteen of these are the Intensive Journal categories, the other four are for the related discipline of *process meditation*. The workbook enables a person to write down in various logs the inner and outer experience of his life and then in a series of exercises called "Journal Feedback," draw his life into focus, enlarge his capacities, clarify where he now is, determine his resources, decide on new directions in the face of transitions or crossroads. It is important to understand that in this work the therapeutic and integrative results are not directly sought. They are, as it were, an indirect outcome of the energies generated by the process of Journal Feedback. Another way of saying this is that working with these exercises enables each of us to understand the meaning of our lives and go on to fulfill that meaning.

It should perhaps be emphasized that a central image of this process is that each of us "goes down his own well" in privacy With the aid of "twilight imagery," process meditation, and working with our dreams, we go down into our depths in a unique way. It is in those depths and not on the upper, superficial levels that we do the exercises of Journal Feedback. Hence we have access to much that we do not know consciously but that we know nevertheless. Nor is what we know merely personal. For going down the well we go beyond the personal into the transpersonal, the shared humanity.

Progoff's is a *holistic* depth psychology. The discipline of this working on oneself is designed to further wholeness and reconstructing one's life. Its therapeutic effects are brought about not by striving toward therapy but by providing the active techniques that enable an individual to draw upon his inherent resources for becoming a whole person. It establishes a person's sense of his own being by enriching his inner life with new experiences of a creative and spiritual quality by means of the Journal Feedback exercises. Since these experiences happen to him and are recorded by him while they are actually taking place, each person accumulates a tangible and factual validation of his personal growth as it is in process.

Progoff refers to Ralph Waldo Emerson's conception of self-reliance as one way of understanding the results achieved by the Intensive Journal process. For Emerson, self-reliance is the basis for human growth and dignity. Emerson says in his essay *Self-Reliance*, "Nothing can bring you peace but yourself." When our reliance is upon things or people outside of ourselves, we are not drawing upon the strengths that are inherent within us, and what is more important, we are not developing our strengths further. The Intensive Journal process provides a practical method by which each individual, at whatever his present level and condition, can experience the active power of self-reliance as an available capacity.

## APPLICATIONS

In the decade since the creation of the Intensive Journal workbook in 1966, some fifty thousand persons were introduced to this method by workshops and the first printings of *At a Journal Workshop*. But implicit from the first was the idea of the Intensive Journal program as one of very broad social outreach, able to serve a great public of all levels of income, age, and education. In 1977 a major step in this direction was taken with the beginning of the National Intensive Journal Program. Responsible local organizations throughout the country have been invited to become sponsors of ongoing Intensive Journal programs in their communities. Protestant and Catholic churches and retreat centers have been particularly responsive as sponsors in the first months of the expanded program.

The Intensive Journal program is taught in a growing number of colleges and universities in both workshops and term courses. Among the applications are its use in college counseling and pastoral counseling. There was a notably successful project in New York State in using the Intensive Journal process in a job-training program in the ghetto. A Women's Institute in the Midwest reports great success in introducing the Intensive Journal program to substantial groups of women convicts in the prisons. In the creative arts there have been successful uses of the process as part of the training of classes of dancers and potters. These examples are indicative of the wide range of applications that are possible.

# Intensive Psychotherapy
## *Richard D. Chessick*

### DEFINITION

Intensive Psychotherapy is best thought of as psychoanalysis with parameters; that is to say, a form of psychoanalytic treatment modified to suit the nature of the patient involved. If we define psychoanalysis as a treatment characterized by a frequency of at least four sessions each week during which a transference neurosis develops and is resolved by proper interpretation, we can compare Intensive Psychotherapy against this procedure. In Intensive Psychotherapy, the patient comes in less frequently, usually twice or at most three times weekly, may or may not lie on the couch, and does not ordinarily form a full-blown transference neurosis. Although strong transference reactions do develop and are usually interpreted, the curative factors in Intensive Psychotherapy are out of a multiple of influences, of which interpretation of transference is just one. In psychoanalysis, on the other hand, interpretation of the transference neurosis is thought to be the major and central curative factor.

### HISTORY

Freud is the discoverer and founder of Intensive Psychotherapy as he was, of course, the discoverer and founder of psychoanalysis. All the principles of understanding and dealing with patients in Intensive Psychotherapy are based completely on the Freudian psychoanalytic point of view, and all interventions in Intensive Psychotherapy are based on our metapsychological understanding of the patient at any given time. All interventions are verbal only; at no time is any form of physical or social contact with the patient ever employed, and the treatment is always of one individual patient with no other person or persons present, except in certain unavoidable emergency situations.

No person should be allowed to practice Intensive Psychotherapy without undergoing several years of Intensive Psychotherapy or, better yet, personal psychoanalysis himself, and with satisfactory termination of personal therapy. Without a deep and thoroughgoing personal treatment, it is impossible to avoid major counter-transference floundering and both exploitation and retaliation against patients. It is easier to exploit patients in Intensive Psychotherapy and to become lost in counter-transference than it is in psychoanalysis, because in the latter the rules are more clear cut, whereas in Intensive Psychotherapy a combination of supportive, educative, and interpretative interventions is often called for, as well as the use of psychopharmacologic agents.

Psychoanalysis was designed by Freud for a very specific type of patient, those with transference neuroses. These conditions, such as certain phobias, obsessions, anxiety states, hysterical symptoms, and the like, were discovered to be based on infantile neuroses formed during the time of the resolution of the Oedipus complex, at around five years of age. Such patients were assumed to have traversed the first three or four years of life reasonably well, and to have a cohesive sense of self and, with resolution of the Oedipus complex, a fairly solid repression barrier, intact ego, and strong superego. Tensions between the id, ego, and superego produced first repression, which was unsuccessful, and then recourse to symptom formation to aid repression. Patients with emotional disorders forming prior to the oedipal period were considered untreatable by psychoanalysis, according to Freud.

The increasing plethora of such "preoedipal" disorders, such as schizoid personalities, schizophrenics, many depressive disorders, certain perversions, borderline patients (Chessick, 1977), and many personality disorders forced psychoanalysts to reevaluate their treatment. One group of psychoanalysts, such as the Kleinians and others, rewrote Freud's theories entirely in order to justify the application of his psychoanalysis to preoedipal disorders; this group has more adherents in England. American pioneers such as Alexander, Fromm-Reichmann, and many others introduced a variety of so-called parameters, modifying the formal rules and regulations of psychoanalysis to fit these patients. For example, patients with personality disorders who engage in dangerous behavior must be warned by the therapist of the consequences of such behavior to themselves, and in some cases the therapist must even intervene directly. This would represent an unavoidable modification or parameter from the classic psychoanalytic paradigm of interpretation of the transference neurosis and compromise the neutrality of the therapist. The development of Intensive Psychotherapy out of psychoanalysis and the historical roots of the various techniques used in Intensive Psychotherapy are traced in my book *Great Ideas in Psychotherapy*, which is understandable to the educated lay reader.

## TECHNIQUE

In the communication with the patient, every detail of the therapist's behavior, office, atmosphere of treatment, and speech has an effect on the patient and fosters pacification, unification, resolution of defects in development (especially of narcissistic formations), and strengthens the adaptive and defensive functions of the ego. In later phases of treatment the procedure resembles more and more a formal psychoanalysis. There is a difference of opinion among authors as to whether the patient should begin immediately on the couch four times weekly even though parameters have to be introduced. Psychoanalysts tend to this latter procedure; psychiatrists and other nonpsychoanalysts tend to see the patient less frequently and sitting up. It remains moot as to which approach is best, as the basic principles of treatment are the same either way. More details of the technique and practice of Intensive Psychotherapy are given in my book *How Psychotherapy Heals*.

## APPLICATIONS

Intensive Psychotherapy is a highly effective procedure for the treatment of a large variety of emotional disorders that are not suitable or amenable for psychoanalysis. It is the treatment of choice for schizophrenia, borderline patients, personality disorders (except for the addictions), and psychosomatic conditions. It is second choice for a large number of patients who cannot afford to find the time for formal psychoanalysis. The goals are less far reaching in Intensive Psychotherapy than in psychoanalysis; the therapist is more satisfied with limited structural change, resumption of normal developmental lines, and better adaptation. Sometimes he must help the patient accept residual deficits and scars from early infancy. The danger of placing such preoedipal disorders in formal psychoanalysis rather than Intensive Psychotherapy lies in raising the patient's hopes for extensive intrapsychic rearrangement, which is often not possible when such profound early psychological destruction has occurred.

# Interactional Psychotherapy

*Sheldon Cashdan*

## DEFINITION

Interactional Psychotherapy is a treatment process that depends almost exclusively on the therapist-client interaction for enacting change. The focus in the therapy is on the maladaptive behavior patterns that the client uses to structure his relationships. Labeled "strategies," these patterns are highly manipulative and lead ultimately to a breakdown in his relationships with others. Interactional Psychotherapy is based on the premise that the client will invoke strategic maneuvers in treatment and attempt to structure his relationship with the therapist in much the same way as he does with other significant figures in his life.

Of the many strategies that exist, the four most commonly seen in therapy are Sexuality, Dependency, Martyr, and Power strategies. Each represents, respectively, the exploitative use of eroticism, help-seeking, ingratiation, and control in human relationships. The task of the therapist is to establish the conditions that allow the strategy to be expressed in the treatment setting. Once this is accomplished and the strategy emerges, the therapist can respond to it in such a way as to help the client interact in new and more adaptive ways.

# HISTORY

Interactional Psychotherapy is a relatively new technique, although its underpinnings can be found in a number of interactional approaches to personality. Eric Berne, Robert Carson, and Erving Goffman are but a few of the writers who emphasize the way human interaction and pathological behavior are related. Interactional Psychotherapy is the natural derivative of such approaches since it articulates precisely how the therapist-client interaction can be used to modify maladaptive behavior.

# TECHNIQUE

The interactional therapy process is comprised of five relatively distinct stages. They are:

> Stage One: Hooking
> Stage Two: Maladaptive Strategies
> Stage Three: Stripping
> Stage Four: Adaptive Strategies
> Stage Five: Unhooking (Termination)

Each stage encompasses a relatively discrete set of techniques and a corresponding shift in the client's behavior. The goal of treatment is to guide the client through these stages to provide him with a series of sequential learning experiences. This in turn leads to the replacement of maladaptive strategies by more adaptive ways of relating.

At the beginning of the treatment process the therapist must establish the conditions that will enable him to become a significant figure in the client's life. Through a combination of support and mild advice giving, the therapist transforms himself from a distant "expert" into someone warm and caring, someone capable of being regarded as a "significant other" (someone who plays an important role in one's life). After this is accomplished, as indicated by the client's wanting to come to therapy rather than feeling he needs to, the first stage of treatment—hooking—is completed.

The client's maladaptive patterns then begin to emerge, marking the beginning of stage two. This occurs as the client comes to view the therapy relationship as one that potentially can gratify relational needs. The client, therefore, begins to use the same strategy with the therapist as he does with other important figures in his life. In the beginning, the strategy is expressed in vague and indirect ways. The therapist's job in this stage consequently is to transform indirect expressions of the client's strategy into clear, unambiguous statements. What this means is that the therapist must allow himself to become the target of the client's strategy. This is done so that the strategy can be dealt with effectively in an experiential fashion.

Stage three—stripping—is the phase of treatment in which the client's strategy is confronted, challenged, and eventually refuted. By refusing to be manipulated while simultaneously affirming the relationship, the therapist chips away at the strategy and "strips" the client of his major way of relating to people. The stripping stage tends to be an extended phase of therapy since clients do not easily give up what they have come to depend upon so desperately. Often it is a tumultuous phase. But unless it is successfully negotiated, the client will not experience what it means to be in a relationship that is strategy-free.

The fourth, or adaptive, strategy stage is marked by self-revelation on the client's part and by transactional feedback on the part of the therapist. For perhaps the first time in his life the client begins to reveal some very basic doubts about himself. Very often these have to do with detachment from others and deep doubts about his ability to care. Almost always, issues of self-worth and self-esteem emerge.

This is the stage of therapy in which issues of identity are delved into in detail. With strategic behavior patterns weakened, the client can now explore more productively how his identity is confirmed in his interactions with others. It is here that therapist feedback has its greatest impact. Because the therapist has become a "significant other," and can now communicate without having to cope with strategic roadblocks (extreme dependency, seduction maneuvers, etc.), he can help the client appreciate how his maladaptive behavior patterns undermine his relationships with others.

The final stage—unhooking—marks the beginning of a letting-go process. The major learning of therapy has already taken place. The client has survived a relationship with a meaningful figure without having to rely so heavily on his strategic maneuvers. Bolstered by this experience and armed with some of the rudimentary interpersonal tools of human interaction, he now is in a much better position to form meaningful productive relationships outside the therapy. As outside relationships become more gratifying and the cost of staying in therapy outweighs the benefits, the therapy comes to a close.

## APPLICATIONS

To the extent that most maladaptive behavior patterns can be depicted in strategic terms, Interactional Psychotherapy is applicable in a variety of contexts. The system has been described in one-to-one terms merely for descriptive purposes. It is equally applicable in group therapy, marital counseling, family therapy, and other therapy settings involving more than a single client. The main difference in multiper-son contexts is that the therapist focuses less on his role as target and more on the way participants target one another. Other differences exist (Cashdan, 1973) but they have more to do with changes in specific techniques than with major alterations in the therapy process.

# Jungian Group Psychotherapy
## Thayei A. Greene

### DEFINITION

Jungian Group Psychotherapy is designed to provide individuals with both interpersonal and intrapersonal experience of the psyche within a group setting. In Jungian theory and practice, the priority of individual analytic therapy, one to one, is explicitly affirmed. Group therapy, therefore, is seen as a valuable adjunct and aid to the central work of an individual with an analyst. The group by its very nature constellates unconscious projections, affective (emotional) reactions, and the struggle for individuality in relation to the collective. The concreteness and immediate experience of group interaction provide an arena within which individuals can encounter their psychological reality. Unconscious dynamics are first confronted, often painfully, and then slowly assimilated through the mirroring effect of group feedback and group acceptance. In this way the introverted and individual bias in Jungian psychology is compensated by the healing potential of creative communal experience.

## HISTORY

Carl Jung himself was profoundly skeptical about the value of group therapy and he never included it in his own analytical practice. His concern and appreciation for the value and uniqueness of the intrapsychic experience of the individual made him wary of the intrusiveness and collective categorizing so typical of much group behavior. It was not until the early 1960s, around the time of Jung's death, that a very few Jungian analysts began to experiment with group process as an adjunct to individual analysis. Group therapy as a treatment modality has become increasingly accepted by Jungians, but even now is practiced only by a minority. Only in the New York Training Center is group therapy included as a required element in the training experience of prospective analysts.

## TECHNIQUE

Group psychotherapy is such a recent development for Jungians that no commonly recognized or agreed upon technique has as yet developed. At this point the particular personality and past group experience of the therapist is liable to determine his technique more than any other factor. There is as yet only the barest minimum of Jungian writing specifically devoted to the subject (see bibliography). One implication of this lack of a substantial history or literature is that Jungians have had to look outside their own school to find models and methods with which to work.

Probably the most important contributions to the techniques used by Jungian therapists in group process have been drawn from the gestalt and encounter group experience. Some therapists also use bio-energetic and sensory awareness methods. In almost every case the method chosen has the purpose of aiding an individual to explore the intrapsychic dimensions of some interpersonal conflict. Two methods used extensively in individual Jungian analysis—namely, dream analysis and creative fantasy—are also frequently employed within the group process. When, for example, a member has had a dream about the group, such a piece of unconscious material is considered most appropriate for group analysis, even though it may also be worked within an individual session. Creative fantasy involves a method of guided exploration and analysis of images emerging spontaneously from the psyche of an individual group member or occasionally from the unconscious material of several group members at the same time. The starting point for such a fantasy may be a dream image, a powerful affective reaction, a significant figure in the group member's life, or possibly an internal image evoked by some other member of the group.

Since Jungians consider the experience of individual analysis to be the result of a unique encounter between two psyches, there is naturally a rather similar attitude toward the role and function of the therapist in a group. Various projections and transference phenomena will inevitably occur that the therapist must deal with in a manner consonant with his own personality and style. The focus of therapeutic leadership in a group is almost never a concentration upon transference and resistance as the primary catalyst for awareness. The therapist is more often one who intervenes only when other resources in the group are not available or when specific professional knowledge and interpretation is needed. Such an approach tends to evoke a transference to the group itself in both positive and negative forms, as nourisher and devourer, as rule giver and liberator.

## APPLICATIONS

Although there is no consistent and widely accepted technique, Jungian group therapists are in general agreement as to the central values and applications of the group process. Absolute priority is given to the legitimacy and integrity of the experience of the individual within the group. Whatever the projections, reactions, distortions of a group member, these are approached with a phenomenological and accepting attitude as that individual's present psychological reality. Positive and negative interactions in the group are first allowed to be played out and fully experienced and then are looked at in terms of subjective meaning and unconscious dynamics. Such an approach provides each group member with a greatly strengthened sense of individual identity and value in the face of social collectivity. Particularly for introverted and socially isolated people, such an experience of individuality within a group can lead to significant therapeutic change in social adaptation. By its very nature a group presents each member with a variety of personalities and psychological types in a way that no one-to-one individual analytic experience can do. Thinking and feeling, sensation and intuition, introversion and extraversion are all present and evoke reactions within the group. In that way the group process becomes a laboratory for the life situation and conflicts of its members in their marriages, work, and other interpersonal involvements. The major complexes, such as mother, father, oedipal, authority, etc., are spontaneously enacted within the group and thereby become available to analytic exploration and individual assimilation.

# Kinetic Psychotherapy

*Robert S. Schachter*

## DEFINITION

Kinetic Psychotherapy (KPT) is a form of group therapy designed for adults, children, and families to help participants look at their patterns of interaction with each other as well as their behavior in various life situations. Additionally, it is a vehicle for learning to identify and verbalize emotion. Behavior is viewed as a statement made in response to a feeling state. Group members have the opportunity to assess if the manner in which they make their statements is effective. They are encouraged to use adaptive behavior and find alternatives to ineffective patterns of interaction.

Kinetic Psychotherapy accomplishes these aims via a series of physical interactive games that imitate real-life situations. An example is "Frustration," in which five participants form a circle and attempt to prevent a sixth member from catching the ball that is passed around. As the play continues, three things occur. First, the excluded member begins to experience feelings. These are projected into the game, as evidenced by different responses of various members.

Second, as feelings become apparent, the individual assumes his characteristic coping response to such a situation. For example, the one who usually gives up when frustrated will begin to give up. The game is stopped at this point and the player is given an opportunity to view his response pattern. If it is effective, the participant is encouraged to use it; however, in the case of the person who gives up, he is aided by the group in finding an alternative coping mechanism that fits with the person's style. Another useful example is that of the person who withholds expression of emotion when angry. As the individual becomes angry in the game and a typical pattern emerges, he has an opportunity to verbally communicate this feeling directly to another. A structure exists in which all emotions can be identified and verbally expressed with the person never being pushed past the point that he can tolerate. As a result, the person *experiences* a resolution of a confrontation.

Third, associations to other experiences of similar feeling tone become conscious and are available for discussion, which occurs at the end of the activity session. This verbal interchange is relatively traditional in its technique. Behavior observed in the activity period is examined and related to behavior in real-life situations.

## HISTORY

KPT was developed by this writer essentially by accident. After observing a number of youngsters interact in a game situation, I found that affective (emotional) responses were more intense and that characteristic patterns of response became evident in a way not possible with traditional verbal or play approaches. I experimented with hundreds of games that have been distilled to the existing fifty activities now used. Each of these is designed to imitate a real-life situation in feeling tone and to stimulate interaction. Experimental studies with children indicate a high rate of behavioral change (80 percent) within a treatment time of six months with weekly group meetings. A 10 percent regression rate was revealed by a two-year follow-up. Work with adults has not been documented experimentally.

## TECHNIQUE

Kinetic Psychotherapy combines the three approaches of the Psychoanalytic, Existential, and Behaviorist schools. After an intensive evaluation, a person is placed in a group of six that is balanced to include several persons of aggressive and several of passive behavioral styles. Psychoanalytic theory is considered as one participates in the activities, and the psychodynamics of this individual are constantly considered within the context of the activity. If he is interested in pursuing the cause of various behaviors, this is explored in the verbal group discussion segment. Here, intrapsychic material that has become available is also examined. The experiential aspect of KPT is fundamental to how a person becomes aware of present patterns and how one can retrain oneself to use new ones. As the game is stopped and the participant focuses on the pattern the instant it is occurring, an experiential awareness occurs in which the behavior suddenly becomes clear. Similarly, as an individual practices a new behavior, this becomes part of the ego functioning and is added to a person's repertoire of responses. The behaviorist orientation is stressed in understanding how new behaviors are reinforced. Since it is a group therapy, feedback based on observed behavior is immediately available to participants. As an adaptive behavior is learned, group members and the therapist are often spontaneously supportive. Additionally, the person usually encounters positive response in life situations as techniques learned in the group are applied. The resulting sense of competency is a strong reinforcer.

In each situation, an individual's style is respected. A person who has been quiet for thirty years is not expected to become a screamer. Defenses are also highly respected. Members are *never* forced to talk about what they don't want to discuss, nor are they forced to participate when they feel resistant. This situation is worked with in the way resistances traditionally are. Hopefully, they are put into some context that helps the person understand the behavior.

### APPLICATIONS

With adults, KPT has proven very effective in work with nonpsychotic cases of depression, anxiety, phobias, social skill training, and general situations where a person needs to learn more effective ways of facing, accepting, and using emotion in interpersonal situations. With children KPT has proven valuable in dealing with cases where behavior ranges from overly passive to overly aggressive. Adjustment reactions, phobias, immature behavior, and emotional problems stemming from learning disabilities all have shown impressive diminution. As a tool for family therapy KPT helps make explicit the family process and facilitates interventions for improved communication.

In summary, Kinetic Psychotherapy is a form of group therapy suited for those who need to face and change current patterns of functioning. By using a range of physical interactive games as its base, KPT allows participants to face their coping systems and aids them in finding alternatives that fit their basic style.

---

# Kleinian Technique

*Ruth Riesenberg-Malcolm*

### DEFINITION

Melanie Klein's technique is a psychoanalytic method used in treatment of children as well as adults.

# HISTORY

Klein began her therapy first in Budapest in 1917, mainly with children. This work enabled her to study early infantile development at firsthand. From this analytic work she obtained her main insights into the functioning of the human mind. These discoveries also helped to shape her analytic technique.

In 1924 Klein moved to Berlin to undergo analysis with Karl Abraham. She came to England in 1926 through an invitation of the British Psycho-Analytic Society. She settled in London and practiced and taught there until her death in 1960.

Her ideas and methods are widely used in the treatment of both neurotic and psychotic patients, and have greatly influenced the thinking of the British School of Psycho-Analysis.

Klein came to realize that the individual is exposed from birth to a conflict caused by the action of the two opposite impulses: love and aggression. She is an adherent of Freud's view on the life-and-death instincts. An early and rudimentary ego also exists from the start and is capable of experiencing those impulses and anxieties, and of creating defenses necessary to defend itself. The impulses, being of a biological nature, cannot directly be perceived as such by the mind. The ego creates fantasies that are psychological transformations of instinctive impulses as well as representatives of the object that satisfies them. The mechanisms of projection and introjection operative throughout life play a central role in the infant's relations to his objects. All these mental phenomena are perceived and expressed in the mind by unconscious fantasy.

# TECHNIQUE

This basic theoretical understanding made Klein and her followers develop certain emphases of analytical technique that are generally thought to distinguish them from other followers of Freud's basic method. First, Kleinian analysts are especially rigorous in using transference as the main basis of formulating interpretations, and they assume that transference operates from the moment the analysis begins rather than as something built up gradually. Second, in evaluating the transference they use not only the verbal contents of what the patient says but also the feelings that he expresses by his manner of saying it and the feelings he evokes in the analyst. Third, they do not necessarily deal with defenses, rather than anxieties, first, as most of the analytical schools do but refer to the anxiety content together with its defense. Fourth, compared with many analytical schools of thought in the United States and on the Continent they interpret more frequently.

However, Klein and her followers maintained the main points of Freud's classical technique: the analyst works with the patient five times a week in sessions lasting fifty minutes, asks the patient to lie down on the couch, to free associate, uses his understanding of transference, and presents his findings to the patient in the form of interpretations with the aim of achieving therapeutic insight. The Kleinian Technique is thus modeled on Freud's method. In a sense it adheres to it with special strictness, since it avoids making any kind of interventions other than interpretations.

To illustrate some of these points I want to describe some material from the initial sessions with a patient. He was a thirty-year-old man, very handsome, cold and distant. He came to his first session and proceeded to tell me that he did not expect much from analysis. In fact, he did not expect anything at all, but just wanted to see whether it might help him with his problem. He added that his main problem was not just psychological. As it happened he was told by his father that he had to get married or he would be disinherited. (His father wanted to make sure of an heir to the family name.) He had never had a real girl friend. He had never been in love and he had never had sexual intercourse. All this was said to me in a very superior way. After a short pause he proceeded to say that he was rather surprised that Kleinian analysts treat adult patients; he had thought they worked only with children, but he was pleased to have chosen a Kleinian analyst. Here I pointed out to him, tentatively, that it seemed to me that he had two different feelings: on the one hand, he expects very little from the analysis; but on the other hand, he is somewhat hopeful that I might be able to help him with the problems he felt to have been with him from childhood. This would explain his remark that I was a "Kleinian" and also his notions that Kleinians work only with children.

Perhaps he hoped that I might be able to help a part of him that might feel like a child and that this might allow him to feel friendly toward a woman and eventually to move toward marriage. The patient mocked a bit, scorned the interpretation, and said that he could not comprehend my point. Then he proceeded to tell me that he had often been out with women; some he found very pleasant but he always felt distant toward them. Usually what happened was that they were very interested in him, and then he dropped them. He proceeded to recount in some detail a particular episode that puzzled him. He was going out with a girl who seemed to be getting more and more attached to him and then, for no reason he could account for, he suddenly left her in the middle of a dinner party. This situation had always made him feel rather uncomfortable and strange. He could not understand it. He said that often he daydreamed about becoming a bishop and building an enormous church. He suddenly asked me when I took my vacations. I suggested that perhaps his attitude played a part in producing his feeling that nothing is to be expected from the analysis. I went on to say that he might fear that were he to allow himself any hope from the analysis this would make him feel unsafe, and that this insecurity would be a torture to him. For example, he might be exposed to the disruption of my going on vacations. I also pointed out that this would explain his question about vacations which otherwise seemed premature, since we were in the beginning of the year. In this interpretation I tried to connect his cold, superior attitude with his attempts to make me feel unwanted. He wanted me to know that he could walk out on me and thus could avoid the bad feelings that he might have if he were placed in the same situation that the girl whom he had left had been placed in.

The patient's response to this interpretation was slightly different from his response to the previous one. He proceeded to dismiss what I said, but he sounded 'more thoughtful and not so patronizing. In the following session he said that he had had a dream where he was sitting in a train feeling terribly frightened; he felt he might lose his way and his belongings. He could not understand this at all. He associated with this a time when he was very young—under seven—and was sent to boarding school. He had felt utterly desolate there, and he tried to phone his parents, but they just would not listen and told him to be a man. Here I was able to interpret how if he did not express his usual coldness and contempt and wasn't patronizing he might feel like this terribly desolate child. I reminded him of the previous day's session, about the vacations, and said how he feared that I might send him away as he had been sent away to school and that led him to put all these vulnerable and frightened parts of himself and his feelings into me, and then he looked down at me as he felt he had been looked down on when he was small and he treated my interpretations as though they were noises from a child who was making too much fuss. Here, for the first time, the patient laughed. He tried to dismiss the interpretation by saying, "Oh, it's quite interesting. I think I understand what you say. Of course it is a parallel, just a parallel, and anyhow, I don't know how it would solve my problem."

In the following day's session he began to tell a dream. In the dream he woke up and tried to recall his dream, but he was interrupted all the time by a very gay, mocking, handsome young man who looked a bit like himself and who kept singing opera very loudly. The moment he tried to speak, the singing grew louder and louder. Here I made the following interpretation with the aid of an association he had given me, namely, that through the dream we could see that there seemed to be a big split between two aspects of himself in his relation to me and to the analysis, and that those aspects were in conflict. Also, I suggested a connection with his saying the day before ". . .I think I understand what you say. Of course, it is a parallel . . ."I remarked that this division in him makes him see things in parallels.

I have brought some instances from the beginning of this patient's analysis to illustrate my mode of interpretation, which is conditioned both by one's understanding of the transference and content of the patient's material, and by one's theoretical conceptions. In his comprehension of the transference and the central role it plays in the analytical work, the Kleinian analyst is much influenced by the idea that object relations exist from birth and by the concepts of the paranoid-schizoid and depressive positions, each with its characteristic pattern of anxieties and defenses. The understanding of the processes that underlie the formation of the transference—that is, repetitive compulsion—and its meanings make a Kleinian analyst watchful for manifestations of it from the very first session, and the analyst tries to understand how the patient first relates to his analyst—what expectations he has, what anxieties he feels, what methods he uses to defend himself. In evaluating the patient's material the analyst takes into account, together with his verbal communications, the total of the patient's behavior; his movements from the moment he enters the room, his tone of voice, the form he speaks in, the way he responds to the analyst's interventions.

Interpretations are given frequently and are formulated as soon as some understanding of what is happening has been reached. They are then modulated and shaped according to the patient's response. To be therapeutic the interpretation has to refer to the patient's feelings, anxieties, and defenses. It has to take into account the external stimuli, the transference situation, as well as the links with the past. It should refer to the role of the internal object as well as the interplay between fantasy and reality. All this would make an interpretation very long. Interpretations are often given in part at first and then gradually completed, generally enlarged by the new material the patient brings and which corrects and enriches the initial approach. The time it takes to complete an interpretation is irrelevant, but it should be completed to be of therapeutic value. Interpretations are not first directed to the defenses, as in many techniques following Freud, but they refer directly to the unconscious conflict. Here, Klein's use of the concept of fantasy plays a very central role as fantasies represent at the same time impulses and their objects, defenses and mental mechanisms, and they are intrinsically connected with feelings. Following these ideas, the Kleinian analyst does not have a preconceived idea of what to interpret first. He will try to direct his interpretation to where the conflict is felt to be more acute and therefore where the anxiety is stronger. The understanding brought by the interpretation usually allows for some modification of the immediate anxiety, which alters the relationship and allows it to proceed for further examination and working through the existing fantasies. As I have said, interpretations in Kleinian Technique are generally frequent and the analytical session has the characteristics of an active dialogue. The Kleinian view is that analytical insight is gained through the modification of misconceptions and faulty relationships and that such modification can be achieved only by active searching for causes and communicated verbally to achieve the understanding of them. The continual projection on to the analyst of the patient's relationship with his internal objects permits the analyst to understand his internal world, which, by being communicated verbally through interpretations, allows the patient to modify his object relations by new introjections and therefore to free the ego from enslavement by continuous conflict.

The conception of projective identification and its different functions has played a very central role in Kleinian Technique. It shapes both the understanding of the patient's projections as well as the formulation of the interpretations. The interpretation of projective identification allows the patient slowly to modify and reintegrate the parts of himself he has projected. A step in this process was made by the patient in the example cited above, when he began to accept at least the idea of a small, frightened part of himself instead of projecting it into the analyst. The understanding of the material in the transference is helped by the analyst's own perceptions of the responses to the patient's that he feels in himself. This counter-transference, though having its roots in the unconscious of the analyst, is greatly influenced and shaped by the patient's projections. To illustrate this process I want to give some material from another patient, a woman.

She was feeling that she had a "rather good relationship" with me; no matter what happened, and despite anything I said, she perceived me as a very good, friendly analyst, and believed she was my favorite patient. At the same time she totally ignored my interpretations. Not only did she not discuss them, she also showed subsequently that she was completely untouched by them. She would say something either long or short and then she would politely stop talking, expecting me to speak. She appeared to listen to me, paused for a moment, and then continued with whatever she had been thinking of before, or during, my talk. While this was taking place, I felt awkward and increasingly more restricted while experiencing a sense of pressure to enlarge my interpretation, to explain things in more detail, or to find different or more elaborate ways to present it to the patient. As I became aware of this I took special care to scrutinize the detail of the patient's responses, coming to the conclusion that she not only had not listened, but that she spoke in an attitude that conveyed her belief that what I said was futile, while her explanations were felt to be fascinating. Slowly I was able to say that while I was speaking she may have heard my words, possibly only my voice, but at the same time she went on thinking her own thoughts. I said that the whole situation did not seem to bother her much and she felt that the most important thing was to tell me what was in her mind. It then emerged that she had been enacting a strong fantasy in which she was inside me and was identified with me as an ideal object that provided everything. She herself became this object. My role as an external object, on the other hand, was to be a place where she could get rid of her trouble and bad feelings. Slowly, the patient began to explain that she was afraid that she would be expelled from the job she held in a research institution. She thought that her employers might already have discovered that she did not care much for the research she was doing and that what she wanted was for them to like and admire her and find her very extraordinary.

I have quoted this example to illustrate the way in which the patient in the transference relationship was responding to me in two ways. First, she was regarding me as an ideal object, inhabited and totally possessed by her. But second, insofar as I was independent of her, she felt me to be bad and persecuting. This "bad me" was quickly split off into an external situation, the place where she worked.

The understanding of splitting processes in early development, both formative as well as defensive, also helps us to understand the appearance and coexistence in analysis of different parts of the personality, feelings and anxieties that originate in different phases of development but which can coexist and certainly do appear in the treatment in no specific order other than that given in the patient's personal history. In my view it is important to maintain flexibility in the understanding of the anxieties with their shift from object to object and defense to defense so that one can take them up as they show themselves in each session or period of work. It is only by dealing step by step that one can help to try to bring the different parts of the patient's personality together and help toward integration through insight into earlier anxieties.

# Learning Theory Therapy

## Irving Beiman

### DEFINITION

Learning Theory Therapy encompasses a wide variety of therapeutic procedures or techniques used to provide the client with learning experiences that promote desirable or adaptive ideational, behavioral, and affective (emotional) responses. The use of such procedures is based upon the assumption that a client's psychological problems are a function of maladaptive learning and are therefore modifiable by new adaptive learning experiences. Thus, psychological problems are not viewed as symptoms of some underlying intrapsychic, genetic, or biochemical disorder. Rather they are viewed as functionally related to current, antecedent, and consequent events, as well as developmentally related to prior maladaptive learning experiences.

### TECHNIQUE

In the initial assessment, the therapist usually interviews the client to determine the problem(s) he wishes to change. After a problem has been identified, sufficient information is usually gathered to determine: 1) the problem's situational context; 2) the frequency, intensity, and severity of the problem; 3) the events that precede and follow the problem's occurrence; and 4) the client's thoughts and feelings before, during, and after the problem's occurrence. The therapist will often gather additional information to determine whether the client's physiological arousal is a relevant factor, as well as whether the client has the necessary skills to perform appropriately in a problematic situation. This information is always gathered at least partially via the clinical interview, but additional methods may also be used, including various questionnaires and rating forms (Ciminero, et al., 1977). Clients are often assigned homework tasks requiring them to record one or more aspects of the above information in a diary or on self-monitoring forms that are then returned to the therapist.

The therapist then uses this information to conceptualize the problem by specifying client-specific functional relationships between the problem and current internal/ external events. A summary of the therapist's conceptualization of each problem is presented to the client, although it is always subject to modification based on additional information. When, for example, enough information is available to formulate hypotheses about etiological factors in the client's learning history that could account for the problem, this information is included in the conceptualization. During this presentation the therapist and client establish mutual agreement regarding: 1) the problem(s) to be addressed and ensuing therapeutic goals, 2) factors currently contributing to or maintaining each problem, 3) the interaction of a client's maladaptive learning history and the development of each problem, and 4) the probable treatment procedures to be used and therapeutic rationale for their effectiveness. Mutual agreement on the goals and procedures of therapy is called a therapeutic contract and may be made in writing.

The principal techniques included in Learning Theory Therapy are classified here according to the type of clinical problems for which they are considered most appropriate: 1) skill deficits, 2) maladaptive approach responses, 3) maladaptive anxiety, stress, and avoidance responses, and 4) maladaptive self-statements, attitudes, and covert responses. See Rimm and Masters (1974) for a comprehensive discussion of the evaluative research and clinical application of these and other techniques.

1.   *Skill deficits.* Clients frequently do not possess the behavioral capabilities (skills) to perform adequately in certain situations. A skill deficit, therefore, may be one factor contributing to the problem when the client frequently avoids certain situations and/ or performs poorly in them. Common examples of such problems include: deficient interpersonal, heterosexual, assertive, or parenting skills. The principles applied to these problems are derived from operant conditioning (Williams, 1973).

After a treatment contract has been established, the therapist performs a task analysis of the target skill in which the desired target responses are conceptually broken down into their prerequisite subskills. The most basic subskills are taught first because this type of therapy approaches deficits by teaching (shaping) the desired complex set of responses in gradual steps (successive approximations) toward the eventual goal (target).

The specific therapeutic procedures used to teach a given skill include: 1) bibliotherapy—the client reading about how to perform a certain skill, 2) verbal instruction by the therapist, 3) modeling—demonstrations of the skill by the therapist, assistants, or via film, 4) prompting/fading—therapist cueing the desired response and gradually decreasing the cues, 5) role playing, role reversal, and behavioral rehearsal with feedback—acting out of relevant interpersonal interactions by client and therapist, with verbal praise and corrective suggestions by the therapist, and 6) homework—assigning the client increasingly complex homework tasks to perform in the natural environment. Therapist praise, encouragement, and corrective suggestions follow the client's performance report in each session. Homework of this nature is almost always used by Learning-Theory therapists in the treatment of all four major types of clinical problems.

2. *Maladaptive approach responses.* Approach responses may be maladaptive because: 1) they are inappropriate in their frequency, duration, or intensity or 2) they are directed toward inappropriate target objects, usually sexual in nature. Examples of 1) include excessive food, alcohol, drug, and cigarette consumption. An example of 2) is sexual responses directed toward target objects that the client and/or "significant others" (people close to the client) consider to be inappropriate or undesirable, as in cross-dressing (transvestism). The principles used to assist the client in this type of problem are derived from operant self-control (Mahoney and Thoreson, 1974) and aversive conditioning (Sandler, 1975). The problem is approached therapeutically by decreasing the likelihood of the undesirable response and increasing the likelihood of responses that are incompatible with, or antagonistic to, the undesirable response.

The principal techniques used for 1) include: self-monitoring, self-reinforcement, contingency management, covert sensitization, and aversive conditioning. These techniques should be utilized hierarchically, moving toward more aversive procedures one step at a time, if necessary. Self-monitoring requires the client to record the frequency, intensity, or duration of the problem after it has occurred. Self-reinforcement dictates that the client reward himself when he has abstained from engaging in the undesirable behavior or has engaged in behavior incompatible with the undesirable response. Contingency management calls for rewards/punishments to be administered by the therapist or a significant other, dependent upon the nonoccurrence/occurrence of the undesirable response. Covert sensitization requires the client's imaginal pairing of unpleasant or noxious scenes with the imaginal undesirable response. Aversive conditioning calls for the application of unpleasant or noxious stimuli soon after the occurrence of the undesirable response.

The procedures used for 2) include all of those for 1) with the addition of masturbatory conditioning. This technique requires that clients pair the pleasurable sensations leading to, and resulting from, orgasm with images of appropriate sexual partners. All of these procedures, with the exception of covert sensitization/aversive conditioning, are typically administered by the client in appropriate settings in the natural environment (home, work, etc.). The therapist instructs the client in the basic technique, monitors progress, and provides individual guidance to maximize therapeutic effect.

3. *Anxiety, stress, and avoidance responses.* An anxiety response may be defined as subjective tension or discomfort accompanied by physiological arousal. Subjective/physiological anxiety responses are often paralleled with the client's verbal/motoric responses to avoid or escape anxiety-provoking stimuli. Maladaptive anxiety can be *reactive* when it is secondary to some other psychological problem; e.g., an interpersonal skills deficit. When this is the case, treatment is directed toward the more primary problem; e.g., interpersonal skills training. Anxiety can also be *self-produced*, when it is primarily

a mediated cognitive response resulting from specific maladaptive self-statements or more general cross-situational attitude responses. When this is the case, treatment often deals more directly with the problematic cognitions through some form of cognitive restructuring (briefly described below). Finally, anxiety can be a *conditioned* response to specific external antecedent stimuli. In this case, some form of desensitization therapy is indicated (Paul and Bernstein, 1973). Implosion has also been recommended, but densensitization seems to be the preferred treatment. Desensitization is historically based upon the combined principles of reciprocal inhibition and counter-conditioning (Wolpe, 1958). According to these principles, conditioned anxiety responses will be permanently weakened (counter-conditioned) if a response incompatible with anxiety, i.e., relaxation, can be made to occur while the client is in the presence of the anxiety-provoking stimuli. The temporary weakening (reciprocal inhibition) of the anxiety response by relaxation occurs during the client's graduated exposure to the negative stimuli.

4.  *Maladaptive self-statements, attitudes, and covert responses.* Learning Theory therapists have historically focused almost exclusively on clients' overt maladaptive behavior, but increasing attention has recently been devoted to clients' maladaptive cognitions. The client's perception of events and self-statements about those events seem to be gaining increasing acceptance as potentially important targets for therapy. Because the basic assumption in this approach is that maladaptive cognitions are a function of maladaptive learning, the problem responses are subject to improved learning experiences through cognitive restructuring.

Cognitive restructuring includes techniques described by Ellis (1962), among others. Whether the problem is a specific maladaptive self-statement in a particular situation or a more general maladaptive attitude that seems to occur in a variety of situations, the initial step is to define the problem and specify the cognitive targets for change. A therapeutic rationale is often presented that explains how the client's maladaptive cognitions developed and how therapy should facilitate their change. In-session treatment often involves the therapist's challenge of the maladaptive cognition in various ways, including consideration of the negative consequences of failing to change, as well as the positive consequences of altering the maladaptive self-statement or attitude. A more adaptive cognitive alternative is then proposed and practiced in the session. Homework assignments usually require the client to record relevant cognitive activity, and require the client to engage in behavior consistent with the adaptive cognitions that are being developed.

In summary, Learning Theory Therapy requires the therapist's application of one or more treatment procedures to ameliorate the client's problems. In- and extra-session learning experiences designed by the therapist lead the client to change ideationally, behaviorally, and affectively in the direction of mutually agreed upon goals. Therapy is terminated when these goals are reached.

# Learning-Based Client-Centered Therapy

*David G. Martin*

## DEFINITION

This work is not so much a different approach to psychotherapy as it is an attempt to explain, within the perspective of learning theory, why the core helping skills of the "therapeutic triad" (accurate empathy, respect and warmth, and genuineness) are effective in the treatment of anxiety-based problems. I argue that the theoretical foundation of client-centered therapy, a belief that humans are innately self-actualizing, is untenable on grounds of both logic and evidence. However, there is considerable evidence that the approach is effective, especially when recent elaborations of Rogers's approach are included. The critical question is: If humans are not innately self-actualizing, how can the client be trusted to direct therapy—how can the client be trusted to talk about the things that he or she needs to talk about? I develop the theoretical answer to this question in a series of steps.

1. *The nature of neurosis.* Neurotic problems are based on anxiety. Either the anxiety itself is the reported problem and/or self-destructive behaviors ("symptoms") develop and become persistent because they are reinforced by anxiety reduction. Anxiety is based on conflict, particularly internalized conflict in which thoughts and feelings have become fear cues, but these thoughts and feelings are also motivated, either biologically (sexually, for example) or because of inconsistent learning experiences (being both rewarded and punished for feeling dependent, for example). These thoughts and feelings are partially repressed and can thus arouse anxiety without being understood by the individual. Consciousness is conceptualized as the degree to which brain processes are symbolic, and repression is explained in neurological-learning terms. The anxious person repeatedly partially thinks the anxiety-arousing thoughts because they are motivated, but engages in avoidance behavior such as repression, obsessive thinking that precludes thinking the "real" fear-arousing thoughts, etc. This avoidance prevents extinction of the fears of the thoughts.

2. *Relieving internalized conflicts-in theory.* The client is continuously approaching the feared thoughts (they are motivated somehow or they wouldn't be causing anxiety) and then avoiding them. If, when the client attempts to verbalize such a thought, the therapist explicitly verbalizes what the client has implied (thought partially), the therapist is preventing the avoidance behavior by holding the client in the presence of the fear cues. The therapist is being deeply empathic—communicating understanding of the client's intended message. If the client is held in the presence of the fear cues in a rewarding setting (most importantly a good relationship), he or she will feel mild anxiety that will then extinguish and/or be counter-conditioned. Thus, thoughts that were formerly anxiety arousing become neutral, and the client is able to approach more closely the elements of his or her internalized conflicts—the client progresses step by step toward a more ac-

curate and thorough understanding of and experiencing of his or her own thoughts and feelings.

3. *The critical theoretical point.* The client will repeatedly attempt to approach the elements of his or her internalized conflicts. The therapist can thus trust the client to try to deal with what he or she needs to deal with. In summary, the logic of the critical theoretical point is this:

a) If there is anxiety, there must be conflict. All of us have thoughts that arouse fear but are not somehow motivated; thus, they cause no anxiety. The thoughts and feeling simply are not performed. If there is anxiety, we know that fear-arousing thoughts must be motivated.

b) If there is conflict, there is an approach tendency active that repeatedly motivates the person to think the thoughts, at least in partial form.

4. *The effects of therapy*, a) *anxiety reduction* —exploring the thoughts and experiencing the feelings leads to extinction of the fears of the thoughts and feelings, thus relieving the conflict, b) *autonomy and increased problem-solving ability*-this is a subtle but critical difference between this approach and more directive, interpretive approaches. The client is the problem solver. By responding to the client's approach responses, the therapist is continuously reinforcing client-initiated thinking. The client's thinking and feeling are being reinforced by the anxiety reduction that follows as the fears extinguish and by other factors, such as attention from the therapist. If the therapist is the problem solver, the problem may get solved, but dependence on the problem solving of others has been reinforced. A deeply empathic approach solves the problem and reinforces independence; c) *symptom relief*—relieving the anxiety removes the reinforcement for the symptom, which is usually eliminated by life experiences when it no longer serves an anxiety-reducing function, because the symptom is by definition self-destructive; d; *increase in self-esteem*—the person is his or her own thoughts and feelings. If what a person is makes the person feel bad, self-esteem is low. Through therapy, what the person is, comes to feel better. Stated coldly, the person is reinforced for responding, so responding ("being") becomes secondarily reinforcing. Stated more attractively, by being accepted and understood while being the person he or she really is, the person comes to accept and understand himself or herself.

## HISTORY

I was trained as a Rogerian at the University of Chicago and developed a commitment and respect for empathy-based therapy. When I taught at the University of Iowa, I found myself increasingly satisfied with the practice of empathy-based therapy and increasingly unable to defend its theoretical foundations. This formulation is an attempt to reconcile the dilemma this created.

## TECHNIQUE

My work doesn't elaborate technique to any great extent, devoting only one chapter to it. Essentially, being deeply empathic involves verbalizing what the client is trying to say and can't quite say; that is, verbalizing the client's intended, implicit message. The therapist's actions center around the belief that the client is the problem solver. Egan

(1975) and others have elaborated on the practice of therapy in a way that I find generally compatible with my theoretical thinking.

## APPLICATIONS

I make a strong plea for an eclectic approach within a general learning perspective. I see empathy-based therapy as most effective for anxiety-based problems, but I also specify appropriate circumstances for the use of behavior modification (still with the client as the problem solver), and argue that this approach to therapy is inappropriate for sociopathic disorders and for problems that are situationally caused, without anxiety as a significant element. I leave open the question whether this approach can contribute to the treatment of psychotic disorders.

# Life Skills Counseling
## Winthrop R. Adkins

### DEFINITION

Life Skills (also referred to as Life Coping Skills or Life Skills Education) is a planned counseling intervention designed to help people learn to cope more effectively with the predictable psychological and social problems, crises, and developmental tasks they face throughout life. Like other counseling approaches, it is aimed at helping people to clarify feelings and values, make decisions and choices, resolve conflicts, gain self-understanding, explore environmental opportunities and constraints, communicate effectively with others, and take personal responsibility for their actions. Yet, unlike those counseling interventions that rely mainly on non-structured verbal exchanges between practitioner and client on a wide range of general problems, Life Skills makes use of preplanned, carefully developed learning programs as well as instructional and counseling methods to help people learn to cope with particular problems one at a time. As such, Life Skills is part of an increasing trend in the field toward programmatic approaches to coping, exemplified by such courses and workshops as Parent Effectiveness Training, Assertiveness Training, communication skills, stress management workshops, and Career Education.

Life Skills can best be understood as an effort to create an alternate and complementary delivery system to provide counseling services aimed at making learning opportunities available to the large number of people who need but cannot obtain counseling. This system is designed to provide a wide variety of learning methods and processes to help people acquire the necessary knowledge, insight, and particularly the behavior for coping successfully with complex, emotion-laden problems. The system consists of a program design and learning model, a set of program development methods, a staff training program, and dissemination and installation processes. This system permits the development of programs for the common life problems of particular populations, such as disadvantaged adults, high school dropouts, women returning to the labor force, the physically and mentally handicapped, and persons facing divorce, unemployment, or retirement. The programs are designed to be delivered by specially trained teachers as well as counselors in a wide variety of educational, training, rehabilitation, mental health, and community agency settings.

Each Life Skills program consists of a cluster of Life Skills learning units, each of which is focused on a specific coping problem, such as how to present oneself effectively in a job interview, or how to avoid escalating marital arguments, or how to listen responsibly to children. The four-stage Structured Inquiry learning model serves as a guide for trained program developers who create a sequence of learning activities and experiences and supporting video, print, and audio materials for each unit. In the design of each Life Skills unit particular attention is paid to such issues as learning readiness, peer group support, inductive and deductive reasoning, small-step learning followed by immediate reinforcement, behavioral modeling, role playing, and simulation with video feedback. The structure of each unit provides for the elicitation of feelings as well as prior experiences, the incorporation of new knowledge, and the translation of knowledge into actual behavior. Once the unit is completed, it is tested, revised, and then published. The Life Skills Educator Training Program prepares staff to deliver the Life Skills Units. The development methods and installation process ensure that excellent units are developed and installed effectively in actual learning centers.

## HISTORY

The Life Skills approach to counseling has evolved over the past fourteen years as a result of considerable trial-and-error learning, research, and development. The initial ideas for Life Skills (Adkins, 1970) were derived from observations made in 1964 in a YMCA counseling and training program about the limitations of middle-class counseling methods for educationally disadvantaged clients. These ideas and observations led to the design of the first Life Skills program, which was tested in Project Try, a $4.5 million anti-poverty training program in New York's Bedford-Stuyvesant area.

The initial program made use of problem-centered, experience-based and behavior-ally oriented learning groups and attempted to employ a mixture of teaching as well as counseling methods to facilitate learning. The development of resources and learning activities that could structure the learning sessions was mainly the responsibility of trained teachers and counselors. It was found, however, that practitioners were not able to create the kinds of resources that adequately met the design requirements for effective learning. The conclusion was that the learning tasks were too complex and the learning activities and materials needed were too difficult to develop on an as-you-go basis. More experimentation was needed. My colleagues and I had, however, worked out some critical concepts and learning methods during that period that later proved useful.

In the years that followed, I moved my base of operations to Teachers College, Columbia University, and continued the development of the program design. Gradually, the present four-stage learning model was developed, incorporating video and other learning methods. A program development process was created to permit the systematic development of Life Skills units by full-time trained developers. In 1971, with funds from the U.S. Bureau of Adult Basic Education, a Life Skills Development project was established and work began on making use of the learning model in developing a 10-unit Employability Skills Program (Adkins, et al., 1975) for adults dealing with the psycho-social tasks of choosing, finding, planning, and getting a job. Three years later a field-tested multimedia program was completed. It was published by the Institute For Life Coping Skills, a non-profit organization.

Recently, steps have been taken to lay the base at Teachers College for the development of new Life Skills programs for other psycho-social problems of other populations. A new R and D Center for Life Skills and Human Resource Development and a new master's and doctoral specialty to train counselors of adults and program developers have been established. A research study (Adkins, et al., 1977) on the life-coping problems of unemployed, disadvantaged adults—documenting the psycho-social problems of career development, marriage, parenthood, relations with others, health, community living, and personal development—has been completed and several experimental videotapes dealing with representative problems have been created. A documentary film on the Employability Skills program and the Life Skills method has been completed and distributed and a book that will describe both the theoretical and operational aspects of a national program for Life Skills is now in progress.

## TECHNIQUE

The Life Skills Structured Inquiry Learning Model is the central core of the Life Skills approach to the delivery of counseling services. Its four stages structure the sequence of learning activities and experiences for learners, and the teaching and counseling functions to be performed by Life Skills Educators. The model also serves as a format for program developers. What follows is a description of how a fully developed Life Skills unit would be delivered by a specially trained Life Skills Educator in a small group of ten to fifteen learners.

A Life Skills group begins with various group-forming activities and with an orientation to the program, frequently followed by a contracting session in which the learning objectives are explained and the roles and responsibilities of both learners and Life Skills Educators are made explicit and agreed to in advance.

*The Stimulus Stage.* Each learning unit begins with a provocative presentation of a problem, usually in the form of a five-minute dramatic, emotion-arousing video vignette that depicts a person such as the clients confronting a difficult situation and making a number of errors. The emotional impact of the tape and the details presented are designed to stimulate and focus discussion.

*The Evocation Stage.* In this stage, usually lasting about forty-five minutes, the Life Skills Educator (or LSE) attempts through a structured pattern of questions to elicit from the group elements of the problem that was presented, to identify the critical issues, and to get the group members to describe similar experiences they have had. The LSE makes every effort to elicit feelings, thoughts, and experiences from all group members in order to get the group to define the problem, to suggest solutions to it, and to identify areas for further inquiry. Through convergent and divergent questioning techniques, and the skills of paraphrasing, reflecting feeling, and summarizing, the LSE endeavors to dignify the learners by helping them to realize how much they already know about the problem. As comments are made, they are recorded on flip charts as closely as possible to the language they are offered. By the end of the session the group will have become aware of what it feels and already knows about the problem, will have had its curiosity aroused, and will have identified further areas for inquiry.

*The Objective Inquiry Stage.* Once Evocation is completed, the learners engage in a variety of learning activities to find out and experience what *others* know about the problem. Through the use of specially prepared video modeling tapes, pamphlets, audio tapes, questionnaires, rating sheets, simulation xercises, and specific learning activities, the LSE aims at expanding group members' awareness about the problem conceptually and to help them gain insight into the problem's origins, its current manifestation and consequences, and what must be done to solve the problem. Prior concepts are challenged, confirmed, and tested by new concepts presented through various exercises. Opportunities to acquire new knowledge about how others view or have solved a similar problem are also provided. The predevelop-ed activities and materials are designed to be used by learne'rs individually or in dyads, triads, or in large group exercises in ways that permit individuals to move at their own pace, make their own decisions, and to gain knowledge and experience in their own preferred style, either through reading, seeing and hearing, experiencing, or discussion. Learners also engage in a number of exercises that are designed to help them incorporate their new knowledge with their previous understanding and feelings and to practice specific subskills required for solving the problem. Video is used where relevant to model solutions, to present new concepts and knowledge, and to monitor and give feedback on the practice of new behavior.

*The Application Stage.* The purpose of this stage is to help the learner to translate his new understanding, insight, feelings, and knowledge into actual behavior in a simulated or real-life situation. Learners engage in role playing or simulation exercises that, where possible, are videoed, rated, and critiqued by themselves, other group members, and the LSE. After appropriate feedback the learners are encouraged to repeat the behavior in simulated situations and then later in real-life situations until behavioral mastery is achieved. Throughout this stage the LSE functions in a manner similar to that of a coach, providing direction, support, and feedback as the learners attempt to gain increasing comfort in incorporating the new behavior into their basic repertoire. Throughout all four stages the LSE makes every effort to maintain a cohesive, supportive learning group and a nonjudgmental climate in which learners have the freedom to express their feelings, ask questions, to disagree, and to make mistakes.

*Development and training.* Over the years my colleagues and I have created specific methods for selecting the coping problems for programming, for defining learning objectives, for designing internally consistent units, for developing, testing, and revising the learning activities and materials, and for evaluating the impact of learning units on the learners. We have also devised methods for disseminating programs and for installing them in existing learning centers in such a way that schedules, facilities, and administrative procedures support the effort. The training program for Life Skills Educators, which is designed to familiarize them with the learning model and the contents of the units, and to equip them with the basic counseling, teaching, and administrative skills to deliver the program, is essential for the success of the program. LSEs are given special training in managing the group process and the learning activities, in adapting the program to the local conditions and individual learner needs. The training program makes full use of small group interactive learning methods, behavioral practice, and video feedback.

## APPLICATIONS

The most extensive application of the Life Skills approach has been in the previously described Employability Skills Series for disadvantaged adults and adolescents. It is now being distributed nationally and has thus far been installed in over a hundred and seventy learning centers (Adult Basic Education, CETA, high schools, women's counseling, mental health, migrant worker, physically handicapped, prisons, drug rehabilitation, YMCA, hospital, and community college) in twenty-six states. Several research studies are in progress and evidence to date indicates that the program is perceived to be helpful and effective by learners, staff, and administrators.

For several years I have taught courses, given presentations and consulted broadly about Life Skills. As a result there have been numerous other applications of the Life Skills model in programs for such groups as middle-class women, Native Americans, Canadian disadvantaged adults, the handicapped, and such occupational groups as teachers, counselors, and managers. Though many of these programs are not fully developed, they do begin to illustrate the potential range of applications. Thus, many new applications of the Life Skills model are anticipated in the years ahead. It should be noted, however, that our popularization of the term "Life Skills" has recently been applied to competency-based literacy programs. Care should be exercised in distinguishing between those Life Skills programs that aim at modifying psycho-social coping skills and those that have other learning objectives. We can conceive of the day when there will be hundreds, perhaps thousands of different Life Skills units on coping problems in such areas as parenting, marriage, health, and personal development. We are currently experimenting with other adaptations and modifications of the learning model and ways of training program developers more efficiently. We are also exploring a variety of alternatives for making use of the new R and D Center and the new graduate program to help others to set up development centers while at the same time maintaining and improving the quality of development and delivery within the framework of responsible research, evaluation and training.

# Lithium Therapy
*Ronald R. Fieve*

## DEFINITION

Lithium, a naturally occurring salt, is the first agent in psychiatry to be specifically effective against a major mental illness. In manic-depressive disorder it calms psychotic manic excitement, usually within five to ten days. When taken on a maintenance regimen it prevents the recurrence of major highs and, to a lesser extent, lows, thus being the first truly prophylactic psychiatric drug. Lithium is of little value in the treatment of acute depression. The ion's mechanism of action is not known.

## HISTORY

Lithium's effect in mania was discovered serendipitously by the Australian psychiatrist John F. J. Cade in 1949. Studies that confirmed his results were soon under way in Europe. However, recognition of the value of lithium treatment was slow in the United States because lithium chloride, used as a salt substitute in the 1940s, had caused a number of deaths and serious poisonings among patients with heart and kidney disease, conditions in which it is now known that lithium is dangerous. The FDA ban on lithium was not lifted until 1970, when it became available for treatment of mania. In the past twenty years numerous studies have established beyond doubt lithium's effectiveness in mania. More recently, several investigators have shown its prophylactic effect in the depressed as well as the manic phase of manic depression, and in recurrent depression. (Fieve, 1978).

## TECHNIQUE

Lithium carbonate is given orally in tablet form. In acute mania, dosage is 1500 to 1800 mg daily in divided doses. Maintenance dosage is 900 to 1200 mg. Blood lithium levels must be maintained in the therapeutic range of 0.8 to 1.5 mEq/Liter. The amount of lithium in the blood is measured by flame photometry, a relatively simple office procedure. Monitoring is done weekly for the first month of treatment and monthly thereafter.

Since lithium easily can become toxic, it is essential that it be administered by an experienced clinician. Diuretics, diet pills, and crash diets are contraindicated, as these upset the electrolyte balance on which safe lithium treatment depends. Patients with heart or kidney disease are usually not recommended for treatment.

Side effects may include hand tremor, weight gain, muscle weakness, diarrhea, gastrointestinal upsets, polydipsia and polyuria, goiter and hypothyroidism, maculo-papular cutaneous lesions, leucocytosis, and mild EKG changes. Most of these subside within the first few weeks of treatment. Patients on lithium report no dulling effect as occurs with the major tranquilizers. They are able to lead relatively normal lives as long as they continue to take the medication. In most cases they find additional psychotherapy unnecessary once their mood swings have been stabilized.

Many patients on lithium also require periodic antidepressant medication, which can be discontinued once their depression subsides.

## APPLICATIONS

Once stabilized on lithium, even the most severe cases of manic depression can be treated on an out-patient basis. Lengthy hospitalization, shock treatments, and extensive psychotherapy are rarely needed. The implications for future mental health care in this country are great. Lithium clinics, based on a medical model, can dispense lithium and other drugs to a large number of severely ill patients. Utilizing paramedical personnel and a few psychiatrists, such clinics can treat patients safely, inexpensively, and effectively (Fieve, 1975). This type of clinic is beginning to appear. Unfortunately, many major hospital centers still lack facilities for dispensing lithium as well as personnel trained in lithium administration. In addition, manic depression and recurrent depression are often misdiagnosed by clinicians (often as schizophrenia), and consequently improperly treated (Cooper, et al., 1972). With increasing knowledge of diagnosis and treatment of affective disorders (of mood and emotion) the outlook for this major mental illness is bright.

# Living Therapy

## Gay Hendricks and Carol J. Leavenworth

### DEFINITION

Living Therapy is a moment-by-moment, day-by-day approach to uncovering the basic processes of effective living. It is a method to be used by individuals in problem solving and in achieving maximum emotional and spiritual growth. It is also a set of principles and techniques used by therapists with individuals and groups. Living Therapy focuses on the following basic processes to achieve its goals:

1. Awareness and observation of the physical, emotional, mental, and spiritual processes of the individual
2. Deep experience of self, particularly in the realm of feelings
3. Love and acceptance of self at each point of the living process
4. Identification and integration of wants and needs
5. "Centering," through awareness and incorporation of the inner core so that harmony occurs at all levels of being.

Living Therapy is a personal approach leading to the transpersonal. By applying the basic processes to the personal issues that arise in living, the individual establishes contact with the inner self, the core from which we have access to knowledge of others and of the universe.

### HISTORY

Throughout his training, which included experience in Behavior Modification, client-centered therapy, and numerous body therapies, Gay Hendricks returned repeatedly to the question: what are the basic elements underlying all therapies that create real growth and change? In 1974, after a period of deep meditation in the wilderness, Hendricks formulated the principles that are the foundation of Living Therapy. Based on the original principles, substantial refinements and additions were made by Carol Leavenworth, M.S. Later they were joined by Gary West, M.S.W., David Hubbard, M.D., and others who have contributed to the development of a comprehensive system.

### TECHNIQUE

Techniques used in Living Therapy are based on the premise that dissatisfaction and ineffective behavior are a result of denial and resistance to one's current experience. Since most of us are seldom in contact with our core self, we often do not recognize many of our deepest needs for contact and unity with our environment. These needs are manifested in progressively more dramatic experiences in order to return focus to the core self. Therefore, we experience unpleasant feelings, bodily stress and disease, ineffective thought patterns, inappropriate behavior, and eventually problems in our environment. All of these are creations of the self, designed to bring us back to our own center.

Living Therapy clients are assisted in returning to the level of awareness appropriate for solving the presenting problem. Most often a person's thoughts and behavior are standing in the way of the experience of certain feelings that need to be recognized and lovingly accepted as a real part of the individual's personality. Clients are taught to observe, experience, and love their feelings. They learn to identify real needs and wants as well as appropriate ways of getting needs met.

They are assisted in learning how to stay centered in the here-and-now in order to enhance actualization of emotional and spiritual growth.

Techniques that facilitate this process are varied and include meditation, body work, and homework assignments, such as observing and listing basic feelings (e.g., fear, anger, sadness, joy) experienced during the week.

## APPLICATIONS

The basic processes of Living Therapy are being used both in an educational setting with teacher and counselor trainees and in psychotherapy. The approach was developed and stabilized with the "normal neurotic" clientele seen in private practice and in community mental health settings. It is now being used on a limited basis with psychotic out-patients. Specific techniques used vary from client to client. The approach is also being applied in education, with the assistance of curriculum materials that teach the basic processes of effective living.

---

# Logotherapy
## *Viktor E. Frankl*

### DEFINITION

Logotherapy, or existential analysis (*Existenzanalyse*) as I, its founder, have also called it, is referred to by many authors as the Third Viennese School of Psychotherapy (after Freud's psychoanalysis and Adler's individual psychology). To me (Viktor E. Frankl) logos means meaning, and Logotherapy, indeed, centers and focuses on my concept of a "will to meaning": that is, the striving to see in life, and fulfill, a meaning and purpose. Today, ever more patients complain of a sense of meaninglessness and emptiness that I have termed "existential frustration" and "existential vacuum," respectively. So far, two test devices have been designed and developed in order to measure an individual's existential frustration; namely, James C. Crumbaugh's PIL Test (1968) and Elisabeth S. Lukas's "Logo-Test." Existential frustration need not but may well result in neurosis, known as a "noogenic neurosis" in contrast to the conventional, or psychogenic, neurosis. According to statistical studies conducted in various countries of Europe and in America, about 20 percent of the cases of neurosis accruing in clinics and hospitals are noogenic. In such cases, Logotherapy is the method of choice. In addition, it also lends itself to the treatment of obsessive-compulsive cases and phobic cases in which anticipatory anxiety has established a vicious circle: a symptom evokes a phobia, the phobia provokes the symptom to reappear, and the reappearance of the symptom reinforces the phobia. A logotherapeutic technique that I described in a paper published in 1939, namely, "paradoxical intention," is devised to break this feedback mechanism by inducing the patient to deliberately "try to do," or "wish to happen," the very things he fears. In other words, the pathogenic fear is replaced by the paradoxical, ironical wish. What thereby is achieved is a complete inversion of the original avoidance pattern of behavior on the part of the patient. Another logotherapeutic technique, "dereflection," counteracts the fact that the more an individual aims at pleasure, the more he is liable to miss it (Frankl 1975). For pleasure is, and must remain, an effect of loving encounter or meaning fulfillment, and is destroyed and spoiled whenever it is made a target. As I see it, frigidity and impotence result from the very attempt of a male patient to demonstrate his potency, or a female patient to prove to herself her capacity for orgasm. As to the treatment of noogenic neuroses, however, it is in no way the job of a psychiatrist to prescribe meanings, as it were. It is rather up to the patient himself to choose his own meanings. Each person does have his own meaning, and so has every situation confronting him. "Man's search for meaning" thus winds up with a *Gestalt* perception, with meaning inherent in each and every life situation. Thus there is no life situation conceivable that really would lack any meaning. Meaning is available first through creating a work, or doing a deed; second, through experiencing something, or lovingly encountering a person. Last but not least, there is a third possibility as well: even facing an unchangeable fate, say, an incurable disease such as an inoperable cancer, man may bear witness of the human potential to turn one's predicament into an achievement. Thus, life is unconditionally meaningful. This contention does not involve moralizing but is based on a phenomenological analysis of the "pre-reflective ontological self-understanding" observable in the man on the street. Recently, Logotherapy's axiology has been validated by empirical research based on computerized data obtained from several thousand subjects.

# Lomi Body Work

*Jeffrey A. Schaler and Renée Royak-Schaler*

## DEFINITION

Lomi Body Work is an integrative psycho-physical therapy in which deep muscular tensions in the body are released through a series of direct physical manipulations. The Lomi practitioner uses his hands, knuckles, fingers, and elbows to stretch the fascia, or sheaths of connective tissue, in the body and to balance the subtle energy flow in the body. The aim is to allow a balanced and unrestricted flow of creative life energy, increased body awareness, postural alignment, and emotional as well as physical integration.

The underlying theory of the work is that personal integrity is expressed in the physical body through awareness, structural equilibrium, muscular resiliency, breathing, and homeostatic vitality. By directing awareness in the present to muscular tension and through restructuring the body in a way that facilitates physical integrity, associated aspects of the mind and emotions may be realized and responded to in a natural and nourishing way. By examining how people support themselves physically, one can begin to see how attitude is reflected in posture and how conscious posture can affect one's experience of life. Lomi Body Work is a holistic application of experiential learning that encourages an individual to investigate, acknowledge, and take responsibility for the many aspects of self.

## HISTORY

Lomi Body Work was originally developed by Robert K. Hall, M.D., and Richard K. Heckler, Ph.D. Hall, a psychiatrist, was a close friend and associate of the late Frederick S. Perls, founder of Gestalt Therapy, and was one of the first people trained in Structural Integration by its founder, Ida P. Rolf, Ph.D. Hall relinquished his traditional role as a psychiatrist through his association with Perls in 1967. He moved from a mechanistic approach to the body toward a vitalist's perspective of the whole person through his association with Perls, Heckler, and Randolph Stone, the founder of polarity therapy. Heckler, a Gestalt psychotherapist and currently a master of aikido, studied polarity therapy under Stone. In 1970 Hall and Heckler synthesized their knowledge and together created Lomi Body Work.

Lomi Body Work has its roots in related holistic methods such as polarity therapy, Gestalt Therapy, Structural Integration, Proskauer breathing, Eastern philosophy, and the principles of aikido and hatha yoga.

## TECHNIQUE

Lomi Body Work involves a series of sessions in which the practitioner and client work together on specific areas of the body. At least seven areas are focused upon during each session. These are: 1) the extent to which a person is physically aware of his body, his strength, his vitality; 2) the form and function of the body section and its relationship to the person as a whole; 3) breathing; 4) personality expression; 5) manipulating connective tissue; 6) tracing and facilitating energy flow; and 7) exercises that allow maintenance.

Generally, the Lomi Body Work technique promotes the understanding that one's physical as well as mental-emotional way of being in the world consists of many habits, which can be changed. Specifically, these habit patterns change through manipulation of connective tissue and through a willingness on the part of the client to observe and correct posture, breathing, and self-presentation.

The skeletal structure is designed to support the body and the muscular structure is designed to move the body. Maximum muscular efficiency is attained when the body naturally assumes a balanced vertical stance, as defined by a plumb line center of gravity. When the body is out of vertical alignment, muscles compensate to maintain an upright stance in response to the additional horizontal surface area of the body exposed to gravitational pull. Muscles lose their tone and develop a bone-like quality in direct proportion to the degree in which the body is off center— and in direct relation to an individual's sense of personal freedom. The Lomi practitioner moves to these areas with his hands and separates the congested fascia while the client concentrates on breathing.

Lomi Body Work uses concentration and attentiveness as a center from which to operate. New realizations and personal growth are the product of a cooperative, interpersonal venture between the practitioner and the participant and not a form of mechanical processing done by the practitioner to an individual. The Lomi practitioner is not concerned with forcing a person to fit a preconceived model of structural alignment and proper function. The work is designed to meet the individual needs of the person, be they physical, emotional, or mental, and to support the acknowledgment and appreciation of one's unique nature of existence.

## APPLICATIONS

Lomi Body Work is valuable for people of all ages and backgrounds. Certain aspects of the work are emphasized according to individual needs. It is for people who want to understand and feel a sense of command over themselves both physically and mentally. It is not for people who are seriously ill and not to be considered a form of medical treatment for disease.

Lomi Body Work has a wide range of applicability, from people who seek to develop a greater awareness and comfort in their body to dancers and athletes seeking improved functional performance. By releasing tension and opening constricted areas of the body through Lomi Body Work, the participant can experience the benefits of more efficient carriage. Structural response to gravity becomes more evenly balanced throughout the body. There is less demand on the body through the elimination of inefficient and unnecessary physiological conflict. As a result, circulation is improved, neural flow is less restricted, breathing capacity is increased, and tension is released, allowing graceful and more fluid movement. In general, the vital systems of the body become more responsive to the needs of the individual.

Lomi Body Work is a valuable adjunct to psychotherapy. Clients are encouraged to develop a personal practice that strengthens their will, reveals the extent to which they exercise responsibility, and aids in understanding the relationship between what they do and how they feel.

Frequently, Gestalt Therapy is used as a medium for assimilating new realizations and changes in consciousness that occur through the Body Work. This is not a necessary aspect of the work. But when feelings emerge while releasing tension and freeing the blocked flow of energy, the participant is encouraged to acknowledge and accept his feelings. Much can be learned by investigating the feelings and memories that have been stored in the body. Often they provide valuable insights into unresolved parts of one's personality and lead to growth and integrity when assimilated. Freedom from the bondage of negativity (tension) is essential for a mature and meaningful life.

# Marathon Group Therapy

## *George R. Bach*

### DEFINITION

As with all effective group psychotherapeutic programs, the Marathon Group Therapy promotes intimate, authentic human interaction. One of the unique aspects of the Marathon technique is an intensification and acceleration of genuine encounter through a deliberate instigation of group pressure focused on behavioral change.

This is facilitated by a time-extended schedule requiring uninterrupted sessions lasting from sixteen to over forty hours.

### HISTORY AND TECHNIQUES

The first paper on Marathon Therapy was presented by the author on May 5, 1964, at an annual meeting of the American Psychiatric Association. In 1963 I learned that the late Frederik Stoller had experimented in a psychiatric hospital setting with time-extended group therapy sessions that would meet nonstop for at least twelve hours. Before I learned about this, I had conducted weekend encounter groups in retreat-like resort settings with traditional workshop hours: nine to twelve and two to five, with possibly another evening session, say, from eight to ten. This kind of broken-up schedule facilitated informal socializing, recreation, rest, and recuperation. However, it seemed that after each intermission, what progress had been made in the preceding work session was to some extent lost, because during the intermissions the people would interact in habitual social ways instead of in new therapeutic ways. I wanted the group members to experience and explore new ways of relating to each other and new ways of feeling about their own identity, self-worth, body image, etc. These social intermissions diluted the environmental cues supportive of growth-stimulating ways of communication. By doing away with socially oriented intermissions and adopting Stoller's time-extended schedule, I found a practical way to prevent this dilution of therapeutic group influence.

In the course of conducting over twenty thousand therapeutic group hours with a great variety of patients, I have observed that for most patients, the fifty-minute individual hour or the one- to two-hour group session is not long enough for them to take off their social masks; i.e., to stop playing games and start interacting truthfully and authentically. It takes a longer session for people in our culture to abandon the marketing stance of role playing and image making, which they habitually practice in the workaday world.

Clinical experience has shown that group-pressure, rather than the therapist's individual interventions and interpretations given privately, can move people effectively and quickly from impression making and manipulative behavior toward honest, responsible, spontaneous leveling with one another. But it takes time for the therapeutic group to generate the pressure necessary to produce behavioral change.

Today, fifteen years after its inception, the number of people (students, clients, patients, even whole organizations) that participate in Marathon Groups and gain self-growth value from such participation can be counted in the hundreds of thousands. In California, a growing number of young research- and writing-oriented psychologists are taking interest in systematically exploring the variables that account for the growth and the experientially proven value of the marathon technique.

The basic objectives and ground rules for the professional conduct of Marathon Groups are as follows:

The Marathon Group is a social interaction laboratory in which participants can free themselves, for a twenty-four- to forty-two-hour stretch, from image making and from manipulative game playing and experience an improved quality of social contact for which the term authentic communion suggests itself.

Having experienced authentic communion with Marathon Group peers, the participants are encouraged to apply what they have learned to their daily lives and to attempt to improve the quality of their contact with "significant others" (people who are important in their lives). This involves a change of interpersonal stance, from manipulation to communion. This learning is, in my opinion, the most urgent social task for psychotherapists to complete.

In a Marathon Group, twelve to eighteen participants interact continuously and uninterruptedly in a secluded setting. The sessions last for at least twenty-four hours and may be scheduled for a longer time. The participants are usually not emotionally disturbed persons who are desperately seeking therapeutic help. Rather, the Marathon experience appeals to growth-seeking individuals who sense in themselves and in others the need to have more authentic interactional experiences than everyday living affords in our marketing-oriented and mechanized society.

The long session is terminated by a "closure party," during which a gradual re-entry into the conventional social atmosphere is made. The entire session may be recorded on video tape and a feedback follow-up is scheduled four to eight weeks later. Possessions are designed to reinforce those decisions for change that have been emerging during the Marathon itself. In our Institute practice, the Marathon retreats for private patients are systematically integrated with the regular therapy program. Most patients are first seen individually and then assigned to a regular two- to four-hour weekly therapy group. Marathon retreat experiences are interspersed at intervals of four to six months. Some Marathons are "specialized" for marital couples, singles, professional training for psychotherapists, etc.

As subjective truths are shared during the Marathon process, irrational or ineffectual behavior appears incongruent, to be dropped in favor of new, more exciting and stimulating behavioral patterns. The latter emerge and are practiced in the course of the Marathon. An important task of the therapist is to maximize group feedback and enhance the opportunity for genuine encountering of, and exposure to, group pressure. For these reasons the Marathon is not unlike a "pressure cooker" in which phony steam boils away and genuine emotions (including negative ones) emerge. Decisions for change and serious commitment to follow through in life action are frankly elicited. Follow-up sessions will inquire into their validity.

## APPLICATIONS

Prospective Marathon participants are not sorted out in the traditional psychiatric-diagnostic sense, but rather on the basis of 1) attitudes toward self-change and 2) group constellation. Before admittance, "Marathonians" must convince one and preferably both professional co-therapists that they are anxious to make significant *changes* in their customary ways of acting and being in this world. This presumes some degree of basic self-understanding of what one *now* is and what one can potentially become. The purpose of the Marathon is to awaken and strengthen further feelings for new directions and movement toward self-actualization in mutual *intimate* concert with others who are growing also.

The Marathon Group-Therapeutic experience is most fully effective with those who wish to exchange their own ways of acting and being in this world and who are ready to quit blaming others and their environment for their present unsatisfactory lot.

# Marital Therapy
## Alan S. Gurman

### DEFINITION

Marital Therapy, generically speaking, is any psychotherpeutic treatment that is aimed at producing change in the relationship between marital partners. A number of treatment formats have been used to this end. For example: individual psychotherapy (of one partner), concurrent therapy (in which each partner is treated by the same therapist, but separately), collaborative therapy (in which each partner is treated separately by two different therapists who communicate with each other about the treatments), conjoint therapy (in which the partner are treated together by the same therapist or co-therapists) and combinations of these arrangements. Conjoint therapy, which is sometimes conducted with groups of three to five couples, is by far the most common treatment format for marital problems. In addition to the research evidence for the superiority of this approach (Gurman and Kniskern, 1978; Gurman and Rice, 1975), there are theoretical reasons for believing that the conjoint method is generally the most appropriate strategy. The most basic and important of these reasons is that the marital therapist does not view psychological dysfunctioning or "psychopathology" as residing *within* individuals only, but as the result of dysfunctional *interpersonal* patterns and styles of adaptation. While viewpoints vary on the issue (Gurman, 1977), most marital therapists are concerned with producing change in both individual partners as well as in their interactions.

### HISTORY

Marital Therapy has been an outgrowth of family therapy, where the husband-wife relationship was focused on as a subsystem of the family. As such, it has been referred to as "a technique in search of a theory." Indeed, it is probably accurate to say that existing theories and techniques that are specific to the treatment of couples have followed rather than preceded the practice of Marital Therapy. The earliest practitioners in the area were referred to as "marriage counselors" and were much more likely to be social workers and pastoral counselors than psychologists or psychiatrists, who are now very active in the field. As with family therapy, there are now relatively few training centers that specialize in the treatment of marital problems, few agreed upon criteria of adequate training, no encompassing national professional organization, and little legal regulation of its practice. Therefore, owing to the history of the field, most marital therapists see themselves as primarily affiliated with other disciplines; e.g., psychiatry, psychology, social work, sociology, and the ministry.

## TECHNIQUE

Marital Therapy, like many psychotherapies, does not have a unified body of techniques but, rather, is represented by a number of theoretical persuasions, among which are significant similarities as well as differences (Gurman, 1977). What these approaches have most fundamentally in common is the belief that relationships are of at least as much importance in the behavior and experience of people as are unconscious intrapsychic events. Three major contemporary approaches to Marital Therapy exist: the psychodynamic approach, the systems approach, and the behavioral approach. The psychodynamically oriented marital therapist is interested in helping both spouses understand intellectually and emotionally how their earlier experiences, especially in their families or origin, influence their expectations of, behavior with, and style of relating to their partners. The psychodynamic marriage therapist also places a good deal of emphasis on each partner's manner of relating to the therapist. Systems-oriented marital therapists are distinguished by their interest in the power dimensions of the marital relationship and in the "rules" that have evolved in a couple's characteristic style of communicating. While it is not true of all systems-oriented therapists, the majority are primarily concerned with achieving symptomatic change in the couple's presenting problem. Behavioral marriage therapists are noted by their interest in pinpointing the specific changes that are desired by each partner in the relationship and by using an educational, teaching approach to help spouses identify sources of satisfaction and dissatisfaction in their relationship, develop effective communication skills, conflict resolution skills and behavior change negotiation skills. Their interventions, based primarily on (social) learning theory, are intended to facilitate couples' abilities to develop the necessary interpersonal skills to carry out their own behavior-change goals in the inevitable absence of the therapist.

While these differences among the major approaches to Marital Therapy are real, they tend only to reflect dominant themes and emphases. Most marital therapists, regardless of theoretical persuasion, borrow heavily from apparently competing and disparate "schools" of treatment. Most marital therapists share an interest in achieving a number of mediating or intermediate goals, such as: 1) the clarification of each partner's individual desires and felt needs in the relationship; 2) encouraging each partner to recognize his/her mutual contribution to the marital discord; 3) the recognition and modification of communication patterns; 4) increasing reciprocity; 5) decreasing the use of coercion and blaming; and 6) increasing cooperative problem solving. In addition, there are a number of ultimate or long-range goals toward which most marital therapists work: 1) increased role flexibility or adaptability; 2) resolution of presenting problems and decreased symptomatology; 3) open and clear communication; 4) a more equitable balance of power and influence; and 5) increased self-esteem and sense of autonomy.

To achieve these short- and long-range goals, a number of common techniques are usually used: clarification of each partner's feelings; redefining the nature of the relationship problems and their meaning; offering focused help in the development of decision making, communication and conflict-resolution skills; examining and changing each partner's expectations of the relationship; working to achieve insight or understanding of the factors that bear directly on the couple's felt satisfaction in their marriage; confrontation of defensive behavior in the session, for example, denying anger toward one's spouse.

## APPLICATIONS

While Marital Therapy is commonly applied to the treatment of straightforward relationship problems (e.g., poor communication; crises, such as a partner's extramarital affair; sexual difficulties; frequent arguing and lack of emotional closeness; disagreements regarding relationships with other significant people, such as each partner's own parents), different marital treatment methods have been used with success in dealing with such apparently "individual" problems as alcoholism, depression, and compulsive gambling. In general, most Marital Therapy deals with one or more of the following fundamental issues in establishing and maintaining a workable and adaptable marital relationship: dependency and autonomy conflicts, achieving a comfortable level of emotional and sexual intimacy, establishing each partner's individuality and separateness, establishing flexible rules regarding decision making and role responsibilities, and establishing equitable means of using power and influence. Clearly, the emphasis on these different issues varies from one theoretical persuasion to another; marital therapists are quite selective about working toward specific goals and dealing with specific themes and issues that have particular relevance for a given couple.

# Mandala Therapy

*Margaret MacRae*

## DEFINITION

Mandala Therapy encourages and directs the making of original circular designs in color. The circle, the Mandala, as a symobl of self provides a ground of being on which to project symbolic relationships of conscious and unconscious dynamisms. As a projective method of centering and balancing personality, it is a meditative and relaxing procedure that reflects or anticipates stages in ego or self-integration and the individuation process.

As a psychotherapeutic tool it involves therapist and client in an insight-directed dialogue similar to dream analysis.

# HISTORY

"Mandate" is a Sanskrit word meaning circle. Most of the literature concerning Mandalas deals with it as a sacred art form of the Orient, as in Tibetan Buddhism. Although there has been no fully developed concept of the universality of Mandala symbolism, contemporary interest, initiated by Carl Jung, has prompted research relating the Mandala to other cultures and traditions. The American Indian sand paintings of the Southwest are closely related in form and content to those of Tibet, as are the circular dance patterns occurring in Dervish monasteries. The spiritual foundations of many diverse religions and philosophical considerations, as in Sufi Doctrine and the I-Ching, include Mandala symbolism, and the reevaluation of such esoteric studies as astrology and alchemy provides new insights concerning its psychological implications.

The history and theory of the Mandala as a universal integrative principle was introduced to Western psychiatric spheres by Carl Jung. It provided the key to his entire system, the basis of analytical psychology. Jung observed that as a psychological phenomena, Mandalas occur spontaneously in dreams and paintings and drawings composed during certain states of intrapsychic conflict. This discovery, and its relationship to findings in his studies of primitive and medieval cultures, led him to abandon the idea of the superordinate position of the ego and inspired him to formulate his theory of the collective unconscious, the self, and its symbol, the Mandala.

The Mandala as a diagnostic and psychotherapeutic tool was researched in the 1960s and 1970s by Joan Kellogg, ATR, at St. Joseph's Hospital in Paterson, New Jersey, and at Maryland Psychiatric Research Center. Patients who had not spontaneously produced Mandalas, when encouraged to compose the circular design, produced self-expressive symbols. Ms. Kellogg's recognition of the common symbolic elements of pathology in these personal Mandalas broadened the possibilities of the use of the Mandala.

# TECHNIQUE

The method of introducing Mandala Therapy varies somewhat according to the kind of population and type of mental health facility in which it is used. Whether or not the person involved in therapy is made consciously aware of the transpersonal potential of the symbol depends upon factors of time, client goals related to degree of disturbance, intellectual capabilities of the client, and the education and training of the therapist.

The simplest application of the therapy is allied with Art Therapy technique in its general approach. The therapist asks the client to compose an original circular design as a means of centering and relaxing. The client is presented with a sheet of white paper large enough to include a circle, inscribed lightly in pencil, or 10 inches or approximate head size and with surrounding ground area approximately equal in proportion to that of the circle. A set of pastels or oil pastels is provided that include a wide range of colors and specifically those colors that are primary in Luscher Color Theory.

The client is asked to choose a preferred color and with it make a center shape of any sort. After coloring in this shape with the outlined color or another, the client is directed to pause and meditate on this center, consider its possibilities as the nucleus of a design, and then begin spontaneously to compose the Mandala. The client is informed that the edge of the circle is a fence but not a barricade and that he may extend or contain his design in whatever manner is pleasing to him. Upon completion he is asked to view his design from all sides and decide which is the top.

If the client is not ready for insight-directed therapy, he is encouraged to continue to make Mandalas that are pleasing to him. If he is an appropriate candidate for psychotherapy, he is asked for comments about his design. The therapist with a knowledge of universal symbolism is able to assist the client in interpreting his Mandala and guide him toward an understanding of his present psychic situation, the growth potential within him, and whatever impediments there may be blocking growth.

## APPLICATIONS

Mandala Therapy is universally applicable. As a psychotherapeutic method, it requires the therapist to be educated and trained in Jungian analytical psychology and knowledgeable in the many allied fields of study that contribute to its theoretical basis. It is a useful means of Art Therapy in psychiatric settings, nursing homes, rehabilitation centers, and private practice. Its transpersonal aspect enriches growth-oriented centers and consciousness-raising programs.

# Buddhist Insight Meditation

## Jack Kornfield

## DEFINITION

Insight, or Vipassana, meditation is a Buddhist system of mental training, based on the Buddhist psychology (Abhidhamma), which uses repetitive mental exercises to foster concentration and nonreactive awareness. Insight Meditation in some form is at the heart of all Buddhist mental cultivation. It combines a preliminary development of concentration—the training of the mind to stay steadily focused on an object—with a further cultivation of "mindfulness." The development of mindfulness involves training the mind to see clearly, and without reaction, the changing process of all experience. The trained mind, collected, concentrated, and alert, can then become free of neurotic habit patterns, fears, and judgments by simply allowing them to arise and pass away without identifying with or acting on them.

## HISTORY

Insight Meditation is based on over 2,500 years of Buddhist tradition, coming from the understanding and teaching of Gotama Buddha. His primary insights concerned the impermanent nature of all experience, the cause of human suffering (which is attachment and "unskillful" desires), and the understanding that there is no fixed or solid self, but rather only a constantly changing process of body and mind. He also taught the principles of habit and of mental cause and effect (karma), i.e., that attachment to reactions and attitudes become the basis for the subsequent strengthening and reoccurrence of these same reactive patterns and their underlying attitudes. He taught many techniques of mental cultivation for the development of concentration, love, compassion, and detachment, and expounded a complex psychology, the Abhidhamma, to explain all elements of mental experience. These teachings have been adapted and translated into many practices that fit into the cultural milieu of most Asian countries, from China, Japan, and Tibet south to Burma and Sri Lanka. Recently a number of skilled teachers have begun to offer this mental training in the West.

## TECHNIQUE

Insight Meditation is a specific sequence of mental training. It begins with learning to concentrate on one's own natural breathing process, a technique repeated for a number of hours until the mind becomes tranquil and composed. This exercise is followed by a systematic training of nonjudgmental awareness on four fields of experience: 1) bodily and sensory perceptions, 2) feelings, 3) objects and images of the mind, and 4) consciousness, or the knowing faculty itself. The mind is trained to fully allow, while being steadily aware of, the experience of any of these four fields of bodily or mental activity. The nonreactive quality of the aware mind allows all experience to unfold without the extreme response of suppression on one hand or of expression on the other. This middle ground, when developed, fosters an openness to experience without a need to act and allows psychic release and integration to occur as a natural part of the silent meditation process. As the mind becomes more skilled in the application of mindfulness, an increased awareness is carried over into all other daily activities. In this way this same release and integration infuse one's daily life.

The Abhidhamma psychology views experience as having three aspects. First is the object of experience, of which there are six classes: sights, sounds, tastes, smells, body perceptions, and objects of mind. Second are the separate classes of consciousness that arise anew in each moment. Thus there are moments of eye consciousness, ear consciousness, nose consciousness, tongue consciousness, body consciousness, and mind consciousness, changing with each new object. Third, there is a whole array (fifty-two in all) of mediating mental factors. These affective (of moods and emotions), cognitive, and perceptual qualities of mind determine how each moment of consciousness relates to its object. They include neutral qualities, such as perception, recognition, will, and basic attention. They also include unskillful qualities, both affective and cognitive, such as greed, hatred, fear, worry, restlessness, and doubt. Finally, there is a group of qualities, such as love, generosity, wisdom, mindfulness, tranquility, self-assurance.

The purpose of the mental training in Abhidhamma terms is to cultivate through repetition the skillful mental qualities that simultaneously inhibit the arising of the unskillful ones (which are seen as the causes of suffering and dissatisfaction). The initial training of concentration brings to the mind tranquility and a reduction in restlessness and agitation. This is followed by the training of this nonjudgmental mindfulness that functions to reduce the other unskillful factors, such as greed and hatred, and fosters the arising of openmindedness, generosity, love, and self-assurance. Ultimately, when these skillful factors become well developed, the mind becomes composed and aware enough to successively abandon some of the unskillful states and neurotic patterns for good. Wisdom, fearlessness, and calm become the predominant mental qualities, and are accompanied by increased self-knowledge and greater empathy, compassion, and understanding.

## APPLICATIONS

Most frequently used as normative psychotherapy, Insight Meditation has been successful in treating neurotic disturbances from severe to mild, some forms of depression, specific behavioral problems, and psychosomatic disorders. It is especially valuable for bringing deep personal and spiritual insight and satisfying the developmental needs of most normal adults.

---

# Meditative Therapy⁵*

## Michael L. Emmons

### DEFINITION

Meditative Therapy is an eyes-closed method wherein the participant enters a naturally occurring altered state of consciousness and allows an "inner Source" to engage in its curative process. Meditative Therapy is an inner-directed, self-unifying or self-healing approach conducted in an altered state of consciousness. This means that the person involved in the process closes his eyes and describes the events taking place throughout one's entire being. As the inner workings unfold, they treat the whole person. The Inner Source deals with mind, body, and spirit adjustments that may need attention. There is a part of us that seems to know everything about us and knows what to do to allow us to go beyond our present state of being, to transform our whole self mentally, physically, spiritually.

There is inside each of us a powerful source of knowledge, a self-contained system of help, an Inner Source. This inner wisdom is a natural, inherent, inborn process that some feel is God directed and others feel is brain directed. It has been given many names throughout the ages: the deeper self, the buddhi, the supercon-scious, the higher self, the biological wisdom, the subliminal self, the God-within, the oversoul, the not-self, the Christ consciousness. The derivation of its power and the actual name given make no difference, because the Inner Source will work automatically to help us reach our full potential in spite of what we call it and where it comes from.

### HISTORY

Meditative Therapy is most closely aligned with the current methods of Autogenic Abreaction from the work *Autogenic Therapy* by Schultz and Luthe. For centuries, there have been natural methods in existence that are similar in nature to Meditative Therapy. These methods are mostly found in one of the basic forms of meditation —mindfulness meditation—as discussed in the ancient Buddhist text *The Vissud-himaga*.

---

5* From *The Inner Source* by Michael Emmons, copyright 1978. Impact Publishers, Inc., San Luis Obispo, California 93406. Reprinted by permission of the publisher.

## TECHNIQUE

There is no specific technique that the therapist employs in Meditative Therapy. The Inner Source is in charge of helping the individual. The therapist's role is to be a nondirective guide and help the individual to patiently allow the inner-directed process to unfold. To begin Meditative Therapy the client simply lies down, closes the eyes, and begins watching and describing out loud any type of experience taking place. The person is to focus on bodily reactions, visual images, and thought processes, allowing the Inner Source to proceed. Within the atmosphere of a patient and noninterfering attitude, the Inner Source will unfold a wide variety of intricate, often beautiful, workings to help the individual.

These curative workings have been catalogued under the name of autogenic discharges by Schultz and Luthe. A wide variety of responses can take place, including tastes, smells, dizziness, floating sensations, colors, patterns, trembling, twitching, singing, heaviness, warmth, anxiety, fear, depression, thoughts, memories, etc. Each Inner Source is unique and will employ these reactions in various combinations to help the client.

Meditative Therapy is conducted once a week for a session of from thirty minutes to two and one-half hours. The Inner Source will begin the session on its own, once the eyes are closed, and will also finish on its own. For this reason, no preset amount of time can be determined for the session to last. For most clients, the main part of therapeutic outcome will take place in five to ten therapist-facilitated sessions, after which the person can be taught self-Meditative Therapy.

Meditative Therapy has the potential to produce dramatic, sometimes frightening, results in a short period of time. For this reason, no one should attempt to use the method on oneself or others without reading the references at the end of this article.

## APPLICATIONS

By patiently allowing the Inner Source to work, one may experience a wide range of positive outcomes. Potential results that often take place are as follows:

1. Relief from psychosomatic complaints
2. Resolution of childhood conflicts
3. Regulation of sleeping patterns
4. Increased ability to relax
5. Lessening of tension and anxiety
6. Reduction of habitual fear responses
7. Greater self-confidence
8. Decreased physical pain
9. Closer alignment to a Spiritual Source
10. Increased tendencies toward inner direction
11. More satisfying interpersonal relationships.

The reason that these results are given only as likely outcomes is because each person has his or her own unique set of outcomes, depending upon what areas of one's life may need help. Generally speaking, the full range of neurotic disorders can be treated employing Meditative Therapy. At this point, there has been no application of the method to the psychoses.

The Inner Source produces its outcomes naturally through the above experiences. The results of Meditative Therapy are *not* largely based on either client or therapist insight or interpretation of ongoing and resulting psychic material.

In summary, although Meditative Therapy is not a cure-all, the method has the ability to produce significant positive changes in a relatively short period of time. Follow-up data, ranging between three and eighteen months, document lasting results on a number of clients for a variety of complaints.

# Meeting Psychotherapy
## *Maurice Friedman*

### DEFINITION

Meeting Psychotherapy is a general name for all those psychotherapies that emphasize meeting—the direct, open, mutual trusting contact between therapist and client(s) as the central, as opposed to ancillary, source of healing. Healing through meeting implies that meeting must also be a goal as well as the means to therapy.

### HISTORY

Freud built direct meeting between psychoanalyst and patient into the very foundations of psychoanalysis. To C. G. Jung, the dialogue in which the therapist must engage and risk himself as a person was an essential part of therapy. Swiss psychoanalyst Hans Trüb, a former Jungian, made healing through meeting his life's work. Others who have contributed to the field are: Swiss existentialist psychoanalyst Ludwig Binswanger, the German-American founder of psychodrama J. L. Moreno, the American psychologist Carl R. Rogers, the American psychoanalyst Leslie H. Farber, the Hungarian-American family psychiatrist Ivan Boszormenyi-Nagy, and the English family therapist Ronald Laing.

In *The Undiscovered Self* (1958) Jung says, "All over the world, it is being recognized today that what is being treated is not a symptom, but a patient." The more the doctor schematizes, the more the patient quite rightly resists; for the patient demands to be dealt with in his uniqueness. In *On Becoming a Person* (1961) Carl Rogers tells how he changed his approach to therapy; instead of asking how he could treat the client, he recognized that changes come about through experience in a relationship. He found that the more genuine he was in a relationship, the more aware he was of his own feelings, and the more willing he was to express his own feelings and attitudes, then the more he was able to give the relationship a reality that the person could use for his own personal growth. Under the influence of Martin Buber, as well as of Soren Kierkegaard and his former mentor Harry Stack Sullivan, Leslie Farber has developed an original theory of "will and willfulness" as the center of psychiatric diagnosis and healing. At the same time,

Farber has gone further than anyone in recognizing the factual limitations of healing through meeting to which Buber pointed in his "Dialogue with Rogers" (Buber, 1965).

Ivan Boszormenyi-Nagy (1973) follows Buber in distinguishing between relationships that are merely functions of individual becoming, normalcy, adaptation, and perspective and relationships that are ontological in the sense that they have a reality, meaning, and value in themselves. This leads Nagy to forceful and repeated emphasis of Buber's distinction between intrapsychic guilt feelings and interhuman existential guilt The traditional therapist often removes certain manifestations of psychological guilt only at the price of increasing the patient's existential guilt; for the reality of a disturbed order of the human world can only be affected by action and existential rearrangement, if at all. In Nagy's family therapy, this means: "The individual can be liberated to a full and wholly personal relationship only to the extent that he remains capable of responding to parental devotion with concern." Thus, what is central to Buber's philosophy of dialogue—learning to meet others and to hold one's ground when one meets them—is central to Nagy's "reciprocity in intergenerational family therapy."

## TECHNIQUE

Meeting is a two-sided event that is not susceptible to techniques, meaning that a therapist does not manipulate the client in order to bring about a certain result. What is crucial is not the skills of the therapist but what takes place between the therapist and the client and *between* the client and other people. In every respect in which the therapist makes an object of the person—"whether by diagnosing him, analyzing him, or perceiving him impersonally in a case history," says Rogers—he stands in the way of his therapeutic goal. The therapist is deeply helpful only when he relates as a person, risks himself as a person in the relationship, and experiences the other as a person in his own right. "Only then is there a meeting of a depth which dissolves the pain of aloneness in both client and therapist."

To embark seriously on healing through meeting is to leave the safe shores of the intrapsychic as *the* touchstone of reality and to venture on to the high seas in which therapy is no longer seen as something taking place *in* the client. Although the client hopefully becomes wholer in the process and the therapist has a special role as initiator, facilitator, and confidant, the healing itself takes place in that sphere which Buber calls the "between."

In his family psychiatry, Nagy espouses a "multidirectional partiality" in which the therapist will be partial at one time to one member of the family and at another time to another. The family therapist must be strong enough to be included in the family system yet remain outside in the role of facilitator for emotional change and growth. Buber says he must have that "inclusion" or "imagining the real" by which he experiences the patient's side of the relationship without losing his own.

The therapist open to healing through meeting will feel that more is demanded of him than his professional methods and role. At the same time he will feel that whether the healing does or does not take place is not a result of *his* success or failure.

## APPLICATIONS

The readjustment and integration of the intrapsychic sphere is a by-product of Meeting Psychotherapy, but the locus of healing is the interhuman, the interpersonal, the social, the cultural, and even the political. Thus, healing is not limited to client alone or even to the relationship between therapist and client. Real healing must enter into all relationships: the interhuman, the family, the group, the community.

# Megavitamin Therapy
## *A. Hoffer*

### DEFINITION
The term "megavitamin" refers to the use of some of the vitamins for prevention and treatment of disease in dosages much higher than required to keep most normal people in a relatively good state of health. "Mega" refers to the dose. There are, of course, no megavitamins, lecular therapy.

### HISTORY
It was inevitable that soon after pure vitamins became available that they would be used for a variety of diseases. In psychiatry vitamin *B3,* the anti-pellagra vitamin, was tried by a few enterprising psychiatrists for depression. Some of these conditions quickly responded. With Dr. H. Osmond, I (A. Hoffer) began the first double blind controlled studies ever completed in psychiatry. (In the double-blind method, neither the patient nor the researcher knows whether the active substance or the placebo is administered.) We compared the only known treatment of that time (psychotherapy and electroconvulsive therapy) and placebo against the same treatment plus three-gram doses of vitamin *B3* each day. Our method has since become the standard method of modern clinical trials.

We found that at the end of one year the vitamin *B3* group had achieved a 70 percent recovery rate, compared with a 35 percent rate for the placebo group. The placebo rate was comparable to natural recovery for acute and sub-acute schizophrenics. After four double blind controlled experiments and after clinical experience on over fifty thousand patients, my orthomolecular colleagues and I have concluded that vitamin *B3* in optimum doses (a better term than megadoses) is an important ingredient of proper treatment for most schizophrenic patients. Osmond and I also used large doses of ascorbic acid for our patients treated outside of these double blind experiments.

Through the research of scientists, including Cott (1967, 1969, 1971), Hawkins (1968), Hawkins and Pauling (1973), Pfeiffer (1975), Rimland (1973), and many others (see Hawkins and Pauling, 1973), other vitamins have been found essential, especially pyridoxine and, to a lesser degree, vitamin B12.

The next major advance was Dr. Linus Pauling's (1968) conclusion about the relationship between brain function (mental health) and the optimum biochemical environment. He defined orthomolecular psychiatry as "the treatment of mental disease by the provision of the optimum molecular environment for the mind, especially the optimum concentrations of substances normally present in the body."

Since then there has been a gratifying advance in the theory and practice of this more advanced form of psychiatry and medicine. A modern orthomolecular therapist pays close attention to nutrition, to supplementation with optimum doses of vitamins and minerals while also using all other chemotherapies that will help and not harm the patient. There are a number of megavitamin pioneers who have, with dedication, advanced knowledge always in confrontation with classical medicine, which has remained ignorant and therefore resistive to nutritional therapy. These include F. Klenner (1971, 1973), I. Stone (1972), and L. Pauling (1968, 1970, 1974), for ascorbic acid. W. Shute and Taub (1969) for vitamin E, and C. Reich (1971) for vitamins A and *B3*. Recently, medicine seriously examined megadoses of vitamin A as treatment for cancer. There is already available very significant data showing that ascorbic acid should be a very important component of any treatment program for cancer.

The controversy over the use of optimum doses of vitamins is not scientific. Not a single opponent to Megavitamin Therapy has any personal experience as a clinician with this form of treatment. Therefore, they depend entirely on sloppy literature reviews and biased conclusions. All new discoveries in medicine are greeted by similar antagonism, and Megavitamin Therapy is no exception. But the controversy will become scientific when critics duplicate the published methods for using Megavitamin Therapy and show it does not work. This has not yet occurred, and Megavitamin Therapy is advancing rapidly. This is the response to a massive demand from thousands of patients and their families who have personally witnessed their failure to recover on orthodox treatment, and the vast improvement when the orthomolecular approach was used.

## TECHNIQUE

1. *Medical model.* Patients, whether schizophrenic or depressed, are considered to be ill. The pure psychosocial models are not used. Psychotherapy is based upon this model. It includes discussion of diagnosis, treatment, and prognosis and calls upon any psychosocial therapies that can maximize the probability of recovery in conjunction with chemotherapy.

2. *Nutrition.* Patients are placed upon a diet that suits them best. This may depend upon trial and error based upon clinical experience. Generally, all orthomolecular therapists advise against nonfoods such as sugar, dyes, and other additives not shown to enhance the nutritional value of the foods in which they are added. In planning diets, the question of allergic reactions must be examined; food allergies can cause any psychiatric syndrome, including schizophrenia and learning and behavioral disorders in children.

3. *Vitamins.* These are used in optimal dose levels. This is determined by beginning with lower doses and increasing them, depending upon the rate of response. The best dose is the quantity that brings about steady improvement and causes no side effects. At these doses there is no medication safer than the vitamins. The common ones are vitamin B3, ascorbic acid, and pyridoxine, but any of the others may be required.

   *a)*   *Vitamin B₃.* Two forms are available; nicotinic acid (medically known as niacin) and nicotinamide (or niacinamide). Nicotinic acid causes facial flushing when it is first used, but in time, in most cases, the flush vanishes or becomes inconsequential. There is no flush with nicotinamide. The dose range is in grams per day. It may require adjustment either way, depending upon the response.

b) *Ascorbic acid.* The optimum dose varies with the patient's degree of illness or stress. The sicker that person is the more ascorbic acid is required and can be tolerated. If the tolerable level is exceeded, there is diarrhea.

c) *Pyridoxine.* Usually less than 1 gram per day is required.

4. *Minerals.* Attention will be given to optimum amounts of minerals. Usually this means reducing levels of toxic metals, such as lead, when they are elevated, or restoring essential elements, such as zinc, when they are low. Pfeiffer's recent book details the kind of attention which is essential.

5. *Other chemotherapy.* Drugs are used as required, but only as adjuncts to orthomolecular therapy; the objective is to reduce the dependence upon drugs, consistent with the patient's response. The goal of therapy is to have the patient on nutrient therapy alone, or with doses of tranquilizers, anti-depressants, etc., so low that there is no inhibiting effect on the person.

6. *Duration of treatment.* This may vary from a few months to a lifetime. It is determined by withdrawing supplements after the patient has been well for long periods.

## APPLICATIONS

1. *The schizophrenias.* Megavitamin Therapy works quickest and best for acute and sub-acute illnesses. Progress with treatment is measured clinically and, if necessary, with tests. Osmond and I have developed two very helpful tests: a) the Hoffer-Osmond Diagnostic Test (HOD) (1975) and b) the Experiential World Inventory (EWI).

2. *Children with learning and behavioral disorders.* I use this broad term because none of the nearly one hundred terms have been shown to be helpful in determining treatment. Etiological diagnosis is more relevant. Under the broad group under this heading orthomolecular therapists include three main subgroups: a) the vitamin dependencies, b) cerebral allergies, and c) mineral imbalances.

3. *The neuroses and depression.* A large proportion suffer from psychiatric manifestations of the saccharine disease (see Cleave, 1975). When tested with a five-hour glucose tolerance test, most show definite abnormalities. Diet correction is a main component of treatment.

4. *The addictions.* These diseases, which include alcoholism and drug addictions, also yield to orthomolecular treatment. Two important recent contributions come from Smith (1974) and Libby and Stone (1978).

5. *Criminal behavior.* Many advances are being made here. This, coupled with general acceptance of the view that psychosocial intervention alone is not very useful, will rapidly expand serious examination of orthomolecular views.

# Mental Hospital as a Psychotherapeutic System

*Louis Linn*

## DEFINITION

The Mental Hospital is an institution for the in-patient care of the emotionally ill, maintained by private endowments, public funds, or both.

## HISTORY

In medieval times, church-sponsored facilities were often models of humane concern. Too often, however, these settings became houses for the care of the indigent and the friendless, and in which treatment and nursing were so poor that few emerged alive. In the late eighteenth century the French psychiatrist Pinel removed the chains from confined psychotic patients. This proved to be a revolutionary act that triggered similar developments throughout the Western World. Dorothea Lynde Dix pioneered in the establishment of the state hospital system in this country. In her day, these were models of so-called moral treatment and of the no-restraint approach to patient care.

In the twentieth century a combination of population growth nd a lack of effective treatment methods led to mental hospital overcrowding. In time, these institutions degenerated into antitherapeutic storage depots for the unwanted. The term "asylum," which once meant a sanctuary or a place of peace, became a term of opprobrium. In 1904, ex-patient Clifford Beers wrote *A Mind That Found Itself*, a manifesto that led to the formation of the National Association for Mental Health and to some beginnings of hospital reform.

## TECHNIQUE

In the 1940s a series of fundamental developments occurred that altered the mental hospital situation. Effective somatic methods of treatment appeared; namely, electroshock therapy (ECT) for depression and mania and insulin therapy (ICT) for schizophrenia. In addition, contributions from group psychology led to the concept of the "hospital as a therapeutic community" and the individual ward as a "therapeutic milieu." In the 1950s new medications appeared with unprecedented ability to control psychotic symptoms. For the first time community-based treatment of the major mental disorders became a practical possibility. In the 1960s, federal legislation implemented this breakthrough with the concept of the Comprehensive Community Mental Health Center that stated that the treatment locale of choice for most mental patients is the community in which they live, in contact with family, friends, and their customary occupational and recreational opportunities. Along with this, psychiatric units in general hospitals became widespread.

We are now in a new phase of mental hospital utilization. It is clear that there will always be chronic, incurable patients whose numbers will increase in spite of the most optimistic therapeutic advances imaginable. These chronic patients must be cared for, some in hospitals and some in community-based sheltered settings that can provide viable alternatives to long-term in-patient care. The plight of the chronic, incurable patient remains a major problem awaiting satisfactory solution.

The acute mental disorders provide a different set of problems. The most important fact about acute psychiatric hospitalization is that it occurs when a previously satisfactory adaptional state ceases to work. For example, a schizophrenic patient may be living in the community over a period of years, a potentially suicidal patient may contain his self-destructiveness, a sexual exhibitionist may control the urge to act out his exhibitionistic desire. All these potential crises may remain quiescent until one day an environmental change occurs. A loss of some kind is usually involved—loss of a crucial love object, a job, a body part, or some other source of self-esteem. At that time, and at that time only, a previously latent psychiatric disorder becomes clinically manifest.

In such instances, hospitalization may play a rescuing role, protecting the patient from his own uncontrolled impulses and from the punitive responses of those who do not understand his predicament. The hospital provides him with a relatively rational input in place of the confusion in his own home, and with medications that ease his suffering and increase his self-control. In short, the hospital functions as an asylum in the finest sense of the word.

In the sheltered setting of the hospital, overt manifestations of mental disorder tend to melt away quickly. In place of the acute emotional decompensation that prevailed on admission, a state of remission sets in during which the patient may even be entirely symptom-free. However, it cannot be emphasized too strongly that this symptom-free state does not reflect a cure. All it signifies is that the patient is able to function in a more or less symptom-free state within the sheltered setting of the hospital. It provides no clue concerning his ability to adapt to his previously traumatic outside environment. No one understands this better than the patient himself, and that is why he is so often afraid to leave the hospital or why he tends to relapse as his discharge date approaches. In view of this, it should surprise no one that many patients discharged at this point in the treatment program relapse swiftly or commit suicide.

This simple sequence of events is subject to widespread misunderstanding. Unless the patient's environment has also been improved, he will not maintain his hospital-induced improvement. It is true that medications and a strongly supportive after-care program may help the patient to be more tolerant of his life stresses. But it makes no sense to omit entirely the environmental factor from the therapeutic equation.

In order for the environment to be more tolerant of the patient, he and his family must learn to relate to each other with more compassion. This requires time and it must be accomplished gradually. Therapeutic leaves of increasing length as well as overnight leaves must be professionally monitored, regulated, and modified as clinical conditions require.

## APPLICATIONS

Admission to a mental hospital usually occurs through one of three routes. With "informal admission" the patient accepts hospitalization of his own accord. The exact same conditions prevail in this circumstance as if he had accepted hospitalization for a nonpsychiatric illness. He is free to leave at his own discretion, even against the advice of the physician. Most admissions to general hospital psychiatric in-patient units are of this type.

In the case of "voluntary admission," the patient voluntarily signs a certificate requesting admission. However, once the patient has accepted admission, the hospital is empowered by law to keep him hospitalized, against his will if necessary. The length of the involuntary stay in this instance is usually in the order of one to two weeks and is carefully prescribed by law. This gives the hospital the opportunity to prevent discharge against medical advice when such an action might have serious consequences for the patient or those close to him.

Finally, "involuntary admission" is used when a patient in need of in-patient care is deemed to be a danger to himself or others but refuses to accept "informal" or "voluntary" admission. "Involuntary" admission occurs, then, when a member of the family or some concerned person in the community applies for help. In this instance one or two physicians (depending on local ordinances) examine the patient at the request of the "petitioner" and decide on the basis of the history and their findings if in-patient care is indeed unavoidable. In this instance, the hospital is empowered to retain the patient as long as the physicians treating him deem necessary. There are a variety of laws that protect the civil rights of these involuntarily confined patients. In actual practice "involuntary" confinement is infrequently used. If properly approached, most patients who require in-patient care can be prevailed upon to accept one of the other types of admission.

# Methadone Maintenance
*Arthur Maglin*

## DEFINITION

Methadone Maintenance is a system of therapy utilized in the treatment of opiate-dependent persons. Almost always, the addiction being treated is to heroin, but the therapy is applicable to persons addicted to such other opiates as morphine, opium, and Demerol.

The opiate-dependent person is given daily doses of methadone, a dependency-forming synthetic opiate, which can eliminate narcotic craving, block opiate euphoria, and allow the patient to function normally. Since a transition to a new and satisfying style of life is the general goal of Methadone Maintenance therapy, an essential and mandated feature of this form of treatment is counseling services.

Since methadone has no direct effect on the potential abuse of other drugs, such as cocaine, barbiturates, amphetamines, and minor tranquilizers, regular monitoring of patients' patterns of drug intake is accomplished by means of clinical observation and analysis of urine samples. Attempts are usually made to screen out polydrug abusers before admission into a Methadone Maintenance program. Counseling techniques are used to prevent new nonopiate addictions from developing once a patient is enrolled in treatment.

## HISTORY

The failure of drug-free counseling programs and therapeutic communities to attract and successfully rehabilitate the majority of heroin-dependent people has led to a continuing search for a chemical agent that could serve as an adjunct to counseling in helping people to break away from the heroin addict life-style. Methadone, developed into a system of maintenance therapy by Vincent Dole and Marie Nyswander during the 1960s, has so far been the most successful of these chemical rehabilitative aids. Others still being researched include Darvon-N, LAAM, naltrexone, and cyclazocine.

The original Dole-Nyswander theory specified that opiate addiction produces a permanent change in body chemistry, which creates a nonreversible need for an opiate. Since clinical trials showed that methadone taken once a day allows an opiate addict to function normally, while heroin taken several times a day does not, Methadone Maintenance became a viable form of drug replacement therapy. However, opiate-dependent persons, according to Dole and Nyswander's original hypothesis, might have to be maintained on methadone for life.

This theory is no longer universally adhered to. Most experts now believe that it is possible for many opiate-addicted people to return to a drug-free state after one or more years of Methadone Maintenance therapy, if they have been aided through counseling in constructing a satisfying new life-style. Usually, this means that the patient has improved family relationships, established new friendships, and become involved in some form of structured full-time activity, such as work, school, or child care. Increasingly, Methadone Maintenance programs contain drug-free aftercare components.

In recent years Methadone Maintenance programs have had to cope with the increasing prevalence of combined addictions. Since methadone taken in combination with heavy or steady doses of such drugs as sedatives, minor tranquilizers, or alcohol can medically endanger the patient, attempts—often not successful—to treat the nonopiate addiction by means of various individual, family, and group counseling techniques have become an important feature of the methadone treatment modality.

Methadone programs fall into two general types: public and private. The public programs are funded almost entirely by governmental sources. They tend to have larger and more qualified staffs than the private programs in which the patients pay for their treatment and which are run on a profit basis. Private programs receive some governmental funding via the Medicaid program. Much of the controversy, though by no means all of it, that has surrounded Methadone Maintenance programs has centered on the practices of many of the private clinics.

## TECHNIQUE

Methadone is given to voluntary patients in uniform daily dosages of 20 to 100 mg. Urine samples are collected and analyzed once a week. A counselor is assigned to the patient and a treatment plan is developed that takes into account the rehabilitation goals to be achieved.

These goals may typically include, in the beginning, helping a patient to negotiate the welfare system in order to establish a legal source of income and perhaps to obtain rent for an apartment. Later goals may include obtaining a high school equivalency diploma, obtaining job training, and seeking employment. Throughout, the counselor attempts to aid the patient in finding new means of coping with problems other than turning to drugs. The counselor will advise against detoxification from Methadone Maintenance before the patient has established a reasonably comfortable pattern of re socialization and will support detoxification after such a pattern has been accomplished.

With some patients, insight-oriented techniques will be utilized. In other cases, *supportive and directive techniques will be seen as more appropriate. Group therapy and family therapy are also frequently employed.*

## APPLICATIONS

Methadone Maintenance is an effective form of therapy with strictly limited applicability. Methadone Maintenance is of no use to persons addicted to substances other than opiates. It is useful only as an aid to improving the functioning of many opiate-addicted persons. Other treatment modalities, such as drug-free therapeutic communities, are more applicable to others.

Out of the tens of thousands of patients for whom Methadone Maintenance has been successful as an aid to improved functioning, it can for many also be a step toward total abstinence from drugs, a goal that most addicts see themselves as working toward.

# Psychoanalytically Oriented Milieu Therapy

*Jacquelyn Sanders*

## DEFINITION

Psychoanalytically Oriented Milieu Therapy is the application of the theory of psychoanalytic ego psychology to the design of all aspects of an environment. The total milieu (including the physical setting, the structure and detail of the patients' lives, and the staff who work daily with the patients) is used to provide the necessary conditions for the patient to resolve inner conflicts and develop strong, healthy personality structures.

## HISTORY

The first effort to apply psychoanalytic understanding to the "life structure" of the patient was made by August Aichhorn, who, after World War I, treated a group of "wayward" youngsters in an institutional setting. In the 1940s further development of this approach took place in various parts of the United States (with Stan Szurich in San Francisco, with Fritz Redl in Detroit, at Southard School in Topeka, at Bellefaire in

Cleveland, and at the schools of the Jewish Board of Guardians in New York). The work of Maxwell Jones and Harry Stack Sullivan was also very influential. In 1944 Bruno Bettelheim became director of the Sonia Shankman Orthogenic School of the University of Chicago and, for the next twenty years, worked with staff, colleagues, and consultants in psychiatry, psychoanalysis, anthropology, and education in developing a model of Psychoanalytically Oriented Milieu Therapy.

## TECHNIQUE

The essence of the therapy is a deep and respectful consideration of all aspects of a person's life with the purpose of understanding how each aspect can be utilized to help the person heal and grow. I will describe this through examples of how it is effected at the Orthogenic School. The physical setting is a potential therapeutic agent, since it is often the most pervasive and permanent element in an institution. At the school, decisions on furnishings are made by the director in consultation with the staff and patients who will be living with those furnishings. When an entire institution is furnished in this way, as beautifully as possible, the residents begin to get the message that they are, and deserve to be, respected. Very little gets broken or damaged.

The structure of the day is also considered and can have a similarly powerful impact. For example, all of the children (forty), teachers, and counselors who are working that day meet at the end of the school day and after lunch on Saturday. Once a week the director comes to the meeting to discuss matters of common interest, such as: redecorating, which condiments should be available at every meal, or why people have difficulty eating. At these meetings, each person is supported by all others, and there is an institutionalized time for the director and all residents to listen to what any patient has to say. This meeting structure again conveys respect, support, and the conviction that each person can influence what happens to himself.

In a therapeutic milieu, the interactions between patients and staff are given the most careful attention. Some of the most significant times for a brilliant autistic boy were when his teacher sat with him while he used the toilet, for a psychotic adolescent it was when he was sick in bed, and for a schizophrenic girl, when she met a dog on a shopping trip and clung to her counselor. Our children are rarely able to communicate their anxieties and fantasies around such critical issues outside of the time when they are actually experiencing them. Therefore, they need to have the therapeutic person available at the time the critical issues are aroused. Since these are the interchanges that are most important, they are discussed at formal and informal meetings with staff, director, and consultant psychiatrists.

The following is a brief indication of some of the implications of the theory of psychoanalytic ego psychology for this therapy. The primary task of strengthening and developing the ego is accomplished by the ego exercising its function of satisfying the demands of the internal and external worlds. We, therefore, try to design an environment where this is possible and which gradually becomes more challenging. For example, in regard to satisfying internal demands, some kind of food is always available to the patient in such a way that he can get it himself; and the bathrooms are very attractive and easily accessible. Thus, because of the physical arrangements and the traditional structure, the patient can, with little difficulty, satisfy his needs.

We at first drastically reduce the demands of the external world so that the patient can have success in meeting them. We gradually impose demands, always trying to have them make sense in the patient's terms. While they do have to live with five or six other people, at first we require only that they not hurt themselves or anyone else. Gradually a meaningful program is developed, in terms of what they are cognitively ready to learn, what will appeal to them psychologically, and what will help them to master their internal and external worlds.

In order to choose appropriate experiences and respond appropriately, the staff has to understand the patients, themselves, and the nature of the unconscious. At the daily meetings with the director and/or consulting psychiatrist, the staff is helped in this understanding. The school is designed to facilitate many other interactions: the staffs meet frequently and the director and senior staff are available for consultation and support. The efforts of the staff in all these meetings are continually to try to understand, reevaluate, and rethink our work so that we can build a world for these patients that can be healing and growing—a therapeutic milieu.

### APPLICATIONS

The principle of considering the psychological impact of all aspects of an environment has very wide application. It has, for example, been very effectively applied to normal classroom situations, from preschool upward.

# Mirror Image Therapy

### Richard E. Frenkel

### DEFINITION

Many years ago, while analyzing a patient, I noticed her facial expression becoming distorted while she free associated material about her mother. Since I found it difficult to accurately describe this change to her, I asked her to look in a mirror.

She was instantaneously shocked: "My God, I look like my mother! It's her mopey look," she retorted.

For many years thereafter, on almost a daily basis, I used a mirror to analyze this patient's transference and resistance until she completed her analysis.

### HISTORY

At that time, the psychiatric literature showed no reference to the use of the mirror as a *diagnostic-therapeutic tool*. However, many articles existed on the mirror for other purposes. I then continued to research the use of the mirror as a diagnostic-therapeutic tool in psychiatry.

### TECHNIQUE

The Mirror Image Projective Technique (M.I.P.T.) is a diagnostic-therapeutic instrument that is in easy reach of any psychotherapist.

The patient is asked to focus on his mirror image. When the patient becomes inducted into a "mirror trance," he is then asked to free associate to his image. Defenses are unblocked and the unconscious mind is permitted to flow, bringing forth vital feelings and thoughts of recent and past experiences. Intermittently, the patient focuses and unfocuses his eyes upon his image, as he ventures from reality to the unconscious and back. He is a participant observer while using the mirror. In some cases, immediate interpretations can be made from the data gathered. Occasionally, primary instantaneous insight is gained by the patient.

While the ordinary "black-and-white mirror" is used for the diagnosis of mental illness, and used as a therapeutic tool, the "multicolored mirror" is employed to decipher the emotional meaning of color for the individual patient. Emotion appears to be directly related to color.

Since the M.I.P.T. accomplished therapeutic change, I termed this treatment Mirror Image Therapy. Sound-recording equipment and videotapes have proved themselves to be invaluable in aiding the therapeutic process. I have found the M.I.P.T. to be applicable to all types of psychopathology. Thus far, in my practice, no type of pathology has been resistant to the M.I.P.T.

## APPLICATIONS

The M.I.P.T. is very useful in combination with other therapy modalities.

Child Mirror Therapy was employed with five child stutterers. The seven-year-old children all took turns using the mirror in the classroom. They free associated to their mirror image rather easily as if it was play therapy. They exposed their problems to their fellow students and teacher. I supervised their teacher, as we reviewed together tape-recorded sessions of the children using the mirror. Many simple problems were solved rather quickly for the children.

Adult Group Therapy with the M.I.P.T. was also readily accomplished. Each patient was asked to free associate to their mirror image before the group whenever it was deemed necessary. Many startling and unexpected thoughts and feelings were brought out in a natural manner before the group. Some remarked that it was like having individual sessions during group therapy.

Family Therapy with the M.I.P.T. also proved to be very rewarding therapeutically-Mentally retarded patients reacted to the M.I.P.T. rather well. The M.I.P.T. helps differentiate between organicity and other nonorganic conditions.

### Symptomatic Treatment

*Depression.* The M.I.P.T. is most useful in decreasing depression. The mirror is an *antidepressant instrument.* At times it will provoke the patient to cry, and thus relieve anger. This reduces the depression in the individual. The patient acquires symptomatic relief from the depression.

*Suicide prevention.* Since the M.I.P.T. decompresses depression, this reduces considerably the chance of the patient acting in a suicidal manner.

*Controlling hallucinations.* The mirror is *antihallucinogenic.* When a patient is actively hallucinating, he is asked to look at his image in the mirror and to constantly focus on his image. Invariably the voices disappear from the patient for a period of twenty-one to twenty-six seconds. Ambulatory schizophrenic patients are taught to carry pocket mirrors with them so that they can control the "voices" anytime they wish.

*Reducing anxiety.* The mirror precipitously reduces a patient's anxiety. Mirror responses "gush out" from the patient and anxiety disappears. I term this the "gushing phenomenon." Panic states are thus obviated. Phobic patients are helped by this mirror maneuver.

### New Horizons in Mirror Research

*A new clinical theory of vision.* From the present data at hand, it appears that the rods of the retina register the visual structure and function of experience. The cones deal with the individual's emotional reaction to experience. Both the structural aspects of experience and the emotional reactions to experience are integrated in the retina. Then these integrated impulses pass through the visual tracts and are deposited in the memory bank of the brain.

The mirror experience causes the unconscious mind to release both the structural (black-and-white mirror experience) and the emotional (colored experience) reactions from the brain via the process of videotape recall.

*Meaning of color in dreams.* The multicolored mirror instrument consists of diverse colors in plastic that move across the surface of a mirror. Seeing one's image in a different color appears to be different from viewing color in the environment. A multicolored image response brings forth strong feelings relating to people and objects. If a specific color represents one's feelings to a definite person, such as a mother or father, then this same color may be color-specific in colored dreams. If further research validates this observation, the meaning of color in dreams could be unraveled.

*The creativity center in the brain.* The ordinary mirror and the multicolored mirror permit the therapist to sense the degree of creativity possessed by the client during the M.I.P.T. experience. A creativity center definitely exists in the brain.

*M.I.P.T., drugs and mental illness.* Future research will combine the use of drugs with the M.I.P.T. so that symptoms that describe mental illness can be reduced. In turn, this might be an indirect way of determining what biochemicals cause mental illness.

---

# Modern Psychoanalysis

## Johannah Segers

### DEFINITION

The first psychoanalytic patient was Anna O., who described psychoanalysis as "the talking cure." Sigmund Freud learned that when his patients talked to him freely, their hysterical symptoms abated and their neurotic conflicts were, to some degree, resolved.

Modern Psychoanalysis subscribes to Freud's concept and Anna O.'s definition of psychoanalysis but has expanded it to include treatment of narcissistic disorders— problems that develop in the first two or three years of the child's life before language has been learned. These are rooted in the preoedipal stage of the patient's development and they are preverbal in nature. Therefore, ways had to be discovered to deal with resistances that make talking freely about them difficult or impossible. Both Modern Psychoanalysis and classical psychoanalysis derived from Freud's belief that talking promotes cure. But specialization in narcissistic problems of preverbal origin has led the modern psychoanalyst to the definition of cure as the *analyst's resolution* of the patient's *resistance* to saying everything. So the emphasis is on the relationship between analyst and patient, including all of the ramifications of aggression and pleasure; love and hate.

The modern psychoanalyst recognizes the importance of concentrating on the patient fixated in the very early stages and others with fixations considered untreatable by psychoanalysts. Traditionally, the psychoanalyst diagnoses the patient and decides whether or not he is treatable. The modern psychoanalyst differs in that he does not base his decision to treat on his diagnosis but rather on the motivation of the patient to get treatment. Modern psychoanalysts, in fact, take responsibility for any failure in working with schizophrenics, although the patient's cooperation is sought and ultimately essential for cure.

## HISTORY

In 1961 Dr. Hyman Spotnitz stated that "special approaches being developed for the treatment of the preverbal personality will facilitate emergence of a more efficient form of psychotherapy for both verbal and preverbal personalities—a modern form of psychoanalysis." Ten years later the Center for Modern Psychoanalytic Studies (now known as the Manhattan Center for Advanced Psychoanalytic Studies) was founded by psychoanalysts who, says Spotnitz, "had for ten to twenty-five years been working as modern psychoanalysts in New York. ..." The term "modern psychoanalysis" describes a specific theory and technique that Spotnitz and his colleagues developed to advance and further the effectiveness of traditional methods. There are now five institutes training modern psychoanalysts.

Although the name was not used until the 1960s and the Center was established as recently as 1971, Modern Psychoanalysis actually began in the 1940s with a program sponsored by the Jewish Board of Guardians. "The Borderline Project," directed by Yonata Feldman with Spotnitz as the consulting psychiatrist, was designed to "investigate ... borderline and schizophrenic children and their families to learn why these patients did not respond to the existing treatment approaches." (Spotnitz, 1976) As a result of "The Borderline Project's" investigation, "articles on schizophrenia ... outlined a new theory of technique for the ego in need of insulation." These writings document the first exploration of modern psychoanalytic techniques in the treatment of schizophrenics.

## TECHNIQUE

Since Freud described it as an "unconscious phenomenon operating in all human relations," transference has been considered the base for the theoretical framework of psychoanalysis. Freud defined psychoanalysis as "any line of investigation which takes transference and resistance as the starting point of its work." Resistance is viewed by the modern psychoanalyst as "a primitive form of communication" that can be used as a major tool in work with preverbal disorders. When the patient is unable to put the nature of his problem into words, the modern psychoanalyst studies the patient's resistance communications. As narcissistic resistances are resolved, cooperation between analyst and patient is achieved and the patient is able to experience object relationships. In narcissism, ego boundaries are blurred.

When the patient is able to define himself and others, the schizophrenic elements that have been a part of his being for so long subside. If this point of development is reached, the patient has reactions to others because they are like themselves, not because he thinks they are the same as him.

In work with schizophrenic patients, classical techniques run into difficulty due to neglect of the hostility that exists in the transference and the defenses against his aggression that the narcissistically disordered patient brings to the transference. But modern psychoanalysts have learned that "hatred can be a therapeutic force ... [that] binds the schizophrenic patient to his transference object even more firmly than love. [This patient is willing] to master his aggressive impulses provided that the danger that he will act on them is kept to a minimum." (Spotnitz, 1969) Modern psychoanalysts recognize that early in the treatment it is necessary to control the amount of stimulation occurring in the sessions as well as to limit pressures that might cause the patient to put his destructive impulses into action rather than verbalize them. The modern psychoanalyst's immediate goal is to provide a comfortable, nonstimulating environment so that the patient's communications can be studied and the pent-up aggression (and eventually all thoughts and feelings) released through resolution of the resistances. One of the techniques developed toward this end is a form of psychological reflection. This can be used in two ways as the following excerpts will describe.

1. *Echoing the ego.* In this method, "The ego's pattern of self-attack is highlighted through the echoing procedure. The therapist uses it to repeat at times with dramatic emphasis—the patient's expressions of low regard for himself. The unequivocal echoing of this ego in the process of 'low rating' itself strengthens his attitude that he is not fit company for a wonderful object. And yet, however black the ego, the object (or therapist) never moves away. It dedicates itself to meeting the ego's constant need for psychological closeness to an object, the kind of object that will stick with the ego through thick and thin. That is the crucial factor. Hypothetically, this procedure may be said to reverse the original process of ego formation, when the infantile mental apparatus failed to release hostile feelings toward its earliest object since the latter was experienced as being too distant. ... As it is repeatedly demonstrated that expressions of hostility do not drive the object away, the patient tends to discharge his aggression more and more freely in feelings and language. . . ."(Spotnitz, 1969a)

2. *Devaluating the object.* "Instead of echoing the ego's complaint about itself, the object can respond 'I'm just as bad' ... resolving another aspect of the infantile defense pattern: the tendency toward object-worship. [Preverbal patients must protect the object at all costs. They are reacting as they did in infancy when the parents survival was the only assurance of their own.] The greatly needed original object which was experienced as too rarely available also came to be regarded as too valuable to attack. Rather than risk damaging such a wonderful object or driving it even farther away, the infantile mental apparatus began to bottle up its aggressive impulses. Generally, the echoing procedure is employed first. ... object devaluation is usually set in train after the patient has acquired

some feeling for the therapist as an external object. After the patient has become fully capable of expressing in the treatment relationship the aggression which objective interpretation may mobilize, the therapist shifts from psychological reflection to interpretation as his judgment dictates." (Spotnitz, 1969a) Modern psychoanalysts do, in fact, offer the patient interpretations as the above statement indicates, but these are made at the patient's request if, in the analyst's judgment, it will aid in resolution of a resistance. It is the patient's interpretations of his problems, showing his own understanding, that are considered truly significant in the modern psychoanalytic process.

The *toxoid response* is another technique developed by modern psychoanalysts to "immunize" patients from their toxic introjects. In the preoedipal phase the child is in a symbiosis with the mother. They are as one. If the infant experiences too much hostility from the mother he may deal with it by incorporating it as part of his own being. When the modern psychoanalyst judges that the patient is ready (later, or final stages of treatment) he will give the patient measured doses of the toxic introject. In effect, the modern psychoanalyst helps the patient extroject the toxic elements within. Specifically, he tells the patient the same negative things about himself that the patient has been telling, either symbolically or directly, his psychoanalyst and the world. As a result of this process the patient is able to expel the poisonous self-image he has derived from negative interactions with the mother. This is done to reduce the patient's disposition to emotional upheavals in the future.

## APPLICATIONS

Classical psychoanalytic technique as discovered by Freud is designed to treat psychoneurosis and is applied in several steps: "1) transference is evoked and transference resistance is studied. [Here, resistance is viewed as [4]the force in opposition to making the unconscious conscious']; 2) countertransference resistance is recognized and analyzed.] Originally it was believed that this aspect of the treatment—the analyst's feelings for the patient—should be suppressed. But subsequent to Freud this notion was reversed.]; 3) transference resistance is interpreted; 4) resistance patterns are worked through; 5) resistance to termination is resolved." (Spotnitz, 1969)

This application of therapeutic principles did not alleviate schizophrenic symptoms because of the defense of the aggression in the patient's transference feelings. Therefore, Modern Psychoanalysis developed some new sequences in applying techniques: "1) narcissistic transference develops and is analyzed (silently). [In the occurrence of narcissistic transference, the patient assumes that his feelings about himself include his analyst—both have the same interchangeable feelings]; *2)* the patient's attempts to contact the analyst are studied. [Responses are used] to control the intensity of the resistance; 3) narcissistic countertransference resistance is recognized and analyzed. [The analyst develops feelings that correspond to his patient's]; 4) narcissistic transference resistance is effectively influenced through joining ... [echoing the ego]; 5) narcissistic transference is worked through; 6) object transference develops and is studied. [The patient has feelings for the analyst as an object separate from himself]; 7) countertransference resistance is recognized and analyzed, [those feelings of the analyst that interfere with the analytic process]; 8) object transference is interpreted. [This corresponds with step 3 in classical technique]; 9) object transference resistance is worked through; 10) resistance to termination is resolved." (Spotnitz, 1969)

Termination is considered when "the long-range task of resolving the defensive patterns of maladaptations that prevented the patient from completing essential maturational sequences" is completed. This process can be summed up by describing two aspects of the task: 1) the problem interfering with the patient's maturation "must be aroused with sufficient intensity to be identified and understood" and *2)* when the analyst understands the behavior repetition of his patients sufficiently he knows how to have therapeutic influence—that which helps the patient to get in touch with feelings long detached from his own awareness.

As a result of causing the original growth problems to reemerge in the transference relationship between analyst and patient, an opportunity is made available to reeducate the patient in more adaptive ways of functioning. This allows further growth of the personality.

---

# Money Therapy
# Through Financial Counseling

### Helen *C. Potter and Virginia B. Jacko*

## DEFINITION

Money Therapy Through Financial Counseling is a learning process by which the patient is enabled to cope with his financial problems and prevent money worries through effective management of money. Patients reduce money worries, not by temporary handouts of money, but by taking appropriate action to handle specific situations. As they learn to plan, set money goals, and realize some of those goals, their worries and negative attitudes tend to be replaced by positive ones.

## HISTORY

Until recently few psychotherapists have dealt directly with the patient's money worries as these were considered mere symptoms of psychological problems and incidental to more fundamental difficulties. Recognition that money problems of patients cannot be ignored was sparked by the 1961 financial report of the Joint Commission on Mental Health. "To enable the patient to maintain himself in the community in a normal manner" was the stated objective of the Joint Commission. This objective cannot be realized unless patients learn to manage the money needed for everyday living. Increased concern for Money Therapy is reflected in money therapists' participation in programs of rehabilitation at some mental hospitals and clinics, a Veterans Administration hospital, and other rehabilitation facilities including a Halfway House. Some private psychiatrists, clinical psychologists, and marriage counselors refer patients to financial counselors for Money Therapy. The Menninger Clinic handles money problems of patients as an integral part of resident therapy and aftercare programs. In their life adjustment training, three mental health centers in Wisconsin and one in Nebraska include some Money Therapy to enable patients to develop shopping skills.

By 1970 the interest of psychotherapists in Money Therapy had developed to the extent that 130 therapists requested reprints of the article by Potter and Stanton, "Money Management and Mental Health," *in American Journal of Psychotherapy*. These and other therapists, including clinical psychologists and alcoholic counselors, were asked in 1973 to answer questions regarding the role of financial counseling in therapy for emotionally disturbed or impaired adults. Eighty percent of the 230 respondents to the mail questionnaire agreed with the survey statement, "Financial counseling can contribute to the mental health of emotionally disturbed or impaired adults who have the capacity to handle money by reducing financial stress." (Jacko, 1975) Seventy-seven percent agreed that "financial counseling can help emotionally disturbed or impaired adults build up defenses against impulsive and compulsive buying." The role of financial counseling in reducing the stress of excessive indebtedness was considered by the respondents to be especially relevant to therapy, as were marital disputes over money. The majority of psychiatrists and clinical psychologists favored giving the regular therapist the major responsibility for Money Therapy, while the other respondents favored a specially trained financial counselor.

## TECHNIQUE

Through his experience and knowledge the financial counselor becomes the intervening medium in the patient's arena of money problems, enabling the patient to better define and achieve money goals. A patient may be assisted in wiping out debt worries by lowering his level of debt through careful planning and greater control over compulsive and impulsive spending. A patient may reduce money worries by learning to shop more carefully, by seeing how he can provide for more of his needs through his own efforts, and by finding ways of increasing his net income.

Mindful of the patient's need for self-respect and freedom, the money therapist assists the patient in recognizing and weighing alternatives. He helps the patient secure the facts, evaluate these, and make choices that give satisfaction and not regrets. Dialogue is cultivated to motivate the patient to acquire more effective money practices. A contract, signed by both therapist and patient, may contribute to the cooperation needed to achieve the goals of the Money Therapy. Case records are important to give direction and present an organized picture of relevant information.

Intervention in a money crisis is short-term therapy. It is exemplified by the alcoholic patient who was too preoccupied with financial problems to cooperate in a resident program of rehabilitation. His repossessed truck contained all his construction tools and equipment to which the creditor had no claim. His repeated phone calls to the creditor to obtain his rightful property were to no avail, but one call by the money therapist brought a prompt return of the tools and equipment.

Achieving better money management requires a longer period of therapy. Once goals and strategies are set, progress is assessed with guidance and encouragement by the therapist until the patient makes money his servant and not his master. While six to eighteen months of therapy are usually sufficient, it was five years before one emotionally disturbed patient was able to save for her annual vacation instead of allowing each vacation to create intolerable debt worries.

## APPLICATIONS

Adults with financial worries tend to respond better to psychotherapy if financial distress is reduced through Money Therapy. Also, the call for help may be initiated by a financial problem that calls for Money Therapy.

Money Therapy is not for those who lack the capacity to manage money, such as the severely retarded or schizophrenics. For alcoholics it is not applicable during the drying-out period, but can be integrated with both in-patient and out-patient rehabilitation. Money Therapy is most effective with those between the ages of sixteen and sixty. However, money crisis intervention is important for the elderly, especially in helping them obtain redress for deception and fraud.

Since money problems have been found to be a factor in over half of all marital disturbances, Money Therapy is also useful in marriage and family counseling. The money therapist who helps a family develop an operative family financial council can bring about improvement in communication between children and parents and thereby reduce family tensions. Money Therapy can contribute greatly to a reduction in mental illness, as a "substantial fraction of all stress factors that precipitate mental illness in American society is economic in origin." (Brenner, 1973)

# Morita Therapy

### Suk C. Chang

## DEFINITION

Morita Therapy is a psychotherapeutic method. It is also called experiential, bed rest, nondiscursive, or work therapy, which describes some aspects of the approach. In this treatment, psychological conflict is resolved through an autonomous interaction between affect (emotions and moods) and idea. This is done by minimizing external and artificial intervention. Implicit in this method is a premise that human psyche is fundamentally purposeful and rational and, therefore, therapeutic (or self-healing), *if* it is allowed to unfold freely.

## HISTORY

Morita Therapy was developed by Morita Shoma in the 1920s and has been practiced in Japan. Since the 1960s, it has drawn increasing and widening attention, and there is a growing amount of literature on the subject.

# TECHNIQUE

Clinically, Morita Therapy is applicable to a wide range of neuroses, where there is a significant subjective anxiety, some psychosomatic conditions, and borderline cases. Its principle can be applied under various circumstances, but its method and mechanism can be better illustrated in an in-patient setting.

The in-patient treatment is generally divided into four stages—absolute bed rest, partial bed rest, partial work, full work. Each stage takes up to a few weeks, except for the first stage, which lasts for one week. It is the absolute bed-rest stage, described briefly below, that is the most characteristic and crucial but least understood.

The patient, severely anxious and dysfunctional, is placed in bed, alone in a room. He is asked to refrain from all unessential diversionary activities (mental and physical) including radio, TV, telephone, visitors, reading, smoking. Therapistpatient contact is regular and supportive, but it is brief, nondiscursive, and nondirect-ive. The patient is told that a solution to his problem ultimately rests with him.

Alone in bed, and deprived of all the usual ways of self-distraction and diversion, and with external disruption minimized, this already sensitive or sensitized person has no other option but to engage in intrapsychic activities. For the first time since the onset of his neurosis he is left alone with the problem that brought him to this predicament: his attention inevitably turns to his neurosis.

Neurosis is an idiosyncratically woven complex of affect(s) and idea(s). Therefore, as the patient's attention turns, say, to a neurotic idea, negative affect, especially anxiety, is aroused. Since anxiety is unpleasant, he automatically calls forth a counter-idea in order to neutralize it. However, this intellectual (or logical) attempt fails, since neurosis is not a logical matter. This failure intensifies his anxiety, compelling him to a renewed effort, but he fails again, and so forth. In short, a vicious circle of neurotic affect and idea is formed, spiraling toward a crescendo and reaching the limit of tolerance. At the height of this conflict, as he is wholly consumed in the struggle, he has staked his life against the problem. In other words, he has brought his neurosis to a direct conjunction with the most elementary and irrefutable fact—his life. This is a reversal of neurotic process and tendency (of avoidance, displacement, escape, rationalization, substitution, and symbolization) to confrontation and struggle. Whereas neurotic conflict is futile, the struggle during the bed-rest period is effective, because the direction of the process is reversed, autonomous, and authentic.

Neurosis is a result of a person's past—unfortunate but inalterable. However, its current psychic representation can be altered, provided that the client is willing to struggle. To suggest that neurosis is easily, mechanically, and painlessly curable is, to say the least, an illusion, since "change," especially for the better, requires overcoming personality structure and trends that are embedded and locked in with one's familial, social, and political environment.

What Morita Therapy provides is the environment and conditions in which this struggle and self-transformation may be made effectively. And an essential condition for this process (an induction, progression, and resolution of neurotic conflict) to occur is a psychological freedom in which one's psychological contents—affect and idea—may interact and unfold authentically and autonomously, or unadulterated and uninterrupted. It is this freedom that is conspicuously lacking today. Consider, for example, that each language characterizes different societies and times, idiosyncratically molding individual perception and categorizing the world—thereby conditioning and structuring one's mind. It is the freedom from this conditioning that Morita Therapy provides by resolving the conflicts or by cleansing psychosocial artifacts from one's consciousness, thus reaching the common ground, lucid consciousness, and clarity of perception.

## APPLICATIONS

Morita Therapy has recently been applied, aside from the indications described earlier, to depressive neurosis. As its mechanism becomes clearer, its indication will be better delineated.

The significance of Morita Therapy, however, rests less in its technicalities and clinical application, which can be modified as time goes on, and more in its still unfolding theoretical implications. For example, the nature of and interrelationships between "affect" and "idea." In this regard, it has been suggested that a premise underlying Morita Therapy indicates that human psyche is fundamentally rational and purposeful. In this context, it has been indicated that the psychology of Morita Therapy is identical to that of meditation.

# Multimodal Therapy
## Arnold A. Lazarus

### DEFINITION

Multimodal Therapy is a technically eclectic approach to psychotherapy. While drawing heavily on communications theory, cognitive theory, and social learning theory, multimodal therapists are willing to apply effective methods and techniques from any discipline. In Multimodal Therapy, the most significant process is a careful and systematic inquiry into seven dimensions or modalities of "personality." Every case is thoroughly assessed for problem areas in behavior, affect (moods and emotions), sensation, imagery, cognition, interpersonal relationships, and also in the biochemical/neurophysiological realm. If the medical or physical modality is subsumed under the term "drugs," a very convenient acronym can be constructed. Taking the first letters from behavior, affect, sensation, imagery and cognition, we have BASIC. The interpersonal and drug modalities give us ID. *Thus, Multimodal Therapy is the assessment and treatment of the BASIC ID.* (It needs to be stressed that the *D* modality encompasses much more than "drugs" and also includes diet, exercise, nutrition, and many other medical/physical considerations.)

A basic premise is that the seven modalities are interactive (a change in one modality will affect all the others to a greater or lesser extent) and yet each modality is also sufficiently discrete to require specific assessment and therapy. In essence, thorough therapy needs to cover the entire BASIC ID. To ignore, bypass, or overlook one or more of these modalities is to practice incomplete therapy. This leaves patients prone to relapses and/or the development of new problems.

## HISTORY

My initial training in psychotherapy was along traditional lines. I was exposed to psychodynamic thinking and most of my clinical supervisors adhered to the principles of Freud, Harry Stack Sullivan, or Carl Rogers. I received some training from Adlerians during my internship and found this orientation, with its emphasis on human dignity and didactic interventions, more appealing and more helpful than the others. But behavior therapy (Wolpe and Lazarus, 1966) offered the widest repertoire of systematic techniques. I found methods like assertiveness training and desensitization far more effective in facilitating observable change than the interpretive methods I was first taught to employ. In retrospect, it is now obvious to me that I made the error of needlessly subscribing to the idea that human neuroses are a result of conditioning, instead of realizing that behavior therapy transcends the constraints of "behaviorism" and is effective for reasons that animal analogues cannot begin to explain (Lazarus, 1977).

While conducting follow-up studies of clients who had received behavior therapy, I found that about 36 percent had relapsed anywhere from one week to six years after therapy (Lazarus, 1971). Subsequent follow-ups were conducted more thoroughly and revealed an even higher relapse rate, especially in cases who were disturbed and maladjusted rather than merely suffering from minor adjustment problems and situational difficulties.

When looking into the reasons behind the disappointingly high number of relapses, it became evident that people were *not* falling victim to unconscious forces welling up from unresolved complexes. Most of the people who relapsed had simply not acquired sufficiently effective coping responses to deal with inimical life situations. The usual behavior therapy approach does not deal in sufficient detail with many aspects of affect, sensation, imagery, cognition, and interpersonal factors (Lazarus, 1976). Most practitioners of behavior therapy do not devote sufficient time to "existential problems," or to issues of self-esteem. They gloss over various values, attitudes, beliefs, and neglect several significant nuances of interpersonal functioning. The conventional behavior therapist is also inclined to disregard important areas of defective learning, despite his avowed allegiance to principles of learning. For example, behavioral approaches do not pay attention to the fact that many clients suffer from a lack of information about their own emotions and motivations. Furthermore, many people are inclined to block thoughts and feelings from their own awareness—another fact that most behavior therapists seem to disavow.

The first series of Multimodal Therapy follow-ups comprised twenty clients after a two-year post-treatment period. Stability and durability of outcomes were clearly established. Only two cases required booster treatments before this period. Their relapses were due to the fact that they had been inadequately prepared to deal with "future shock" (i.e., various inevitable changes in life's circumstances). This problem is probably best handled through imagery (Lazarus, 1978). A second series of follow-ups is presently under way. Initial impressions of the data seem to confirm the fact that Multimodal Therapy produces enduring, positive results.

# TECHNIQUE

After establishing rapport, conducting a thorough assessment (which, at the very least, includes a Life-History Questionnaire and a functional analysis of all presenting complaints), and administering any tests deemed necessary, a Modality Profile is constructed. Here is the Modality Profile of a forty-year-old woman whose presenting complaints were: "I drink too much and I worry too much."

| MODALITY | PROBLEM | PROPOSED TREATMENT |
|---|---|---|
| **Behavior** | Excessive drinking | Self-monitoring + Aversive imagery |
| | Carries out various compulsions | Response prevention |
| **Affect** | General anxiety | Relaxation training Positive imagery |
| | Bouts of depression | Positive reinforcement |
| | Holds back anger | Assertiveness training |
| **Sensation** | Tension headaches | Relaxation training |
| | Low back pain | Orthopedic exercises |
| **Imagery** | Scenes involving her mother's criticisms | Role playing + empty chair method |
| | Nightmares about failure (mostly work related) | Images of mastery |
| **Cognition** | Morbid thoughts | Thought stopping |
| | Categorical imperatives (shoulds, oughts, musts, etc.) | Rational-Emotive Therapy |
| **Interpersonal** | Withdraws from many social situations | Social skills training (preferably in group) |
| | Quarrels with husband | Couples therapy |
| **Drugs** | Overweight | Self-monitoring/ self-control |
| | Possible biological depression | If necessary, have M.D. prescribe antidepressant medication |

Comprehensive therapy at the very least calls for the correction of deviant behaviors, unpleasant feelings, negative sensations, intrusive images, irrational beliefs, stressful relationships, and physiological difficulties. Durable results appear to be in direct proportion to the number of specific modalities invoked by any therapeutic system. Lasting change is a function of systematic techniques and specific strategies applied to each modality. Patients are usually troubled by a multitude of *specific* problems that tend to require a similar multitude of *specific* treatments. Multimodal Therapy encompasses: 1) specification of goals and problems, 2) specification of treatment techniques to achieve these goals and remedy these problems, and 3) systematic measurement of the relative success of these techniques.

## APPLICATIONS

Multimodal Therapy has been applied to individuals, couples, families, and groups. Target problems include depression, anxiety, psychosomatic difficulties, obesity, sexual inadequacy, and mental retardation (Lazarus, 1976). Other practitioners who use the multimodal approach are encouraged by the results. For instance, I launched a Multimodal Therapy Institute where four of my associates have treated a variety of people with different problems in several settings. Furthermore, in collaboration with Dr. J.J. Shannon of Seton Hall University, a controlled research project is being planned. And finally, Dr. Lillian Brunell has been using Multimodal Therapy on hospitalized patients at Essex County Hospital Center with most promising results.

In essence, Multimodal Therapy provides a useful framework for detailed assessment, one that is open to validation, and one that permits a problem-centered treatment plan to emerge within the context of patients' needs rather than within the constraints of therapists' theoretical predilections.

---

# Multiple Therapy

## Jerry A. Treppa

## DEFINITION

Multiple Therapy refers to the multiplicity of relationships possible when two therapists, preferably a man and woman, are affectively (emotionally) and interde-pendently involved together in individual, conjoint, family, or group therapy. The essence of Multiple Therapy lies in the emotional relationship and affective exchange that exists between the two therapists that they bring to bear in their therapeutic interventions with the client(s). The nature of this relationship is the crucial dynamic in Multiple Therapy. The more the therapists' relationship is characterized by feelings of basic trust, emotional harmony, and a commitment to enhance and facilitate each other's growth, the more they will be able to utilize their relationship in a therapeutic way. When this emotionally reciprocal relationship exists, this form of therapy serves as a powerful catalyst for facilitating interpersonal change and growth. The degree to which these characteristics are absent in the relationship reduces the power and intensity of this therapeutic approach.

The major difference between Multiple Therapy and other approaches that employ two therapists is in the nature of the interaction between the therapists, which influences the therapeutic conditions offered. It cannot be emphasized enough that Multiple Therapy is more than having two therapists with a client in a room together. To assume that any therapeutic situation that employs two therapists is synonymous with Multiple Therapy is not only erroneous but also blurs its distinction from these other methods (i.e., co-therapy, role-divided therapy, three-cornered therapy, joint-interview, co-operative therapy, and dual leadership) (Treppa, 1971).

# HISTORY

The earliest utilization of two counselors in a therapeutic setting dates back to the 1920s, when Adler and his associates employed this method as a means of overcoming emotional blocking and resistance in children. Their utilization of two therapists was limited to the therapists' discussing the child's problem in his presence and did not involve an interaction between the therapists and client as it is currently practiced in Multiple Therapy.

By the mid-1950s, a number of articles appeared that discussed the applications, merits, and disadvantages of using two therapists. This technique was discussed in terms of its value in: teaching, training, and supervising new therapists; promoting the professional growth of experienced therapists; overcoming therapeutic impasses; enhancing specific therapeutic outcomes; and facilitating the process of full-term psychotherapy. Of these writings the contributions of Dreikurs, Whitaker, and their colleagues were the most significant in furthering the use of this technique.

Although Dreikurs, an Adlerian, is responsible for the term "multiple therapy," his approach of employing two therapists used a structured consultive model, which the present author believes is the precursor of Co-Therapy. While Whitaker and his associates borrowed the term multiple therapy from Dreikurs, their approach is different from his and parallels the definition used here in describing Multiple Therapy. The contribution of Whitaker and his associates to the development of Multiple Therapy was their emphasis on the relationship between the two therapists and the emotional interchange possible in this modality.

Mullan and Sanguiliano have elaborated on the phenomenological and interpersonal processes involved in Multiple Therapy. The most significant aspect of their work lies in their attention to the phenomenological processes involved in establishing and maintaining an effective Multiple Therapy team. Recently, a number of significant dimensions in Multiple Therapy that have not been discussed extensively before were brought to the attention of the professional community as a result of the work of Kell and Burow. Their contribution is particularly important in that they discuss not only the phenomenological processes of Multiple Therapy in detail but also the multiplicity of interpersonal relationships that can be used in a dynamic manner in Multiple Therapy to facilitate therapeutic change. In their approach, one sees the power of Multiple Therapy when it is skillfully applied.

# TECHNIQUE

Six dynamically distinct relationships are possible when two therapists interact with one client in Multiple Therapy; more relationships are possible when more than one client is seen. Multiple Therapy involves the skillful use of these relationships. With one client, these relationships are: (1 & 2) that between the client and each therapist separately, (3) that between the two therapists, (4) the client's interaction with the relationship between the therapists, and (5 & 6) each therapist's interaction with the relationship between the client and the other therapist (Kell and Burow, 1970). The existence of these relationships facilitates the generation of conflicts that can be clearly felt and observed in the therapy session and also provides the forum for resolution. For example, one therapist, by interacting with the client, often facilitates the expression of a conflict with the parent of the same sex. The other therapist, observing this interaction, strives to understand the dynamic sources of the conflict, works with the client toward resolving it, and endeavors to facilitate the relationship between the client and his/her co-therapist.

Multiple Therapy is helpful in teaching an individual about the meanings of healthy interpersonal relationships: child-parent(s), friend-friend, and man-woman.

This is true because the interrelationship between the therapists models a relationship in which dependency, autonomy, appreciation, and collaboration are manifested.

In Multiple Therapy it is common for the therapists to experience the therapeutic process differently from each other. For example, one therapist may be attuned to the feelings connected with the client's experience while the other therapist may attend to interpersonal aspects of that situation. Or one therapist may be talking to the client about some innocent prank the client engaged in and the other therapist has a fantasy in which he/she sees the client in serious physical danger. These differing responses between the therapists can be used to: facilitate the client's self-differentiation; teach the client about the impact of his/her feelings, thoughts, and behavior; clarify the client's ambivalence; anticipate acting-out behavior; enhance the client's sex-role identity; support and confront the client simultaneously; enhance regression so that a positive outcome occurs, etc.

Multiple Therapy is a complex method of psychotherapy requiring the therapists to: 1) work on their relationship continuously, 2) emotionally and intellectually understand the complexities of this approach, and 3) capitalize on the multiplicity of relationships that are available to them to augment constructive changes.

## APPLICATIONS

The benefits of Multiple Therapy have been observed in a variety of situations (Treppa, 1971). Its application is particularly helpful in overcoming therapeutic impasses that occur with one therapist. Further, its value in fostering the professional and emotional development of the therapists is considerable in that the effectiveness of this approach is directly related to the psychological maturity of the therapists and their interaction.

In terms of its application to full-term psychotherapy, every client could profit from Multiple Therapy. The method is seen as effective in promoting intrapersonal and interpersonal differentiation and facilitating an integration of the phenomenolog-ical, interpersonal, and rational aspects of an individual's functioning so that a constructive and growth-producing balance is achieved.

Multiple Therapy is a particularly effective therapeutic approach in treating severely disturbed clients (psychotics, psychopaths, and suicidal individuals), families, groups, and individuals with specific interpersonal difficulties (the distrustful client, the client with identity problems, the deprived client, and the emotionally unstable client) (Treppa, 1971; Treppa and Nunnelly, 1974).

# Music Therapy
## George L. Duerksen

### DEFINITION

The music therapist uses music and musical activities to help accomplish specific therapeutic aims in diagnosis, restoration, maintenance, and improvement of mental and physical health. The music therapist, using music systematically, attempts to bring about desirable changes in behavior. The process attempts to help the individual undergoing therapy develop better understanding of self and environment and become increasingly competent in adjusting both for best health.

### HISTORY

Although references to music in medical practice appear in literature from the earliest times of Western civilization, psychiatric Music Therapy received great impetus during World War II. Over two hundred U.S. psychiatric hospitals maintained active music programs in 1944 (National Music Council, 1944). University curricula designed specifically to prepare professional music therapists were initiated in the mid-1950s, and university research accelerated development of the profession's data base. A group of practicing music therapists and college teachers organized the National Association for Music Therapy (NAMT) in 1950. In 1954 the NAMT recommended a curriculum for preparation of music therapists, and soon began a registry of individuals who had completed this curriculum. In 1977 the NAMT listed fifty U.S. academic institutions accredited to prepare music therapists, and 109 clinical institutions accredited for Music Therapy internships. Professional organizations of music therapists also exist in England, on the European continent, in South America, and in Australia.

### TECHNIQUE

Music Therapy techniques apply individual and cultural functions of music in a variety of contexts. These techniques require knowledge of the influence of music on behavior. Music's influences stem from 1) the individual's genetic and experiential makeup, and personality structure; 2) the cultural and social environment; and 3) the physical and acoustical environment.

Music, as well as the other arts, fills basic physiological and psychological needs for pattern, form, sensory stimulation, and sensory elaboration. Music is an artistic way of controlling and adjusting the auditory environment; a way of making that environment more suitable.

Evidence from anthropology and sociology indicates few cultures that do not have music. Almost all cultures attribute great power to music. Although a few believe music to be evil, and attempt to repress it, most use music for important constructive functions. Music almost always is used when man attempts to transcend everyday reality—when he participates in his most sacred and most important activities. It almost always is used to identify and unify groups. In most cultures, music is used for physical stimulation and sedation.

There are few individuals for whom some sort of music does not have a strong attraction. Thus, it can provide a focus for therapeutic activity and motivate and reinforce extended participation in therapeutic relationships. Music also provides a vehicle for nonverbal communication. Musical stimuli evoke and induce feelings that cannot be obtained through other means. Musical activity provides a healthy and socially acceptable way of expressing feelings. Music promotes psychological closeness, and allows that closeness to develop without the need for words, or the feeling of threat. In most cultures, individuals will express with music the words they are hesitant to say in nonmusical contexts. Musical stimuli provide a vehicle onto which feelings may be projected, and then examined in retrospect.

Music tends to dissipate feelings of aloneness. During active music making or listening, music distracts—from pain and from attention to unpleasant parts of the environment. Musical stimuli tend to free imagination and feeling. Music reduces aloneness by helping the individual become more unified in feeling with the group. It reduces hostility among individuals and permits (in some cases even encourages) physical contact.

Musical stimuli, and the activity required to produce them, provide structured reality. Auditory stimuli are real, and provide grounds for discussion and agreement or disagreement. Participation in musical activity objectifies behavior, and the participant's contact with musical reality becomes directly observable.

Part of the unique motivational and reinforcing value of music stems from its gratifying quality. For most individuals there are some musical stimuli that simply "sound good." In many cases, these individuals prove willing to devote much time, effort, money, and behavioral change to the pursuit of this music. Musical performance also provides gratification; successful performance allows development of self-esteem and the esteem of others.

Music provides a Gestalt (a perceptual whole) of individual and group activity. It elicits individual responses according to various psychological and physical needs; it integrates psychological, affective (emotional), cognitive, and psychomotor activity in a complex behavior characteristic of the well-functioning human being. Group musical activity coordinates these individual patterns into a goal-oriented activity that may combine cooperation and competition, precisely organize group physical behavior, and stimulate affective and psychological unity among group members.

Musical control of behavior pervades ordinary life.. Activities signaled by musical stimuli become folkways; thus, music is nearly always directly influenced by custom. Examples of this include the physical command to "stand up" that the "National Anthem" communicates, the affective meanings conveyed by the song "Happy Birthday to You," and the sophisticated patterns of conversation and eating that are encouraged by the complex stimulus of proper background music, lighting, table setting, individual attire, and other artistic aspects of the formal dinner. In addition to these musical persuasions based on custom, certain structural characteristics of musical stimuli tend to elicit physical stimulation while other characteristics elicit physical sedation.

Music's adaptability allows it to serve individuals or groups of various sizes. Musical activity is adaptable to a variety of locations, materials, and environments. The physical and psychological needs of several individuals may be met by a single musical activity, and that activity can be adapted to individual differences among the participants. Music may be used as foreground, a stimulus on which to focus attention; it may also serve as background, where it can influence without attracting attention.

## APPLICATIONS

Psychiatric Music Therapy takes place in mental hospitals, geriatrics institutions, community mental health centers, and private practice. There is also a mental health aspect to Music Therapy practice in orthopedic hospitals, general hospitals, and in special education.

Most Music Therapy applications involve processes from one or more of the following categories: experience within structure (behavior inherent in, or required by, the musical experience itself); experience in self-organization; and experience in relating to others (Sears, 1968). Therefore, applications are approached through individual or group participation in musical activity, through use of music as a reinforcer or motivator, and through specifically programmed foreground or background music for nonmusical activities.

Applications of Music Therapy include using musical situations for cognitive development, including development of self-knowledge and academic learning; using musical situations for psychomotor development, including physical coordination, flexibility, dexterity, motor control, and reduction of speech disfluency; using musical situations for social development, including reduction of antisocial behavior, stimulation of socializing behavior, and development of group *esprit*; using musical situations for perceptual development, including auditory discrimination and concepts; and using musical situations for affective development, including self-esteem, the esteem of others, good feelings for others, and relevant attitude formation.

# Mutual Help Groups
## Phyllis R. Silverman

### DEFINITION

There is an increasing awareness of the growing number of special interest groups formed to provide mutual help to their members. All people participate in helping interactions and networks in which each individual can sometimes be recipient and/or sometimes helper. When a helping network is developed in order for people to share their common experience in coping with a problem, we have a mutual help exchange. These exchanges become "formal organizations" when the process of institutionalization creates a formal organizational structure. After the process of formalization occurs, an organization or program has typically been referred to as a "self-help group." Since the helping exchange almost invariably goes both ways, the term mutual help is more descriptive.

Levy, Killalae, and Silverman all provide similar definitions of a mutual help organization:

- Their membership is limited to people with a common concern or problem.

- Helpers have had experience in solving the problem, and utilize this experience in helping new members.
- Where the founding members have left a legacy of problem-solving methods, these were based on their own personal experience in successfully coping with the problem at hand.
- Help is offered in an informal manner and helpers are able to respond quickly to members' needs.
- Members may utilize knowledge and processes developed in other settings but make their own determination about how to integrate this information into their programs.
- Policy and resources rest with the constituents of the organization, who are both providers and recipients of service.
- The group enables and encourages members to move from the role of recipient to that of helper, a movement that is in itself part of the helping process.

The purpose of Mutual Help Groups is to enable members to behave differently, to adapt to life changes, or to overcome problems. Individuals join such groups during periods of transition in their lives and as they accomplish the goals of the group they either become helpers to new members, become involved in other aspects of the organization, or leave entirely to go on to other things.

## HISTORY

The quality and quantity of formal human services available has been an important influence on the formation and growth of Mutual Help Groups.

Over the last century the development of formal human service agencies was accompanied by a professionalization of the helpers involved. Helping became regularized and procedures were developed to make the help more consistent with the current scientific thinking about the cause of psychological problems. In many instances the founders of Mutual Help Groups have sought such professional help and found the assistance offered either inadequate, inappropriate, or unsuccessful. Mutual Help Groups, such as Alcoholics Anonymous, the Association for Retarded Citizens, and the National Association for Autistic Children, developed in response to professional failure. Groups such as these were founded by people who had been treated for many years in various formal clinical programs without successful outcome. Such groups often restrict the involvement of the professional human service community and tensions between the two care-giving systems occasionally develop (Silverman, 1977).

Mutual Help Groups also come into being because of technological advances. For example, people with cystic fibrosis now live into their early twenties and sometimes marry. Victims of extensive burns now survive who formerly would have died from their wounds. Consequently, afflicted persons may form Mutual Help Groups to develop appropriate procedures for dealing with their new situations.

Mutual Help Groups also develop in times of rapid social change, when established reactions and coping patterns are often found to be inadequate, and when new knowledge cannot be rapidly translated into common practice. Today the family cannot keep up with the changing needs of its members and is losing its function as the major interpreter of society and educator to future generations. Role vacuums can exist as people move through normal transitions in the life cycle. For example, the bereaved do not know how to mourn when a death occurs in the family. Mutual Help Groups such as the Society of Compassionate Friends (for bereaved parents) and Widow-to-Widow programs develop to not only augment the role of the family, but sometimes to function in lieu of the family or other transitional care givers. Mutual Help Groups such as the Associations for Childbirth Education and La Leche League began when couples became aware of data regarding the value of family-centered, nonmedicated childbirth, and the value of the nursing relationship between mother and child. As these Mutual Help Groups insist on implementing these new approaches to childbirth and child care, they are bringing about change in professional practice and in societal mores (Silverman, 1977).

Although tension often accompanies the interactions between the mutual help system and the formal human service system, they should be seen as complementary rather than competing modalities. Gottlieb, citing Saranson and Speck's discussion of network theory, calls for an exchange of resources between mutual help networks and the professional system.

## TECHNIQUE

Three aspects of a mutual help experience can be identified. The individual first recognizes that he has something in common with other members of the group; next he develops a sense of common cause with the group; and finally, he is concerned with the group's continued existence and may become a helper. The characteristics correspond to the nature of help needed in the stages of any transition. The stages of transition are impact, recoil, and accommodation. In impact the individual has to accept himself as someone in a new situation. The ability to acknowledge this is facilitated when he meets members of a Mutual Help Group with whom he can potentially identify. In recoil he needs someone to teach him how to cope with his new situation. Members of a Mutual Help Group develop a unity as they share their common experiences; they no longer feel deviant or alone. Their feelings are legitimized, their problem is typical, not unusual. They feel hopeful. They learn how someone else dealt with the problem. This learning becomes possible when there is someone who provides a role model, and who can provide specific information about ways to cope. Finally, the individual can change roles from beneficiary to provider of help. The interaction in a mutual help exchange is like that of siblings where the same experience has been shared, but not at the same time. The helper is potentially a friend, and the relationship can become reciprocal. To ask help from a professional can reinforce an individual's sense of weakness since he is always in the role of recipient in a client relationship. Mutual Help Groups meet in homes, churches, or other similar local facilities since they depend on members' donations to cover operating costs. Some national organizations provide detailed guidelines to local chapters, others are a loose federation with no central control of local activities. Help is provided through individual contacts, regular group meetings, "hotlines," and in some groups out-reach to potential members. Helpers are always volunteers chosen for their abilty to share their experience with others. The fact that the recipient can change roles and become a helper reinforces his sense of competence and adequacy as well as gives meaning to his previous experience.

# Mutual Need Therapy

## Jesse K. Lair

### DEFINITION

Mutual Need Therapy occurs when two or more people recognize their mutual need for each other and disclose their deeper and more private feelings about themselves to each other.

### HISTORY

Mutual Need Therapy is my attempt to describe and make explicit a therapeutic process that so commonly occurs in life. Two natural "experiments" are primarily responsible for directing my attention to this area. The first involves the method commonly used to test outcomes of psychiatry· or counseling. People presenting themselves for treatment are randomly assigned to one of two groups: the members of one group receive treatment, the other (control) group members do not. Often there is little evidence that treatment has had much effect. A major contaminant might be the Mutual Need Therapy that occurs. When patients present themselves for treatment, their defenses have usually begun to break down. Both the treated and untreated groups probably talk to some "significant others" (people who are important in their lives). So there are possibly from one to ten people involved in the treatment of the subjects. The effect of the presence or absence of psychiatrist or counselor in the treatment, then, might easily be blurred.

The other natural experiment studied by the author and the major contributor to the development of the theory is the self-help movement of Alcoholics Anonymous. Though not an alcoholic, I was able to participate in AA over a ten-year period. The best description of what occurred in AA to free the alcoholic from his addiction was Mutual Need Therapy.

### TECHNIQUE

In Mutual Need Therapy there is very little technique. For the two participants there are only a few basic guidelines that are helpful.

I. *Mutuality:* The first prerequisite is that there be a mutuality between the two people: they need to like each other just as they are; they cannot have any program to improve each other.

2. *Mutual need.* Each person in the relationship must see his need for the other person rather than feel the other person needs him. So it is.a relationship of equals. each admitting his need for the other.

3. *Openness to a higher power.* The people involved need to be accepting of each other's views of a higher power, God, or a supreme being. As with any feeling, the feelings about some higher power are not to be argued with or disputed. 4. Each person is an expert only in his own feelings. No judging, criticizing, or analyzing is to be done.

5. *The participants, except for the above few guidelines, are free to say and do what seems appropriate.* The other participant or participants are free to listen to the feelings and support the person. In this format, there is only one way for someone to give counsel to another when asked: to tell how ·he faced a similar problem, what he did and how it worked for him. But the overwhelming emphasis is on listening to and accepting the other person, as well as enjoying his presence.

## APPLICATIONS

I use Mutual Need Therapy in working with people presenting themselves for counseling when there is an adequate amount of mutuality in the relationship. I also advocate that all people seeking better relationships establish some mutual need relationships in order to benefit from the therapeutic effects that come from a deep acceptance of a person just as he is.

# Mutual Storytelling Technique

## Richard A. Gardner

## DEFINITION

The Mutual Storytelling Technique is a method of therapeutic communication with children. In it, the therapist elicits a self-created story from the child, surmises its psychodynamic meaning, and then creates a story of his own using the same characters in a similar setting. The therapist's story differs from that of the child in that he introduces healthier resolutions and maturer adaptations.

## HISTORY

Eliciting stories is a time-honored practice in child psychotherapy. From the stories children tell, the therapist is able to gain invaluable insights into the child's inner conflicts, frustrations, and defenses. The techniques described in the literature on child psychotherapy and psychoanalysis are, for the most part, attempts to use such stories therapeutically. Some are based on the assumption, borrowed from the adult psychoanalytic model, that making the unconscious conscious can itself be therapeutic. My own experience has revealed that few children are interested in gaining conscious awareness of their unconscious processes, let alone utilizing such insights therapeutically. Children do, however, enjoy both telling stories and listening to them. Since storytelling is one of the child's favorite modes of communication, I wondered whether communicating to him in the same mode might not be useful in child therapy. The efficacy of the storytelling approach for the imparting and transmission of values and insights is proved by the ancient and universal appeal of fable, myth, and legend.

# TECHNIQUE

It was from these observations and considerations that I developed the Mutual Storytelling Technique—as one solution to the problem of how to utilize the child's stories therapeutically. In this method the child first tells a story; the therapist surmises its psychodynamic meaning and then tells one of his own. The therapist's story contains the same characters in a similar setting, but he introduces healthier adaptations and resolutions of the conflicts that have been exhibited in the child's story. Since he speaks in the child's own language, the therapist has a good chance of "being heard." One could almost say that here the therapist's interpretations bypass the conscious and are received directly by the unconscious. The child is not burdened with psychoanalytic interpretations that are often alien to him. Direct, anxiety-provoking confrontations, so reminiscent of the child's experience with parents and teachers, are avoided. Finally, the introduction of humor and drama enhances the child's interest and pleasure and, therefore, his receptivity.

Drawings, dolls, puppets, and other toys are the modalities around which stories are traditionally told in child therapy, but these often restrict the child's storytelling or channel it in highly specific directions. The tape recorder (audio or visual) does not have these disadvantages; with it, the visual field remains free from contaminating and distracting stimuli.

I introduce the game by asking the child if he would like to be guest of honor on a make-believe television program on which stories are told. If he agrees—and few decline the honor—the recorder is turned on and I begin:

Good morning, boys and girls. I'd like to welcome you once again to Dr. Gardner's "Make-Up-a-Story Television Program." On this program we invite children to see how good they are at making up stories. Naturally, the more adventure or excitement a story has, the most interesting it is to the people who are watching on their television sets. Now, it's against the rules to tell stories about things you've read or have seen in the movies or on television, or about things that really happened to you or anyone you know.

Like all stories, your story should have a beginning, a middle, and an end. After you've made up a story, you'll tell us the moral or lesson of the story. We all know that every good story has a moral.

Then after you've told your story, Dr. Gardner will make up a story, too. He'll try to tell one that's interesting and unusual, and then he'll tell the moral of his story.

And now, without further delay, let me introduce to you a boy [girl] who is with us today for the first time. Can you tell us your name, young man?

I then ask the child a series of brief questions that can be answered by single words or brief phrases, such as his age, address, school grade, and teacher. These "easy" questions diminish the child's anxiety and tend to make him less tense about the more unstructured themes involved in "making up a story." The child is then told:

Now that we've heard a few things about you, we're all interested in hearing the story you have for us today.

At this point most children plunge right into their story, although some may feel the need for "time to think." I may offer this pause; if it is asked for by the child, it is readily granted. There are some children for whom this pause is not enough, but nevertheless still want to try. In such instances the child is told:

Some children, especially when it's their first time on this program, have a little trouble thinking of a story, but with some help from me they're able to do so. Most children don't realize that there are millions of stories in their heads they don't know about. And I know a way to help get some of them out. Would you like me to help you get out one of them?

Most children assent to this. I then continue:

Fine, here's how it works. I'll start the story and, when I point my finger at you, you say exactly what comes into your mind at that time. You'll then see how easy it is to make up a story. Okay. Let's start. Once upon a time—a long, long time ago—in a distant land—far, far away—there lived a—

I then point my finger, and it is a rare child who does not offer some fill-in word at this point. If the word is "dog," for example, I then say, "And *that dog*—" and once again point to the patient. I follow the statement provided by the child with "And then—" or "The next thing that happened was—." Every statement the child makes is followed by some introductory connective and an indication to the child to supply the next statement—that and no more. The introduction of specific phrases of words would defeat the therapist's purpose of catalyzing the youngster's production of his own created material and of sustaining, as needed, its continuity.

This approach is sufficient to get most children over whatever hurdles there are for them in telling a story. If this is not enough, however, it is best to drop the activity in a completely casual and nonreproachful manner, such as: "Well, today doesn't seem to be your good day for storytelling. Perhaps we'll try again some other time."

While the child is engaged in telling his story, I jot down notes, which not only help in analyzing the child's story but also serve as a basis for my own. At the end of the child's story and his statement of its moral, I may ask questions about specific items in the story. The purpose here is to obtain additional details, which are often of help in understanding the story. Typical questions might be: Was the fish in your story a man or a lady? Why was the fox so mad at the goat? or Why did the bear do that?

## APPLICATIONS

The technique is useful in the treatment of a wide variety of psychogenic disorders of childhood. It is generally useful for children between the ages of four and twelve. It is contraindicated in the therapy of children who resort significantly to fantasy, especially those who are psychotic. Such children need reality-oriented therapeutic approaches rather than those that encourage fantasy formation. Some of the specific psychiatric disorders for which the method has been shown to be useful are listed in the bibliography.

# Mythosynthesis

## Ann O'Neil Enscoe and Gerald Enscoe

### DEFINITION

Mythosynthesis is a mode of growth and development therapy using personal and social myth as a means of discovering important and hidden aspects of the personality. It is based on the observation that human beings in the maturation process create frames of reference, belief structures, which become for them patterns of reality. These belief structures make sense out of their world and become almost like an envelope of assumptions through which reality is filtered and limited. This frame of reference is both personal and cultural, created by the person out of both unique experiences of the individual and the accumulated experience of the culture. We call this frame of reference a *myth*, and the mythic envelope through which here and now experience is filtered is the *mythosphere.*

We use the term "myth" not in the sense of anything false or misleading, but as a creative ordering of the world. All human beings exist within their own mythosphere, and in that sense we create the world we live in. It is not a question of having or not having a mythosphere; it is only a question of how well our mythospheres function in helping us get our needs met and enhancing our lives and potentials.

Because each individual creates his or her own mythosphere, the individual can reorder or re-create it once it has come to awareness. Since the original mythosphere is created at a very young age, say, before the age of six, and because many old patterns are now obsolete, the mythosphere is frequently based on inadequate or distorted external information. It may have been the best the child could do with the data he or she had then, but it becomes a limiting and inadequate system for dealing with the here and now.

Mythosynthesis works with bringing the mythosphere to awareness using fantasy, imagery and metaphor to make the world picture concrete; and in a nurturing small group setting invites the person to look at his/her myths, value her/his creativity, and to own and enlarge the mythosphere, bringing it up to date as he/she chooses. Any decisions can be affirmed in the group.

### HISTORY

We developed Mythosynthesis after teaching poetry for some years and doing psychotherapy in which our primary model is Eric Berne's Transactional Analysis. We accept Berne's tripartite structure of the personality, and find the concepts of the Parent, Adult, and Child very useful in our work. We focus a great deal on the Child ego state with its own three-part structure: the Free Child, the Little Professor or Creative Child, and the Adapted Child. And we find the language of poetry, which is concrete, imagistic and metaphorical, to be the language of the Child.

Mythosynthesis has some grounding in Carl Jung's concepts of the integrated personality and the archetype. It is also indebted to Fritz Perls' Gestalt Therapy and to the work of A. Maslow and R. Assagioli. Also important is the redecision work of Robert and Mary Goulding. The term *Mythosynthesis* and the concept of the mythosphere are our own and will be more fully developed in a book length manuscript we are now preparing for publication.

## TECHNIQUE

Mythosynthesis works best in a small group setting, either in an on-going therapy group or in special weekend or weeklong intensive work. The mythosphere is created early in a person's life and the energy holding it together is Child energy. For that reason* significant redecisions about the content of the mythosphere are made in the Child ego state by the Creative Child, i.e. Little Professor. Therefore, the technique of Mythosynthesis requires cathecting the Child ego state and encouraging Child creativity. It is a form of controlled regression centered around words, images, developing metaphors and defining one's space through stories, drawings and poetry.

Since we work with cathecting the Child ego state it is important that the therapists provide a nurturing and protective environment and have their Adult available. The members of the group provide a variety of personal myths and models of reality, which helps in expanding, and modifying individual mythospheres. It is important that the group and the therapists do not pressure the individuals to change; rather the atmosphere and the techniques must invite and allow for change and affirm the individuals' O.K.ness and ability to make their own decisions. Conflicts within the group are seen as differences in individual mythospheres, each member being reminded that her/his mythosphere is self-created and therefore he/she is responsible for its contents. We also stress that the myths are valuable and creative, not to be denied but possibly to be changed and enhanced. The oyster doesn't get rid of the sand; rather it builds a pearl from it.

By bringing the mythosphere to awareness, the client can claim it and her or his own creative powers. The desired result of the Mythosynthesis techniques comes about when the client accepts the mythosphere as his/her own creation, makes a decision to change it, modify it, or keep it, and accepts the responsibility for living in the world of his own making. A synthesis is achieved between what she/he wants and what he/she believes is possible.

## APPLICATIONS

Mythosynthesis is a mode of therapy which helps people to realize more of their own potential and to achieve greater awareness and self-acceptance. It has proven effective in helping people change destructive and self-defeating neurotic patterns of behavior. It is growth oriented and is firmly based on Maslow's assertion that all neurosis is a failure of personal growth. It has not been tested with severely disturbed or psychotic clients; but if one assumes that some psychoses are manifestations of severely distorted mythospheres, there is no reason to believe that it could not be a helpful adjunct in treatment. The techniques are very useful in raising the level of self-esteem and self-acceptance as well as encouraging personal responsibility for the conduct of one's life.

# Narcoanalysis

## Burke M. Smith

### DEFINITION

Narcoanalysis is a procedure in which a patient is given a drug to facilitate communication with the therapist. A closely related procedure is called narcosynthesis. Currently the most frequently used drugs are Sodium Amytal (Amobarbital Sodium) and Pentothal (Pentothal Sodium), although other barbiturates and even other classes of drugs, alone or in combination, have been used. The general purpose of Narcoanalysis is the evocation of suppressed or repressed memories, feelings, and impulses, and the reintegration of these into consciousness.

### HISTORY

Horsley (1943) introduced the term "narcoanalysis" and described his procedure, but the antecedents of the method go back to the earliest use of alcohol, herbs, mushrooms, and other natural substances to loosen tongues and release inhibitions. Various anecdotal accounts of the disinhibiting effects of numerous anesthetic, narcotic, and stimulant drugs are to be found in the literature.

Horsley had observed, in 1931, that some uncommunicative patients became cooperative and conversational under the influence of Nembutal, but that by the following day they had forgotten what they said. He followed this observation with experimental attempts to develop narcosis as an alternative, or a supplement, to hypnosis. He found that small doses (of Nembutal) injected slowly would produce an altered state of consciousness. If the therapist maintained verbal contact with the patient throughout the procedure, the uncovered content could, in many instances, be integrated into the conscious level. He first conceptualized the phenomenon as narcotic hypnosis but later described four distinguishable phases of the total process: 1) light narcosis (drug induced), 2) hypnosis (verbally induced), 3) analysis (recall), and 4) synthesis (reintegration). Horsley used his technique with a wide variety of in-patients and out-patients, including the so-called shell-shock cases from World War I. He observed many individual differences among the response patterns and found that the procedure had to be sensitively monitored and modified with each patient.

The next significant publications dealing with Narcoanalysis and narcosynthesis were by Grinker and Spiegel (1943, 1945). These military psychiatrists reported on the use of this procedure with selected battle casualties in the Tunisian Campaign of World War II. The patients found to be most responsive to this technique were those who were in an acute anxiety state following a psychologically traumatic experience that had been repressed. Grinker and Spiegel found that under the influence of a slowly administered intravenous injection of a barbiturate (they preferred Pentothal over Amytal because of its faster action and faster metabolism) the patient not only could remember the precipitating incident, but that he often "relived" it with the full emotional intensity of the original event. They also found that the constant interaction between patient and therapist, the repressed material could be "synthesized," i.e., integrated into consciousness with subsequent relief of anxiety.

The technique, in one variation or another, has been used clinically during the past three decades but there have been few published reports. No systematic, controlled investigations were reported until Hain, Smith and Stevenson (1966, 1970) published the results of a comparison of the efficacy of three "active" drugs (Sodium Amobarbital, Hydroxidione, and Methamphetamine) with a placebo (Saline). This investigation was done under conditions that were quite different from the usual clinical circumstances. An anesthesiologist administered a predetermined dose of a randomly selected drug; neither the interviewer nor the patient knew which drug was administered. The interviewer was not the patient's primary therapist and, in fact, had seen the patient only once, if at all, prior to the interview. The interviews were conducted in a laboratory with various recording devices, and were observed, through a one-way mirror by two or more observers (with the patient's knowledge and consent). In most cases, the results indicated that the drugs, as opposed to the placebo, facilitated the ability of the patient to talk about some of his problems. No dramatic abreactions (a reliving of past events) were observed but this may have been not only because of the stark laboratory setting but also because most of the patients' problems were long-standing and rarely attributable to an identifiable trauma.

## TECHNIQUE

Narcoanalysis must be done by a person licensed to perform injections (i.e., a physician), and it should be done in a setting where emergency resources are readily available in the event of untoward reactions. The usual medical-legal precautions, including a signed consent, are taken. The interview itself may be conducted by a nonphysician therapist.

The probability of effective results is enhanced if the drug is administered by the therapist who has already established a reasonably trusting relationship with the patient, and if the interview is conducted in a quiet, relaxing atmosphere, with the patient reclining on a bed or couch.

Amytal and Pentothal are the drugs most frequently used for this procedure and the choice is made by the physician. Amytal is somewhat slower acting and its effects last longer than do those of Pentothal, but it is safer. After the preliminaries are completed, the drug is injected very slowly while the therapist maintains continuing verbal interaction with the patient and simultaneously monitors the effects of the drug. When the patient manifests relaxation, slight slurring of speech or errors in counting backwards, the injection is stopped (the needle may remain in place for subsequent additional medication). The content of the therapist's remarks will be relevant to the individual patient, his problems, and his personality, and may be supportive or challenging as the situation dictates.

Once the desired level of narcosis is reached, the therapeutic interview proceeds, again highly individualized. At the close of the interview, the patient is allowed to rest until the therapist is assured that it is safe for him to leave. For the patient who has had Amytal, it is recommended that he have an escort for twelve to twenty-four hours.

## APPLICATIONS

Narcoanalysis is a useful technique for a variety of conditions and purposes. It may be used to relieve acute anxiety, tension, or agitation. It may be useful in dispelling acute hysterical amnesia. But it is most frequently used as an adjunct in the exploratory phases of psychotherapy by enabling the patient to reveal suppressed and/or repressed material (facts and feelings), and in breaking through an impasse in the therapeutic course. It can often be useful in firming up the patient-therapist relationship. In general, the therapeutic effectiveness of Narcoanalysis is greatest when used with patients whose symptoms and concerns are of recent onset. The technique has been of little value in treating long-standing syndromes.

The use of Narcoanalysis is not without risk, medically and psychologically. The therapist should be especially alert to idiosyncratic and synergistic (especially with alcohol) reactions. Among the psychological risks are the activation of suicidal behavior, the release of paranoid ideation, hallucinations, or other psychotic manifestations. Patients with organic brain syndromes in remission may regress and develop confusion, disorientation, and other symptoms.

# Natural High Therapy
## Walter E. O'Connell

### DEFINITION

Natural High Therapy is a here-and-now optimistic behaviorally oriented therapy designed to teach about chronic and crucial constrictions of self-esteem (feelings of worth and significance) and social interest (feelings of similarity with others and belonging in the universe). The two variables of self-esteem (SE) and social interest (SI) are the only two qualities over which persons have absolute control, but only actualizers have learned to be aware of this basic truth. Only those individuals who are alerted to this phenomenon are in control of its growth benefits.

People spend most of their time and energy unwittingly attempting to overcompensate for the damage precipitated by continuous invidious comparisons, creatively arranged in the service of protecting learned and cherished identities or life-styles. Only actualized life-styles are not constrictive. Discouraged life-styles represent both irrational demands and negative nonsense, which narrow the inner . and outer movements of SI. On the cognitive and behavioral dimensions, isolated monadic behavior is fostered rather than dyadic other-concerned movements. All humans need and get power (or influence). Such idiosyncratic inner and outer movement is stabilized by the life-style constrictions. Persons may develop tremendous power with little SE. Such are considered our problem people: the lower the SE, the more the need for psychiatric hospitalization.

A natural high experience follows from ceasing one's constrictive efforts, halting devaluations of self and others. When one's goals and roles are truly realized one may feel unique, similar, and significant. This state is the natural high. The supernatural high, feeling one's innate worth and inherent connectedness without the need for external proof, is the ultimate goal of Natural High Therapy.

## HISTORY

Natural High Therapy is the product of my (Walter E. O'Connell) work in the mental health field in the last twenty-five years. Natural High Therapy is the only psychotherapy to develop out of humor studies. The growth of the humorous attitude toward life still remains the hallmark of the super-natural high.

Since the 1950s I have been both borrowing and inventing concepts and techniques to teach man that he is an active agent (hence, response-able) and not the passive victim of past, present, and future circumstances that he yearns to be. Natural high methodology has-always been wary of iatrogenic "illness" (types of discouragement introjected from cynical authorities). Hence, man should learn and practice a theory that "makes sense," is self-reflexive (and so can "explain" his own constrictions), and must be practiced like any other skill or sport.

Early clinical papers described positive goal states of therapy, another area of psychiatry so often neglected in our emphases on pathology and the externals of counting, weighing, and measuring. In 1963 references to psychodrama were relabeled as "action therapy" because my colleagues and I were not Moreno trained and were concerned with goals, self-induced constrictions, and the movements of encouragement, beyond catharsis itself. Action therapy became the chief vehicle of Level I (self-constriction). My experience as researcher on a patients' training lab ward, using Lewinian theory, led me to incorporate the didactic-experiential methods to Level II (learning dyadic encouragement through practice). Level III (the Trans-personal) relies on meditation, contemplation, guided imagery, and Jungian active Imagination. A vital premise of the natural high theory is that levels must be mastered sequentially. Problems of hyperdependency, active and passive competition, and human ignorance, unless learned from Level I and II training, block the efforts needed to actualize the deep, inner potentials. Since 1972 the focus on humanistic identification has undergone a semantic change. Research, training, and therapy with drug addicts has led to a less abstract and more motivational term, the Natural High. Throughout the history of the democratic optimistic educational venture there is an indebtedness principally to Alfred Adler and Rudolf Dreikurs for the insights of Individual (Adlerian) psychology. Other informal teachers from various schools of therapy were C. G. Jung, Kurt Lewin, Abraham Maslow, Albert Ellis, J. L. Moreno, and Ira Progoff. I consider Natural High Therapy to be part of a tradition, exemplified by the works of the before-mentioned therapists, called humanistic depth psychology. The thrust of that endeavor is on self-training for self-actualization, with constant concern for contributions to SI growth.

Some therapists have suggested that Natural High Therapy be placed under the rubric of neo-Adlerian therapy. Such a switch is impossible since there is no Adlerian change of emphasis that would negate earlier works of Adlerian psychologists. What Natural High Therapy does is to expand the usual Adlerian work on the social dimension to phenomenological and transpersonal facets also. The community goals beyond the typical doctor-patient interactions are highlighted. Adlerian concepts are interrelated and translated into behavior in the natural high theory. Positive personality goals can be reached via self-education in Natural High Therapy. The latter radically expands Adlerian theory and practice but does not clash with its basic SI tenets.

## TECHNIQUE

Natural High Therapy uses a great variety of techniques to teach response-ability: that persons can and must take responsibility for SE and SI enhancement, without blame, punishment, and individious comparisons. Action therapy has been a resource of Level I where people experience their constrictive cycles. From inadequate SE and SI comes the "demandments," the I-must and You-must of controls, goals, and roles ingrained early in life. From demandments come frustration, and the subsequent blame of negative nonsense. People blame self, others or life. We are so creative that we arrange, provoke, and selectively find "reasons" and proof for our deadly blamegames. Then comes misery.

Level II spells out in action the encouragenic movements. For example to be a healthful significant other we must practice stop, look, and listen; paraphrasing and guessing at feelings; interested postures; self-disclosure; the movements of basic feedback; telling others how they could encourage us and guessing at how we could do so to them; not rewarding useless goals or seeking them ourselves; and, of course, learning to develop and use the sense of humor. Level II fits Adler's implications about courage as being active social interest. Encouragement is difficult because in its essence it doesn't focus on externals or a perma-smile approach to pathology. Encouragement means teaching ourselves and others that we and we alone constrict our worth and belonging no matter how discouraging the environment.

The teaching of the encouragement process was modeled on didactic-experiential interactions, using group feedback as vehicles for learning the Lewinian model. Natural high goes beyond simple feedback of feelings into a feedback on goals, or "how" and "why" people, usually without awareness, chronically constrict themselves, then sicken with blame, our chief social disease. Natural high focuses on persons rather than techniques and says in effect that unless teachers and therapists learn to become soul-makers to themselves, they will continue to misuse techniques.

Level III is radically different from the preceding individual emphasis; it is the experiencing of ideas in which man becomes more than just a replaceable object in a callous, static universe. Teilhard de Chardin saw love as creating radial energy for universal evolution. Carl Jung saw man as responsible for the acceptance and expansion of the pattern of universal synchronicity and self-actualization of the God within.

Meditation, contemplation, active imagination, and guided imagery can all be in the service of developing ultimate athletes in the game-of-games: those who know that, together with all others, they are response-able for creation of their supernatural highs, and for contributing to such growth in others.

Like encouragement process, Level I (action therapy) and Level III (guided imagery) later played a part in the didactic-experiential focus on death. At the request of the Veterans Administration, my colleagues and I created death and dying labs (once again based upon the encouragement model of Level II) for thousands of professionals. Initially, these methods were employed to desensitize death fears in those who worked close with terminal patients. I later discovered that such simulated experiences of death can become actualizers for anyone. Death labs accentuated feelings of SI and help people to look at where their true strength (SE and SI) and power (Level II encouragement) were centered. I then formulated the natural low: a sense of compassion toward others and a mourning of our own deaths catalyzed by death and dying labs. The natural low complements the natural high and both are needed for actualization.

## APPLICATIONS

Throughout its evolution, Natural High Therapy has been taught and demonstrated to groups of every possible classification: psychiatric, educational, business-industrial, and religious. The psychosocial tenets of love-self, love-neighbor, and love-God (Levels I, II, and III) are discovered and practiced in terms of human movements and purposive goals. The incorporation of the spirit and techniques of Adler and Dreikurs within the natural high practice makes the latter appropriate for the reeducation toward democratic principles through home and class councils. Both Dreikurs and Adler aimed beyond the doctor-patient model to the teaching of the community through positive principles. Such is the fond hope—and practical application—of Natural High Therapy also.

The Institute for Creative Community Living (ICCL) at the University of St. Thomas, Houston, focuses on tutoring in ego-interpersonal and self-actualization. College credit and certification is offered for natural high coursework within the Adlerian frame of reference. At ICCL, education is above all for self-realization rather than to prepare professionals narrowly in the orthodox disease model.

# Negative Practice

## Daniel B. Fishman

## DEFINITION

Negative Practice is a behavior therapy technique. It consists of having a client actively and deliberately repeat an undesirable, "automatic," "involuntary" habit— such as a tic, nail biting, or stammering—while paying careful attention to the behavior being practiced. The goal of negative practice is to become more aware of the habit and, ultimately, to reduce the habit.

## HISTORY

This technique was formulated by Dunlap and presented in his 1932 book, *Habits, Their Making and Unmaking*. It was not widely disseminated, however, until 1958, when Yates was able to relate the procedure to "reactive inhibition," a well-known concept of Hull's popular learning theory, and to document its efficacy in the treatment of tics. While it has not generated a large number of published studies, it is considered a basic tool in the behavior therapist's repertoire, as illustrated by references to it in a variety of recent books written for behavioral practitioners and consumers.

# TECHNIQUE

At first glance, Negative Practice appears to be a paradoxical technique: the client deliberately engages in a behavior in order, ultimately, to reduce that behavior's frequency. However, upon reflection, it becomes clear that a behavior that is deliberately and consciously practiced is not the same as one that is automatically and involuntarily performed. In fact, one of the therapeutic uses to which Negative Practice can be put is simply to bring an automatically performed habit into awareness (Watson and Tharp, 1962). This is helpful because it is very difficult for clients to change a behavior of which they are not aware. Thus, clients can first deliberately practice habitual behavior while consciously paying attention, so that they learn to pay attention to the behavior while performing it. Once this new behavior of "paying attention" when the habit begins is learned, it becomes easier to develop an additional intervention plan to eliminate the undesirable behavior. For example, once the client becomes aware of beginning to engage in an undesirable habit, this awareness can be used as a cue to perform an incompatible, desirable behavior.

In addition to functioning as a preliminary step to other intervention techniques, Negative Practice can be effective in itself because effortful activity eventually generates a negative state of pain and fatigue, which Hullian theory calls "reactive inhibition." Under the buildup of such a negative state, and in the absence of any positive reinforcement of the behavior, *not* engaging in the activity will avoid the aversive effects of fatigue and thus be effectively reinforced. Furthermore, from the point of view of Pavlovian conditioning, the aversive fatigue that develops in association with the undesirable behavior becomes conditioned to the behavior. In other words, the client associates the behavior with an unpleasant feeling, and thus a conditioned inhibition of the habit is learned.

# APPLICATIONS

While Negative Practice is applicable to a variety of undesirable "involuntary" habits, its most documented use has been in the treatment of tics. For example, Yates (1958) applied the technique to a female client with multiple tics and found it particularly successful when the client practiced them for as long as one hour, followed by prolonged rest. Clark (1966) treated two adults, both of whom manifested explosive repetition of obscenities ("verbal tics") along with various motor tics, which were interfering with their jobs and social relationships. The therapist instructed the clients to repeat the verbal tics as often as possible until they could no longer emit them. This technique successfully eliminated the verbal tics, and at the same time, the motor tics disappeared spontaneously. Browning and Stover (1971) successfully eliminated a severe eyebrow-raising tic in a schizophrenic teenager with seventeen Negative Practice sessions spread over a four-week period.

A number of published reports describe other applications for Negative Practice. For example, Gambrill (1977) describes a forty-five-year-old woman who found herself frequently vacillating between the kitchen and the living room if either her son or husband was speaking. To eliminate this problem, the therapist instructed the woman to imagine three times a day that her son and husband were talking while she was in the doorway, and she was to deliberately vacillate by walking back and forth through the doorway ten times on each occasion. Although the imagined scenes were obviously not identical to the actual problem situations, this approach was found to be successful in eliminating the original "vacillating" behavior. As another example, Beech (1960) applied Negative Practice to the treatment of a writer's cramp of five years' duration, which had proven unresponsive to over two years of previous psychoanalysis and hypnotherapy. Whenever the client grasped a pen, the index finger would contract and the wrist would bend sharply, causing severe pain, fatigue, and immobilization of the hand. The client participated in seven Negative Practice office sessions with interspersed home practice sessions, with each session consisting of repeated effortful finger contractions. As a result, there was a rapid and progressive decline in the incidence of finger contraction, along with a similar decrease in the untreated wrist spasm.

In addition to the above behaviors, Negative Practice has been shown to be useful in changing such habits as stammering, thumb sucking, nail biting, exhibitionism, talking too loudly, overeating, habitual typing and spelling errors, and self-scratching during sleep (Watson and Tharp, 1962).

In closing, it is important to stress that Negative Practice is a very specific technique that can be successful only in the context of a total psychotherapeutic relationship. Factors important to the success of Negative Practice are the motivation of the client to eliminate the behavior; development where necessary of a more adaptive alternative response to the behavior to be changed (e.g., the stutterer must know the correct mode of speech and the poor speller the correct spelling of misspelled words); the similarity of the habit as practiced to that of the real-life habit; and the elimination of factors that might continue to reinforce the undesirable response (Lehner, 1960). Moreover, it must be remembered that the major documentation of the effectiveness of Negative Practice consists of single case studies, and better-controlled research is needed to further delineate the nature of this technique's therapeutic effectiveness (Bandura, 1969).

# Neuro Linguistic Programming

## John O. Stevens

### DEFINITION

Neuro Linguistic Programming (NLP) is a detailed operational model of the processes involved in human behavior and communication. This model is still being rapidly developed, defined, and adapted to specific contexts. NLP is not itself a psychotherapy. Its principles can be used to understand, and make changes in, *any* realm of human experience and activity. However, it has been applied to therapeutic concerns, and the result is a powerful, rapid, and subtle technology for making extensive and lasting changes in human behavior and capacities. This technology is detailed and explicit, and can be easily taught and learned. A client can learn enough basic skills in a weekend or two to make his therapy much faster and more effective. Of course it takes longer to become fluent and subtle in these skills.

## HISTORY

NLP was developed within the last four years by Richard Bandler, John Grinder, Leslie Cameron-Bandler, and Judith DeLozier. Their background includes extensive training in cybernetics, mathematics, and linguistics, and their specialty is the ability to make models of information-processing systems (linguistics models language, cybernetics models computers, and mathematics models the economy). One of the first systems they chose to model was gestalt therapy, and their first book, *The Structure of Magic*, is a detailed and explicit model of how language can be used to elicit a complete verbal representation of a person's experience. They also show how that complete verbal representation can be used to reevoke the full experience and be instrumental in reevaluating that experience. A second volume, *Magic II*, is a further extension, with substantial theoretical and technical developments.

They next chose to model Virginia Satir's Family Therapy and then Milton H. Erickson's Hypnotherapy. In each case they have modeled the observable communication/behavior processes (verbal and nonverbal) and have abstracted the useful and productive patterns and relationships. They have left behind those parts of the process that are not useful, and also left behind most of the practitioners' own theories about what they do.

Besides their keen observation of other researchers' therapeutic work, they have been exceedingly creative in observing and specifying the patterns of minute observable behavior that constitute the external expression of a person's internal state. For instance, they are able to reliably determine whether a person's moment-to-moment internal experience is visualization, kinesthesis, or audition from the following observable variables: direction of gaze; pupil dilation; breathing pattern; voice pitch, tonality and tempo, minimal head movements and hand gestures; changes in facial color, tones, and symmetry; lower lip size, etc.

NLP also borrows ideas from neurology, including particular information about hemispheric dominance and specialization of function in the brain.

## TECHNIQUE

All internal processing of experiencing can be described as being represented in neurological channels that correspond to the major sensory channels: visual, kinesthetic, auditory, and, to a lesser extent, olfactory and gustatory. Our thinking, deciding, remembering, and all other behavior can be described as a sequence of internal representation (usually partly or entirely outside awareness) that has a pattern as well as a content. Like a program in a computer, this pattern limits the possible ways that any content can be processed and utilized. It is possible to work directly with these patterns. By modifying, redesigning, adding to them, or replacing them, it is possible to give the person more flexibility and new capacities and abilities.

For instance, if you are a good speller, you probably represent a word visually and check this picture with a kinesthetic feeling to know that it is correct. (To verify this in your own experience, represent a familiar word visually, and notice how your body feels when the word is spelled correctly, compared to how it feels when the word is spelled incorrectly.) If you represent a word auditorially, however, you will have difficulty spelling words that are not spelled the way they sound. A poor speller can become a good speller as soon as he learns the program or pattern of representing visually and checking kinesthetically. This kind of learning is often very rapid, and quickly becomes unconscious. (If you have been a poor speller, you may have become a good one simply by reading this.) Everyone already has lots of stored pictures of words; it's simply a matter of putting them to appropriate use.

Many of the problems that bring people to therapy are as simple, structurally, as the spelling example above. People *do* have the resources to behave in more satisfying ways; they simply are not using these resources in ways that are appropriate to their needs and the outcomes they want.

In one of the basic processes, called reframing, you can learn to communicate directly with parts of another person (or yourself) that are functioning outside of awareness. Using reframing and other basic processes, it is possible to elicit "deep-trance" phenomena without any hypnotic induction. It is possible, for instance, to utilize unconscious resources to have a person temporarily forget his name using reframing—a cheap trick, but one that demonstrates the power of this method to elicit responses from parts of the person that are not in awareness. Another basic tool, anchoring, can be used to reconstruct a person's personal history by, for example, connecting a feeling from a pleasant situation to a memory or situation that previously elicited unpleasant feelings. It is even possible to create entirely new episodes of "history" that can serve as personal resources.

An experienced NLP practitioner can deal with most phobias and many other simple problems in a half hour or less. Probably at least half the other symptoms that bring people into therapy can be dealt with in a one-hour session or two. But the NLP practitioner treats more than symptoms: he goes to the functional (not the historical) root of the symptom and makes the changes at that level.

## APPLICATIONS

As mentioned previously, NLP can be applied to any area of human behavior and communication. Although NLP can be applied to remedial, psychotherapeutic tasks, it is actually a *generative* model that specifies what new capacities are possible. It is possible to study a person with an exceptional skill, abstract the pattern of that skill, and give this pattern to someone else so that it functions unconsciously to give him the foundation for the same skill. NLP can also be used to calculate and generate *new* behavior and skills, or new combinations of existing ones.

A few of the areas (other than psychotherapy) in which NLP has developed specific applied technologies are: learning languages, learning sports, speed reading, remembering, business management, advertising, medical problems, and education.

# Neurotone Therapy

*Aris W. Cox*

## DEFINITION

Neurotone Therapy is a treatment modality whereby small amperage, uni-directional electrical current (usually one milliamper or less) is applied, through saline-soaked cotton electrodes attached in two pairs, to the head.

## HISTORY

Neurotone (or electrosleep) Therapy was developed in the Soviet Union by Liventsev, and this treatment modality became known in Western Europe and the United States after a symposium was held in Graz, Austria, on the topic in 1966 (Wageneder and St. Schury). Neurotone Therapy devices are now commercially available in the United States.

## TECHNIQUE

The person to receive the treatment is usually in a reclining position. The electrodes that are attached to the device are soaked in saline so that they will provide current transmission. They are then attached to the points over both mastoid processes and above both eyes. At this point, the machine is turned on and the dial that controls the milliamperage of current to be delivered is adjusted upward until the recipient reports an uncomfortable stinging or tingling sensation under the electrodes. The dial is then turned back until the recipient reports no discomfort and the current is left at this setting for the remainder of the treatment, which is usually of thirty minutes' duration. A usual experience is that the tolerance for the amount of current delivered increases over time so that milliamperage levels that were initially reported as uncomfortable become tolerated by the patient after a week or two. The treatments are given in intervals of every other day or three times a week for varying periods of time until certain target symptoms are improved. In my (Aris W. Cox) experience, several patients have purchased neurotone devices for themselves and have become able to treat themselves on an as needed basis for certain target difficulties, which are discussed below.

## APPLICATIONS

The usual results of neurotone treatments are reports of relaxation, lessened anxiety, and objective improvements in sleeping for most patients (Rosenthal, 1972). The negative side effects sometimes encountered are difficulty in concentration and easy fatigability. From these reported effects, therefore, it follows that this form of therapy is helpful in the treatment of chronic insomnia, acute and chronic anxiety states, and mild to moderate depressive reactions.

Sleep disturbances at this time probably form the primary indication for this form of treatment. Insomnia usually responds quite effectively to a series of nine to twelve neurotone treatments spread over a period of three to four weeks. In the treatment of acute and chronic anxiety states and depressive reactions, there are no hard and fast rules to follow as to duration of therapy. The patient may be treated until reported improvement occurs or until one month has passed with no improvement. At this time, it is appropriate to give up this form of therapy as of little benefit. Data about the effectiveness of Neurotone Therapy is difficult to come by. Usually three-fourths of the population of properly selected patients will report benefit.

Neurotone Therapy is also of help in the induction of a hypnotic trance. The use of the machine at current of comfortable levels produces a state of relaxation and heightened suggestibility more quickly than ordinary hypnotic suggestion alone. In addition, in mild to moderate withdrawal states, especially those associated with alcohol abuse, Neurotone Therapy is of use in tranquilizing patients and in diminishing the amount of psychotropic medication necessary to prevent delirium tremens.

## Contraindications and Side Effects

No serious side effects to Neurotone Therapy have been described. As noted previously, uncomfortable symptoms of difficulty in concentration and easy fatigability are noted by some patients after treatments. These symptoms clear rapidly with the cessation of therapy.

Obviously, Neurotone Therapy is a symptomatic form of treatment useful in ameliorating certain target symptoms. In its use, therefore, as in the use of any symptomatic treatment, careful diagnosis is important. To delay the institution of proper therapy for serious psychiatric conditions, such as endogenous depressions or emerging paranoid psychoses, and to use Neurotone Therapy instead is to court disaster. Therefore, a careful psychiatric examination is necessary to ascertain whether or not sleeplessness is due to a severe underlying depression or to a more benign situation disturbance. Likewise, it is important to ascertain whether the anxiety is occurring in the background of a well-organized personality or in one undergoing a psychotic dissolution.

Neurotone Therapy by itself will not suffice for the management of withdrawal states. It is meant to be, in these conditions, purely supportive and ancillary. It should not be relied upon as a treatment of choice or as a sole modality of therapy. As an aid to hypnosis it will enhance the hypnotic suggestibility of a proper candidate for hypnotherapy. It will not produce a suggestible state in a guarded and suspicious paranoid person or in other individuals who are not initially suitable candidates for hypnosis.

## Conclusions

A criticism of electrosleep therapy present from its introduction has been its efficacy. These questions have not been resolved completely and the issue is still open as to whether or not Neurotone Therapy produces its beneficial effects because of suggestion or because of placebo effect or whether it exerts true therapeutic effects on the central nervous system of the subject. Reigel, et al. (1969), at the University of Wisconsin, were able to demonstrate lessened gastric acid secretion in individuals with peptic ulcer disease after a series of neurotone treatments. They theorize that this was due to some effect on the cerebral phase of gastric acid production. Rosenthal (1972) performed a series of controlled studies measuring the therapeutic effects of Neurotone Therapy on certain clinical syndromes and on certain physiologic parameters. He found Neurotone Therapy effective in the treatment of chronic anxiety and depressive states when compared with no treatment at all. In addition, they found alterations in plasma thyroid hormone levels, which they felt were the result of neurotone effects on the hypothalamus (1978).

Cox and Heath gave a series of neurotone treatments to a patient prepared with deep and surface electrodes for the treatment of temporal lobe dysrythmia. The neurotone device sedated and calmed the patient in a manner much more effective than psychotropic drugs and without producing the contaminating effect on the EEG recordings that psychotropic medications create. The Neurotone Therapy also produced EEG changes that correlated with great improvement in the patient's clinical state. That is to say, the patient noted feelings of well-being, and tranquility following the Neurotone Therapy. It should be reiterated that Neurotone Therapy is a symptomatic form of treatment only. The benefit of this form of therapy is that it may obviate the necessity for the use of psychotropic medications that have potential addictive and toxic side effects. In summary, therefore, Neurotone Therapy is a safe and probably effective form of symptomatic treatment primarily for insomnia and chronic anxiety states. It has limited usefulness in the treatment of mild to moderate withdrawal conditions and as an adjunct to hypnotherapy. Much data, however, remains to be collected before its usefulness can be fully documented.

---

# New Identity Process

## Daniel Casriel

### DEFINITION

The New Identity Process (NIP) is a totally new psychiatric delivery system necessitated by the clinical observations uncovered while using the technique of scream therapy. The NIP deals with the ABC's of experience (A = affect, B = behavior, C = cognition), exercising feelings to effect changes in behavior and attitudes. Suppression, repression, or under utilization of feelings, which originally comes from cultural and parental impositions, can act as a block to happiness throughout one's adult life.

It takes a strong discharge of these built-up emotional tensions to permit a person to really be aware of their influence, to see the difference between the painful smothering of feelings and emotional well-being. With screaming, an emotion is exercised until it is fully expressed. The scream exercises take place in groups, where confrontation by and relationship with one's peers can act as a catalyst for getting to feelings.

As little time as possible is focused upon symptoms, but more time and effort is channeled into the reeducation process. As the emotions pour out, insights pour in. "I exist," "I need," and "I'm entitled [to my feelings/to fulfill my needs]" are the basic principles that replace old attitudes. In learning to feel entitled, an individual gains a new sense of identity, hence the name NIP.

The human potential movement has contributed at least three important concepts to which the NIP is also committed. They are: 1) man is not innately evil, or born with an excess of aggression, 2) a person has the power to change himself, and 3) a person can enrich the quality of his life with new experiences. To these the NIP concepts are added:

a) Human beings have a biologically based need for emotional and physical closeness with others, which I call "bonding."

b) Emotions are *real* (as biologically and chemically proven) and can be useful and meaningful when experienced and understood for what they are.

c) Emotions have their own points of reference (pain and pleasure), their own standards by which to be judged, as opposed to intellectual ones.

Emotionality is an integral part of being human, something we all have in common, something we all need to share. When, instead of letting emotionality be our common ground, we try to hide and protect our feelings, we are depriving ourselves of the bonding experience. Emotional openness or the flexibility allowing us to open (and close) is a prerequisite for an ongoing bonding experience, and is necessary for fulfillment. Accepting or letting in pleasurable feelings can itself be a step in the right direction but the best proof of man's innate sociability is the fact that his pleasure is most valued when it is shared. Emotional groups are a first step toward sharing feelings, all feelings, whether it's for the fist time or it's a relearning process.

## HISTORY

I have been developing the NIP since 1962, when I was greatly influenced by my involvement in Synanon, a residential facility for the treatment of drug addiction. There I observed how verbal confrontation helped speed up therapeutic progress. In the fall of 1963 a Synanon-styled, hostile-provocative encounter group was introduced to a selected group of patients from my private analytic practice. I had no idea the group process would be so effective with these middle-class neurotic, but nonpsychopathic, patients. Within six years it was necessary to move three times to larger quarters to accommodate almost six hundred patients (in groups) per week. My current quarters, a six-story building in the heart of Manhattan, additionally houses residential patients in AREBA (Accelerated Reeducation of Emotions, Behavior and Attitude).

I have been aided by a gradually enlarged staff of professionals and paraprofessionals whom I trained experientially through the process into which they entered in the role of patients. Since the publication of my most recent book in 1972, the NIP model has become educational and not medical. I do not consider the patient-student "sick" but rather unhappy, a state reached through conditioned maladaptation of the ABC's. The NIP attempts to teach them how to be and to *feel* happy.

If one wants to relate the NIP to traditional psychoanalysis, one must look to Freud's earlier work involving hypnosis. The patient was induced to reexperience traumatic feelings in what is called an "abreaction." In NIP this mechanism is paralleled by the discharge of emotions in screaming and a few other expressive exercises. This is sometimes spoken of as the "ventilation" of feelings, and its importance in therapy has been acclaimed by only one other worker, Arthur Janov, whose version of "scream therapy" is somewhat similar, but upon close examination, in more ways different from my process. Of course, the NIP has evolved beyond Freud's hypotheses, for instance, in its effectuality with the severely character disordered personality of the drug addict.

## TECHNIQUE

The technique we use to help a person get to his feelings is screaming, which is the full-bodied expression of an emotion. Pain, anger, fear, pleasure, and the need for love are the basic human feelings that may have been unacceptable elsewhere, but one is free to express in groups. One learns in groups that it's not dangerous to show feelings, that they won't kill you or overwhelm you. Group members demonstrate that you will not be condemned or disliked for having the feelings you have, and furthermore, their actual responsiveness and empathy reassure you that what you are experiencing is not abnormal.

Many of the problems that people are seeking to change in therapy are symptoms of character-disordered and neurotic personalities. Such symptoms as alcohol or drug abuse, overeating, inability to maintain good relationships, and self-alienation and estrangement are self-defeating patterns of behavior that the patient is told to drop. Until he has replaced his old habits with a new outlook and a correspondingly new strategy, he is told to "act as if" he doesn't need the crutch or escape he is used to. He is not allowed to hide from his emotions. It may be hard, because the only reward one gets for his efforts is growth. On the other hand, once a person gives up his symptoms, he will have all his old feelings coming up again, and he will start to make some real headway in the groups, with support and encouragement from group members.

Once inside the group, a person is told to drop his defenses completely, to express what he feels in inexpressible, either because of embarrassment or taboo. If the person is resisting help, blocking out others, or simply feeling blocked and noncommunicative, this is when confrontation or prompting by group members cuts down time. For example, constant complaining about another's behavior without acknowledging feelings of hurt and anger would be an indirect expression of one's needs. Experienced group members would recognize at least one of the several messages that this person is giving: the person may be afraid to admit "I need love"; he may be afraid to get angry with someone he cares about (as most of us are); he may be worried that he will be judged as weak if he shows his pain. Confrontation helps bring these underlying feelings into focus. Each person will have specific thoughts and experiences contributing to such attitudes, and one's work in groups consists of finding out what these thoughts and attitudes are so that they can be discarded and replaced by adaptive, positive attitudes. One must practice in applying the new attitudes outside the groups.

A person learns gradually to operate upon the three basic attitudes—I exist, I need, and I'm entitled—and he practices taking what he needs with entitlement. If he is working toward these positive goals, group members will encourage and reward him with warmth and genuine affection, without even thinking about it, without judging him, without asking for anything in return. He will find that these feelings make him better able to deal with others, to be loving and confident that his love is a pleasure to those who receive it. A more satisfied person is not vulnerable as often as someone who is distressed. A well-adjusted person has learned that it is healthy to be vulnerable sometimes, to feel pain or loss when necessary, so as not to be paying an emotional price of guilt or remorse after the events are long over.

## APPLICATION

The NIP deals not only with the mild or "normally" unhappy or disturbed, but with the most severely disturbed who do not have brain damage. That broad diagnostic range encompasses the severe neurotic, the severe character disordered (delinquent, alcoholic, addict) and the so-called borderline, functional (not organic) schizophrenic.

# Nutrition-Based Psychotherapy

## *Alfred L. Scopp*

### DEFINITION

The purpose of nutritional therapy is to create an optimal molecular constitution of the body. This includes supplying the concentration of nutrients the body needs to maintain peak psychological functioning. Since proper mental functioning requires the presence of many different nutrients in the brain and nervous system, psychological symptoms may result if proper levels of nutrients are not maintained in the human body. Also, certain foods can result in psychological symptoms, and it may be necessary to eliminate them from the diet.

Human beings can be conceived as an equilateral triangle consisting of psychological, body-structural, and nutritional components. Frequently, nutrition can be an important and sometimes critical link in improving psychological functioning.

The use of nutrition as an adjunct to psychotherapy in the treatment of emotional and mental disorders is based on a number of assumptions:

1. Nutritional deficiencies manifest themselves through emotional symptoms long before acute deficiencies result in medical symptoms. For example, Newbold found that, though they showed no symptoms of physical illness, over one-third of his psychotherapy patients had low levels of vitamin B12. They improved substantially when they were given supplemental B12. Krehl has found that patients with mild deficiencies of magnesium had the following symptoms: alarm from unexpected movement or noise (100 percent), disorientation (83 percent), mental confusion (77 percent), hallucinations (44 percent), and convulsions (22 percent).

2. Just as there are wide variations in personality, there are wide variations in individual needs for various nutrients. Stress also increases the need for certain nutrients. Roger Williams calls this key concept in nutritional therapy "biochemical individuality." VanderKamp found that schizophrenics metabolized ascorbic acid at a rate ten times that of a control group of normal individuals. He gave six to eight grams of ascorbic acid every four hours to ten schizophrenics and all of them showed clinical improvement. The wide variation in individual needs for nutrients explains why some people may need dosages of

B6, niacin, C, B12, or B1, or other stress-related vitamins in quantities hundreds of times greater than the minimum daily requirements in order to function at their psychologically optimal level. Other people may meet their nutritional needs on a well-balanced diet alone. The purpose of nutrition counseling is to facilitate the client's discovery of the best nutritional program for him.

The average American diet is neither well balanced nor nutritionally adequate. Soil depletion of trace minerals and the refining of foods has resulted in the removal of about 80 percent of some nutrients critical for psychological wellbeing, such as chromium, magnesium, and the B-complex vitamins. I (Alfred L. Scopp) have found that 90 percent of my psychotherapy clients do not meet minimum daily requirements of two or more nutrients according to a computer diet survey completed by the clients. The Senate McGovern Commission report confirmed these results for the general population. Over 25 percent of the caloric intake of the American diet is from white sugar, a food devoid of any vitamin-mineral value. Kugler found that 90 percent of respondents taking tranquilizers had inadequate dietary intake of magnesium, a natural tranquilizer.

## HISTORY AND TECHNIQUE

Megavitamins, such as niacin and vitamin C, were used in the 1950s by Hoffer and Osmond for hospitalized schizophrenics. Feingold and later Rimland found that when food additives, preservatives, sugar, and/or excessive refined carbohydrates were removed from the diet of hyperactive or learning disabled children, behavior dramatically improved. Pfeiffer has found three subcategories of schizophrenia with distinct biochemical and personality profiles as well as appropriate corrective nutritional therapy. The Northern Nassau County Mental Center has treated five thousand schizophrenics and alcoholic clients using nutritional psychotherapy with a high success rate. Treatment consists of an individually tailored program of vitamins, minerals, diet, and avoidance of specific "cerebral food allergies" that can create a variety of mental and emotional problems such as depression, irritability, and confusion.

The following diagnostic aids can be used by psychologists to facilitate greater nutritional awareness:

1. *Computer diet survey.* The client records all foods eaten over a period of a week. The results are then computer analyzed to determine the intake of vitamins, minerals, and nutrient factors in comparison with minimum daily requirements or optimal daily allowances. If the client's diet lacks certain nutrients, foods high in these nutrients may then be added to it.

2. *Hair analysis.* A small amount of hair is cut from the nape and analyzed by atomic absorption spectrography to determine mineral levels in the hair in comparison to norms. Ashmead and others have found a correlation between hair mineral levels and various psychopathologies. Mineral imbalances can be corrected through mineral supplements or by diet modifications and typically give a sense of increased self-confidence and sustained balance energy.

3. *Applied kinesiology muscle testing.* George Goodheart has observed an empirical relationship between specific nutrient deficiencies and right-left strength imbalances of specific muscles. The muscle strength imbalances can be used as a diagnostic indicator for

nutrient needs, and nutritional recommendations are based upon muscle-testing indications rather than on theoretical formulations or symptoms alone.

Based on right side versus left side change or imbalances in muscle strength of specific muscles, the following determinations can be made:

a) What vitamin mineral, enzyme, and glandular extract is needed

b) How many tablets for each deficiency are needed

c) What brand is compatible to the person's chemistry (the brand chosen may make a difference in the success of the program)

d) What foods they must eliminate from their diet.

4. *Careful diet diary and systematic diet variation* can be used to identify "provocative" foods and food-behavior relationships. Provocative foods, also known as "cerebral food allergies," are any food that an individual, as a result of his biochemical individuality, cannot metabolize properly and that consequently results in psychological symptoms. Provocative foods are usually eaten frequently or craved. Common provocative foods are wheat, sugar, dairy products, chocolate, soy, or citrus. Provocative foods may also be identified by a change in pulse rate of at least eight beats per minute after exposure to the food, dramatic behavior changes, or by a weakening in muscle tone as revealed by applied kinesiology muscle testing.

## APPLICATIONS

Nutritional therapy is especially recommended whenever symptoms are chronic, when other treatment modes have not been successful, or when fatigue, anxiety, depression, or poor concentration are an important part of the clinical picture in the absence of any organic basis.

Whenever corrective vitamins and minerals are used to replace body reserves depleted by abnormally high stress, high biochemical individual needs, or inadequate diet, the client's physician should be informed of any planned nutritional therapy program. Close liaison with the physician is important if the client has any major medical problem. Nutritional therapy programs seldom work well when only one or two nutrients are added to the diet. Since the body is a complex ecological unit and many nutrients act synergistically with each other, nutritional therapy is generally more successful when all the factors of diet, vitamins, and minerals are taken into consideration.

A Nutrition-Based Psychotherapy is a potent adjunct to other psychotherapies, especially in chronic depression, anxiety, hyperactivity, learning disabilities, and psychosis. Nutritional therapy can be considered successful when the patient obtains the mental clarity, energy, vitality, and sense of well-being that enables him to function effectively in psychotherapy and in his life. About 80 percent of my clients report they are "highly satisfied" with the changes they experience on the above critera as a result of an individually tailored nutrition program.

# Object Relations Therapy
*Vincent Frein and Carole Dilling*

## DEFINITION

In his book *Schizoid Phenomena, Object Relations and the Self,* H. Guntrip states, "I cannot think of psychotherapy as a technique but only as the provision of the possibility of a genuine, reliable, understanding, respecting, caring personal relationship in which a human being whose true self has been crushed by the manipulative techniques of those who only wanted to make him not be a nuisance to them can begin at last to feel his own true feelings, and think his own spontaneous thoughts, and find himself to be real."

To expand on this definition:

1. An analyst can't guarantee a therapeutic relationship *or* a relationship with a therapeutic result or, in fact, a relationship. He can only provide time and provide for the possibility of some kind of genuine relationship developing in which the patient is able to be helped with his subjective difficulties.

2. What the analyst sees in an adult as psychic flaws represents the efforts of a child to deal with terror and fear, to make whatever adaptations were necessary to survive and to preserve relations within his original family.

3. Analysis and cure demand of the analyst a readiness to be more a "scientific researcher" or a "professional" or a "therapist." He must be able to become personally and emotionally involved in a unique relationship with *this particular individual.*

4. It is within the context of this caring and personal relationship that the patient will have the courage to begin to experience the analyst as possessing the same qualities as the parental figures who originally interfered with spontaneous and healthy growth. Rather than discouraging this misperception, the analyst helps the patient to experience and relive these feelings in relation to him. The analyst also helps the patient understand the childhood origins of the feelings, and the way in which they have been internalized and are projected into all present relationships (transference analysis).

5. When the original failures of childhood are uncovered and understood, the patient stands face-to-face with needs that were never met. At these deepest levels of regression, the analyst must, now especially, be more than a projection screen or scientific researcher and must (symbolically or actually) meet these needs that are no less real in the present than they were in the original childhood situation. The failure of the analyst to meet these needs is equivalent to a repetition of the original trauma of childhood. It is only when the analyst is able to supply the human provision needed in childhood that the patient is able to grow in a real and spontaneous way that was formerly impossible.

In essence, with all of his symptoms and defenses, a patient comes to analysis to find *someone* who, in taking the place of the parents, will enable him to grow. Psychotherapy ultimately depends on the analyst's ability to supply this human provision.

# HISTORY

Although a study of object relations theory would have to begin with Freud *(Mourning and Melancholia; The Ego and the Id)*, Freud's thinking did not emphasize the object but rather remained basically an understanding of personality in terms of drive theory. Freud saw the satisfaction of the impulse or inhibition of impulse as the primary determinant in early development, and he pointed to the significance of various erotogenic zones in the evolving personality structure. In this framework thumb sucking in earliest infancy would be seen as an attempt to satisfy a sucking impulse. In object relations theory, the shift is toward an emphasis on the object; all libidinal strivings are seen as the seeking of an object rather than satisfaction of impulse. In this case the erotogenic zone becomes merely a pathway to the object. The infant's desire is for the mother. The mouth is merely a channel of contact with the object—the mother's breast. Here thumb sucking can be seen as the infant's attempt to provide a substitute object (the thumb) for his natural object (mother-breast).

The shift from a theory of libido to a theory of object relations has been in process since the late 1930s, even though object relations theory has only recently begun to achieve popularity in the United States. The major theoretical contributions have been from British analysts, especially Klein, Fairbairn, Winnicott, Gun-trip, Kahn, Milner, and Balint. While object relations theory can be considered a school of thought, it is important to note that there is no one founder. It is rather a body of theory that has been developed by many analysts, each doing his own independent thinking and each making his own unique contribution. The common theme that emerges in the work of each of these contributors is the focus on the importance of the object relation in the earliest stages of human development. It is their enormous contributions to the understanding of the earliest beginnings of life that lead them to important implications for therapy and the patient-therapist relationship.

# TECHNIQUE AND APPLICATIONS

The words "technique" and "application" are more suited to the sciences than they are to persons and personal relations. Technique or application are words that could apply to some kinds of therapy—chemotherapy, shock therapy, desensitization techniques, goal-directed short-term therapies, and the various forms of behavior modification therapies. All of these aim in some way for a regulation or modification of behavior where the individual can easily be seen in impersonal terms.

When we look at the personal, we realize how unsuited thinking in terms of technique becomes when we start to talk about what is human, unique, and individual. It is clear that for human development what are essential are the qualities of the parent and who the parent is in relation to the child. Similarly, the goal of psychoanalytic training should be not to teach a theory of a technique but to allow the analyst to develop into a fairly self-aware, well-related, integrated, empathic human being who desires to and is able to enter a relationship with another person, enabling that person to overcome his fears and discover his own individuality. It is with this understanding that Winnicott concludes that "the ultimate outcome of psychotherapy depends not on what the analyst does in relation to the patient but rather on who the therapist is unself-consciously in relation to the patient." (1958)

# Occupational Therapy

## Diane Shapiro

### DEFINITION

Occupational Therapy is a health and rehabilitation profession concerned with helping individuals reach and maintain their maximum level of functioning. Clients learn modified ways of behaving as a result of participating in an activity directed by a qualified occupational therapist.

### HISTORY

The notion of activity as a therapeutic modality goes back in the history of civilization to the ancient Egyptians who "treated" the emotionally ill by assigning chores to them. Throughout the history of psychiatry, reference is made to diverting patients or keeping them busy. Early in this century, mental institutions employed staff specifically to occupy patients' long days. In 1917, a group of nurses, psychiatrists, and therapists formed the American Society for Occupational Therapy. The two world wars increased the need and scope of Occupational Therapy. The American Occupational Therapy Association now represents over twenty-three thousand occupational therapists who work with emotionally, physically, and developmentally disabled clients of all ages. The application of activity as a therapeutic modality has developed beyond "busy work" in the past several decades. Activities are used by occupational therapists to assess a client's functioning and to change behavior and feelings.

### TECHNIQUE

Dysfunctional behavior often causes a client to seek psychiatric treatment. Frequently, for example, emotionally disturbed individuals cannot adequately care for themselves or their family. They may spend excessive amounts of time sleeping, be late for work, or be truant from school. Or, on the other hand, they may overwork, allowing no time for leisure. Such imbalance likely results in overall dysfunctioning which then affects the lives of their family and friends.

Occupational therapists assess the daily routines of clients so that new skills can be learned or adjustments in the personal and physical environment can be made. The assessment always involves the client's participation in an actual activity. The client's skills in executing various tasks are analyzed. An activity program is then assigned to allow the client to develop the skills necessary for living adequately and productively within the most practical environment.

The specific techniques employed by Occupational Therapy are dependent upon a therapist's given theoretical orientation, the client's needs and interests, and the amount of time available for treatment. Although the specific activities used to evaluate and treat clients may vary, some type of activity is always used. Both evaluation and treatment occur in individual or group sessions.

Three examples of how Occupational Therapy techniques are applied are offered in the next section. Each example is based upon a different theoretical orientation to illustrate how and why some activities are used by occupational therapists.

## APPLICATIONS

1. *Skill acquisition approach.* A program designed to help a client acquire new or different skills is based upon the assumption that by knowing how and being able to do basic life tasks, clients can change their behavior and function in a more satisfying way.

If, for example, a client were poorly groomed, socially remote, and unable to attend to any task with sufficient skill to secure and keep a job, the occupational therapist would use a battery of evaluative activities to identify existing assets. An interview and interest test would then help the therapist to match assets with possible job and leisure activities. The client would be instructed in specific job skills and perhaps assigned simulated work or referred to a sheltered workshop. When the client learned to perform work tasks, the therapist would then teach grooming skills and help the client to find a job. Instruction would be given, for example, in using classified advertisements, employment agencies, preparing for an interview, and writing a resume.

The therapist using such an approach is not primarily concerned about why the client is, for example, socially remote. The emphasis is placed upon how the client should be functioning, given his position and responsibilities in life. Skill acquisition activity programs are usually graded at levels that maximize the chances for success.

2. *Sensory integrative approach.* A pattern of physical symptoms is observed in a specific group of psychiatric clients. The familiar symptoms are: a) an exaggerated 5-shaped spinal curve—head dropped forward with face downward, b) a shuffling gait, c) weakened flexor muscle tone, d) absence of eye contact, and e) a generalized clumsiness. These clients respond favorably to simple activities that provide for nonjudgmental, non competitive gross physical movements, such as yoga. For some as-yet-unknown reason, the stimuli provided by these types of activities help not only the above-mentioned symptoms, but improve self-care and interpersonal behavior. It is hypothesized that this type of treatment may facilitate neurosensory development.

3. *Psychoanalytic approach.* Psychoanalytic principles can be applied to therapeutic activities. A client's art experiences may be used to identify conflicting feelings through his finished product. Art media allow for the capturing of expressions that can be studied and discussed with the client. Projective techniques are valuable for clients whose dysfunctional behavior is caused by disturbed feelings and who are capable of engaging in insight-oriented treatment.

A group art project is sometimes assigned to several clients or to a family to help them to see and understand how they relate to one another. Not only is an opportunity provided to understand interaction, but a sequence of group art projects permits members to act upon their insight by experimenting with new behavior.

All Occupational Therapy programs are concerned with the client's total lifestyle. Each prescribed activity is part of a program that may also include recommendations to modify or change the environment. An occupational therapist may refer clients to instructional and vocational programs or to other community resources.

# Office Network Therapy

## Max Sugar

### DEFINITION

Office Network Therapy, which may also be called self-selected adolescent peer group therapy, is used with adolescents who are in a crisis or have massive resistances in ongoing therapy. Network Therapy counters the usual withdrawal of peer support and isolation that often are factors in adolescent psychopathology. The patient selects his own peers as members of his therapy group to come in with him when, and as often as, he wishes their presence. These sessions are continued for as long as the adolescent needs them but usually six to ten sessions suffice. The number of peers assembled at each session is up to the adolescent, and sessions take place in the usual office setting (Sugar, 1975).

### HISTORY

I first used this technique around 1967, after learning of Speck's innovative work with network intervention with adults (1965). His therapy used the patient's social network, or arranged one, to learn of the hidden puppeteers and other significant relationships contributing to the patient's dynamics. His arrangement consisted of: multiple generations, or adolescents, in large numbers meeting in a large space such as the patient's home, a gym, or church in the evening; an attendance of forty or more; sessions of about four hours; the therapist and several auxiliary therapists. The application of the concept to the office setting involved consideration of his experiences and narrowing the focus to the adolescent and one generation in a regular office setting during regular hours for a forty-five-minute appointment with only one therapist.

### TECHNIQUE

The technique is applied when there is a sufficient amount of control and cooperation available from those in the patient's environment (parents or guardians) as well as a minimum of cooperation and self-control from the adolescent himself. The adolescent is asked to consider having a therapeutic club or a therapy group of his own. If interested, it is explained to him and his family, and if they agree, it is initiated. The therapist explains that many of the friends the patient has brought into the waiting room with him or whom he has discussed in sessions, as well as others so far unmentioned, may have data about him that might be helpful in furthering his therapy. These individuals are viewed as part of the patient's network of involvements with people who have some particular meaning to him. From a dynamic standpoint, they may bring some revelations and contributions to the therapy. The therapist may then tap into this field of potential information that may expand his understanding of, and be helpful to, the elucidation of the patient's dynamics and his progress in his therapy. The sessions are arranged so that the patient and his peers may manage as conveniently as possible to attend. The patient's other therapy sessions may be continued or decreased as the therapist deems necessary. One particular session is maintained for the peer network sessions on a weekly basis, but if the youngster wishes to have more than one network session during the week, that may also be arranged. The fee for the sessions is that charged for the individual sessions to the patient and no fee is charged to the peers.

The patient selects which, and how many, peers he wants to accompany him to each session by explaining to each of them his need for their presence, and their importance to him. He also explains that this is not therapy for them, that there is no confidentiality about what they say to each other but that confidentiality about what is said will be kept by the therapist. During the sessions he and his peers may speak about anything they wish. It is up to the patient to inform each of his peers about the time and place of the sessions and for which session he wants them.

When a peer first attends a session he is asked to identify himself and briefly discuss his relationship and attitudes to the patient. The basis for procedure is group process with the patient as the focal point. This allows the patient and his peers to interact, exchange information, bring up historical data or current problems, which the therapist notes, as well as the dynamics and transference aspects. The therapist then may comment or ask questions according to the needs of the situation during each session. The number of peer group sessions usually is not more than ten and has varied from one to ten, but it is left up to the patient to determine when to discontinue them. He may show up without any peers to have an individual session and subsequently have network sessions interspersed, instead of on a weekly basis.

## APPLICATIONS

The presence of peers in the waiting room with an adolescent may be used as an indication that this patient may have some unconscious wish to have a protector, helper, or benefactor in the sessions with him. If alert to this, the therapist may utilize it as a springboard to invite the companions into the sessions for a particular need of the patient, if the patient wishes to do this. In family therapy there is often, especially by youngsters, a fear of reprisal by some member of the family. This may cause some inhibition or deliberate withholding of material, as does fear of exposure or shifts in power or status which may develop in family therapy (Ackerman, 1958). The approach to a crisis in an adolescent's life has varied, from the consideration by Langsley and Kaplan (1968) using the twenty-four-hour-a-day team approach to avoid hospitalization to the use of partial hospitalization or hospitalization while continuing ongoing therapy.

I have found Office Network Therapy for the adolescent to be useful particularly in dealing with three types of conditions: 1) when a youngster is in a crisis that seems to be indicative of a developing disorganization, 2) when he is a suicide risk, and 3) when a youngster has massive resistances in therapy that are not responding to the usual efforts to deal with them. In assessing whether a youngster might be able to respond to Office Network Therapy, a risk is quite evident in all three categories. In the first here is a possibility of the youngster developing further disorganization and dysfunction, while in the second the threat to survival is obvious. In the third application there is the threat that the youngster may discontinue therapy prematurely or act out in other ways.

The office network arrangement utilizes the natural tendency for groups of the same sex to form in adolescence. It allows the youngster to deal with his difficulties in the presence of peer support in a friendly "living room" away from home.

Parental cooperation is necessary and has to be quite evident throughout the time the adolescent is in Office Network Therapy. The parents may see the therapist as a threat when he has a symbiotic relationship with the youngster. The goal is to not threaten the tie to the parent but to loosen that bind and strengthen the bonds to the peer group. If the parents are cooperative, the venture has a much greater chance of being successful.

Office Network Therapy seems to be most easily accepted by adolescents who have a strong need to conform to their own subculture; many adolescents have a great need for conformity and clinging at this point in their lives.

# Operant Conditioning Therapy
## *Virginia Binder*

### DEFINITION

The term "conditioning" conjures up, in the minds of laymen and some professionals as well, visions of *1984 or A Clockwork Orange* in which humans are manipulated like machines. A closer look at Operant Conditioning Therapy* reveals that it functions more like the good parent or good teacher in using consistent rewards and occasional punishment, clear instructions, patience, and concern to teach educational and socialization skills. The primary distinction between the operant therapist and a good parent is that the therapist can specify what he is doing and how it works. As a complete definition of Operant Conditioning Therapy requires more space than that allotted, let it suffice to say that the operant therapist can be identified by an attempt to apply principles derived from the learning laboratory, by a focus on behavior rather than underlying hypothetical constructs, and by an emphasis on results demonstrable through evaluation research.

### HISTORY

For centuries man has attempt to control the behavior of others through rewards (high salaries, praise, and official titles or honors) and punishment (fines, loss of a job, or even torture and imprisonment). Usually, however, these attempts have succeeded with some of the people and been ineffective with many others. Such attempts are generally haphazard, not tailored to the needs of the individual, and rely too heavily on the use of punishment. Only since Skinner's extensive laboratory work, which he began in the 1930s, has man systematically studied ways to maximize the effectiveness of reinforcement (reward and punishment). The potential for the therapeutic use of operant conditioning was recognized in the late 1940s and 1950s with a few demonstrations of limited behavior change in psychotic patients. The movement blossomed in the 1960s and 1970s, so that now most therapists are familiar with its uses, and about 10 percent

---

* May also be called (or makes up a large component of) behavior therapy, behavior modification, contingency management, and/or social learning.

of psychological therapists in a recent survey identified themselves as behavior therapists—an impressive figure when you consider the number of therapies described in this volume. The first practical uses involved operant experimental psychologists working on a one-to-one basis with severely disturbed individuals. Then considerable group work took place, and most recently the principles have been taught to parents, teachers, and even the clients themselves. Thus operant therapy constitutes an integral part of the contemporary community mental health movement.

## TECHNIQUE

The operant therapist enters into a four-stage process when working with a client.

1. *Identify and describe.* With the goal of therapy being a change in behavior rather than the understanding of unconscious conflict or emotional catharsis, it is critical to pinpoint the target behavior (the behavior to be changed) precisely. For example, instead of stating one of a schizophrenic's problems as a morbid preoccupation with death, the operant therapist might observe that all of his conversation centers on murders and funerals. Thus the therapist can tell when the patient talks less of funerals whereas he would be less able to detect a decrease in a morbid death preoccupation. Similarly, if parents claim their child is uncooperative, the therapist may ask them to translate that to a statement, such as the child never complies with requests until threatened with a spanking. This type of clear description makes it possible to determine what reinforcement contingencies in the environment are maintaining the behavior.

2. *Record.* Because of the therapist's interest in evaluation, baseline measures of the frequency of the target behavior are recorded, and the situational context in which the behavior occurs is noted. Thus, when specific consequences are introduced, the recording is continued and it becomes readily apparent whether any change is occurring within a reasonable time period.

3. *Initiate treatment.* To change behavior, one rewards those actions that should be encouraged and is careful not to reward those actions that are to be discouraged or eliminated. The basic rule is simple. However, implementation is more complex, as the therapist must select the most potent reward(s), determine how and when rewards should be given, and make provisions for the new behavior to occur and continue outside the treatment context. Furthermore, some behaviors are not even part of the client's repertoire, so they must be established before they can be rewarded. To do this, the therapist tries to "shape" the behavior by breaking it down into small steps and rewarding successive approximations of the desired behavior. For instance, when teaching a child to swim he can be taught to stroke, kick, float, and breathe properly before combining the steps. Or the desired behavior can be modeled so that the client can copy it to obtain the reward.

One stereotype of the operant therapist is that he does not talk to the client and may spend weeks shaping a behavior that the client could perform immediately if only requested to do so. This is not the case. To the extent that the client is able, he can enter into active collaboration with the therapist in determining treatment goals and the means of achieving them.

4. *Evaluate.* To decide whether the treatment has been effective, the frequency of the behavior during and after treatment is compared with the frequency during the

baseline period. If there has been a change in the desired direction, the therapist may then want to withdraw and reintroduce the treatment to rule out the possibility that some other event has caused the change. It should be noted that the effectiveness of the treatment is determined by inspecting the data—not by the subjective opin-ions of the therapist and/or client.

## APPLICATIONS

Operant treatment methods have been used with a wide range of client problems. On one hand, severely disturbed individuals can be helped: autistic children have been taught language, retarded children have been taught self-help skills, and chronic psychotics have been returned to the community. On the other hand are those with milder problems: weight loss and smoking reduction have been common target behaviors.

Two broad applications of Operant Conditioning Therapy are the token economy in educational and mental health settings and contingency contracting. In a token economy, target behaviors are determined for a group of individuals who receive points or tokens when they perform the desired behaviors. The points or tokens are then redeemable for a wide range of commodities. The tokens can be seen as analogous to a paycheck. In contingency contracting, two or more individuals specify behaviors they would like the other(s) to change and which rewards they would be willing to give in exchange for the changes. This direct communication of needs can then be formalized in a contract. Such a procedure has often been adapted by couples and families experiencing conflict, and has recently been shown to be effective in families having a delinquent child.

# Organic Process Therapy

## Dan Miller

## DEFINITION

Organic Process Therapy is an intense feeling therapy integrating the separate energies of contemporary (primal, gestalt, encounter) and traditional (Freudian, Reichian) forms of therapy into a single energy stream. It states that the body is a warehouse containing within itself all the real and symbolic events and personalities experienced in the past with their emotional connections to fear, anger, love, joy, and pain.

It advocates that the healthy part of the organism is always striving to regain the state of somatopsychological homeostasis (organic unity of body, feeling, mind, and spirit) in which we were born, and which had been fractured by life experiences. For healing, self-fulfillment, and the sense of well-being to occur it is essential to recapture this unified state. To unify the Somatopsyche, people are urged to feel what is happening in their bodies. A pain, a feeling of sickness, or a headache can be the signs of a long-suppressed emotion trying to crash through the defense barrier. "Feel your body," "Let your body talk to your mind," "Trust your body!" are expressions that recur constantly. The participant who trusts his body during the course of an "organic" session finds that it can lead him down a new path toward hidden feeling, toward birth, and beyond birth, to the transpersonal and creativity. Trusting your body ultimately leads to self-healing.

Connections are established within the Somatopsyche by reaching the Organic Self, which is the pivot of organismic intelligence in Organic Process. The Organic Self lies buried in the interface of body and mind. Oversimplified, it is the sum of the basic, original feeling of true Self. During the course of life's traumas there are accumulations of bioneurotic blocks underneath which the Organic Self becomes encapsulated to the extent that we lose conscious awareness of its existence. However, it is the natural tendency of the body/feeing/mind/spirit (the Somatopsyche) to strive ceaselessly for self-expression and for liberation from the chains of infantile repression.

When the homeostasis of the person is dangerously disturbed the Organic Self provides the person with messages that may become transformed into dream images, physical and emotional stress in illness, or disturbed interpersonal relationships.

## HISTORY

Organic Process Therapy was developed by myself (Dan Miller) as a synthesis of my experience and thoughts during my practice and research as a psychologist over eighteen years. My concepts retain Freud's guiding theme that the combination of repressed infantile emotions and defense systems erected by the individual in order to survive in hostile, anxiety-arousing environmental conditions creates many neurotic formulae for living. To this was added concepts from Wilhelm Reich regarding body armor and muscular and sexual withholding of impulses, while studies in the physiology of emotions in schizophrenia (Hoskins), and normative physiological functioning, (Cannon, Selye, Goldstein, Lehninger) provided the physiological focus.

My views regarding society's contributions to neurosis come from Fromm, Sullivan, and Reisman and were crucibles in the development of a social matrix of understanding, while the applications of techniques received the most impetus from gestalt, encounter, psychodrama, and primal therapy.

## TECHNIQUE

By gradually opening a person's defenses and fixations through deep breathing, body feeling, sound and movement, trauma, which were initiated as early as birth and perhaps before, are recovered and the real emotions of the Authentic Self are felt. Changes that take place are durable and focused rather than haphazard and temporary, because it is a participatory therapy rather than one that is dependent on an expert's authority. The competence of the therapist enables him to work with the level of motivation and defense brought into it by the participant. He attempts to make the patient aware and responsible for his defenses rather than attempting to remove them by attacking the ego. The participant is not left infantilized with a heavy charge of unintegrated emotional material. It is therefore an extremely effective way of dealing with the potentially dangerous outcome that sometimes follows from the loss of defenses in deep regression therapies.

Activation of primals (regression and catharsis of childhood trauma) in Organic Process Therapy can take place in several different ways: through workshops lasting a weekend to three weeks, a three-week individual intensive, or single individual sessions. Workshops provide a mixture of regressive experiences and "here-and-now" encounters. The combination helps participants establish connections between past and present, separating and distinguishing between experiences that belong to the past and what is relevant for daily life. This occurs particularly effectively in group interactions, when a very emotional encounter with another person triggers a particularly deep regression. A participant, through this flow of feelings, discovers his formerly blocked emotion in the encounter, dissolves it in the regression part of the session, and returns to interact with new awareness, a new sense of his responsibility for himself, and fresh energy for his life.

## APPLICATIONS

The therapy works best for persons who are willing to take up an exploration of dimensions of their life experience as a whole, taking risks to uncover emotions they thought were closed to them. The age range of persons most frequently seeking it out are in their early twenties to late fifties, couples as well as individuals. Some successful exploration has been done with teen-agers, but they are carefully screened. There has been no serious attempt to use it in the psychoses, but instances of treatment with borderline and ambulatory schizophrenics have shown some marginal changes. It is counter-indicated when severe acting out occurs in group and individual sessions with the person showing little ego strength to cope responsibly with the reality of the situation.

At present there are centers and therapists practicing Organic Process Therapy in Livingston Manor, New York; Middletown, New Jersey; Pittsburgh, Pennsylvania; and Washington, D.C.

# Medical Orgonomy

*Elsworth F. Baker*

## DEFINITION

Orgonomy is the science of the functional laws of cosmic orgone energy that comprises all natural phenomena, from living things to the universe itself. Medical Orgonomy is the part that deals with the functioning of man and the illnesses he suffers from.

## HISTORY

This science was developed by Wilhelm Reich, M.D., who was born in Galicia, a part of the Austro-Hungarian Empire, on March 24, 1897, and who died in 1957. Reich was Freud's most important pupil and, when he was still in his twenties, had already made many important discoveries in the understanding and treatment of the neuroses. He insisted that Medical Orgonomy was the logical extension of Freud's clinical findings. For a long time Reich considered this work to be within the realm of psychoanalysis even after Freud, who at first admired Reich's ability and fresh ideas, could follow him no further and became upset over some of his findings and theories. Reich's technique became more active than the usual Freudian psychoanalysis, emphasizing and keeping in the forefront the negative transference and also describing the attitudes and expressions of the patient rather than using the typical analytic free association. He could thus mobilize more emotional response and produce faster cures. He called his technique Character Analysis, since he was analyzing character rather than dealing with symptoms.

Studying patients who were cured and those who were not successfully treated, he found consistently that those who recovered had developed a satisfactory sexual life while the failures remained unsatisfied sexually or quickly reverted to their previous unsatisfying sexual life. He postulated that to cure a patient, libido stasis must be overcome and further prevented by adequate sexual outlet. Reich therefore set about to ascertain just what was an adequate sexual outlet. He found that sexual activity in itself did not guarantee this but gratification in the sexual act did. Reich called the capacity for gratification "orgastic potency." Here the act ended with total convulsions of the body followed by complete relaxation and a tender, grateful attitude toward the partner. This meant that the libido must be more than a psychic concept, as Freud postulated; it must be a real energy. Reich called it "orgone energy," from organism. It is built up in the organism by the intake of food, fluid, and air and is also absorbed directly through the skin. It is discharged by activity, excretion, emotional expression, the process of thinking, and by conversion into body heat that radiates to the environment. Also it is used up in growth. In the usual course of events, more energy is built up than is discharged. Thus, to maintain a stable energy level, excess energy must be discharged at more or less regular intervals. This is the function of the orgastic convulsion. This must not be confused with what is popularly called "an orgasm," meaning that the man has had an ejaculation and the woman a clitoral climax. These produce only incomplete satisfaction. Reich determined that a person who develops truly adequate sexual release cannot maintain a neurosis. Neuroses exist only on repressed excess energy or stasis. Reich thus developed a concept of health based on energy metabolism of charge and discharge which he called "sex economy."

He noted, however, that in our society the child is not permitted to function naturally. Starting from birth, the environment that greets the newborn is mostly unfriendly; it is cold compared to the warm uterus. The baby is treated roughly, it is separated from the mother whom it continues to need for warmth and contact, placed on regimented feedings, subjected to early toilet training, and blocked from any sexual pleasure. The barrage of forbidden activities require the child to hold back his feelings and expressions, which is accomplished by holding his breath and tightening the muscles of his body until finally he goes through life with restricted breathing and a rigid body. Reich called this the "armor." The permissive upbringing popular in the last decade or two amounts to parental abdication of any role in guiding or disciplining and produces intense anxiety in the child; it can result in even more damage than when inhibition is inflicted.

The armor binds energy, removing it from normal functioning. It interferes with the free flow of energy through the organism and especially to the pelvis and genitals so that it cannot be discharged adequately, if at all, through sexual activity. This is the somatic side of repression. In this Reich disagreed with Freud. Reich felt that society was wrong in imposing these restrictions on the individual, believing him to be capable of self-regulation if allowed to grow up naturally, while Freud felt the restrictions were necessary to avoid a chaotic society. However, with such restrictions the individual becomes erectively impotent, premature, anesthetic, or otherwise lacking full sexual pleasure. Reich termed this "orgastic impotence" and found that the majority of both male and female individuals suffered from this condition. Energy, therefore, continues to build up, producing stasis and eventually overflows in the form of neurotic symptoms.

Reich began working on the muscular armor as well as on the character. He called this "character analytic vegetotherapy." It was even more effective than character analysis alone. This technique produced many vegetative reactions in the organism, such as blanching of the skin, sweating, pallor, blushing, etc., manifestations of the vegetative nervous system that was being affected in therapy. Investigation led to his formulation of the basic antithesis of vegetative functioning. Excitation of the sympathetic nervous system causes muscle contraction, felt as anxiety, while excitation of the parasympathetic nervous system produces expansion which is felt as pleasure. To overcome the contraction, which causes the armor, anxiety has to be faced and overcome.

As emotions eventually came to mean the manifestations of a tangible bio-energy and character as specific blockings of that flow of energy, Reich found that it was possible to change character directly by freeing bio-energy rather than indirectly through the use of psychological techniques. The latter was not ignored, but its importance depended on the particular case. He now called his technique "medical orgone therapy."

Through reactions of the body during the process of dissolving the armor, Reich discovered that the body was functionally divided into seven muscular segments, each of which reacted as a unit and was to a certain degree independent of the other segments. The seven segments are the ocular, oral, cervical, thoracic, diaphragmatic, abdominal, and pelvic. They are usually freed in that order except that the chest is most often mobilized first so that it can be used to build up energy in the organism and provide additional inner push to help in both revealing and removing other blocks. Any one segment may fail to respond completely until further segments are freed.

## TECHNIQUE

The principle of therapy is quite simple, merely to remove the restrictions to the free flow of energy through the body and restore normal functioning. In other words, to remove the armor. In practice it may be extremely difficult and complex. There are three avenues of approach, the importance of each depending on the individual case, although all three are necessary tools in every case. They are:

1. Breathing, which builds up energy and exerts an inner push on the blocks. It may overcome lesser holding and does help reveal and overcome more severe blocking. The patient is asked to breathe fully without forcing and allow himself to develop a rhythm that soon becomes easier and freer.

2. Directly attacking the spastic muscles to free the contraction. The contraction of the skeletal muscles can be worked on directly, the organs and tissues only indirectly. To mobilize the contracted muscles, the therapist must first increase the contraction to a point that cannot be maintained. This is done by direct pressure on the muscle by the thumb or by otherwise irritating it. Of course the muscle will only contract down again unless the emotion (or idea) that is being held back is released and expressed. For

this reason groups of muscles that form a functional unit in holding back emotions are worked on together.

3. Maintaining the cooperation of the patient by bringing into the open and over-coming his resistances to therapy and/or the therapist. This last is extremely important because the patient will in every way endeavor to maintain his immobility and try desperately not to reveal himself. Behind this is intense fear of expansion and movement. When the patient begins to feel his own restrictions and gains sufficient contact with his organism so that he knows that he is holding back and why, he can be very helpful in his therapy. His lack of contact is one of the most difficult problems to overcome. It must be pointed out so that the patient is made aware of it.

Anxiety is the basis for repression and is behind all contraction. The organism is always trying to control anxiety and cure is effected by forcing the patient to tolerate his anxiety and express his forbidden feelings. The most important emotion to elicit is rage, and until this is released he cannot experience the softer feelings of love and longing.

The therapist works from the head down, removing the layers of armoring from superficial to deep. There are three basic layers in every armored individual: 1) the social facade; 2) the secondary or great middle layer where the sum of all the repressions has built up, resulting in destructive forces such as rage, hate, contempt, spite, etc. There are usually many subsidiary layers; 3) the healthy core that expresses itself when all blocking has been removed.

In development the organism is subjected to repeated restrictions of its natural and even secondary functioning. Each prohibition becomes part of the character through fear of punishment or rejection and is retained in the armor. There is an increase in inner tension that produces harshness and expresses itself as hate. This must again be repressed so only modified expressions, such as contempt or disgust, are allowed to come out.

The second or great middle layer is usually very complex, many sublayers pile one on another until a social adjustment has been reached. This is the social facade. This may be comparatively stable or unstable, depending on the effectiveness of the defenses in the middle layer and the degree of satisfaction the organism can still attain. The social facade contains one or more basic character traits that cause the patient to react the same way to each problem he meets. It becomes the main character defense. Reich called it the "red thread." It must be recognized and understood to properly evaluate the patient. The basic character trait is never dissolved but remains always an integral part of the personality although it may be modified. It may be socially acceptable, such as modesty or reserve, or socially unacceptable, such as dishonesty, cunning, or cheating.

The three layers are dealt with in each segment as they are mobilized until the final core of unitary vegetative functioning is reached. The depth of the layer on which one is working is recognized by the extent to which the organism is involved in the response, and the ability of the patient to function. If the first four segments are free, one is always working at a deep layer.

When one reaches the pelvis, which is always freed last, the main danger in therapy presents itself. If the pelvis is freed early, as is done in some body-oriented therapies, the individual cannot handle the sexual impulse and either confusion and disintegration follow or else earlier problems, such as sadistic impulses, are carried into the sexual life. One exception is with depressives, where the low energy and great inhibition make early freeing of the pelvis safe. Freeing the pelvis is called the end phase of therapy. It is especially dangerous if the main block has not been dissolved. The end phase begins with the full flow of energy into the pelvis and the totality of the organism begins to function. The danger is in the sudden rise in energy level. Previously the person functioned by binding energy, and since now he no longer can, he may react dangerously to the high level of energy.

At first the patient feels he is right back where he started. Symptoms reappear, sometimes stronger than before. One source of danger is a tenacious block that shows where the danger will occur in the end phase. If the block is in the diaphragm, for example, somatic symptoms and collapse must be watched for. The more tenacious the block, the more trouble can be expected. The main block plus orgasm anxiety that occurs at the end of the end phase may make the situation insoluble. Suicide, psychosis, even murder or other criminal behavior may occur. Organic symptoms may also appear and require surgery, such as appendicitis, ovarian cyst, fibroids, and even cancer may develop. The organism must develop tolerance to this new functioning and terror give way to pleasure in the accomplished freedom. The final problem is to structuralize the patient's health. He is kept under observation and assisted until he is secure against regressing. This may take one or two years.

Orgastic potency is always the goal but cannot be attained in most cases. However, the majority will attain a satisfactory degree of health and functioning with the overcoming of all major symptoms. Where stasis can be prevented or overcome and the environment adjusted satisfactorily one can expect the patient to continue to improve for years after therapy has been discontinued.

## APPLICATION

Orgonomic technique is less dependent than most therapies on verbal communication from the patient and is very effective in attacking the neurotic structure. Thus, it has a very wide application. Besides the usual neuroses, it is especially effective in treating schizophrenia, epilepsy, and the somatic biopathies, such as asthma, gastric ulcer, hypertension, spastic colitis, and many types of headache. However, not every case can be treated and a few can only be made worse. It is important to recognize these cases early and discontinue therapy.

---

# Paraverbal Therapy

### *Evelyn Phillips Heimlich*

## DEFINITION

Paraverbal Therapy is a term applied to a method of observation, diagnosis, and treatment. It uses a variety of expressive media that are on a common level with words. This provides many alternative channels to establish both verbal and nonverbal communication. The method employs a multisensory approach in the treatment of disturbed patients (children and adults) who cannot be reached by traditional discursive means or conventional adjunctive therapies, such as art, music, or dance therapies. Such inaccessible patients require treatment that decreases maladaptive behavior while maintaining a therapeutic relationship.

Paraverbal Therapy, based on psychiatric principles, uses alternate means of communication to achieve therapeutic goals. This multisensory approach can be used when necessary, as a distance, or as a bridge between patient and therapist. It is achieved through improvisational and nontraditional techniques. Media are not used for the purpose of mere creative expression, but as metaphoric symbols for particular behavior.

Paraverbal communication consists of the following:

1. Statements in the form of non-verbal or verbal dialogues
2. Speech cadences
3. Unconventional use of body movement as well as unconventional use of music components (rhythm, tempo, accent, pitch)
4. Improvised or familiar melodies and lyrics (sometimes used projectively)
5. Projective use of psychomotor maneuvers, mime, dramatizations, and art.

Inherent to Paraverbal Therapy are improvisational techniques. These provide patients (in both group and individual treatment), with needed concrete experience in the areas of sensory-motor skills, object relations, and cognitive enhancement. This is done through the use of the patient's intact and preferred means of communication—whether it be auditory, visual, kinesthetic, or tactile. Basic to the improvisation used in Paraverbal Therapy is the fact that a variety of modalities can be used interchangeably as needed, in swift succession. These changes are instituted in response to the ease and shared pleasure of the therapist and patient. This is helpful in building the trust so difficult to achieve with inaccessible patients. Effective behavioral change can only occur if the strategies evolve from an assessment and observation of the patient's presenting emotional status. The paraverbal method affords the therapist, as participant-observer, many choices of communicative channels that make him less threatening to the patient. The metaphoric expression of material, through many channels, allows them safe symbolic representation of problems, and the development of the therapeutic relationship. This is crucial in reaching inaccessible patients, with numerous shifting defenses. On this account, preconceived notions of which modality is to be used in a session are contra-indicated.

Paraverbal techniques, through their communicative channels, provide interaction on a range of levels. Synchronous and reciprocal response to strategies concretely reveal a measure of the patient's state of development to the therapist.

## HISTORY

Paraverbal Therapy had its inception at two institutions where I taught. One was an experimental elementary and junior high school. There I used body movement, music, art, and drama as vehicles for childhood expression and development. The other was Sarah Lawrence College, where I taught student teachers the techniques of using the arts for early childhood development. While observing my demonstrations with the children at the college nursery, staff members, including Dr. Lois Gardner Murphy, as well as the school doctor, Dr. Benjamin Spock, were impressed with the therapeutic effect of my work with special children. They suggested that I embark on a didactic psychoanalytic course in order to utilize my techniques for therapeutic purposes.

I did this and then obtained a position at Edenwald School for Retarded and Disturbed Children, where I did therapeutic work with children who had communication difficulties. Results were satisfactory, but I felt the need for additional training so that I could become more specific in my therapy. I then went for further training to N.Y. State Psychiatric Institute. Under the supervision of Dr. H. D. Dunton, I treated and researched five hundred cases of inaccessible and disturbed children. The results of this work led to the formulation of the concepts of Paraverbal Therapy. For help in the development of these concepts, as well as for the creation of the name "Paraverbal Therapy" itself, I am deeply indebted to Dr. Sydney G. Margolin, of the University of Colorado Medical Center.

## TECHNIQUE

Intimacy and trust are basic to each session. To achieve intimacy, the therapist positions himself as close as feasible to the patient(s). Techniques for achieving trust are noted throughout the following description.

The therapist uses a variety of instruments to arouse curiosity, orient patients, as well as to command and expand attention. Used are bongos, tambourine, hand drum, floor drum, castanets, autoharp, guitar, a variety of bells. In addition, there may be an easel and chalk, jump ropes, and balls of various sizes. The patient is encouraged to select the instrument of his choice, as a first step in establishing trust and an atmosphere of acceptance.

Paraverbal Therapy has proven useful as a technique for communication with children having the following diagnoses:

1) Elective mutism, hyperkinesis
2) School phobia
3) Schizophrenia
4) Gilles de la Torrette syndrome
5) Learning difficulties
6) Autism
7) Acting-out behavior
8) Depression
9) Minimal brain damage
10) Blindism

The children varied in age from three to sixteen years. They were seen and treated in one-to-one sessions, in mother-child dyads, on occasion with their families, and in group sessions. From a cultural point of view, the technique is useful not only with children from average American families, but as a bridge to children and parents from low-income minority groups.

Their communication needs stem partially from deprivation as well as cultural differences.

While Paraverbal Therapy can be an enriching therapeutic experience for any disturbed child, it is not a treatment of choice for those patients who can make use of traditional therapeutic approaches.

Neutral nonverbal dialogue begins in one of the following ways: the patient improvises (at random) a simple rhythmic pattern, which the therapist immediately imitates four or more times, varying expression with loud, soft, fast, slow, etc, or the therapist may initiate the dialogue by tapping out the syllables of the patient's name: *JENN I FER*. The patient is encouraged to imitate on his instrument. (For mature patients, popular names of cars, foods, TV programs, etc., are substituted.) The therapist then suggests "Let's tap together."

The therapist constantly needs to reappraise the response of the patient. It is of the essence that the therapist observe and then administer just the amount and kind of stimuli needed to maintain the communication basic for treatment. (There are some patients who can utilize only a limited amount of ongoing stimulation from any *one* specific communication channel.)

The sound of the unusual auditory stimuli coming from the tapped instruments orients the patient and commands attention. It organizes, helps establish identity, and gives recognition as well.

If attention wanders, the therapist then introduces a change in body posture so communication can continue. Changes may vary from sitting to standing, to rhythmic walking, hopping, clapping, and rhythmic chalking to music.

The next technique, improvisation, can be used to move the patient into more intimate communication. Improvisatory use of lyrics, melodies, mime, and dramatization, can provide cognitive, as well as projective, material.

With these paraverbal techniques, therapists and patients can go from the neutral phase of drum tapping, to the more personal phase of body movement, to the still more personal phase of improvisation. For example, in the use of the common folk song "Nobody Knows the Trouble I've Seen," the therapist and patient can deal projectively with such themes of loneliness, sadness, alienation— or the cognitive aspects of *up* and *down* ("Sometimes I'm up and sometimes I'm down").

Participation, reciprocity, flexibility, and resourcefulness are essential aspects of the therapeutic structure.

# Partnership Therapy

*Ben C. Finney and Norma Crockett*

## DEFINITION

Partnership Therapy is the sharing of the same therapist and therapy session by two or three clients who did not have a prior relationship. It is similar to group therapy in that it puts strangers together to develop relationships that become a part of the therapy, but it differs in that with only two or three clients there is more time for each person and more relating in a one-to-one way with the therapist.

## HISTORY

Partnership Therapy arose out of a wish to extend the duration of the therapy experience beyond the maximum of ten sessions, which the staff of the Counseling Center at San Jose State University had agreed upon. Staff member Finney had a group that had dwindled down to two members and he noted the increased intimacy and psychological movement between members. This provided the idea for deliberately setting up a group of two—a partnership. Since each client would use only half of the whole hour session, the number of sessions could be doubled. When tried, it was found that rather than diluting the therapy experience, the shared time and interaction between the partners enriched it. Another staff member, Crockett, tried it and found it worked well for her. A number of therapists have used it and found it to be productive, giving some of the advantages of client interaction that group therapy provides and yet retaining the more focused client-therapist interaction of individual sessions.

## TECHNIQUE

In the selection of partners, clients are chosen who are reasonably similar in age and value systems, although it has been found that different people can develop a trusting and productive relationship. Usually the idea of partnership sessions are introduced after the therapist and client have met together for a session. The advantages and disadvantages of the structure are explained and the clients are assured that they can ask for individual sessions or terminate the partnership if they wish. Since one or other of the partnership usually misses a session or so, the need for individual sessions does not need explicit arrangement.

Experience with this approach indicates that two and even three partners are able to develop mutual trust and intimacy rather quickly and talk about personal topics more rapidly than in group therapy. With only two or three clients, each has time to talk adequately about his personal concerns and feelings, and is usually able to discuss private material as readily and deeply as in individual sessions. The partners take turns talking to the therapist, who controls how long each talks, shifting back and forth. He may also encourage the partners to interact with each other as they would in a group. All the familiar therapeutic processes occur in much the usual way, and the process does not appear to be attenuated but has the added dimension of a shared experience.

The advantages of the partnership technique are:

1. When a client is able to risk the exposure of some of his most sensitive and shameful feelings with a peer and finds they are accepted, he has made a step toward accepting these feelings within himself and in being able to share himself more openly in other relationships.

2. The feelings of one client will bring out similar feelings in the other— feelings he may have been overlooking or minimizing.

3. The pace allows a client to stop and digest what he has just said or discovered— while his partner talks.

4. The client has the opportunity to test out a new behavior with a peer—e.g., saying how he feels toward another person in a protected situation.

5. The therapist can focus on the interaction between the clients and help them see how they interact and affect others.

6. When the amount of therapy time is limited, it makes it possible to extend the number of hours. When the waiting list gets too long, more clients can be seen. In private practice clients who can not afford full fees can handle a split fee with a partner.

7. When a therapist is not able to make an appointment, the partners can work together. Sometimes partners who would like more frequent times or therapy over a longer duration are trained to work together with a therapist. The therapist gets them to interact more in the therapy hour and plays an increasingly less active role, then meets with them every other time and finally at infrequent checkup sessions. This system of working alone is the basis of Harvey Jackins's successful system of Co-counseling (Jackins, 1965).

The disadvantages are:

1. Strong negative transferences may develop between partners (this is when one partner shifts negative feelings about a significant person in his past to the other partner). Usually these can be worked through, but sometimes a partnership has tobe dissolved.

2. Sensitive material may be withheld, such as embarrassing sexual thoughts.

3. A special problem exists in structuring contacts between partners outside these ssions, especially opposite-sexed partners. The hazards and difficulties are pointed out, and an agreement reached that all contact will be open to inspection during the therapy hour. However, sometimes emotional attachments do arise and then the therapy becomes couple therapy, or may even need to be dissolved so the partners can talk about their feelings toward each other in a neutral setting.

## APPLICATIONS

Partnership Therapy seems to be applicable to most therapy styles, except where the therapist feels that developing an intense client-therapist transference relationship is important. Similarly, a wide variety of clients can be handled in this structure, probably as wide as the range of clients treated in group sessions. Both individual and group therapy have particular advantages, and partnership combines the advantages of both. Between the one person of individual therapy and the six to fifteen of group, there are a number of combinations and the two or three of partnership adds another modality to psychotherapy.

# Paradigmatic Psychotherapy
### *Renatus Hartogs*

## DEFINITION

In Paradigmatic Psychotherapy, which is psychoanalytically based, the therapist presents himself to the patient as a model for identification and introjection ("setting forth an example"). He adopts the roles of the significant personalities in the past and present life of the patient, with their varied viewpoints and temperaments, in order to free the patient from being controlled by disabling memories and regressive habits. In this fashion, the therapist permits the patient to correct defective precepts of reality and at the same time demonstrates to the patient those ego functions that the patient does not possess or misuses. He thus provides the patient with the much-needed opportunity to learn to cope with crucial and stressful life situations. To achieve this purpose, the therapist acts as a paradigm of the world, in which the patient must learn to move and to survive.

## HISTORY

Marie Coleman Nelson, in collaboration with social scientist and historian Benjamin Nelson, originated and developed the technique known as "Paradigmatic Psychotherapy." The first complete presentation of her method appeared in the journal *Psychoanalysis* (Vol. 5, No. 3, 1957) under the title "Paradigmatic Psychotherapy in Borderline Treatment," co-authored by Benjamin Nelson. This approach was originally designed to provide the therapist with a new, effective procedure for overcoming stalemates encountered when the classical approach of psychoanalytical interpretation proved to be inadequate in the treatment of borderline cases. One year before this article, Mrs. Coleman Nelson reported her early experiments in a paper entitled "Externalization of the Toxic Introject" *(Psychoanalytic Review,* Vol. 43, No. 2, 1956). Her work and scientific contributions led to the establishment of the Paradigmatic Behavior Studies Seminar in New York, devoted to research in strategically selected types of role playing and model functioning as well as the deliberate reprojection of the patient's pathological and healthy motivation.

## TECHNIQUE

Paradigmatic Psychotherapy is designed to provide the patient with an interpersonal experience that reveals to him his misperceptions of inner and outer reality. This goal is achieved through the application of any of the following approaches:

1. *Analysis of resistances.* By active mirroring (either imitative or exaggerated joining of resistance); by duplicating reported interpersonal experience.

2. *Analysis of introjects and images.* By assuming the role of the self-image (patient's idealized, hated or unconscious self); by assuming the role of the introject (patient's idealized, toxic, or unconscious introject); by assuming the role of a "stranger" (alien, uncomprehending, distant).

56. *Analysis of fantasies and transference.* By entering into ongoing fantasy; by following the patient's own recommendations of procedures for the analyst to follow ("self-dosing"); by adopting any of the methods listed under resistances and introjects.

Thus, through presenting the patient with paradigms, he is systematically exposed to an active form of mirroring, permitting him a direct recognition of his projections (his attributing his own behavior, attitudes, etc., to someone else) and resistances, their nature and origin, and allowing him to externalize them and to repudiate all toxic introjects. This technique leads to the development of a degree of ego-strength, which ultimately makes paradigmatic tactics superfluous and permits the therapist to conduct the final phase of the treatment in a more classical fashion.

## APPLICATIONS

While originally designed primarily for the treatment of borderline patients, this method and procedure has been sufficiently developed to be used for the therapeutic management of all adult as well as adolescent patients, in whom the toxic introjects have created overwhelming anxiety, hostility, and helplessness and have led to the development of paralyzing misperceptions, parataxic distortions, compulsive indecision, and faulty reality testing.

# Past Lives Therapy
## *Morris Netherton and Nancy Shiffrin*

### DEFINITION

Past Lives Therapy is a technique for using reincarnation in psychotherapy. It brings past lives into alignment so that the individual lives appropriately in the present. Other therapies assume that the past is alive in a troubled present in the form of early childhood trauma. Past Lives Therapy differs only as to how far back we are willing to go—to the dawn of civilization.

### HISTORY

Reincarnation, the idea that the soul is reborn over and over into different bodies, is not new. Two of the world's oldest religions, Hinduism and Buddhism, assume reincarnation as fact. Isolated sects of other religions, e.g., the Druze, a Muslim sect, and the Jewish Kabbala, also assume its validity. Reincarnation was part of Christian theology until the reign of Justinian and Theodora. Since that time it has existed in a kind of mystical underground in the Western World, though the American Transcendentalists believed in it. In Past Lives Therapy, Oriental thought joins mainstream Western psychology to provide an effective way of dealing with this life's pain.

### TECHNIQUE

The therapy works by tracing self-destructive patterns through several lives. Using the presenting material in a given session as a starting point, the client builds up a picture of the past life. The therapist focuses the client's attention so that he actually reexperiences the traumatic events. Intellectual discussion is discouraged at this point.

Four things have to happen in the sessions for the inappropriate behavior to be erased. The phrase that fixes the inappropriate behavior must be repeated until intensity and attachment are gone. Traumatic deaths must be fully reexperienced along with the events that lead up to them.

The events of any given past life must be placed in chronological order. In the initial session they may seem muddled and fantastical to the client. It is important to keep going over them until the client is clear about the order in which they happened. This lends some reality to the situation.

A journey through the prenatal and birth of the current life is vital to the therapy's success. Phrases spoken by the mother and by those around her affect the fetus, determining which past lives will affect this one. Without this journey through the prenatal, the session is useless, as the traumatic past lives will continue to dominate the client's actions.

The working through of the birth trauma has an additional benefit. At birth the individual learns to handle stress. The way the mother handles that very painful situation becomes the individual's models for life. Once a person experiences this, and separates his actions from his mother's, he finds he's handling the problems of everyday life better than ever.

A case example illustrates this. A client, whom we will call Elaine, delivered a child by Caesarean section then refused her husband sex for eleven years. "He's too big for me," was her complaint. With that phrase as her starting point, Elaine relived many deaths by rape, and a number of deaths during pregnancy. In the incident that seemed to be the cornerstone of her problem, she found herself in medieval England. She was fourteen and pregnant by an important nobleman who needed an heir, through she was not married to him.

At that time deliveries were a public matter. At a certain point it seemed clear to the midwife that it was necessary to choose between mother and baby. Without a second thought the nobleman chose the baby's life over the mother's. Elaine died hearing the words, "He's too big for her." During the prenatal of this life we found Elaine's mother thinking, about her father, "He's too big for me." During birth, we found the doctor saying (of Elaine, to her mother) "She's too big for you." All of this worked together to ensure that the phrase "He's too big for me" would dominate Elaine's adult sex life.

## APPLICATIONS

Past Lives Therapy is effective with numerous behavioral and psychosomatic difficulties, including marital and sex problems, childhood and adolescent difficulties, migraines, incipient ulcers, drug and alcoholism abuse. It cannot repair tissue damage. It can, however, give people with such physical problems as cancer, nephritis, and epilepsy a better understanding of their conditions, thus enabling them to cooperate with medical treatment.

# Pastoral Counseling

*Edgar N. Jackson*

## DEFINITION

Pastoral Counseling is a specialization engaged in by clergymen who have had special training in counseling under supervision. Because most of the training has been in clinical settings, the practice is usually marked by some of the characteristics of clinical relationships. That is, Pastoral Counseling is usually done in a counseling room on a one-to-one basis at appointed times and with at least minimal objectives concerning desired psychological movement.

## HISTORY

Religious guides and counselors have from ancient times worked with troubled people to help them meet the problems of life. Originally, the main objective was to aid in resolving moral and spiritual problems and the main interest of the counselor was in this area of inner stress or outer behavior. Traditionally, the priest or pastor used the authority invested in him to manipulate people toward generally accepted codes of morals or patterns of religious practice.

In recent years there has been modification of the practice of Pastoral Counseling. The recent history of the behavioral sciences, particularly psychology, has thrown light on the casual factors that lie behind observed behavior. This has led to a reassessment of the pastor's role in working with people. Instead of the authoritative and manipulative role, the counselor has been increasingly concerned with antecedents of behavior in the family history and the personal history of the coun-selee. This has led to specialized training, usually in a hospital or other institutional setting. Much of the instruction has been from persons with extensive psychological training but limited religious insight and understanding. This has led to a change in the focus of Pastoral Counseling. It has become increasingly clinical in its stance and the basic concerns of religion as it has been traditionally understood have been held in abeyance.

## TECHNIQUE

The recent history of Pastoral Counseling has had a major impact on the techniques employed. Many of those who have been certified in clinical pastoral education find that their special skills seem to be out of place in the parish context. They tend, therefore, to seek employment in institutional settings, where the limited, protected, and authoritative role of the clinical counselor is preserved. Much Pastoral Counseling is done in hospitals, penal institutions, homes for the handicapped, and on college campuses. However, in more recent years, there have been numerous cooperative ventures among churches to set up community counseling centers that have many of the characteristics of mental health clinics. People aware of needs make appointments and see a counselor for their appointed hour. The length of the relationship may vary with the nature of the problem and the method of intervention used by the counselor.

## APPLICATIONS

Probably the major problems that appear at the pastoral counselor's office have to do with interpersonal relationships, usually spouses or child-parent relationships with an increasing number of concerns of how to manage the aging. Depressions seem to lead the list of emotional problems. Often the first contact concerning a social problem is made with a pastoral counselor, who may refer the client to the appropriate social service agency. In specialized settings, the setting tends to determine the role of the counselor. The hospital chaplain focuses on identity, anxiety, problems of suffering, and finding a meaning for the experience of pain and anxiety. The penal institution tends to center on the problems of stress in a restricted and hostile environment. The mental hospital offers the opportunity to try to achieve relationships where they have been shattered by personal tragedy or social accident. Pastors with special training who remain in the community have a broader range of opportunity to work with people.

Training in Pastoral Counseling is carried on under qualified supervisors in hundreds of hospitals and other training centers throughout the country. Thousands of pastors have had this form of supervised clinical education for periods usually ranging from three months to two years. They may represent the first line of defense against mental and emotional illness not only because of their training in diagnosis and emergency therapy but also because they have developed skills in how to refer, and to whom referral may be wisely made.

# Pharmacotherapy

## Andrew E. Slaby

### DEFINITION

Pharmacotherapy is defined as the treatment of disease by the use of drugs. The term "psychopharmacotherapy" more explicitly refers to the treatment of psychiatric illnesses with medications. While Pharmacotherapy alone is seldom considered sufficient treatment, for the treatment of some psychiatric disorders it may be the most important single component in the control of the disabling symptoms. Today lithium carbonate, for instance, is considered the most essential part of the treatment of the recurrent mood swings of patients with manic-depressive illness. Comparably, one of the members of the major classes of antipsychotic drugs—the butyrophenones, the phenothiazines, or the thioxanthenes—is considered necessary for the management of symptomatic behavior of severely disturbed schizophrenics, especially if it is hoped that they be managed outside a hospital context. The most optimum care, even of the most severely disturbed patient, would always include an integrated program of Pharmacotherapy, psychotherapy, and sociotherapy.

### HISTORY

Most of the major psychotropic drugs used today did not come into use until the middle of this century. Lithium carbonate was introduced for the treatment of manic-depressive illness in 1949 by an Australian named Cade, who found in some studies with uric acid that lithium had a calming effect on patients with labile (changeable) moods. Although the drugs's potential for the management of manic states was recognized early, it did not come into wide use in this country until the late 1960s and early 1970s. This was probably due in part to the fact that it was discovered in far-off Australia. In addition, patients using it became easily toxic unless carefully regulated, and in this country at the time of its discovery, the psychoanalytic movement was at its zenith. Use of drugs was disparaged as second-class treatment.

The first major antipsychotic drug to be used was Chlorpromazine, introduced in 1952. It was synthesized in an attempt to make a better antihistamine. When it was observed to produce tranquilization without sleep, it was given to a group of schizophrenics and found to be a potent antipsychotic agent.

The antidepressants were also first put into use in the 1950s. The drug Iproniazid, used in the treatment of tuberculosis, was found to have a mood-elevating effect on patients taking it, and in independent studies it was found to be effective in the treatment of depression. Because Iproniazid was found to have several undesirable effects in addition to its antidepressant quality, efforts were made to find other drugs of the same general group that had fewer side effects but the same mood-elevating effects. Iproniazid and related compounds interfere with the enzyme monoamine oxidase, which is responsible for breaking down compounds such as dopamine and norepinephrine in the brain. Depression is thought to be related to reduced amounts of norepinephrine and dopamine at critical central nervous system sites. The other major group of antidepressant drugs, the tricyclic antidepressants (so-called because of their chemical structure), were developed about the same time.

## TECHNIQUE

Skillful use of psychotropic drugs entails an awareness that they are not useful in all the forms of a given disorder and that even with individuals for whom they are appropriate and effective, dosage varies, and at times even the most chronic of severely ill patients may be relatively symptom-free without the use of drugs. Adept use of psychotherapeutic and sociotherapeutic techniques will often minimize the need for medication, even with psychotic patients.

Psychotropic drugs provide symptomatic relief, and it is the management of symptoms that the clinician aims for. Lithium carbonate is used for the treatment of cyclic mood disorders and appears particularly effective in the management of mania. The antidepressants are not effective for the treatment of all depressions. They appear most effective in instances where there is a sleep disorder, appetite and weight disturbance, a reduction in libido, and a diurnal variation of mood. The antipsychotic agents do not appear to affect, in a major way, long-term social adjustment in chronic schizophrenics. They do, however, help reduce paranoid ideation, hallucinations, delusional thinking, and other disturbances of thought that interfere with functioning.

All the drugs must be used with considerable caution as there are a number of long-term and short-term side effects. A decision must be made early in the course of a patient's illness to ascertain whether the benefits to be gained by Pharmacotherapy outweigh the side effects that may result. The patient and his family, together with the psychiatric clinician, play a role in the decision. Sometimes the benefits are clearly apparent. A patient who is profoundly depressed may avoid hospitalization, continue to work, and not attempt suicide. Other times effects may be less apparent or a psychotherapeutic technique equally or more effective. In all instances it is good medicine not to continue Pharmacotherapy longer than is clinically indicated.

## APPLICATIONS

Pharmacotherapy has been used in the management of all so-called psychogenic psychoses and for many organic brain syndromes. In addition, milder disturbances of behavior such as enuresis (bed-wetting) and the phobic-anxiety-depersonalization syndrome have also responded to drugs in many instances. Lithium carbonate is used in the treatment of manic-depressive illness, cyclothymic mood disturbances, and in some instances of episodic violence. The phenothiazines, butyrophenones, and thioxanthines are used in the management of psychotic symptomatology whether it is part of a schizophrenic reaction or an organic brain syndrome. In affective disorders (affecting mood or emotions), they may be used together with an antidepressant if a patient is paranoid or severely agitated. In chronic organic brain syndromes, small doses of the antipsychotic agents are sometimes effective in symptomatic management. Imipramine, a tricyclic antidepressant, has been used effectively in the treatment of enuresis and the phobic-anxiety-depersonalization syndrome. Haloperidol, a butyrophenone, is used in the treatment of Gilles de la Tourette's syndrome. The minor tranquilizers, such as the benzodiazepines, are used predominantly for insomnia, anxiety, and some alcohol withdrawal. The last mentioned group of drugs are probably much overprescribed, although when indicated, they can provide considerable relief.

# Phenomenological Psychotherapy
## *Donald E. Polkinghoine*

## DEFINITION

Phenomenological Psychotherapy is a treatment approach developed by Husserl, Heidegger, and Merleau-Ponty. It is based on their understanding that (1) human beings organize their experiences and give meaning to them through particular conscious attention and through focus upon aspects of the world; (2) behavior is the result of choices grounded in personal experience; and (3) the therapist can assist clients and patients in clarifying and bringing to awareness the patterns which are used to interpret their life experiences and make them meaningful. Phenomenological Psychotherapy is not a body of systematized techniques. It is a basic approach to clients and patients, and within this approach techniques can be used that have been developed in various therapeutic systems.

## HISTORY

The historical roots of phenomenological psychology lie in the "act" psychologies which were developed in Germany in the late nineteenth century. The "act" psychologies studied mainly human consciousness (an interest which was later abandoned by American behaviorism) and postulated that consciousness consists of the appearance of objects—appearance which results when one "acts" or focuses attention on particular outer or inner objects. The "act" psychologies were opposed to the generally accepted associationist theory which held that consciousness is the mere accumulation of sensory experiences linked by mental laws of association. Thus, "act" psychology proposed that consciousness is constructed by a person's specific active attention, not through the passive reception of sensory input. In short, people attend to and act on the world so as to create meaning and organization.

Two major programs refined and developed the study of consciousness as proposed by "act" psychology: Gestalt psychology, as practiced by Wertheimer and Koffka, and phenomenological psychology, founded by Husserl (1895–1938). While Gestalt psychology concentrated on perceptual patterns of organization, phenomenological psychology emphasized the study of the ways in which consciousness organizes itself to produce the meaning-laden experiential world in which we exist and through which we know ourselves, others, and our physical environment. Husserl's major contribution was the development of a special method for studying these processes of consciousness. He believed that the methods used by science to study objects in the physical-temporal world were inappropriate for studying human experience, and his method employed disciplined intellectual exercises in order to establish a standpoint for observing one's own conscious activity. One of the most significant contributions made through the use of this method is a description of the human experience of time. Husserl found that conscious time is experienced as a merging of anticipations of the future and the fading of the immediately previous experiences, not as a continuous flow of present moments.

Although Husserl believed that his method allowed consciousness to be viewed from a perspective which transcends one's personal history, the most significant developers of phenomenological psychology after him—Heidegger (1962), Sartre (1956), and Merleau-Ponty (1962)—believed that one could not step outside of one's own existence to study consciousness. They maintained that we remain situated as historical and bodily beings even as we study ourselves. They retained Husserl's focus on consciousness and the need for phenomenological-type methods for studying human existence, but they emphasized that consciousness itself is shaped by givens of human existence. Because of their emphasis on the human situation as the base on which consciousness organizes itself and its objects, their work is referred to as *existential phenomenology* to distinguish it from the "pure" phenomenology of Husserl. Most of the significant psychotherapy contributions to develop out of phenomenology have come from followers of this group—for example, Binswanger's (1963) studies of schizophrenia and love, Boss's (1957) study of dreams, Minkowski's (1970) work on time consciousness, and Strauss's (1963) work on sense experience.

More recently, there has been a growing emphasis within phenomenological psychology on the role of culture in shaping the organizational patterns and meaning-giving structures of consciousness. Studies concerned with language and speech, cultural values, social and economic systems, and historical settings have provided insights into the means by which consciousness interprets and forms its experiences. Examples of this recent work are Ricoeur's (1970) analysis of Freud's focus on the archaic, Ricoeur's (1967) exploration of the cultural symbols of evil, and Gadamer's (1975) investigation of human existence as grounded in interpretation. The term applied to this kind of work is *hermeneutic (interpretive) phenomenology.*

Although phenomenology originated in Europe and remains primarily a European phenomenon, it has had significant impact in the United States. The translation of texts made the work of the European writers accessible to American psychotherapists as early as the 1930s, and there has even been some emigration of phenomenologists to America—for example, Alfred Schutz (1973). Major interest was also aroused by the translations of existential-phenomenological texts which were published in *Existence* by May and his associates in 1958.

An American psychotherapy centered in the experience of the client was developed by Rogers during the 1950s. His work—along with the work of others more specifically oriented to phenomenology, such as Snygg and Combs (1949) and Gendlin (1962)—brought the attention of American psychologists to the study of consciousness, and this American development paralleled the basic approach to therapy which was then being developed by the European phenomenologists. The American version, however, grew out of the practice of therapy as an alternative to psychoanalysis and behaviorism, and it was not the result of philosophical awareness as was typically the case in Europe.

Currently, the basic approach of phenomenology—a focus on the created experience of the client rather than on underlying unconscious forces or on behavior without consciousness—is being integrated into the client-oriented or humanistic American therapies by providing a philosophical foundation. The impact of the European writers on American psychotherapists is increasingly evident in the content and citations of American research articles, in the formation of several American journals devoted to phenomenological psychology, and in the development of doctoral programs in psychology—at Duquesne University, at the University of Dallas, and at the Humanistic Psychology Institute—which emphasize phenomenological psychology.

## TECHNIQUES

Phenomenological Psychotherapy does not provide clearly delineated techniques for working with clients. It does not have any equivalent of the transference of Psychoanalysis, the anxiety hierarchies of Behavioral Modification, or the reflective listening of Client-Centered Therapy. Nevertheless, the general phenomenological understandings do imply ways of practicing psychotherapy.

Therapists and clients (patients) face each other as responsible persons who have come together to engage in dialogue in order to bring about the clarification of experiences and to uncover the structures of meaning through which they are interpreting the events of their lives. The therapist is equipped with general understandings of the operations of consciousness which have been gained through study and training in phenomenological psychology. Using these understandings as a base, the therapist focuses the therapeutic dialogue so that the basic structures through which the client's world is given meaning come into focus. By exploring the areas of the client's experience of his/her bodily location as well as the spatial distance between aspects of the self and between others and the environment, by exploring his/her experience of participation in time, and by exploring the experience of the meaning patterns used for interpreting other people, the therapist and the client—come to greater awareness of the general ways in which the person exists in the world. This awareness provides a phenomenologically based diagnostic which identifies the particular areas of constricted meaning which can then be explored in greater depth. The purpose of the exploration, in sum, is to provide the client with a greater repertoire of meanings so that his/her sensitivity to the differing aspects of self, others, and the environment can be increased.

The interaction between the client and the therapist is centered in the conscious experiences of each other. As they share and explore alternative possible interpretations of each other, the client's experience becomes fuller. The archaic and unconscious aspects of existence are acknowledged in the therapy, but the focus remains in the telic or purposive dimensions that are open to the client. The client is understood to be a creative subject, capable of solving problems and making decisions that will allow for a fuller, less restricted experience and, on the basis of this experience, capable of making choices and acting to affect and change the world. The therapist helps the client to identify and to clarify the decision points and meaningfulness of the possible choices. The emergence of clear and precise understanding provides the client with a greater power for decision and enactment than was previously the case when the client's experience was delimited by restrictive meaning patterns or when the experience was confusing because it did not offer a clearly focused view.

## APPLICATIONS

The primary application of Phenomenological Psychotherapy has been in the development of a deeper and fuller understanding of the lived experiences which clients and patients have. The understanding of another's experience is an important— perhaps the most important—tool that therapists bring to their work with clients. By being sensitive to and appreciating the client's particular way of experiencing the world, the therapist can come closer to understanding the world from the client's perspective. One example of this major application of phenomenological psychology is Minkowski's (1970) work in uncovering the changes in one's experience of time during an episode of depression. During a period of depression, the experience of time changes so that there is no propulsion to the future. The future becomes blocked off, and there is no openness to new and different possibilities. Instead, one experiences a future which merely holds a closed repetition of the past. Another example is Binswanger's (1963) careful analysis of five cases of schizophrenia, which has opened the way for a deeper appreciation of the constricted meaning structures available within a schizophrenia-type existence.

A second significant application of phenomenological psychology is the alternative approach to diagnosis which it provides. Instead of categorizing clients according to their various symptoms, phenomenological diagnosis concentrates on the ways in which the clients organize their experiences (Keen, 1975). This alternative offers a more meaningful and more useful system of treating and understanding mental illness than the present symptom-based system.

Phenomenological Psychotherapy has been used in working with people whose experiences are organized in a neurotic way or in a severely psychotic manner. It has also been used to help people making life decisions, giving them assistance in identifying and clarifying their meaning patterns. Its primary and most important application, however, derives from the therapist's awareness of the client's various approaches to transforming his/her experience into an ordered and meaningful system.

# Phenomeno-Structural Psychotherapy
*Robert Mucchielli*

## DEFINITION

Phenomeno-Structural Psychotherapy is based on phenomenology and on structural psychology. It is a method used to treat neuroses and psychosomatic diseases. It is a face-to-face and a uniquely verbal psychotherapy. During the sessions (one or two per week, each lasting one or one and one-half hours), the patient expresses as spontaneously as possible and as authentically as possible his personal way of experiencing various life situations—what he feels, and how he reacts to them. He is free to choose his starting point, his way of expression, and direction. Verbal interventions of the therapist are comprehensive and nondirective. From the patient's speech and from his nonverbal observed attitudes or behavior, the therapist —without suggestion or interpretation, explication, advice giving or investigating causes, or making any diagnosis, but persevering in the intention to clarify themes— interprets the constants of the imminent organization of the patient's unique universe and of its structures of meaning.

The method is phenomenological because it is centered on the life of the patient. It excludes intellectual constructs and all etiological research—thus, there is no reference to nosology (disease classification), to clinical a priori tables, or to any explicative metapsychology such as psychoanalysis.

The method is based on structural psychology in the sense that it supposes coherent organization between the meaningful structures that are nonconscious for the patient but which are working on his perceptions.

The coming back to health is conceived—in the Phenomeno-Structural Psychotherapy—as liberation of the Ego (or *Ipse*) with respect to pathological thematization, which inhibits or restricts the Ego's dynamism and potentialities.

Opposed to the Freudian classical psychoanalytic theory of the Ego, the phenomenological anthropology (Anschauung) considers the Ego and the personal consciousness as dotted with its own creative energy, capable of love and project, ontologically included into interhuman relationships and temporality.

## HISTORY

Phenomeno-Structural Psychotherapy is linked with the ideas of Eugene Minkowski (inspired by Bergson's anti-intellectualism) on one side and with Ludwig Bins-wanger on the other side (inspired by the phenomenology of Hiedegger), creator of Daseins-Analyse. The Phenomeno-Structural Psychotherapy is, because of this, a variation of existential analysis.

The name "phenomeno-structural" was proposed by Minkowski and the method is part of existential analysis practice of Binswanger (Switzerland), Roland Kuhn (Switzerland), Medard Boss (Switzerland), Rollo May (U.S.A.), Henri Ellensberger (Canada), Cargnello (Italy), and others.

Let's talk of the historical influence from the nondirective psychotherapy of Carl Rogers, of which the principle is also the comprehension of the patient's lived universe without reference either to nosology, or anamnesis (a remembering), or to any explicative a priori concepts. However, Dr. Rogers mistakes the conception of the pathological universe as meaningful-for-the-subject, a universe dotted with internal logic, with structural imminent organization.

Historically, structuralism comes from 1) linguistic conceptions (de Saussure), which considered the language as system, and 2) anthropological conceptions (Levi-Strauss), which considers all social organization as unconscious structure giving a meaning to observable expressions at the level of social behavior and values. Structuralism is applicable to psychopathology in so far as the entire mental illness universe may be considered a *system.*

The unconscious, in this method, is not at all the Freudian set of dynamic impulses pressing on an Ego, reduced to an awakeness oriented toward the external reality. For us, the unconscious is always present in the subject's life, and it is the whole of the structures giving their meaning to perception-objects and to behavior. It is a set of patterns *(Gestalten)* without its own contents but structuring all informational or reactional content, in the way of an unvarying assimilator.

## TECHNIQUE

The first preparatory session is concerned with the organization of the psychotherapy and informing the patient about the method. The rules of the patient's behavior are then clearly formulated: he must tell his feelings and discuss his life in everyday situations as well as in the therapeutic situation itself. Generally speaking, he must make the therapist understand what he feels, direct acting is prohibited (the patient must verbalize his impulses without acting out). He begins with what he wishes and goes on to spontaneous expression; if uneasy, he has the right to stop, but he must describe the uneasiness. The interventions of the therapist are also an object of information during the preparatory sitting: the therapist says that he will not be the first to break the silence, that he endeavors to try to understand what will be said, and says that he will be available even between sessions in case the patient feels anxiety or confusion. The therapist answers all the patient's questions (during the preparatory sitting) without forgetting to formulate the attitude implicated in the question itself in a climate of security and confidence.

Security and confidence are two fundamental values to be protected throughout the therapy. Confidentiality is affirmed. Reminding the patient of those agreements will be useful later if the patient forgets them.

The sittings are face-to-face in a simple and friendly room, not too large or too small. The therapist's and patient's armchairs are identical and at a distance of one or one and one-half meters, set in a way so that they form an angle broad enough to permit the avoidance of direct face-to-face contact in order to reduce the possible uneasiness of unavoidable staring.

The initiative is always with the patient. The therapist's interventions are mostly like Rogerian reformulations, but as soon as the therapist (owing to content-analysis of the client's speech and observation of meaningful attitudes and postures) has enough *existential context,* he tries to single out themes, constants, and meaning-giving substructures.

These later become more and more linked between themselves, toward the nonconscious fundamental structures.

The language of the patient is very important. The point is to understand his words with their personal connotations. The "semantical interrogation" (e.g., What do you mean by...?, What does that mean for you...?, What do you want to say . . .?) are used even for apparently simple words. It is necessary in the reformulations to use again the subject's words with their explicit meaning.

As in Rogerian psychotherapy, the patient's agreement is required for any reformulation, because that is the guarantee that the therapist has remained "inside the universe of meanings" of the patient and has avoided "interpretation." The patient feels strong emotional states, similar to abreactions (reliving a past event), when central structures are discovered and formulated (conceptualized).

As with semantic psychotherapy, the insight of a previously nonconscious subjective meaning's structure is the cause of what I call "new DEFINITION of concept" *(redéfinition du concept)* by the reflexive consciousness and the auto-critic Ego. That phenomenon is very much like the "reality confrontation" used by all psychotherapy. Feelings called "transferential" are analyzed as soon as they appear and cannot be used as a principal medium for the therapy. In other words, the experience of a true and satisfactory interhuman relationship (the interpersonal relation born from the dialogue of the conscious thoughts) becomes paradigmatic, and interferes powerfully in the process of Ego's liberation.

### APPLICATIONS

The typical indications are neuroses, psychoneuroses, and psychosomatic diseases. This psychotherapy is not applicable to psychoses without help of neuroleptic drugs capable of reestablishing communication. Phenomeno-Structural Psychotherapy is not indicated for diseases associated with mental debility or loss of mental capacity (mental deterioration, cerebral damage or dysfunction, aging). It is not applicable in cases where the patient has constructed a life pattern satisfactory for him, even though pathological. These clients do not feel the need for help—for example, homosexuality, which is well organized and accepted, or the structured sociopathies of recidivist criminals. It is applicable to adolescents and children more than ten years old.

# Philosophical Psychotherapy
## *William S. Sahakian*

### DEFINITION

Essentially a cognitive-type psychotherapy, Philosophical Psychotherapy effects behavioral change and emotional control through one's thoughts, philosophical outlook, or attitude. Our beliefs, intellectual posture, or perspective on life can and does affect our personalities as much (if not more) than our physical environment or the external stimuli to which we respond. Often it is our philosophical attitude toward the world around us that governs how we will tend to respond to a particular situation or to a given set of stimuli.

To alter personality it is necessary to effect changes in a person's philosophy of life. While a certain type of philosophy predisposes one to pessimism, depression, or moroseness, another philosophical view on life can dispose a person toward being optimistic, exuberant, and content. What is so remarkable about Philosophical Psychotherapy is that it often succeeds when a number of other psychotherapeutic techniques have failed.

## HISTORY

The birth of Philosophical Psychotherapy is traced to two patients who did not respond to the expert psychotherapeutic care accorded them by several psychiatrists. Because conventional methods of therapy proved futile, it was necessary to resort to novel techniques in these two cases.

One of these clients strove in vain to eliminate an incorrigible neurotic symptom. Neither he nor his therapists could uproot the symptom that he interpreted as an ominous sign of failing mental health. Convinced that his sanity would be debilitated if the neurotic symptom were not conquered and expunged from his personality, he rallied every fiber of his being to eject this unwelcome invader from his personality. The results were disastrous. Rather than finding any relief, he merely compounded his troublesome condition by exhausting himself emotionally in his vain attempts to gain mastery over his neurotic symptom. His succession of failures left him demoralized, depressed, and emotionally depleted. Without realizing it, he had navigated himself into a position where his neurosis was not the important issue, for the seat of his distress had now become the huge sum of emotion expelled to dominate a neurotic symptom that he felt would damage him mentally if left uncontained.

It was at this point that Philosophical Psychotherapy was introduced. He was advised to stop fighting his neurosis, to accept it—to be philosophical about it. To accept it with an air of indifference. If other people with handicaps accept theirs and yet continue with the business of life, why could he not do the same? Rather than fighting his neurotic symptom, he was told, why not accept it as part of his personality? His attitude of philosophical indifference proved a turning point in his well-being. Immense amounts of energy were no longer wasted on rallying his forces to attack his neurotic symptom but were now used constructively in productive living. No longer emotionally depleted, demoralized, or depressed, he felt that he was a well man. What was remarkable was his insistence that he was cured of his neurosis, when all that actually took place was relief from emotional exhaustion.

The efficacy of philosophy as a therapeutic agent was first noticed when a number of students regularly reported "feeling good" after certain lectures. They derived more than a conveyance of information from the lectures; they felt as if they were more suitably equipped for confronting life's problems and crises. A reassessment of the lectures that proved therapeutic as well as informative found them to be of a certain type. Many were stoical in character. A person was encouraged to face life's problems philosophically—to face them with stoical indifference. If a situation cannot be changed, then one must change one's attitude toward it. If you cannot achieve what you would like to attain, then like what is within your reach. There is nothing in heaven or earth worth losing your composure, for a tranquil state of mind is a priceless possession.

## TECHNIQUE

It is important to explore the patient's philosophical attitude in order to ascertain whether it is supportive or counterproductive to wholesome mental health. Often a person's philosophical stance, belief, or outlook adversely affects his emotional or mental health. To be in this predicament, a person need not be brainwashed by some nefarious group; it may result from self-administered brainwashing. People can and do think and talk themselves into a philosophy or philosophical attitude or a belief that causes anxieties.

After determining that the client's philosophical beliefs are counterproductive to constructive responses or wholesome living, it is necessary for the therapist to act in the role of facilitator to change them for desirable ones. The therapist aids the client in changing his attitude or assists him in becoming more philosophical about his condition—even in cultivating an attitude of philosophical indifference.

In the case of the man mentioned earlier, our dialogue proceeded as follows:

You have told me of some of your neurotic symptoms and you say that you want me to help you to eradicate them. Why? I asked.

What do you mean, Why? he replied. Any normal person would want to get rid of them. They are tormenting problems and disturb me terribly. They have made me miserable for a long time.

Have you ever tried to live with them? I asked. Some crippled people have learned to live with their ailments. They do not spend every hour of their waking day or an entire lifetime striving to gain mastery over their problems. They accept their plight and learn to live with it, as do many other people who are handicapped victims. Some persons with the loss of an arm or with a heart condition learn to live within the limitations of their handicap; they do not waste their time and exhaust themselves vainly combatting their problem. Is it not possible for you also to do something comparable?

After staring at me with a meaningless look for almost a minute, the patient's eyes and face lit up, and he smiled broadly and said: "Why didn't the other psychotherapists tell me this long ago? Of course I can accept it and live with it. In fact, I feel better already. It is most ironic," he added, "that I should come to a therapist, requesting that he cure me, and then have him tell me to keep my problem."

## APPLICATIONS

Philosophical Psychotherapy is most effective in those recalcitrant cases that do not yield to other forms of therapy. Its value is best appreciated in dealing with those long-term cases where common forms of psychotherapy have proved fruitless.

Other applications include cases in which more fundamental forms of personality change are sought—where a complete change of life-style or a new attitude on life will benefit the individual. Those with various emotional problems—especially people plagued with anxieties and other fears and those facing life's crises and other distressing situations—benefit most from Philosophical Psychotherapy. It is a boon to so-called normal people seeking to maintain their slim hold on "sanity." It comes as a relief to neurotics of long standing.

# Philotherapy

*Emery Breitner*

## DEFINITION

Philotherapy is a religious form of psychotherapy based on love, faith, and acceptance of one's self. Its aim is helping the patient to be himself in his own environment. To find himself and his place in his world without guilt, pretense, or role playing.

The goal of Philotherapy is for the patient to accept himself the way he is. To help him to live without hiding, fighting, or pretense. To make him see that he has a basic experience in life, a place, an attitude, a role that he has to accept. That success, health, longevity are not up to him. The aim is to remove the false illusion that he is responsible for everything that is happening to him and around him. To recognize that there are powers stronger than him. That he does not have to control that which is beyond him. That he can find peace in himself within his own world.

## HISTORY

Philotherapy evolved from my (Breitner) dissatisfaction with the conventional, intellectual, insight-oriented psychotherapy. Anyone following the recent developments and new trends in therapy can see a deluge of new ideas, new doubts and confusions, and can see that we are experiencing a crisis in psychotherapy and in the field of mental health. Many explanations and many theories have been presented recently, but none have brought any solution. One might wonder if any logical approach can be helpful to solve an illogical problem.

After many years of practice, I realize that it makes very little difference how much we know about our problems, since understanding of a problem is not going to change it. Intellectual insight is not going to help us. The therapy I describe is based on an induced regression and intense emotional involvement. It is experiential and existential, rather than intellectual. Because this form of therapy is based on regression, acceptance, and love, I call it Philotherapy.

Philotherapy is based on an assimilative theory of neurosis. That is, we assimilate, incorporate everything—good, bad, and indifferent alike—from our environment. We assimilate love, faith, fear, doubt, and other feelings. They are superimposed on our genetic makeup. This way, we can see neurosis as an assimilated, incorporated, negative experience. The amazing thing about this negative experience I call neurosis is that it stays with us. The experience is painful and unpleasant but we still repeat it. It seems that it is the only meaningful link we have with our parents.

## TECHNIQUE

Our study extended over a period of five years, including 184 patients. Our technique was based on a strong emotional and supportive relationship between therapist and patient. But the basic question remained: why did it help in one case and not in another? What was the principal therapeutic factor? I have found that those patients who developed acceptance, faith, and an ability to regress showed an improvement during therapy. To be exact, 152 patients showed definite signs of emotional regression, increased acceptance of themselves and their basic experience of life. And faith in God. That is why I would categorize Philotherapy as a religious form of therapy. The technique itself uses self-hypnosis, pharmacotherapy, hypnotherapy, and biofeedback to go back to this basic experience.

## APPLICATIONS

Selection of patients was the first step. We used M.M.P.I., T.A.T., Rorschach, and other projective techniques to choose patients who had ability to develop regression and faith. We have found that Philotherapy was most effective in interpersonal, anxiety-related problems. It was also effective in stress-related disorders, psychosomatic problems, such as peptic ulcers, hypertension, colitis, and anxiety states, with or without psychosomatic symptoms.

We found our approach least effective in obsessive-compulsive and sociopathic character disorders, where the symptoms were detached from the individual and where patients used denial and reaction formation as a defense.

---

# Photo Counseling

## F. William Gosciewski

### DEFINITION

Photo Counseling involves the utilization of family photographs or snapshots in any phase of the counseling process for the purposes of facilitating communication, enhancing client-therapist understanding of problems, and supporting client changes in therapeutically desirable directions. Photo Counseling is an adjunctive therapeutic process used within the context of a broader treatment orientation or program. It allows the therapist to enter more meaningfully into the client's extratherapeutic life space and, by so doing, to "see" the client in his home, his neighborhood, his recreational pursuits, and so forth. Photo Counseling is, therefore, a process of investigating, clarifying, and modifying various adjustment states with the aid of photographs that are, as Oliver Wendell Holmes noted some years ago, like mirrors with memories.

### HISTORY

The technology of photography has, of course, been available to the general public for many years, and the practice of snapping pictures to commemorate special occasions and to capture special moments has become a great American pastime. The vast majority of people have available to them stacks of photos, if not boxes of slides or reels of film. It is surprising that in the therapeutic arena so little use has been made of this rich source of personal history. Traditionally, variations of counseling or psychotherapy have been predominantly verbal phenomena, and the old adage "A picture is worth a thousand words" has fallen on deaf ears.

A few years ago, in my (Gosciewski) capacity as counseling psychologist at the St. Vincent Community Mental Health Center in Erie, Pennsylvania, I had occasion to work with some clients who were, for one reason or another, resistant to the counseling interchange. By chance, one client brought with him one day some snapshots recently taken at a family outing. In sharing these photos with that client I noted a significant change in the quality of interchange between us, leading to increased openness, better understanding, and a generally improved therapeutic relationship. In the years since that fortunate discovery, I have continued to utilize this approach and to encourage others to do likewise. The results thus far have in all cases been positive and, in some instances, impressive.

## TECHNIQUE

In using Photo Counseling, the therapist requests that the client bring into the counseling session a random selection of family photographs portraying himself and other members of his family at varying times in his past. While such a request can be made at any point in the counseling process, it is most often found to be valuable early on, as it tends to facilitate improved communication and relatedness at the outset. The integration of the Photo Counseling technique can be done initially, occasionally, or regularly over the course of psychotherapeutic treatment, depending on its demonstrated utility, availability of photographs, and client responsiveness.

Once the client has brought in the requested photos, the therapist proceeds to share with him the experiences or circumstances conveyed by the pictures. This is an open-ended procedure wherein the therapist enables and encourages the client to relate past experiences to present ones, toward the end result of greater understanding and continuity in life experience. Just how this is done depends ultimately on the personal style of the counselor as he relates to the client. Some productive variations include making then-and-now comparisons, noting similarities and differences with significant others (important people in the client's life), interpreting for the client's consideration indicators of positive and/or negative relationship factors, and focusing on physical and selected environmental features considered to be of particular significance in the client's self-perception.

## APPLICATIONS

To this point, Photo Counseling has been found to be of particular value in three broad areas of the counseling process. First, the pictures can be used to establish and build rapport. Sharing with the new client in experiences on such a close and personal level provides an excellent starting point in a less threatening structure.

Second, analysis of photos aids in the diagnostic process wherein the focus is on accumulation and integration of information about the client. Pictures can be used to verify or alter the client's version of problematic concerns; specific photos can lead to investigations of emotionally charged and perhaps highly defended areas of concern; and photos can be utilized in a psychometric manner by, for example, asking the client to tell stories about them, write captions for them, and the like. Finally, photos can be used progressively over several sessions as a way of assessing gains, resistance, and therapeutic changes of all types. In this respect the use of Photo Counseling can give indications of the need for progressive changes in counseling emphases.

Photo Counseling can be used in many settings, at all age levels, and with clients of most descriptions. It is best conceived of as an adjunctive therapeutic approach that facilitates any therapeutic endeavor dependent on rapport, communication, and increased self-awareness as requisites to improved adjustment states.

# Placebo Therapy
## Jefferson M. Fish

### DEFINITION

Placebo Therapy is the name for the deliberate application of principles of social influence, such as those involved in faith healing and the placebo effect (when a patient responds favorably to a placebo), to psychotherapy.

There has been a proliferation of new schools of therapy, which is exemplified in part by the need for a book such as this. While these schools have persuasive theoretical rationales for the techniques they employ, the courses of action they recommend are often mutually contradictory. If opposing methods can lead to positive results, it may well be that it is the client's belief in the therapist's role as a healer and in the efficacy of his methods, rather than their actual effectiveness, which is the common ingredient in their success.

The implication of this point of view is that it is possible to view psychotherapy as a social influence process. Doing so enables one to detect the strong and weak points of various therapeutic approaches in influencing people to change. Even more important, it makes it possible to construct a framework for the conduct of psychotherapy that maximizes the impact of these persuasive factors. Since the social influence process is present in all therapy, whether therapists recognize it or not, it seems reasonable to structure therapy to take advantage of it—rather than ignoring it and risk its working against the therapeutic strategy.

### HISTORY

The publication in 1961 of Jerome Frank's *Persuasion and Healing* was perhaps the most important of the antecendents of Placebo Therapy. The book viewed psychotherapy from the broad perspective of behavior change, and found elements in it that are common among religious healing, shamanism in primitive tribes, brainwashing, experimental studies of persuasion, and the placebo effect. In developing the clinical framework for the conduct of Placebo Therapy, important influences came from Jay Haley and the communications therapists, Milton Erickson and his directive and hypnotherapeutic interventions, and Arnold Lazarus's Broad Spectrum Behavior Therapy as well as his advocacy of technical eclecticism. Important theoretical influences were Leonard Krasner and Leonard Ullman's formulation of social learning theory, Theodore Barber's studies of hypnosis, Martin Orne's concept of demand characteristics, and a variety of theories, effects, and concepts from social psychology, such as attitude change, attribution theory, cognitive dissonance (including the effort justification hypothesis and reactance), expectancy, and role theory. I integrated these various theoretical and clinical elements in *Placebo Therapy* (Fish, 1973).

## TECHNIQUE

Limitations of space allow for a description of only some of the more important features of the social influence framework of Placebo Therapy.

People who come for therapy are usually suffering from a more or less vaguely defined misery as well as beliefs about that misery, such as "I'm crazy," or "I'm a hopeless case." The assessment process is aimed at defining the patient's misery as consisting of a number of concrete problems, such as anxiety in the presence of authority figures, fear of rejection by members of the opposite sex, or lack of conversational skills. By defining the goals of therapy as solving problems such as these, the therapist communicates "You're not an incurable neurotic, you merely have problems A, B and C." The patient must eventually accept this sort of communication, since if he says that there is more to what bothers him than A, B, and C, the therapist simply responds by working with him to define the "more" in terms of other concrete problems, perhaps D and E. Eventually, by agreeing on the goals of therapy, the patient must give up his self-defeating beliefs about the hopelessness of his condition. In addition, as part of the assessment process, the therapist tries to find out about the patient's strongly held beliefs, or faith.

The therapist then devises specific treatments, or healing rituals, for each of the patient's problems. Such treatments should be clearly related to the problems, and this relationship and the rationales as to why the treatments work should be explained in a manner based on, or at least consistent with, the patient's beliefs. Doing so heightens the patient's expectancy of success, and in this way makes success more likely. Wherever possible, the techniques should involve something that the patient does himself. This encourages the belief that he is not out of control, but rather is able to regulate his own behavior.

As the patient undergoes the healing ritual (e.g., conversing in prescribed ways with people of the opposite sex), any improvement that occurs can be used by the therapist to demonstrate progress, and thereby initiate the positive cycle of hope, leading to improvement, leading to more hope, greater efforts, and more improvement. This is the opposite of the negative cycle that characterizes most people who come for therapy: hopelessness that leads to halfhearted efforts at change that leads to failure that confirms the hopelessness, and so on.

## APPLICATIONS

Among the applications of Placebo Therapy, the clearest are the various forms of directive therapy, such as hypnotherapy and behavior modification. In the former, hypnosis as a potent form of socially sanctioned magic offers an ideal medium for Placebo Therapy. However, many therapists who use hypnosis depend on their role as a magician who uses his secret power to cure people. Unfortunately, this stance does nothing to encourage the patient's belief that he can control his own behavior. In fact, to the extent that it works, such hypnosis confirms his belief that he is out of control. Actually, hypnosis research indicates that individuals vary in their hypnotizability. Hence, treatment can be presented as a self-cure process, in which the therapist tests the patient to see how hypnotizable he is, and to the extent to which the patient is capable of it teaches him self-hypnosis and devises a way for him to use it in a healing ritual. In this manner, the patient gains a feeling of self-control by using one of his valuable abilities (the ability to hypnotize himself) to regulate another aspect of his behavior. In a similar way, by explaining behavior modification techniques in terms of patients' beliefs—instead of using conditioning concepts, which frequently evoke *1984* imagery—behavior modifiers can add the placebo effect to any treatment effect associated with their techniques.

# Aesthetic Plastic Surgery as Psychotherapy

John Ransom Lewis, Jr.

## DEFINITION

Plastic surgery has as its purpose the improvement in functioning and the improvement of appearance. Aesthetic Plastic Surgery, or cosmetic surgery, deals primarily with the improvement of appearance. However, even this branch of plastic surgery cannot be definitely separated from reconstructive and reparative surgery that also deals with appearance along with the repairs and reconstructions. The psychological implications of this are numerous and varied, but the primary psychological purpose of the surgery is improvement in appearance in order to improve the patient's own self-image.

## HISTORY

A history of Aesthetic Plastic Surgery is a history of plastic surgery in general and goes back many centuries to the early Indian and Egyptian "healers." It began perhaps in the sixth or seventh century before Christ, when Sushruta developed methods of reconstruction of the nose, amputated as a punishment for criminals or the inhabitants of conquered cities. Much of this early knowledge was lost for a long time, but probably gradually found its way through the Arab, Persian, and Greek civilizations and finally to Rome through Jewish scholars. It was later practiced with somewhat different techniques by members of certain Italian families. The most notable of these was the Branca family, whose members developed reconstruction of the nose and other types of plastic surgery, passing the techniques down to younger members of the family. Gaspre Tagliecozzi of Bologna further advanced the cause of plastic surgery, including reconstruction of the nose. Plastic surgery received a great impetus during World Wars I and II.

## TECHNIQUE

The concept of plastic surgery as a method of treating psychological problems or to supplement psychologic management of the patient may be sound if the patient is properly evaluated and is properly motivated. In short, psychotherapy by Aesthetic Plastic Surgery may be a successful method of treatment if there is an imperfection that contributes to the patient's unhappiness, either as a deterrent or as a distraction to the individual's adjustment to other problems and situations. It may sometimes be important that the decision be made by a consultation of psychologist or psychiatrist and plastic surgeon.

However, not all patients for Aesthetic Plastic Surgery need to have psychological screening. Many patients come with very well-considered reasons for having surgery, the defect or deformity is easily recognizable, and the motivation for correction is considered logical. However, the patient who blames all his unhappi-ness, business failures, and marital difficulties on a physical abnormality is raising a red flag for the plastic surgeon to see. He should beware of this patient unless the patient is properly cleared by the psychologist or psychiatrist.

The patient should not be allowed to expect more than a reasonable result, and must realize that patients vary in their ability to heal. The disappointed patient may be made worse psychologically than if no surgery had been performed. Therefore, it behooves the surgeon and other consultants to judge the real need for the surgical corrections and to make clear to the patient the degree to which these deformities and defects will be corrected. A reasonably motivated patient who has a significant problem and who has emotional stability will benefit from plastic surgery in nearly every instance. However, there may be instances where a less emotionally stable patient may be helped if there is cooperation between the surgeon and the psychologist or psychiatrist.

## APPLICATIONS

The applications of Aesthetic Plastic Surgery are broad and encompass all areas of the body. Imagined defects and deformities are rarely if ever successfully operated upon, though minor defects may often cause considerable improvement psychologically if the patient's expectations are realistic. To achieve a desirable self-image (a feeling of being beautiful or at least normal), so important to most people in giving them a feeling of assurance, one considers surgery in various areas of the body for correction. The corrective rhinoplasty for correcting the nasal contour, the corrective otoplasty for correcting deformed ears, deformities of the chin to correct the "Andy Gump" chin or an overly prominent chin (prognathism) may be performed often with local anesthesia. Correction of droopy eyelids can give a much more pleasing appearance and correction of droopy eyebrows may eradicate the angry look on the patient's face. Face-lift procedures, including support of the neck, cheeks, temples, and usually combined with eyelid corrections, help to eradicate the aging of the face and is one of the most common procedures for which the plastic surgeon is called upon to perform. Corrections of the breasts for under-development is done with reasonable simplicity, and reduction of overly large or sagging breasts is carried out commonly by the plastic surgeon. Procedures such as these increase the comfort of the individual as well as improve appearance. The abdomen, which has been stretched and is redundant because of multiple pregnancies, or which is obese and redundant due to excess fat, may be corrected along with any attendant separation of the muscles or hernias that may be present. Thus, one combines functional problems and problems of appearance in correcting both. Reshaping in the hips, buttocks, and thighs is also relatively commonly done, but patients should always be aware that scars are the result of any surgery where an incision is made.

An important aspect of Aesthetic Plastic Surgery is reconstruction of the breasts. When the disease is cystic mastopathy without malignancy, a subcutaneous mastectomy is carried out with reconstruction of the breasts immediately using breast implants. This leaves a reasonably normal-looking breast with a reasonable soft natural feel in most instances. Reconstruction of the breasts following simple or radical mastectomy is also possible and is more commonly performed. The woman who has lost a breast frequently is compared in her attitude to the man who has been castrated. It is quite a blow to her feeling of femininity and often, the possibility of reconstruction is almost as important to the patient as the actual reconstruction itself. Obviously, one cannot completely duplicate the normal opposite breast, but a reconstructed breast can be very reasonable with the bra on and a satisfactory match in most instances even without the bra. The patient who knows of this possibility before her surgery can face the prospect of losing a breast surgically with much more confidence and with much less distress. The actual reconstruction can be carried out for those patients who desire it after the proper eradication of the malignant lesion. Usually this means a wait of some time when the lesion is an invasive malignancy, but often for the early malignancies, an early reconstruction is possible.

# Play Therapy
## Justin S. Psaila

### DEFINITION

Play may be employed in analytically oriented child psychotherapy as a specific therapeutic technique. Play therapy, a useful tool at the disposal of every child therapist, is based on the fact that play is the child's natural medium of selfexpression. It is the therapist's window into the child's fantasies, thoughts, and feelings. Also, as Erikson (1972) observed, play is the child's method of thinking through difficult experiences and employing a setting in which to resolve them.

Play Therapy is no longer exclusively employed in child psychoanalysis; rather, it is utilized by therapists with diverse theoretical backgrounds. Regardless of orientation, the therapist can make use of Play Therapy to aid the child in: 1) expression of fantasy and imagination; 2) release of energy and aggression; 3) opportunity for social learning; 4) opportunity for creative activity; and 5) acquisition of physical skills.

### HISTORY

Child psychoanalysis, as pointed out by Gardner (1972), is one form of child psychotherapy. It refers to analytic treatment approaches based on the theories and principles of Sigmund Freud, and used by Anna Freud, Melanie Klein, and their followers.

Freud (1908) first introduced play theory. He defined play as fantasy employing the use of real objects (toys) in contrast to pure fantasy (daydreams).

H. Hug-Hellmuth (1921) introduced play into child analysis. She was the first to appreciate adequately the value of play in the treatment of emotionally ill children. She observed that several symptoms and conflicts can be recognized by the study of play activities.

Melanie Klein (1932) elaborated on the use of Play Therapy. She modeled her treatment of children on adult analysis, and substituted free play for free association. She developed a play technique in which she translated every action of the child as having an underlying symbolic function and interpreted the unconscious content to the child.

Anna Freud (1928) considered Play Therapy an indispensable tool for familiarization with small children. She took issue, however, with Melanie Klein in that the child has not the same purposive attitude as an adult. She rejected Melanie Klein's posit that transference does not take place. Anna Freud employed Play Therapy primarily to gain the child's confidence and to establish a positive relationship. She employed direct interpretation sparingly, and was critical of the value of direct interpretation as employed by Melanie Klein.

In the last forty years much has been contributed to our knowledge of Play Therapy by child therapists in every field, and of diverse schools of thought.

## TECHNIQUE

Adults keep their egos tuned to reality by fantasy within themselves and verbalization with another. Erikson (1950, 1963) observed that, in modern Play Therapy, the way the child keeps his ego tuned to reality—that is, to make up for defeat, frustration, and suffering—is through toys and an adult (therapist) for himself.

The play situation offers a unique opportunity for the development of a therapeutic relationship between the child and the therapist. Anna Freud (1964) saw this relationship—or as she called it, "a real dependence on me"—as all important in child analysis. Play offers a timid child with few resources an opportunity to do something with the therapist. Play material offers an external medium of support while the child is discovering who the new person (therapist) is, and what they can be/do together.

A guiding principle to keep in mind while establishing a relationship and throughout the duration of therapy is that what the child is doing is less important than his freedom to do something, as long as the something is within the limits set down by the therapist. It is agreed that the setting of limits in Play Therapy is necessary. While some significant differences were found in the types of limits used, a considerable body of limits was employed by all. Limits investigated were in the areas of: 1) physical aggression against therapist; 2) physical aggression against equipment; 3) safety and health; 4) playroom routines; and 5) physical affection.

In psychoanalytically oriented child psychotherapy play may be used as a diagnostic tool. Through observation of the child at play the therapist can gauge the areas and the degree of the child's problems. Through play the child gives clues as to his rigidity, his inhibitions, his preoccupations, and his perceptions of people. It follows that play contributes to our knowledge of the patient's attitudes and feelings about himself and about others.

Through the play medium, the child takes the first step toward an organized and meaningful expression of himself. The naturalness and spontaneity of Play Therapy, as emphasized by Virginia Axline (1947), allows the child to safely display anxiety, fear, and anger; by use of his toys he gives the therapist concrete evidence of his feelings.

Play provides the child the opportunity to act out his fantasies and conflicts. Negative and anxious children are thus helped to externalize their aggressive feelings through play activity. The child's activities and his conversations can very often be easily translated from their symbolic meaning to his actual fantasies and imaginations. If the therapist is a Kleinian, he may take this opportunity to interpret the child's unconscious conflict (Klein, 1975). If he is a follower of the Freudian (Anna) method, the therapist may utilize this knowledge of the psychodynamics of the child in other ways, such as providing the child with certain experiences that can also be therapeutic (Gardner, 1972).

Cathartic use of play as put forward by Carr (1902) can relieve the child of psychic tension and aid him in sublimating his contained drives. Through play activity the child learns to change socially unacceptable impulses into socially acceptable behavior. Destructiveness and sadism may find overt outlet in sports and athletic activities.

It is readily apparent, then, that Play Therapy is of definite value in the treatment of emotionally ill children.

## Role of Therapist

In the play situation, as in all therapy, the therapist himself is the principal therapeutic agent. Each therapist must select from the wide array of techniques and ideas those which coincide with his own personality, and with which he feels comfortable. It is important that these techniques allow the child to know he has found a person who is interested in his feelings, and who will not condemn him because of them. This relationship, as Allen (1966) points out, is a very special one as it is begun with a goal of ending it.

It is entirely up to the therapist if, and at which time, he will use controlled play, structured play, directive or nondirective play, or place the child in a play therapy group. The therapist will determine this by the problems the child presents.

## Tools

Ginott (1960) has attempted to establish a rationale for selecting toys in Play Therapy. He considers the value of any toy, object, or activity in child therapy depends on its contribution to the realization of five objectives. A treatment toy should: 1) facilitate contact with the child; 2) evoke and encourage catharsis; 3) aid in developing insight; 4) furnish opportunities for reality testing; and 5) provide media for sublimation. Play material, then, must be chosen to serve a variety of needs. However, too much material and too wide a diversity tend to defeat the basic purpose. The main consideration is simplicity.

Toys that allow both for creative activity and destructive purposes should be available. Dolls and household toys allow children of both sexes a chance for imaginative play that introduces the element of relationship. Sutton-Smith and Rosenberg (1961) tell us that the types of games and toys used by children of both sexes have become more common over the past years. They feel this points to increasing similarity of the sexes.

Soldiers, toy guns, and similar toys offer material for aggressive expression and enable children to be more daring with their feelings than is otherwise possible.

Paints and drawing materials are most valuable. Finger paints allow a child an unusually wide scope for his movements. A child may tell his story graphically when he is unable to verbalize the feelings expressed in the drawings. A piece of paper, a few crayons, and, in modeling, a lump of clay offer the child a handy means of self-expression (Kanner 1935, 1948, 1957).

Although Gardner (1972) prefers a tape recorder to competitive games, a few competitive games, such as checkers, dominoes, or chess, may be useful. Mechanical toys and complicated puzzles have only occasional use. If the child becomes very absorbed in the thing he is doing, the fact that he is doing it with another may be lost. In this case the activity becomes too much of an end in itself.

## CONCLUSION

There have been a variety of approaches in Play Therapy with disturbed children that have been found effective. These approaches are similar in that they contain human values that the therapist attempts to communicate. All agree that play is the child's natural medium of expression and means of communication. Approaches differ in their philosophies and in their theories of personal dynamics. However, a substrate of common thinking is present among child therapists above and beyond their ultimate theoretical beliefs. It is important that one does not get bogged down in speculations about clinically unproven unconscious processes. However, a frame of reference appears necessary for conducting therapy even if it serves only the avowed interest of the therapist. It is only natural that what Erikson (1950, 1963) called the child's sense of mastery should follow from play, for to the child, play is a serious business of life (Mitchell and Mason, 1935).

---

# Poetry Therapy

## Jack J. Leedy and Sherry Reiter

### DEFINITION

Poetry Therapy is a therapeutic process in which poetry is used for the purpose of personal growth and emotional healing.

### HISTORY

Despite its recent recognition, Poetry Therapy is hardly a novel or new method of healing. It is believed that shamans and witch doctors of prehistoric times used rhythmic chants to control environmental upheaval and heal the sick of their tribe. Documented evidence proves its use as early as the fourth millennium *B.C.*, when Egyptian chants were written on papyrus and then ingested by the patient so that the power of the words would have immediate effect. The Bible fleetingly mentions the use of poetry and music by David to soothe the savage breast of King Saul about 1,000 B.C.

Considering the historical link between poetry and healing, it is not surprising that the ancient Greeks worshipped Apollo, the dual god of medicine and poetry. About 330 B.C., Aristotle, in Poetics, introduced the theory of catharsis, which became of monumental importance in the fields of therapy and art. The first official poetry therapist on record dates to the first century A.D., when a Roman physician by the name of Soranus treated the mentally disturbed by having his patients enact scripts in poetic form.

During the centuries that followed, poetry was used by individuals primarily for aesthetic purposes; recognition of the healing properties of poetry lay dormant till the twentieth century. Freud, the father of psychoanalysis, became fascinated with the similarities of dreams and poetry, as links to the unconscious. In 1959, the first formal Poetry Therapy program was instituted in the Psychiatric Division of Cumberland Hospital, Brooklyn, New York, by Dr. Jack Leedy, and the late poet Eli Greifer.

Ten years later, the Association for Poetry Therapy was founded. One of its major goals is the maintenance of standards in the training and certification of poetry therapists. The Association serves as a link and information source for about four hundred poetry therapists, including educators, mental health professionals, and recreation leaders who use Poetry Therapy in their work. In recent years, other centers for Poetry Therapy have sprung up across the country to train poetry therapists and serve the public.

## TECHNIQUE

Ideally, Poetry Therapy is used as an ancillary group therapy in conjunction with individual sessions. It is suggested that co-therapists of opposite sex conduct the session to encourage maximum manifestation of transference . The current training of poetry therapists who are knowledgeable in the fields of poetry, as well as psychology, is an encouragement to those psychologists, psychiatrists, and therapists who are hesitant to implement such a technique by themselves. The poetry therapist is, in one client's terms, "not one of us or one of them," but serves as a stepping stone or link between doctor and peer.

When a person identifies with the pain or joy of the poet, emotions that may have been previously repressed are released. The poet, whether alive or long dead, is a kindred spirit whose written expression reassures the client that he is not alone. By examining the thoughts and feelings in the poem rather than the patient directly, the client remains unthreatened and retains the objectivity necessary for gaining new perspectives.

Whether the therapist brings in written material or the clients themselves write on a given theme, poetry becomes the vehicle for a dynamic group or individual session. After sharing written material, discussion of feelings and associations follow. With the release of "emotional clutter," new insight and understanding is attained.

It is the responsibility of the poetry therapist to choose his material carefully, encouraging maximum identification and participation. The "isoprinciple," choosing a poem because its mood is identical to that of the client, is one effective guideline. Rhythm, meter, rhyme, and other poetic devices all contribute to the emotional affect of the poem, and must be taken into consideration.

Poetry utilizes the same mechanisms as dreams—symbolism, condensation, and displacement. These disguises allow the client to comfortably express what might otherwise be inappropriate or unacceptable to society. The contents and form of a poem may be examined, just as a dream is. Frequently the poem is more reliable, since its written form is complete and intact. Like the psychiatric symptom, poetry provides valuable information for the therapist, and simultaneously serves to bind and reduce anxiety.

## APPLICATIONS

As an added dimension to the total treatment plan, different forms of Poetry Therapy are used in almost all types of emotional as well as physical disorders, with all age groups. Successful groups are currently being conducted in hospitals, schools, mental health clinics, methadone treatment centers, prisons, recreation centers, and geriatric homes. It has been proven effective with neurotics, psycho-tics, retardates, drug addicts, alcoholics, and the suicidal.

Methods and techniques will necessarily vary according to the particular population. When a group has limited verbal ability, as in a retarded or preschool population, poems may be acted out or spoken, rather than written. Or a group may dictate to the group leader, which is a technique popular with adolescents in six hundred schools.

Poetry Therapy enables the client to honestly communicate what he may not be able to express in any other form. For this reason, Poetry Therapy is often successful when other therapies have failed.

# Positive Therapy

*Allen E. Wiesen*

## DEFINITION

Positive Therapy is the systematic selection of life over death. Existential in nature, it assumes man's capacity to recognize thoughts, feelings, and actions that will promote a positive outcome versus a negative one, and to choose the positive course. Well-established principles of human behavior, including cognitive and behavioral principles, are subsumed under the principle of human control. Thus, deep relaxation techniques, biofeedback, cognitive methods, and rational-emotive methods can be accounted for by the principles of Positive Therapy itself. Positive Therapy, then, may be seen as a "master system" under which many long-established concepts can be viewed within a positive existential framework. Positive Therapy is at odds only with negative therapies or negative aspects of therapies that counter man's ability to choose. Psychoanalysis and deterministic models are rejected by the positive therapist.

## HISTORY

Positive Therapy has a diverse history with strong roots in William James's pragmatism, Albert Ellis's Rational-Emotive Therapy, modern self-control principles, European existentialism, and contemporary understanding of human physiology. I have developed it over a period of thirteen years of clinical practice, and, it provides a very consistent framework within which to understand a very wide range of human thoughts, feelings, and actions.

## TECHNIQUE

The method of practicing Positive Therapy is best described in the book *Positive Therapy: Making the Very Best of Everything*. The positive therapist operates always with the understanding that "life offers but two alternatives: positive and negative." The therapeutic approach enables the individual to make predictions as to the outcome of his thoughts, feelings, or actions and to select those that will have a foreseeable positive outcome in his life. This aspect of Positive Therapy is derived from William James's pragmatic orientation. There is minimal involvement with the client's history, and the focus is on the present and the future. The relationship between the client and the therapist is as client to consultant rather than doctor to patient. More specifically, the therapist facilitates the client's awareness of negative thoughts, feelings, and actions and provides him with techniques to convert them into positive thoughts, feelings, and actions. Fundamental to Positive Therapy is the concept of the "trap circuit." This is the primary unit of self-destructive thinking, feeling, or acting. Negative thoughts (in the form of sentences or "movies") fall within the category of TC I (trap circuit type I). TC II is a designation for behavior that will produce a negative outcome in the individual's life; TC III describes negative emotional states. These three components, thoughts, feelings, and actions comprise a system in which each component reinforces the other. The positive therapist, then, helps the client become aware of the system within which he is operating, helping him abandon a negative system for a positive one.

## APPLICATIONS

Positive Therapy is broadly applicable to most aspects of mental and emotional existence. The principles are very useful in the treatment of anxiety, depression, psychosomatic disorders, marital difficulties, parent-child relationships, and so on. This wide application is possible because of the concept of the positive versus the negative system. For example, psychosomatic disorders, such as headaches, are treated through a combination of cognitive changes, relaxation techniques, and specific behavioral changes oriented toward reducing stress. Interpersonal conflict is viewed within the perspective of low-tension versus high-tension communication. Positive Therapy, then, enables the therapist to approach a very wide range of human concerns within the framework of a highly consistent model.

# Primal Therapy

## E. Michael Holden

### DEFINITION

Primal Therapy is a psychotherapy in which patients vividly reexperience intensely painful events of infancy and childhood. Such reexperiences are called Primals. A Primal is a two-phase response pattern, which starts with intense suffering and a sympathetic nervous system crisis. The first phase is a crescendo of involuntary panic during which one cries or screams in agony. This reaches a peak and is abruptly followed by a parasympathetic recovery phase. At the start of the second phase one has a vivid reexperience of an early-life painful event. The recall is total and organismic. The recalled memory is typically visual, but any or all of the sensory modalities may be included in the reexperience. At the end of a completed Primal one is slightly euphoric, very lucid, and profoundly calm.

Primal therapists consider Primal Therapy to be neurosis in reverse. Neurosis comes into being because children are hurt. They respond partially to that hurt. The parts of the pain responses not felt (completely experienced and expressed) in childhood are the basis for neurosis in adults. In Primal Therapy complete responses to early pains occur, and neurosis dissolves.

### HISTORY

Dr. Arthur Janov saw his first Primal in 1967, as described in his first book, *The Primal Scream*. By 1977, approximately 1,400 people had had Primal Therapy.

### TECHNIQUE

The techniques of Primal Therapy have never been published. There are many mock-primal clinics in the world and we have learned from patients at those clinics that Primal Therapy is extremely dangerous when attempted by those without training. If a patient at a mock-primal clinic obtains excessive access to early Primal Pain, the result is mental fragmentation and suicidal impulses. Because Primal Therapy deals with Painful *feelings* rather than *words* about those feelings, it should not be attempted by those without appropriate training. (Pain is not learned as an idea, but rather as a total experience; thus, it is unchanged if approached only with words.)

#### Research

Neurosis is a psychophysiological disorder involving the brain and body. We cannot measure Primal Pain but we can measure the way it is physiologically processed.

In a completed Primal, the first phase includes marked elevation of pulse rate, blood pressure, and EEG voltage, and an increase of 2-4°F in body temperature. At the end of a completed Primal (and physiologically, its definition), all the vital signs and EEG voltage are below baseline values. Over many months in Primal Therapy there are sustained decreases in pulse, blood pressure, and EEG voltage, and a 2-3°F decrease in core body temperature. Recent studies of plasma epinephrine and norepinephrine in Primal patients have disclosed 10 to 80 percent decreases in the levels of these hormones. Preliminary studies of plasma lipids have also indicated decreases in plasma triglycerides and cholesterol.

## APPLICATIONS

Our experience indicates to us that there is but one neurosis—the individual's response to unintegrated childhood pain. Because a wide variety of disorders are but many individual responses to pain, the classification of many "neuroses" is in fact artificial. Anxiety, depression, thought-fragmentation, preoccupation with death, etc., are all partial responses to Primal Pain.

Excessive smoking, drinking, and all the addictions are responses to Primal Pain. The sexual dysfunctions, some hormonal disorders, and all psychosomatic disorders are responses to Primal Pain. Full reexperience of the early Pain, the Pain which is the *raison d'etre* for neurosis, is the way to reverse neurosis. Asthma, colitis, hypertension, and migraine are particularly responsive to Primal Therapy. When neurosis fails—as a group of mechanisms for dealing with childhood Pain—the result is psychosis. Although it takes much longer, Primal Therapy can also reverse nonorganic psychosis.

# Privation Psychotherapeutic Technique

## Joan Erdheim

## DEFINITION

The Privation Psychotherapeutic Technique was expounded by Sandor Ferenczi, one of Freud's closest colleagues and personal friends. This technique of bringing about frustration for the purpose of growth was thought by Ferenczi to be an active psychoanalytic technique. In contrast to the typical passive stance assumed by the analyst (one where the patient's free associations are not interfered with except for the purpose of making interpretations), the analyst adapting the privation technique introduces the recommendation that the patient cease certain behavior. The rationale is that this behavior, masturbatory in nature, has become a resistance to treatment. Only by its cessation, Ferenczi suggested, could the tension that this behavior dissipated be allowed to build. More tension would promote the awakening of significant early memories and fantasies. These dormant events, holding the key to the resolution of the patient's pathology, were previously unknown to the patient and therapist. They had been unconsciously acted out via this masturbatory behavior and thus not remembered nor talked about. The behavior

Ferenczi considered to be a masturbatory equivalent, worthy of prohibiting, includes women rubbing their thighs together when on the couch, men sticking their hands in their pockets, urinary habits before sessions, flatus activities, sphincter play in general, handling of the face, movement of the legs, tics, and shaking of the body.

## HISTORY

Like many of the innovative analysts, Ferenczi made his historical discoveries about treatment in his work with patients, the patients he most fervently struggled to cure. He speaks of a patient with whom he had reached an impasse; that is, until he discovered her to be masturbating on the couch via pressing her thighs together.

Ferenczi claimed, "I must confess—and this is characteristic of the slowness with which an incipient new point of view erupts into consciousness—that even then it was a long time before I hit on the idea of forbidding the patient to adopt this position." According to Ferenczi the eventual effect of this privation was "staggering." The patient to whom customary genital discharge was inaccessible, experienced intense bodily and psychological pressure, ultimately leading to long-forgotten memory fragments (i.e., childhood events that permitted the discovery of the most important traumatic causes for her illness). Ferenczi claimed significant progress (i.e., the capacity for genital orgasm).

This case was written up in a paper entitled *Technical Difficulties in the Analysis of a Case of Hysteria (Including Observations on Larval Forms of Onanism and "Onanistic Equivalents") (1919)*. The paper greatly stimulated Freud's opinions on active privation in the treatment situation. In his 1919 paper entitled *Lines of Advance in Psychoanalytic Therapy*, Freud referred to Ferenczi's ideas, raised some questions about them, then proceeded to enunciate his own fundamental rule of privation.

Freud stated that developments in psychoanalytic therapy will no doubt proceed along new lines, "first and foremost along the one which Ferenczi in his paper on treatment of hysteria has termed the active approach." Freud questioned, "Are we to leave it to the patient to deal alone with the resistances we have pointed out to him? ... Does it not seem natural that we should help him by putting him into the mental situation most favorable to the solution of the conflict which is our aim? ... Should we hesitate to alter external circumstances by intervening in a suitable manner?" He concluded, "I think activity of such a kind on the part of the analyzing physician is unobjectionable and entirely justified." Freud continued, "I shall not attempt today to introduce you to this new technique which is still in the course of being evolved, but will content myself with enunciating a fundamental principle which will probably dominate our work in this field. ... Analytic treatment should be carried through as far as possible under privation, in a state of abstinence."

Other historical analysts, such as Theodore Reik, seemed to subscribe to this general privation rule. Reik likened the psychoanalytic process to the workings of a machine. In order for both to run well, some degree of friction was indispensable.

Debate about whether therapy should take place in an essentially depriving or a gratifying milieu has gone on and still continues. Ferenczi himself later changed his mind and felt that what really is needed for growth is love (i.e., indulgence from the therapist).

## TECHNIQUE

The technique is one where the analyst is on the lookout for masturbatory behavior (e.g., the female patient rubbing her legs together) or what might be highly sublimated masturbatory equivalents (e.g., playing with one's hair). This is especially important to do when the analyst feels therapy has reached a stalemate. This behavior is then forbidden; tension in the patient rises and the tension gets converted into his (the patient's) conscious awareness of libidinal wishes. These wishes then can get traced back to early traumas. The analyst thus has new material to interpret to the patient, the material that will lead to resolution of the neuroses. The impasse has been bypassed.

## APPLICATIONS

According to Ferenczi, the privation technique should not be used in the beginning of treatment before a solid working alliance has been given time to develop. The patient might be prompted to break off treatment if the analyst's introduction of this command is premature. At the end of treatment this technique is often necessary. It frequently induces the last presentation of unconscious material.

Beginning therapists are advised against using it. They may easily go wrong in their application and may furthermore lose the necessary insight into the dynamics of the neuroses.

All neurosis, especially obsessional neuroses and anxiety hysterias, are conditions where the privation technique might be applied. Anxiety neurotics suffering from sexual inhibitions (e.g., women with frigidity problems, men with premature ejaculation and involuntary emission disturbances) might be especially helped. Neurastheniacs, patients suffering from chronic diffuse fatigue, and patients with psychomotor symptomology such as tics, are good candidates for this technique.

Therapists of all types today take their stand on the principle of privation. Robert Langs, an innovative psychoanalyst, strongly believes in creating and maintaining a privation-type therapeutic situation (he terms it a "secure frame"), where both patient and therapist must be responsible for controlling their acting-out behavior. Likewise est, a therapy as diverse from Langs's psychoanalytic approach as is any, introduces deprivation behavior for the purposes of facilitating a quick catharsis.

# Provocative Therapy

*Frank Farrelly and Jeffrey M. Brandsma*

## DEFINITION

Provocative Therapy is a system of verbal psychotherapy wherein the therapist engages in a wide range of behavior, largely in the role of the Devil's Advocate. Through the use of several provocative and humorous techniques, paradox, and nonverbal acceptance, the therapist attempts to elicit, often through the client's resistance, behavior that is self- and other enhancing.

## HISTORY

Therapists and theorists have long noted the utility and influence of humor, paradox, provocation, and play in selected ways with various cases. The systematizing of this form of therapy occurred in the experiences of co-author Frank Farrelly, as he worked at the Mendota State Hospital in the psychotherapy research project with Carl Rogers from 1961 to 1963. The basic parameters and techniques were conceptualized and defined in the clinical experiences of the following years, resulting in a book to communicate its status in 1973- 1974.

## TECHNIQUE

Many techniques are employed to elicit the following behavior from clients: 1) affirmation of self-worth, both verbally and behaviorally; 2) appropriate assertiveness in tasks and relationships; 3) realistic defensiveness; 4) psychosocial reality testing and discrimination learning; 5) risk taking in relationships, especially with regard to feelings of anger, vulnerability, and affection.

Some of the most common sets of techniques are as follows: 1) provocative (and paradoxical) verbal communication, wherein the therapist amplifies and encourages self-defeating behavior, ideas, and attitudes in a humorous context; 2) nonverbal (often qualifying) communication, such as a twinkle in the eye, selective use of touch, smiling, intonation, and so on. Nonverbal communication combines with the provocative verbal communication, which means that at least two levels of communication often occur, therefore, at times, contradictory messages are sent, such as saying one thing and meaning another. These qualifiers often convey the therapist's empathy for and contact with the patient; 3) humorous techniques that include banter, exaggeration, reduction to absurdity, ridicule, sarcasm, irony, and relevant jokes. Despite humorous denials verbally, humor is one of the chief mechanisms of conveying sincere warmth and caring; 4) confrontation and feedback both in terms of the social consequences of one's attitudes and behavior and in terms of the immediate subjective perception of the client by the therapist. This can be done directly or indirectly, in straightforward or metaphoric terms; 5). dramatic techniques, such as role playing various fantasized scenarios, with the therapist modeling the patient's negative behavior and playing along with the client in "larger-than-life" fashion, suggesting ridiculous solutions to problems.

Provocative Therapy has identifiable theoretical roots in Client-Centered and Rational-Emotive Therapy, but with very different application. There are some descriptive, theoretical, and practical conceptions similar to those of Victor Frankel, Jay Haley, and Watzlawick, Beavin, and Jackson. These are more fully explored in the book *Provocative Therapy.*

## APPLICATIONS

In clinical practice there have been no restrictions on age, sex, educational background, social class, or degree of problem. Settings have ranged from traditional ones to less formal encounters. The therapy has been employed in groups, individually, and with families and couples. This approach, in addition, was developed on state hospital in-patients and employed with persons having diagnoses from all the functional diagnostic categories. In the hands of a competent therapist, it is thought to be particularly appropriate for character disorders, psychotics, and the inarticulate.

# Psychedelic Therapy
### Kenneth E. Godfrey

## DEFINITION

Psychedelic Therapy utilizes psychedelic substances (e.g., LSD-25, psilocybin, and mescaline) to facilitate therapeutic change. The success of the therapy depends on knowledgeable selection of the patient, with subsequent responsible supportive orientation, administration, guidance, interpretation, integration, and termination of the therapeutic process with the patient.

## HISTORY

In 1943, five years after he synthesized LSD-25, Dr. Albert Hoffman discovered its mind-altering capabilities. As a model psychosis-producing drug, it was studied until A. K. Bush and W. C. Johnson wrote of it as an aid to psychotherapy. A. Hoffer and H. Osmund, utilizing it as a therapeutic treatment for alcoholism, described its characteristic reaction and defined it as "psychedelic"—"mind manifesting or revealing." Since that time, thousands have received psychedelic treatment for scores of psychiatric illnesses or conditions in varying ways and with differing results.

Prior to the early 1960s, work with LSD-25 was largely by and with scientists. However, since that time it spread to the "street culture" and found itself the center of heated, emotional controversy in the lay as well as in scientific circles. Some scientists (prohibitionists or panaceans) contributed to the unscientific and irresponsible propaganda surrounding uses of hallucinogenic substances. Such reaction affected the scientific work with the drug, and scientific research into and treatment with LSD-25 was largely discontinued. There is no doubt in my mind (Godfrey) that LSD-25 is a most powerful and mind-altering drug. It therefore deserves great responsibility, knowledge, and caring on the part of those employing it. To be licensed to administer the drug, one must first contact the Food and Drug Administration.

## TECHNIQUE

Selection of the therapeutic team, the principal therapist, co-therapist, and others working in the area is of paramount importance. Qualifications of the therapist include: emotional maturity, thorough grounding in the theories of human development, knowledge of health and illness in relationship to the whole person, experience in conducting psychotherapy, capacity to deal with very primitive material in the patient and self, strength of convictions, a secure self-image and identity, a reality orientation, persistence, and versatility. The therapist should have, during the therapeutic process, the ability to smoothly change from the role of supportive to interpretive, physical to psychological, subjective interpretive to objective and vice versa, yet still hold the therapeutic relationship. These above attributes cannot be too strongly stressed.

All members of the team need to understand and agree to the basic philosophy of the therapy yet also retain their individuality. A man and a woman should be working together as principal co-therapists with each individual patient. These principal co-therapists must know the importance of their role and practice it to provide genuine human contact of a quality that most patients have not been previously open to receiving. All team members must commit themselves for the duration of treatment.

Selecting the patient to be treated should be done by the treatment team. The patient ideally will be intelligent, with a secure enough ego to be able to withstand loss of ego boundaries, he will utilize, work with, and integrate the symbols of the experiences, commit himself to the process and the team, and be dedicated to gaining health. All these are seldom found in one individual patient.

Within a treatment setting, which is informal (homelike), supportive, aesthetically pleasant, comfortable, and accepting, one should train the therapeutic team (at least two per patient) to include all personnel within the treatment area in a therapeutic psychological set. This includes open, positive attitudes of acceptance and reinforcement of values of great human worth, caring, protecting, helping, relating in a loving, empathetic manner, with a view to finding health within the individual.

Initially one works with each patient to attain understanding of his personality and illness, to establish a positive rapport, to define goals, attain a commitment to the therapeutic agreement, orient the patient to the specific treatment modality and substance to be utilized. After these conditions are fulfilled, the technique of treatment is chosen to accomplish the goal(s) of treatment with the least expenditure of time and personnel.

Several aspects of the process of psychedelic treatment are common to most treatment centers. Of these are: 1) an informal, supportive setting, 2) a therapeutic, psychological set, 3) a comfortable lounge or bed for the patient, 4) a cover for the eyes, 5) stereophonic high fidelity headphones, 6) a program of music, 7) a red rose or carnation, 8) a two-sided hand mirror, 9) pictures of people, especially those significant to the patient, 10) food and drink in due time, 11) a team of two (man and woman) therapists who are strong and committed to the treatment program.

After thorough psychological testing, a period of time to get well acquainted, to answer questions, the time for the first psychedelic session is agreed upon. The team (including the patient) then begins its assault on the patient's illness. On the agreed upon morning, the team gathers in the treatment setting. The drug (LSD-25) is soon taken orally by the patient. Conversation, looking at pictures, feelings of closeness, support and caring are there to be experienced. As soon as some visual or other perceptual changes are noticed by the patient, he is fitted with blindfolds and stereo headphones and lies down to listen to the music selected to assist through the experience. Both therapists are in the psychedelic therapeutic setting at all times to support, protect, interpret, console, orient, and do whatever is called for to enlighten and help the patient to discover genetic roots, mistaken ideas, fears, love, acceptance, intrinsic worth, relationships, and other significant truths toward health.

In the experience, multitudinous symbolically significant things occur. With and from these symbolic occurrences, one can progress to health. The treatment team assists the patient to interpret, consolidate, and integrate the experience into the patient's own life.

Psychedelic treatment helps one to grasp the extent of one's mind, its relationships to others, to things, to thoughts and to 'The Light," which is often felt to be God. One or more (up to one hundred) experiences may be used to treat one individual patient. The size dosage for each usually runs from 50 micrograms to 400 micrograms LSD-25. The larger dose tends to produce a more psychedelic experience, while the smaller seems to encourage an analytic-type experience.

## APPLICATIONS

Psychedelic Therapy is used for the treatment of: 1) neurotic illnesses; 2) character disorders (homosexuality, criminal characters); 3) addictions (alcoholism [sedativism], opiate addiction, other drugs); 4) terminal illnesses (cancer); 5) some psychoses (schizophrneia—paranoid type, manic depressive psychoses).

Most therapists having had experience utilizing psychedelic drugs as adjuncts or tools of therapy feel it speeds up the therapeutic process in all areas of illness. In cases of homosexuality, criminal character disorders, schizophrenia, and other psychoses, it is felt to possibly be the best help to a permanent normality, though it has not yet received a fair trial in those areas. Isolated instances can be found to strengthen that point.

Terminally ill cancer patients undergo immense suffering, as do those close to the patient. The victim tends to be held in an isolation manufactured by fear, pain, perfidy, denial, guilt, anger, grief, fantasies, and beliefs about death and dying. Hopelessness pervades. After psychedelic treatment, the majority need much less opiates for pain; they tend to face reality and work through the process so as to lose the fear of death, anger, and isolation. The immediate family profits and grows as well in being helped to work through its own grief process. If for no other reason than that of terminal illness, Psychedelic Therapy should continue.

# Psychic Healing

## Stanley Krippner

## DEFINITION

"Psychic healing" and "paranormal healing" are terms used to describe the alleviation of physical or psychological problems when there appears to be no adequate medical, physiological, or psychological explanation for the healing. It is one example of a variety of alleged events categorized as "psi phenomena"—interactions between organisms and their environment (including other organisms) that cannot be explained by currently held scientific models of the universe.

Psychotherapy, the treatment of problems of mental health, can be defined as a structured series of contacts between a socially sanctioned healer and a patient who seeks relief, and who acknowledges the ability of the healer. Using this definition, any number of unconventional practitioners can be regarded as psychotherapists, whether or not they are also called *curanderos*, faith healers, folk healers, medicine men, shamans, spiritists, or witch doctors. All of these individuals purport to alleviate symptoms, change behavior, and improve personal functioning through procedures that are not consistent with currently held scientific models. As a result, these individuals are often called "psychic healers," even though it is not actually know if psi represents any part of their treatment. Thus, the use of the term "psychic healer" does not imply that the practitioners so described actually possess paranormal abilities.

## HISTORY

"Psychic healers" have no common historical tradition, as they have operated throughout history in virtually all parts of the world. Krippner and Villoldo (1976) divide "psychic healers" into four categories, admitting considerable overlap:

1. *Shamans.* In the strict sense, shamanism is a historical phenomenon of Central Asia where the term originated. Later, similar developments were observed elsewhere. The shaman is, among other things, a magician and a "healer." He (or she) specializes in altered states of consciousness in which the soul is said to leave the body, ascending to the sky or descending to the underworld.

2. *Spiritists.* Shamans control their "spirit allies" without becoming their instruments. Spiritist "healers," however, claim to be taken over by "spirits" during "healing" ceremonies. The nineteenth-century French spiritist Allan Kardec wrote several instructional books that have been especially influential in Latin America. However, "spirit incorporation" also takes place among spiritist "healers" in Asia and Africa.

3. *Esoterics.* Esoteric "healers" follow various "hidden" teachings, such as alchemy, astrology, the Kabbalah, radionics, tantra, and Yoga. The writings of such esoteric teachers as Alice Bailey are also used as the basis of "psychic healing" by some.

4. *Intuitives.* The intuitive "healer" undergoes no special training or initiation, responding instead to a "call from God" or simply beginning to "lay-on" hands. Olga Worrall and Ruth Carter Stapleton are examples of intuitive "healers."

## TECHNIQUES

Treatment procedures instigated by "psychic healers" do fulfill the four basic components of psychotherapy as outlined by Torrey (1972).

1. Therapists name what is wrong with, their patients and the very act of naming it has a therapeutic effect because the patient's anxiety is decreased by the knowledge that a respected and trusted therapist understands what is wrong. The identification of the offending agent (a traumatic childhood experience, violation of a taboo, possession by an ancestral spirit) also may activate a series of associated ideas in the patient's mind, producing confession, abreaction, and catharsis.

2. Personal qualities of the therapist constitute an important component of psychotherapy. Rogers (1957) has conducted research demonstrating that "accurate empathy, non-possessive warmth, and genuineness" are of critical importance in producing effective psychotherapy; these traits appear to be more important than the specific techniques used by the therapists or the type of training they have had.

The selection of therapists in other cultures is handled by criteria other than academic achievement; for example, through heredity, "supernatural" designation, self-designation, and/or the automatic designation of individuals who are different (orphans, the blind, the crippled, those who report "visions," etc.). Much has been made of the allegation that some primitive cultures select their "healers" from the ranks of the emotionally disturbed. However, Torrey (1972) has produced data that indicate that "most therapists in other cultures are unusually stable and mature individuals."

3. Along with a shared world view and the personal qualities of the therapist, patient expectations are an important part of the therapeutic process. Frank (1974) concludes that the apparent success of healing procedures based on various ideologies demonstrates that the healing power of faith resides in the patient's mind, not in the validity of its object.

4. Psychotherapeutic procedures represent the fourth component and Torrey reports that the "techniques of therapy all over the world are found to be the same. ... Over all the similarities in the techniques used by witch doctors and psychiatrists far outweigh the differences." How effective are the procedures used by "psychic healers"? Torrey has surveyed the existing data and concludes that they have about the same success rate as that obtained by Western psychiatrists.

Psychic healers, of course, use a number of techniques and ascribe to several concepts foreign to traditional Western psychotherapists. It is these procedures that are purportedly paranormal. No single technique or concept characterizes all psychic healers, but the most common are: discarnate entities, Divine intervention, life after death, "out-of-body" experience, "laying-on" of hands, magical remedies and ceremonies, "subtle bodies and energies," and psi phenomena (e.g., psychokinesis).

## APPLICATIONS

In cultures where there is no access to Western medicine, native "healers," typically, are totally responsible for health-care services. However, in countries replete with so-called psychic healers as well as physicians and psychotherapists, the advice usually given is to see both a conventional and an unconventional practitioner.

As Western psychotherapy attempts to explore alternative approaches to diagnosis and treatment, the psychic healing traditions deserve to be examined. Kiev (1968) has concluded that native or "folk" psychotherapy is "important not only as a form of prevention which contributes to lower incidence, but as a form of treatment agency whose presence leads to a reduced flow of people going to hospitals." In other words, an intensified study of Psychic Healing may well produce important practical as well as theoretical results.

# Tibetan Psychic Healing

## Ven. Norbu L. Chan

### DEFINITION

Because so many people insist on accepting the world of their own making, or what Vajrayana Buddhism calls the illusion projection of the mind, it is no wonder that the cases that could be treated by what is termed as mind healing are plentiful.

### HISTORY

In approximately *A.D.* 724, Padma Sambhava, a famous Indian Buddhist Tantric Master, was invited to Tibet to teach Tantra healing techniques, as well as Buddhism, to the king and people of Tibet. These techniques include extraordinary insight of a keen nature developed by much meditation. This insight delves into the causes of the afflicted person's illness. Mantras and incantations are utilized along with special musical instruments and yogic movements of special exercises, such as Kum Nye, which relax the body and mind. A final and very important understanding of the component nature of beings in this universe—how the molecular structures come into and go out of existence—has to be obtained by the practitioner. Since the training for these skills is so strict, only Tantra Lamas have been effective in practice.

Padma Sambhava made this prediction: "When the iron bird flies on horses with wings, then the Vajrayana Path will go to the land of the red man." In other words, when the West has achieved a certain technical ripeness, the Vajrayana Path will be open to them.

### TECHNIQUE

The reasons for disease can be many. They include life-style, diet, temperament, and heredity. All of these factors come from the same place: the patient's mind.

The success of treatment depends solely on the patient's willingness to follow the plan of the Tibetan mind healer. The ideas of the West toward materialism are very damaging to the maintenance of health. Most patients suffer from an extreme fear of death, which has been thrust upon them by constant rejection of the elderly, commercial marketing schemes to boost youth, and the falsehood that man and his body are immortal. What man, the thinking being, truly is is immortal, but his body is not.

In order to get the mind at peace and rest, the patient must develop an insight, through the guidelines of the Lama-physician, as to what is indeed real and what is not—what he really is and really is not. The patient is further instructed that all material things around him have only a temporary nature. This includes his own material form, this planet, and all that dwell within this universe. At first the patient is either horrified or depressed when he finds that everything that he has given a reality to has no real existence—that no self can exist apart from another self. The patient then must become the student and the "debriefing" of this illusionary world begins.

Tibetan mind healing was taught only to devoted *trapas* (students) of Lamas in Tibet. The teachings were passed along by oral transmission, which was known to be "secret" merely because the Lama insisted on such rigid devotion and sincerity. The Lama becomes the complete dictator of the student and all other goals have to be discarded. Few individuals wish to follow such a stringent path, and therefore, consider the teachings "secret." The basic teachings are those of Vajrayana Buddhism, which extend far beyond an intellectual level of "word understanding," but reach into depths of the Oneness of all beings—beyond all opposites.

The present mind that we are calling "mind" is none other than an accumulation of thoughts, opinions, and reactions to those thoughts and opinions that based on the proportion of greed, anger, and attachment that man has foolishly accepted as his "individual reality." Man has been conditioned to accept all that he sees as real and solid, which, of course, is not true. No one can deny that the material world surrounding us is made up of atoms revolving at a speed according to the vibrational level of its existence. The reasons for each material being's vibrational level is Karmic and can be altered only when the person has learned to control his Karma—or when the person is fortunate enough to become acquainted with a Lama and mind healer who can teach him how to control his Karma. Counseling is one of the main applications in mind healing, along with sincere love and no regard for time consumption. Energy patterns are also altered by a physical exchange of energies from the Lama to the patient. The techniques of this energy exchange are very traditional and stated in symbols and terms that are so profound that words without experience cannot give an accurate rendering of their effect.

## APPLICATIONS

Diseases that have been considered terminal have been "cured" by Tibetan mind healing. However, the Lama psychic healer carefully counsels his patients that their deaths have been only "momentarily postponed" and that by the very fact that they have been born, they must eventually die.

Sociological, cultural, and religious blind belief contribute to the sickness of man. Man tends to accept the phenomenal realities of these beliefs without understanding that they are, in fact, the results of past actions that appear as molecules now arranged in what appears to be forms that make our senses tell us an "object" has appeared. We react to that "object" according to our conditioning behavior. The psychic healer teaches the patient to doubt his senses. Once the patient begins to understand the true nature of the Universe and the force that brought him into and out of existence, he will begin to see that all life, all thoughts, opinions, and concepts are quite transitory, illusionary, and without any real substance except for the mind that perceives them. The ultimate goal is the attainment of the Oneness beyond the hypnotic world of shape and form—beyond birth, old age, and death.

As the patient approaches a deeper insight, he will begin to understand that: "If there is a world of being, of birth, old age, and death, good and evil, sorrow and happiness, pain and pleasure, hate and love, then there must be an opposite state that is inconceivable to express by spoken or written word—a state that is called the deathless state—beyond the confinements of the present material world."

# Psychoanalysis

## Howard H. Schlossman

### DEFINITION

Psychoanalysis is a psychological science based on the theory that there is causal relationship between present mental activity of wish, thought, or behavior, with their conscious and unconscious components, and all past experience. This has been called "the principle of psychic determinism": nothing occurs by chance, each psychic event is influenced by preceding episodes. The affect (emotion) laden and energy-charged linkage of the present with the past is governed by a structure of mental apparatus, process, and function originating in hereditary elements. These mature along pathways of psychosexual development molded by environmental stress, thereby structuring by their mixture individuals of unique character and personality.

### HISTORY

In approximately eighty years of application, Psychoanalysis has become a method of treating mental illness, a technique for scientific investigation of the mind, a general human psychology and philosophy contributing added clarity to every human experience. The term itself owes invention to Sigmund Freud, who, in conjunction with his followers developed the science. Freud's early experimentation with hypnosis as an attempt to free patients of psychic symptoms and suffering led to the frustrating awareness that many subjects were not hypnotizable. In a variation of technique, Freud found that a firm insistence on communication of all thought without any conscious censorship produced data of repressed material similar to that obtained under hypnosis. This, the investigative procedure of "free association," had the great advantage of far broader applicability than hypnosis and the involvement in the treatment of the conscious, reality-oriented judgment of the patient. The doctor and patient working together establish a "therapeutic alliance," where their joint efforts are directed to understanding and mastering the conflicts inherent in the psychic pathology. Having begun as a medical procedure, the initial goal was treatment. Through the recognition of similarities in content and structure found in psychological symptoms, dreams, character types, myths, and religion, Psychoanalysis became a general human psychology some years later.

As an evolving science, it has gone through a number of theoretical changes as new data came to light from practice and experiment. The present theory, the structural theory, is based on the psychic model of id, ego, and superego. The id is the most primitive structure of the mind. It is the repository of the sexual drive (the libido) and the aggressive drive, called collectively "the instinctual drives." These are expressed through urges arising from biological needs; they are loosely structured and easily displaced because the energy is not bound to a particular wished-for person or thing represented in the mind. The ego is the mental portion that is in contact with external reality and the other portions of the mind, the id, and superego. It "occupies a position between the primal instincts, based on the physiological needs of the body and the demands of the outer world." Through its structural ability to restrain and channel, the ego can mediate between the demands of inner psychological reality of wishes and urges of external reality. The superego, the last portion to develop, does so through identification with the attitudes of parents and internalization of the ethical standards of society. It represents moral attitudes, social and sexual standards, and personal ideals and values. By means of provoking anxiety and guilt feelings in the ego, the superego can interfere or assist the ego in its functions of mediating the expression of instinctual drives within external reality.

Conflict both within and among the major components described above leads to compromises of energy and apparatus and results in symptom, character formation, and/ or sublimation with or without pathological distortion. The form of the compromise is individual. As mentioned earlier, it is a product of the early interactions of biologically base instinctual drives and inherited mental structures with the environment. In turn this form influences the capacity for adaptation of the early psychic organization to the external world. By perceptual feedback, memory, and integration, learning and development proceeds to yet another level of compromise leading to enhanced coping with the inner world of fantasy and urges and the outer world of society. It might be conceptualized as an ascending spiral with many vertical or resonant lines of connection among the rungs.

## TECHNIQUE

The technical procedure that distinguishes the classical, or "Freudian," psychoanalysis is "free association." Within this unique rule of treatment, all data of dreams, fantasies, urges, slips, and so on are communicated. The purpose is the recognition of the unconscious thoughts and withheld affects that shape the conscious communications. By examining the interrelationships of the conscious communications and repressed data, we can infer the operative force of unconscious fantasy and wish. The analyst, for his part, maintains a neutrality, refrains from introjecting his own associations, and does not educate. He interprets the data of protective mental mechanisms or repressed thoughts as it is necessary in order to draw attention to unconscious resistance impeding the analytic work. Free association, then, with its freedom of expression and unjudged acceptability, ultimately reestablishes in the perceptions and feelings about the therapist the childhood constellation of wishes, injunctions, and compromises that were originally directed to the parents and assists in understanding the core of the subsequent psychopathology. This phenomenon is called "transference"; i.e., the childhood constellation is transferred onto the therapist. The major childhood organizer of character structure is the triangular relationship of mother, father, and child, called the "Oedipus complex." Its manifestation during the analysis is the largest contribution to the content of the transference. The analysis and understanding of the transference manifestations, of which the patient has been consciously unaware, is made possible by the neutrality and accepted objectivity of the analyst. This adds the necessary sense of conviction concerning the unconscious that facilitates change and symptom relief. As though in turning on a light in the dark unknown, the terrors are exposed as empty and anxiety is no longer needed as a signal of danger.

In view of the universality of the unconscious, the psychoanalyst also has transference attitudes and desires of which he is unaware. They may be completely outside of consciousness or well rationalized and thus acceptable to conscious judgment. Therefore, in order to maintain objectivity and prevent these needs from interfering in the treatment of the patient, the analyst must himself be thoroughly analyzed. This brings about a two-fold gain of the resolution of neurotic inhibition and bias in the therapist and prevention of the patient being used for the therapist's needs, called 'counter-transference.'

## APPLICATIONS

At first, the application of Psychoanalysis was in the hysterical and obsessive-compulsive neurosis—pathological mental states with clear ego-alien symptoms. Following the development of ego psychology that led to the analysis of defenses, character disorders, narcissistic states, and psychoses also became available to treatment. The technique has been successfully applied in children as young as two and a half and adults in their sixties. However, the ideal psychoanalytic patient would be an adult of twenty to forty who suffers with ego-alien neurotic symptoms and has a strong curiosity about mental function.

# Psychoanalytic Group Therapy
## Marvin L. Aronson

### DEFINITION

Psychoanalytic Group Therapy refers to the application of psychoanalytic principles to the treatment of individuals in small groups. The goals of this form of psychotherapy are to elicit and ultimately to work through the core conflicts of each member of the group.

### HISTORY

Although several percursors appeared in the 1920s and 1930s, analytic group psychotherapy did not emerge as a major therapeutic movement until World War II. At first, it was regarded simply as an expeditious way to treat a suddenly expanded patient population and not at all comparable—in depth or effectiveness—to individual analytic psychotherapy. However, its practitioners quickly realized that it not only constituted an important treatment modality in its own right, but that it offered certain technical advantages that were not available to the individual analyst.

Analytic group therapy is now practiced extensively throughout the United States. A burgeoning professional literature has accumulated and a good deal of clinical research has been carried out. The field has also reached a high level of development in Great Britain and in a number of Latin American countries, especially Argentina and Brazil. Although there are many exceptions, the Americans tend, both in theory and in practice, to focus on the psychodynamics of the individual in the group, whereas the British and the South Americans are more likely to address their interventions to the group as a whole. In recent years, European therapists have become quite interested in analytic group therapy, and there is every reason to believe that its clinical APPLICATIONS there will greatly expand in the near future.

Important figures in the history of analytic group therapy in the United States have included: Nathan Ackerman, Helen Durkin, Edrita Fried, Henriette Glatzer, Asya Kadis, Emanuel Schwartz, Samuel Slavson, Arlene Wolberg, and Alexander Wolf. In Great Britain, its leading exponents include: Wilfred Bion, Henry Ezriel, S. H. Foulkes, Malcolm Pines, Joseph Rey, and A. C. R. Skynner. Leading figures in South America are Bernardo Blay Neto of Brazil and Leon Grinberg and Raul Usandivaras of Argentina.

## TECHNIQUE

Group patients are instructed to interact with each other and with the therapist as openly and nondefensively as they can. In the course of their interactions, three major types of communications manifest themselves: 1) accurate observations of and responses to events and personalities within the group, 2) transference reactions (transference occurs when a patient shifts feelings about a significant person in his past to other patients), and 3) projections and/or more primitive projective identifications.

Each patient inevitably reveals the patterns of feeling and acting he developed in his original family and that he still maintains in his intimate relationships outside of the group via the network of multiple transferences he establishes in the group. Concomitantly, he projects unacceptable aspects of himself onto individual members, the therapist, or the group as a whole. (Projective identifications are more likely to characterize patients with severe ego disturbances, but they also appear, although to a lesser degree, in the communications of neurotics and character disorders.)

The analytic group therapist employs repeated interpretations of the emergent transferences and projections in order to bring their unconscious determinants into awareness. As in individual analytic therapy, he systematically interprets relevant aspects of the patient's fantasies, defenses, and security operations. He has the added advantage in group therapy of being able to point out the precise interpersonal impact that each patient's behavioral patterns has on others.

By the middle phases of anlyatic group therapy, the members typically ally themselves with the therapist's goals and begin to interpret each other's behavior and to deal with individual and group resistances. They also establish a group culture that rewards those members who demonstrate a willingness to experiment and to change. This benign peer pressure is extremely salutary in prompting patients to take the emotional risks essential for translating insights into more adaptive actions.

Elicitation and working through of core conflicts proceed most effectively if group resistance is maintained at an optimal level. One of the most crucial skills required of the analytic group therapist is that he be able to resolve any group resistances that threaten to impede untrammeled communication within the group.

Acquiring this skill necessitates specialized training; preferably, such training should come after the therapist has mastered the intricacies of individual psychoanalytic therapy.

Most American authorities agree that analytic group works best in conjunction with individual therapy, conducted either by the same therapist (combined therapy) or by a colleague (conjoint therapy). Ideally, patients should be seen individually for at least fifteen to fifty sessions before they enter a group. The reason for this is that individual therapy is much better suited for establishing a working alliance. Clinical research has shown that the majority of premature dropouts from group therapy are caused by insufficient attention to the establishment of a working alliance in the early phases of the therapeutic process.

## APPLICATIONS

The indications for Psychoanalytic Group Therapy are essentially the same as for individual analytic therapy. Preferably, patients should be of at least average intelligence, have had some gratifying experiences in small groups during their formative years, and possess a minimal capacity for expressing their thoughts and feelings in words.

Initially, analytic group therapy was mainly used for treating neurotics and character disorders. In recent years, modified versions of it have been extensively utilized for the treatment of borderline and certain schizophrenic patients in a variety of in-patient and day-hospital settings. Current developments in object relations theory and in ego psychology have been of considerable help in adapting analytic group therapy to the clinical needs of these patients.

# Psychobiological Psychotherapy
*George Mora*

## DEFINITION

Adolph Meyer's psychotherapy can be viewed as a rather loosely structured and flexible approach to the treatment of mental disorders in the context of his so-called psychobiology. Such an approach resulted from the conglomeration of many trends expressed by various psychiatric schools. Though obviously quite influential in the period between the late 1910s and the early 1940s, Meyer's psychotherapeutic approach—probably because of its very broad comprehensiveness and eclecticism— has been progressively forgotten. Yet, many of its tenets are still quite pertinent to today's psychotherapeutic scene.

## HISTORY

The history of psychobiology is intrinsically related to the life and work of its founder, Adolf Meyer (1866– 1950). Born near Zurich, he graduated from the medical school there and then received training in Germany, France, and England. He was especially influenced by the Darwinian ecological orientation of Thomas Huxley and by Hughlings Jackson's basic concept of the individual person as functioning on progressive levels of integration in the context of the evolution and dissolution of the central nervous system.

Upon emigrating to the United States in 1894, Meyer worked first in mental hospitals in Illinois and Worcester, Massachusetts (1894– 1902), then in New York City at the Pathological Institute of New York State (1902– 1909), and, finally, at the Henry Phipps Clinic of Johns Hopkins University (1909– 1942). It was here, in Baltimore, that, as professor of psychiatry, he established the most important psychiatric center in the world for the training of psychiatrists.

Among the main trends that contributed to Meyer's psychobiology are: 1) the acceptance of the American philosophical pragmatism (Charles Pierce, William James, John Dewey, George Mead, Charles Cooley), with its emphasis on a concrete, pluralistic view of the individual and his society and on a basic optimistic outlook toward human nature; 2) the formulation of a holistic biological concept of the human personality, to be conceived of as a chronological unfolding of events resulting from the relation between habit, situation, and pathology (as typically represented by schizophrenia, a twisted maladaptation caused by habit disorganization or deterioration); 3) a recognition of the validity of many of the Freudian concepts, accounting for the explanation of pathological personality reactions as regression to former, previously protective, phylogenetic reactions that are incompatible with adaptation in later life; 4) a pioneering involvement in the prevention movement of mental hygiene (through his association with Clifford Beers, the author of *A Mind That Found Itself* [1908], and, the following year, with the organization of the National Committee on Mental Hygiene), which led to his clear anticipation, in the early 1900s, of the tenets of today's community mental health movement.

## TECHNIQUE

Central to psychobiology is the study of the individual person, who Meyer defined as a biological unit, functioning either alone or in a group, maintaining an internal and external homeostatic equilibrium in coping with new situations, and capable of a high range of differentiation in capacity and function and of a relatively high degree of spontaneity and responsiveness.

In contrast to hypothetical psychological and metapsychological concepts brought forward by many schools, Meyer stressed as basic for psychobiology the observation of objective facts, the formulation of predictable conditions in which these may occur, and the testing and validation of methods for their controlled modifications. The biographical approach to the personality offered a practical and specific guide for gathering individual data, a means of organizing that data, and a method for checking and reevaluating data elicited under varying conditions. For Meyer the clinical psychiatric examination included the following components: 1) present motives and indications for the examination as emerging from the biographical study; 2) related personality traits, factors, and reactions; 3) physical, neurological, genetic, and social aspects of the personality; 4) differential diagnosis; 5) individual therapeutic plan. Dissatisfied with the limitations of one-word diagnoses for the complex field of human behavior, Meyer initially used the terms "reaction set" or "reaction type" in diagnostic classification. Later on, in the 1920s, he used the word "ergasia" (from the Greek word for work, *ergon*) to describe the general concept of behavior and mental activity and its plural, "ergasias," to denote specific behavioral units.

Thus, he called organic brain reactions "anergasia," toxic psychoses "dysergasia," and so on. This classification, never accepted in psychiatric nomenclature, was in direct contrast to Meyer's overall emphasis on the common-sense approach in psychiatry.

Regardless of the diagnosis, the initial interview was to focus on the situation that required immediate therapeutic intervention. In fact, for Meyer, treatment began at the time of the initial contact, with the patient's exposition of the problem. Paramount for the success of the treatment, especially at the early phase, was the cooperation of the patient's better self; that is, the healthier part of the patient's ego. In fact, these healthier aspects of the patient's personality were considered as the starting point for treatment. Also, in the initial stage of treatment, it was important to define the difficulties—involving eating and sleeping habits and other daily routines—in concrete terms familiar to both the therapist and the patient.

From this chief complaint, the attention progressively shifted to the nature and extent of the disturbance in the context of the patient's overall functioning, his previous medical history, and the role played by his constitution, development, and environment. Problems were approached mainly on a conscious level, in a face-to-face sitting, beginning with the experiences undergone by the patient in the interval since the last interview. Eventually, deeper sorts of material were brought to the surface with the help of spontaneous associations (a term that Meyer preferred over that of "free associations"). This unconscious material, in addition to information supplied by his family, supplemented the psychiatrist's efforts and facilitated the understanding of the situation. Ample support was to be given to the patient, so as to help him to function adequately between interviews, the intensity and frequency of which were flexible according to circumstances. With the help of the therapist, the patient was to be able to formulate his life story by means of a chart, to demonstrate understanding of the origins of his difficulties and appropriate means to ensure their resolution and prevent their repetition. Eventually, the point was to be reached where the patient would analyze his personality problems and their relative importance (distributive analysis) and then reconstruct the origin of his concepts and devise healthier behavior patterns (distributive synthesis). In essence, "habit training"—that is, the modification of unhealthy adaptation to achieve personal satisfaction and proper environmental readjustment—was to be reached by using a variety of techniques, such as guidance, suggestion, reeducation, and direction.

## APPLICATIONS

In contrast to most of the well-known psychiatrists contemporary to that period—notably Pierre Janet, Freud, and many others—Meyer shied away from detailed presentations of case histories of patients treated by him. Yet, there is plenty of evidence that his psychotherapeutic approach based on his optimistic and melioristic philosophy of psychiatry was successful in many cases.

Early in his career, at the dawn of our century (in contrast to Kraepelin's pessimistic view), he was already emphasizing the possibility of recovering from schizophrenia by overcoming faulty habits, notably withdrawing. Around the same time, he proposed correct plans for the intervention and prevention of the patient's illness with the help of his family, school, and community. In line with this, Meyer should be given credit for the first application of the principles of social work, of occupational and recreational therapy, and of aftercare programs for convalescent patients as early as 1904 at the Manhattan State Hospital West.

Later on, as psychobiology became better defined, he emphasized the importance of collaboration by the members of the therapeutic community—physician, patient, nurse, and ward group—and the patient's family in providing a setting to safeguard the integrity of the patient's personality functions.

Particularly important is the fact that, in contrast to the emphasis on the treatment of neurotic patients by the various psychodynamic schools, Meyer stressed that Psychobiological Therapy was especially valuable for psychotic patients. This may account for the tradition of psychotherapy of psychoses, which was carried on for a few decades in the Washington- Baltimore area by representatives of various Freudian and neo-Freudian schools. On a wider scale, such an orientation was pursued by some of the most well known of Meyer's pupils, such as Charles MacFie Campbell, David Henderson, Wendell Muncie, Oscar Diethelm, W. Horsley Gantt, Alexander Leighton, Franklin Ebaugh, Edward J. Kempf, John Whitehorn, Leo Kanner, J. Masserman, and Theodore Lidz.

In view of the predominant role that Meyer played in psychiatry in this country and abroad (more than one hundred of his pupils became professors of psychiatry), it is puzzling why so little is known today of Meyer's contribution. Several reasons may account for this: the arduous style of his writings, the lack of systematization of his thinking in favor of a rather provisional and pluralistic approach, the disregard for presentation of clear and comprehensive clinical histories of patients, and finally, the challenge offered by the great depression of the early 1930s to his fundamental optimistic orientation of life. Psychoanalysis—a well-organized movement—was soon to present the greatest impact in academic circles, psychiatric settings, and in the culture by and large. Yet Meyer's philosophy opened the way to the psychodynamic thinking and, later on, anticipated today's community mental health approach.

# Psychodrama
## Lewis Yablonsky

### DEFINITION

Psychodrama is a natural and automatic process. Everyone at some time has an inner drama going on in his mind. In this confidential setting you are the star of your Psychodrama session and play all of the roles. The others you encounter in your monodrama may be your parents, an employer, a God you love or one who has forsaken you, a wife, husband, or lover who has rejected you or demands more than you are willing to give. The others, or, as they are called in Psychodrama, "your auxiliary egos," may not be actual human adversaries but some ideal someone or something you want but cannot have—an unfulfilled dream, or perhaps an obsession for fame or wealth.

Many people are able to act out these internal psychodramas in the reality and activity of their external life. For such people, Psychodrama is not a necessary vehicle except as an interesting adjunct to their life experiences. But for most people, Psychodrama can provide a unique opportunity for *externalizing* their internal world onto a theatrical stage of life; and, with the help of the group present at a session, emotional conflicts and problems can often be resolved.

In Psychodrama a person is encountering his conflicts and psychic pain in a setting that more closely approximates his real-life situation than in most other therapeutic approaches. A young man in conflict with a parent talks directly to a person as an auxiliary ego playing his parent. The fantasy (or reality) of his hostility or love can be acted out on the spot. He can experience his pain (in one context, his "primal emotions") not in an artificial setting but in direct relationship to the "father", "mother," or other person who helped build the pain into him, since his enactment takes place as closely as possible to the pertinent, specific core situations in his life.

The resolution of his pain or conflict does not necessarily require an extensive analysis or discussion because he is experiencing the emotions *in situ*, in action. Often, when someone has had a deep psychodramatic experience, there is no need for lengthy group discussion—sharing—or analysis. The protagonist has learned about the mystery of his problem in action; he feels better immediately, and it is not necessary to go beyond that point.

People develop problems, conflicts, and psychic pain in the normal course of their day-to-day life scenarios. To be sure, extensive one-to-one or discussion group therapies help to unravel a person's emotional mystery; however, at some point the person involved must enact his discoveries or insights in life. The logic of Psychodrama is that the person and the group learns or relearns best in action that most closely approximates life and that is in Psychodrama. In many cases, the combination of individual counseling or verbal group therapy in concert with Psychodrama maximizes therapeutic results.

Another important aspect of Psychodrama is that it is a mirror of life, not only for the central protagonist or star having a session, but for the group present at a session. Group participants are encouraged to witness aspects of their own lives that became manifest in the session, as if watching a dramatic play that projects their own behavior onto the stage in front of them.

## HISTORY

The origin, development, and meaning of Psychodrama is intrinsically part of the life history of Dr. J. L. Moreno (1889-1974), founder of Psychodrama, sociometry, and the group psychotherapy movement. Moreno, in his early years, planted the roots of Psychodrama in the rich philosophical and psychological soil of Vienna around the turn of the century. During that period, Moreno's goal was to develop a "theatrical cathedral" for the release of the natural human spontaneity and creativity that he believed existed naturally in everyone. As early as 1910, Moreno was preoccupied with the development of this concept of a humanistic theater of life. In that period, Moreno's Theatre of Spontaneity was a place where people in groups had the opportunity to act out their deepest dreams, frustrations, aspirations, moods of aggression, and love; in brief, the range of their human emotions. Moreno's early dreams have substantially materialized into the psychodramatic form that is practiced today around the world.

In the early period of Moreno's Theatre of Spontaneity, he had a limited concern with fostering "therapy" or "mental health." These positive consequences were noted by Moreno only as side effects of the psychodramatic process, which he saw as an opportunity to free the spontaneously creative self.

Moreno came to the United States in 1925 to promote an invention he was then working on, a machine for the recording and playback of sound on steel discs. He decided to remain in the United States, was licensed, began medical-psychiatric practice in New York. Immediately, he set out to introduce Psychodrama into the mental health professions and into American culture in general. He began psychodramatic work with children at the Plymouth Institute in Brooklyn and also became involved with the Mental Hygiene Clinic at Mt. Sinai Hospital. In 1929 he began the first regular program of large-scale "open" Psychodrama in America three times a week in an Impromptu Group Theatre at Carnegie Hall. He later continued his work and practice with his wife and colleague, Zerka, at the Moreno Institute, Beacon, New York. Zerka continues his work at the Moreno Institute, the center of a worldwide Psychodrama movement.

## TECHNIQUE

Psychodrama has considerable adaptability and flexibility. All that is required for a session is the conflict (philosophical or concrete), the group, and a psychodramatist. The freedom for a group to act out its problems is represented by the freedom of space on a stage, or any open space.

All Psychodrama sessions have several intrinsic elements: a *director*—the catalyst of the session; a *subject* or *protagonist*—the individual who presents a problem and represents the group in the session; the *auxiliary ego(s)*—who plays the role required by the protagonist for presenting the problem; and techniques such as *role-reversal*, the *double*, *mirror*, and the *soliloquy*.

The group present is crucial to a Psychodrama because all members are considered participants. The group is not an audience as in a theatrical production. Many members will participate actively at some point in a session as auxiliary egos, but even those who sit through a session without speaking are expected to be empathetic and identify with the protagonist and the problems being presented. The group and the director enter the protagonist's world with him, even though at a later session they may attempt to introduce the consensual reality of the group present or the larger societal viewpoint. According to Moreno, "The person's enactment of their reality comes first—their retraining comes later." In this regard, Moreno advocates allowing the protagonist as much as possible to pick *his* scene, *his* place, and *his* auxiliary ego in order to enact *his* problem.

It is an assumption of Psychodrama that a protagonist learns and relearns more effectively when he is deeply involved in a crucial scene from his life than if he simply talks about a situation. It involves "insight in action." Often, the protagonist who has experienced the insight may experience it on a subconscious level. When this happens, it is usually unnecessary for him to have to verbalize his insight or catharsis. It is his, he has already experienced it in action. As Moreno stated, "Even when an interpretation of an act is made, the action is more primary. There can be no meaningful interpretation without the act taking place first."

There are three phases to a Psychodrama session: 1) the warmup, 2) the action, and 3) the post-discussion. The warmup and the action of a session are vital, and the post-discussion is also highly significant. This is the portion of a session during which the group members *share* their empathy and experiences with the protagonist. For example, in the session revolving around the engagement, many members of the group revealed their own uncertainties about accepting the boundaries of marriage. This has the honest effect of apprizing the protagonist that he is not alone in the dilemma. It also provides the group members with the opportunity to reflect openly about their involvement in the session and to synthesize their responses. There is ample room for analysis in Psychodrama, but the basic principle is that analysis should always follow the action and the post-discussion. In the post-discussion phase, the director must draw from the group their identification with the protagonist. This process produces group insight, increases cohesion, and enlarges interpersonal perceptions.

## APPLICATIONS

Many people, after their first participation in Psychodrama, raise the question, "Isn't it painful to enact a difficult experience even in the controlled environment of a Psychodrama?" Sometimes it is, but the basic premise of the question is not accurate. *It is impossible to exactly relive any experience.* What is usually produced in Psychodrama is the person's *here-and-now* mental picture of an important past scenario of his life. The concept of the *here and now* in Psychodrama thus encompasses past and future projections of significant life events as they currently exist in the person's internal monodrama.

An important aspect of Psychodrama is that all of these time states are explicated in action. Some of these issues are revealed in the case example of a series of Psychodrama sessions I ran with a young man incarcerated in a state hospital for the so-called criminally insane. Ralph, at eighteen, was in custody for blacking out of control and attempting to kill his father. The verbal interactions he had with various therapists in the hospital about his "past behavior" had admittedly been of limited help in reaching him. His immediate therapist requested that I direct a Psychodrama session with Ralph to help him explore some of Ralph's psychodynamics in action. In this case, Psychodrama became a valuable adjunct to Ralph's individual therapy.

In addition to Ralph's potential for violence, another symptom that he manifested was a body tic. According to a medical report by a doctor who had examined Ralph, there appeared to be no physiological basis for the tic. In the first Psychodrama session I ran with Ralph as the protagonist, I noted that the tic was enacted and accentuated whenever there was reference to his father, or sometimes even when the word, "father" was used.

In the session, Ralph led us back to a basic and traumatic scene in his life with his father. He acted out a horrendous situation that occurred when he was eight: his father punished him by tying him up by his hands to a ceiling beam in their cellar—like meat on a hook—and then beat him with a belt.

We determined from several sessions with Ralph, and my consultations with his therapist, that the traumatic experience of the whipping and other parental atrocities produced his tic. The tic seemed to be a way he controlled striking back at his basic antagonist, his father. In brief, Ralph had two extreme postures that emerged from his parental abuse: one was the tic that incapacitated him from the other—extreme, uncontrolled violence.

In the final scene of one Psychodrama, we had progressed to a point where Ralph accepted a male nurse as an auxiliary ego in the role of his father. In the Psychodrama scene, Ralph would alternately produce the tic or attempt to attack his "father." There was hardly any verbalization of Ralph's rage—he required an action form to express his emotions.

After Ralph had physically acted out much of his rage, I finally improvised a psychodramatic vehicle that facilitated a conversation between Ralph and his auxiliary ego "father." I put a table between him and his "father." At the same time he talked to his father, I gave him the option and freedom to punch a pillow that he accepted symbolically as his father. This combination of Psychodrama devices enabled Ralph to structure in thought and put into words his deep venom for his father. He blurted out much of his long-repressed hatred in a lengthy diatribe. Finally, we removed the props, and after his rage was spent, he fell into his "father's" arms and began to sob, "Why couldn't you love me? I was really a good kid, Dad. Why couldn't you love me?"

Although he went through several phases of his hostility in several sessions, he could not go all the way and forgive his father, a symbolic act that I had determined would help to relieve him of the ball of hostility in his gut that produced his violent acting-out behavior.

In a later session, we had him play the role of his father, and he for the first time began to empathize with the early experiences in his father's life that brutalized him. Ralph's grandfather—who beat his son—was the original culprit and Ralph was indirectly receiving the fallout of his father's anger toward his father, or Ralph's grandfather. When Ralph reversed roles and returned to himself, it diminished his hostility towards his father and he, at least psychodramatically, that day forgave him.

A central point in explicating Ralph's extreme Psychodrama experience is to reveal that the learning-in-action on his part, combined with his private sessions, was effective. Ralph could not just *talk* about his anger. He required a vehicle such as Psychodrama that gave him the opportunity to physically and psychologically reenact the scenarios of the early parental crimes against him in their bizarre details. In my experience with Psychodrama, this seems to be the case for most people. Although most people's problems are not as extreme as Ralph's, at times we all require an action-oriented psychodramatic experience for catharsis from and insight into an emotional problem.

Most people require an active vehicle for expression, either exclusively or as an adjunct to an individual-verbal approach. It is apparent to many individual therapists that many clients, when embroiled in the discussion of deep emotions, either have the urge or actually get up off the therapeutic couch or chair and begin to physically move around. It is precisely at this point of action that Psychodrama comes into play. There is no real conflict between verbal analysis and role playing; there is, however, ample psychodramatic evidence that most people could benefit from some form of learning-in-action as an adjunct to their verbal-discussion therapy-

# Psycho-Imagination Therapy

*Joseph E. Shorr*

## DEFINITION

Psycho-Imagination Therapy uses imagery as a vehicle to bypass the conscious censor to reveal the individual's self-image, areas of conflict, and strategies for coping with the world. The imaginary situation provides the therapist with a window into the world as it is seen by the client.

Clinical experience has shown that there are specific Imaginary Situations that can reveal in a nonthreatening manner the kinds of information that a person needs to facilitate change. The basic theoretical formulation of Psycho-Imagination Therapy appears in my books, *Psycho-Imagination Therapy* and *Psychotherapy Through Imagery*.

Imagination is viewed as the central kernel of the consciousness and an important way of access to the unique inwardness of the individual's subjective world. The active introduction and conscious use of imaginary situations is found to be a stimulating investigative tool, a way to open up action possibilities and a facilitative therapeutic approach. It allows the individual to explore more safely and openly; to differentiate; to experiment with and to integrate fantasy and reality, reality and potentiality, self and not-self, and choices of action all within the context of a cooperative therapeutic alliance and encounter. Projecting the ego in imagined situations constitutes a fantasy experience of self-agency that opens the way to real being-in-the-world.

No technique is used without reference to the self-other theories of R. D. Laing and Harry Stack Sullivan. The phenomenological approach to humans, or how a person views his world, can be appreciably enhanced by knowledge of his waking imagery. It is phenomenology in action.

## HISTORY

Psycho-Imagination Therapy was initially developed in 1965. Emphasis in the therapeutic interaction is on separating one's own view of oneself from the attributed self as defined by the significant others in one's childhood. Ideally, the "true" identity is helped to emerge while the "alien" identity is eliminated.

When this theoretical stance is combined with the ubiquitous imagery of the person it brings about a more immediate increase in awareness of conflicts by both patient and psychotherapist.

The roots of the use of imagery as a therapeutic tool extend back to S. Freud, C. G. Jung, R. Desoille, H. Leuner, G. Bachelard, et al.

## TECHNIQUE

The two basic premises of Psycho-Imagination Therapy are: (1) everyone needs to make a difference to someone, and (2) everyone seeks confirmation of acknowledgement of himself. These needs occur contemporaneously. When they are not fulfilled, the child develops false positions. If a person is not confirmed for his true self then he develops strategies to secure confirmation for a false self. The security operations he involves himself in serve to maintain his identity even in the absence of true acknowledgement.

The interpersonal and intrapersonal interactions, as well as the individual's strategies within the self-other relationships, are best seen through the systematic use of waking imagery. A person's imagery can show how he organizes his world, his style of action, and the marked individual differences to which the therapist should be attuned. Imagery provides a primary avenue through which thoughts, wishes, expectations, and feelings can be most effectively reactivated and re-experienced. Imagery, unlike other modes of communications, usually has not been punished in the past and is, therefore, less susceptible to personal censorship in the present.

The active and systematic introduction of categories of therapeutic imagery, such as Spontaneous Imagery, Self Imager Imagery, Dual Imagery, Body Imagery, Task Imagery, Parental Imagery, Sexual Imagery, Cathartic Imagery, and other imaginary situations; the finish-the-sentence technique; the self-and-other question; and the most-or-least questions are specific treatment procedures.

### APPLICATIONS

Psycho-Imagination Therapy is essentially for general, as well as neurotic, populations; certain obsessive-compulsive persons; and some schizoid persons.

# Psychomotor Therapy
## Albert Pesso and Diane Pesso

### DEFINITION

Psychomotor Therapy is an action-oriented form of therapy that includes information presented by the client's body tension, overt and covert actions, reports of physical sensation, as well as emotional sounds and verbal content regarding feeling states and ideas. This information is processed in a highly organized interaction called a structure. In a structure the information, both verbal and nonverbal, is related to on both concrete and symbolic levels. A structure may start with the motor recapitulation of a past event.

We Albert and Diane Pesso observed that emotion is part of a continuum of Emotion-Action-Interaction, and that all three parts were intimately related to one another. It was concluded that the emotion contained the seeds and information about its outcome as action. And the action contained the seeds and information about its chosen target, the interaction.

In a structure, the target figures of emotional expression are polarized into negative or positive figures. Negative accommodators stand in for the negative aspects of real-life figures, such as parents, peers, siblings, and so on, and respond in a manner indicating defeat and destruction to the rage reactions of the client. Positive accommodators respond with the wished-for behavior while usually in the role of ideal parents. These responses provide powerful new positive learning experiences for the clients, which is, in a sense, a reprogramming.

## HISTORY

Psychomotor Therapy developed out of our desire to create methods to help actors and dancers to become the best possible movement communicators of honest human feelings. Our individual training and explorations in physical movement started some thirty-five years ago.

It is difficult to list the experiences that made our discovery and development of this method possible. Some of them were: the observing of our own bodies/selves and our students as we let them express unconscious emotions into feeling states; training in the movement techniques of Isadora Duncan, Stanislovsky, Martha Graham, Jose Limon, Martha Hill, and Barbara Mettler; readings of Freud and various psychologists; working with Charles Pinderhughes, M.D., Leo Reyna, Ph.D., and many others.

We taught large numbers of people, of all ages, in our studio and at several colleges. One of our most important observations was that when people expressed emotion through movement without anyone responding to them for long periods of time, it frequently resulted in feelings of futility and loneliness. This made us want to explore what it would feel like for them to have their movements responded to in a validating and gratifying way.

We found that the best way to encourage free expression of emotions so that more parts of the self could come forth was to have other people role play the category of person (positive mother, father, etc.) for the desired response. This provided the greatest satisfaction and flow of emotion. We called this precise, controlled way of role-playing reactions, "accommodation."

Early groups in Psychomotor drew the attention of Charles Pinderhughes, M.D., a psychiatrist who invited one of us (Albert) to participate in a research program on Psychomotor at the Boston V.A. Hospital (where he was director of psychiatric research) over a five-year period.

Then we both began to work with patients in Psychomotor at McLean Hospital (the psychiatric division of Massachusetts General Hospital). Al conducted many introductory groups for members of the staff of McLean.

We also continued to develop Psychomotor in our private practices. The Psychomotor Institute, a nonprofit organization, was founded in Boston, and Al headed up the program for training psychomotor therapists. Currently, the institute administrates the predominantly post-doctoral psychomotor certification training programs for practicing psychotherapists. There are fully trained, certified psychomotor therapists in Massachusetts, Georgia, Florida and the Netherlands.

## TECHNIQUE

Preparation for psychomotor structures has three stages. The first stage deals with training the client to become sensitive to his own motor impulses. The second involves sensitization to the effects of the spatial placement of others in their visual field. The final stage deals with the handling of emotional feelings and events, using the skills of the first two stages, in structures.

The first stage is basically intrapsychic. The goal is to give the group member skills and tools to comprehend how he feels and behaves under the stimulus of different motor impulses. In Psychomotor Therapy motor impulses are grouped in three different categories: reflexive, voluntary, and emotional. Attempts are made to move purely in each one of these modalities as self-diagnostic techniques to determine the state of the emotions.

The second stage is basically interpersonal. It teaches an individual to be more aware of the emotional impact of gesture and the placements of one or more individuals. In this stage accommodation is taught.

The third stage is both intrapsychic and interpersonal and handles the emotional expressions involved in structures.

### APPLICATIONS

Psychomotor Therapy is being applied in psychiatric hospitals and clinics in the United States and Europe and in drug treatment centers, chronic-pain units, schools for disturbed adolescents, etc. In private practice, it is being applied in groups and one-to-one sessions with a wide range of clients, including clients with psychosomatic problems. Some therapists have adapted psychomotor techniques and have evolved procedures whereby traditional psychotherapy is offered in conjunction with psychomotor techniques and structures.

Psychoanalytically oriented therapists, gestalt therapists, transactional analysts, bioenergetic therapists, and psychodramatists find many elements of Psychomotor Therapy compatible with their systems and have included Psychomotor techniques in their overall practices.

---

# Psychosurgery

## H. Thomas Ballantine, Jr.

### DEFINITION

Surgery for psychiatric illness has been defined by the National Commission for the Protection of Human Subjects of Biomedical and Behavioral Research in its report to the Congress as: ... brain surgery on (1) normal brain tissues ... or (2) diseased brain tissue of an individual if the primary object of the performance of such surgery is to control, change, or affect any behavioral or emotional disturbance of such individual." (1977) By the use of the phrase "affect any behavioral or emotional disturbance" the National Commission has emphasized that any such surgical procedure must be performed solely for therapeutic purposes. In other words, these surgical approaches are methods of treatments that are reserved for those unfortunate individuals who are disabled by psychiatric illness and have been treated over a long period by generally accepted nonoperative psychiatric methodologies without success.

The term "psychosurgery" is frequently used to define this form of therapy but, unfortunately, often brings to mind the radical frontal lobotomy introduced by Egas Moniz more than forty years ago, and occasionally conjures up fears that Psychosurgery has been or could be used for social or political purposes. The original frontal lobotomy has long since been replaced by techniques that are restricted to the placement of small, discreet lesions in carefully selected regions of the brain. Modern psychiatric surgery has evolved to such a degree that it bears no relation to the type of operation that was first introduced, and any attempt to use Psychosurgery as a form of "mind control" would be ethically indefensible and logistically impossible.

## HISTORY

In 1936, the distinguished Portuguese neurologist Egas Moniz published the first clinical study of frontal lobe white matter for the treatment of psychiatric illness. This procedure was soon modified in the United States by Freeman and Watts, who sectioned the inferior portions of both frontal lobes (at about the level of the tragus). Somewhat later James Poppen further restricted the operation to the medial white matter (just anterior to the anterior horns of both lateral ventricles).

About thirty years ago, Scoville in the United States and Geoffrey Knight in England introduced the so-called orbital undercutting procedure. At about the same time, acting upon the suggestion of John Fulton, professor of physiology at Yale University Medical School, Sir Hugh Cairns at Oxford and Professor Jacques Le-Beau in Paris undertook to interrupt the white matter in a procedure which was termed "cingulectomy."

In 1960, Knight, as a result of his observations of orbital undercutting patients, began placing radioactive "seeds" in certain brain regions. In 1962, Foltz and White published their experiences with an approach they called "cingulumotomy," and which has subsequently been widely employed for the treatment of psychiatric illness.

Although the "open" operations of bimedial leucotomy of Poppen and the orbital undercutting advocated by Scoville are still employed, the most widely used surgical techniques for the treatment of psychiatric patients involve the placement of small lesions (produced either by heat, cold, or radioactivity) under stereotactic control.

These surgical refinements stem directly from a search for a surgical therapy that will produce an improvement in the psychiatric status of patients so treated with a minimal risk of undesirable side effects. Furthermore, the use of stereotactic techniques has enabled the surgical approaches to be extended from the frontal lobes into other regions of the brain: the subcaudate region, the cingulum, the amygdala, the thalamus, and the hypothalamus. Finally, some surgeons have reported favorable results from combined lesions (such as those involving the amygdala, the cingulum, and the subcaudate regions).

## TECHNIQUES

In the so-called open operations (bimedial leucotomy and orbital undercutting), the surgeon exposes the region he desires to interrupt through a small craniotomy. Then, under direct vision, the white matter is progressively and selectively interrupted.

Space does not permit a detailed description of all the "closed" stereotactic procedures, but a typical approach is the one that has been used at the Massachusetts General Hospital since 1962 for bilateral cingulotomies:

Under either local or general anesthesia, two burr holes allow access of special ventricular needles. Under continuous X-ray monitoring, the ventricular needles apply radiofrequency current to an area of the brain (ungulate bundle) for the production of lesions. The volume of tissue interrupted measures 2 cm in length by 1.3 cm in diameter. It is essential to interrupt the lower-most fibers of the cingulum that enter the corpus callosum.

## APPLICATIONS

It cannot be too strongly emphasized that surgical therapy for psychiatric illness must be reserved for those disabled patients who have been judged failures from all other accepted forms of nonoperative psychiatric therapy. These procedures are truly "surgical approaches to the treatment of *psychiatric illness*" and must never be used for social or political purposes. The same ethical and moral restraints operate in this sphere as they do in all other forms of treatment of illness. This point of view was emphasized by the National Commission for the Protection of Human Subjects of Biomedical and Behavioral Research in its recommendation that such surgery "be used only to meet the health needs of individual patients."

In general, these surgical procedures for psychiatric illness are applied primarily to individuals suffering from the so-called affective disorders, such as depression, disabling anxiety, anorexia nervosa, obsessive compulsive neurosis, and germ phobias. Patients suffering from thought disorders without emotional involvement, particularly if the symptoms are of early onset and long duration, are not so likely to benefit from psychiatric surgery. Moreover, the best results are generally to be found in those individuals who give a HISTORY of having functioned effectively in society at some period in their lives. There are several other important points in selecting patients for surgery, and the protocol to be described, which is followed at the Massachusetts General Hospital, can be used as a guide to other physicians and institutions who wish to employ this form of treatment:

First, no patient is considered for an operation unless referred by a psychiatrist who agrees to follow the patient post-operatively. Moreover, the patient must have a sympathetic relative or close friend who agrees to be supportive in the postoperative period. The patient is then seen by the neurosurgeon who carefully and candidly explains the risks as well as the possible benefits of the surgical procedure. The patient is then interviewed by an independent psychiatrist and a neurologist, both of whom are not otherwise concerned with the care of the patient. Only if all three specialists agree that the surgery is appropriate is it then offered to the patient. Facilities must be available for extensive psychomotor testing pre-operatively and post-operatively. Finally, the patient and those around him must agree to a period of observation stretching into years after surgery.

In properly selected patients a conservative estimate of the results is as follows: 20 percent of the patients are able to function effectively in society without need for psychiatric care; another 60 percent are significantly improved but require varying degrees of psychotherapy and the administration of psychotropic medications. Finally, 20 percent of patients will not benefit from the surgery. The risk of undesirable side effects is minimal. In a series of 154 patients treated at the Massachusetts General Hospital, who were carefully studied post-operatively, there were three instances in which patients had one seizure. In no instance was there evidence of a reduction in cognitive ability nor were there any neurologic complications. (Ballantine, et al., 1977)

It is of great importance to have these operated patients followed (and treated when necessary) by the referring psychiatrists. Surgical treatment of psychiatric illness should be thought of as an adjunct to rather than a substitute for conventional psychiatric therapies. In this context, surgery for psychiatric illness can be considered as an accepted form of therapy that can be of great help in the treatment of disabled psychiatric patients.

# Psychosynthesis

## H. C. Tien

### DEFINITION

Psychosynthesis is a therapeutic process of combining individual elements of the mind to form a whole personality. Classical Psychosynthesis, as defined by Assagioli, is the system of psychotherapy that recognizes the central core of the *self,* or the persisting "I-consciousness," as distinct from the changing biological, emotional, and mental states. Classical Psychosynthesis has three connotations: 1) It is a principle underlying the reality of life; 2) it is a method including different techniques from psychoanalytical procedures, suggestion, will training, music therapy, symbolic learning, sublimation, and meditation; and 3) it is a goal-oriented therapy to achieve a person's highest humanistic aspirations.

Cybernetic Psychosynthesis, as defined by myself (Tien), combines the ideals of Classical Psychosynthesis with modern medical technology and information theory for personality development. The holistic definition of Cybernetic Psychosynthesis is a unified system of the eclectic elements of classical psychoanalysis and Psychosynthesis, based on traditional family medicine, psychotherapy, electrotherapy, behavior therapy, and group dynamics, with television technology (videology) as the natural instrumentation to realize the humanistic aspirations for world community mental health.

### HISTORY

The term "psychosynthesis" has been used by Maeder in 1927, by Bierre in 1925, and by Janet in 1889. This brief historical citation should include the ancient psychosynthesist Wu Chengen, a fifteenth-century Chinese writer (*Journey to the West*).

Psychiatrically, Freud stated in 1924 that "I cannot imagine ... that any new task for us is to be found in this Psychosynthesis. If I ever could permit myself to be honest and uncivil, I should say it was nothing but a meaningless phrase." In 1927, Assagioli developed Psychosynthesis as a critique of the limitations of psychoanalysis in his doctoral thesis. Classical Psychosynthesis is another splinter from Freudian Psychoanalysis, and remained obscure until 1965, when Assagioli published *Psychosynthesis: A Manual of Principles and Techniques.*

In 1969, I published my first paper on modern Cybernetic Psychosynthesis in *The American Journal of Psychotherapy*, entitled "Pattern Recognition and Psychosynthesis." (Tien, 1969) I traced the modern development of Psychosynthesis as a natural evolution from Classical Psychoanalysis and Classical Psychosynthesis, both occidental and oriental, and also from the cybernetics of Norbert Wiener, the information theories of Shannon and Weaver, together with modern neurophysiology of Pavlov and Sherrington. The historical development of Psychosynthesis has been well recorded in the *World Journal of Psychosynthesis* since 1969.

## TECHNIQUE

In Classical Psychosynthesis, Assagioli advised that "the best training for practicing Psychosynthesis (as in the case of psychoanalysis) is a 'didactic Psychosynthesis.' When this is not possible, it is most advisable that the therapist undertake an auto-psychosynthesis (self-synthesis) by applying the techniques to himself before, or at least while, applying them to others."

In Cybernetic Psychosynthesis, I recommend video techniques and video therapy for both auto-analysis and auto-synthesis, made technically possible through electronic technology. Instead of interpreting dreams and free associations, the modern psychosynthesist can analyze himself and others by video and effect synthesis of self and others by "telefusion" techniques.

In Classical Psychosynthesis, the techniques include catharsis, critical analysis, self-identification, dis-identification, will training, imagery training, auditory evocation, creative imagination, ideal models, symbol utilization, intuition, music therapy, and the transmutation and sublimation of sexual energies, together with spiritual psychosynthesis, including the exploration of the superconscious.

In Cybernetic Psychosynthesis, I use all the classical techniques, but also attempt to integrate psychotherapy with behavior therapy, electrotherapy, chemotherapy, marital therapy, and family therapy.

In short, all techniques, both medical and psychological, are utilized to transform an inferior personality to a higher personality, based on the *two-personality theory*, which states that every personality has at least two personalities. The theory is based on the following conceptual postulates:

1. The ego-consciousness is a single scintillating form of self-creating time series in the cortex of the brain (i.e., imageries of self)

2. A personality is a time series of scintillating frames of the conscious neuron patterns (i.e., ego-consciousness)

3. Every time series may be divided into two time series, the first ego-consciousness is observing the second one (e.g., when one personality is watching oneself via videosynthesis).

In the practice of videosynthesis, the person is usually analyzed into two personalities. All the therapeutic techniques—analysis, interpretation, behavior therapy, medication, electrotherapy, biofeedback, etc.—are videotaped and fed back to the individual to control his current, less adaptable personality (i.e., inferior ego state) to develop his future, more adaptable personality (i.e., a higher ego state) as the therapeutic goal.

## APPLICATIONS

In the classical application of Psychosynthesis, the techniques are used widely to treat or to prevent neuroses and personality disorders. It may be fruitfully used in education to develop superconscious functions, especially in interpersonal and group dynamics. Classical Psychosynthesis may be applied as in psychoanalysis to accelerate the integration of the personality and also for its self-actualization. Assagioli hoped "to see develop over a period of years—I certainly do not claim it has been achieved— ... a science of the self, or its energies, its manifestations and how these energies can be released, how they can be contacted, how they can be utilized for constructive and therapeutic work." That was an authoritative statement by Assagioli in 1965, but by 1969, I introduced the hoped-for video techniques with the needed scientific instruments, which have enabled us to transfer these energies of information directly from the synthesist to the patients. In the application, the family physician may become a family psychiatrist who works with other therapists, psychologists, social workers, technicians, and all community mental health professionals to advance the idea of Psychosynthesis of a healthy mind, in a healthy body, in a healthy community.

Psychosynthesis is applied to the practice of family medicine and psychiatry, with special emphasis on the total health needs of the individual and his family, by making therapy available not only at the curative level—to treat the neurotic, psychosomatic, psychotic, or psychopathic disorders—but also to prevent the development of neurosis, psychosis, and personality disorders, which may feed into the destructive conflicts of the individual, his family, his community, his nation, or our world. Also, Psychosynthesis provides the budding concepts of creative service for the individual, his family, and our mental health community, so that we can direct, integrate, and develop our own highest personalities for the creative, harmonious, historical development of mankind.

# Psychotheatrics

*Robert D. Allen and Nina Krebs*

## DEFINITION

Psychotheatrics (PT) is a process based on theories and techniques from theater and the practice of psychotherapy. PT is action oriented, focuses on individual responsibility, enhances the discovery of options, and helps the individual create a design for behavior change.

The primary person involved in change (client, student, group member, trainee) functions much like a theater director, directing action or emotional scenes relevant to his needs for change. These may be past, present, or future scenes—real or fantasy. Psychotheatrics may be used as a therapy modality, educational process, theater process, or awareness process. As options for new behavior evolve, the process is structured to provide the primary person with the opportunity for testing them.

# HISTORY

Psychotheatrics was originated by Robert D. Allen and developed in conjunction with Nina Krebs at California State University, Sacramento. From 1973 to 1977, extensive research was conducted with PT there; at one time this involved ten mental health clinics and one child-care center, making this study one of the most thorough ever enacted. A three-condition design was used: 1) PT, 2) regular treatment (traditional therapies used in each agency, having a wide range, from Gestalt, Psychodrama, Reality Therapy, to Values Clarification, etc.), and 3) no treatment. Psychotheatrics was found to have a more beneficial impact on clients than the other two conditions in every area of study: alcohol abuse, drug abuse, day treatment, children, interpersonal relationships, and awareness. During this period of time, PT was constantly being refined, resulting in a process that is easily used in a wide variety of settings. In 1976, the Association for Psychotheatrics (AP) was formed to provide a forum for the exchange of ideas among persons interested in PT, to encourage the training of qualified individuals in PT, and to maintain high standards in the training and practice of PT. In line with its purpose, AP has established a registry, a list of registered PT professionals that ensures professional recognition and public protection. The Association is dedicated to the development of PT in the fields of mental health, education, and theater.

# TECHNIQUE

PT has been developed in three forms:

*Playwright.* For work with individuals; usually a one-time event as part of some other process. Individual directs relevant situations and deals with options that emerge.

*Spectator.* For work with groups of people who have a common variable. May be used as a one-time workshop process or as format for ongoing groups.

*Environmental.* For work with an individual who has specific behavioral change goals. Occurs in controlled setting with other people who are in the same change process.

Here is a simplified description of the PT process:

1. Primary Person describes a relevant feeling fantasy or real situation.

2. Facilitator helps primary person conceptualize situation for immediate performance.

3. Primary Person directs situation with Facilitator, associates, group members, or available others serving as "players" to act scenes.

4. Primary Person suggests options for change. Facilitator may add to these.

5. Primary Person may direct players through several options.

PT is mainly a way of providing a setting where someone can gain a new degree of objectivity or understanding about whatever process he is in that is of interest or concern. This ability to view oneself at a distance using behavior that was never dreamed possible has high impact. Whatever the PT action phase application, the process can be thought of in three broad steps toward behavior change: 1) the individual observing and understanding his behavior; 2) developing options for more effective behavior; 3) experimenting and assessing newly uncovered options. The three steps toward behavior change parallel the central focus of most action-oriented therapies and educational processes. The PT action phase is designated to shorten the length of time required for major changes to occur. The PT impact— combining the powerful forces of producing, directing, and actualizing—provides a synthesis for the individual that other techniques do not offer in the same way. The integration of producer and director dynamics is reflected by actualizing.

Although dialogue is used as part of all three PT elements, the emphasis is not on words alone. Integration of thoughts, words, movement, and feelings is important. Educationally, this has implications for many people whose strengths are in nonverbal areas often missed in typical academic settings. A deaf workshop participant pointed out that PT has great possibilities for communication and education among people who cannot rely on hearing.

Since PT can be used with individuals (Playwright), groups (Spectator), and individuals in a controlled environment (Environmental), the facilitator, teacher, or lay person has choices about which form would be appropriate for his needs.

## APPLICATIONS

Psychotheatrics is a contentless process and is thus adaptable for many purposes in a variety of settings with people of different levels of sophistication. Some areas of usefulness include:

1. In-service training for professionals: empathy training, interpersonal communications, decision making, diagnosing conflict, perception checking, experimenting with new options.

2. Direct services to students or clients: group process, individual behavior change, defining individual responsibility, teaching skills and concepts.

3. Personal awareness: decision making, understanding conflict, options development.

# Puppet Therapy

*Eleanor C. Irwin*

## DEFINITION

Puppetry, a form of drama in which human figures or fantasy creatures imitate life, can be a valuable tool in therapy with children, as it provides a nonthreatening and spontaneous means of communication.

## HISTORY

From the "string pullers" of early Greek literature to the "Cookie Monster" of today, puppets have been a popular form of theater as well as a favorite child's toy. Woltmann, one of the first to explore the psychological rationale and therapeutic use of puppetry, has traced the development of Casper, his main puppet character, to an East Indian shadow puppet in 5000 B.C. Woltmann produced carefully designed puppet shows for the inpatient child audience at Bellevue Hospital, and thought of his shows as representing universally accepted prototypes of all people that were projective in nature.

It has not been the marionette, however, but the hand puppet that has been popular in child therapy. The ease of manipulation combined with the richness of the symbolism of the spontaneously enacted drama has led to the use of puppets in diagnosis and treatment with children as well as families. Currently, puppets seem to be available in most playrooms, but are often not used in a planned way that could take advantage of their usefulness as projective tools.

## TECHNIQUE

For many youngsters, talking is difficult, but communicating through puppets is easy and nonthreatening. Children seem to identify readily with the puppet characters, which have a unique potential for eliciting conflict and action. Additionally, as the child is caught up in the action, there is a wealth of nonverbal behavior that can aid in the understanding of the child's difficulties. Thus, the spontaneous stories not only give valuable information, but the pleasure and catharsis that accompany the play experience can promote a positive attitude toward treatment, aiding the formation of a treatment alliance.

For diagnostic purposes particularly, it helps to have a range of puppets available, from realistic to fantasy ones, as well as an adequate choice within each category. While some young or emotionally immature children use only animal or symbolic characters, most utilize a variety, from real to fantasy figures, aggressive as well as nonaggressive types. Providing a variety of materials can help elicit the expression of both acceptable and unacceptable impulses in physically safe, disguised play. Therefore, categories could include: realistic as well as royalty family figures; wild as well as tame animal puppets; and symbolic character types, such as the devil, witch, or ghost. Quantity is not important, but choice (in terms of specificity and degree of disguise) and range of materials are crucial considerations.

### Puppet Diagnostic Interview

If puppets are to be used to gather diagnostic information, the child's spontaneous communications and nonverbal behavior are carefully noted as he begins to select from among the puppets placed on the floor in a random pile (Irwin and Shapiro, 1974). When the selection is complete, the child is invited to go behind a stage, or to some other comfortable spot, and begin by "introducing" the selected characters, as though performing a "real" puppet show. With an overcontrolled or undercontrolled child, the therapist might wish to lengthen the "warm-up" and engage in friendly dialogue with the puppets, thus helping the child to feel less anxious and more comfortable.

Once the characters are introduced, the therapist can announce the beginning of the show and become the audience/observer. According to style and preference, some therapists tape record the session; others take notes on dialogue, character, action, and conflict; while others are able to capture and recall the essence of the session without the aid of either.

Once the child has spontaneously enacted his story, the therapist can extend the format of the show by interviewing puppet and/or puppeteer, thus eliciting further associations that can help to unravel the story's symbolic meanings. Not infrequently, this post-play dialogue produces rich associations that help to clarify some of the numerous messages within the story. The story material in some ways can be likened to the manifest content of a dream, while the associations can expand upon some of the possible latent meanings. Sensitive questioning that encourages the child to be introspective about the play can aid in the assessment of the child's observing ego and capacity to think symbolically and abstractly.

## Examining the Form and Content

Puppet material can be looked at in terms of both form and content. The latter is often easier to identify, being reflected in the characters, plot, themes, setting, overall affective (emotional) tone, and ending. In following the sequences within the material, one can often see "self" and "other" representations, as well as the conflict between impulse and defense. The therapist's understanding of the material comes from the verbal, nonverbal, and symbolic information expressed in such facets as setting, names of characters, slips of the tongue, etc.

The content may give some idea of the nature of the conflict, while the form often gives clues about how the child is handling the conflict, in terms of ego defenses, perceptions of self and others, general developmental level, etc. The form of the play—i.e., the level of organization and structure, process and sequences, perceptual and motor behavior, as well as verbal and cognitivie capacities— is important in understanding how the child is integrating inner and outer demands. Together, form and content form a multilayered picture of the child, just as the puppet interview complements the social history and other clinical data, aiding in the formulation of a diagnostic recommendation.

## Using Puppets in Ongoing Treatment

Generally, puppets are used in the treatment context in the same way that other relatively unstructured materials are used, with the child free to choose what he wishes to use and how. Frequently children play with particular puppets over many weeks or months, almost as though the materials become an externalized part of them, a kind of self-symbol. In following the ongoing symbolic play, the therapist can keep track of the ever-shifting psychic currents, the transference, and the degree to which the child is able to accept and integrate interpretations. Some children seem able to "hear" interpretations given via the puppet play before they can hear the connections to their own lives. Carl, an inhibited and frightened child, could acknowledge the puppets' wish/fear of acting aggressively against the father figure; this afforded cathartic relief and led to the gradual recognition and working through of his own fears of aggression. Rambert (1949) has described how she dealt with resistance and introduced specific themes into treatment via puppet play. In general, therapists seem to utilize puppets in the context of child therapy or play therapy, operating within their own theoretical framework.

## APPLICATIONS

Puppets have been used educationally and therapeutically for many purposes with families as well as preschoolers, physically ill and emotionally disturbed children, and in in-patient and out-patient settings. While some writers have discussed the presentation of puppet shows or the making of puppets, this article has focused on techniques that can elicit fantasy through spontaneous storytelling, using ready-made hand puppets. The material that emerges can then be used within the therapist's own theoretical framework, in diagnosis or treatment.

# Radical Therapy

*Arthur Maglin*

## DEFINITION

Radical Therapy is not so much a technical approach to therapy as it is an attitude toward the therapeutic process as a whole. The premise of Radical Therapy is that all therapy is laden with social and political value choices. Since the values of the client in the therapeutic process are influenced—often profoundly—by the values and attitudes of the therapist, it is incumbent on the therapist to fully analyze the values he holds rather than to either ignore them or take them for granted.

Radical Therapy understands that the origin of psychic oppression is contained in the nature of institutions that participate in the formation of inner emotional conflict. These institutions include the isolated authoritarian nuclear family, the educational system, the mass media, the religious establishment, the regimented workplace, and the organs of state power. These institutions produce and reproduce class divisions, racism, sexism, self-seeking, alienation, authoritarianism, submis-siveness, cynicism, and a host of other value orientations and emotional conditions. Feelings and behaviors of inadequacy, impotence, inferiority, lack of self-worth, anxiety, and so forth can be traced to the institutions, processes, and ideologies of capitalist society.

Hence, as much as is possible within a genuinely therapeutic context, radical therapists seek to encourage the spirit of rebelliousness rather than to belittle it as "adolescent," and to encourage the spirit of social idealism rather than to crush it as "grandiosity."

Radical Therapy views psychology as having society-wide implications. Psychotherapeutic pronouncements exert a profound influence on everyone. They affect the way we raise children, envisage love, marry, educate people, experience sex, view ourselves, and distinguish abnormal behavior from normal. Therapists are the priests and gurus of our time—experts whose words are accepted as truth. So the radical critique of therapy is seen as implying the need for a counterweight to the support that mainstream social work, psychology, and psychiatry have lent to the status quo.

It may easily be seen that there are a great variety of therapeutic techniques and theories that can be made compatible with a Radical Therapy approach. Hence, there are radical psychoanalysts, radical transactional analysts, radical Gestalt therapists, and even radical body therapists.

## HISTORY

Radical Therapy can trace its origins to almost the very beginnings of modern psychotherapy. Almost as soon as the Freudian psychoanalytic movement was launched, Otto Gross, a German anarchist and psychoanalyst, was developing a synthesis of psychoanalysis and radical theory. Alfred Adler, while still a psychoanalyst, made the first attempt to integrate psychoanalysis and Marxism. In the early 1930s Wilhelm Reich headed up the Sexual-Political Association.

There have since been numerous writings that have attempted to integrate psychological insight and a radical political perspective by such people as Frantz Fanon, Herbert Marcuse, Norman O. Brown, R. D. Laing, and many others. Significantly, these works have been written by people who have not been sympathetic to the Stalinist bureaucratic regime in the Soviet Union. Soviet psychological writings since the 1920s have been arid, unimaginative, and one-dimensional. Ironically, they often have much in common with American behavioral psychology-

The recent history of Radical Therapy can be dated as beginning in 1970, with the first issue of a journal called *The Radical Therapist*, a product of the previous decade's radical ferment. *The Radical Therapist* is now renamed *State and Mind*. It has been joined by other journals, such as *Issues in Radical Therapy* and *Catalyst: A Socialist Journal of the Social Services*. Radical therapists practice privately, in independent collective groups, and in established agencies. The Radical Therapy movement has its own internal controversies, but basic cohesion remains around the proposition that the politics of the therapist—whether conservative, liberal, radical, or hybrid—is a potent element of the therapeutic process and the social impact collectively made by psychotherapeutic authority.

## TECHNIQUE

For Radical Therapy, knowledge of the points at which the various psychodynamic psychotherapies influence emotional and behavioral change is key. These points include suggestion, persuasion, emotional support for approved trends, information about alternatives, and approval-disapproval cues. These are necessary parts of the process, but they are anything but value-free. An understanding of the fact that these elementary techniques are laden with social meaning and impact allows the radical therapist to use himself in a conscious way. A clarified analysis of social problems becomes intrinsic to the therapist's knowledge base when it is understood that, in a cumulative way, values concerning competition, personal ambition, sex roles, sexual orientation, class and racial biases, and so forth are a prominent part of therapy.

When the therapist is not aware of what he is doing in the area of values and world view, then the influence will be covert, but it will remain. Therapies that believe they have a neutral value in a political sense or that the personal is not political can only encourage attitudes that are accepting of the status quo.

## APPLICATIONS

Aside from the differences that might exist between, say, a radical psychoanalyst and a radical Gestalt therapist, there are three main trends discernible within the radical movement as to how to apply the basic insights of Radical Therapy. These may be called aggressive radical therapy, defensive radical therapy, and social radical therapy.

Aggressive radical therapy holds to the notion that people can (and perhaps even ought to) be radicalized through the therapeutic process. When all values are made explicit—sometimes through actual didactic sessions—then the client will see that the solution of emotional conflict and the raising of political consciousness are synonymous. The difficulty with this approach comes first of all with the self-selection of clients who are almost always radical or radicalizing people.

Defensive Radical Therapy views the therapeutic process as a survival enterprise. The attempt is to begin at the client's present state and to use as much encouragement as is possible to aid the client in seeing the social reinforcements of his problems, the lack of uniqueness, and the combative, assertive attitudes that are necessary to keep oneself from self-defeating behavior. The role of therapy is seen not so much as to create pervasive radical consciousness as the mode of mental well-being—which is, in any case, considered generally impossible in the therapeutic context—but to create sufficient social awareness as one tool in helping people to cope with a nonsupportive, oppressive, authoritarian social order.

Social Radical Therapy tends to give up on the notion of individual, group, or family therapy in favor of seeing society as the patient. Social radical therapists in their purest form tend toward dissolving into the larger radical political movement, except insofar as by their origins as therapists they tend to have a special interest in protesting mental hospital abuses, in helping mental patients to organize politically, in doing community-based organizing, and in incorporating psychological insight into political analysis.

A possible synthesis is to view aggressive Radical Therapy as frequently useful to radical clients, defensive Radical Therapy as often useful to nonradical clients, and social Radical Therapy as a necessary dimension of the radical therapist's view of how to uproot the conditions that cause emotional oppression.

# Radix Neo-Reichian Education
## Charles R. Kelley and Julie Wright

### DEFINITION
"Radix" is an archaic term meaning "root, or primary cause," and is used at the Radix Institute in the same sense that "life force" is used. The radix is not energy, but a substratum that is the source of both energy and feeling. The radix flow is experienced as feeling or emotion and is expressed in the spontaneous expressive movements of the body. Chronic muscular tensions (the muscular armor) block the flow of the radix and the feelings expressed through the flow. Radix Neo-Reichian Education, then, is a form of personal growth work based on loosening the muscular armor, and so freeing the radix flow. The process is experienced as an opening of the capacities for feeling.

### Radix Neo-Reichian Education HISTORY
The Radix "education in feeling" process is a development growing from the work of my (Charles Kelley) teacher, Wilhelm Reich. Reich was a psychoanalyst who began his work with Freud. He began to find that blocks to progress in analysis were held in bodily tensions. Out of this observation came his two major discoveries. First, he discovered and described the existence of the muscular armor, that is, how blocked emotion is

held in the chronic patterns of tension in the body. Reich's second major discovery was expressed in his concept of "orgone energy," the tangible life force we call the radix. The Radix Institute was founded in 1960, three years after Reich's death, to do scientific and educational work with Reich's concepts.

## TECHNIQUE

Our primary approach in using the radix to free the armor is the Radix Intensive, which is performed by one teacher and one student, usually in the presence of a small supportive group. The student is invited to deepen his breathing and to allow whatever happens. He is not to force any feelings, but to allow whatever feelings arise, or if none come, to accept it. The teacher will work to expand the breathing and to help the student release the tensions and blocks to expressive movement and to feeling expression as they appear.

The Intensive is experienced as a freeing of feelings, an expansion of awareness, an opening of consciousness. A course of Intensives is an extended trip done without drugs, the goal of which is the growth in the capacity to experience and express deep feeling. The Intensive frees feeling that is blocked by muscular armor, opens feelings that are buried, and softens and releases feeling that is held for fear of explosion. As connections are made with the feelings, awareness of the body grows. The body feels increasingly alive and integrated in its movement and expression.

The student is not taught what to feel but how to release the feelings that are already there. Usually this involves first the surrender to some painful emotion, such as grief, fear, or anger, which must be experienced before the emotions of joy, love, and pleasure can emerge and deepen. We are not free to choose what to feel, only to choose whether or not to feel. Radix education in feeling is a process of coming alive emotionally.

## APPLICATIONS

Dramatic changes occur as a result of this process repeated over time. The voice can drop, the eyes become less tense and more seeing. Men often regain the capacity to cry and women often regain the capacity to be angry and assertive. The frenetic person can become focused and centered; the withdrawn person can become more open and in contact with others. The sexual experience can change profoundly as the capacity for full sexual surrender develops.

The fundamental form of the Radix Intensive is the small supportive group. Being present as others start "feeling" and helping them emotionally are highly important parts of the work. Effective group work can be done on a weekly basis, in a sequence of monthly workshops, or in an extended residential program workshop. The more blocked the individual is in feeling, the greater the value of the extended concentrated residential work. Day after day feeling work has a powerful cumulative effect. An excellent introduction is a one- to three-week residential "feeling" workshop. Most students will eventually participate in some individual sessions as well. The advantage of individual sessions is simply to provide more concentrated expert time to an individual's special problems than is possible in a group situation.

The Radix Intensive is also an effective way to work with couples, each working in the presence of the other. The couples' Intensive helps mates to experience their relationships on the deepest level, whatever that is for them. When existing feelings are opened and experienced in this way, couples tend to come together strongly or to separate, based on the way they feel. They seldom stay in the uncertain, unresolved, unsatisfying limbo that characterizes so many man-woman relationships.

One of the innovations of Radix work is the development and synthesis of group techniques from many sources to deepen and support the Intensive experience. Body awareness exercises, Feldenkrais exercises, encounter techniques, bioenergetic stress positions, Branden sentence completions, Gestalt techniques, and other exercises are integrated with Reichian body work and used along with the Intensive to deepen and expand the feeling capacities of the student. Many of the exercises are designed to help integrate the student's expanded feeling capacities into his life and his actions. There is a sharing on a deep feeling level, often developing among group members, that can be a profoundly moving experience. The group allows a high level of participation, since much of the support work is done all at once, in dyads or in small sub-groups. At no time is everyone just watching the leader work with one person. This has two advantages. As everyone works together, there is a lot of freedom to allow feelings to come and to give and receive support from other group members. When emotional support for the work comes from other group members, there is a tendency to form close connections among group members rather than to develop a dependent relationship with the group leader, wherein he represents a father or authoritarian figure. To us this is as it should be.

# Rational-Emotive Therapy
## *Albert Ellis*

### DEFINITION

Rational-Emotive Therapy (RET) is a theory of personality and a method of psychotherapy; it is based on the hypothesis that an individual's irrational beliefs result in erroneous (or "crooked") and damaging self-appraisals. RET attempts to change these faulty beliefs by emphasizing cognitive restructuring (or "philosophic disputing"), in accordance with its ABC theory of emotional disturbance and of personality change. This theory holds that when a highly charged emotional Consequence *(C)* follows a significant Activating Experience or Activating Event *(A)*, *A* may importantly contribute to but only partially "causes" *C*. Rational-emotive theory hypothesizes that emotional difficulties or Consequences are largely created or "caused" by *B*—people's Belief System about *A*.

RET contends that when undesirable emotional Consequences occur at point C, these Consequences (such as severe anxiety, depression, hostility, or inadequacy feelings) can almost invariably be traced to people's irrational Beliefs *(iB's)*. It also holds that these irrational Beliefs can be most effectively Disputed (at point *D*) by using the logico-empirical method of science. When disturbed individuals do this kind of Disputing, and thereby change or eliminate their absolutistic, illogical, and anti-empirical thinking, their undesirable emotional and behavioral Consequences (that is, their neurotic symptoms) diminish or disappear and eventually cease to reoccur. RET, perhaps more than any other system of psychotherapy, emphasizes the philosophic Disputing of clients' self-defeating Beliefs. But this cognitive restructuring is done in conjunction with a variety of other emotive and behavioral methods, because it holds that cognitions, emotions, and behavior all significantly interact and have a reciprocal cause-and-effect relationship. RET is therefore a comprehensive method of psychological treatment that is pronouncedly cognitive but that concomitantly stresses and utilizes affective (emotive) and behavioral modes of basic personality change.

## HISTORY

Rational-Emotive Therapy (RET) was created by this writer (Albert Ellis), a clinical psychologist, in 1955. I had been first a pioneer sex therapist and marriage and family counselor and then trained as a psychoanalyst, and for several years practiced psychoanalysis and psychoanalytically oriented therapy. When I found psychoanalysis to be woefully inefficient because of its neglect of the philosophic sources of disturbance, its obsession with irrelevant historical material, and its ignoring of behavioral methods of change, I went back to philosophy and science, amalgamated their findings with modern humanistic thinking, and started to practice RET. I emphasized the importance of 1) people's conditioning themselves to feel disturbed (rather than their being conditioned by parental and other external sources); 2) their biological as well as cultural tendencies to think "crookedly" and to needlessly upset themselves; 3) their uniquely human tendencies to invent and create disturbing beliefs, as well as their tendencies to upset themselves about their disturbances; 4) their unusual capacities to change their cognitive, emotive, and behavioral processes so that they can: a) choose to react differently from the way they usually do; b) refuse to upset themselves about almost anything that may occur, and c) train themselves so that they can semi-automatically remain minimally disturbed for the rest of their lives.

## TECHNIQUE

RET therapists almost invariably utilize a number of cognitive, affective, and behavioral methods of therapy, and do so quite consciously on theoretical as well as practical grounds. Unlike many "eclectic" therapists, however, they do not unselectively use almost any procedures that work with a given client, nor do they emphasize, as do classical behavior therapists, symptom removal. Instead, they strive for the kind of profound personality change that tends to accompany radical philosophic restructuring.

In terms of emotive methods, RET therapists use several procedures, including these: they fully accept clients despite their poor behavior, and they practice (as well as directly teach) an unusual degree of tolerance, or unconditional positive regard. They use many affective exercises, such as the well-known RET shame-attacking and risk-taking exercises. They employ rational emotive imagery, originated by Dr. Maxie C. Maultsby, Jr. (1975). They use verbal force and vigor in their encounter with clients, in order to powerfully help uproot these clients' self-sabotaging ideas and behavior. They clearly distinguish between clients' appropriate (goal-achieving) and inappropriate (self-defeating) feelings and show these clients how to enhance and practice the former, and how to minimize the latter. They at times use special emotive methods, such as rational humorous songs, to help clients change their disturbed thoughts and feelings.

Behaviorally, rational-emotive therapists use almost all the regular behavior therapy methods, particularly operant conditioning, self-management principles, systematic desensitization, instrumental conditioning, biofeedback, relaxation methods, modeling, etc. They especially favor *in vivo* desensitization and have pioneered in assertion training, skill training, activity homework assignments, and other forms of action-oriented desensitizing procedures. In using both emotive and behavioral methods, however, RET practitioners don't just try for symptom removal, but also strive to help clients to effectuate a profound philosophic as well as behavioral change.

Cognitively, RET shows clients, quickly and forthrightly, exactly what it is they keep telling themselves that makes them emotionally upset; and it teaches them how to change these self-statements so that they no longer believe them and, instead, acquire a sensible, reality-based philosophy. In this respect, RET hypothesizes that "emotional" disturbances almost invariably include a strong element of absolutistic thinking, and that if clients fully acknowledge and surrender their shoulds, oughts, musts, demands, commands, and necessities, forego their childish grandiosity, and stick rigorously to wanting, wishing, and preferring rather than direly needing they will eliminate most of these disturbances.

More concretely, RET shows clients that they have one or more major irrational Beliefs (iB's), which stem from: 1) their human condition and their innate tendency to think "crookedly," and from 2) the exacerbation of this tendency by their social and cultural learning (Ellis, 1977a; Ellis and Grieger, 1977; Ellis and Harper, 1975). These basic irrationalities can be reduced to three main forms, which virtually all humans hold to some degree but which disturbed individuals hold more intensely, extensively, and rigidly:

*Irrational Idea No. 1:* "I MUST be competent, adequate, and achieving and MUST win the approval of virtually all the significant people in my life; it is *awful* when I don't; I *can't stand* failing in these all-important respects; and I am a *rotten person* when I don't do what I MUST do to act competently and to win others' approval." When people strongly hold this irrational Belief and its many correlates and sub-headings, they tend to make themselves feel inadequate, worthless, anxious, and depressed and to develop phobias, obsessions, compulsions, inhibitions, and similar disturbances.

*Irrational Idea No. 2:* "Others MUST treat me kindly, fairly, and properly when I want them to do so; it is *terrible* when they don't; I *can't bear* their acting obnoxiously toward me; and they are damnable, worthless people when they don't do what they MUST do to treat me satisfactorily." When people have this irrational Belief and its correlates, they tend to make themselves feel intensely and persistently angry, condemning, bigoted, violent, feuding, vindictive, and homicidal. They can also become grandiose and depressed.

*Irrational Idea No. 3:* "I need and MUST have the things I really want; and the conditions under which I live and the world around me MUST be well ordered, positive, certain, and just the way I want them to be, and they MUST gratify my desires easily and immediately, without my having too many difficulties or hassles. It is *horrible* when conditions are not this way; I *can't tolerate* their being uncomfortable, frustrating, or unideal; and the world is a rotten place and life hardly worth living when things are not as they *should be* in this respect." When people devoutly believe this irrational idea and its correlates, they make themselves angry, self-pitying, and depressed; they inwardly or externally whine; and they have abysmal low frustration tolerance, along with its concomitants of avoidance, goofing off, lack of discipline, and procrastination.

Rational-emotive therapists quickly and efficiently try to show their clients that they have one, two, or all three of these irrational Beliefs (iB's) and perhaps many of their corollaries and subheadings. They try: to teach these clients that their emotional problems and neurotic behavior are the direct and indirect result of such Beliefs and in all likelihood will not diminish or permanently disappear until they clearly see and acknowledge these Beliefs, actively and cognitively Dispute them, force themselves to emote differently while undermining them, and use a number of behavioral approaches to change the actions that accompany and that keep reinforcing these absolutistic, self-sabotaging Beliefs. Rational-emotive therapists mainly use the cognitive restructuring methods of science and philosophy to help uproot their clients' disturbance-creating ideas. But they also may use a number of other cognitive techniques, such as the teaching of positive self-coping statements; thought stopping; cognitive diversionary methods; semantic and linguistic analysis; self-monitoring procedures; the analysis of false attributions and expectancies; didactic instruction; skill training, effective methods of problem solving; etc.

## APPLICATIONS

I originated RET as a method of individual psychotherapy but soon developed a group therapy procedure, which includes the training of all group members to use RET with each other (as well as with their friends and associates outside the group). This is to help them become more skilled at talking themselves out of their own irrationalities and at working at their homework assignments, which are to be done in real-life situations. Group RET likewise includes a good many shame-attacking and risk-taking exercises, active confrontation, role playing and behavior rehearsal, and verbal and nonverbal feedback.

RET also favors large-scale group processes: such as lectures, workshops, live public demonstrations of RET, seminars, courses, etc. More than most other forms of therapy, it strongly encourages several bibliotherapy and self-help procedures: including the reading of books and pamphlets; listening to recordings, films, radio, and TV presentations; the use of charts, signs, and posters; vicarious therapy; the regular filling out of rational self-help forms; and various other psychoeducational methods. RET has also pioneered in rational-emotive education through the teaching of RET principles to children in their regular school classes, taught by teachers especially trained in RET, rather than by psychologists or psychotherapists.

In the treatment of clinical problems, RET has led to reports and studies on anxiety, depression, hostility, character disorder, psychosis, sex, love, and marriage problems, child rearing, adolescence, assertion training, self-management, and other important areas (diGiuseppe, et al., 1977; Ellis, 1977; Murphy and Ellis, 1978).

RET has achieved success and popularity in a number of self-help books (for example, Maultsby, 1975), and RET materials have, in addition, been incorporated into literally hundreds of other books and pamphlets on assertion training, self-management, personal adjustment, and do-it-yourself therapy. RET materials have also been embodied (with or without due credit) into many other forms of psychotherapy and personality training procedures.

# Rational-Emotive Group Psychotherapy
## Richard L. Wessler

### DEFINITION

Rational-Emotive Group Psychotherapy is simply Rational-Emotive Therapy (RET) conducted with groups of people instead of with a single individual. It is an approach that seeks to help people change their self-defeating and goal-defeating emotions and behavior by identifying their self-disturbing beliefs and assumptions, and by teaching them how to change such ideas and values.

RET is based upon the general assertions that humans respond primarily to cognitive representations of their environments and not to their environments per se; that humans disturb themselves by making unrealistic demands upon themselves, other people, and the world; and that the demand for individual perfection, in particular, contributes significantly to human unhappiness.

The goals of RET emphasize the individual's enjoyment of life, made possible by freeing oneself from self-evaluations of all kinds, from unrealistic anguish about unalterable reality, and by increase toleration for one's own and other people's imperfections.

### HISTORY

Rational-Emotive Group Psychotherapy began almost as early as individual Rational-Emotive Therapy (RET). In 1955, Albert Ellis, a clinical psychologist and psychotherapist already well known as a sex and marriage counselor, became dissatisfied with the results he obtained from employing the psychoanalysis principles in which he was trained. As he describes it, he then took the bold step of directly confronting his patients with their self-defeating philosophies, actively arguing against their irrational ideas, and assigning behavioral and cognitive homework assignments for them to practice their newly adopted ways of thinking and acting (Ellis, 1962).

His theoretical position has undergone some refinement since then (Ellis, 1973), as RET has increasingly converged with other behavioral and cognitive approaches that emphasize cognitive control of behavior and/or emotions.

RET rejects the idea of unconscious motivation of behavior and control of behavior by past and passive conditionings. RET assumes that beliefs and behavior are learned, that some dysfunctional beliefs are very easily learned (probably due to a human's biological tendencies to learn them), and that humans can employ their conscious thought processes to their own benefit by solving their problems and rethinking the self-defeating assumptions about other people and their own perfect-ability.

## TECHNIQUE

RET uses an educational model of therapy rather than a medical, emotional-release, relationship, or conditioning model. A therapy group consists of two or more people, up to whatever maximum the therapist wants (Ellis prefers to work with about twelve clients at a time). Typical group sessions begin with problems brought up by individual members. The therapist and other group members question and offer comments to the focal client to help clarify the problem, to uncover irrational ideas, and to dispute their validity.

The therapist is usually very active and provides a structure along which the discussion proceeds. Often the therapist will explicitly employ the ABC model of emotions, a mnemonic device to remind people that emotional consequences (C) are determined by one's evaluation of or beliefs (B) about activating events (A). To change negative emotional consequences, the therapist focuses the attention of the client and of other group members upon irrational beliefs—those that lack factual bases and consist of absolutistic demands (often revealed by words like "must", "should", "ought").

While the therapist encourages group members to accept each other (i.e., to avoid positively or negatively rating each other's worth as people), excessive amounts of mutual support are discouraged because such support may interfere with the group members confronting one another's irrational beliefs. Further, it may contribute to a client's disturbance by satisfying his self-defined need for love and approval. Nevertheless, people in RET groups behave like people in other voluntary groups; they develop group cohesiveness and often strong feelings for one another.

From time to time, most RET group therapists introduce exercises to the group. These exercises are similar to those used in other groups, and are intended to help people become more aware of their feelings, behaviors, and the impressions they make on others. In addition, the therapist helps clients get insights into the beliefs, assumptions, and personal philosophies that cause the feelings and behavior, and to develop plans to change them.

The goals of RET group therapy are the same as those of RET individual therapy (Ellis, 1975). These include teaching clients how to change their disordered emotionality and behavior, and to cope with almost any unfortunate events that may arise in their lives. To achieve these goals, the therapist very actively teaches people to think more clearly. Both therapist and group members give homework assignments to clients, some of which (such as speaking up in group) may be carried out in the group itself. Role playing, risk taking (such as disclosing ordinarily hidden experiences and feelings), and experimentally interacting with other people can be done in a group far more effectively than in individual therapy.

RET principles can be presented in large groups, and while individuals do not get much opportunity to discuss their personal problems, they may learn what ideas in general lead to extreme anger, depression, anxiety, guilt, and other self-defeating emotions.

With such information, they may engage in self-counseling and get insight into their own irrational beliefs and begin to work to change them.

## APPLICATIONS

RET may be used with any group of people except those who are intellectually deficient or very withdrawn.

Hospitalized patients present a challenge to the therapist's creativity, since they cannot easily try new behavior, and the range of homework assignments is necessarily limited.

Although relatively few people may achieve what Ellis terms "an elegant solution" (philosophic restructuring), many people can learn to clarify misconceptions, accept themselves more fully, blame themselves and others less, and substitute more adaptive coping statements for self-defeating ones.

# Rational Stage-Directed Therapy and Crisis Intervention

## D. J. Tosi and D. M. Eshbaugh

### DEFINITION

Emotional crises occur when an individual's appraisal or interpretation of situational events reflect certain cognitive distortions or irrational ideas. Rational-Emotive Crisis Intervention Therapy (RECIT) was developed to correct irrational ideas and cognitive distortions. While many crises intervention approaches focus mainly on removing a person from a difficult situation, RECIT places a priority on assisting persons to reinterpret their situational experiences in a more rational and adaptive way. The client is exposed to an ABCDE model that puts into rational perspective the present crisis events (A), associated beliefs and appraisals (B), emotion affects, or emotional responses (C), bodily effects (D), and behavior (E). Criteria for rational thinking and behaving have been outlined by Ellis and Harper (1975) and Tosi (1974). A systematic exposition of basic irrational ideas may be found in Ellis and Harper (1975).

### HISTORY

Tosi and Moleski (1975) formulated Rational Emotive Crisis Intervention Therapy (RECIT), an outgrowth of standard Rational Emotive Therapy (RET). The main theme of RECIT was to manage the clients' cognitive processes or beliefs about what is happening during a crisis situation. Tosi and Moleski proposed a model for understanding the person-in-crisis situation—The ABCDE's of Crisis Intervention. This early model depicts (A) the situational or environmental conditions and events that elicit (B) the person's interpretation (beliefs, ideas, appraisals) of the situation, (C) his emotional reactions to the A and B events, (D) physiological responses, and (E) behavioral responses to any of the preceding events.

Recently, however, my colleagues and myself (Tosi, 1974; Tosi and Marzella, 1975; Tosi and Eshbaugh, 1976; and Reardon and Tosi, 1977) have developed and conducted numerous research and case studies on Rational Stage-Directed Imagery (RSDI) and Hypnotherapy (RSDH). While primarily psychotherapies, they also add a new dimension to RECIT. RSDI and RSDH maintain essentially a cognitive-behavioral orientation but are also heavily experiential and stage directed. The therapist 1) trains the client in the use of cognitive-restructuring; 2) induces a deeply relaxed or hypnotic state in the client; 3) instructs the client to focus attention on relevant ABCDE processes; 4) assists the client via imagery to restructure self-defeating cognitions, affect (emotions), bodily responses, and behavior; and 5) directs the cognitive restructuring processes through the developmental stages of *awareness, exploration, commitment* to rational action, *implementation* of rational thought and action, *internalization*, and finally *change*. The client is directed to experience via imagery the crisis intervention process at each stage while being in a deeply relaxed or hypnotic state.

The use of imagery or hypnosis in crisis intervention in particular and psychotherapy in general facilitates 1) the focusing of the client's attention on relevant problem areas; 2) cognitive restructuring; 3) cognitive control over bodily states— i.e., heart rate, blood pressure; 4) self-awareness; 5) gaining a realistic problem perspective; 6) deep muscular relaxation; and 7) the use of positive suggestions for future action.

## TECHNIQUE

The ABCDE model in crises intervention permits the therapist to determine the area(s) of the person's functioning which need to be managed or brought under control. The therapist then must raise several questions. First, what aspects of the crisis situation are modifiable? Second, what are the client's beliefs or ideas about the situation? Are they distorted or irrational? To what extent is the client aware of his beliefs? Third, what are the associated affective and physiological responses? Fourth, is the client's behavior in the situation appropriate or inappropriate? Therapists using RECIT need to attend to every aspect of the model, although they may be required to focus on some areas more than others. In RECIT the therapist most always tries to help clients gain an accurate cognitive perspective of their difficulties.

RECIT with RSDI and RSDH permits a systematic expansion of awareness of thought (cognitive awareness), affect (emotional awareness), bodily responses (physiological awareness), action (behavioral awareness), and the environment (environmental awareness). Through imagery and relaxation or hypnosis a person can more vividly experience the relationships between the social-psychological influences of the past, the here and now, and the future.

## APPLICATIONS

RECIT with RSDI and RSDH has broad applications in the area of crisis-related disorders. Whether these are affective (i.e., depression, emotional disability, anxiety, etc.), psychophysiological (i.e., palpitations), or behavioral (i.e., suicide), the use of the cognitively oriented RECIT is potentially helpful in symptom reduction and crisis resolution. A case history would be beneficial in understanding RECIT with RSDI and RSDH.

Karl A., a thirty-year-old white male, exhibited a serious agitated depression. Initially, Karl was encouraged to relate the situational event, A, that had "caused" his emotional crisis. Karl was deeply involved with a woman, who abruptly left him six months prior. He promptly became hypomanic depressed. Thus, the A was established. As the assessment continued, the behavioral aspects, E, of his hypomanic depression were found to be multiple and markedly self-defeating. For example, Karl quit his job and spent his days either talking obsessively to people or being in total isolation, ruminating about his loss. Drug use was prominent, and he tended to alienate people with his hostility. During periods of excessive rumination, he would entertain homicidal and suicidal ideas. The psychophysiologic aspect, D, could not at that time be assessed, and it was felt that it played a secondary role to the depression associated with Karl's homicidal/suicidal ideation.

Therapeutic intervention focused upon the belief or attitudinal system, B, associated with the hypomanic-depressive syndrome. Karl believed that it was awful that the woman should reject him and that she should be punished for this "crime" committed against him. Karl's narcissistic rage, however, was frequently turned inward. On a more covert level, Karl believed himself to be quite worthless as a human being. Rejection of any sort affirmed that he was weak, dependent, and incapable of being able to live a normal life. At this point, the ABCDE analysis was sufficiently complete to relax/hypnotize the client. Using imagery and relaxation, Karl was made aware (awareness stage) of the relationship in relation to the situational event, his beliefs, his emotions, and his behavior.

The therapist then proceeded to help Karl explore (exploration stage) more constructive alternatives to his present crisis state. Cognitive restructuring was introduced here. Though initially resistive, merely getting Karl to focus attention on more constructive thoughts, feelings, and behavior tended to reduce his distress. The therapist helped Karl explore coping beliefs, such as "I am not a weak, dependent and worthless person just because one person rejects me"; "Believing that she must love and approve of me at my demand makes me depressed, so it would be in my best interest to believe that if she doesn't love me it is not a catastrophe"; "Her rejecting me is not the cause of my problem, it's really my belief about her rejecting me that is causing the problem", and "I cannot change her to make me feel better, but I can change my beliefs to make me feel better and accept my situation as it is." After exploring these and many other beliefs, Karl was guided into the commitment stage. Rational beliefs that he seemed to respond most favorably to were repeated again and positively reinforced by the therapist. As Karl's distress gradually subsided, he was asked to see himself (via imagery) becoming committed to the implementation of more desirable ways of thinking and acting. Then he was asked to visualize himself implementing (implementation stage) more rational ways of functioning in real crisis situations. Finally, the therapist asked Karl to see and to feel himself internalizing (internalization stage) these more adaptive behaviors and bringing about substantive changes (change stage) in his behavior.

To assure maintenance of Karl's behavioral change, the therapist recommended that he come in the next day, which he did. He showed markedly fewer depressive symptoms. Noticing that Karl was in a more elated mood, the therapist suspected that Karl's hypomanic defenses were returning. The therapist recommended longer term therapy, because of Karl's cyclical tendencies to become excessively depressed/ hypomanic. Confirming this, Karl decided to enter therapy. Essentially the same therapy was used as in the crisis intervention, except that more situations were used. In about six months, Karl was more able to cope with rejection, to minimize feelings of worthlessness, and was able to obtain employment in a sales job with moderate success (three months after therapy terminated). Homicidal and suicidal ideation was absent. The excessive rumination about his former woman-friend was markedly diminished, and drug abuse ceased. Finally, Karl's interpersonal hostility became less prominent and he entered into more substantive relationships.

---

# Reality Therapy

*Alexander Bassin*

## DEFINITION

In simple terms, Reality Therapy is based on two principles. They are that man is driven by 1) a need for love, a meaningful and reciprocal relationship with a responsible person. According to Dr. William Glasser, the founder of Reality Therapy, "In all its forms, ranging from friendship through mother love, family love, and conjugal love, this need drives us to continuous activity in search of satisfaction." 2) A need for a feeling of self-worth, self-esteem, self-respect. "Equal in importance to the need for love," Glasser adds, "is the need to feel that we are worthwhile both to ourselves and to others. Although the two needs are separate, a person who loves and is loved will usually feel that he is a worthwhile person, and one who is worthwhile is usually someone who is loved and who can give love in return." The reality therapist works actively with the client to help him meet these needs, and the emphasis in treatment is on here-and-now events in the clients' life, rather than on past events (as in psychoanalysis).

## HISTORY

Dr. William Glasser received his psychiatric training at the West Los Angeles V.A. Neuropsychiatric Hospital and UCLA. During his internship he began to question the basic tenets of classical psychoanalytic theory and practice. Building 206 of the VA hospital, which was directed by Glasser's mentor, Dr. G. L. Harrington, exposed Glasser to a typical chronic ward of psychotic patients. The patients in this ward were confined an average of seventeen years, and the average discharge rate was about two patients a year. When Harrington and Glasser introduced the nuclear concepts of Reality Therapy, the ward was quickly transformed from a custodial storage tank for people waiting to die into a lively therapeutic community that returned most of the patients to a constructive existence in the community.

Glasser's first important assignment (in 1956) as a full-fledged psychiatrist was with the Ventura School for Girls, an institution operated by the State of California for the treatment of seriously delinquent girls. Here he introduced and refined the ideas and techniques used in Building 206, with the same gratifying results. In 1961 Glasser published his first book, *Mental Health or Mental Illness?*, which laid the foundation for the emergence of Reality Therapy.

Glasser first used the term "reality therapy" in April 1964, in a formal paper delivered at a criminological convention, and a year later Glasser's seminal volume, *Reality Therapy–A New Approach to Psychiatry*, was published by Harper & Row. The book is notable for its scrupulous freedom from jargon, its dedication to common sense, and a clear and determined rejection of the prevailing psychodynamic mode of psychotherapy. Soon after its publication, Glasser established the Institute for Reality Therapy in Los Angeles, where he conducts training programs for qualified practitioners.

Students of Reality Therapy note that a spiritual ancestor was Paul DuBois, a Swiss physician who urged in 1909 that the doctor treat his patient as a friend rather than a "case," and provide him with a positive, healthy outlook on life. Dejerine and Gaukler (1913) in France and Joseph H. Pratt, the group therapy pioneer in this country, expressed many of the same ideas. Alfred Adler and the founder of the so-called psychobiological school, Adolph Meyer, likewise echoed a number of Reality Therapy sentiments. However, it should be recognized that at the time Glasser began to formulate his theories and techniques, he could not have been directly influenced by these people.

## TECHNIQUE

Although Glasser's theory has become increasingly complex during the period 1962–1977, the technology of practice has remained relatively consistent, easy to understand in principle, but devilishly hard to do.

1. *Involvement.* A warm, friendly, personal relationship is the foundation for the successful practice of Reality Therapy. One cannot crack the lonely armor of the failure/identity person by being aloof, impersonal, or emotionally distant. The client must become convinced that another human being cares enough about him to discuss his life philosophy, his values, his hopes for the future as well as politics, sports, sex, and religion in an honest and transparent fashion. Any subject that both therapist and client consider worthwhile and interesting are appropriate for conversation. When the therapist can get the client to joke and laugh with him, progress is being made.

Very soon the client presents a problem that is bothering him. The therapist listens as the client usually thrashes about, blaming his miserable childhood, his unfeeling parents, his boss, his wife, society, fate, etc.

2. *Behavior.* The therapist does not argue about the client's self-serving analysis of his troubles. Instead he firmly moves (once the involvement is strong enough to stand the strain) to get the client to examine his behavior. "What are you doing?" is a favorite RT question. Glasser proposes that no one can gain a success identity without being aware of his current behavior.

People in trouble often avoid facing their present behavior by speaking at length about their feelings. Of course, feelings are important, but for a relationship to be successful, how we *behave* is what counts. So, if a depressed woman comes to Dr. Glasser's office and laments at length about how upset, worried, and miserable she feels, he might respond, "I believe you. You have convinced me that you are depressed, and I appreciate that you are upset. *But what are you doing?*"

3. *Evaluation.* After his behavior has been held up for scrutiny and described in detail, the therapist gently asks, "Is it doing you any good? ... Is it the best available choice for you? ... Is it in the interest of your wife, your children? etc." This self-evaluation feature of Reality Therapy is frequently misunderstood. The therapist does not act as a moralist; he does not deliver sermonettes; he does not tell a patient his behavior is wrong and that he must change. The judgment "I ought to change" belongs solely to the patient.

4. *Plan.* It is not sufficient that the person declare that his behavior is counterproductive. The therapist must help him work out a plan that will bring him involvement and self-worth. The tact, creativity, and ingenuity of the therapist is tested at this stage of the therapeutic process. He must avoid a plan that is beyond his client's ability. A failing person needs success. Glasser says, "The plan should be ambitious enough so that some change, small though it may be, can be seen, yet not so great that failure is likely." A plan that calls for small, success-assured increments of change is better than one that is grandiose. The plan should be concrete, specific, with no loose ends or uncharted contingencies.

5. *Contract.* The legal profession discovered centuries ago that a commitment, a contract, helps a wavering client stick to his resolution. Glasser was a pioneer in adapting this notion to his therapeutic technique. It is characteristic of people with failure identities that they avoid committing themselves, initialing a contract. Perhaps, in their loneliness they are convinced that no one cares, and if they fail they will be exposing themselves to more pain. But insisting on a verbal commitment, even a written contract, intensifies involvement. It verifies that the therapist is concerned about him and provides him with the strength to carry out a minimal plan that may lead to more ambitious projects in the near future.

6. *Follow-up.* It is well that we recognize that the failure identity person may agree to a plan, make a commitment—and then do nothing. Therefore, the reality therapist leaves as little as possible to chance. He may say, "You have this plan, and you've made a contract to carry it out. But how will I know that you did it?" This approach is an additional sign of the therapist's concern and involvement. He may accept the suggestion that the client will telephone, or report in person about fulfilling the contract.

7. *No excuses.* In the course of the follow-up, the reality therapist is not amazed if the chronic failure person does not carry out the plan. Invariably this client will present a whole array of excuses. In Reality Therapy, once a commitment has been made, the therapist does not accept excuses. He does not discuss excuses. He does ask why; he says, "Let's not waste time arguing about excuses. What counts is accomplishment. Do I still have your commitment? Perhaps the plan was too hard for you. Should we make it easier or leave it as it is? When will you carry it out? Will you initial this contract? How will I know if you've carried out the plan?" Excuses and rationalizations disrupt involvement and have no place in Reality Therapy.

8. *No punishment.* Successful people have an exaggerated regard for the value of punishment because they believe that a great deal of their own success stems from a fear of punishment. But the reality therapist is aware that with failure-oriented individuals, punishment, the use of mental or physical pain to modify behavior, generally does not work. Incompetent and irresponsible people are punished over and over again through-

out their lives, but instead of changing for the better, they tend to become even more fixed in their failure identity. The rule of Reality Therapy is: no punishment, but no interference with natural consequence. Therefore, the therapist does not scold, curse, ridicule, or denigrate people; he uses praise in large measure instead.

9. *Never give up!* Finally, the reality therapist must appreciate that his clients are often content with failure and want him to give up on them. Then their world view will be confirmed: "I'm no good. It's no use trying. Nobody expects me to accomplish anything." The reality therapist mobilizes his own strength and patience to persist in maintaining an involvement despite failure after failure.

Although these steps are presented here in a somewhat mechanical form, their correct application in real life requires great flexibility, creativity, patience, and humor on the part of the therapist.

### APPLICATIONS

In contrast to conventional psychodynamic therapy, which seems to be effective only with people who suffer from what may be called the YARIS syndrome *(Young, Articulate, Rich, Intelligent,* and *Successful),* Reality Therapy frequently works with those populations that are beyond the parameters of conventional treatment: the failures, the criminals, the addicts, the whole army of poor and ineffectual people that most therapists will not touch.

# Realness Therapy
## Charles McArthur

### DEFINITION

Year by year, as we develop, we each give away pieces of our authenticity. We are hostages of family constraints and confined to the actions permitted by our culture. To survive, we have denied our own realities, sometimes before we knew them. For the neurotic, the psychotic, and the character disordered, too much that was precious has been forsworn. Such patients' realities surface intermittently, as their disowned, fragmented selves come back to haunt them. Ironically, these haunted people must learn to embrace their own, often very scary, ghosts, in order to exorcise them and reclaim authenticity.

The job of the realness therapist is to midwife the patient's denied realities, to conjure up and speak in behalf of the patient's ghosts and so, by gentle means, enable the patient to exorcise them. Only then can the patient take full possession of his self, the core of being we all have but so seldom know. The therapeutic relation becomes the kind of special place we all might gladly find where, by vindicating our own lost reality instead of continuing to deny it, by quietly letting it have its say, we might discover and recover what was once our birthright: a self of our very own.

Metaphor? No, more like an operational definition. All therapists elect those techniques that express their therapeutic metaphor. It is their metaphors that differentiate them.

## HISTORY

If someone had come to existential psychology by way of formal study of the underlying philosophies, mastered the psychodynamic awareness of Freud and his modern descendants, watched the human farce with the eye for motives of a professional writer, lived a lifelong adventure story, then settled into the compassion that ennobles passion in maturity, that someone would be the inventor of Realness Therapy. That is the history of Dr. Paul Stern. Born in Germany, he attended the universities of Brussels and Zurich, then, emphasizing psychology more than philosophy, did graduate work at the University of California in Los Angeles and Harvard, where he took his Ph.D. In between, there was a war, life on three continents, and writing that ranged from intellectual pieces to covering Hollywood antics. After a short stint in Harvard's student health services, Dr. Stern began private practice in Cambridge, where his Center for Humanistic Therapy teaches the realness orientation, as will his new Centers in New York City and Greenwich, Connecticut.

## TECHNIQUE

The ritual aspects of therapy create a stable, trustworthy situation in which patient and therapist can risk emotional "trips." Realness Therapy has quite usual ground rules, though with supportive variations. The patient's willingness to risk his realness must be matched by the therapist's readiness to be available when badly needed. The lonely trip into one's inner self must not be made unattended.

The therapist unswervingly takes the side of the patient's disowned remnants of self: his fantasies, visions, intuitions, and dreams. He helps the patient to embrace them, then to withstand their impact, and so at last to make them part of his lived reality, which then becomes richer. The consulting office gives officially disapproved realities sanctuary, where two can share "a charmed mystery tour" of inner space.

The basic truths of lost selves are always simple—simple as deepest feelings. The therapist emboldens the patient to toss aside the complexities of logic, the strictures of common sense, the systematization of our world by Descartian or Freudian cosmologies. (Complexity, Dr. Stern points out, is our worst culturally patterned disorder.) The patient is transported to surreal landscapes where the rules of common sense are suspended. There is a magic that therapy practices on space and on time. The unlived past replaces the empty present. There are bolder and bolder leaps "in a multidimensional life space no longer subject to the astringent laws of Newtonian physics." The patient is on a self-trip.

Yet all this is done without announcing the itinerary ahead in doctrinaire interpretations. To the objection "But I don't know if all that was real," the therapist says, "Never mind; let's hear about it!" To the observation that "When I awake my dream seemed to make no sense after all!" the therapist may say, "Yes, but how did it feel while you were dreaming?"

Gently. Above all, the therapist says these things gently. In a sanctuary, one must suffer no abuse. Of the violent therapies that seem part of our Zeitgeist and seem also to "work," Stern tartly remarks, "So does torture!"

Realness Therapy runs counter to those in which the well-trained patient is taught to pour his feelings into a plaster-cast of systemaization. There is, Stern points out, "no pre-arranged highway" to *this* patient's reality. At any one crisis, there is no correct road for the therapist to take. Indeed "the notion of the correct road itself may be absurd." He tries to encourage the therapeutic trip along whatever road the patient seems readying himself to take. If that dead ends, they must seek another. The roads are many. The patient will show them both many wonders along each way.

If that sounds easy, regard this description of a realness therapist:

Of course, whether the person in therapy can reach his goal and gets hold of his own reality depends, in the end, on the realness of the therapist. The demands on him are enormous. In order to do his job of midwifery well, the therapist ought to be a paragon of contradictory virtues. He ought to be sensitive but robust, kind but not easily seduced, warm without being seductive, a seer of ghosts who has his feet firmly on the ground, flexible as Proteus yet endowed with integrity. He ought to have the improvising touch and the radar antennae of the artist who discovers and makes visible what is invisibly present rather than indulging in arbitrary invention. He simply cannot go by the book and the rules of orthodoxy, but must improvise his way over an ever-changing, only partly mapped terrain full of pitfalls that make continuous demands on his ingenuity.

## APPLICATIONS

Every one of us has the right to a self of our own. Realness Therapy therefore has a general application. The limitations are of human resource rather than of method: every helper finds a limit to how many and how heavy his cases may become. While clearly a treatment of choice for neuroticism, Realness Therapy has more than usually constructive things to say to the psychotic and the character disordered. It shares with some existential approaches a view of violence as attempted reclamation of the self. This leads to treatment with respect, something not often offered to violent individuals. Above all, it views not only psychosomatic, but "purely" somatic ills as outcroppings of the unreclaimed self and seeks to free us from being dehumanized by an anachromanistic Newtonian medical paradigm.

---

# Rebirthing

*Lark*

## DEFINITION

The initial goal in the process of Rebirthing is to heal the damage done to the breathing mechanism at birth, when the child is cut off from its supply of oxygen through the premature cutting of the umbilical cord and forced to learn to breathe with lungs that are filled with fluid, under circumstances that seem to say, "Breathe or die." The initial panic or terror in which the child learns to breathe is then reinforced on a subconscious level every time it takes a breath, until the person learns either to release it or it simply remains stored in the body and the subconscious as one of these nameless fears.

In the process of Rebirthing, a person learns to release whatever tension is blocking the breathing mechanism from its full, efficient working, and then, as the healing takes place, to be able to use the breath as a completely supportive and creative part of daily life. It is an ongoing process, and the effects can range from dramatic life changes to very subtle feelings of contentment; it is usually a direct and very powerful experience of personal power. Rebirthing is one of those experiences where it is almost as difficult (and sometimes more) to talk about afterward as before.

## HISTORY

The founder/discoverer of Rebirthing, Leonard Orr, spent a lot of time with other psychological techniques during the years prior to his experimenting with the use of the hot tub in inducing altered states. One technique was staying in the bathtub for long periods of time, and he noticed significant revelations occurring when he did. Finally, around 1974, he began to experiment with friends, suspending them in a redwood hot tub with a snorkel and a pair of nose plugs, and he found that many of them experienced significant realizations about patterns that were basic and generally destructive in their lives. A lot of his friends also began to reexperience their own births during the process, and Orr began to realize that many of the effects were due to his presence. He concluded that he had released enough of his own birth trauma that people felt safe to experience and release theirs with him in the hot tub.

Some of his friends began to work with him, Rebirthing other people, working with transforming the blocks and patterns as they became conscious, and Rebirthing spread slowly and steadily. Then another breakthrough occurred about a year later, when Orr tried working with the breathing pattern that happened in a rebirth, without the environment of the hot tub. It became obvious that it wasn't only the warm water that was responsible for the effects, but also the presence of the rebirther and the method of breathing.

## TECHNIQUE

The emphasis, then, in a rebirth is on the breathing, and having the person come to a place where the breathing is relaxed and even, rhythmic and balanced, with no pauses between exhales and inhales, and no holding patterns that limit the movement of the ribs and diaphragm.

The importance of having the rebirther present in the initial stages has to do with the nonverbal communication to the rebirthee that the experience is safe and beneficial, and also with the verbal suggestions that the rebirther will make to guide the rebirthee in letting the breath be relaxed and connected. The reexperiencing of the fear and panic surrounding that initial breath, no matter how brief, can be overpowering without the presence of another person who's secure in the knowledge of the safety of the process.

Once a person heals the damage done to the breathing mechanism, taking on the average of three to ten two-hour sessions, the change is permanent, and the breath can then be used as a tool to release specific patterns in the body and mind. At that point people begin Rebirthing themselves if they wish, so any dependency on the rebirther as therapist is short-circuited. The initial part of a person's rebirthing process is usually done out of the water, because it was discovered that Rebirthing in the hot tub first was usually overwhelming and often impeded the process of release and integration.

## APPLICATIONS

Since Rebirthing releases deep body tension and thought patterns, it can be useful to anyone who's interested in becoming more aware of who he is. Many people experience spontaneous remission of diseases during the process. Breathing difficulties are the most obvious maladies that can be affected, and there are a number of ex-asthmatics who are rebirthers; just about every disease, from chronic lower back pain to cancer, has been released by people. A breathing cycle can be used either to short-circuit colds, sore throats, and other allergic-type reactions or speed up the healing process. Since the natural tendency of the body and mind is toward health, Rebirthing seems to simply speed up that tendency. Experience of psychic capabilities also increase and expand; indeed, Rebirthing simply seems to expand people's awareness of their capabilities.

# Relationship Enhancement Therapy
## Bernard Guerney, Jr. and Edward Vogelsong

### DEFINITION

Relationship Enhancement Therapy (RE) attempts to eliminate dysfunctional patterns of interpersonal interaction by teaching participants skills that will enable them to relate more effectively and constructively with each other. This technique is designed to build a relationship that is harmonious and that will provide an enduring climate for the positive development of the social unit and the individuals within it. RE aims to alter the ways in which each individual views the deepest emotions and most important interpersonal behavior of himself and of other significant people in the interpersonal environment. Similarly, it seeks to alter far into the future the ability of each individual to bring into consciousness emotions and behavior that had previously functioned outside of awareness, and to express such emotions in a manner constructive to self and others. Achieving this ability (especially if the other significant individuals in the interpersonal environment have made similar gains) permits the individual to make fundamental changes in interpersonal systems that are important to him and to influence positively his own life and the lives of his intimate associates. The systems approach used in RE therapy deliberately aims at replacing the *vicious cycles* operating in the system with *auspicious cycles*. In essence, the goal is to have each person learn to be honest and compassionate with the people who are important to him, and to elicit honesty and compassion from them. The theoretical underpinnings of RE derive much from Carl Rogers, B. F. Skinner, Albert Bandura, Harry Stack Sullivan, and Timothy Leary.

## HISTORY

Development of the RE therapies began in 1962 with Filial Therapy, wherein parents were taught in groups to conduct therapeutic play sessions with their seriously disturbed, but not psychotic, children under direction and supervision, and were taught to transfer the therapeutic attitudes and skills into their daily interactions (see Filial Therapy). The children showed steady and marked improvement. Moreover, parents reported their ability to improve relationships with spouses through application of therapeutic attitudes and skills. Therefore, in the mid-1960s conjugal therapy was developed, wherein husbands and wives with troubled relationships were successfully taught to employ therapeutic skills with one another (e.g., Rappaport, 1976). The view was presented that paraprofessionals, and particularly intimates, might prove to be a significant postive force in the delivery of therapeutic services (Guerney, 1969). Experience with this approach led to an even firmer belief that methods pioneered by mass education provided a more viable model than the medical model for developing and delivering individual and group psychotherapy. The success of this method of service delivery had an important effect on the systematic development of procedures to use Relationship Enhancement Therapy with other populations.

RE therapeutic methods were then made available, in an abbreviated form, to families with milder problems and to families that wished to learn therapeutically derived skills in order to *prevent* problems or to *enrich* relationships that were already satisfactory. The RE method, therefore, was used as a preventive mental health program with premarital couples (Guerney, 1977), with parents and adolescents working as dyads (Coufal, 1975; Guerney, 1977; Vogelsong, 1975), and in larger family units. Films and tapes were made to explain and demonstrate the methods of Relationship Enhancement to professionals and prospective clients.

## TECHNIQUE

Relationship Enhancement Therapy teaches specific skills that improve interpersonal communication and problem solving. The participants learn to express themselves in constructive ways to avoid arousing defensiveness and hostility in others. Participants practice stating their own feelings about issues rather than making accusations or analyzing each others' motives. They are taught to express underlying positive feelings associated with implied criticisms and to state their desires and wishes as a basis for negotiating problem/conflict resolution. The program participants learn to interact with others through understanding and acceptance rather than by argument and hostility. They learn to discuss and resolve important relationship issues in such a way as to increase harmony, trust, empathy, and mutual satisfaction.

These skills are incorporated into the participants' behavioral repertoires by way of systematic leader demonstration and exemplification, and by having the participants practice the skills under intensive and extensive supervision by the therapist. Participants receive individual instruction from the leader and strengthen their learning by teaching others in the group while they themselves are learning. Specific suggestions are provided for daily practice and maintenance of the skills in the natural environment, and specific skills are provided and practiced to promote generalization.

The participants learn the following sets of behavioral skills or modes of behavior.

1. The *Expresser* mode is designed to increase the participants' awareness of their own feelings, perceptions, and desires as they pertain to the relationship. The Expresser is taught to communicate this awareness in a way that will increase the possibility of being understood and responded to in a compassionate way. Participants learn six guidelines that enable them to formulate good Expresser statements.

2. The *Empathic Responder* mode is designed: (a) to focus the attention of the participant on the essential content and emotions of the Expresser in order to reach the deepest possible level of compassionate understanding of the Expresser's statements, including the implications the statement has for the relationship and (b) to communicate this understanding and compassion to the Expresser. The effect of such communication is to help the Expresser better understand his own emotions and desires within the relationship and to make it easier to express them in a still more fundamental and honest way in the next communication.

3. *Mode Switching* is a behavioral skill that involves: (a) the ability always to keep in mind which of these two modes of behavior is being employed at any given time, (b) the ability to know when to employ one mode and when the other, (c) how to move from one mode to another in a way that is coordinated with the other person, and (d) when and how to switch from one mode to the other in order to facilitate problem solving and conflict resolution.

4. In the *Facilitator* mode, participants learn the kinds of principles, skills, and behavior employed by the leader to teach the other three sets of skills. This mode is used (a) to facilitate the learning of other group members during the instructional program and (b) to enable the participants to help others they interact with to use the skills whenever it is appropriate to do so in everyday life.

5. *Problem/Conflict Resolution* involves a set of six skills which are designed to ensure that clients: (a) take a suitable amount of time in an appropriate place to consider their problems separately and jointly; (b) take steps to assure themselves, before they push for a solution, that they understand all the important emotional and interpersonal aspects of the problem; (c) seek solutions which are aimed at maximizing *mutual* need satisfaction; (d) propose, receive, and react *intellectually* to the proposed solutions of another with a high degree of operational clarity, and react *emotionally* in such a manner as to further encourage careful and fair problem solving; (e) attempt to foresee the consequences and difficulties of any suggested solution in order to permit careful and realistic refinements at the outset; and (f) make plans for a systematic reassessment of the agreements reached in order to make such revisions as may later be found necessary.

6. *Generalization and Maintenance* skills are taught by explaining, for example, the importance of cues, of self-monitoring, of a relatively high success rate, and of receiving reinforcement (from self-statements as well as from others) when attempting to abandon old and/or to acquire new attitudes and behavior. Special logs are used not only with the intention of helping clients to better incorporate RE skills, but to help them acquire some skills for generalizing and maintaining any new attitudes or behavior.

These skills act together to prevent discussion from degenerating into unproductive digressions or into accusations and counter-accusations; they act instead to focus the discussion into more and more fundamental aspects of the problem and of the relationship. Other skills taught include those of knowing (a) when to try to generate specific suggestions for problem/conflict resolution, (b) what kinds of suggestions to make, and (c) how to use the four behavioral modes to arrive at mutually satisfying problem/conflict resolutions.

The skills and procedures are taught and practiced systematically in accord with social-learning and reinforcement principles. The therapeutic procedures are always supportive and are flexible enough to cover the individual needs and personalities of a very wide range of individual differences in degree of disturbance, intelligence, and socio-economic status.

## APPLICATIONS

The method can be applied with and for single individuals, dyads, small groups of individuals, families, or other social groups. It can be applied with in-patients as well as out-patients. Relationship Enhancement has been tested by outcome and follow-up research that has demonstrated its durable effectiveness with a variety of populations, including married couples, dating couples, fathers and their adolescent sons, and mothers and their adolescent daughters. It has been shown to be effective in improving the skills of the participants and enhancing relationship satisfaction and adjustment in all these instances (Guerney, 1977). The method also has been adapted and successfully used in high school (Hatch and Guerney, 1975) and in business contexts. The method has been judged extremely promising in the rehabilitation treatment of addicts in residential and halfway-house settings and with out-patient alcoholics and their wives.

# Relaxation Training

## Ian M. Evans

### DEFINITION

Relaxation Training refers to a variety of procedures designed to induce in an individual a state of relative muscular relaxation with concomitant subjective feelings of tranquility and calm. Physiologically, this state, which has become known as the relaxation response (Benson, 1975), can be identified by decreases in blood pressure, heart rate, and respiratory rate and by increases in skin resistance—all homeostatic changes controlled by the autonomic division of the nervous system. The relaxed state is also characterized by decreased tension in the skeletal muscles and by increased percentages of alpha wave activity in the EEC

The most common Relaxation Training procedures are progressive muscle relaxation, which will be the focus of this article; autogenic training, in which the individual concentrates on self-suggestions of warmth and heaviness in the limbs; hypnosis, in which suggestions of relaxation and mental calmness are provided by the hypnotist; bio-feedback, in which one of the physiological systems mentioned above is monitored and the signal fed back to the individual; and various methods of meditation, such as Zen, Yoga, or Transcendental Meditation, which involves passive concentration on a word or symbol in a quiet, comfortable environment. More detailed descriptions of these procedures may be found in Evans (1975).

## HISTORY

Meditative and contemplative methods have been an accepted part of both Eastern and Western religious practices for centuries. However, as a psychotherapeutic technique, Relaxation Training was pioneered in the 1920s by Edmund Jacobson (1938), who devised a procedure known as progressive relaxation to teach hypertensive individuals to relax. Jacobson's procedure became widely known only when Joseph Wolpe adopted the training method for his anxiety-reducing technique, systematic desensitization (Wolpe, 1958). As a result, Relaxation Training became an important part of behavior therapy during the 1960s. About the same time, popular interest in Eastern religions, meditation, and altered states of consciousness attracted the attention of the scientific community to the benefits of meditation for inducing the relaxation response and for bringing responses of the autonomic nervous system under voluntary control (Wallace, 1970).

## TECHNIQUE

All Relaxation Training procedures share certain common elements, which may be the reason that comparisons of their relative efficacy typically show few differences. Ideally the training takes place in quiet surroundings with the individual resting comfortably on a reclining chair or bed. Suggestions that the individual will feel relaxed but not tired are common and some instruction is provided that directs the individual's attention towards internal feelings. The purpose is that the recipients will learn the training procedure and be able to implement it themselves.

The advantage of progressive relaxation training is that by focusing on *muscular* relaxation, the individual's new relaxation skills can be used in a variety of situations. During the early stages of training, the individual is first asked to tense a muscle, to hold that tension until the muscle or muscle group involved is easily identified by slight discomfort (between five and ten seconds), and then to let go, or relax, that muscle. The release may be either gradual or abrupt, with gradual release being easier to continue beyond the normal resting point. The trainee is encouraged to notice the difference between the tension and the relaxation. This simple procedure is repeated with the other muscle groups in a systematic order, usually arms, trunk, face, lower limbs. The trainee is asked to notice what is done to relax a muscle and then to keep doing that beyond the normal resting level. Typically a single training session requires about twenty-five minutes of instruction.

Audio-taped relaxation instructions are widely available (e.g., Budzynski, 1976). However there is some evidence that live training is more effective. What is probably most advisable is to provide the client with an audio tape of the instructions for practice at home, which should be daily. The trainee should also be encouraged to implement elements of the relaxation in everyday situations, such as relaxing facial muscles while driving a car. Sometimes it is useful to teach individuals to cue their own relaxation by having them say "relax" to themselves as they release muscle tension; accompanying this with the exhalation of a deep breath is also effective.

## APPLICATIONS

A major application of Relaxation Training is as a component of Systematic Desensitization. In this procedure for treating phobic anxiety, the client is trained to relax and while relaxed is asked to imagine vividly situations or events that usually provoke anxiety or fear. It appears from numerous experimental studies that the exposure of the client to the fear/anxiety-provoking scenes is more important for treatment success than the relaxation. However, Relaxation Training does result in significantly lowered levels of autonomic arousal, the physiological component of anxiety, and therefore may be necessary to calm the phobic client sufficiently to confront the feared situation.

Because it does have this inhibitory effect on anxiety, the implementation of deep relaxation can be very useful to individuals exposed to unavoidable fear-provoking or stressful situations in real life. Thus, for instance, the person who fears public speaking is taught to relax and encouraged to implement the relaxation prior to delivering a speech. If the real-life exposure is carefully graded—i.e., the task requirments are more and more anxiety-producing ones—this procedure is identical to systematic desensitization, but conducted *in vivo* instead of in imagination. More recently, however, it has been suggested that when applied in this way relaxation serves as a self-control technique whereby the individual can use self-relaxation as a deliberate method of controlling anxiety in a wide variety of settings. Thus, the client is taught not just how to relax but when to use relaxation as an active coping skill (Goldfried and Trier, 1974).

If Relaxation Training is thought of as imparting a useful skill for self-control, then numerous additional applications suggest themselves. For instance, self-induced relaxation can be very helpfully implemented by people with insomnia while they are waiting to fall asleep. Self-induced relaxation is particularly valuable in dealing with anxiety-related disorders that specifically involve extreme muscle tension, often in one or a few specific muscles, such as tension headaches (here the individual would be taught to maintain less tension in neck and forehead muscles throughout a stressful period), writer's cramp (the individual would be taught to relax immediately prior to a writing task, such as signing a check), bruxisms (teeth grinding), and vaginismus (spasm of the vaginal muscles preventing intromission). Where discrete muscles are involved the general Relaxation Training procedure may be enhanced by biofeedback of muscle potential signals (EMG feedback). Because muscular tension exacerbates the pain of uterine contractions during labor, Relaxation Training is an important component of preparation for natural childbirth.

Finally, relaxation may be taught to individuals who have difficulty in controlling their anger or their rising tension levels in frustrating situations. For example, in one investigation in my (Ian M. Evans) laboratory it was shown that women who were taught relaxation skills and also taught to implement them in stressful situations became less tense when exposed to repeated baby cries, an aversive experience that is often the trigger for explosive aggression by abusive parents.

# Restricted Environmental Stimulation Therapy

*Peter Suedfeld*

## DEFINITION

Restricted Environmental Stimulation Therapy (REST) or sensory deprivation therapy involves the use of severely stimulus-reduced environments. The patient is alone for up to two days, usually in a completely dark, soundproof chamber or immersed in a tank of water. Environmental restriction may be combined with messages or other inputs.

## HISTORY

Reduced stimulation was a component of various folk medicines, and is related to the use of solitude and meditation for religious and self-actualizing purposes. In some cases, as in Morita Therapy (used in Japan since the 1930s), these cultural practices have evolved into formal medical therapies.

The first report of controlled clinical use appeared in 1959. Hassan Azima and his collaborators used the sensory deprivation chamber to produce deep regression on the part of the patient, enabling him to relive problems of early life and to liberate himself from the residue of the problems that interfered with his adult functioning ("anaclitic therapy"). John C. Lilly and J. T. Shurley, two psychiatrists who developed the water-immersion technique of sensory deprivation, have used the technique tc enhance self-insight and to reach higher levels of consciousness. Henry B. Adams and his group pioneered the use of room confinement and therapeutic messages with hospitalized psychiatric patients. More recently, a research team headed by this writer (Peter Suedfeld) has used the technique as a method of behavior modification, combining it with informative and persuasive messages, relaxation training, relevant visual stimuli, and biofeedback training to produce changes in dysfunctional habit patterns.

At present, sensory deprivation therapy appears to be a small but growing approach. Applied research is being carried out in Canada, the United States, West Germany, and Japan. Some clinical facilities using the Restricted Environmental Stimulation Technique (REST) have also been operating.

## TECHNIQUE

The most frequently used techniques of recent years minimize absolute level of stimulus input. In room confinement, which has been explored the most fully in clinical contexts, the client lies on a bed in a dark and soundproof chamber; in water immersion, he is either completely submerged or floating in a tank of body-temperature liquid.

In the typical procedure, the client is thoroughly oriented to the chamber or tank and related equipment. He is shown how to use the life-support items and how to terminate the session. A monitor is always present nearby, listening through the intercommunication system to ensure that the client is following the instructions and is not experiencing major discomfort or stress. The period of confinement is from a few hours to two days, comfortably completed by the great majority of participants.

## APPLICATIONS

Azima's group found that anaclitic therapy had beneficial effects on a number of psychiatric patients, particularly depressives. The only contraindication was that the technique seemed to have negative effects on obsessive-compulsive neurotics. Later studies have found positive results with neurotic and psychotic patients in a wide variety of diagnostic categories. Reduced stimulation in conjunction with more traditional psychotherapeutic techniques has been helpful with autistic children. Scattered reports have shown good results with anorexia nervosa, persistent infantile colic, hypochondriasis, esophoria, and with a number of behavioral disturbances where brief periods are used as time-out from positive reinforcement and social contact.

Sensory deprivation with messages has been reported to increase clients' openness and self-esteem, and to decrease symptomatology, both observed and measured by clinical scales. It has also been used to increase hypnotizability, and may therefore enhance hypnotherapeutic procedures.

In the area of habit control, sensory deprivation therapy can reduce smoking rates for as long as two years after a twenty-four-hour session. The same treatment, combined with messages and preceded by tallying and satiation smoking, has produced complete abstinence in 80 percent of clients six months after the session, a very high rate compared to other techniques reported in the literature. A parallel technique has been successful with grossly overweight patients. Replicated findings have shown the usefulness of sensory deprivation in ameliorating snake phobia, and there is some pilot work using it with biofeedback and relaxation training for patients suffering from essential hypertension.

Sensory deprivation therapy seems to be most successful with those patients whose symptoms are the most severe, and is strikingly effective with patients of relatively low socioeconomic and educational background. Other favorable data are: the reduced environmental stimulation situation is found to be pleasent for a variety of patients (prominently including schizophrenics and alcoholics); the lack of side- or after-effects; and the ease of constant monitoring and immediate modification or termination of the session, if desirable.

So far there have been very few contraindications of the use of the technique. Sensory deprivation is apparently harmful for obsessive-compulsive neurotics; more obviously, patients who have abnormal needs for stimulation or a fear of dark, enclosed places will find the experience dreadful. Monitoring and quick release can reduce the problems of people who first discover that they are claustrophobic when they begin the session. Post-release interviewing with a sympathetic counselor is desirable: clients who quit typically feel that they have failed and may require reassurance, while those who have completed a scheduled session are eager to discuss their experience.

The method requires minimal therapist and patient time. The monitor can be a nonprofessional with brief training. The facility needs only a dark, silent room or tank, and a control space with intercommunication set. Chamber furnishings are a bed, chemical toilet, food container, and water bottles. Thus, an adequate facility can be set up at relatively little cost.

There are four main uses: to enable people to gain greater insight, a clearer understanding of their problems, and some ideas about appropriate resolutions; to induce rapid,
deep regression; to foster rapport with the therapist and reduction of symptomatology;
and to bring under control reactions that the client himself recognizes as injurious to his
health, but which he cannot extinguish without assistance. It appears desirable to increase
the use of sensory deprivation therapy in those situations where its success has already
been demonstrated and to intensify research testing the limits of its effectiveness.

# Role-Acting Therapy

*Robert F. Ostermann and Sarah Donahue*

## DEFINITION

Everyone acts out various roles in everyday life. Personal roles arise primarily from internal, individual forces, including various ego states, whereas social roles are prescribed
primarily by external, social forces. These two forces do not act independently and the
well-adjusted individual is one who can effectively actualize his personal roles within the
context of appropriate social behavior.

Roles are at times inadequately or incorrectly conceptualized, and at times undiscovered, untried, or unused. Some cause great anxiety and give rise to defensive behavior, or
are avoided. Acting is an important life function, for it is through acting that one learns
how to adopt a socially prescribed behavior and how to be oneself "appropriately." One
who attempts to live his personal self in all situations and at all times is likely to experience as much maladjustment as one who attempts to become whatever others require.

Role-Acting Therapy, then, is a group process whereby, through prepared scripts,
the individual learns a pattern of behavior that is adjustively sound in social situations.
There is, however, a distinction between role-playing therapy, spontaneous improvisation,
and Role-Acting Therapy. The latter helps a person act, while the former helps a person
become. Frequently the two merge, and acting and being are one. When the two cannot
merge, the therapeutic objective is effective interpersonal relationships without disowning
self. This requires role acting. An important characteristic of the therapeutic process is that
prepared scripts are used. These scripts provide clearly conceived social roles and socially
effective role behavior for the client to learn, practice, and "try on for fit."

## HISTORY

The history of Role-Acting Therapy is not yet distinct in the history of group therapy, since role acting has occurred as a part of a more comprehensive process. It is clear
from anthropological evidence that role acting as human behavior has been employed
for centuries for various cultural purposes. Psychologists have observed that the taking
on of the behavior of others cognitively and affectively (emotionally) occurs as part of
the normal growth process as early as age three. Children's games of "Let's pretend we

are . . ." reveal ego role states and games of "I must and you must ..." reveal social role prescription. Schoolteachers engage children in role acting, although not primarily for therapeutic purposes. However, role assignments frequently serve to reinforce some apparent personal characteristic or teach appropriate social behavior.

Moreno, in formally employing dramatic techniques in therapy, not only created psychodrama, but pioneered the process of group therapy. Traces of his work with respect to role playing and Role-Acting Therapy can be found in the theories and techniques of Perls, Kelly, Glasser, and Berne.

Yablonsky cites a recent, typical rehabilitation project that employed Role-Acting Therapy as the principal technique of therapy with eighteen antisocial, underachieving adolescent boys. Through the coaching they received, the boys showed improvement in school attendance and classwork as well as in self-control and social relationships.

Role-Acting Therapy is a technique compatible within the theoretical context of a number of therapies. In Reality Therapy, role acting is the acting out of the proper behavior, not the acting out of personal experiences and feelings. Glasser sees the latter as tending to reinforce "irresponsible behavior," thereby the client is confronted with the moral issues of right and wrong. In the context of Transactional Analysis, role acting actually teaches the client scripts and games, but as scripts and games he owns consciously. In this way the client becomes autonomous and authentic. Role acting provides a warm-up or preliminary step for those who "cannot" role play in psychodrama. In Gestalt Therapy, role acting sharpens the awareness of social role and personal role disparity. For the behavior therapist, role acting is a form of group learning laboratory whereby the clients shape new, socially acceptable modes of behavior, experience the positive reinforcement of social approval, and develop their own "kinesthetic" sense of the new role.

Criticism of Role-Acting Therapy arises from theorists found at opposite extremes of the continuum of other-directed versus inner-directed behavior. Those who emphasize the outer, socializing forces see a tendency for identification with imaginary or fantasied characters, leading to role confusion or the reinforcement of unreal behavior.

The retort, however, maintains that behavior that is exclusively inner-directed or exclusively outer-directed is illusionary to begin with. Adjustment consists of the "trade-offs" that are made between personal and social forces. For all individuals, that rests at different points on the continuum, and for the same individual it rests at different points on the continuum at different stages of growth. To be able to *act*, distinct from *being*, and to discover new modes of being through acting is the therapeutic goal of Role-Acting Therapy. It is not a matter of either-or, and monitoring this balance with sufficient reality testing is the critical job of the therapist, as it is with any technique employed.

Those therapists who prefer therapy that involves their client's intuitive and spontaneous reactions will find Role-Acting Therapy procedures cumbersome and restrictive. For those who prefer a systematic approach and for the beginning therapist who needs some structure to start with, Role-Acting Therapy appears to be a useful tool and an appropriate starting point.

## TECHNIQUE

Role-Acting Therapy is structured as a group process in which passages from play scripts present the actual dialogue or monologue to be spoken and acted within the interpersonal dynamics of the group. Participants function in either therapeutic or process roles.

1. *Therapeutic roles.* The *principal* is that group member on whom the script and group activities are focused. The *co-principal* or *auxiliaries* (a term borrowed from psychodrama) act out other roles in the selected script but, unlike psychodra-ma, they act these roles as they perceive them and not as perceived by the principal.

2. *Process roles.* The *director* coaches, models, drills, encourages, restrains, corrects the principals and co-principals. In a word, the director is the main direct force in the group process. The *critic* represents the conditions of social approval and the critic's reaction serves as reinforcement. The remaining members of the group serve as an active *audience*, heightening the awareness of social presence, providing reinforcement and feedback after the performance.

The tasks of the therapist are: 1) to heighten group responsibility for the process and its effectiveness, 2) to provide information regarding appropriate role conception and behavior, 3) to overcome process blocks, 4) to serve as observer, critic, and director with respect to all the process roles in the group process, and 5) to introduce other techniques, such as guided fantasy, role playing, role reversal, etc., as they seem appropriate to the therapy process.

The role-acting scripts are short passages from a play. A basic script library includes passages highlighting those social roles, interpersonal situations, and emotions most frequently encountered in the "good life" and in maladaptive behavior, as well as those that present positive growth opportunities. The search for appropriate script material and script writing are suitable extensions of the group process. The group process follows this course:

1. *Designate principal and principal's role.* A period of exploring an individual member's role problems and readiness.

2. *Select script material.* A group problem-solving session that prompts a fuller discussion of the specific role difficulty and the criteria for appropriate behavior.

3. *Designate process roles.* The therapist casts the process roles in order to maximize the growth process for all involved, not just the principal.

4. *Rehearsal.* In this phase the director coaches the principal and the auxiliaries. The rehearsal usually begins with reading the script and proceeds through reading with emotion, walking the lines, and finally, acting with a full incorporation of script language and body language. Emphasis is not placed on memorization of lines. Improvised props and/or costume help the principal "get into the role." The director is coached by the therapist.

5. *Performance.* As a distinct phase in the process it provides an air of criticalness and detachment for the principal.

6. *Process feedback.* In this phase the group members share observations and introspective reactions, not only to the principal's role acting but also to the process roles acted by the other group members. Feedback can redirect the process back to an earlier phase, lead to wider processing, such as others role acting the same script, or to a deeper processing, such as the principal improvising his personal role-script spontaneously.

## APPLICATIONS

Some of the major applications of role acting are: 1) learning how to act out personal roles and social roles in a socially acceptable way, 2) expanding personal and social-role repertoire, 3) resolving role conflicts, 4) overcoming blocking, 5) discovering new personal roles and shaping these roles toward actualization, and 6) giving voice to repressed personal scripts.

# Roleplaying Therapy

*Raymond J. Corsini*

## DEFINITION

Roleplaying Therapy may be defined as a rehearsal or recapitualization of any event, actual or imagined, for the purpose of amelioration of any real or conceptualized situation. Putting this a bit differently, psychotherapy may be seen essentially as a learning process devoted to changes in behavior, thinking or feeling, but usually all three, and one way to achieve these changes is to actually "do" what is called for. Thus, a person who is afraid to ask someone for a job, may learn to overcome his fears and learn the technique of dealing with a job situation through rehearsing such a scene with a friend, or with a stranger in a safe situation. What we have, then, is a kind of rehearsal, a tryout in a situation in which one cannot fail. Similarly, if one has a lot of anger toward some person, he might discharge that anger by "having it out" with that person (which would be reality), or by roleplaying, that is, dealing with someone who represents that person.

Consequently, Roleplaying Therapy says in effect that one way of getting psychological benefit is through actually acting out a problem in a safe situation with people who themselves will play other roles, and in this way vicariously experiencing emotions, gaining skills, and obtaining information.

It is this writer's opinion, based on considerable knowledge of a variety of psychotherapeutic techniques (Corsini, 1973), that of all psychotherapeutic methods, none of them is more powerful—and consequently more difficult and more potentially dangerous in the wrong hands—than psychodrama, the general name for Roleplaying Therapy.

## HISTORY

While we can be sure that roleplaying has been used for a wide variety of purposes throughout the centuries, including psychotherapeutic uses, generally the development of roleplaying as a psychotherapeutic technique is attributed to J. L. Moreno (1946), an Austrian-born psychiatrist who first experimented with theater-in-the-round and then began to treat patients on the psychodrama stage, having them explain their psychological difficulties to others, who might include the therapist and assistants, and then act out the problems with the help of the assistants under the therapist's direction.

This technique, first used in the 1930s, became quite popular. Under Dr. Moreno's direction, a society, The American Society of Group Psychotherapy and Psychodrama, and a journal, *Group Psychotherapy,* were established, and the procedure has now been more-or-less accepted by many eclectic therapists as an ancillary therapeutic method, both for individual and for group psychotherapy. A number of books explain the system. Moreno's book (1946) may be too specialized for many people. One by Corsini (1966) and one by Starr (1977) may be more suitable for the general reader.

## TECHNIQUE

The technique is essentially that simple: the patient (known as the hero) plays his own role in a situation that may have taken place in the past, or that may be a current situation, or one that is anticipated in the future. He may now act out his role alone, or in interaction with other people who play other roles. Thus, the person acts as though he were actually in the situation portrayed and that the others were actually those in his real life.

Many variations exist. Thus, after finishing a scene, the person may change roles with someone and experience how others react to someone playing himself; or he may watch how someone else plays the role he played in the same way he played it. The first is called "switching" and the second, the "mirror technique." There are dozens of variations, but these are the principal ones.

Roleplaying Therapy can take place alone: that is, if one rehearses a speech in the privacy of one's bedroom, this is a kind of roleplaying. Masturbation can also be seen as Roleplaying Therapy, if the person imagines he is with another person. Roleplaying can take place in a one-to-one situation with the therapist perhaps playing the role of the client's mother or wife. It can take place in a group therapy situation, in which group members can play a variety of roles to meet the needs of other members. And, it can take place in a situation specifically designed for psychodrama, with a stage, a director, an trained assistants. Such psychodrama situations are found at the Moreno Institute in Beacon, New York, and at several other locations in this country and abroad.

## APPLICATIONS

The applications of Roleplaying Therapy have been very wide. It can be used for practically any problem, though it seems especially valuable for dealing with delinquents and criminals. It also has considerable value, when used properly, in marriage difficulties. In terms of specific problems, the considerable literature shows that it has been applied to almost any kind of situation in which psychotherapy can be used.

Also, roleplaying is employed in situations closely allied to psychotherapy, for example, education (Wells, 1962), nursing training (Fein, 1963), industry (Corsini, et al., 1968; Maier, et al., 1975), and in the home (Lippitt, 1947).

Psychodrama may be viewed as a technique that can be used with any therapeutic theory, a general procedure, much like the interview, and consequently its use does not mean any acceptance of Moreno's sociometric theory. It may also be seen as the method of choice and be employed exclusively. It can be used on a very "light" basis, such as: "Let's see how you talk to your child when you want him to go to bed," or it can be used on a very "heavy" basis, with a whole team of assistants who will act as representatives of people in a patient's life.

# Say It Again—An Active Therapy Technique

*Ben C. Finney*

## DEFINITION

Say It Again is an active technique for releasing feelings, bringing out insight, and changing behavior. It uses *repeating*, in which the client is asked to repeat each sentence several times before going on to the next sentence; *prompting*, in which the therapist, like the stage prompter, provides lines for the client to say; and *directions* where the therapist, like the drama director, directs the client how to act and express his feelings.

## HISTORY

I (Ben C. Finney) developed Say It Again gradually in a trial-and-error way. I found that it elicited intense emotional catharsis, and that the abreaction (reliving) of traumatic experiences, especially early childhood experiences, produced insight, behavior changes, and reduction of personal discomfort. Other therapists have used it and they too have found it productive. It can be employed easily and then stopped without disruption when another method seems preferable.

## TECHNIQUE

*1. Repeating.* In repeating, the client is instructed to repeat each sentence he says several times before going on to the next phrase, letting it "echo" andr ecruit feelings and associations until a new sentence comes to mind. He is also asked to repeat this new sentence several times before saying the next one, which is repeated in turn. He is encouraged to "listen" to what he is saying and to try to feel the emotional impact rather than to think about what he is going to say next. When he stops talking because he is blocked or trying to sort out what he is thinking, he is urged to keep on repeating the last sentence until a new one emerges.

2. Repeating a sentence over and over has several important effects. Forcing such a novel mode of expression disrupts the familiar thought patterns and encourages new ways of thinking. Second, it is difficult to repeat long and complex sentences, and of necessity phrases are short, direct, and childlike, and the usual defenses against feelings of intellectual abstractions are blocked. When a phrase contains emotions, repetition allows the person's feelings to be recruited and amplified, rather than avoided by his jumping to a new topic.

3. Preserving emotional momentum is important. Insisting that the person keep talking—repeating the last phrase he said if nothing comes to mind— helps keep up the momentum. Another way to keep one momentum going is for the therapist to repeat over and over the last phrase the client said before he stopped. If the client is right on the edge of strong feelings, this will push them over into discharge. The therapist can also amplify the feelings that have been expressed by the client by repeating the feelings with

more intense emotional expression. By using the voice and expression to intensify feelings, the therapist can draw out more emotion from the client.

4. *Prompting.* In prompting, the client is offered a phrase to say that is not one he has previously said, but one close enough to what he is ready to express that he could accept it as his feeling. He is asked to repeat it at least once to see if it feels correct. If the phrase does not express the client's thought or feeling correctly, he should then change it so that it does. It is similar to an interpretation, in that the therapist is directing the client's attention to some feeling that he has not been immediately aware of; it differs in that prompting can be used repeatedly to push the client with frequent small nudges, whereas interpretations are used less frequently and usually involve larger steps.

5. *Directions.* In directions, the therapist acts like a director who tells the actor not only what to say, but how to say it and how to move and gesture. As director, the therapist can tell the client to act or talk more assertively, to clench his fist, pound a pillow, or to shake with fear. These physical actions often help intensify a feeling or to make it more real.

The following is a typescript of part of a session illustrating these techniques. The client has connected with the "child" in herself and is talking to her "father".

> Client: You don't show your love to me. You don't show your love to me. You don't show it. [*repeat*]
>
> Therapist: *Louder!* "You don't show your love to me." Say it louder. [a *direction*]
>
> Client: *You don't show it! You don't show it. You show it to that baby* [a shift, introducing the baby]
>
> Therapist: "You show it to that baby and not to me!" Say that! [This *prompt* involved a very small step; the "You don't show it" and "You show it to that baby" are combined.]
>
> Client: You show it to that baby and not to me! *You show it to that baby and not to me!!!* [increasing anger] IT'S ALL GONE!!
>
> Therapist: Pound the pillow! [a *direction*] Say, " *You took your love away and gave it to that baby!* Say that!; [This *prompt* amplified the feeling "It's all gone" and "You show it to that baby."]
>
> Client: You took your love away and gave it to that baby. *You took your love away and gave it to that baby!*
>
> Therapist: Say, "*You took your love away and gave it to that baby and it hurts!* Say it loud!! [a *prompt*, putting the pain in her expression into words, and a *direction* to say it loudly with feeling]
>
> Client: YES! IT HURTS!! YOU TOOK YOUR LOVE AWAY AND GAVE IT TO THAT BABY AND IT HURTS! [The client begins crying.]

## APPLICATIONS

Say It Again can be introduced when the client needs to get to feelings, or it can be used on a regular basis. Most clients accept it comfortably, but some are threatened and it is not used. Except for an occasional client who complained that the strong feeling kept on reverberating after the session and threatened to get out of control, I have not had adverse reactions to the technique. While my experience has been limited to adult maladjustment problems and neurotic conflicts, other therapists have reported good results with schizophrenic clients.

It can be used in couple therapy, in which the two talk directly to each other, but in the Say It Again structure the therapist controls the interaction. It seems to slow the interaction down so that each can hear what the other is saying.

In groups, one style is to put a member on Say It Again structure for a dozen phrases and then to stop and let another member react and say how they are feeling. The new member is kept on Say It Again for a bit and then it is shifted to another member. With the use of *directions* and *prompts* an interaction can often be made to be more feeling and productive.

Another style is to take a volunteer and have him lie down, with the group sitting close and touching him. The person is kept on Say It Again until some abreaction develops. When a suitable place to stop is arrived at, then the other members are encouraged to express the feelings they had as they listened. Usually one member seems to have strong feelings, and he in turn is focused on with the Say It Again structure.

# School-Based Psychotherapy
## *Monica Holmes*

### DEFINITION

School-Based Psychotherapy is treatment delivered to teen-agers by mental health professionals in the school. Individual, group, and family therapy are all available in the school setting. Mental health staff have access to firsthand observations of their clients in a variety of settings, and can work not only to modify the client's maladaptive behavior but also provide consultation to teachers in an effort to make them part of a therapeutic team.

### HISTORY

The in-school mental health program was initiated by our agency (Community Research Applications, Inc.) in 1968, in one junior and one senior high school in low-income areas of New York City. Originally designed as a screening program in which student problems would be diagnosed and referred, it became apparent that appropriate referral sources were unavailable or unacceptable to our client population. This client population, with many youngsters showing poor impulse control, low self-esteem, aggressiveness, or marked withdrawal, was in need of clinical services. Because they would not accept referrals to mental health agencies, the treatment unit was developed in the school.

### TECHNIQUE

A whole range of therapeutic techniques is involved. Students are referred by teachers, but may come on their own. They know the staff, have seen them around the school and are willing to seek help on their own. The diagnostic process involves talking with the student, observing him in a range of different classroom situations, and talking with teachers and parents, as may be appropriate. Following this, the student may be seen either with his parents for a few focused family therapy sessions, or in a group, and/or individually. Group sessions are focused primarily on reading, as many of these children read four to five years behind grade level, a factor that contributes to their low self-esteem and disruptive classroom behavior. Each therapeutic reading group has six children who work each day with a mental health professional. The reading groups have proved to be especially effective in working with impulse disorders. These reading groups also engage in considerable game playing. Board games for four or more children, monitored by the therapist, represent a particularly useful technique for learning ego-adaptive skills. Behavior therapy with frequent brief contacts during the day for positive reinforcement have also proved to be especially effective in working with impulse disorders.

The referral process is different from the traditional clinic setting because clients already know the staff and do not feel that they are being asked to speak with a stranger. The diagnostic process is different from the traditional clinic setting because the staff has the opportunity to make extensive firsthand observations. The therapeutic process is different from traditional psychotherapy because much reliance is placed on helping with reading as a technique to foster ego-adaptive capabilities and group process. The accessibility of clients also makes it possible to do behavior therapy to provide consistent reinforcement.

## APPLICATIONS

The model is useful in any situation in which children show maladaptive school and interpersonal behavior but are unlikely to accept a referral to a mental health facility. Based on experience, our agency personnel believe that mental health professionals who want to be helpful to children from low-income families should get out of the clinics and into the schools.

# Sector Therapy

### William F. Murphy

## DEFINITION

Sector Therapy is a "short-term" psychotherapy based predominantly upon the theories and clinical experience of modern psychoanalysis. It differs from those that use "minimal interference" in lieu of "free association" inasmuch as the interview material in each session is kept within a sector concerned with the origin and development of the presenting symptoms or problem by means of a special verbal feedback technique.

# HISTORY

The original technique was developed by Felix Deutsch in 1939 at Beth Israel Hospital in Boston because of difficulties encountered when "minimal interference" techniques were used with psychosomatic cases and psychoneurotic conditions that could be seen only infrequently, or were unable or unwilling to cooperate due to shame, fear, or mistrust. The original method was called "The Associate Anamnesis." In 1946 Dr. Deutsch became a consultant at the Cushing V.A. Hospital where this original method of exploration was developed into a technique of psychotherapy and used for the treatment of psychiatric and psychosomatic problems in World War II veterans. It was then called "Sector Psychotherapy." In 1954 Dr. F. Deutsch and this writer (Dr. W. F. Murphy) published two volumes describing this method of therapy in full, illustrated by recorded interviews which were completely explained, and discussed. Later I modified this technique so that it could be used with various types of patients suitable for psychoanalysis but who cannot obtain it. A textbook explaining and illustrating these modifications was published in 1965.

# TECHNIQUE

Minimal interference techniques were originally an outgrowth of psychoanalysis. Originally a *contract* was made with the patient to reveal all his thoughts and feelings. In psychoanalysis a major task of the analyst is the detection of various methods of *resistance* used by a patient to evade this contract. When these "resistances" are analyzed and interpreted correctly the patient learns how he dealt with himself and others, and why, in the past and present. Minimal interference does not lead to free association, with or without a "contract" (or "therapeutic alliance"), and in most patients seen less than three times a week transference states and their interpretation are usually unreliable and evanescent. In many cases minimal interference leads to minimal activity on both sides and to minimal progress. Sector Therapy avoids these problems by encouraging patients to associate to their own material. This is accomplished by questioning the meaning of words that are ambiguous, obscure or highly charged emotionally. This method also allows the therapist to guide the associations and confine them to any chosen *sector*, usually one centered around conflicts and symptoms or difficulties with major figures in the present and past. The first person mentioned in connection with the original complaints is often found to be connected with the *origin* of the symptoms in many ways and the relationship with this person is explored in depth and usually found to be one that was highly ambivalent.

By expanding words related to *time*, such as "always" or "usually" or "never," the patient is guided back into the past so that the present can be understood in context with its antecedents, a variation of Santayana's dictum that those who have forgotten the past are condemned to repeat it in the present. When confronted with past and present similarities in terms of *relationships, desires, symptoms* and *fears,* the patient is often able to realize that as an adult he has more independence, choice, and control than he had as a helpless child, and that acting and feeling as he did is childlike, habitual, and destructive to his adult self-regard. The adult side is then encouraged to make a better solution than had been made before.

The *words* selected for this feedback process are obviously the crux of this technique. Those concerning *time* and strong *feelings* have been mentioned. Some are words used *repetitively* by the patient; these words are idiosyncratic and especially meaningful to him. Others are double-entendres, slips of speech, or those *symbolic* of important areas of conflict or concern. Many such words, phrases, or sentences are obviously ambiguous and a clue to ambivalent relationships, past and present.

Use of the patient's own language usually leads to the development of *transient* positive transference states, which can be reinforced in many cases by respecting certain attitudes of the patient, i.e., being easygoing with similar patients and more reserved with more formal patients. In this sense the therapist acts as a "narcissistic mirror image" (Kohut, 1971).

With this method, neurotic and psychosomatic patients often lose their symptoms or obtain great relief from feelings of pain, hate, intense longings, anxiety, and depression; it can often be demonstrated that these *affect* states (of mood or emotion) were derived from old personal relationships displaced over the years onto other persons or, as in the case of psychosomatic illnesses, onto parts of the body. These relationships were obviously traumatic and of great intensity and ambivalence. When a reconciliation or settlement is made the symptoms become minimal or disappear.

A large number of complete and fully expanded Sector Therapy interviews transcribed from tapes have been published and are available for study. These illustrate fully the role of language in making conscious unconscious meanings and associated affects connected with everyday speech.

The introduction of new words into the chains of associations of the patient, and his acceptance of them, tends to change his emotional attitude. Modification of emotional attitudes is central to all psychotherapy. In this sense the unconscious is treated as if it were similar in structure to, and part of, a patient's language and feelings. (Lacan, 1975).

During the first few interviews the therapist should obtain a thorough history concerning the present and past family constellations, with special attention to names and dates. In many cases a preliminary autobiography is of great value. Reporting of dreams is encouraged as they are full of ambiguities and key words in need of development. Questions can be asked at any time when structured into the context and continuity of the interview. Medication can also be used when pain, anxiety, and depression are overwhelming.

In the initial and in succeeding interviews there should be an introductory stage where key words are collected, fed back, and expanded until the main persons and affects in the present situation are revealed. Then there is a middle stage where the patient is guided back into the past and kept there until the origin of these affects and their relation to the present is suggested or, at times, plainly revealed. Finally, there is an end stage in which the patient is returned to the present, and its relationship to the past is made obvious. With some patients and in some circumstances, it is necessary to go back and forth from the present to the past a number of times. This weaving together of times makes unconscious relationships conscious, integrates and strengthens the patient's ego, increases historical self-awareness, diminishes anxiety by spreading it over a large segment of time, and encourages a rational solution to existential problems. It also reveals to the patient how correctly or falsely he categorizes persons or things, perceives relationships in time and space, how he thinks of agency and causation, and how he conceives of his own body and self-image, all in a more profound way than before.

## APPLICATIONS

Although based on psychoanalytic theory, Sector Therapy minimizes the need to interpret transference resistances and emphasizes the cognitive aspects of psychotherapy. It is therefore especially useful in the following cases:

1. Those too *easy* or too *difficult* for psychoanalysis, i.e., patients with mild symptomatic disorders of short duration, and mild psychotics.

2. Severe borderline disorders, especially those suspected of having a latent psychosis

3. Cases with psychosomatic problems

4. Mild to moderate character disorders, especially narcissistic characters

5. Cases suitable for psychoanalysis who cannot afford the time or cost. This is especially so when the therapist is well acquainted with psychoanalytic theory and practice, and when transference problems are too intense, as Sector Therapy can readily be transformed into psychoanalysis by increased use of transference interpretations.

# Self Psychotherapy

## Albert Steinkirchner

### DEFINITION

Self Psychotherapy is a natural psychological process of self-emergence that is activated by "spontaneous introspection," a technique of looking into one's own mind. The subject turns his attention internally to observe those mental images that appear by their own power across his internal psychic screen. This activates a dynamic psychological process that completes any undone steps in personality development and maturation.

### HISTORY

Self Psychotherapy has its roots in the psychoanalytic techniques of "free association," and introspective technique in which the subject turns his attention internally to his feelings, images, and ideas. This type of introspection, as used in classical psychoanalysis, focuses especially on those images, feelings, and ideas that refer to the relationship between the psychoanalyst and the subject. Self Psychotherapy takes this freedom of association a step further in that the subject is free to become emotionally involved with *any* spontaneous images without restriction.

# TECHNIQUE

To begin self therapy, the subject simply looks internally at the mental images that come spontaneously across his "mind's eye." He closes his eyes, clears his mind of thinking and daydreaming, looks straight ahead, and focuses internally on those pictures that appear on their own power (Steinkirchner, 1974).

This spontaneous introspection is similar to turning on a television set without knowing in advance what program is scheduled for that time. You flick a switch and simply watch the screen for whatever picture appears. You do not cause the picture to appear; it comes from inside the television apparatus. Suddenly, on the screen you see an image, and only then do you know what it will depict.

In precise parallel, the subject turns on his psychic set by closing his eyes and looking intently for whatever mental pictures that begin to appear spontaneously on his internal psychic screen. This deceptively simple technique activates the process of Self Psychotherapy.

The basic psychology of this spontaneous introspection is that it starts with definite mental pictures. From these psychological images come ideas, meaningful insights, and emotional reactions. When people first attempt this unique introspection, they often err by turning their attention to random ideas or thoughts to produce significant imagery. Actually, unpremeditated pictures themselves stimulate the production of thoughts that are significant to self psychotherapy. Thus, the rule of thumb for the subject is: look, don't think. He should look for the spontaneous picture in his mind's eye, for this is the precise technique that activates the Self Psychotherapy process.

Visual images are usually the first to be observed. However, during the course of Self Psychotherapy, images from all of the senses show themselves: sights, sounds, conversations, things smelled, tasted, eaten, touched with pleasure or pain, heat or cold, etc.

From these spontaneous images come ideas, associations, judgments, and later reasoning. There are important emotional reactions to the imagery and its meaning.

After about three hours of this introspection, the imagery will begin to show a particular theme from the subject's childhood. This feels like a "settling into" a childhood situation, a feeling as though part of the psyche is living in the situation pictured in the imagery. This is when strong emotions are felt—emotions that are quite appropriate to the scene observed. Gradually, the imagery becomes clearer, less disguised. As the subject forces himself to concentrate on the imagery, the story being played out develops and opens up more completely in its meaning. He begins to relive an emotional conflict from his childhood that has become conscious.

During the first part of Self Psychotherapy, the most important disruptions to the personality development and maturation emerge. These emotionally charged issues erupt from the unconscious part of the personality in a global or gross form. As psychotherapy proceeds, the psyche deals with separate parts of these major conflicts as they affect development and maturation of each psychological function.

After this initial phase of therapy, we begin to see the emergence of just two different kinds of conflicts: 1) those dealing with issues of development or 2) those involved with conflicts of personality maturation.

Maturational conflict occurs between several functions; e.g., between intellect and emotion, and the resolution is always toward some kind of getting together and balancing of the conflicting functions.

Developmental conflicts are solely involved with individual psychological function; e.g., memory, the emotion of anger, etc. A developmental conflict is concerned with a more basic step in personality growth because it focuses, simply, on the functioning of an individual psychological faculty, such as the oral function of taking nourishment. This will come up in psychotherapy, for example, when there is guilt blocking the pathway between oral desire and food, which is its natural object. The developmental conflict is resolved by therapeutic efforts that remove the guilt that stands between the oral faculty and its object, food (Aquinas, 1946).

Maturation and development both contribute to personality growth and are the natural emergence of the personality potentials. They are the important dynamism (along with conscious determination) that cause the Self Psychotherapy process to proceed successfully.

## APPLICATIONS

This technique is limited to the resolutions of the psychoneuroses. It is not applicable to the resolution of psychoses or borderline states because in these disturbances the personality is not strong enough to tolerate the reliving and resolution of unconscious, primary emotional conflicts.

# Self Therapy

## Muriel Schiffman

### DEFINITION

Self Therapy consists of five concrete structured techniques, any one of which enables a person to experience a hidden (unconscious) emotion by exploring, on a feeling level, the apparent (defensive) emotion that covers (represses) it.

### HISTORY

Thirty years ago I (Muriel Schiffman) renewed a relationship with my mother from whom I had been alienated since childhood, and inadvertently stumbled on the basis of Self Therapy. During a series of monthly visits that flooded me with long-hidden, painful emotions, I lost forever a long-time recurrent depression.

In the ensuing years I explored the value of experiencing hidden feelings in the relief of painful and/or inappropriate emotions and found myself changing self-defeating behavior and outgrowing various problems: a peptic ulcer symptom, several phobias, etc. Later, Gestalt self therapy was an outgrowth and modification of my work with Frederick Perls.

I have been teaching Self Therapy through lectures, workshops, and books for the past twenty years. Follow-up studies indicate that people can learn to use and profit from Self Therapy, some with and others without professional help.

# TECHNIQUE

There are five paths to a hidden feeling: 1) thinking it through, 2) talking it out with a good listener, 3) writing, 4) a "back door" to the unconscious, and 5) Gestalt self therapy.

1 & 2. *Thinking it through* and *Talking it out.* a) Recognize an inappropriate or too painful reaction (hating a loved one, obsessive thinking, depression, anxiety, etc.); b) *feel* the apparent emotion; c) ask, "What else did I feel just before *b?*"; d) ask, "What does this remind me of?" This should arouse a new feeling, different from the one with which you began. This hidden feeling should last only a brief time and the apparent emotion disappears; e) look for the pattern: in such situations you usually cover up *this hidden* feeling with *that apparent* emotion.

3. Writing. While experiencing an inappropriate and/or painful emotion describe it, and signs of physical tension, in longhand. Write questions and answers: "What happened just now? What might I have been afraid to feel? What does this remind me of?" until you evoke a new feeling. You are not looking for an explanation of your irrational reaction; merely trying to experience a new emotion. Try different ideas on for size, dropping any one that does not provoke a new feeling.

4. *A "back door" to the unconscious.* Notice any strong emotion evoked by an aesthetic experience (drama, music, literature, ballet, natural beauty, etc.). Try to stay with that feeling and ask yourself, "What does this remind me of?"

5. *Gestalt self therapy.* There are three different techniques for Gestalt self therapy: a) imaginary *encounter with a person* who has aroused an inappropriate or painful reaction, b) exploring a *known inner conflict*, and c) exploring a recurrent or disturbing *dream*.

a) Dramatize an imaginary *encounter with a person* in your present life toward whom you have an inappropriate and/or painful reaction. Enact both roles, beginning with the reality situation. Then exaggerate each role until you can feel an intense emotion. Now ask yourself, "Who did this to whom?" and play an imaginary scene from your past. Use your body: hit or cuddle a pillow, break a carton, stand tall or crouch low. Caricature each side until you provoke a new (hidden) feeling.

Now play the other person of the original encounter sympathetically. Try to understand how he feels. Ask yourself, "When have I felt this way myself?" This person to whom you overreact represents (unconsciously) not only someone from your past but also a part of *yourself.*

b) Notice how you react to certain situations and/or people in a stereotyped, irrational way, alternating between two *opposite attitudes:* rage versus pity, helplessness versus control, love versus hate, rebellion versus dependence, etc. Dramatize a scene involving some present-life problem and/or person, enacting alternately each of two opposing emotions. Exaggerate each side, going back to the past, if possible, until you can experience intensely the irrationality of *both* sides.

c) To explore a recurrent or disturbing *dream*, play every role in the dream. When it comes alive, dramatize some scene in your present or past of which this emotion reminds you. Each role represents an aspect of yourself. Have an encounter between two irrational parts of yourself represented in the dream.

In "real" life we are able to experience only *one* side at a time of inner conflict, so we act out in self-defeating ways. Each time we live out one side we frustrate the other side. We live on an emotional seesaw. But each time we practice Gestalt self therapy and experience *both* sides of the conflict we are free to make some rational compromise in solving the immediate problem, some decision that avoids tormenting either side. With continued work in this area the conflict gradually diminishes, the differences grow less extreme. Eventually the two sides tend to merge into a more rational middle ground.

## APPLICATIONS

Experiment with all five Self Therapy techniques to find which best suits your temperament. Those who crave privacy prefer *thinking it through* and *writing*. Some want a good listener and will do well by *talking it out*. Others need dramatization to come alive and they choose *Gestalt*. For people with too much resistance to begin exploring their own problems, the *"back door"* usually works.

Self Therapy is a tool for coping with daily problems, a technique for avoiding self-defeating behavior and a relief from intense emotional pain. These short-term goals apply especially to the first four techniques: thinking, talking, writing, and the "back door." These four methods can be used only when the apparent emotion is still intense. They are best for everyday living.

Gestalt self therapy is the only technique that can begin in "cold blood," after the apparent emotion has cooled off. Dramatization brings it to life once more.

Gestalt self therapy, exploring inner conflicts, is essential for the long-term goals of Self Therapy: to see reality without distortion, to fulfill one's true potential, to become more like the kind of person one wants to be.

---

# Self-Puzzle:
# A Diagnostic and Therapeutic Tool
## *Chalsa Loo*

### DEFINITION AND HISTORY

To the patient, diagnostic testing is frequently a mysterious anxiety-provoking experience. The patient often is unaware of either the purposes of the tests or the meaning of his responses. Moreover, since diagnosis is often a separate process from therapy, the patient usually never sees the tester again once the evaluation is completed.

The autocratic role of the examiner is another source of anxiety during diagnostic testing (Schafer, 1954). The dominating aspects of the tester's role allows for little sharing of control with the patient. Relinquishing control can be very threatening to the patient, particularly when there is no ongoing relationship between him and the examiner.

It seems especially regrettable that the patient often receives no direct gain from his participation nor feels any real involvement in the process. In developing diagnostic tools that can be integrated into the therapeutic process, continuity of person through the processes of assessment and therapy can be achieved. This notion is evidenced elsewhere, as in Art Therapy. Rubin (1973) reports agreement that "there is much to be said for an activity which is a pleasant kind of cathartic or expressive projective technique, serving both therapeutic as well as diagnostic purposes." The Self-Puzzle is a tool that has potential diagnostic usefulness for the therapist and therapeutic usefulness for the patient.

## TECHNIQUE

The patient is provided with color crayons containing a large variety of colors and a large plain white piece of paper. The instructions to the patient are:

In some ways everyone is a puzzle, consisting of many different parts. You are a puzzle with parts that are special just to you. In many ways therapy is a process of understanding ourselves, the parts of ourselves, and how the parts fit together. I would like you to think about yourself and then draw a puzzle with parts that are labeled that best describe you, as you see yourself now. The number of parts, the shape of the parts, the colors of the parts, and the positioning of the parts are all up to you. They should, however, be used to represent yourself as descriptively as possible. The purpose of this puzzle is to help you understand yourself better, to help me understand you better, and to help us in working out problems in our therapy sessions together. There are no right or wrong answers. This Self-Puzzle is your own creation, and you are to use as much self-understanding as you can. I would like you to create this on your own time, with no one else's help, and you may take as long as you wish.

Each Self-Puzzle must be extensively followed up with as much material that can be of therapeutic value to the patient and diagnostic value for the therapist. The patient should be encouraged to talk about his Self-Puzzle, what it means to him and what associations arose when he created it. The therapist should treat it with the same interest and respect that he accords the patient.

The most prominent benefit of the tool for the patient is that it encourages *introspection*, which leads to greater self-definition.

The Self-Puzzle helps patients make their feelings concrete by labeling and drawing them, leading to greater control and ownership over such feelings and thoughts. The patient achieves a sense of distance when he draws his feelings and thoughts out on paper. When parts of their puzzle are relevant to therapy, the therapist can comment on what is happening and how he sees the patient functioning. In the case of one fourteen-year-old client, it served to objectify the client's emotions. The therapist did not need to impose a purely verbal interpretation, but instead was able to refer the client to the Self-Puzzle. Seeing his emotions in the context of his own self-made puzzle aided in greater control and ownership of his feelings and thoughts (see illustration, p. 592).

## APPLICATIONS

The Self-Puzzle is especially useful with *patients who have difficulty verbalizing* the feelings they are experiencing. Where a patient is disturbed or inhibited by interpersonal contact, the Self-Puzzle, which can be created when the patient is alone, encourages the patient to share more of himself without necessarily having to verbalize it first. Thus, it is a tool that encourages closer contact between patient and therapist. As with art therapy, when "patients picture such inner experiences they frequently become more verbally articulate." (Naumburg, 1966) This was the case with a twelve-year-old selective mute, where verbal therapy seemed impossible. The Self-Puzzle allowed her to pictorially express and then talk about her anger.

The Self-Puzzle provides a method for *charting changes* that occur within the patient or throughout the therapeutic process by using repeated administrations of a Self-Puzzle, modifications of an original one, or the inclusion of aspects of therapy in the Puzzle.

The Self-Puzzle can also be used as a vehicle for *sharing perceptions between people*. The therapist and patient can create and then share both a puzzle of themselves and a puzzle of the other. The Self-Puzzle can be utilized in group therapy as an exercise to encourage feedback between members.

Several factors must be taken into account in analyzing the Self-Puzzle: the number of parts of the puzzle (indicative of complexity of self-perception, degree of defensiveness or openness), the central dimensions of the puzzle and their respective weights (indicative of self-perception, range and description of affect (moods and emotions), motivating factors, critical issues or events, interpersonal relationships and values), and the qualities of the drawing in terms of boundaries between parts, their positioning and size, and in terms of color.

(Further description of the Self-Puzzle with illustrative examples are contained in Loo, 1974.)

---

# Separation Therapy

## Grace Kirsten and Richard C. Robertiello

### DEFINITION

Separation Therapy is based on an attempt to produce a separation in our consciousness between the adult and the child within all of us. The purpose of this is to prevent the child part from sabotaging our rational effective adult functioning and, concurrently, to prevent the adult part from putting restraints on the childlike, fun-loving, free-spirited, creative emotional parts of us. We feel it is the lack of a clear separation between these two parts of us that creates many of our difficulties both in functioning and in enjoyment.

### Separation Therapy HISTORY

Though there have been many other psychotherapeutic systems that have employed the idea of a split (e.g., Freud's id, ego, and superego and Berne's parent, adult, and child), this system did not evolve from an intellectual continuation of these or other systems. Actually, it evolved clinically. A patient in group therapy spontaneously began to conceive of his problems in terms of this conflict and began to initiate dialogues between the child and the adult parts of himself (somewhat similarly to some Gestalt therapy techniques). The idea was picked up by some other group members and supported by the therapist. Within a short time many of the members of the group were employing this technique—sometimes within the group, but mainly by themselves at home. Many patients, some of whom had had years of psychotherapy, reported remarkable results from the use of this technique. It grew and finally evolved into a specific conceptualization of a theory and technique by the authors.

## TECHNIQUE

This is the most novel contribution of Separation Therapy. The person using the technique imagines himself as a child, from birth to age five, standing at his "weak side" (left if he is right-handed), about five feet away from him. He imagines the effective adult part of himself at his strong side, about five feet away. Then he commences a dialogue between these two parts. When he is a child, he speaks in a child's voice and tilts his head up. When he is an adult, he speaks in an adult voice and tilts his head down. Out of these dialogues he gets a better understanding of the needy and happy child in himself and also of the effective adult. Actually, these two parts may have been so intertwined as to preclude a clear awareness of either of them. Having a consciousness of their existence, he may subsequently be able to improve his functioning as an adult and increase the gratification of his emotional needs as a child.

## APPLICATIONS

This technique has been used only in out-patient work. It has not been used in hospitalized patients, though there is no reason to believe it might not be effective there. It has been used in nonpatient groups (such as the wives of compulsive gamblers) and in patients whose diagnoses ranged from neuroses or character disorders to borderline personalities or chronic schizophrenia. It has not been used with drug addictions, psychophatic personalities, or organic brain damage problems.

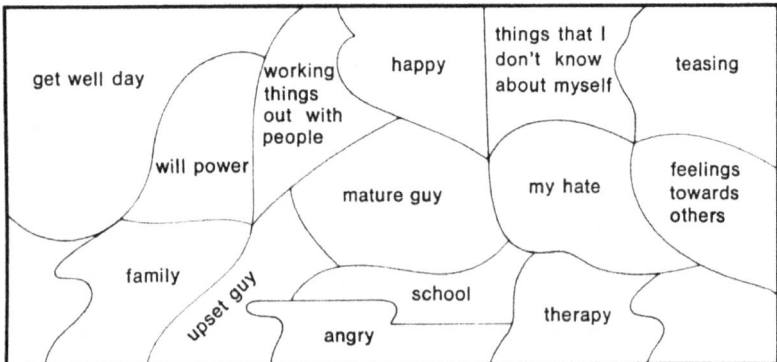

# Sexual Therapy of Masters and Johnson

*Alexander Runciman*

## DEFINITION

Before the publication of Masters and Johnson's books *Human Sexual Response* (1966) and *Human Sexual Inadequacy* (1970), therapy for sexual dysfunction was basically the same as for any other psychological dysfunction: it dealt with the individual's early childhood conditioning and with repressed emotional trauma. The research reported in *Human Sexual Inadequacy* provided a factual basis for a form of short-term therapy that was unique and more effective than previous approaches. Basically, treatment involves a sequence of sexual tasks to be followed by *both* partners of a couple. The treatment is used for impotency, nonorgasmic response, premature ejaculation, vaginismus, or ejaculation incompetency.

## HISTORY

The treatment procedures evolved from the physiological studies of human sexual response done by Masters and Johnson at the Reproductive Biology Research Foundation. The therapy itself does not fit neatly under the heading of any of the current forms of therapy, although most professionals associate it with behavior therapy.

In years past, therapy for sexual dysfunction in a marital unit was often provided for only one of the partners. This approach was seldom successful. For example, if a man goes through analysis for a long period to try to solve his impotence problem and his wife is not included in the treatment, he obviously keeps returning to the same marital situation that contributed to or even caused the impotence in the first place.

## TECHNIQUE

The basis of success of treatment is that the couple is treated as a unit. The second principle is that there be a male-female therapy team. This is for the purpose of having someone of the same sex with whom both the husband and the wife can identify. They need to feel that there is someone there who can understand their unique feelings as a man or a woman.

The first step in therapy is usually for the male therapist to take a thorough medical and sex history of the husband and for the female therapist to do likewise with the wife. On the second appointment this process is reversed—the woman therapist takes the husband's history and the male therapist takes the wife's. This is not a repeat of information but provides a means of checking to make sure that nothing has been left out, and of identifying attitudes that may be expressed differently, depending upon whether the therapist is a male or a female. This may be important in determining unrecognized or unspoken attitudes. For example, if a wife is able to talk freely with the woman therapist, and becomes nervous, inhibited, and tense relating to the male therapist, this expresses her degree of comfort or anxiety with persons of her own or the opposite sex.

A medical examination is a standard requirement before sexual therapy. It is important to determine use of medications or any physiological problems that could affect the central nervous system. The vast majority of sexual dysfunctions in both sexes result from psychological rather than organic factors.

After the sex histories and the medical examinations are completed, there is a roundtable discussion. During this session, the male and female therapists discuss with the couple their initial opinions of the marital interaction. This does not necessarily deal with sexual function, but primarily concerns how the husband and wife are seen to affect each other by their attitudes and actions in the overall dyad situation. This information is used as the basis for the specific program of therapy appropriate for each particular couple.

At the roundtable, the parties have the option of disagreeing with the therapists' observations. There is no obligation for them to continue; in fact, the therapy cannot be beneficial if they don't agree that changes are needed in the relationship itself.

Following the roundtable, the couple begins a program of sexual tasks, the first stage of which is called "sensate focus." This is used with every couple, no matter what the presenting problem. Sensate focus simply consists of learning to touch one another and to communicate what feels good or what doesn't feel good. During this stage the couple is told specifically to avoid intercourse, and the touching of genital regions or the breasts of the female is prohibited. The purpose is to allow the husband and wife to discover the numerous sensitive and sensual parts of the their bodies, other than genitals and breasts, and to begin to communicate with each other about the parts of the body that may be easier to talk about than the genital areas. The therapists need to carefully evaluate when a couple is ready to proceed to the next stage.

The second stage, after the couple has learned how successfully to communicate what is pleasurable to them, consists of mutual stimulation of the genitals, but again without any attempt to engage in intercourse. The wife and husband are specifically told not to strive for orgasms but to learn to communicate with each other what feels pleasurable in regard to genital stimulation.

After a couple has completed these two stages, the therapy can take various directions, depending upon the presenting problem.

In the case of impotence there is a series of procedures used in which the female learns to stimulate the penis in specific ways as instructed by the therapist. When her partner does get an erection, it is she who makes the insertion. The woman learns what to do and when to initiate insertion and movement. In this way the pressure to perform that leads to impotence is reversed—i.e., the woman assumes some of the responsibility. This release form performance pressure enables the man to relax and enjoy, and, incidentally, "perform" successfully.

For premature ejaculation, the "squeeze technique," which requires communication and cooperation between the partners, has been found to be very effective. With the squeeze technique, the man must let his partner know when he is about to ejaculate. She then squeezes the tip of the penis, thereby inhibiting ejaculation. This process can be repeated as many times as needed. Couples usually have to use the squeeze technique for several weeks before the male's tendency toward premature ejaculation is reversed.

If the presenting problem is a nonorgasmic response in the female, there is a step-by-step process the couple is instructed to follow. At the third step the female takes the superior mounting position. The reason for this is that many women have been passively underneath their partners, and have never really learned to know what their response system requires. In this step, with the penis fully erected and the vaginal area well lubricated, the woman inserts the penis under instructions to remain still and experience the pleasurable feel of vaginal insertion without orgasmic demand. The process continues over days of repetition through phases of mild female thrusting, mild male thrusting under female verbal control, mutual thrusting with a period of separation for general caressing, and attempts to break the pattern of unilaterally initiated and demanding pelvic thrusting.

The central theme in the Masters and Johnson therapy program is the necessity for continued communication between the partners. While physical instruction and practice are important elements, greater stress is placed upon the relationship between the partners and reeducation of the ways of satisfying sexual functioning. These elements of the therapeutic process are in evidence from the start of history taking and discussion, but they come into focus when some improvement has been shown as a result of the physical practice, when the couple has overcome certain negative feelings and becomes amenable to this focus.

Perhaps another key to success of this type of therapy is that the therapists consciously take the role of authority figures. When patients' sex histories indicate ignorance, misinformation, and negative conditioning—and everyone who comes for therapy falls into this category to a degree—the therapists make a point of identifying these sources of difficulty and then explaining that the patients do not need to let these things from the past continue to be negative influences.

And, as necessary, attitudes and mutual behavior are explored in such areas as religious and early childhood conditioning, drinking habits, general inadequacy and dependence, use of sex as a weapon or as a tool for ulterior purposes, and unrealistic sex fears.

## APPLICATIONS

In their treatment of impotency, Masters and Johnson (1970) reported a 73.8 percent success rate. Premature ejaculation is the easiest of the male dysfunctions to treat; treatment has resulted in a 97.8 percent success rate.

Of 342 nonorgasmic women, Masters and Johnson reported a success rate of 80.7 percent. In some of the failures the marital relationship was considered hopelessly destructive.

High success rates were reported, too, for two sexual inadequacies not covered in this description: ejaculatory incompetence (the inability to ejaculate while the penis is in the woman's vagina)—82.4 percent, and vaginismus (a condition in which any sexual approach produces a powerful and often painful contraction of the vaginal muscles)—100 percent.

*The therapy has the best application with couples who view the problem as a shared one and are willing to cooperate as a team in reversal of the inadequacy.*

# Sexual Attitude Restructuring

*Ted McIlvenna and Loretta Mason Haroian*

## DEFINITION

Sexual Attitude Restructuring (SAR) is a process of education/therapy designed to help individuals and couples examine their beliefs about human sexuality and change from a negative to a positive point of view about sex. The SAR process is based on the following assumption:

1. Sex plays a very important role in every person's life. Sexual fantasies, desires, and behavior should be recognized as valuable and integral parts of each person's total self.

2. Sex can and should be discussed casually and non-judgmentally. Individuals have a right to know the facts and can enrich their lives by learning about the full range of sexual behavior.

3. Everyone has the right to have a good sex life, including persons who have physical or mental disabilities (paraplegics, diabetics, amputees, heart patients, the mentally retarded, emotionally disturbed, etc.).

4. Sexuality is one of the most individualistic parts of a person's life. It is up to each person to determine and then to assume responsibility for his own style of sexual expression.

5. To experience a healthy and fulfilling sex life people need to learn about and appreciate their bodies, know their feelings and their own sexual response cycle, become sensitive to the needs of others, and develop meaningful and intimate contact in their sexual relationships.

## HISTORY

The SAR process grew out of a project in the early 1960s designed to determine the needs of young adults. In response to the findings of that project, the National Sex Forum was established in October 1968 for the training of professionals in sex education, sex therapy, and sex counseling. Shortly thereafter, the programs were opened to the patients/clients of the professional participants for personal sexual enrichment. Today over seventy thousand people have participated in the SAR process and more than half have been members of the helping professions.

In 1970 the National Sex Forum began making sexually explicit films of all aspects of human sexual behavior for use in the SAR process. There are more than sixty films currently being used in sex education and sex therapy programs in over two thousand schools and agencies around the world.

In June 1976, as an outgrowth of the research of the National Sex Forum and a growing demand from members of the helping professions, the Institute for the Advanced Study of Human Sexuality was founded. It is a graduate school totally devoted to the academic and practical study of sexuality.

## TECHNIQUE

The SAR process is an examination of the broad range of sexual behavior and of individual feelings about what people do sexually. The long, absent permission to know about sex dramatically aids people in their ability to focus on and reconcile their sexual belief system.

The educational/therapeutic methodology consists of desensitization to sexual myths and resensitization to sexual facts through lecture, media (films, slides, and video) and small and large group discussions. Ten years of research shows that the use of sexually explicit films is the most important agent in attitudinal change. The SAR process includes:

1.  Endorsement (it is all right to be sexual, to know all there is to know about human sexuality)
2.  Information giving (the history of sex research; what we know about human sexuality, and about our bodies and how they respond sexually)
3.  The development of sexuality from birth to death
4.  Masturbation (the way most men and many women make their first commitment to sexuality)
5.  Homosexuality (and bisexuality) in the female and male
6.  Desensitization and resensitization (banishing sexual myths and replacing them with facts)
7.  Female and male sexuality
8.  Sexual enrichment (how to have a better sex life)
9.  Special problems (medical, religious, cultural, legal, etc.)
10. Sexual therapy for specific dysfunction (impotence, premature ejaculation, preorgasmic women, physically or emotionally disabled persons, etc.)
11. Cultural expression of sexuality, both historical and contemporary (art, film, dance, music)
12. Legal aspects of sexual behavior

## APPLICATIONS

Accurate sexual information has long been unavailable to many professionals and most of the general public. Therapy for specific dysfunction was virtually unheard of and such complaints were subsumed under other therapies with questionable results.

The SAR process, based on every person's right to acquire sexual knowledge, provides the most current factual sexual information, helps the individual to make an aware choice of his sexual life-style, and offers the most effective therapeutic procedures for the treatment of specific sexual dysfunction.

The format of the SAR process in large groups emphasizes the educational aspects, using films, slides, lectures, and large group discussions. Small group discussions are sometimes used and individual therapeutic consultation is available if needed.

The format of the SAR process in small groups emphasizes the therapeutic aspects, using video cassettes, a written manual (*The SAR Guide for a Better Sex Life*) for home assignments, and personal sharing in a small group. Participants may be referred to the group for specific sexual dysfunction or for personal sexual enrichment.

# Shadow Therapy

## Mary Robertson

### DEFINITION

Shadow Therapy is a two-dimensional method of therapy for children. The method of treatment consists of involvement in three environmental alternatives and in a focus on inner-psychic experiences. The therapy environment consists of three environmental potentials that are under the control of the child: 1) darkness, 2) candlelight, and 3) full light. These therapy environments mimic dusk, dawn, and the day/night environment.

The inner-psychic potentials consist of: 1) objects, 2) shadow of objects, and 3) inner images.

This two-dimensional approach was developed by the author as an expanded concept of Shadow Therapy. It offers a varied environmental structure for access to subconscious and unconscious material and increases the potential for child and therapist to communicate.

### HISTORY

Shadow Therapy originated because of a disturbed, isolated child's needs and because of the author's childhood experiences watching shadow plays in Chengtu, China. I integrated the child's needs and my childhood recollections into a method of therapy.

I initially reported on this method of treatment at the International Congress for the Further Scientific Study of Mental Deficiency held in Copenhagen, Denmark, August 1964. I have continued to expand the use of environmental variants as well as focused on a broadened concept of image processing.

### TECHNIQUE

Shadow Therapy is conducted in a windowless room where darkness can be achieved. Chairs for patient and therapist are available along with a small table. There are no toys, puppets, doll houses, etc., as are usually found in a play therapy room. Placed on the table are a candle, matches, paper and pencils, and crayons and pen (these vary, depending on the needs of the child). Prior to the beginning of the session, the candle is lit. The patient is then brought into the room, and the therapist faces the child toward the wall saying, "Look, there is your shadow."

In the initial sessions of Shadow Therapy, this method of procedure continues. However, autonomy is soon established, and the child chooses darkness, candlelight or a regularly lit environment. The length of time in each type of environment varies according to where the child is in therapy and what environmental needs the child has. Reporting on self and the environment through drawings also varies. The child has autonomy to chose the medium of communication both environmentally and inner-psychically. The therapist responds to the level of communication the child uses in the different environments. Most children reveal more primitive types of material when in the darkness environment. Changes in times spent in the different environments appear related both to inner-psychic feelings as well as to known traumatic events that have occurred at some time prior to the specific therapy session. Usually, if patients find the darkness environment too difficult to handle, they turn on the light or ask to have the candle lit. Regression is easily documented in Shadow Therapy both by recording environmental choices and by the behavioral manifestation in these environments. Fear of primary processing following external trauma frequently results in maintaining a candlelight environment for one or more sessions. Difficulties in self-concept may result in displacement by patients onto their own shadow or onto the shadow of the therapist. Shadows frequently become symbolic representations of people or events the child is unable to handle directly.

## APPLICATIONS

This method of therapy is particularly effective with depressed children, with children with delayed mourning, with isolated, abused, and psychotic children.

# Short-Term Anxiety-Provoking Psychotherapy

## Peter E. Sifneos

### DEFINITION

Short-Term Anxiety Provoking Psychotherapy (STAPP) is a psychotherapy aimed at helping neurotic patients with circumscribed symptoms and/or difficulties in interpersonal relations to solve the conflicts underlying these difficulties over a brief period of time, and to overcome their presenting complaints.

### HISTORY

This type of treatment was developed at the Massachusetts General (1956- 1968) and the Beth Israel hospitals of Harvard University Medical School. Since then several studies dealing with the outcome of STAPP, two of which involved the use of control patients, have demonstrated not only that it is an effective therapy but also that it is the treatment of choice for those candidates who fulfill its selection criteria. These are the following:

# TECHNIQUE
## Evaluation and Selection Criteria

The patient must have a circumscribed chief complaint and must give a history of having had a meaningful or altruistic relationship during his early childhood. He should demonstrate an ability to interact flexibly with an evaluator and have an access to his feelings during the evaluation interview. In addition, there should be evidence that he possesses an above-average psychological sophistication as well as a high motivation to change, and not only to have a symptomatic relief.

The psychological conflicts that underlie the complaints of the patient who fulfills the above-mentioned criteria must be demonstrated to be Oedipal in nature. This implies that the difficulties that have been encountered originated during the patient's childhood, when he was struggling to make a choice between one parent at the expense of another, even though both parents were loved. The ensuing problems and compromises, having been maladaptive in nature, gave rise to the neurotic difficulties encountered during the patient's adult life, and were instrumental in bringing him to the therapist for help.

By the end of the evaluation, which involves a systematic history taking, it should be clear whether or not the patient fulfills the criteria that have been outlined, and whether he has Oedipal conflicts underlying his difficulties. If this is the case, the therapist must present his own formulation of the psychological problem and must obtain the patient's cooperation to work jointly with him in order to resolve it. This technical maneuver is referred to as the therapeutic "contract."

## Technique of STAPP

The interviews are face-to-face, once a week, lasting for forty-five minutes. No time limit is set, in contrast to other kinds of brief therapy, which are limited to a special number of interviews or specify a final date for termination. The open-ended system gives a greater flexibility to the patient to overcome his difficulties. It is emphasized, however, during the evaluation that the therapy will last only "a few months." Having reviewed the length of STAPP over the last few years, we found that the majority of the cases were treated over a three- to four-month period, of twelve to sixteen interviews.

The technique of STAPP involves the rapid establishment of rapport with the patient so as to create a therapeutic alliance and set the stage for the development of what Alexander calls "a corrective" therapeutic experience. The patient's transference feelings which are positive in nature are discussed explicitly and early. In addition, the therapist, by a judicious use of clarifications, confrontations, and questions that are anxiety provoking in nature, keeps the patient within the therapeutic focus that has been outlined previously. This, in turn, enables him to make repeated parent-transference connections that are vital technical maneuvers, and help make the therapist-patient interaction "alive," so to speak, during the interview.

Every effort is also made by the therapist to avoid getting entangled into pregenital characterological issues, which the patient uses defensively to avoid the anxiety aroused by the discussion of the therapeutic focus, and which prolong the therapy unnecessarily.

If enough progress has been made in the resolution of the patient's psychological problem, as evidenced by tangible examples that new behavioral attitudes have been developed, and that the patient is able to deal with his interpersonal relations in a more mature way, then plans should be made for termination of the treatment.

## Outcome

From several studies mentioned already that dealt with the results of STAPP, my colleagues and I (Peter E. Sifneos) have discovered that the most striking improvements occur in such parameters as the patient's self-esteem, his self-understanding, and his interaction with key members of his environment. In addition, the development of novel behavioral patterns, new learning and problem solving, which are utilized by the patient long after the therapy has come to an end, are good indications that he has freed himself from his neurotic chains.

## APPLICATIONS

What is our most impressive conclusion about STAPP, however, is the fact that it sets into motion the machinery for new patterns of psychological functioning. The patient, who is relatively healthy but who has been selected to receive this kind of treatment because he suffers from circumscribed psychological problems involving Oedipal conflicts, keeps on using these new patterns effectively to resolve any new psychological difficulty that he is likely to encounter in his life. In this sense, this therapy can be viewed as being truly preventive, and because of this it can be considered to be an invaluable learning experience for the patient.

---

# Structured Short-Term
# Therapeutic Intervention

*Richard A. Wells*

## DEFINITION

Structured Short-Term Therapeutic Intervention involves the employment of specific behavioral and personal change methods over a planned period of time with the goal of bringing about beneficial changes in the client's current life.

Additionally, the helping process is aimed at relieving the often painful stress that accompanies disruptions and difficulties in the client's intimate interpersonal relationships, important social roles, and significant personal functioning.

The therapist and client select one or two major areas of difficulty as the focus of the helping intervention and agree to work on these problems for a predetermined length of time, usually no more than fifteen weekly sessions. The therapist chooses the particular change techniques that he judges will be most useful in achieving the desired goal and instructs and encourages the client in their application. The change strategies employed are structured in the sense of comprising a sequence of steps or phases that break the process of change into component parts and thereby help guide the activities of both therapist and client. Many such techniques are now available in the clinical literature covering a wide range of common social and interpersonal situations. The therapist's efforts throughout the helping process are directed toward making problem and goal definitions as clear as possible, supporting the client in systematic, sequential problem solving, and using the pressures of an explicit time limit as a key factor in facilitating change.

## HISTORY

Brief forms of treatment actually have an extensive history. It is well known that psychoanalysis, prior to its introduction in the United States, was a method requiring months, rather than years, of therapeutic effort. For example, one reported therapy intervention by Freud took only seven interviews. Despite this trend toward increasing the length of therapy, psychodynamic theorists have made important contributions to the philosophy and methodology of short-term treatment. Otto Rank, for instance, wrote extensively on the power and potency of time-limited contacts while Franz Alexander pioneered brief methods of treatment emphasizing the corrective emotional experience inherent in the therapist-patient relationship. In addition, therapeutic schools as seemingly divergent as gestalt therapy, client-centered methods, psychodrama, and rational-emotive therapy have all experimented with short-term methods and contributed to its rationale and technique.

Structured Short-Term Intervention represents an integration of two major influences in the helping field; namely, the behavior modification methods based upon social learning theory and the time-limited approaches stemming from crisis intervention. Behavior modification has demonstrated that people can achieve significant changes in their lives through structured methods that emphasize the identification of desired behaviors, the step-by-step acquisition of change through imitation and practice, and generalizing such change into real life via homework tasks and assignments. Crisis intervention, on the other hand, has not only recognized the impelling life stress that frequently motivates people to seek help but also has identified the importance of time in the process of change. That is to say, a crisis can be seen as a time-limited event in the life of its victim that will resolve itself (for better or worse) unless effective help is received within its natural time span.

Both behavior modification and crisis intervention are aimed at direct change in the immediate and current life of the individual seeking help. They share a common belief that human difficulties are most usefully conceptualized as problems in living—disruptions in ongoing daily life, dissatisfaction in the quality or quantity of interpersonal relationships, deficits in the skills needed to manage one's life—and that the focus of treatment should be on remedying these gaps.

## TECHNIQUE

Obviously many specific techniques can be utilized in Structured Short-Term Intervention as long as they are relatively standardized in their operation and are relevant to solving immediate problems in living. For example, assertion training, systematic desensitization, structured communication training, the sexual counseling procedures of Masters and Johnson, relaxation exercises, and such re-educational methods as bibliotherapy, as well as a wide range of techniques stemming from behavior therapy, may be selected for employment within the intervention. Much of the skill of the therapist lies not only in his knowledge of a variety of change methods but also in his ability to choose an appropriate technique and to sensitively adapt it to the particular needs of his client.

It may well be helpful, however, to sketch out the overall model of time-limited intervention in order to illuminate the role of particular change techniques within this framework. Time has already been emphasized as a key element in short-term treatment. Thus, the contact between therapist and patient can be conceptualized as comprising three distinct phases, each with explicit time boundaries. The first phase is a one- to two-interview sequence in which problem(s) and goal(s) are defined; this is followed by the main interventive period of up to fifteen sessions in which one or more change procedures are utilized and active treatment is terminated; finally, after a follow-up period, two to four months in length, intervention is concluded by a final interview in which progress is reviewed.

The therapist not only spells out the time limits of each of these phases to the client but also adjusts his own efforts to fit within their defined boundaries. This results in highly positive pressures on both therapist and client to identify the most pressing problem and to work productively on bringing about the desired changes. Implicit in the short-term helping process is the belief that change will most likely ensue from a concentrated effort on a single—but significant—problem in living. In order to emphasize this process the therapist will insist that the client with multiple problems choose the one or two of highest priority for intervention. Most short-term work terminates at the end of the contracted time period; yet it should be noted that it is always possible for client and therapist to negotiate, at the end of a particular helping sequence, an agreement to concentrate on a new problem area. Additionally, if short-term treatment does not achieve its goals within the expected time, therapist and client may agree to move into longer-term treatment.

## APPLICATIONS

Many therapeutic methods have unfortunately based their techniques and strategy on clinical experience and research with a socially and emotionally advantaged clientele. Indeed, a number of therapies either directly or indirectly screen out clients who are not intelligent, highly verbal, relatively affluent, and managing their current lives well enough that they are prepared to enter a lengthy therapeutic experience with little immediate hope of benefit. Yet there is no doubt that a great many very ordinary people seek help only at a point where emotional stress has assumed major proportions. Such potential clients have little concept of therapy as a process aimed at wide-ranging personality change, over a period of years, and tend to drop out of treatment rather rapidly when its goals appear vague or irrelevant and the expected time commitment endless. Other clients can become dependent upon the helping relationship and stay within its protective confines long past any point of real gain.

Structured Short-Term Intervention can be seen as offering the helping professional-and many needy clients — a legitimate alternative method of achieving change. In this sense it should be viewed not as a substitute for longer-term helping but as an effective approach to assisting large numbers of troubled people who neither desire nor are suitable for traditional treatment methods. Such an approach to helping is particularly needed in the many community clinics and family service agencies that function in the front lines of the helping professions, offering service to an often both distressed and advantaged clientele.

# Elavil Sleep Therapy

*Thad J. Barringer*

## DEFINITION AND HISTORY

Elavil Sleep Therapy is a method of treatment for certain non psychotic reactions in which amitriptyline (Elavil) and a phenothiazine (Sparine) are utilized to maintain almost continuous sleep or dozing for a period of three days.

There is historical precedent for this method. Noizet in 1854 wrote of the beneficial effect of sleep lasting three days, and Liebault when it lasts a "considerable time." Janet reported the relief of hysterical paraplegia with four days of hypnotic sleep. These methods seem to coincide with this technique more than those of a Swiss physician, Wetterstrand, who formulated a hypnotic sleep system lasting a three-week period or more.

The method of sleep therapy is to be differentiated from the rest approach, which was formulated by an American, Samuel J. Jackson, and developed and applied by S. Weir Mitchell in 1875. This rest approach utilized rest, massage, and super feedings and became quite popular and fashionable in America. Its use spread to Britain and France and was applied and theorized there at the turn of the century.

Controversy occurred with these rest-sleep methods. Cabot thought that mental disturbances were caused by emotions and not overwork. Morton Prince thought that these methods would foster the neuroses. Dubois pointed out the difference in those conditions of stress reactions and those of the severe pathologic state.

Janet seemed to be aware of all of these things and was not so simple as to think that prolonged sleep would cure every thing. But he clung to the sensibility of the rest-sleep approach: 'The patient has been exhausted by undue activity. Very well, then, let us prescribe rest. Let us, as far as possible, suppress every form of activity. The subject is not rich enough to bear the cost of the life he is leading. We need not trouble to enquire which items in his expenditure are excessive and ruinous; it will suffice if w~ simply prohibit every kind of expenditure, for then we shall be quite certain that the patient will have to economise his energies. " (Williams and Webb, 1966).

## TECHNIQUE

Following a history taking physical examination, and diagnosis, the patient and the family are told that sleep therapy will be utilized in order to ameliorate the symptomatology. They are told this is symptomatic therapy and is analogous to methods utilized for "combat fatigue" during war (Black, 1970). They are given a description of the procedure and told that this is an initial approach rather than a specific treatment for a specific disease. _

The patient is told that his responsibility will be to sleep, doze, relax, dream, daydream, to get up only with aid, eat what he wishes, and drink abundant fluids. He is warned about dry mouth, postural hypotension, loss of accommodation, and constipation. He is told that no problems will be discussed for the next three days but will be taken up thereafter. He is separated from all responsibility and decision making. For example, if a patient is worried about the children's care or finances, he is told this is the spouse's or family's problem, and it is not discussed further.

Visiting privileges are based solely upon the anticipated effect upon the patient.

When allowed, it is kept to a minimum with an appropriate, cooperative, supportive, knowledgeable person. Visits should be brief (fifteen to twenty minutes) and occur at mealtimes when the patient is awake (noon or 5:30 P. M.).

The amount of drugs utilized varies, dependent upon weight, previous use of drugs and/or alcohol, and age. In general, the following is ordered:

1. Elavil 25 mg 1M q6h
2. Elavil25 mg p.o. q6h (0-10-25 mg may be ordered)
3. Sparine 100 mg p.o. q6h (50-75-150 mg may be ordered)
4. Valium 10 mg IM/PO p.r.n.
5. The patient is allowed to get up only with aid
6. Blood pressure and pulse q6h (prior to medication)
7. Colace ii h.s.

Sometimes Dalmane (15- 30 mg) or Quaalude (150- 300 mg) can be substituted for Valium. About 50 to 100 mg of Thorazine or Mellaril can be substituted for Sparine.

The nursing care is extremely important. Medication must be varied in order to maintain sleep without excessive hypotension. Blood pressure is taken prior to medication and rechecked as indicated. The nurse needs to control firmly and consistently the program relating to visitation. The most important aspect of nursing relates to the nurse's attitude; a nurse who is comfortable emotionally with this treatment approach is an absolute necessity.

*Post-sleep phase.* On the fourth day, this regime is discontinued. PO medication is started as is appropriate. Commonly, Elavil (10-25 mg t.i.d. and 75- 100 h.s.) and Valium (2-5 mg t.i.d.) or Tranxene (SD 22.5 mg) at 8:00 A.M. is utilized. Dalmane (15-30 mg h.s.) can be utilized as a sedative if needed. Mellaril (25- 100 mg h.s.) can be used when indicated. The type medication depends on the target symptoms and basic personality type.

Rehabilitation is carried out on a gradual basis. On the fourth day the patient is up in the room in bedclothes. Meals are served to him in his room. A midmorning rest, a one hour nap following lunch, a half hour rest about 4:30 P.M., and bed by 9:00 or 10:00 is ordered. This is continued for the next few days and decreased as appropriate.

On the fifth day the patient is up and around the unit, usually dressed, and has meals in the dining room. About the sixth day occupational therapy and/or physical therapy is begun as is indicated. Trial visits outside the hospital, with or without home visits, can be ordered as appropriate.

During this post-sleep period, exploratory interviews, conjoint interviews, psychological testing, and further laboratory procedures, as needed, are carried out. It is during this time that a genetic and dynamic diagnosis can be added to the clinical diagnosis and further treatment plans formulated. This may vary from any of the psychotherapeutic techniques, chemotherapy, marital counseling, or combinations thereof.

The total time involved is usually one to two weeks when dealing with an acute stress reaction with a good home situation, and perhaps ten to twenty days with more neurotic symptoms and/or difficult home situations. Appropriate out-patient follow-up is recommended.

## APPLICATIONS

This technique is utilized for those reactions usually classified as a stress reaction, one of the neuroses, or one of the psychosomatic disorders. It is contraindicated in the psychoses or more severe borderline states. It is of greatest use in crisis intervention, whether the symptoms are primarily those of anxiety, agitation, tension, depression, obsessions, or are psychosomatic. The depression that responds the best is that classified as reactive in type. This method is utilized as a beginning rather than as a definitive "treatment" or "cure." What follows varies as to the individual patient at that particular time.

The following problems sometime occur:

1. Allergic type reactions to Elavil, in particular, may occur with agitation and hyperactivity. Sometimes a delirium type acute brain syndrome may develop ("central anticholinergic syndrome"). Elavil must be decreased significantly or discontinued. Valium and Thorazine are good substitutes for the Elavil-Sparine combination.

2. Overt passive-agressiveness—whether in hysterical, passive-aggressive, or emotionally unstable personalities—leads to a poor result. This patient resists being "put to sleep." When this occurs, the method is discontinued and the patient is told why. Often the patient then will ask for a repeat of the method which will then be effective.

3. In severe borderline patients, a psychosis may be precipitated, either schizophrenic or manic in type. (For this reason, an anti-psychotic drug is always used.) In a suspected borderline type, the amount of Elavil is reduced and the phenothiazine is increased (Thorazine or Mellaril is used).

4. Some people are threatened by dreams. They may erroneously think that we are going to analyze dreams, or that dreaming is bad or a weakness. They are encouraged to dream.

# Soap Opera Therapy

### Anne F. Kilguss

## DEFINITION

I first became interested in soap operas when a patient resistant to therapy claimed she had no life choices, did nothing with her time outside of therapy, and had nothing to discuss. When the focus was put on her daily routine, she told of spending hours watching soap operas; the themes she related were the issues with which she was struggling. Through discussing soap operas with her and other

patients, I began considering how women use media psychologically, and in particular, how they use the soap operas.

I am a bit reluctant to call the therapeutic use of soap operas a therapy. I consider it to be a therapeutic tool for opening up discussion and as a path to the patient's unconscious. I use it in collaboration with more traditional dynamic psychotherapeutic techniques with both individuals and groups in out-patient and in-patient settings.

## HISTORY

Soap operas are watched by thirty-five to fifty million women (Nielsen, 1972). They are a major cultural phenomenon. Their wide appeal indicates that they are actually an example of myth and the collective unconscious in the tradition of Jung and Campbell (Jung, 1964; Campbell, 1968). Folklore and myth have long been used as a means of airing and purging collective wishes and impulses. They might also be compared to the morality plays of the Middle Ages in which social mores and ethics were delineated and reinforced.

Myths are catalytic in the continual reworking of internal conflicts and identities. The concept of identity is too strongly associated with adolescence; identity formation is a lifelong process.

An individual can actually assume only a given number of roles at any one time, but through imagination and role playing he may try on personae from all stages of life. Art, drama, media, and other vehicles enable the individual to try on this multiplicity of roles and rework his singular and group identities. Soap operas offer such a forum.

Periodically I have monitored soap operas and analyzed their themes, which emphasize incest, suspicion, distrust, victimization, dependency, loneliness, joyless-ness, and fear. Their masochistic tone stresses that women can only endure the pain in life. Sexuality and aggression are externalized. Character formation is split like that of a borderline character into the good and the bad, the weak and the strong. They fail to portray ambivalences and conflicts within an individual. The guilt from taboo wishes, such as incest and murder, are conveyed by an atmosphere of doom and depression, a lack of spontaneity, attack on innocents, and unrealistic portrayals of psychiatric disorders. Professional women are seen as being neurotic, and the stable characters are the older women who have devoted all of their energies to their families. In general, there is an inability to sublimate drives. Although many of the characters are upper-middle-class professionals, the programs give scant information about the work that is being done. The doctors, lawyers, nurses, and secretaries spend most of the time getting in and out of personal relationships. This observation is psychologically important because sublimation can be used to take the edge off these drives. The principal characters are unable to be alone or independent, and this is seen by the immediate replacement of mates after a death or divorce.

Sex is also dealt with unrealistically on these programs. Modern birth control is unheard of. When an affair takes place, a pregnancy is bound to follow, because for these characters pregnancy is one or the few sources of pleasure, joy, and gratification. Clinically, it is known that some pregnant women feel important, even if they do not feel values in and of themselves. On a more primitive level, they may feel full and satisfied. Although the programs value pregnancy, once the child is born, viewers do not see the diapers and the midnight feedings. Instead, they are given a portrayal of the ideal baby.

Soap operas show few relationships involving a mutually satisfying sexual relationship. For both men and women, the emphasis is on procreation. Although abortion is the only sexual issue that is developed at all, the primary concern is with the infantile wish for a child. As Ellen Peck has noted, twelve of the sixteen programs aired in 1972 have strong reproductive themes; pregnancy is a way of being important and holding on to a man. Few plans for abortion are carried out. Abortions are not presented as complicated solutions to conflict-ridden decisions.

The older, wiser, conflict-free woman is another popular character. She does not demonstrate the problems of aging. If it were not for her confused children, she would have little to do in life. She is invariably well groomed and able to attract younger men.

In regard to problem solving, the soap operas repetitiously portray women as being victimized. They forget or ignore the existential dilemma that by not doing anything one may be doing a great deal.

How then are we to understand the power and influence of the soap operas? Television creates a unique intensification of affect, or emotional response, in viewers. When listening to avid fans' discussions of their favorite soap operas, I have been impressed with the feeling that the characters are real people with whom the viewers share their daily lives.

## TECHNIQUE

While working in a community mental health center, I was impressed by the number of young, depressed, borderline female patients. Many were heads of households with young children and were nonintellectual, if not nonverbal, compared with the neurotic patients many practitioners were taught to treat in graduate school. When approaching such patients, I reexamine their life-styles and values and recall the old adage of beginning where the patient is. If women watch soap operas, the discussion of such programs can open a path to the patient's unconscious and fantasy life. From the program, one works back to the individual and her concerns. This method may be comparable to using play therapy with children. Freud believed that dreams and jokes were the most direct routes to the unconscious. I propose that the individual's use and interpretation of media is another.

Many viewers use soap operas as peer groups. For the individual who is constantly trying to keep up with a world he was not raised to understand, media offer advice on how to cope with this gap.

Patients should be encouraged to bring their immediate outside lives into therapy. After attending numerous case conferences and seminars, I postulate that mental health professionals and their patients denigrate such contemporary phenomena as media and soap operas as being unworthy of discussion in the therapeutic situation. By such myopic professionalism, they are cutting off avenues to their patients.

### APPLICATIONS

I have used this technique effectively with in-patients and out-patients, in group and individual settings, with female and male patients from a wide range of socio-economic strata. The technique has been most effective with female borderline patients and with depressed females.

# Social Casework
## David G. Phillips

### DEFINITION

Social Casework, like the field of social work as a whole, has grown out of a variety of specializations in diverse fields of practice. Current casework theoreticians are not working in the direction of creating a unitary theory or definition of casework; no attempt at such a definition could possibly be accurate or adequate. Social Casework is a general heading for a number of different treatment approaches utilized by caseworkers in different settings. A recent volume entitled *Theories of Social Casework* contains not only chapters on the three major approaches that have developed in casework, but on four other major treatment approaches utilized by caseworkers; behavior modification, family therapy, crisis intervention, and adult socialization (Roberts and Nee, 1970).

In spite of this diversity, there are important characteristics that tend to unify and define any form of casework practice and that are central to the tradition from which casework has grown. These characteristics include:

1. A commitment to understand, differentiate, and to act for and with the individual
2. A traditional role in promoting individually satisfying and socially constructive living
3. A commitment to a base in the behavioral sciences
4. A commitment to the operation of the humanitarian values of the social work profession.

# HISTORY

The modern practice of Social Casework originated with the "friendly visitor" in the Charity Organization Society of the late 1800s. Since the Charity Organization Society was concerned with moral reform, as well as the alleviation of poverty, the friendly visitor was utilized to separate the "worthy" poor who were deserving of assistance from the "unworthy" poor who were not entitled to help.

By the turn of the century, the simplistic and moralistic distinctions between "worthy" and "unworthy" poor had begun to break down. There was growing recognition that the poor were often victims of social circumstances beyond their control, and with this recognition came a change in the function of the friendly visitor or caseworker. The caseworker still went to the homes of the poor but now the job was to gather relevant facts about the case, develop an appropriate treatment plan based on these facts, and present the treatment plan to the family to be carried out. It was seen, however, that families often did not cooperate with even the most carefully developed treatment plan. In an attempt to deal with this difficulty, the process of fact gathering became more and more complicated and attention also shifted to the establishment of a friendly relationship that would help to insure eventual cooperation with the treatment plan. With these developments professional preparation began to be important, and by 1904 a full eight-month training program was being offered at the New York School of Philanthropy (now the Columbia University School of Social Work).

All through their history, social workers have dealt with the most needy and disadvantaged members of the society. Under the pressure of massive individual and social problems, development of theory in the field has often lagged behind the implementation of pragmatic techniques of practice. This was particularly true in the early years of the field and the first attempt to define Social Casework did not come until 1915. This first definition was offered by the great, early theoretician Mary Richmond, who saw social casework as "...the art of doing different things for and with different people by cooperating with them to achieve at one and the same time their own and society's betterment."

Although many basic principles and values were beginning to be articulated, the actual process of casework remained in the dead end of advice giving until World War I. The treatment of "shell-shocked" soldiers began to popularize the concepts of Freudian psychoanalysis, and in a short time these concepts swept casework.

The idea of "resistance" now made it possible to explain the impasse that caseworkers had reached with their clients. The emphasis shifted in casework to an interest in psychological development and "psychotherapeutic" modes of treatment. These ideas continued to dominate casework all through the 1920s and the social reform tradition in social work was pushed to the background (Briar and Miller, 1971).

During the I 920s caseworkers continued to move into more and more diverse areas of practice, such as "medical" social work and "psychiatric" social work. This increasing diversity gave rise to an attempt in the field to articulate the generic principles that underlie all of casework practice. The first great milestone in this attempt was the Milford Conference of 1929. But neither the work of this conference nor that of subsequent theoreticians has laid the issue to rest. The current trend in casework is in the direction of acceptance of the diversity of casework theory and practice.

The 1930s were a time of particular importance and complexity in the development of casework, and a number of the events of that decade have had profound and lasting effects. In 1930 the first great theoretical split in casework as introduced by the publication of Virginia Robinson's book A Changing Psychology in Social Case Work. Robinson's book announced the "functional" point of view that had developed at the School of Social Work of the University of Pennsylvania in opposition to the psychoanalytic concepts that dominated casework in the I 920s; the controversy of the "functional" versus the "diagnostic" approaches was to permeate casework theory for many years.

Another long-standing controversy in casework has been that of a "social reform" approach versus an individual treatment approach: One of social work's greatest traditions is rooted in the social action history of leaders such as Jane Addams of Hull House. During the 1920s, the social reform tradition in casework was pushed into the background by the psychodynamic concepts that dominated the field at that time. The Great Depression of the 1930s renewed the awareness of caseworkers of the inextricable interrelatedness of society and individual, and revived their interest in bringing about social changes that would benefit the individual. The social change versus individual treatment issue was not laid to rest, however, and it has continued to echo throughout the years. A current, and extremely promising, resolution of this issue lies in the direction of discarding those concepts and classifications that have proved to be so problematic. In this conception, "treatment" intervention can be at either a social or an individual level, depending on which is most relevant and appropriate (Siporin, 1975).

The introduction of the concepts of ego psychology in the late 1930s was of particular importance for social casework and these concepts have started to provide a point of rapprochement for many of the theoretical splits in the field. An immediate effect was that the concept of the ego as the bridge between inner and outer reality started to provide a theoretical synthesis for Social Casework's dual concerns with the "social order and the psychological depths" (Briar and Miller, 1971). The gradual spelling out of the treatment implications of developmental ego psychology has resulted in some lessening of the theoretical diversity between the three major casework approaches: "psychosocial," "functional," and "problem of the unconscious. The functional approach centered around the School of Social Work of the University of Pennsylvania and was deeply influenced by the ideas of Otto Rank, who had served on the faculty of that school. The term "functional approach" comes from the emphasis that this method places on the use of agency function as basic to the helping process in casework.

There are three central and defining characteristics of the functional approach:

1) The functional school works from a psychology of growth. It sees the center for change as residing not in the caseworker but in the client, with the worker's method consisting of engaging in a relationship process that releases the client's own power for choice and growth. The functional group emphasizes man as "determining himself from himself and from the relationships and external conditions of his life and as acting on and using relationships, including a potential relationship with the caseworker in the continuing creation of himself...

2) The purpose of the social work agency is viewed as a partial or concrete instance of social work's overall purpose and as giving focus, direction, and content to the worker's practice. Casework is not considered a form of psychosocial treatment...but a method for administering some specific social service...

3) The functional school developed the concept of social casework as a helping process, through which an agency's services are made available; the principles involved are those having to do with the initiating, sustaining, and terminating of a process in human relationship. This means that the worker enters into the relationship with an avowed lack of knowledge of how it will turn out...only client and worker together can discover what can be done with the help offered. The worker's responsibility is for control of his part in the process, not the achievement of any predetermined end. ... (Smalley and Bloom, 1977)

The functional school does not deny the existence of the irrational or the unconscious and the potentially crippling effects of traumatic early experiences. The psychological base for functional practice is, however "....a view that the push toward life, health, and fulfillment is primary in human nature, and that a person is capable throughout his life of modifying both himself and his environment according to his changing purposes and within the limitations and opportunities of his changing capacities and changing environment." The purpose of social work then is "... the release of human power ... for personal fulfillment and social good and the release of social power for the creation of the kind of society, social policy, and social institutions that make self-realization most possible for all men." (Smalley and Bloom, 1977).

## The Problem-Solving Approach

This casework approach was developed by Helen Harris Perlman of the University of Chicago in the mid-1950s. Although this approach branched off from the "diagnostic" approach, which was dominant in casework at the time, it is not a radical departure and is still rooted in psychodynamic theory. The problem-solving approach has drawn from concepts of ego psychology, from certain perspectives of the functional school, and from philosophical views of existentialism (Perlman, 1977).

The core assumption of this approach is that human living is a problem-solving process and although people coming for casework help have specific problems, their fundamental difficulty is in their method of solving problems. The focus of casework therefore is not on the specific problem, but on the problem-solving capacity (ego functioning) of the client as revealed through the problem and the attempts at solution.

The actions of the problem-solving approach have the following aims:

1.  To release, energize, and give direction to the client's motivation, that is, to minimize disabling anxiety and fears and provide the support and safety that encourage a lowering of disabling defenses ... and a freeing of ego energies for investment in the task at hand.
2.  To release and then repeatedly exercise the client's mental, emotional, and action capacities for coping with his problem and/or himself in connection with it....
3.  To make accessible to the client the opportunities and resources necessary to the solution or mitigation of the problem—those opportunities in his environment that are essential conditions and instruments for satisfactory role performance (Perlman, 1977).

The problem-solving model emphasizes the importance of the understanding of the person in the social and interpersonal context, and there is an assumption that the problem will be experienced as a difficulty in person-to-person or person-to-task relationships rather than as an intrapsychic difficulty. The problem-solving approach is similar to the psychosocial approach in its emphasis on the centrality of the relationship between caseworker and client as the context in which the problem solving takes place. There is a similarity to the functional approach in the emphasis on the client, rather than the caseworker, as carrying within himself the potential for recognizing the nature of the difficulties and resolving them; the process of casework aims at helping the client to mobilize and utilize these potential capacities.

In the problem-solving approach, two major categories of help are offered to the client:

One is to make necessary resources available or accessible and to facilitate the client's use of them by interceding with or modifying the attitudes of those who control those resources. The other is to guide and stimulate the person's use of his own faculties in working over the feelings, thinking, and behaviors that may cause or ameliorate his problem (Perlman, 1977).

# Social Influence Therapy

*John S. Gillis*

## DEFINITION

Social Influence Therapy is concerned with altering clients' views or perspectives about themselves, their relationships with others, and the quality of their life in general. To accomplish this the therapist attempts to gain a position of influence, and then to use this position to deliver a therapeutic (attitude-changing) message. The therapist borrows freely from other disciplines, those persuasive techniques that are of demonstrated or potential value. Such strategies are adapted mainly from social psychology. Thus, the therapist attempting social influence incorporates ideas and tactics from such areas as attitude change and interpersonal attraction. The literature on placebo effects in medicine also serves as a source of tactics. Influence attempts by the therapist are the primary strategies of treatment and are initiated and controlled by him. It is, in fact, the position of those sympathetic to this view that most contemporary therapies involve strong components of influence; social influence therapists simply attempt to identify these and then maximize their efficacy through careful pretherapy planning.

In most instances, such techniques will be used as adjuncts to more traditional therapeutic approaches. For example, a therapist may use primarily rational-emotive techniques but also use the counter-attitudinal strategy of requiring clients to express attitudes contrary to their own, if their own are seen as maladaptive.

Similarly a therapist may favor a nondirective approach but use a variety of tactics to build his client's expectations of benefit from treatment.

Succinctly, then, Social Influence Therapy is an approach to treatment that attempts to change the clients' attitudes or perspective by employing a range of persuasive tactics adopted from areas outside of therapy.

## HISTORY

Notions of the therapist's role as an influence agent have been abundant in the literature of psychotherapy for some years. Only very recently, however, have attempts been made to define this as a primary function of the therapist or to suggest the tactical implications of this role definition. If one considers the historical background to include those writers who have recognized that therapists function as influence agents, antecedents would include J. D. Frank's *Persuasion and Healing* (1968); several of Goldstein's papers but most prominently *Psychotherapy and the Psychology of Behavior Change* (1968) by Goldstein, Heller and Sechrest; and a variety of papers on power, influence, and expectation effects in counseling and psychotherapy.

Despite the frequency of such views, few of those who have expressed them would regard themselves as social influence therapists. A major attempt to bring this diverse literature together and conceptualize therapy primarily in these terms was this writer's 1974 paper (Gillis). While few of the views presented were original, I urged that the tactical implications be taken seriously and described an array of maneuvers that might facilitate therapists' influence attempts. An equally important function of this paper was that it called attention to an extensive literature in social psychology that had relevance for treatment.

This paper was followed by my students' attempts to empirically demonstrate the application of social psychological conceptions to therapy (Berren and Gillis, 1976; Childress and Gillis, 1977; Friedenberg and Gillis, 1977). Gillis and Berren (1977) also collected major articles relevant to the topic in an edited book, currently in press. A major item in this collection is a monograph that attempts to present a systematic view of therapy as an influence process.

## TECHNIQUE

As noted, Social Influence Therapy borrows its techniques freely from areas traditionally considered remote from counseling and psychotherapy. For purposes of discussing tactics, influence therapists have found it convenient to consider therapy as a four-stage process: 1) enhancing the client's belief in, and commitment to, treatment; 2) establishment of a position of influence; 3) the use of this position to deliver the therapeutic (attitude-changing) message; and 4) provision of evidence that change is taking place. A number of techniques may be employed for each of these purposes. Because of space considerations, only examples of tactics from stage 1 will be given here.

Research on cognitive dissonance reduction suggests that individuals come to value highly those things that they have worked hard to attain. Clients may thus be required to make some sacrifices to gain admission to therapy. One way to accomplish this is to have clients complete an extensive testing battery before beginning treatment. In an effort to enhance clients' beliefs in the value of therapy they are sometimes referred to reports of successful cases or required to discuss their upcoming treatment with patients who have recently had a successful therapeutic experience. Because of evidence that individuals often tend to adapt attitudes that they have publicly voiced, clients are sometimes asked to deliver a prepared therapeutic message to other persons having similar difficulties, or, in other words, to serve as counselors. In most cases, clients entering treatment will first be given a pretherapy interview. While one purpose of this session is to provide information about therapy, its major function is to point out the value and effectiveness of treatment.

## APPLICATIONS

Most of the efforts of those who espouse this view have gone into developing a new conceptualization of therapy. Applications have been relatively few. Influence strategies have been successfully used with several clinical cases, however, including phobias, paranoid delusions, passive-dependent disorders, and general family distress.

# Social Network Intervention

*Ross V. Speck*

## DEFINITION

Social Network Intervention is a clinical approach to difficult problems within a person or within his family, utilizing a professional team of two or more members as the catalyst, and from forty to one hundred friends, kin, or neighbors as the therapeutic agent. Certain editors have labeled the approach "network therapy," but there is a consensus among workers in this field that network intervention is a more accurate term, in the same sense that crisis intervention is preferred to "crisis therapy."

I define a social network as that group of persons, family, neighbors, friends, significant others who can play an ongoing important role in supporting and helping an index person or family. It is the layer surrounding the family unit that mediates between the family and the larger society. It is the remnants of the tribe in primitive societies. More modern equivalents are those people who assemble at family reunions, cousins' clubs, weddings, and funerals.

## HISTORY

I began working with schizophrenic families in their own homes in 1958, on a National Institute of Mental Health (NIMH) demonstration project, "Family Treatment of Schizophrenia in the Home," with Alfred S. Friedman, Ph.D., as program director. During the next seven years our co-therapy teams saw several hundred families, each with one or more diagnosed schizophrenic family members. The goal was to study and treat the family on a regular basis, avoid hospitalization, and in the great majority of cases to use no medication. We were testing the efficacy of family therapy.

In about 80 percent of cases we were able to modify the social shared psycho-pathology and prevent hospitalization. However, in about 20 percent of cases the problems of double binding, mystification, sick-role reinforcement, scapegoating, etc., seemed to arise from outside the family. We found in these cases that a family member would be absent from the sessions in the home as a potent resistance against family change. John C. Sonne, M.D., Jerome E. Jungreis, M.S.W., and I named this resistance "the absent member maneuver." We also found that there were extended family members or other members of the family's social network who played the same absent and powerful role. For example, a family's lawyer had been giving personal advice to the family for years. When invited to participate in the family therapy he refused on the grounds that his relationship to the family would be altered, and he felt needed in his leadership position.

In another case the mother's sister's husband made a contract with the family that in exchange for financial help, they would come to his house for a debriefing after each family therapy session. He would tell them what to accept and what not to accept from therapy.

We began to see that difficult problems such as symbiosis (a relationship of mutual dependency), suicidal preoccupation, marital impasse, or schizophrenia often stretched beyond the family into larger extended family groupings. It became apparent that treatment failure often had to do with working with too small a unit—such as the family. Therefore, we began to invite significant family relatives and friends to the family therapy session in the home.

In 1964, at the suggestion of Erving Goffman, Ph.D., I read *Family and Social Network* by Elizabeth Bott, Ph.D. She had done a research project in London in which she carefully studied the social networks of twenty "ordinary" British families. The concept of the social network has been developed in 1954 by John Barnes, a British professor of anthropology.

The work of Barnes, Bott, and Edward Jay supplied a theory and a construct that enabled me, a clinician, to develop a technique of working with the network or tribe. By 1966 I had assembled the first social network of a schizophrenic person and was conducting weekly network meetings aimed at modifying the family pathology and alleviating the chronic distress and crisis.

Since then my colleagues Joan Lincoln Speck, Carolyn Attneave, Ph.D., Uri Rueveni, Ph.D., and others have done Social Network Intervention on over fifty networks, and have supervised the process in many more. As networks vary in size from forty to two hundred persons, we have used the technique with several thousand people.

## TECHNIQUE

Techniques evolve with experience, trial, and error. In the first network intervention, I met with the network in the index family's home for weekly sessions of two or three hours over a nine-month period. I did not realize then that I was operating with one foot on the accelerator and one foot on the brake. However, this long first experiment did expose me to practically every emergency, trial, or continuum that a network intervenor (my term instead of therapist) might encounter. Most subsequent network interventions have been accomplished in one to six long evening sessions, with two or three meetings being the most frequent series.

We meet in the home of the family who requests network. The technique is very energetic and hence is only used when other methods—individual, group, family, hospital treatments, etc.—have failed. It can be used to avoid hospitalization.

The intervention team has a leader—intervenor—an encounter expert, and two or three other team members we call consultants. The team huddles, wanders about, picks up gossip, group process, and affect (moods and emotions) and is the catalytic agent that keeps the network group moving to its task. The team's role is analogous to shaman or medicine man—not tribal chief. The network members are encouraged to do the work of helping change the family.

When the family decides to try the network method, they are told to pick a date within the next week, set a time (usually 7:30 p.m.), and then call all the people they know—relatives, neighbors, friends—support systems for every member of the family. From four hundred to one thousand telephone calls result. They tell the network that they are having a tribe meeting in their home, with professional psychotherapists present, to get help with tough family problems. Curiosity and mild paranoia ensure that forty or more people will attend. By experience, I do not like to work with less than forty persons and I so inform the family. Usually fifty or sixty show up.

The intervention team meets with the family for one or two hours—sufficient time to clarify in simple terms what the family wants—a job for an unemployable person, separate living arrangements, prevention of suicide, change in behavior patterns, etc. Then the team meets to plan structure and strategy for the meeting, with alternate plans as well in case of resistance and stalemate.

We conceptualize the network as the tribe a person belongs to. The industrial revolution created a large middle class with separate smaller homes, and destroyed the Western medieval extended family living system. The remnants of feudal society where people lived in large groups have survived in the somewhat invisible social network.

In all old, simpler, more primitive tribal societies, the tribe effectively solved problems of living for individual members. The American Indians, the Hawaiians, African tribes, the Eskimo, and many others had healing ceremonies for personal problems.

1. Thus, the network intervention begins with a retribalization. When the network has assembled (by 8:00 p.m.; the team gets to the home at 7:30 p.m. to move furniture, get acquainted, watch sub-groupings and group affect), the intervenor calls for silence, then gives a short (three-minute) talk about tribes and the reasons for the assembly. Then the network is asked to stand up and begin humming until a tune or song appears. There are many ways to transform a crowd into a working group. I prefer to war-hoop and jump up and down with the network for a couple of minutes. Then I get everyone to close eyes, hold hands, and silently sway. This is hypnotic. You now have the group's attention and they are aware of a common bond.

2. We call the network process the network effect. Its next phase is *polarization*, which is accomplished by setting up competing sub-groups—inner and outer, with the family telling what they want, the rest of the network responding. People polarize over issues, such as generation gap, conservative-liberal, power-powerless-ness, male-female, etc. Polarization increases the energy of the newly formed group. The team instigates active debate and watches for the innate group leaders whom we call the activists.

3. Polarization leads to *mobilization* of the activists, who will help the tribe formulate goals and plans. They will also help organize and lead support groups for each of the family members. Between network members they are available for crises or consultation.

4. The fourth phase of the network process is common to all large groups. It is called *resistance-depression*. The intervention team helps to resolve this recurrent phase by brief mini-encounter methods, encouragement, and other retribalization or polarization techniques.

5. When network goals are reached, the whole tribe feels breakthrough has occurred.

6. This is followed by a feeling of accomplishment, elation, and exhaustion.

## APPLICATIONS

Network intervention is useful in many human situations where a plateau or stalemate has occurred. It has been successful in preventing suicide and hospitalization. Difficult paranoid and other schizophrenic situations can be alleviated. No claim for cure is made here. Networks are the best employment agencies. I know of no better solution for problems of symbiosis.

We have used network intervention on professional organizations looking for change and in some professional racial-ethnic stalemates. Some political groups are using network principles to expand or consolidate their groups.

---

# Social System Psychotherapy

## E. Mansell Pattison

### DEFINITION

This paper focuses on clinical methods for intervention, collaboration, and co-ordination with the social systems that comprise the social matrix of an identified patient. The conceptual basis for these methods derives from the field theory of social psychologist Kurt Lewin. He proposed that a person exists and acts with a field of social forces. Change in behavior may occur in two ways. We may seek to change the structure and function of the person, so that he acts upon and interacts with his social matrix in a different fashion. This is the modus operandi of traditional psychotherapies. In contrast, social system therapies focus on changing the structure and function of the field of social forces, such that the person is provided a more healthy social matrix of existence. In turn, the changed social field impacts upon the individual to produce a changed repertoire of individual behavior.

There is not one social system therapy, but rather a spectrum of therapeutic strategies that involve various social systems of the individual. The basic science methods of social anthropology are used to define these social systems (Boissevain, 1974). They have shown that a person can and does relate to a finite number of persons, about fifteen hundred.

These people can be arranged in what is termed *zones*. These are like a series of concentric circles about the person, arranged in terms of intimacy, importance, and basis of relationship to the person. The *first order zone* contains the nuclear family of the person with whom there is regular contact, intimate relationship, and high degrees of instrumental and affective (emotional) exchange. The *second order zone* comprises close friends, neighbors, co-workers, and relatives who are of high significance to the person and with whom there is a high degree of structured and expectable exchange of affective and instrumental resources. The first and second zone comprise what I (E. M. Pattison) call the "intimate psychosocial network" as it is critically related to mental health function. The *third zone* consists of persons with whom one has less regular contact, such as distant friends and relatives, or people whom one sees frequently but does not value highly, such as neighbors or co-workers. This is a network of potential relationships. As one makes geographic moves, changes jobs, or enters different life stages, people may move between these three zones of the person. The third zone is important as a recruitment area for mobilizing social resources for a person. The *fourth zone* is the "effective" zone. These are people who are strategically important, so relationships are maintained and can be a resource. These might include a family doctor, business acquaintances, and neighbors. The *fifth zone* is the "nominal" zone. This consists of people known only casually or through others, or representative of agencies of services. Such people are linked to the person only in terms of specific needs. Examples might be a minister, caseworker, or information provider.

Another means of analysis is by the definition of *set*. Consider the metaphor of an oriental tapestry. One can look at the tapestry in terms of various *sets*. That is, we can look at the floral arrangement, the geometric patterns, the blue areas or the red, follow individual colored threads through the weaving, etc. In other words, we use different set criteria to perceive different patternings in the same whole tapestry.

In like manner, we can use different *criteria set* to determine different social networks among the fifteen hundred people in a person's life. The *personal set* is the egocentric subjective network. This is how a person perceives and defines the relationship of himself to the fifteen hundred people in his life. The *categorical set* is people arranged by an objective criteria according to a given category. An example is a family network where the objective category is legal kinship. An *action set* is defined by people linked by a common course of action together. An example would be a mental health team conference about a patient that involved mental health, school, police, welfare, probation, and church representatives who meet to conclude a common course of collaborative action on behalf of the patient. The *role-system set* are people linked by specific role relations, although their actions may be various. Examples would be members of a therapeutic community, or patients and staff of a day-care center. The social network relationships are defined by the organizational structure. The *field set* is determined by content of common interest. Examples would be the common interests that bring together a church group, members of a sailing club, or participants at an old-age activities center.

## HISTORY

Social system therapies have several antecedents. First is the extension of family therapy from work with just the nuclear family, to psychotherapy of the extended family of grandparents, relatives, and other family members living in the home;

and psychotherapy with multiple family groups. A second contribution comes from family sociology that has demonstrated that not only blood kin, but "functional kin" who are friends and neighbors may comprise the functional extended family. A third contribution comes from the recognition in community mental health of the value and utility of mobilization of community support systems. At present there are a wide variety of clinical methods being reported in the literature, although they have not been heretofore systematically collated.

## TECHNIQUE AND APPLICATIONS

From a system point of view the issue is not what is or is not therapy, but rather it is a question of definition of social system boundaries, specific system contracts, and types of system interventions.

### The Personal System—First Zone Interventions

The first zone consists of the nuclear family constellation. Family therapy would be the social system intervention here. Married couples group therapy and multiple family therapy are corollary methods. The professional is therapist of the social system.

### The Intimate Psychosocial System-First-Second Zone Interventions

This social system has been usually defined by the "category" set; namely, who is related to the nuclear family by blood or marriage. The clinical method is an extension of nuclear family therapy applied and modified to meet the needs of a modified kinship family structure, which may include the extended family system, or may be expanded to include such functional kin as neighbors, co-workers, community residents, etc.

My colleagues and I (Pattison, 1973; Pattison, et al, 1976) approach direct psychotherapy of the psychosocial kinship unit comprised of those in the personal network of the defined patient. In contrast to the above, which use a "category" set, I use a "personal" set to define the psychosocial kinship system. This technique is addressed to changing neurotic social systems.

Finally, there is the "network intervention" of Speck and Attneave (1973). They also use a "personal" set. However, they differ from me in that they do not necessarily attempt to change the structural function of the psychosocial system. Rather, they define their work as mobilizing the system to effectively respond to the patient. Further, they do not limit their work to the intimate psychosocial network of first and second zones, but may work briefly with a group of up to two hundred people, which includes third- and fourth-zone people. Their method is addressed to changing psychotic social systems. Nevertheless, we still have the therapist directly meeting the ongoing social system.

### The Temporary Psychosocial System—Quasi-First-Second Zone Interventions

Here we deal with situations where there is no adequate psychosocial system available, so a temporary whole system is constructed. Examples are the therapeutic community devised by Maxwell Jones to treat sociopathic disorders, the therapeutic communities and Synanon for the treatment of drug addicts, and the hospital and day-care social rehabilitation programs for schizophrenics. The therapist here does not treat the patient, but "directs the system."

## The Ecological System—Third-Fourth-Fifth Zone Interventions

This social system is not a face-to-face interactional group, but rather a linkage of persons who provide a discrete set of services. That is, those who are linked to a patient, or can be linked to a patient in order to catalyze the provision of useful affective and instrumental support. The intent of this type of system intervention is to assemble an effective response network. Thus, people in zones three to five may be assembled in one place to organize and plan an effective response to the patient. Such a conference might include a psychotherapist, a probation officer, a schoolteacher, pastor, neighbors, family, and relatives. The aim is to achieve communication and congruence of goals among all the people with whom the patient may have contact through explicit linking of the patient with each person in each ecological niche in the community. The professional here is a "system coordinator."

## The Kin Replacement System—Third-Fourth Zone Interventions

Here we face the problem of the patient who lacks an available number of people to recruit into his social network, to provide affective and instrumental care. Hence, part-time replacements are necessary.

*Sub-type A: The ongoing partial replacement system.* This system is best exemplified in self-help groups. The self-help group does not become involved with the totality of the person's life, but does provide socialization, support, guidance, and assistance around specific life problems, such as alcoholism, child abuse, divorce. The self-help group does not involve the totality of possible life actions as in the intimate psychosocial system. But it does provide ongoing network relations so long as the person remains identified with the problem behavior.

*Sub-type B: The time-limited substitution system.* In this type of system the person is offered a more total relationship to meet an intercurrent stress or crisis, but the system is available only on a time-limited basis to substitute for the lack of a personal social network. Examples here include Big Brother and Big Sister programs, widow-to-widow programs, and crisis intervention groups.

In both sub-types of kin replacement, the professional plays the role of "system collaborator," in which one aids the patient to become involved in such a replacement system.

## The Association System—Fourth-Fifth Zone Interventions

These social systems offer instrumental and affective support on a less intimate and less global basis. They are voluntary associations. Examples would include ad hoc systems such as tavern groups, street-corner gangs, and school cliques, and organized systems like church groups, book clubs, social clubs, service organizations, and recreational associations. Although such voluntary social systems have other social aims and functions aside from psychological support per se, they also provide a rich social matrix for less intimate but nonetheless important human relationships. These systems of voluntary associations became a replenishment resource. The professional relates to these systems as a "system cooperator."

In summary, I do not wish to define each of these systems as "treatment systems." For each system is not a treatment system, nor does the professional have a mandate to treat each system (Pattison, 1976). But I have tried to illustrate how the professional plays different roles vis-a-vis the system so that the patient can appropriately participate in and utilize each social system.

---

# Sociotherapy

## *Ellen K. Siroka and Dominick E. Grundy*

### DEFINITION

In its present form Sociotherapy is traceable to the concept of milieu therapy developed in the United States and Europe after World War II. Milieu therapy has been characterized as using "social psychological forces" in shaping the social organization of a treatment program (Rossi, 1973). The authors of this article prefer Sociotherapy to milieu therapy because the prefix of the former has wider implications, reaching into the dynamics of interaction and association, while "milieu" connotes only the environmental aspects of the technique. The sociothera-plst is a psychotherapist who intervenes knowledgeably and supportively in the patient's life outside the patient-therapist dyad.

### HISTORY

Writing of a concept loosely called "social therapy," Elliott Jaques in 1947, at the Tavistock Institute, showed how therapy of the individual and the group, as well as therapy for the resolution of intergroup tensions, were all related to each other. In the hospital setting a leading proponent of Sociotherapy is Maxwell Jones, whose therapeutic community was a far-reaching attempt to create a milieu responsive to patients' needs (Jones, 1968). Sullivan, Fromm-Reichmann, and Anna Freud each contributed to Sociotherapy's conceptual framework through exploration of links between patient behavior and treatment setting. However, the hospital is not the exclusive domain of Sociotherapy; the emphasis on the social interactions of the patient in natural groupings builds also on the work of those such as Karen Horney and Erik Erikson, who stress the individual's cultural and psychosocial field. Marshall Edelson's *Sociotherapy and Psychotherapy* (1970) is a very important contribution, though its perspectives are shaped by a particular example, the residential therapeutic community, described in a companion book, *The Practice of Sociotherapy* (1970).

### TECHNIQUE

Edelson thinks of the sociotherapist as a clinician whose orientation is "to the situation of social system rather than the personality system." In this sense he develops a theoretical separation between the inner and outer provinces of psychotherapist and sociotherapist:

Psychotherapy is concerned with an intrapersonal system, with intrapersonal states, conflicts between intrapersonal structures, and the specific intrapersonal determinants of motion; and with direct attempts to intervene in, and alter, this intrapersonal system. Sociotherapy is concerned with the situation; with the social system and social conditions; with the reality of available social, physical, and cultural objects; with the world of means, opportunities, facilities, media, values and norms; with the relations, especially the strains, between entities (persons or groups) as these play different parts in achieving the shared goals of the social system; and with direct attempts to intervene in, and alter, this social system. (Edelson, 1970)

Yet this schematic distinction is less valid in practice. The sociotherapist uses his concern with the social system and social conditions as means of making "direct attempts to intervene in, and alter, this intrapersonal system." He designs the setting to be a basis of interpersonal systems that will facilitate the patient's individual development.

## APPLICATIONS

Psychological problems are often connected to estrangement and isolation. Intact relational activities that could offer support, such as the extended family, have withered away in our mass urbanized society and patients entering therapy often suffer from pronounced social handicaps. Institutional life, like that of the ward, belatedly provides a kind of network, but hardly anyone would choose it voluntarily, since apart from intrinsic deficits, the stigma of "mental patient" is a severe burden. Thus, regardless of diagnostic category, many patients seeking psychotherapeutic treatment voluntarily also need an interactive and ego-restorative environment, a world that is neither unreally sheltered nor a sea of unknown faces. A lack of mastery, of integrity, of vocation and the inability to relate satisfactorily to other people may all be linked impairments.

Sociotherapy is thus strongly indicated for patients whose ego deficits have resulted in an impoverished, fragmented, or rigidly protected network. Core emotional problems can be explored in depth in the therapist-patient dyad, while the void or chaos in which the patient lives can be addressed in the sociotherapeutic realm through specific activities or goal-directed tasks in continuous feedback. In the full sense treatment involves the dyad as well as what lies beyond it; both interact with each other.

Initially, patients may resist Sociotherapy for various reasons (anxiety, fear of apparent loss of an exclusive relationship with the therapist, etc.). These contraindications, however, have to do with issues of individual case management rather than with nosology. With cases of paranoia and extreme ego fragility, sociotherapeutic intervention would also have to be monitored slowly and carefully.

# Somatology

## Thomas Hanna

### DEFINITION

Somatology is a theoretical science of somatic process; as such, it is a science of living bodies as they change and adapt during the course of time. Somatology seeks to determine the consistent functional-structural patterns displayed by an organism as it adapts itself to the environment and the environment to itself.

The word "soma," designates any living organism, whether plant, animal or man, whether a single cell or a multicellular individual. The Greek word *soma* refers to the living body seen in its wholeness. Thus, the soma is not simply a "body" but is the unitive functioning of "mind", "body", and "emotions." In all instances the phenomenon of life exists uniquely in the form of the soma, i.e., as a whole, embodied process whose combined elements relate, first of all, to themselves and secondarily to the environment.

Somatology understands that the full nature of the soma (i.e., the life process) can be observed only *in vivo*. Because the soma is a stabilized process of constant change, its center and periphery are always indefinite; however, the presence of a functional centrum within a surrounding membrane is a somatic constant.

The functions and structures of somas have evolved as direct reflections of the electrical, chemical, gravitational, and mechanical laws of the physical universe. Each species of soma has evolved its own specific reflex mechanisms and fixed motor patterns reflecting these universal laws.

More generally and informally, somatology may refer to the living functions and structures of human somas, i.e., to the self-regulatory and balancing mechanisms that guarantee the homeostatic integrity of human life. As a human science somatology seeks to provide a common theoretical ground for the integration of such fields as psychology, physiology, anthropology, and others. This integration becomes possible because somatology's holistic, process-oriented viewpoint transcends the mind-body metaphysics that has been a traditional part of these sciences.

### HISTORY

The word "somatology" was first employed as early as the late sixteenth century by O. Casmann to refer to a general science of living bodies, as contrasted to physics, the general science of matter. For well over two centuries the word was used to designate the anatomical and physiological properties of living bodies.

Somatology, as the science of bodily functions as well as structures, was born in 1872 when Charles Darwin published *The Expression of the Emotions in Man and Animals*. Although Darwin did not then use the term somatology, *The Expression* provided the conceptual framework for a century of research by biologists, geneticists, ethologists, anthropologists, biochemists, neurophysiologists, linguists, and psychologists.

The contemporary sense in which the word somatology is now used was spelled out by Thomas Hanna in *Bodies in Revolt: A Primer in Somatic Thinking* (1970). Here it referred to a general scientific field toward which many of the above-mentioned sciences were converging: the study of the complex of genetically based functions that each species, including the human, has at its disposal. Some of these functions are phylogenetic, others are ontogenetic. Integrating these two aspects into a systematic account of the functional repertory of each species has been the general concern of Somatology from its Darwinian origins to the present.

## TECHNIQUE

Although it is not a technique, as a theoretical science Somatology serves as a theoretical guide for certain applied techniques. In general, Somatology recognizes two areas where techniques can be applied for changing somatic process: techniques that directly intervene in the soma's individual process or indirect techniques that intervene in the environment of the soma. The former techniques are clinical and educational, the latter are social and environmental.

Since its major concern is for the self-regulating and self-balancing mechanisms of the living being, Somatology provides a common ground for interventionary techniques that make use of these mechanisms. Any authentically *somatic* technique—whether clinical, educational, or other—seeks to enhance and facilitate the functional efficiency of the living being by means of operations on the self-regulatory mechanisms of that soma.

Because it is focused on the embodied process of individual life, Somatology is the common ground for all interventionary techniques that deal with the individual *in vivo*—never *in the abstract*. Each individual somatic process is unique, and thus somatic education or therapy is authentic if and only if it intends to improve the given individual process. Therefore, somatic techniques are unique for each individual .

## APPLICATIONS

Although the distinction between clinical and educational techniques may not always be clear, we can designate the following traditions of contemporary therapy and training as *somatic:* The organismic therapy of Wilhelm Reich and Alexander Lowen, the Functional Integration of Moshe Feldenkrais, the Sensory Integration of Jean Ayres, the neuromotor education developed by Carl H. Delacato, Robert J. Doman, et al, the Alexander Technique of F. Matthias Alexander, the Structural Integration of Ida P. Rolf, the Sensory Awareness of Charlotte Selver, biofeedback training and the Client-Centered Therapy of Carl Rogers, whose "nondirective" techniques assume certain self-correcting mechanisms in the individual.

The most general characteristic of all these somatic techniques is that the changes evoked are systemic and holistic, typically showing effects that are simultaneously physiological, psychological, and emotional.

# Strategic Therapy

## Jay Haley and Cloe Madanes

### DEFINITION

The main characteristic of this therapy is that the therapist plans a strategy for solving the client's problems. The goals are clearly set and always coincide with solving the presenting problem. That is, instead of emphasizing the growth and development of the person, the goal of this therapy is to solve the problem that the client offers, and the therapy is considered to have failed if this problem is not solved, no matter what other changes have taken place. Problems are conceptualized in terms of at least two people; the therapeutic unit is usually the family or the couple. Interventions take the form of directives and the emphasis is on communication in the present.

### HISTORY

Strategic Therapy has its origins in communication theory, which developed around mid-century. In 1948 Norbert Wiener published *Cybernetics* and through the next decade all the sciences began to emphasize homeostatic systems with feedback processes that caused the system to be self-corrective. This theory appeared in the field of therapy in the 1950s as part of the development of family theory.

Although the ideas became evident in a number of therapies, the communication approach became most well known through Gregory Bateson's research project on communication, which existed from 1952 to 1962 (Bateson, 1972). The idea of the double bind was published in 1956 (Bateson, et al.) and influenced many therapists to begin to think from a communication point of view. The approach suggested that the interchange of messages between people defined relationships, and these relationships were stabilized by homeostatic processes in the form of actions of family members within the family. The minimum unit was two people, since there was a sender and a receiver of messages. The therapy developing out of this view emphasized changing a family system by rearranging how family members behave, or communicate, to one another. It was not a therapy related to lifting repression or bringing about self-understanding, nor was it based upon a theory of conditioning. The past was dropped as a central issue because it was how people were communicating at the moment that was the focus of attention. In the 1950s the unit shifted from two people to three or more people as the family began to be conceived of as having an organization and structure. The unit became more and more a child in relationship to two adults, or an adult in relation to another adult and grandparent, and so on. The emphasis was upon analogies in one part of a system for another part, so analogical communication was emphasized more than digital (although these terms themselves were introduced by Bateson as a way of classifying any communication).

In the early family therapy, with this approach, awareness was still thought to bring about change and so interpretations were used because other therapy techniques had not developed to fit the new ways of thinking. By the 1960s therapists using the communication approach were not making interpretations and were not educating the family. It was assumed that new experiences, in the sense of new behavior that provoked changes in the family system, brought about change. Directives were used in the interview to change communication pathways, such as requiring people to talk together who had habitually not done so. There were also directives used outside the interview, particularly with the influence of Milton Erickson's directive therapy on the communication therapists (Haley, 1973). The tendency in the early days was to be growth oriented because of a concern with encouraging a wider range of communicative behavior in the family system. Some adherents, influenced by Milton Erickson, focused more on the presenting problem, but even then it was a way of increasing complexity in the system. However, the presenting problem was never dismissed as "only a symptom" because symptomatic behavior was considered a necessary and appropriate response to the communicative behavior that provoked it. There was little emphasis upon hierarchy in the early stages; family members were encouraged to communicate as equals. Later there was a developing concern with status in the family organization. Jackson emphasized the structural aspect of parental authority when young people were defined as psychotic. Parents and young people were not interviewed as peers as they would be in a therapy based on free association or individual self-expression. The Strategic Therapy that developed out of the communication approach emphasized organizational structure and focused on the repeating sequences on which structures are based.

## TECHNIQUE

In this therapy every problem is defined as involving at least two and often three people. The therapeutic unit is usually the family or the couple, but the issue is not how many people are actually seen in the interview; it is how many people are involved in the therapist's way of thinking about the problem. A psychiatric problem is understood in terms of a contract between at least two people. For example, if a woman is depressed, the therapist with a unit of one person will try to understand her and help her in terms of her feelings, perceptions, and behavior. The therapist with a unit of two will assume that her depression is related to her husband. His unit will be husband and wife, since he will assume that the problem is part of a marital contract. With a unit of three, it is possible to think in terms of coalitions and in terms of hierarchical structure of an organization. For example, a wife who is depressed might be thought of as caught in a conflict between her husband and her mother.

The therapy is planned in steps or stages to achieve the goals. The therapist must first decide who is involved in the presenting problem and in what way. Next, the therapist must decide on an intervention that will shift the family organization so that the presenting problem is not necessary. This intervention usually takes the form of a directive about something that the family is to do both in and out of the interview. Directives may be straightforward or paradoxical, simple and involving one or two people, or complex and involving the whole family. These directives have the purpose of changing the ways people relate to each other and to the therapist.

It is assumed that a problem or a symptom in a person are ways people communicate with one another and protect one another. For example, a child may develop a problem that will keep his mother at home to take care of him and in this way the mother may not have to face the issue of looking for a job or of confronting her husband who does not wish her to work. It is assumed that a symptom analogically, or metaphorically, expresses a problem and is also a solution, although usually an unsatisfactory one for the people involved.

Since this therapy focuses on solving the presenting problem, it is neither growth oriented–nor concerned with the past. The emphasis is on communication in the present. People go through new experiences as they follow the therapist's directives, but the experience is not a goal in itself. Nor is there an emphasis on working through something or insight or being aware of how communication takes place; if the people involved can get over the problem without knowing how or why, that is satisfactory. The goal of the therapy is primarily to prevent the repetition of sequences and introduce more complexity and alternatives. For example, a typical sequence is one where the child develops problems when the parents threaten to separate. The parents stay together to deal with their problem child, and as the child behaves more normally, the parents threaten separation again, which leads to the child developing problems. The task of the therapist is to change this sequence so that improvement of the child is unrelated to whether the parents separate or not.

There is a concern with hierarchy in this approach. Parents are expected to be in charge of their children, and cross-generation coalitions, such as one parent siding with a child against another parent, are blocked. There is also a cautious concern about where the therapist is in the hierarchy so that he does not inadvertently form coalitions with members low in the hierarchy against those who are higher. It is assumed that therapy must occur in stages and the presenting problem cannot be solved in one step. Similar presenting problems can require different therapeutic plans that must be designed for each particular one.

## APPLICATIONS

Strategic Therapy has been used for a variety of problems: symptomatic and misbehaving children, adolescent problems; lonely single young adults, marital difficulties, and problems of old age. It does not necessarily entail interviewing a whole family; it is an interpersonal approach that is used also with single persons. It is used with neurotics, psychotics, psychosomatic problems, delinquents, addicts, etc. There are no contraindications since specific therapeutic strategies are designed for each particular problem.

---

# Street Psychotherapy
## *Dan Kiley*

### DEFINITION

The primary goal of Street Psychotherapy is to improve the survival skills of the client. Concerns about the mental health of the client are always expressed in terms of the pragmatic day-to-day behavior that reflects the person's ability to maintain a source of legal income and humane shelter. Under these circumstances, the use of any ethical technique of human intervention is acceptable.

Street Psychotherapy differs from other systems of psychotherapy on two crucial points. First, the setting in which the therapy occurs is not the traditional office. The setting can be a poolroom, a bar or an alley, wherever the client, *not the therapist*, is comfortable. The therapist must go to the client since the client will not come to the therapist.

Second, the street therapist does not have the controls afforded by structured time, secretaries, and tests. In more ways than one, the therapist must work within the controls imposed by the client. This calls for a flexibility not found in most professional circles.

## HISTORY

The first street therapists might very well have been Socrates and the Chinese thinker Mencius, both of whom employed unconventional methods of initiating behavior change.

More recently, federal and state projects have often focused on the use of indigent workers to organize and carry out self-help programs in depressed areas. The belief underlying these projects is that people who live in a situation can do more to change the situation than outsiders. Unfortunately, the indigent workers often had the motivation for change and understood what needed to be changed but lacked the preparation and willingness for ongoing training and supervision.

Professionals have often worked in "storefront"* clinics or within gangs to change destructive, violent influences. For the most part, they have not been accepted as equals by academicians, researchers and traditional clinicians, If street therapy can be seen as a viable "profession" for a certain breed of therapist, the wisdom of street survival can support, not detract from, professional therapy.

## TECHNIQUE

Street therapy is both difficult and dangerous. It is difficult because the therapist has to alter his style (in contrast with internship experiences) to accommodate the technique. It is dangerous because, unless carefully implemented, saying the wrong thing at the wrong time can result in physical injury.

There are three parts to the technique itself. They are: Survival, Modeling, and Teaching.

In the first stage, Survival, the therapist must learn the nature of the environment in which the therapy will be done. Understanding the "streets" and the needs of the people who live there is best accomplished by accepting the guidance and teaching of a leader in the streets. With minimal "psychologizing" or analysis, the therapist must learn to survive on the streets. It is a different environment and most middleclass therapists are too fearful and/or ignorant to survive without guidance. Thorough understanding of the rules of survival can minimize physical danger.

The second stage, Modeling, is most difficult. It is where most aspirants fail. The aspiring street therapist, in order to be a success, must find a personally satisfying and professionally sound manner of modeling survival skills that are better than the ones street people possess. That is, the therapist has to be able to survive in the streets better than the street people. Showing the street people how to handle a racist policemen without self-deprecation or getting arrested will earn him the respect and praise of the street people. This respect can and does lead to the development of a confidential relationship in which persons will seek more answers to their respective problems. Modeling alternatives to difficult situations permit the therapist to attain a special rank among the street people. This rank has various labels, all of which are respectful: "cool dude," "on-time mama," "friendly old freak," and (the one I prefer) "street shrink."

The final stage, Teaching, is a very gratifying part of street therapy. Lonely, frightened, and disturbed people seek out the therapist to receive warmth, knowledge, and better survival skills. They are diligent and responsive students. If the street therapist is constantly aware of the need to learn about the changing conditions on the streets and create new alternatives to old problems, his relevance can have a long life.

## APPLICATIONS

There are many people who feel disenfranchised from society. They may not have had a primary family unit or may find their family irrelevant to their needs. Street therapy can apply to any person who is living under outcast conditions in which he finds little or no comfort in the institutions (including the family) held in esteem by most people. Street therapy knows no economic barriers. Many street people have money in the bank but no home for their heart. In this view, no one is excluded from street therapy because of socio-economic level.

The therapist who wishes to practice street therapy will find that the client "population" will have some type of police record. In fact, many of the survival skills that must be taught center on reducing the risk of contact with law enforcement agencies. Thus, the street therapist must be prepared to deal with drugs, gambling, theft, gunrunning, pornography, and even violence. The major obstacle for the therapist is the person's self-image, which says, "I'm one of the 'bad' people in life. I must accept that; then I can work to be the best of the bad."

---

# Structural Integration

## *Ida P. Rolf*

### DEFINITION

Structural Integration (or rolfing, as it is often called) is not primarily a psychotherapeutic approach to the problems of humans, but the effect it has had on the human psyche has been so noteworthy that many people insist on so regarding it. It is an approach to the personality through the components of the physical body. As an approach, it integrates and balances the so-called other bodies of man, metaphysically described as astral and eteric, now more modernly designated as the psychological, emotional, mental, and spiritual aspects.

## HISTORY

Structural Integration, developed by myself during the 1930s and 1940s, reflects my observations on the physics of human structure and the violation of the laws of physics evidenced in all too many "average" human bodies. I believe that as human structures conform more strictly to the reality that physics would describe as competent, a great deal of the bioenergy of the human can be conserved.

The amazing psychological changes that appeared in individuals following Structural Integration were completely unexpected by me. They inevitably suggest that behavior on any level directly reflects the physical energy level of the initiating physical structure.

There is a hierarchy of behavioral needs, ranging from a bare minimum for the use of the individual to a generous overflow applicable to cultural requirements. In traveling up this hierarchy, behavior manifests itself as more altruistic and less aggressive only as the amount of energy available in the physical body can permit it.

## TECHNIQUE

It is impossible in an article of this length to give a description of the technique other than to say that the basic law of rolfing is the same in any situation. The rolfer, trained to see deviations from the template of the body, through directed pressure brings deviant myofascial connective tissue components toward their normal position, as defined by the template. He then requires the part to move in its physiological pattern. Such movement may be gross and conscious, as in the legs walking or knees bending, or more subtly refined and less consciously controlled, as in the chest and abdomen in respiration.

To this extent, rolfing is a manipulative technique dependent on the rolfer. In that it requires the client's active willingness, conscious cooperation, and control in movement during the brief time of the process of change, it demands responsibility on his part and recognition of his goal and purposes. The psychological effect of rolfing is far greater than one would expect to induce in this brief encounter of ten hours of work (the normal cycle for integration as seen by rolfers). This effect, however, can be understood if we see it as the emergence of a different behavior pattern resulting from the very much greater competence of physical myofascial organization.

The degree of correlation here has not yet been studied. But it is reasonably well established that these behavior changes are not linked one-to-one with local areas, but demand an improved level of operation of the whole human. In other words, Structural Integration can be seen only as a holistic approach to greater competence in the human being.

## APPLICATIONS

Rolfing postulates on the basis of its observation that a human is basically an energy field operating in the greater energy of the earth, particularly that energy known as the gravitational field. As such, the individual's smaller field can be enhanced or depleted in accordance with the spatial relations of the two fields. Rolfing, in integrating structure, changes the individual's field in such a way that it is supported and enhanced by the greater field of the earth (gravity).

Since the energy field of the earth acts as a vertical at the earth's surface, to be supported the physical body of the individual must be balanced around a vertical. Any deviation from the vertical either as a whole or in localized segments allows the gravity field to act detrimentally with respect to the human being. Fortunately, this physical body is a plastic medium, thanks to the quality of its collagen structure. By pressure it can be forced away from its original position, as happens in experiences involving physical trauma. But equally through the application of pressure, it can be restored to the spatial relation that coincides with and accepts the energy field of the earth, the gravity field.

At this point it would seem appropriate to state that following Structural Integration, (rolfing) a man's greater awareness suggests to him that his energy has been increased. In fact, rolfing has simply made his energy more available. His greater structural competence makes it possible to utilize his energy more efficiently.

Rolfing is not intended as a medical technique nor as a solution to medical problems. Rather it is a most fundamental nonsymptom-oriented method for the growth and development of human competence and potential on any level.

---

# Supportive Psychotherapy
## David Stafford-Clark

Supportive Psychotherapy is not a scientific subject, at least at present. It is an art with a technique, a procedure with various rules that can be learned and which, indeed, can in some degree be passed on, and this must be the object of this contribution. But no work that has as yet been published gives a scientific basis either for its administration or indications; for the selection of any particular technique through which it is given; nor for the results when compared with any other therapeutic technique, by any scientific assessment that can be made.

This is not to say that attempts have not been made, and will not again be made, to fit a procedure that is ultimately so dependent upon individual human relationships into the objective mold of inanimate or predictable living responses. Nevertheless, it is essential to be clear from the outset that in my (David Stafford-Clark) opinion such attempts as have been made have been entirely irrelevant to the practice of the subject. The purpose of this article will therefore be simply to record a report on experience of a little over a quarter of a century; during which time I have practiced this technique through trial and error—error in particular. Supportive Psychotherapy is never easy.

In the final analysis the merits or demerits of psychotherapy, while arguable in terms of results, remain, at least so far, impervious to scientific enquiry. You cannot calibrate the burden of a desolate heart, count the loss of a broken spirit, nor reckon the cost in time and energy of their repair or restoration: yet such are the raw materials of Supportive Psychotherapy.

## DEFINITION

Supportive Psychotherapy may be defined as the creation of an effective bridge of communication and therapeutic relationship with people too distressed to achieve this for themselves. The pragmatic justification of Supportive Psychotherapy is simply that it works, and thereby fulfills a function indispensable to, although still far too often totally neglected by, the proper practice of medicine as a whole.

## HISTORY

It has existed as a need since medicine began; but has been conceived as a practical technique only during the last fifty years.

*Function and Practice.* Psychotherapy is in essence the treatment of the human mind. As a term for a form of activity directed toward that end, it covers all forms of communication between the professional therapist and the patient, including exchange of ideas, discussion, reasoning, and emotion. It represents the effort to reach out into the mind and world of a sick person and, by comprehending it, to make it comprehensible to him: even to enable him to see it in a different way, and to modify his behavior along lines governed by a deeper and wider understanding and by an increased confidence.

The contribution of psychiatry to a fuller understanding of the principles and practice of medicine must ultimately be to underline a single fundamental truth: the essential wholeness and dignity of man. For although the technique of psychiatry as part of the training of a medical student is of great importance throughout the entire complicated field of human relationship, and of mental health and sickness, it is in this bridge between what are commonly regarded as essentially medical, surgical, pediatric, gynocological, or obstetric disorders and their emotional aspects and manifestations that the whole truth of medicine begins best to be understood.

Confronted by any sick, frightened, disturbed, or unhappy person, the doctor can always remember this simple precept: "Attention must be paid to such a person ..." Once a patient realizes that you care about how he feels, then you have given him a bridge that he can cross to meet you and that you can cross to meet him. Good doctors have always recognized the necessity for such a bridge and the best have discovered something of the way to build it for themselves and their patients. In this sense the better the doctor, the fuller will be his recognition of his own need for psychiatric knowledge and skill; and the more complete his attainment of these objectives, the better doctor will he yet become.

No good doctor can afford to be totally ignorant of Supportive Psychotherapy. Many good doctors believe that they practice it, but lack perhaps a precision in recognizing its indications and a clear grasp of some of those techniques upon which it rests; whole basic principles are now considered.

## TECHNIQUE

The essence of Supportive Psychotherapy can in practice be summarized under four headings:

1. Unreserved and unconditional acceptance of the patient as a separate and equally human being in his own right
2. Sensitive elucidation of the patient's world view and experiences in the light of his disability

3.  Deliberate but unobtrusive construction of a flexible bridge between the patient and the rest of the world (including the therapist), which the patient can then cross to meet it, and which the therapist can cross to meet the patient
4.  Use of this bridge to enable the patient to make what changes are possible in his personality, and to accept what changes the patient may recognize as wise (and practical) in his environment.

### APPLICATIONS

These four principles are the key to Supportive Psychotherapy and its applications. Apart from the first interview, which may require an hour to an hour and a half to establish rapport, subsequent interviews should require no more than forty-five minutes, at an initial frequency of one a week, declining to twice a month, and eventually monthly, every third month and finally, twice a year, as progress is made—and maintained.

It is advisable when closing treatment to make a open offer to return if and when necessary, as judged by the patient. It is unusual for patients to abuse this privilege.

In conclusion, Supportive Psychotherapy is not the same thing as brief psychotherapy, counseling, behavior or group therapy. It is essentially individual, skilled, and flexible. More detailed accounts are contained in the BIBLIOGRAPHY. But its final essential indication is for the patient for whom no one else will or can do anything.

# Supportive Care Therapy

*Robert E. Allen*

### DEFINITION

Supportive Care is both a technique and a philosophy for providing the lifelong continuity of psychiatric treatment necessitated by chronic mental illness. The model was developed primarily as an intervention in the lives of individuals with schizophrenia, and most of the following discussion will deal with the use of Supportive Care in that disease. However, it may also be applied to the psychological management of other chronic psychiatric disorders.

Supportive Care encompasses both biologic and experiential models of schizophrenia. The biology, or the illness, is viewed as a given that can be managed but not "cured." In this sense Supportive Care views schizophrenia in a rehabilitative mode and seeks to maximize function within a disability that in itself cannot be altered. Organic interventions, such as medication, are seen as necessary, but only as a first step in allowing an individual to function at the best possible level. The aim of therapy is not to remove the illness, which is not considered possible, but to remove many of the difficulties caused by the illness. This rehabilitation is accomplished by focusing on the experiential effects of the disease.

Psychologic intervention is aimed at the three fundamental areas of dysfunction that supportive care theory considers nuclear in all individuals with schizophrenia. These are:

1. *Failure of anxiety management*—anxiety is poorly managed, diffuse, and consumes a large amount of energy and effort

2. *Failure of interpersonal transactions*—relationships are clumsy and seen by other as inappropriate, the outcome is often disastrous

3. *Failure of past experience*—there is no ability to use lived personal history as a basis for making judgments and decisions in the present moment

Efforts to manage these disabilities form the core of the application of the theory of supportive care.

## HISTORY

Supportive Care was developed by Werner M. Mendel, M.D., from his experience in treating patients with schizophrenia over many years. He has personally followed over five hundred individuals, some now for over twenty years. The experiential focus of the theory stems from his interest and expertise in existential psychiatry; the rehabilitative focus is primarily from the application of Supportive Care in a project on a group of patients treated at Los Angeles County- University of Southern California Medical Center.

Historically, the medical intervention in the lives of individuals with schizophrenia tended to be acute and episodic. Much effort was given to hospital treatment and less concern to the patients between episodes or in the prevention of future episodes. Supportive Care focuses on continuity, views acute episodes as exacerbations of an ongoing condition, and seeks to provide support, a therapeutic alliance, and prevention of future exacerbations. In this sense it anticipated current thinking as to the importance of aftercare and community psychiatry.

## TECHNIQUE

To understand the techniques of Supportive Care one must be acquainted with the natural history and progression of schizophrenia as it affects an individual's life. Schizophrenia usually begins insidiously in adolescence or early adult life. At some later time it reaches psychotic proportions, causes crisis, and is identified. Its natural tendency is to wax and wane, with periods of relative remission followed by further exacerbations. While early psychiatric notions foresaw a downhill course leading to inability to function, current thinking holds that 50 to 80 percent of individuals with schizophrenia, will, with proper treatment, be able to live relatively functional lives.

Supportive Care involves a constant intervention in the patient's life to minimize the disruptions caused by the nuclear disabilities. Anxiety, often helped by medication, must constantly be brought into awareness both as to its effect on the individual and its causes. Repetitive coaching on interpersonal relationships is best implemented by role rehearsal and actual modeling of appropriate behavior in a variety of social situations. Past patterns of behavior, unavailable to the individual because of failure of historicity, must be identified and used to make reasonable decisions. For example, a mechanic who has been unable to deal with the anxiety and interpersonal demands associated with being made foreman on previous occasions, may again be considering accepting that promotion. He will need the prior problems pointed out and should be aided in perhaps not accepting the new job, assessments that he cannot make on his own.

Because of the recurrency of the disease and the failure of past experience, the techniques of Supportive Care must be repeated constantly. As indicated above, interventions deal with the here and now. Insight models of therapy are not only useless but contraindicated. The therapist should come to view himself as a teacher and as a "life manager" who treats by direct intervention, example, and environmental manipulation.

## APPLICATIONS

Since most individuals enter treatment in crisis, the initial contact should be based on crisis intervention and restitution of function. As the crisis clears the nuclear disabilities are identified in a matter-of-fact fashion and areas of healthy functioning are strengthened and expanded. The initial few years of treatment generally require the most effort as patients may suffer exacerbations and the therapeutic process must begin anew.

As the therapeutic alliance strengthens, the patient becomes more able to cope with his disabilities. Life decisions constantly need to be made and often involve taking the patient off the hook. As time passes contact can be reduced but should never be terminated. Exacerbations can then often be predicted and more frequent contact and perhaps more medication can be used to prevent them. Thus, a patient may be seen frequently for several months, infrequently for a few years, and then frequently again as needed.

Supportive Care is a lifelong process that once begun will never end. If properly applied the technique provides relief from pain and suffering as well as markedly improved comfort and function for the patient.

---

# Sullivanism

*Leston L. Havens*

## DEFINITION

Participant Observation, or Sullivanism, refers both to a general proposition that can characterize all psychotherapy and to certain technical suggestions for working in the social field; both spring largely from the work of Harry Stack Sullivan. The general proposition is that clinical psychiatric work precludes observations of the patient alone; the relation between observer and observed is so interactive that statements about the one must include statements about the other. In short, every clinical observation involves a system of at least two persons.

The specific technical suggestions that also comprise Participant Observation arise from this interactive nature of psychotherapy. Patient (and therapist) are in part responding to the ideas each develops about the other; many of these ideas are projections (parataxes or transferences); the projections may in turn cause anxiety and other symptoms. Therefore management of the projections is, first, a critical goal of the interview and, second, a means of diminishing the patient's symptoms over the longer run.

## HISTORY

Sullivan's was a social psychiatry; that is, he located the causes of mental disturbances in social experience. As a result, it was of central importance to discover what had actually happened in the patient's life. Sulivan believed that the principal obstacle to this discovery was not an intrapsychic process of repression but the inhibitions to frank disclosure that came from projecting on the interviewer various parataxes or transferences. Social patterns learned early in life repeat themselves in the interview; it is often as difficult to remember and tell the truth to therapists as it was to parents. Furthermore, the behavior of many therapists serves to reinforce the pathological patterns. In contrast, the purpose of Participant Observation is to counteract and extinguish the patterns.

## TECHNIQUE

The method has two chief technical innovations: means for getting at what Sullivan called the patient's "social geography" and statements "kicking at the underpinnings" of his pathological ideas.

1. By "social geography" Sullivan meant how things would have looked if the therapist had been sitting there with the patient. He believed that the study of facts should precede the study of fantasies. To this end he sometimes literally sat beside the patient, both to avoid staring at shy people and to direct attention "out there," to the world of social experience he believed had been pathogenic. Directing attention "out there" also had the effect of directing the patient's attention away from the therapist, and so reducing projections on the therapist.

Sullivan would also help his patients reconstruct their historical scenes; he would not, for example, await free associative reconstructions. His implication was that many patients cannot remember alone; they need someone actually on their side to face the forbidding historical figures. He emphasized that assisting patients accurately to reconstruct scenes from their lives requires considerable knowledge and clinical imagination.

2. The purpose of "kicking at the underpinnings" of pathological ideas is to keep transference phenomena under control; they are not to be allowed so free a development as in classical analysis. Sullivan's anecdotes suggest a number of ways of controlling transference development. The principal one to be discussed here is what I (Leston Havens) have termed counter-projective statements.

Counter-transference statements aim to reduce or eliminate projections placed on the speaker; more exactly, these statements aim to deflect the projections away from the speaker to "out there," where their origin can be examined in the patient's experience. Essentially they imply: "I'm not father or mother; father or mother is there." (Note that interpretation of the patient's misunderstanding is avoided; instead the misunderstanding is directly reduced.)

There are three characteristics of counter-projective statements. They refer directly to the past person being projected on the therapist; they talk about father or mother, for example. Second, they *point*, again deflecting the projections away from the therapist. Third, the feeling with which they are expressed must match the patient's feeling, if the therapist is to be with the patient and looking at the difficult figures, rather than being one of the latter himself.

## APPLICATIONS

These techniques are most useful in clinical situations dominated by transference distortions (transference psychoses); for example, in dealing with paranoid patients and with the great expectations of many borderline patients. In both these instances the clinical atmosphere can be rapidly improved by strong counter-projective statements.

Therapists would be wise to have these techniques at hand in many other clinical situations, too. Distancing oneself from the projection of difficult parental introjects is frequently useful during critical juncture points in psychotherapy (and analysis). It is also well to have in mind that many transferences and transference neuroses are much more solidly imbedded than the word neuroses would suggest. Finally, these techniques can greatly facilitate the recovery of actual traumatic events and relationships.

---

# Sullivan Group Psychotherapy

*George D. Goldman*

## DEFINITION

Since Harry Stack Sullivan did not address himself to the problems of group psychotherapy, I am going to apply my personal understanding of Sullivanian principles to this therapeutic approach. For me, a therapeutic group consists of approximately ten persons of both sexes whose ultimate goal is to understand their interpersonal behavior in order to effect changes in it. Group treatment is an adjunct to individual treatment as I practice it. I adhere to a basic Sullivanian principle, which is: present-day interpersonal behavior that is persistently maladaptive and constantly repeated is probably a parataxic mode of operating. By parataxic is meant the carrying over intactly into the present of a mode of behavior that was learned earlier in life in order to cope with significant others (people who play important roles in the patient's life). It is roughly the equivalent of the Freudian concept of transference.

## HISTORY

I see Sullivan as having been quite concerned with what psychiatric problems are, and what they are not. While it surely is one's task to help people and, more specifically, to help people understand their behavior, there are many ways in which this can be done. One could give direct advice, or even be the warm, loving, giving parental substitute who would make up for all the deprivation the patient had suffered. Sullivan, however, felt that the most respectful role, as well as the most scientifically and empirically correct role, was that of an expert at understanding those events that would clarify for patients the processes that involve or go on between people. The patient, of course, was the expert on his specific history of significant interrelationships. Sullivan felt that the analyst could function most effectively by sampling those events that are characteristic of the patient's interactions with other people. What better laboratory to observe and document these dynamic events than in the therapy group, where the analyst is, in the fullest sense of Sullivan's usage of the term, a "participant observer" of human interaction?

## TECHNIQUE

The method of this analytically oriented approach is initially to acquaint my patients with their present parataxic behavior, then to explore with them the origins of this parataxically repeated behavior, and finally to help them find alternative interpersonal behaviors that are not parataxically distorted. What group therapy seems to do best is to make patients aware—vividly, intensely, and emotionally—of how they are behaving in ways that get them into difficulty, ways learned in childhood that are inappropriate to the present and their current adult status. The group therapy is, therefore, most effective in handling the initial phase of treatment as outlined above.

## APPLICATIONS

The goal is basically to catch the person in the act of being himself in his interactions with other people in the group. Human beings tend, if they are not psychotic, to be fairly consistent in their behavior, and so patients are most likely to act out in the group setting their characteristic methods of handling other people or defending themselves against anxiety. As one group member detects such behavior and points it out to another, people see themselves as others see them. Hopefully, they become increasingly convinced of the difficulties that their maladaptive behavior creates for them. Such realization provides impetus to the wish to change oneself. A patient can then bring into individual treatment all the insights gained in group, and explore the historical antecedents of a particular piece of behavior. In the setting of individual therapy, an attempt is made to reexperience the origins of parataxic distortions. Then the patient is freed from the necessity of repeating parataxic behavior blindly and without choice. The next step for both patient and therapist is to work on creating better methods of meeting one's needs and of interacting more effectively in the present-day interpersonal world.

In summary, the way I apply this technique of group psychotherapy is as an adjunct to individual analysis or individual psychotherapy. If the analytic process is designed to find out "What am I doing in my current life that is inappropriate?" "Why am I doing it?" and "What are the alternatives?" then the technique of group psychotherapy is best used to answer the first question. The "why" part of the process as well as the "alternatives" are worked out in individual treatment.

# Systematic Desensitization
## *Gerald Groves*

### DEFINITION

Systematic Desensitization is a therapeutic procedure for overcoming fearful responses or anxiety in certain situations. It consists of graded exposure to fear-provoking stimuli under special conditions, so that emotional reactions other than fear or anxiety predominate. This technique belongs to the family of techniques based on learning principles called behavior therapy.

### HISTORY

The technique of Systematic Desensitization is attributed to Dr. Joseph Wolpe, who devised it following the conclusion of a series of experiments during the 1950s in which he made cats fearful of certain situations by applying repeated electrical shocks to them. He noted that the neurotic cats exhibited fearful behaviors as well as the inhibition of certain appetitive behaviors, such as eating in the situations in which they had been shocked. He noted further that if such cats were induced to eat in situations that somewhat resembled those in which they had received the shock, and then further induced to eat in situations gradually approximating the original shock situation, then they would gradually lose their neurotic fears and inhibitions. To explain these observations, Wolpe elaborated on the theory of reciprocal inhibition that states that neurotic fear may be overcome by eliciting in the fear-provoking situation behaviors or emotions incompatible with and stronger than the fear. In 1924, utilizing identical principles, Mary Cover Jones described the successful treatment of a neurotic child, using eating as the reciprocal inhibitor.

Systematic Desensitization is frequently used in the behavior therapy treatment of neurosis and is the most researched psychotherapeutic technique.

### TECHNIQUE

Systematic Desensitization consists of four operations: 1) behavioral analysis; 2) relaxation training (or training in developing another reciprocal inhibitor); 3) hierarchy construction; and 4) hierarchy presentation.

Behavior analysis subsumes a complete psychiatric evaluation with an emphasis on stimulus-response relationships. This indicates whether anxiety habitually occurs in response to inherently innocuous stimulus situations. If it does, then Systematic Desensitization is frequently indicated.

Relaxation training is usually effected by a modified version of Jacobson's Progressive Muscle Relaxation Method. This involves the deliberate and sequential contracting and relaxing of skeletal muscles, the goal of which is a subjective sense of complete muscular and psychological relaxation.

To enable the patient to quantify the degrees of relaxation, he is introduced to the subjective units of distress scale, given the acronym SUDS. This scale ranges from 0 to

100. The 0 point represents total relaxation; the 100 point represents panic—an anxiety as intense as the patient imagines he can feel. The 50 point represents a subjective sense of unpleasant emotional tension accompanied by some muscular tension, sweating, palpitations, or "butterflies in the stomach."

Each relaxation training session in the office lasts ten to fifteen minutes. Typically, training begins with clenching of the fists, followed by relaxation. Tension lasts five to seven seconds, relaxation lasts approximately twenty seconds. This is repeated two or three times and followed by tensing and relaxing the biceps, triceps, and shoulders. The subject is instructed to practice ten minutes twice a day at home between sessions. At the subsequent session, the muscle groups done previously are quickly reviewed and new muscle groups essayed. Training proceeds until the patient can reliably reach zero on the SUDS scale. At this point, he is ready for a presentation of the hierarchy.

## Hierarchy Construction

One frequently observes that the clinically relevant anxiety-provoking situations may be sorted into families, or potential hierarchies on the basis of themes. Each of these themes forms the basis of a hierarchy that typically consists of six to twelve situations, which are briefly described, and vary in anxiety-provoking potential from a low of 5—10 SUDS to 90–100 SUDS. These are arranged in ascending order of SUDS level with an interval of ten to fifteen SUDS between successive items.

## Hierarchy Presentation

The patient is instructed to become completely relaxed and to signal attainment of this state. When this has been accomplished, the patient is asked to repeatedly imagine the first item, or situation, until it no longer evokes any anxiety. Between presentations of each scene, the patient is instructed to relax completely. The same is done for each successive item. Whenever possible, the patient should be instructed to expose himself in real life to situations already overcome in the office.

Alternatively, Systematic Desensitization may be effected *in vivo* where the nature of the hierarchy and the environment allow. *In vivo* exposure is superior to imaginal exposure.

## APPLICATIONS

Most nonbehavioral professionals perceive Systematic Desensitization as an effective treatment for phobic neurosis only. However, if one views neurosis as a habitual anxiety response to inherently innocuous stimuli based on learning, then a great majority of all neuroses may be seen to have "phobic" elements. Consequently, Systematic Desensitization may be applied in the treatment of most neuroses, frequently as one of a number of interventions. Agoraphobic and obsessive-compulsive neuroses are best treated by methods other than Systematic Desensitization. Systematic Desensitization may be useful in: phobic, anxiety, and depressive neuroses; sexual dysfunction; sexual orientation problems, such as homosexuality and pedophilia; alcoholism; drug abuse; and also psychosomatic problems, such as tension headaches, muscle tension, asthma, hyperacidity, and dyspepsia.

### Key Issues in Relation to Other Therapies

Systematic Desensitization was the first psychotherapeutic procedure amenable to a simple operational description. It is a widely researched psychotherapeutic technique and the majority of studies have shown it to be superior to placebo, supportive, and other nonbehavioral therapies. It has an easily recognizable end point: when the last item on the last hierarchy has been completed, then the Systematic Desensitization treatment is finished. Furthermore, the procedure is easily taught to novices.

---

# T-Groups

## Robert T. Golembiewski and Gerald J. Miller

### DEFINITION

T-Groups constitute a set of experiential, educational designs for understanding the self in relation to others, with the small-group membership providing both the context for learning as well as crucial feedback and emotional support for the learners. T-Group designs can vary significantly (Golembiewski and Blumberg, 1977), and are viewed as a major species of the genus "laboratory approach to learning" (Benne, et al., 1975). Often referred to as "sensitivity training," T-Groups usually are trainer-led, but can be member-led experiences that employ tape-recorded instructions.

Here-and-now events in T-Groups permit individuals to experience and test their awareness of self and others, of group processes and culture. This requires developing a temporary community with appropriate norms, a unique social order in whose psychological safety participants can test how they come across to others. Members also often consciously seek to expand the choices available to them, through experimenting with new behavior; they develop skills useful in diagnosing group and organizational behavior; and gain insight about the conditions that inhibit or facilitate effective group functioning.

T-Group is definitely not shorthand for Therapy Group, although trainers must be alert to the possibility of psychologic trauma. T-Groups focus on educational experiences in which participants must experiment with and improve interpersonal skills while therapy often emphasizes the genesis of ideas, feelings, and behavior. Hence, ethical solicitation for T-Group participants should routinely advise caution for those experiencing unusual stress due to significant problems in everyday coping. The experience could produce information overload because the T-Group can be emotionally arousing—although tolerably so for most—and because it deals with the full range of events in a particular group's life, sometimes mercurially, and often at multiple levels. Finally, T-Group training neither preaches openness as a life-style nor prescribes disrespect for those who opt to be reserved. Both charges can be legitimately leveled against numerous varieties of "let-it-all-hang-out" experiences. T-Groups would focus on the choice between degrees of openness or closedness by specific individuals, and on the consequences of that fundamental choice.

## HISTORY

Under the basic sponsorship of the National Training Laboratory, in Bethel, Maine, T-Groups impacted on the world's consciousness after 1947. In fact, no less an observer than Carl Rogers sees the T-Group and its variants as the most significant educational development of the twentieth century. Today, group experiences are available widely; pop-health variants abound in diverse growth and encounter centers; and quality-control issues loom large. To provide guidance for consumers, as well as to develop certification policies and procedures for the growing number of professionals, the International Association of Applied Social Scientists was founded in 1971. Applicants seeking certification periodically undergo a review process testing their knowledge, experience, and philosophy.

## TECHNIQUE

The major elements of the T-Group process are well known (Blumberg and Golembiewski, 1976), and a large battery of exercises exists to facilitate their emergence and analysis (e.g., Pfeiffer and Jones). Basically, that process is conceptually rooted in Kurt Lewin's observation that behavior and attitudes suggest an equilibrium, often reinforced by groups, whose common costs include inflexibility and infrequent experimentation. Lewin proposed a three-step process for choice or change that acknowledged *and* used his core observation:

- *unfreezing* or altering the forces acting on the individual, especially by reducing some of the threat in choice or change via a supportive group
- *testing* old or new attitudes or behavior in a safe environment
- *refreezing* or the integration of the changed or rechosen attitudes or behavior into one's relationships, as reinforced by group resources

Essentially, the T-Group process rests on the formation of a temporary group with specific norms that support choice or change. Unfreezing begins early, as trainers generally refuse to play the conventional leadership role, and as members seek to establish their identities in a new setting. As interpersonal liking and attraction to the group develop—aided by trainer interventions that highlight central processes and values—participants typically loosen their defenses, develop trust in fellow group members, and acknowledge ownership of behavior.

Testing begins after the movement from fear to trust has progressed sufficiently, the two central features being disclosure and feedback. Disclosure tends to increase the capacity to relate to others, helps individuals isolate areas of concern, and also raises the probability that others will provide data necessary for effective problem solving. Feedback reduces an individual's blind spots. By increasing the availability of inputs from others, one may learn more accurately the consequences of his actions and behavior (Golembiewski, 1972) and might choose to adopt the behavior or attitudes the he comes to see as effective and personally beneficial.

# APPLICATIONS

T-Groups have been used in many environments for diverse purposes, as standard references illustrate (Golembiewski and Blumberg, 1977; Solomon and Berzon, 1972). Complex organizations have hosted most applications, although the present trend favors the use of such spinoffs of the laboratory approach as a team building, role negotiation, and confrontation designs (Golembiewski, 1972). T-Groups also have dealt with a broad range of issues in the classroom, race relations, community relations involving police, schools, and jobs programs, and conflict among nations.

The diffusion of the T-Group strategy raises two concerns, the first being unintended effects or casualties. The trainer's style often contributes, perhaps even with unique force, by overstimulating or inadequately protecting members. Casualties vary from substantially less than 1 percent of group members in most cases, to an astounding rate in one study of approximately one of six participants.

The transfer of any learning to back-home sites constitutes a second major issue raised by the diffusion of the T-Group strategy. Transfer is a function of several intervening variables. We can give only a sample here.

First, characteristics of the individual seem central in transfer. Persons most likely to carry back skills and to maintain learning seem to have a healthy regard for self, a willingness to accept affection, a positive view of friends, and a willingness to risk, in order to gain further understanding.

Second, participants successful at transfer tend to develop strategies that maintain their drive to learn. The strategies include:

1. Experimenting with new behavior
2. Refining new responses in the light of the reactions they evoked
3. Talking with others in depth about the changes they have experienced
4. Taking an active stance toward important events in one's life (Lieberman, et al., 1973).

Third, the degree of transfer of learning also depends upon the back-home situation. An individual's high status, tenure, and authority or autonomy often will help maintain learning, but great differences between the back-home and learning environments can cause learning fade-out. Essentially, forces inhibiting change will tend to become more prominent when the individual leaves the training situation, and practitioners and theorists must find ways to compensate for these barriers to applying the skills or behavior learned in T-Groups.

# Theme-Centered Interactional Groups

*Ruth Ronall and Bradford Wilson*

## DEFINITION

The Theme-Centered Interactional (TCI) system of group leading has its roots in psycho-analytic group therapy, teaching, and communications theory. One to TCI's main theses is that individuals learn, grow, and heal best when they are totally involved; this means they are thinking, sensing, feeling, and intuiting within a milieu that aims at keeping these functions in balance. TCI calls this "living-learning." Based on humanistic prem-ises, TCI is a cooperative rather than competitive approach to group interaction aimed at promoting personal growth and creativity as participants meet for the avowed purpose of sharing their ongoing thoughts and feelings about a previously agreed-upon theme. The theme, then, is considered central to the group's involvement. TCI emphasizes, however, a balance between focus on individual needs, the group-as-a-whole, and the theme (or task). Its chief advantage resides in its unique suitability for use by and for people without previous background in group psychotherapy and for its ability to blend the intellectual/cognitive validity of a rap session with the emotional honesty of an encounter group while avoiding the pitfalls of both.

## HISTORY

TCI was developed by Ruth Cohn in 1955, and is currently taught at the Work-shop Institute for Living-Learning (W.I.L.L.), which maintains training facilities in New York City, Atlanta, Pittsburgh, Michigan, Florida, Toronto, and Europe.

## TECHNIQUE

Cohn describes the process of TCI as follows:

> Group interaction is graphically described as a "triangle in the globe." The triangular points designate the functions of the individual (I), the group (We), and the them (It). The *I* comprises the awareness and activity of the individual in interaction with the group; the *We* designates the concern of each person for all others and the theme; the *It* is the purpose for which the group convenes. The globe is the time-space and other givens of the environment—be they school, organization, community, country, the network of purposes, or mo-tivation inherent in the outside-of-the-group population. The in-side group interaction is co-determined by the glove; thus the TCI group brings values and influences of the university, town, parents, and political-historical situations into the group interaction (Cohn, 1969– 1970).

## The Leader's Role

The TCI leader is a *participant*-leader who functions both as chairman of his own self and of the group process. Similarly, TCI participants are encouraged to "chair" themselves, thus, gradually learning to observe the group process and to participate in its leadership. To facilitate this process, TCI's ground rules and structure have to be made as explicit as possible; axioms, postulates, and auxiliary rules for *communication* are introduced early in the life of a group and are frequently reiterated.

TCI is a highly *structured* system of group leading based on the belief that a firm structure enhances energy flow within the group process rather than restricting it. Here the leader's primary function is that of achieving a dynamic balance between foci, which constantly shift back and forth between the "I," the "We," and the

"It" while at the same time maintaining an overall balance within the "Globe" (the environment in its myriad manifestations).

## Axioms, Postulates, and Auxiliary Ground Rules (Cohn, 1975)

The TCI system is predicated upon the following humanistic axioms:

1. Human beings, as discrete psychobiological units within a unified cosmos, are seen to be simultaneously autonomous *and* interdependent.

2. Life, growth, and the decision-making processes involved in their unfolding deserve respect. Whatever promotes this respect is regarded as humane, whatever this does not as inhumane.

3. Free decision making is bound by both internal and external limits. These limits are expandable.

The foregoing axioms have in common the paradox of *freedom within dependence* from which are derived the following postulates:

*1. Be your own chairperson.* Basic to TCI is the standing invitation to "be your own chairperson"—i.e., not to wait for another's initiative before asserting yourself. However, personal chairmanship is not carte blanche to "do your own thing" without regard to others.

*2. Disturbances take precedence.* Unacknowledged personal distractions (whether internally or externally based) have a stifling effect on both individual and group process unless brought into the open. One cannot be fully *present* so long as one's preoccupation remains hidden. Where such disturbances are external to the group ("I fought with my boss today") a simple factual statement is often enough to enable one to "be with" the group and its theme. Disturbances arising *within* the group, however, must be brought out and attended to.

These two concepts embody the essence of TCI; they represent the recognition of existential phenomena and their translation into teachable and learnable postulates. We are indeed our own chairpersons—autonomous and interdependent, but neither omnipotent nor impotent. Disturbances do indeed take precedence; if unrecognized and not dealt with, they impede our life processes.

As aids to the facilitation of these postulates TCI has developed several auxiliary *ground rules of communication*:

*1. Represent yourself.* Speak in the first-person singular—as opposed to using generalizing pronouns like "one," "we," "everybody," "you"; they only serve to evade personal accountability. On the other hand, speaking for oneself supports responsible statements, avoids projections, and prevents the disowning of one's creativity and fallibility.

2. *When posing a question, state your reason for asking it and what it means to you; avoid the "interview."* Authentic questions seek information necessary in order to understand something or to continue processes; they become clearer and more personal if the reasons for asking them are stated.

3. *Be authentic and selective in your communications.* Be aware of what you think and feel, and choose what you say and do. If you say or do something because you "must" or "ought" to, you are not acting autonomously, because your own evaluation of this action is missing.

4. *Give your personal reactions first and hold off interpretation of others for as long as possible.* At their best, accurate and well-timed interpretations can help to crystallize what the other person was already groping toward; they do not harm. Ill-timed interpretations, on the other hand, often involve hidden intentions and create resistances.

5. *Be sparing with generalizations.* They tend to interrupt the group process, although they can be useful in dynamic balancing or as a bridge to a new subtheme.

6. *When describing your perception of another person's characteristics or behavior, acknowledge it as such and state what they mean to you.* This, together with #2 above, helps to prevent scapegoating. Your opinions of another person, however accurate, are always subjective—with no claims to general validity. Stating what your opinions and/or questions mean to you promotes genuine dialogue.

7. *Side conversations have precedence.* Inasmuch as they are a form of disturbance, they are usually important and very often related to the theme. A participant talking to his neighbor may need help toward further and more open participation in the group process. It is important that this rule be conveyed not as an imperative but rather as an invitation ("Would you tell us what the two of you have been talking about?").

8. *Only one at a time, please.* Nobody can hear more than one statement at a time—verbal interactions have to be consecutive. By the same token, nonverbal communications, such as gestures, grimacing, and sub-grouping, can be equally disruptive and need to be picked up on and brought into the stream of things.

9. *If more than one person wants to speak at the same time,* let each make a brief statement about what he has in mind.

## The Theme

In the words of Gordon and Liberman (1972), the purpose of having a theme is "to declare the group's focus in a clear, simple, inviting way. Like the title of a book or play, it has to attract its clientele, or at least not discourage them initially." They also explain what a theme is not: "A theme is not a *topic* ... is not an area of *subject matter* ... is not an *agenda* ... is not a *point of view* ... is not a *panacea* proclamation such as Joy or Growth."

A theme may be specific in its focus (as, for example, "Creating New By-Laws for Our Organization"—a typical task-oriented group theme) or quite open-ended ("The Challenge of Change," or "Turning On to Learning"). In any case, *sub*-themes are sure to arise that must be dealt with and brought to closure in order to continue developing and relating to the *central* theme.

TCI group sessions usually last one and a half to two hours within ongoing (weekly) or intensive (single weekend or week-long) workshops. In a "one-shot" workshop, a time-span of two and a half to three hours is preferable.

## APPLICATIONS

Applications of the TCI method are wide-ranging in their scope. Organizational meetings and other task-oriented groups come alive when this particular style of leading is employed. Classrooms (ranging from kindergartens to doctoral seminars) have profited from its use, as have political rallies, parent-teacher-community meetings, managerial brainstorming and training programs, police-neighborhood collaborations, etc. It has been used for time-limited groups (Buchanan, 1969), orientation groups, and personal-growth groups in a variety of settings.

Finally, TCI has recently come into use in experiential psychotherapy—both group and diadic—thus coming full circle from its origins in the humanistic and experiential psychotherapies. This development springs from TCI's underlying humanistic philosophy, whereby helping people and clients work together in a reciprocal and collaborative relationship on whatever theme comes into focus. Last but not least, the core concept of chairmanship—awareness of one's responsibility, autonomy, and interdependence—embodies, after all, the prime goal of any psychotherapy.

# Therapeutic Community

## Robert W. Siroka and Amy Schaffer

### DEFINITION AND HISTORY

The concept of a community intentionally designed to maximize the well-being of its members is an old one. This concept has found expression throughout the centuries in numerous religiously or politically inspired Utopian communities. The systematic application of this concept for the benefit of the mentally ill, however, did not appear, with few exceptions, until much more recently. One exception was the Belgian community Gheel, whose residents have "adopted" mental patients into their homes since the seventh century. Another was the "moral treatment approach" of the late eighteenth and nineteenth centuries, which treated mental patients by providing an optimally structured and humane social environment.

It was in the 1930s and 1940s that the scientific manipulation of an individual's social environment began to emerge as a treatment modality. Harry Stack Sullivan, observing in 1931 that schizophrenic patients behaved in a less psychotic manner when ward personnel were sympathetic, was an early contributor to this approach. The Menningers in 1960 carried his work further, prescribing interpersonal environments designed to maximize the therapeutic progress of each patient. J.L. Moreno experimented with and recommended the regrouping of members of residential institutions on the basis of their sociometric connections. In the late 1940s Maxwell Jones began to experiment with redesigning the mental hospital social structure, attempting to create a social environment that would produce therapeutic change. Jones (1953) called this environment a "therapeutic community." Although the term "therapeutic community" is usually attributed to T. F. Main, the concept is most closely linked with this pioneering work by Jones.

Although all therapeutic communities are different, most of those modeled on Jones's work share a number of features. Most important, patients play an active role in their own treatment. The patients in the organization meet usually daily, in face-to-face meetings. The authority pyramid is flattened so that the traditional power hierarchy diminishes and all members of the community, both patients and staff, can contribute to ward administration. Thus, as patients assume more responsibility, roles become blurred and the communication process becomes an open one.

Since Jones's early work, therapeutic communities have proliferated. Many applications of the concept, however, bear little resemblance to the method developed by Jones. To clarify the resulting conceptual confusion, Clark has offered the distinction between the "therapeutic community proper" and the therapeutic community approach. The therapeutic community proper is the type of community described by Jones. The therapeutic community approach is a more general one that includes features such as encouragement of patient freedom and responsibility, wards with open doors, active rehabilitation, and increased community involvement.

## APPLICATIONS

Therapeutic communities (and therapeutic community approaches) have been used in many settings with a variety of populations. Probably the most consistent application has been in the psychiatric hospitals—perhaps because the more traditional hospital organization has been increasingly seen as "anti-therapeutic." Sometimes an entire hospital is considered a therapeutic community, but more frequently a ward or group of wards is given that designation. Within hospital settings such communities have been established with many types of patient populations, including psychopaths, alcoholics, schizophrenics, and adolescents. (For an overview of therapeutic communities within institutions see Rossi and Filstead, 1973.)

Another widespread application of the concept has been in the treatment of drug abusers. Residential treatment centers, such as Synanon and Daytop Village, are therapeutic communities designed specifically for the rehabilitation of drug abusers. Features such as reward systems based on increasing member responsibility, "attack" groups, and the use of program graduates as staff members are characteristic of these communities.

Psychiatric hospitals and residential drug treatment centers are total institutions that serve individuals whose problems are so severe that removal from society into such institutions may be preferred. Jones (1968) has encouraged the extension of therapeutic community concepts out of such total institutions and into larger societies. Such programs do now exist. Day-hospital therapeutic community programs have become numerous. The application of therapeutic community concepts within a psychoanalytic private practice has been described (Freudenberger, 1972). A number of nonresidential therapeutic communities (see the Sociotherapy article) have been created. These are "part-time" communities for functioning members of society who use community activities and groups as laboratories in which they can study and change their own social behavior (e.g., Siroka and Siroka, 1971).

The growth of the therapeutic community has occurred within the context of the "third psychiatric revolution" in which social psychological explanations and treatments of psychopathology have prevailed. Corresponding with the emergence of the therapeutic community has been the proliferation of many related or overlapping group methods, such as family therapy, network therapy, milieu therapy, and sociotherapy. Like other new treatment methods, which are initially applied enthusiastically but somewhat indiscriminately, the therapeutic community will benefit from systematic study and evaluation. Outcome studies performed to date are generally inconclusive. More productive have been a number of investigations of the processes of the therapeutic community (e.g., Rapoport, 1960; Almond, 1971), as well as theoretical analyses of these processes (e.g., Edelson, 1970). Future work in the field should include more systematic evaluations of therapeutic communities, further study of how they work, and continued application in new settings.

# Therapist Disclosure

*Myron F. Weiner*

## DEFINITION

A psychotherapist's deliberate use of self-disclosure to facilitate psychotherapy is a relatively new technical innovation. It involves disclosure, by appropriate means, of the therapist's thoughts, feelings, and certain other personal data as they become relevant to the demands of the therapeutic process. Rational use of this technique demands that the therapist have distinct therapeutic goals and be aware of patients' psychological assets and liabilities, interpersonal needs and skills. It also requires an approach to psychotherapy that recognizes unconscious needs, wishes, and feelings in therapist and patient alike.

## HISTORY

Deliberate personal openness with patients began with the existential psychiatrists, for whom it served to close the gap between patient and therapist. The existentialists postulated that man's emotional difficulties stem partly from his attempts to objectify his universe, rather than fully participate in it and bear its uncertainties. In this system, breaking down the barrier of objectivity between patient and therapist is an important step in helping the patient become more in touch with his intrapsychic and interpersonal worlds, instead of fleeing from living in the here-and-now.

Humanistic psychology has also advocated personal openness by the therapist, largely as a protest against the "dehumanizing" psychoanalytic approach with its allegedly over-intellectualized emphasis on the past and on psychopathology. The humanistic psychologist deemphasizes the importance of dealing with the past and helps patients mobilize their assets to deal with life as it needs to be lived today.

Jourard and others have found that disclosure begets disclosure in social and laboratory settings, but there is no evidence from studies of psychotherapy that self-disclosure per se is a useful therapeutic tool. Asking direct questions ordinarily elicits more information than talking about oneself. The objective data that support the potential usefulness of personal disclosures by the therapist derive from studies of human social development and the development of gender identity. These studies suggest that identification plays as great a role in personality development as conscious or unconscious conflict. If this is true, identification with some attribute(s) of the therapist might be as important for some patients as the resolution of conflict.

Bandura has concluded that psychological and interpersonal skills formerly thought to have been developed through trial-and-error are much more likely to have developed through identification with valued adults and peers. He has found that certain fears in children can be alleviated by a valued person "modeling" desired behavior; i.e., fearlessly picking up a mouse to help a child overcome a mouse phobia.

## TECHNIQUE

As noted above, there is a little therapeutic helpfulness in self-disclosure per se. Most patients have little interest in getting to know a therapist personally as they are more interested in symptomatic relief. The best way to obtain information from patients is to ask direct questions. If a patient will not answer direct questions, it is better to explore his reasons for being evasive than for the therapist to take the lead in disclosure and hope the patient will follow. Ordinarily, the latter approach leads to an exploration of the therapist's personality instead of the patient's problems in life; one of which may be his unwillingness to face himself. Therefore, self-disclosure by the therapist has a limited role in psychotherapy. Most patients learn what they need to know about the therapist by observing his willingness to listen, his ability to understand, and his commitment to help.

As a technique, Self-Disclosure is governed by the parameters that govern all forms of psychotherapeutic intervention; they must be made in appropriate context and in an appropriate amount. Among the factors that govern dosage and timing are: the type of psychotherapeutic treatment employed, the ego strength of the patient, the nature of the alliance between therapist and patient, and the feelings of patient and therapist about one another.

Treatment techniques that aim primarily at enhancing reality testing use personal disclosures by the therapist to help the patient distinguish his projected fears and wishes from the therapist, and to consensually validate the patient's correct observations of reality. These are the techniques useful for the patient who is severely ego impaired.

Self-disclosures of another kind are useful to patients for whom the primary focus of treatment is their interpersonal relationships, with particular emphasis on heightening awareness of unperceived emotional reactions toward, and behavior with, others. In this situation, the therapist can disclose his emotional reactions to the patient's behavior in the therapy session as a form of interpersonal feedback. Interpersonal feedback by the therapist is useful not only for its informational content, but as a model of healthy interpersonal behavior.

Self-disclosure by the therapist is indicated in psychoanalysis or psychoanalytic psychotherapy on those (hopefully rare) occasions when the therapist makes a technical error detected by the patient, or when neutrality would serve only to confuse the patient about a current, important issue between patient and therapist. At times, a self-disclosure can be useful in resolving a particularly tenacious transference resistance.

In general, the greater the patient's degree of ego impairment, the greater is his need for awareness of the therapist as a real person. Concomitant with the ego-impaired patient's needs to know something of the therapist as a real person is his greater difficulty in usefully integrating such information, and his greater degree of vulnerability. Well-integrated patients are not likely to be damaged by therapist disclosures. Therapists often relax, are themselves, and establish friendships with their healthier patients. The disadvantage, in this instance, is that the therapist and patient gain a new friend at the expense of the patient's potential ability to explore his unconscious. And having terminated therapy with a patient and having entered a friendship relationship with him precludes further psychotherapeutic work, should the ex-patient experience further psychological difficulties. When he enters a mutually gratifying relationship with a patient, the therapist becomes unable to maintain his objectivity and his neutral advocacy of the patient's treatment needs.

The therapist needs to be aware of the nature of his alliance with a patient; whether he is at a given moment aligned with the rational aspect of his patient, with his instinctual drives, his superego, or with one of his pathological ego defenses. Awareness of the nature of the alliance allows the therapist to know what type of disclosure is appropriate. The therapist does not, for example, offer himself as a model of high achievement at a time when the patient is engaged in severe self-criticism. This can only heighten the patient's negative valuation of himself.

## APPLICATIONS

In certain situations, self-disclosures by a therapist are necessary. If a disclosure will preserve the life of the patient or the therapist, therapeutic neutrality must be put aside. When there is a significant alteration in the psychotherapeutic relationship as a result of events in the therapist's outside life, the patient has a right to know that the change is not due to interaction with the patient. When some aspect of the therapist's personality interferes with therapy, the therapist must acknowledge where the responsibility lies. Although he does not owe the patient a full exposition of his own inner workings he does need to acknowledge that he is the source of the problem in treatment.

Self-disclosures can be useful under other circumstances as a means to reach certain therapeutic goals. Disclosures by the therapist can help patients with marginal reality testing to define the therapist as a real person and to delineate the real patient-therapist relationship instead of leaving both to the patient's imagination. By conveying respect, the therapist can heighten patients' self-esteem and facilitate identification with the therapist's healthy attributes: his reasonableness, calmness, and interpersonal skills.

There are numerous contraindications to disclosure by the therapist. The chief caveat is to avoid disclosures whose content will tantalize the patient into an exploration of the therapist's personality rather than his own. A thorough knowledge of the patient will establish which disclosures are likely to be distracting and which are likely to be helpful. It is unwise to make disclosures about oneself in an attempt to seduce an unprepared or unmotivated person into therapy, or to manipulate a patient's feelings once he has become engaged in therapy. Disclosures that primarily meet the therapist's social, sexual, or psychological needs without reference to the patient's treatment needs are by DEFINITION nontherapeutic. Therapists are often tempted to self-disclose as a defense against recognizing their own feelings toward, and technical difficulties with, their patients. Such activity by the therapist can increase the patient's push for more direct involvement with the therapist as a real person, can make it difficult for the patient to terminate therapy, push him into inappropriate action outside of therapy, or lead to identification with an aspect of the therapist that is not in the patient's best interest.

The best rule of thumb regarding personal disclosures to patients is to wait when in doubt about disclosing, or when there is a strong push to disclose by patient or therapist. The psychotherapist and his patient generally need the protection afforded by therapeutic neutrality.

---

# Therapy via Telephone
### *John A. Chiles*

## DEFINITION AND HISTORY

Since the advent of the telephone, the use of this device between patient and therapist has played an increasing role in the therapeutic process. Often, initial contact with the therapist is made via the phone, and first impressions are established on both sides of the therapeutic fence. Telephones can allow a patient access to the therapist at moments of emotional intensity and crisis. Telephone calls can be an integral and planned part of individual or group therapy. Telephone contact is used exclusively for therapeutic contact when distance or medical problems are present.

Finally, crisis centers dealing with problems of suicidal intentions, drug abuse, and alcohol have made widespread use of twenty-four-hour-a-day telephone service for crisis intervention and support. Telephone Therapy, then, offers a technique that lacks visual contact and the controls of an office setting, but does provide the patient with much easier access to the therapist. This article will discuss some of these uses of the telephone.

## TECHNIQUE

Telephones are used in both structured and unstructured ways in psychotherapy. An unstructured format is as follows: the patient is given the therapist's phone number and encouraged to call "when you feel bad." The "bad feeling" should be defined as explicitly as possible; e.g., "I feel like hitting my kids," or "I feel like drinking again." At times, the patient's anxiety is immediately relieved. He has been reassured that support is close at hand. The therapist, for his part, has stated he is capable of handling emergencies and is not afraid of a patient's anxiety needs.

The telephone so offered will be used by patients in various ways. A patient who feels dependent can get support, at times, in place of acting out mechanisms such as pill taking. Some patients will attempt a pseudo-intimacy by phone, discussing material they have not brought up in regular sessions. The phone helps by blocking the nonverbal overload of the conversation, and by providing a safety valve for the patient—he can always hang up. Patients with significant interpersonal difficulties, such as schizoid individuals, will use the telephone to achieve closeness while simultaneously maintaining distance. Individuals with difficulty controlling hostility will use the phone to express anger at the therapist. The telephone allows a safer anger, one that is at a distance. Finally, and often late in therapy, some patients will call to talk things over with the therapist. They discuss decisions, ask advice, and in general borrow from the ego of the therapist.

All of these occurrences can provide useful input into therapy. The patient is able to document what heretofore have been vague episodes and can often conceptualize his problems in a manner that is helpful to him. The job of the therapist is to bring the material into the total therapeutic setting: to convert a crisis to a process.

If a patient abuses the use of the phone, the therapist should discuss this directly with him. Is he aware of the inconsiderate side of his personality, and can he bring it under control? Often, it is helpful to set up a regular time for telephone sessions, and to work out a fee for them. In my (John A. Childs) experience, patients rarely abuse telephone access.

The telephone as a planned part of therapy has several aspects to it. Telephone follow-up techniques are routinely used for alcohol and drug abuse problems. Patient and therapist have used the phone exclusively when illness or distance rules out face-to-face contact. Our clinic has frequently used the phone as a planned, daily part of therapy designed to enhance the self-image of patients by asking them to report a behavior they considered, prior to the onset of therapy, as beyond their capacities. An example of this technique is given in the "Applications" section.

A discussion of these telephone techniques must include the person who calls in a crisis and is unknown to the therapist. There are two things he must do. First, he must get identifying information: name, phone number, address. Second, he must speak to the side of the ambivalent patient that is positive. A person with a gun at his bedside or one who has just taken an overdose is calling the therapist because the outcome is uncertain. The therapist might tell him, in the case of an overdose, that he is now hanging up to call an ambulance, that the "client" open the door, and that he will call him back immediately. The therapist should act positively. A crisis call is not a good time to weigh pros and cons.

## APPLICATIONS

In addition to those applications discussed above, here is a more specific example of how telephone use can be of benefit. The following case was handled in an out-patient clinic, where the majority of the therapists were psychiatric nurses.

A fifty-two-year-old woman was referred to the clinic by another agency as a "psychotic telephone user." She had had a twenty-year history of multiple inpatient and out-patient runs at treatment and was currently on the phone many times a day with various doctors and social services, voicing multiple somatic complaints. She was talking to everyone, and in therapy with no one.

The initial interview revealed a chronically depressed and quite angry individual. She was in a very dependent relationship with her thirty two-year-old son and felt explosive and bitter toward her lover of about ten years. She had few ways of coping with these two men. Her days consisted of lying in bed until noon, fitfully calling various people until the evening, fighting with the men in her life until late at night, and drinking herself to an uneasy sleep. She needed ways of expressing anger, ways of dealing with those who made her angry, and, above all, a structure to her life that would make it seem useful.

The patient was instructed to call the clinic daily to express her complaints and anger, and it was agreed with other agencies that this was the only place she would call. The time for her daily phone calls was set at 8:00 A.M. with penalties—fines the first two times and then discontinuation of therapy—for missing the call. Quickly she was able to achieve the hitherto "impossible" task of getting up in the morning. Concomitantly, a new problem was created: what to do with these four morning hours that had appeared in her life? Twice-weekly sessions at the clinic dealt with structuring this time, and for a while she was charged with making daily phone reports at 10:30 A.M. on the progress of mutually agreed-upon tasks. After three weeks the patient was seen in joint therapy sessions with her lover and her son; after several months this resulted in greater freedom and satisfaction among them all. After a year the patient was working and reported a happier life. Although when she first came to the clinic she was taking several psychiatric drugs, she was not on a well-kept schedule. She therefore came to the clinic about once every four weeks for drug follow-up and was continuing to telephone daily. The calls lasted from about 8:00 until 8:05 A.M. and she talked to one of four or five staff members, all of whom she had come to know quite well.

# Token Economy
## Alan E. Kazdin

### DEFINITION

The Token Economy refers to an incentive system in which clients receive tokens (in the form of points, tickets, marks, credits, etc.) for engaging in preselected behaviors. The tokens can be exchanged for a variety of rewards and operate in much the same way that money functions in ordinary life. Typically, the Token Economy is a way of providing positively reinforcing consequences to a number of individuals in institutional, rehabilitation and educational settings. Several therapeutically relevant behaviors can be focused upon with many clients simultaneously. The use of tokens allows restructuring the entire therapeutic environment so that desired behaviors and diverse incentives in the setting are expressed in terms of token earnings and expenditures.

### HISTORY

Antecedents to the Token Economy can be traced to applications in educational and prison systems in the 1800s. These applications provided the equivalent of tickets to students or prisoners for desired behaviors. The tickets served as a medium of exchange for privileges and tangible rewards in the setting. For example, a widespread program in England, beginning in the early 1800s, was based upon providing students with tickets for making progress in academic areas. The tickets were exchangeable for prizes as well as being associated with social recognition.

Despite the historical antecedents, contemporary programs can be traced directly to the development of operant conditioning principles pioneered in the work of B. F. Skinner. Animal and human laboratory research established principles and findings pertaining to the influence of positive reinforcement on behavior, variables that determine the effectiveness of positive reinforcement, and the means of establishing events as reinforcers. This research has served as the experimental basis for contemporary token programs.

Token economies as such developed in the United States in the early 1960s. The development was part of a larger movement of applying research findings from psychology to clinical problems, an area known more generally as behavior modification. Early applications of token economies were conducted with hospitalized psychiatric patients and mentally retarded children in a special education classroom. These early programs demonstrated dramatic behavior changes. For example, in controlled experiments, psychiatric patients were shown to increase in their performance of self-care behaviors and jobs in the hospital, and retardates were shown to increase their academic accomplishments in the classroom. Since these early successes, the Token Economy has proliferated in terms of the populations studied and complexity of behaviors altered.

## TECHNIQUE

The Token Economy consists of providing positive reinforcers (tokens) that have attained their value by virtue of being exchangeable for a variety of other rewards. In a token economy, tokens can be earned only by performing preselected and well-specified behaviors. The specific behaviors focused upon in treatment and the events for which tokens can be exchanged vary with the treatment population and setting.

Actually, the Token Economy is not a unitary technique. Token economies vary widely across a range of dimensions, including who decides what behaviors earn tokens, who administers the tokens, the extent and range of events for which tokens can be exchanged, whether tokens are delivered for an individual's performance or for the performance of the group as a whole, and others. Also, token economies may not only provide tokens for appropriate behavior but also withdraw tokens for inappropriate behavior, a variation that tends to be more effective than merely presenting tokens. Ideally, individuals who receive tokens (e.g., patients, clients, inmates) have some influence in deciding either the behaviors to be focused upon or the events that will serve as rewards.

## APPLICATIONS

The Token Economy requires only specifying the behaviors to be changed, a medium of exchange (tokens) to be provided for these behaviors, and incentives for which the tokens can be exchanged. Hence, it is an extremely flexible technique. Indeed, this is evident in extensive research that has demonstrated the efficacy of token economies in altering diverse behaviors of psychiatric patients, the mentally retarded, children in institutional and educational settings, delinquents, and adult offenders. In addition, the Token Economy has been applied to alcoholics, drug addicts, geriatric residents, and other populations. Individualized token programs frequently are used on an out-patient bbasisto alter the behaviors of children and adults in everyday situations, such as the home or at school.

Although the token program has been effective in changing behavior in a plethora of well-controlled studies across different treatment populations, relatively few studies have compared the Token-Economy with alternative techniques. With a few exceptions, the available evidence has shown the Token Economy to be more effective in altering behavior than verbal psychotherapy, milieu therapy, and routine ward care with psychiatric patients; more effective than pharmacotherapy with hyperactive children and the mentally retarded, and more effective than routine educational practices in "normal" and special education classrooms.

An important issue in the application of Token Economy is the durability and transfer of behavior changes. Behavior changes achieved in token economies are not automatically maintained and do not usually transfer to settings outside of treatment after the program is discontinued. Specific procedures, such as gradually phasing out the program, need to be implemented after behavior change has been achieved to ensure enduring and widespread changes. Currently, research is focusing on techniques to sustain behavior changes when programs are withdrawn.

# Transactional Analysis

*Jon G. Allen*

## DEFINITION

The theory of "ego states" is the cornerstone of Transactional Analysis (TA). Ego states are coherent organizations of thought, feeling, and behavior that are classified into three categories: Parent, Adult, and Child. Parent ego states are internalizations of the parents' behavior in relation to the child, often subdivided into the "critical" (e.g., punishing) and the "nurturing" (e.g., protecting). Child ego states are residues of childhood that are reexperienced in later life, wherein the most intense feelings and need states are expressed. The Child ego states are typically subdivided into the "adapted" (i.e., under the influence of parents, whether compliant or rebellious) and the "natural" (i.e., autonomous from parental influence).

The Adult ego state is the objective data processor; it is attuned to external reality and mediates between the Parent and Child ego states. This theory of ego states highlights the parallel between internal conflict and interpersonal behavior and reflects their origin in family interaction patterns. For example, conflict between the adapted-compliant Child and the critical Parent may be manifested internally in guilt feelings, or interpersonally in ingratiating attempts to please authority figures; these in turn might be traced to the child's early response to an over-controlling parent.

TA assumes that interpersonal interactions are motivated by a need for "strokes" in the form of recognition and contact. On the basis of the intensity and quality of strokes involved, several types of interactions have been distinguished: withdrawal (e.g., isolation), rituals (i.e., stereotyped interactions, such as greeting rituals), activity (i.e., Adult-Adult transactions, such as cooperative work), pastimes (i.e., more extended transactions than rituals), rackets (i.e., attempts to elicit strokes for expressing feelings, such as crying to obtain sympathy), games (typically, defensive interactions with ulterior motives that yield intense, if negative, strokes), and intimacy (i.e., genuine, Child-Child relatedness). Patterns of time structure thus described reflect the person's "existential position," of which there are four major varieties: I'm OK— You're not OK (e.g., intimacy), I'm OK—You're OK (e.g., the TA game of "Now I've got you, you S.O.B."), I'm not OK—You're OK (e.g., the TA game of "Kick me!"), and I'm not OK—You're not OK (e.g., autistic withdrawal).

On the broadest level of analysis, TA employs the concept of "life script," that is a life plan formulated by the Child as a compromise accommodation to parental injunctions. The injunctions are typically restrictions on behavior that are conveyed repeatedly to the child through various nonverbal behaviors. For example, "Don't think for yourself!" might be communicated by overprotective nurturing, and the life script adaptation might be alcoholism. Oftentimes a defensive "counterscript" is organized to protect the person from acting out the script decision (e.g., compulsive overwork as a means of avoiding failure and dependency).

# HISTORY

Eric Berne (1920-1970) was a psychiatrist who parted with psychoanalytic tradition as he developed TA in the late 1950s. He was interested in lay education, and TA couches much traditional psychodynamic thinking in simple language that can be employed by therapists and patients alike. Thus, TA and psychoanalysis share much in common. The concept of ego state is itself psychoanalytic, and the Parent, Adult, and Child are parallel to the Superego, Ego, and Id. Further, both approaches assume that internal and interpersonal conflict have their origin in family dynamics, and both employ insight-oriented treatment. But TA also shares features with several other therapeutic approaches: for example, with humanistic schools, an emphasis on intimacy, spontaneity, and emotional experience, characteristic of the natural Child; with behavior therapy, an emphasis on behavior change and therapeutic contracts; and with Psychodrama and Gestalt, the techniques of role playing and portraying dreams and fantasies in action rather than words alone.

# TECHNIQUE

TA is a theory of personality, not a method of treatment, and the theory has been incorporated into relatively standard treatment modalities. TA is especially well suited to group psychotherapy (and marathon groups) because of its emphasis on the analysis of interpersonal transactions. In general, standard interventions are employed, such as confrontation, explanation, and interpretation. But somewhat unique to TA is the practice of teaching the theory to the patients; many attend workshops in TA theory as they begin treatment. Thus, much of the therapy is conducted in the language of the theory. Patients learn to understand and label their ego states as such, and they analyze their interactions with others in those terms. They learn to identify their games, rackets, existential positions, parental injunctions, script decisions, and so forth. These didactic aspects of TA place a high premium on the role of the Adult ego state as a means of self-regulation and change, but TA therapy is not necessarily a "cognitive" approach. In fact, there is great variation among TA therapists in their emphasis on thinking (e.g., analyzing), feeling (e.g., expressing Child emotion), and action (e.g., practicing new behavior). Indeed, the comprehensiveness and broad applicability of TA concepts allow for their integration into a wide range of therapeutic approaches and styles.

# APPLICATIONS

In light of its broad scope and direct appeal, TA has an extraordinarily wide range of applications (see the *Transactional Analysis Journal*). It has been applied to a great variety of clinical problems (e.g., sexual dysfunctions, alcoholism, drug addiction, child abuse, anorexia nervosa, exhibitionism, schizophrenia, and phobias). It has also found many nonclinical applications (e.g., parent counseling and organizational development consulting) and has been employed with a number of special populations (e.g., geriatric patients, prisoners, and the blind). Its popularity as an educational tool is reflected in the large number of workshops and courses given at various educational levels. The International Transactional Analysis Association has also set forth comprehensive standards for its practitioners. An especially effective training method is the supervision group, in which members are therapists in training who alternate roles as therapists and patients, with the leader supervising the treatment *in vivo*. This forum puts into practice the assumption that personal growth and the development of professional competence go hand in hand.

# Transactional Analysis Group Therapy
### Melvin Boyce

## DEFINITION

Most therapists using Transactional Analysis would agree with the words of Eric Berne, M.D., the founder of TA, who wrote in 1966:

"Group treatment is used ... to refer to the treatment of psychiatric patients [by] a trained psychotherapist or properly prepared trainee under supervision ... when the leader meets in a specified place for a specified period of time with a small number of (about 8) patients ... experimental groups, discussion groups, alternate meetings, multiple therapy, and group work are not TA group treatment." Group treatment, in Berne's mind, suggests a more active, directed, and conclusive process than does the term "therapy

## HISTORY

In 1945, while Consultant to the Surgeon General, Dr. Berne was asked to set up one of the earliest programs for group therapy on the West Coast, at Fort Ord, California, for soldiers, some with combat experience. Different from the group work and group therapy of the East Coast, as characterized by Slavson and others, Berne brought psychoanalytic processes to the group, and probably was doing one-on-one therapy in a group setting. By 1958, Berne had developed a distinctive kind of group treatment, complete with its own language: Parent, Adult, Child, Decisions, Position, Transactions, Games, and Scripts were and are terms invested with special meanings to express concepts about personality and behavior. By the time of Berne's death in 1970, the system had become a movement, with thousands of therapists being trained. However, individualism was the hallmark, rather than closely following a standard, as is the case with Freudian, Gestalt, or Jungian therapy. Many compatible group therapy procedures have been adopted by TA therapists. In fact, only a few negative treatment modalities are excluded. Heavy medication, electroshock treatment, and long-term therapy have low priority, abusive and degrading methods are avoided.

## TECHNIQUE

Most TA practitioners mix TA with more action-oriented techniques, so long as they coincide with TA principles. The client and therapist do and say whatever is beneficial; that is, whatever helps the client achieve the goal, or "fulfill his contract."

The therapist emphasizes the awareness of Parent-Adult-Child ego states, and urges the client to understand his own transactions with outside people through interaction with the therapist and group members. "Games" (transactions with hidden ulterior motives), "Scripts" (lifelong patterns), and early Childhood Decisions (conclusions arrived at under pressure) are explored and the client is asked to reset his focus on positive outcomes. Many techniques are found useful, such as regression to relive childhood traumas and/or revisit the time and place of early "Decisions" by the young child about himself and about life. Other techniques used are confrontation, role playing, psychodrama, social experiments, and consciously cathecting different ego states. The Self is identified and is seen as the characteristic expression of each Ego State.

The therapist is active, along with group members, and many summarize or clarify important points, make specific interventions, limit "story telling," and confront passivity, contradictions, or negative behavior.

## APPLICATIONS

With the development of the system, and the different perspectives of persons from a variety of backgrounds, TA has found ever-wider applications in mental health. Private therapists, workers in clinics and hospitals, and other institutions have quickly adapted TA to their settings. Quite often therapists will combine several approaches. New clients (patients) may be brought together in large groups to learn the principles of TA in a classroom, then are assigned to groups led by one therapist, or two. Individual therapy is sometimes made available as an adjunct, and most clients are expected to continue their work, or parenting, or education, as well. In residential programs, the therapeutic community meeting may be conducted TA style by staff and/or with outside therapists, with the rehabilitation program conducted along TA guidelines. Government agencies have sought out TA practitioners and consultants to some degree. Business has accepted the pragmatic procedures, largely based on the aware, self-motivating, positive outcome features. Churches have adapted the therapeutic, educational, and inspirational aspects of TA, feeling compatible with such TA authors as Harris, James, Jongeward, and Barnes.

By 1977, TA practitioners were active throughout the United States and in forty five other countries, often melding TA with gestalt process, bioenergetics, reality therapy, and rational-emotive procedures, as well as developing further theoretical concepts.

# Transactional-Semantic Psychotherapy
*Theodore Chemodurow*

## DEFINITION

Psychotherapy depends upon communication between the therapist and his patients, and the therapist's tools of trade are verbal and nonverbal language. Transactional-Semantic

Psychotherapy treats the individual in terms of his total communicative functioning. It is a dynamic technique the therapist can use to discover and reveal critical interactions quickly and objectively, which enables him to select and focus on overt interactions and on those crucial nonverbal, covert, subtle, disguised, or concealed influences that determine what is going on in a person and the reciprocal process between people. The therapist then can effectively correct specific areas of the patient's communicative process that prevent or interfere with his having meaningful interpersonal relationships.

Transactional semantics is concerned with the individual's thoughts, feelings, and behavior as they relate to reaction, interaction, and transaction through verbal and nonverbal language, and emphasizes the "transactional whole" of communication. It utilizes syntactics, semantics, pragmatics, general semantics, and incorporates the concept of "transaction in process," while recognizing the organized patterned communicative processes that surround and influence the individual.

Compared with other types of psychotherapy, psychiatric, and psychological treatment, Transactional-Semantic Psychotherapy greatly increases the psychiatrist's efficiency. In this writer's experience in private psychiatric office practice during the past several years, seven out of ten persons previously requiring hospitalization can now be treated on an out-patient basis, with treatment time shortened, and the cost reduced by about 50 percent for the individual and for couples with marital problems.

## HISTORY

The dynamics of communication and of the interactions between therapist and patient have been thought of in terms of isolated separate, independent elements. In 1968 this writer developed a unifying theory of human behavior and therapy entitled "Transactional Semantics," which clearly defines *how* the patient's development is influenced.

The goal of Transactional-Semantic Psychotherapy is to unify concepts of the influence that interact dynamically through verbal and nonverbal language with the individual, bringing them together into a single concept of the total transactional process. "Transaction" describes the continuing exchange of communications between individuals, groups, or other systems with continuous ongoing feedbacks, resulting in changes and developing patterns from the subsequent responses of each person or system. The emerging communicative pattern determines context and, in turn, influences meaning. A "system" is a process that influences the individual through its repetition of communicative pattern, composed of interrelated parts or "subsystems." At this point, the individual may be viewed as a "system in process of communicative transaction."

In studying human interactions through communication, general semantics correlates and integrates syntactics, semantics, and pragmatics into a unified whole, emphasizing the influence of language on thinking, social and individual behavior, and the influence of communication upon throughts, feelings, and actions of both the sender and the receiver.

Studies in kinesics indicate that body motion and linguistics are equally important infracommunicational systems. The linguistic, kinesic, and ethologic relationships, with each other and with comparable systems from other sensory modalities, make up the communication system and are interdependent functions of an integrated process. While language includes all of these part-processes, their relative importance, significance, and meaning vary. Context conveys meaning. This point becomes more obvious and understandable when the entire family and its process system of communication is studied as a unit, often revealing that a twitch, frown, or grunt controls all of the family members.

## TECHNIQUE

The therapist and his patient must "speak" the same language, conveying their thoughts and feelings to each other with the same words (signs, symbols), meaning the same to both. But in therapy, conveying the same mutual understanding of meanings is not enough. The therapist and patient must have the same convictions about their meanings.

In the process of formulating clear, precise thoughts, we use language. In communicating, our language conveys the contents of the thought processes, and formulates thoughts in the process of reflecting objective reality through subjective cognition and the social communication of one's thoughts about reality, attended by his subjective related feelings, actions, connotations, and meanings from experiences within a particular (family-social-cultural-economic) context.

This definition of language emphasizes the connection between language and thinking, the functions of language in the process of reflecting objective reality in the external material world (extra psychic) and the world of man's intrapsychic experiences. Language also serves a communicative function in the sense of a social transmission of results from the cognitive process and the person's subjective thoughts, feelings, actions, experiences. In the intrapsychic sense, language gives one the ability to conceptualize, think, predict, plan ahead, and communicate, which is fundamental to learning and to the structuring of personality.

Language and communication transmit the influence of dynamic events of various patterned systems processes in transaction with one another, reflecting the objective reality of extrapsychic events through subjective cognition and the intrapsychic. The ego functions as a final common pathway into and out of the person, with language as the dynamic relating and integrating force between the intrapsychic and extrapsychic.

"Semantic positioning" describes all of the transactional communicative forces that set up and control the behavior of the individual and family group, including all the verbal and nonverbal forces that are consciously or unconsciously applied within a family to determine each member's reactive behavior. Characteristic and specific interactional patterns for semantic positioning emerge from these operating forces as they structure the framework and boundaries within which the individual operates and develops.

To institute and maintain family unity and solidarity, the dynamic vectors of the family communicative system train, mold, station, and maintain each of its members in a designated position within the system. An individual's relegated position within the family's interlocking pattern decides his status, dominance, and his control by other members. Often, the most powerful determinants are nonverbal (facial expressions, tones of speech, gestures, groans, hesitations, silences). These communicative forces govern what each individual member of the family actually feels, thinks, and does.

The interpersonal relationships of a family often set up a system of communicative patterns that determine the future behavior of the individual. Throughout his life span, a person may tend to seek out only those he might train in the reactive responses that allow him to function within a framework of communicative patterns stemming from his semantic positioning during infancy and childhood. This search for familiarity may govern him in selecting a mate, friends, and associates in later life. Characteristic interactional patterns of communication set the individual patient apart and constitute *diagnostic categories* for various types of psychiatric disorders.

## APPLICATIONS

The art of psychotherapy is governed by the therapist's personality, orientation, and communicative competency (whether verbal or nonverbal, active or passive). The therapist should be aware of what he is, what he is doing, and what is actually going on in the therapeutic situation, rather than using an intuitive approach or to unknowingly influence by chance. His influence upon the patient must follow a logical and planned course of treatment. To manage, control, and direct the therapeutic process, the therapist should be trained to be aware of all the critical transactional-semantic interchanges during treatment.

The focus of the therapeutic effort in individual therapy is on developing the communicative process between therapist and patient. In therapy with married couples, the focus includes both partners as well as the therapist. In treating a multiperson system or family, the focal point is on interlocking and interactional patterns of communication within the family system as well as with the therapist. In each of these different situations, focus must also include each patient's communications with his system of relationships, recognizing the interplay, feedbacks, and resulting effects each has with the other. Understanding the total complex of these various and continuous transactional, interrelated communicative system processes constitutes transactional semantics.

An accurate appraisal of the nature and quality of this transactional-semantic system and its technical mastery is necessary to achieve therapeutic progress. The psychiatric patient's intrapsychic communication and his communication with others are impaired. The therapist, too, may have problems with his communication and be unaware of some of his own nonverbal messages. His own conscious and unconscious attitudes and values are conveyed to the patient (even if he consistently tries to hide them), as well as his overt intentions, nonverbal intentions, and his reactions to the patient's reaction to him. The spoken word is only a part-process in the extremely complicated reciprocal patient-therapist relationship. The context and nonverbal language is of equal or even greater importance.

The therapist is much more involved in the therapeutic process than previously recognized, especially with his nonverbal communications. To achieve his maximum effectiveness in Transactional-Semantic Psychotherapy, the therapist must understand and become more aware of his own personality and communicative process, making them essential, therapeutic tools—selectively, consciously, and deliberately applied. The transactional communicative processes between patient and therapist should be a conscious target for improvement, instead of being overlooked or merely incidental.

All forms of psychologic treatment are shortened when the therapist recognizes crippled communications and directly improves and corrects them consciously and specifically. Transactional semantics can be utilized for intensive short-term therapy-

# Transcendental Meditation

*Harold H. Bloomfield*

### DEFINITION

Transcendental Meditation (TM) is a simple, natural, mental technique that produces deep rest on the level of the body and clarity on the level of the mind. The TM program is particularly suited to active people who want the benefit of medication without adopting a new life-style. It is neither a religion nor a philosophy and requires no lengthy course of study, intellectual capacity, or any special powers of concentration. TM is taught in every major American city at centers associated with the TM World Plan Executive Council, a nonprofit educational organization.

### HISTORY

Maharishi Mahesh Yogi, the exponent of TM in its modern form, first introduced it to the United States in 1959, and since then over a million people have begun the practice.

Until Maharishi began teaching the TM technique in the West, people were skeptical of claims that the practice of meditation could result in increased energy, clarity of thinking, emotional stability, greater health, and decreased drug abuse. But since an article appeared in 1970 in *Science*, "Physiological Effects of Transcendental Meditation," a convincing body of physiological, psychological, and sociological data from research centers around the world indicate that the TM program does indeed produce profoundly beneficial changes.

More than just a technique of relaxation, the TM program has as its goal systematically unfolding the state of enlightenment, full human potential. Historically, the hallmark of the TM program is the synthesis of age-old knowledge from the Indian Vedas—one of the oldest traditions of knowledge in the world—and modern scientific technology, in order to explore the furthest reaches of human consciousness.

### TECHNIQUE

TM spontaneously and effortlessly takes its practitioners beyond the familiar level of their wakeful experience to a state of restful alertness. The TM technique can be learned in a few hours and is then practiced for only fifteen to twenty minutes each morning and evening. The technique is a specific method of allowing the activity of the mind to settle down, while one sits comfortably with eyes closed. This mental process triggers a physiological response conducive to both deep rest and increased wakefulness.

TM students have a mantra (sound which has no meaning but whose effects are known) specifically chosen for them. Thinking the mantra is effortless, as it uses the natural tendency of the mind, and involves no concentration. Because learning to meditate does not necessitate cultivating a new skill, but instead simply involves allowing an innate ability of the nervous system to unfold, it requires no particular attitude, preparatory ritual, special setting, or unusual postures. Though the technique is usually practiced at home, it may be done in any place where a person can sit comfortably without being disturbed. Many busy individuals meditate on planes, trains, subways, buses, or in waiting rooms.

Though sense impressions, feelings, or thoughts may be present during TM, meditators report brief or sometimes extended periods of "pure awareness, transcending," "being awake inside with nothing going on," "not being asleep, but not being aware of anything in particular." Our daily experience is made up of an unending cascade of thoughts, emotions, sensations, and perceptions. TM creates an opportunity for two brief daily periods of effortless disengagement from these continuous impressions. The result is a very efficient, self-generated "psychological housecleaning," which leaves the individual feeling refreshed and renewed.

## APPLICATIONS

In the current edition of the *Comprehensive Textbook of Psychiatry*, Dr. Louis J. West, chairman of the UCLA department of psychiatry, has suggested that TM may be the best of the nonprofessional psychotherapies. Since maladaptive anxiety is the common denominator of almost all mental illness and since TM has been shown to reduce anxiety, there has been increasing interest in the psychiatric community as to whether TM may be useful in the treatment of a wide range of diagnostic categories. Numerous reports indicate that clinicians are finding TM valuable as an adjunct to the treatment of anxiety neurosis, obsessive-complusive symptoms, chronic low-grade depression, identity crisis, psychosomatic illness, and even some psychotic disturbances.

A major positive effect of TM seems to be the increase in self-reliance. Unlike medication or psychotherapy, TM is exclusively under the control of the patient. If he feels better, the result is due not to a pill or his relationship with a therapist but to a natural process under his own control. Drugs may help the patient feel less anxious but may make him feel listless and groggy, and may become addictive. TM has no adverse side effects and can promote what pills cannot—natural psychological growth.

Drug abuse also appears to improve with the TM program. A study of nearly two-thousand meditators showed a drastic reduction in their use of marijuana, narcotics, and other illicit drugs. And in a controlled study published in January 1974 in the *American Journal of Psychiatry*, Mohammed Shafii, Associate Professor of Psychiatry, University of Louisville Medical Center, showed that the longer one practices TM, the sharper the decline in marijuana use.

Many other studies confirm the greater psychological health of persons as a result of TM practice. For instance, a study by William Seeman, Sanford Nidich, and Thomas Banta at the University of Cincinnati found that a meditator's sense of innerdirectedness increases, as does his ability to express feelings in a spontaneous manner, his acceptance of aggression, and his capacity for intimate contact.

The most significant contribution that TM might make to the health field is in the area of primary prevention. To avoid illness altogether and to allow each individual to unfold his full potential has always been the highest goal for those concerned with human welfare. If systematic research continues to substantiate the preliminary findings, the TM program has a good chance of becoming a significant adjunct to psychotherapy and medical care.

# Transference-Focused Therapy
## Joseph Rechetnick

### DEFINITION

Transference-Focused Therapy is used in this article to refer to the treatment of acutely disturbed patients in an in-patient service. The methodological issue confronting the clinician in the acute treatment service is how to appropriately utilize transference phenomena so that effective, brief, analytically oriented treatment can be accomplished.

Transference here is defined as the displacement of patterns of feelings and behavior, originally experienced with significant figures of one's childhood, to individuals in one's current relationships. This is an unconscious process that brings about a repetition, not consciously perceived, of attitudes, fantasies, and emotions (of love, hate, anger, etc.) under many different circumstances. The parents are usually the original figures from whom such patterns are displaced, but in many instances siblings, grandparents, childhood teachers, and doctors may be contributing figures. In the treatment of exacerbated psychotic symptoms, it is important to distinguish, with Glover (1958), between the transference manifestation which, in spillover fashion, confronts the clinician during the first few sessions, from transference neuroses or psychoses (Searles, 1965), which develop as a consequence of long-term analytic treatment. The judicious use of early transference manifestation constitutes the important technical problem I (Joseph Rechetnick) will discuss here.

### HISTORY

A number of people have made significant contributions to the treatment of psychotic patients by means of psychotherapeutic interventions. Among them, Brody (1952) makes the point that in establishing contact with schizophrenic patients, the therapeutic activity should be directed at clarifying the central issues through interpretation, giving the patient ego support, and making "therapeutic utilization of the transference situation." Freda Fromm-Reichmann (1952) stresses the fact that an intensively charged relationship can be established between the schizophrenic patient and the therapist. This general notion of the healing properties of a positively charged transference experience has been stressed by Sechehaye, Jacob-son, and Winnicott. Arlow and Brenner (1964) stress an additional element, which has contributed great measure to the therapeutic approach to schizophrenia. They state that by interpreting defenses, we approach more directly what is upsetting the patient, namely, anxiety.

## TECHNIQUE

The approach to the patient is to utilize the transference and attempt limited insight-oriented psychotherapy in treating short-term patients. In so doing, an attempt is made to focus on one or two critical themes and not to try a more comprehensive psychotherapy. Using this technique it is necessary to identify critical themes rapidly with each patient. These themes include repressed and suppressed hostility, excessive dependency, symbiotic relationships, etc. The treatment strategy is to select aspects of transference manifestations that maximize the insight into the acute exacerbation of symptoms, with which the patient comes to the hospital, and to utilize the selection theme to effect a more integrated consolidation of the patient's resources. Many disturbed patients are ready to relate to a person they consider a special figure as soon as they are admitted to the hospital. This attitude is used by the therapist to help patients in a constructive direction. In addition to fostering the development of the transference, the therapist should interpret the nature of the transference to the patient in the course of treatment. It should also be mentioned that the greater the empathic ability of the therapist, the more likely he will be able to establish a strong transference. The transference with such patients is utilized to enable them to look at internal conflicts, to become aware of their problems, and to encourage the patients to make changes in behavior, attitudes, and so on.

## APPLICATIONS

This article is based on the treatment of patients in an open ward of a general hospital. In each case, an early development of transference was fostered and the transference manifestation was utilized to interpret anxiety and defenses against anxiety by the patient. The following is a brief description of a patient who was so treated.

The patient was a thirty-year-old married student with two children. He had a psychotic episode in a foreign country where he was attending school. Immediately after this episode, he returned to the United States and was hospitalized at this hospital. He had delusions of persecution involving one of his professors with whom he was disappointed because this professor had demanded payment from the patient in order to help him pass his courses. He became enraged at his professor, whom he initially saw as a giving and affectionate father. In this rage, he developed a belief that the professor was pumping gases into his apartment. Evidently this belief reflected his guilt over his anger and hostility toward his previous idol. Throughout his life, he had sought a fatherly, positive relationship with various men in his life. Yet he would become furious if these protective relationships were withdrawn and he was dealt with in a man-to-man way. While he was a student in the United States, the patient had a personal relationship with a college teacher whom he would ask for advice on personal problems. In his own family, he had a passive, "nonexistent" father and a dominating, controlling mother.

In the brief three-week treatment program covering seven sessions, three distinct phases of intervention, while overlapping, could be delineated. (Although these phases are essential constituents of Transference-Focused Therapy, they do not necessarily occur in the following sequence.) The first dealt with the interpretation of the panic underlying a disappointing "parental" experience. His need for a father figure who would be affectionate and giving was explained to the patient, as well as his disappointment and rage when this need was frustrated (as he experienced with the professor's demand for payment). This theme was selected for interpretation not only for its central position in the patient's pathology but also in view of its potential use for transference interpretation.

A second phase was the evocation of a positive transference. The therapist seemed to take the place of the patient's former college teacher and elicited the same feelings of protection that the patient wanted to get from his foreign professor. The issue of timing is critical here. Without waiting for the patient to make an explicit connection between his expectations of his professor and of the therapist, this connection is made for him. He developed confidence in the therapist whom he saw as a nonthreatening, nonpunitive person who did not deny his paranoid delusions as his family did.

The third step involved the utilization of this transference experience in the decision-making process revolving around disposition. The patient requested the therapist to see him privately and was disappointed when this could not be done. The therapist showed him that this disappointment could lead to anger and hostility toward him; this would result in a negative attitude toward the therapist and to the same type of situation as when the patient attributed to his professor harmful intentions toward him. He regularly saw men as either treating him like a giving father or wanting to harm him. This ambivalence manifested itself when the therapist referred him to someone else for private treatment. After this conflict was explained to him, the patient was able to accept this referral without feeling that the therapist was rejecting him or meant him harm. In this phase of treatment, the transference experience was utilized to help the patient accept a referral to another therapist. This decision could be made in the context of a weakening in the delusional system that made it clinically possible and desirable for the patient to embark on an out-patient treatment program.

# Transpersonal Psychotherapy

*James Fadiman and Kathleen Speeth*

## DEFINITION

The *Journal of Transpersonal Psychology* defines the domain of transpersonal psychology as "meta-needs, transpersonal process, values and states, unitive consciousness, peak experiences, ecstasy, mystical experience, being, essence, bliss, awe, wonder, transcendence of self, spirit, sacralization of everyday life, oneness, cosmic awareness, cosmic play, individual and species-wide synergy, the theories and practices of meditation, spiritual paths, compassion, transpersonal cooperation, transpersonal realization and actualization, and related concepts, experiences and activities."

Those who practice psychotherapy within this general context are transpersonal psychotherapists. Transpersonal Psychotherapy includes the treatment of the full range of behavioral, emotional, and intellectual disorders as in traditional psycho-therapies. It also includes uncovering and supporting strivings for full self-actualization. The end state of psychotherapy is not seen as the successful adjustment to the prevailing culture but rather the daily experience of that state called liberation, enlightenment, individuations, certainty or gnosis according to various traditions.

## HISTORY

Transpersonal Psychotherapy can be said to have evolved, in the broadest sense, as the inner or esoteric teachings of all the great spiritual traditions. Within psychology, the major transpersonal thinkers include William James, who first systematically explored states of healthy and higher consciousness; Carl Jung, who conceived of psychotherapy as building a bridge between the real self and the personality, and Roberto Assagioli, who translated Eastern practices into workable psychotherapeutic tools.

The influx into the Western world of Eastern wisdom, in the traditions of Zen Buddhism, Tibetan Buddhism, Yoga, and Sufism—through individuals like Aldous Huxley, Alan Watts, and Ram Dass, and through the universities and growth centers affected by the "human potential movement"—has had the general effect of enlarging the scope of psychotherapeutic practices and goals toward the realm of the transpersonal.

Another major force has been research into voluntary control of internal states from Western biofeedback laboratories, which has shed new light on ancient yogic accomplishments and on the possibilities of the human mind and body. In addition, the work on altered states of consciousness developed most extensively by psychedelic researchers has influenced the thinking of psychologists to include the transpersonal domain.

Growing public understanding and acceptance of paranormal phenomena both reflects the trend in psychology toward the transpersonal and furthers it.

## TECHNIQUE

Transpersonal Psychotherapy can be conducted individually or in groups, may be brief or long term, and may, in some cases, not even be called psychotherapy. It may be characterized as a human interaction aimed toward the goals or end states given above, a Western sadhana of self-knowledge replacing or augmenting traditional religious forms. It leads past (or through) the personality to the realization described in the religious traditions. It is not limited to nor defined by any specific techniques.

## APPLICATIONS

Transpersonal Psychotherapy is indicated where behavioral therapies are least likely to be helpful, where the problems are not encapsulated symptoms, and where the issues include questions of personal values, the meaning of one's life, and the desire for more than average adjustment. A sizable proportion of clients are functioning well in work and love and are striving for more inclusive world view and a clearer idea of their own orientation.

Transpersonal Psychotherapy with psychotics has been done by Laing, Silverman, and Perry, each of whom provided an environment free of stigma, restraint, and drugs, where individuals could reintegrate themselves with the support of those who saw their condition as an opportunity for higher understanding rather than shame.

Recent developments include Grof's work with the terminally ill, as well as the restructuring of business and therapeutic environments along lines first suggested by Abraham Maslow's *Eupsychian Management.*

# Triad Therapy
## Charles W. Slack and Eileen N. Slack

### DEFINITION

Triad Therapy involves three active social roles in treatment. The triad consists of: those who personify the problem, who have it now—(called P); those who personify the absence of the problem, who never had it or had it so long ago that it doesn't matter—(called N; and those who personify the solution to the problem, used to have it but now do not—(called EX).

Ns are often members of some helping profession, but not always so, and there is no absolute reason why professionals cannot play other roles in the triad, that is, either have the problem or be EXs.

When social roles are defined as P, N, and EX in terms of the principal therapeutic problems, then most traditional psychotherapies are readily seen to be dyadic: P and N are in communication but EX is missing. Struggling self-help groups may represent P and EX with an insufficient strength in N.

Well-balanced triads, professional and amateur, have two therapist roles (EX and N) that can disagree as regards P (and other important issues). Such disagreement is not felt to constitute a disadvantage, i.e., N may strongly feel that P should apply more willpower, whereas EX holds the opposite view that willpower isn't necessary. The resulting impact of these seemingly contradictory philosophies, however, is to focus on change and to convince P that change both should and will come.

### HISTORY

Although the entire mental hygiene movement was launched, single-handedly, by an ex-mental patient,[7*] the role of EX began to lose status and influence through the ramifications of professionalism that followed. The history of successful self-help groups such as Alcoholics Anonymous can profitably be studied in terms of triads that contain a few understanding professionals playing the key N role. Other professionals have at times attacked fledgling amateur efforts, forcing them to turn to more understanding segments of the community that offer N support.

---

7*Clifford W. Beers, founder (1909) of the National Committee for Mental Hygiene and (1928) of the American Foundation for Mental Hygiene. Author of *A Mind That Found Itself.*

The earliest implication of three-role theory of rehabilitation is contained in the "law of retroflexive reformation" of Cressey (1955), which states: When criminal A joins with noncriminals to rehabilitate criminal B it is A who is rehabilitated the most. This formulation has become fundamental to systematic understanding of self-help of all kinds but fails to provide equal insight into the primary question as to whether "criminal B" gets rehabilitated at all.

In 1960, Slack published a study that involved paying the patient and reversing the usual client-counselor roles. Dramatic success in cooperation and identification with the therapist (employer) was achieved with otherwise unreachable cases. In 1972, Triad Theory was formulated as a general theory and as a method of therapy and rehabilitation (Slack, 1972), and in 1976, it was documented as a method for "turning around" an Alabama reform school (Slack, 1976).

## TECHNIQUE

Triad Theory can be used to correct weaknesses in existing groups or to construct new groups. In either case, persons representing all three roles must convene regularly. To convert a traditional P-N dyadic therapy group into a triad, the therapist must add several individuals who, in his opinion, have achieved personal solutions to the basic problems of the group. These EXs can then restate and delineate the problems using their own backgrounds as examples; they can act as role models to personify the desired change in Ps, and can suggest techniques and solutions based on firsthand experience. Note that none of these functions can be served by the therapist as N. His role, a vital one, is to support EXs to prevent backsliding and to maintain focus on the presenting personal problem. N must also help maintain a supply of Ps. Without N, EX and P might never get together: N is often the social engineer of the encounter. N should also work to encourage access to the prerequisites of his own role by EXs, since shift from EX to N motivates P to EX. For example, wise drug-rehabilitation programs (as in Daytop Village, for example) will routinely give the ex-addict many management privileges and responsibilities that would otherwise be reserved for nonaddict professionals and other hired staff. Shared authority provides a powerful incentive for the newly admitted, not-yet-ex-addict to stay drug-free during the difficult early period (Slack, 1974).

Method and technique depend on role: EX can do and say many things to P that N wouldn't think of saying. After all, EX has "been there" and knows, firsthand, what P is going through. Yet, without N to provide affirmation and support for EX, P may conveniently fail to see any advantage in EXs role over his own. It sometimes seems to N that EX need not worry about technique at all but just has to be true to himself to succeed. On the other hand, EX may feel the need to improve N's therapy technique, i.e., instruct N on how not to be taken in by Ps rationalizations.

One decided advantage of Triad Therapy is that each role has one other to turn to for advice on how to deal with the third. The "therapist" has a "supervisor" and the "patient" an advocate. These checks and balances improve the performance of all members. Dyadic instruction (such as this essay) is not as effective in developing therapy technique.

Personal problems are often misunderstood by those who have never lived through them. The same holds for states of being, such as "poverty" and "delinquency." Unchangeable conditions, such as blindness, chronic illness, or mental handicap, may seem to be personal problems to outsiders, but insiders know that these are givens not problems. If one labels one's own brain damage as "a problem," then one is likely to look for solutions to it. If, on the other hand, one accepts the damage, one can move on to find solutions to the real problems that are the consequence of the damage—problems that other brain-injured persons have solved in their own lives.

Likewise, being too short or too tall, being foreign born, having a high I.Q., having an alcoholic father, being a homosexual, having a physical handicap, being an orphan, or becoming bald are not, strictly speaking, "problem roles" for triads since, defined this way, few if any persons can be found who "used to have the problem and now do not." However, such states of being as homosexuality or belonging to a discriminated minority are excellent reasons for banding together in triads to deal with problems caused by the unchangeable state of being. Many of these *resulting problems* have excellent solutions personified by persons in the respective states. Thus, homosexuality is not itself a problem because there are no EXs, but alienation, haughtiness, and shame are problems from which many homosexuals have totally recovered.

As triadic organizations mature, more and more EXs move into the N role, getting totally away from the personal problems and stigmas of the problem role. Being an N, then, is not the same thing as the literal fact of never having had the problem. The role of N encompasses those who, to the extent to which it is possible, are indistinguishable from those who never had the problem. Perhaps these recovered Ns are better off (i.e., more self-actualized) than those who never had the problem. Mature self-help groups need not recruit outsiders for the key N role but can fill it from their own ranks.

What causes therapeutic change within the triad? Is it due to imitation, to the rewarding of behaviors or the development of trust and understanding? As outsiders, we would rather not say. In triads, persons are entitled to explain what is happening in their own terms, whereas "objective" explanations might not fit particular internal happenings.

Like dyads, triads must be free to choose their own theories and to organize themselves for any reason whatsoever. Professionals must try not to "control" triads. Free speech and assembly are required. That speech may be very free and assembly very frequent does not mitigate the rights involved.

## APPLICATIONS

Because it organizes groups to solve problems, Triad Therapy has the opportunity to improve the larger social microcosm as well as enable the individual to change his role.

Triad methods were employed at a teen-age reformatory in Alabama where they enabled the elimination of a notorious "detention" facility and the misuse of solitary confinement on a mass basis (Slack, 1976). Currently the methods are being applied at a community treatment program for delinquent boys in Melbourne and at a Victorian Youth Training Center for girls, both in Australia. Also, plans are under way for application in an adult correctional institution in New York.

# Vector Therapy

*John G. Howells*

## DEFINITION

A vector denotes a quantity that has direction. Force, including emotional force, is a quantity with direction and therefore can be represented by a vector.

Vector Therapy is a readjustment of the pattern of the emotional forces within the life space (environment) to bring improvement to the individual or family within the life space.

Vector Therapy is supported as a procedure by the observation that neurosis often spontaneously dissolves without psychotherapeutic intervention. Investigation revealed that this was due to a spontaneous readjustment of a field of forces to the advantage of the individual or the family. Vector Therapy seeks to *direct* a resolution by a skilled assessment of the forces, and by realigning these forces to the benefit of the individual or the family. Creativity through evolution is essentially a repatterning of phenomena in such a way as to allow a more harmonious patterning of the phenomena. Vector Therapy also relies upon our capacity to reshape patterns of forces, but in a systematic, directed fashion.

Psychotherapy means treatment employing psychic or emotional influences, and thus Vector Therapy is a psychotherapeutic procedure. But the beneficial psychic influences operate outside the interview; the interview is employed to assess and guide the psychotherapy in progress outside the family.

## HISTORY

My (John G. Howells) twenty-five years of work with families at the Institute of Family Psychiatry, Ipswich, England, has brought to light cases in which the morbid process of neurosis was resolved or improved by extra-interview procedures complementary to, or divorced from, interview psychotherapy. Clinical work and research supported the hypothesis that therapeutic factors were at work outside the psychotherapeutic interview and efforts were made to identify these factors. Careful assessment supported the belief that the most significant pattern of forces is that within the family, although occasionally the pattern outside the family may also be powerful. It followed that when these forces were producing psychopathol-ogy, changing them would remove or attenuate the trauma. More emphasis was placed on the therapist's capacity for reshaping the pattern of forces in the life space of an individual or a family in a systematic and purposeful fashion. Having arrived at a rational theory of Vector Therapy, its application in a systematic fashion developed into a useful and economical technique.

## TECHNIQUE

Faced with a disintegrated individual, reintegration is possible by mobilizing a set of influences in the present that may still nullify the effects of the previous adverse influence. This can be done (1) by the mobilization of intense, precise, beneficial emotional influences in the interview situation, under the direct control of a therapist, i.e., by interview psychotherapy; or (2) by mobilizing less intense emotional influences of a general nature known to be beneficial over a long period of time outside the interview, i.e., by Vector Therapy. Thus, for example, a child disintegrated by being deprived of the right kind of care is, instead of being subjected to psychotherapy, placed in a foster home selected for its ability to provide the right care. Reintegration comes from a new set of beneficial vectors able to act over a long period of time.

Vector Therapy can involve:

1. A change in the magnitude of the emotional force, e.g., father's aggression may be diminished.

2. A change in the direction of the emotional forces with no change in its magnitude, e.g., a father abuses the mother instead of the child.

3. A change in the length of time during which the emotional force operates, e.g., father works away from home, spends less time at home and his aggression has less duration.

4. A change in the quality of the emotional force when one force replaces another, e.g., father is kind to his son instead of being aggressive.

## APPLICATIONS

The essential steps in application are:

1. Family diagnosis through family group interviews

2. To use family group diagnosis to clarify the pattern of forces at work in that family

3. To bring understanding of its set of forces to the family

4. To move the family to accomplishing a change in its adverse set of forces through a supportive relationship

5. To put the family in touch with community agencies that can help facilitate the change

6. To create community agencies geared to effect changes in family psychic patterns.

Vector Therapy can be used when there are few or no facilities for psychotherapy in the usual interview setting. This situation is common in many countries. Vector Therapy is effective when interview psychotherapy is unlikely to be effective, e.g., with a hard-core or problem family, or when the situation demands an urgent solution, as, for example, when a child at risk in his own home cannot wait for interview psychotherapy to change his mother's attitude and needs to be removed without delay to a safer milieu. Again, quicker results can be obtained by combining Vector Therapy and interview psychotherapy.

# Videotherapy

## H. C. Tien

### DEFINITION

Videotherapy is the practice of psychotherapy with television techniques as an integral process of videology. A videologist, like a radiologist, is a physician who uses technology (video) extensively in diagnosing, treating, and preventing diseases. Videology is the science and art of using medical television for the evaluation and diagnosis of diseases, for the treatment and prevention of disorders and for the education and promotion of physical and mental health. A videotherapist may be a videologist or any qualified member of the mental health profession who uses videotechniques.

### HISTORY

On June 27, 1923, John Baird published the following notice (which no one answered) in the London *Times:*

*Seeing by wireless-inventor of apparatus to hear from someone who will assist (not financially) in making a model.*

Since that day, television technology has advanced by leaps and bounds and has been spreading to the private practice of psychiatry, to the teaching of medicine in medical schools, and to the medical centers throughout the country. Because of the capacity for immediate feedback of the video image, Videotherapy naturally began with confrontation psychotherapy as used by Berger (1965), Alger (1967), and other pioneers (Berger, 1970), echoing the spirit of the Scottish poet Robert Burns:

O wad some Power the giftie gie us
To see oursels as ithers see us!

In 1969, this writer (H.D. Tien, 1970) presented the first unified theory of Videotherapy at the International Congress of Cybernetics, London, England. I formulated a scientific model, the TV-Cybernetic System of Psychotherapy, for the practice of Videotherapy. Berger (1970) edited the first book on videotechniques in 1970. The rapid advancement of Videotherapy culminated in the publication of the *American Journal of Videotherapy* and the founding of the American Society of Videotherapy in 1977.

### TECHNIQUE

In Videotherapy, the psychocybernetic techniques may be used in individual, marital, family, or group therapy. Regardless of any specific type of Videotherapy, the techniques are based on the PERF model. The PERF model (an acronym for *Program—*

*E*rase—*R*eprogram—*F*eedback) is a psychotherapeutic guide for communication and personality development. Theoretically, the PERF model can be represented as follows:

$$E_i\,(E_s) \rightarrow E_o$$

$E_i$ = input of the video image, $E_s$ = stored video image on magnetic pattern; $E_o$ = output of video image on the TV monitor.

In 1961 Wiener said: "There is therefore nothing surprising in considering the functional mental disorders as fundamentally diseases of memory, of the circulating information kept by the brain in the active state." A practicing videologist should take special interest in this remark, that functional mental disorders, psychosomatic diseases, neuroses, and psychoses are due to distorted information that may be analyzed, edited, reprogrammed, and fed back to the patient for his personality correction and development. The technique of the PERF model also extends duplicating the video image of the therapist on television so as to maximize the therapeutic contacts with individuals, couples, families, and also members of the community.

In 1972 I extended the techniques of the PERF model to the techniques of the POPF model. The techniques of the POPF model (an acronym for *P*rofessional contact—*O*n (television)—*P*rofessional contact—*F*eedback) emphasizes the duplication of the therapist on television. The POPF model led to a new generation of videotechniques, namely, the telefusion techniques, which can be classified into three types:

*1. Primary telefusion technique.* The therapist and the patient are simultaneously videotaped in two different rooms, and are also videolinked with immediate feedback through television. This, of course, enhances the privacy of the patients (for example, especially for couch therapy or marital therapy). The primary telefusion technique creates a master videotape, which the videologist can use with other patients, in making video-synthesis available on a mass scale through the ordinary telefusion technique.

*2. Ordinary telefusion technique.* Here the therapist has an opportunity to offer therapy on videotape with both his personal contact at the beginning and at the end of each session according to the POPF model. At the end of the ordinary telefusion session, the videologist reappears to deal with any immediate and medical problems. The routine information and therapeutic instructions may be systematically and clearly transferred to the proper patient efficiently and effectively, according to his diagnosis and medical needs, via the master videotapes.

*3. Booster telefusion technique.* This is similar to the ordinary telefusion technique except there is a delayed feedback. For example, the family physician could write a prescription of four weekly sessions for a patient on diet therapy. The patient will see the doctor on television alone for such a series and then at the end of one month, the physician would discuss the course of diet and nutrition. The power of booster telefusion technique becomes evident when time, cost, and continuity become important factors of therapy.

The key to the telefusion techniques is the master tape. It is clear that the master tape with the image of the therapist (on video) induces transference, positive or negative, and overcomes or mobilizes resistances for later primary therapeutic work (in person) of individual sessions. Two or three telefusion sessions, either ordinary or booster, can intensify and supplement one weekly primary psychotherapeutic session at 50 percent or less of the cost. Apart from the obvious benefits of economy and time (which are necessary but not sufficient conditions for the success of any type of psychotherapy), Video-therapy augments the theoretical underpinnings of psychoanalysis based on the patient's *free association with the free communication* of the therapist. The master tape technique completes the feedback loop of the patient's random output (free association) with the therapist's random input (free communication) for the individual to reorganize his own thoughts, feelings, and images with the two streams of information—his own and the therapist—to merge in his mind as one to develop a higher consciousness of behavioral alternatives and personality development.

Telefusion techniques are effective not only in family psychiatry, but, in fact, any family physician can apply the same POPF model to the general practice of medicine.

## APPLICATIONS

The following clinical situations will serve as excellent examples of the application of Videotherapy:

1. Medical histories can be standardized and effectively applied with the use of videotechniques. Videotaped histories, of course, have high medico-legal value.

2. Initial visits to the physician can be easily recorded for progress and follow-up.

3. Videotechniques can be used for initial family history or mental status examination that can be saved for accurate reference as occasions require in objective documentation.

4. A physician can instruct patients personally, through his own video image, in order to offer his special therapeutic programs or instructions. For example, a physician on video can tirelessly and carefully explain the same procedures regarding diets, contraceptive techniques, etc.

5. Video programs that are pretaped *by the physician himself* tend to be more persuasive in the instructions of his patients.

6. The use of videotapes can resolve time conflicts in scheduling of appointments or family conferences, such as medical diagnostic review that can later be shown to the absent family member.

7. Videotechniques can be used for preoperative demonstration before the patient is hospitalized, in order to prepare the patient physically and psychologically for the procedure.

8. Video programs can offer either preoperative instructions or post operative exercises, so that the patient can be active in his own recovery, for example, in physiotherapy.

9. The use of videotechniques to record informed consent and to satisfy medicolegal requirements should be obvious to any practicing physician.

10. The patient's videotape serves as a part of his medical record, like his written history and physical examination, laboratory and X-ray reports, and are protected by the same professional confidentiality in the traditional doctor-patient relationship.

The above list is only a brief introduction to the various applications of Videotherapy and videotechniques as they can be applied to the practice of medicine, psychiatry, and psychotherapy.

# Vita-Erg Therapy

## S. R. Slavson

### DEFINITION

The basic psychotic process consists of the withdrawal from reality and the creation instead of hallucinatory distortion of actuality as well as adopting illusory defenses. Most often these defenses are mobilized against incestuous urges fed by unwise or pathogenic parents with which the ego of the potentially psychotic patient cannot deal and against murderous hostility toward parents, especially the mother and other persons as substitutes for them. The resulting states are either perpetual fear and overwhelming anxiety, which render the patient periodically frightened and submissive, or rage.

Ideally, the therapeutic requirements of such patients are 1) restitutive and rehabilitating efforts in the life setting of the patients, 2) appropriate chemotherapy reversing psychic energies from inward (centripetal) flow to outward (centrifugal) flow, and 3) increasing the patients' capacities (and tolerance) for human relationships, which are at a low ebb and often nonexistent. The general nature of therapy for patients on the mental hospital wards must be of a type that would *activate* them to respond to external stimuli, for *self-initiated* activities and responsibilities which they would voluntarily choose. Of equal or perhaps greater importance is their relationship with the professional staff and particularly with the "attendants" with whom patients have the most prolonged relationships.

The totality of these multifarious influences I have given the name "Vita-Erg Therapy." (The term is derived from the Latin roots for life and work.) Vita-Erg Therapy consists of a life setting in which patients are viewed and treated as persons, rather than individuals to be cared for, protected, directed, and served as though they were children. However, it is important that this setting and relationships do not replicate the insurmountable pressures and intolerable stresses of the complex family and social setting that caused the patient to withdraw and create a fantasy life.

### HISTORY

The techniques and procedures of Vita-Erg Therapy were initiated by myself (S. R. Slavson) at the Brooklyn State Hospital (New York City) with two "disturbed" locked wards each housing sixty-five of the hospital's most intractable as well as the most inaccessible female patients. While the hospital generally was under liberal directorship, with open wards and freedom of locomotion on and off the grounds, these two wards on the top floor of the building remained locked and patients were restricted from leaving them for any reason. Among, them were patients who hadn't left the wards for two or three decades. They all looked disheveled and unkempt, bearing facial expressions characteristic of mentally deteriorated individuals. The majority were uncommunicative and many were to varying degrees manic and assaultive. A number were in a permanent state of stupor and varying degrees of catatonia. No activities or occupations of any kind were provided for the patients excepting for making their own beds in the dormitory under authoritarian supervision of attendants who were ordinary, uneducated, and unschooled women. The relationships between these women and their charges has been that of strict, demanding mothers and obstreperous children. The latter were punished for the slightest transgression or oversight. In fact, on the wall of the nurses' office there was a list of the type of punishment to be applied to each of the patients.

## TECHNIQUE

The approach to solving the problem was twofold; one was to alter the environment on the wards where patients could otherwise do nothing but sit and stare; the other was to change the attitude of the ward staff toward the patients, including the nurses and doctors, and create possibilities for active involvement with them rather than simply functioning as "baby nurses." The extent of this attitude is dramatically revealed by the fact that I found that about twenty-four adult patients had been spoon-fed by attendants for years. When asked why they did this the reply was, "Because they can't feed themselves." In a discussion of this situation in one of our weekly seminars I suggested that they place these patients in line with the others in the dining room to fetch their own trays and food, which they did without any problem or difficulty.

We installed an electric kitchen on the ward in which cooking and baking could be done; an electric laundry in another small room; a third room was equipped for beauty culture with mirrors on the walls where patients could primp themselves voluntarily; a fourth room was equipped for quiet conferences both for the ward staff and, most importantly, for patients (with a staff member present whenever they became disturbed). This prevented the infectiousness of psychotic outbreaks and conflicts that used to be seriously punished by being locked up in these rooms, as well as a free use of camisoles (straightjackets). It must be noted that these rooms were unused before for any purpose except as "lock-ups." A visit to the women's toilets revealed eight toilet bowls lined up against one wall and four facing them against the opposite wall with no partitions for privacy. This condition was rectified by building partitions with swinging doors. Similarly, in the showering room, no provision had been made for privacy for women taking showers and dressing and undressing. This was easily corrected by installing separating curtains.

On the main body of the ward we had established "four centers of activity" by doubling up tables and surrounding them with chairs. The materials placed on these tables served as *visual suggestion* and could be used for serving and knitting of pot-holders, hats, sweaters, and dresses. Materials such as crayons, watercolors, drawing paper, and brushes; materials for cutting, pasting, crocheting, clay work, tiling, and other arts and crafts that are standard in occupational therapy. Two sewing machines were provided so that patients interested in larger projects could find an outlet.

Music and dancing were part of our program. For this a movable piano was made available exclusively to the two wards; also, much later in the program one of the recreation therapists assigned to our project, introduced group composing of plays that most often included music and dancing; from time to time performances were given to the occupants of both wards and a few times a year for the entire population of the hospital. Also, trips were arranged to places of interest in the nearby community and at times to Manhattan. During the summer, patients who so desired were taken in a hospital van to

Coney Island where they swam, galloped, and helped and protected each other. It is of interest to note that only a few of the patients more in contact were given the opportunity for these experiences to expand their reality. Only the more regressed went on these swimming excursions.

The second major part of the Vita-Erg Therapy—namely, the change of attitudes and functions of staff in relationship to patients—was conducted through weekly seminar for attendants specifically gathered around a large executive office table with the top staff sitting apart around the room. The content was drawn from my brief visits to the wards where I saw the improper reactions of the attendants to patients. Without, of course, revealing the names of the persons involved, discussions of how situations could have been dealt with more constructively always brought to the fore the patients' feelings.

One seminar a month was devoted to an in-depth study of one particular patient who was most puzzling or most difficult. This has never been done anywhere before. Such studies were in the past reserved for psychiatrists only. In these special seminars the social worker read the background history of each patient, the family relationships, the type of parents. We then identified the dynamics that resulted in, and the contributing events to, the patient's psychotic break.

## APPLICATIONS

It is apparent that the basic *content* of the program we have introduced in rehabilitating these highly disturbed and regressed long-term patients is neither original nor new. The very impressive results that we have obtained lay in the alteration of the treatment of patients as though they were normal people, and the spontaneous arousal of wants and inner responses through the stimulation of the total program helped patients return to reality; supplying them with suitable activities unsupervised by staff. Instead, we relied upon the *spontaneous* choices of patients for activities and interests. Perhaps one episode will illustrate this. A member of HEW was making an inspection visit to our two wards (the project was financed by HEW) and was impressed by a woman who was busily and interestedly doing cleaning. He asked her, "Why do you do this?" Her response was, "Because I live here."

Vita-Erg Therapy obviously has its basic roots in Activity Group Therapy and Activity-Interview Psychotherapy for children and adolescents as well as from Progressive Education of which I had had an extensive experience some sixty years ago.

# Wholistic Therapy

*Herbert A. Otto*

## DEFINITION

Briefly stated, the wholistic treatment program has seven components and is based on the health model perspective of the person. Using group plus individual sessions, the focus is on working with both the psyche and soma (body work) while actively utilizing all possible resources and vectors in the life space (environment) of the person seeking help. Wholistic Therapy, as its name implies, is a holistic approach to applicable treatment, regardless of the theoretical base (Neo-Freudian, eclectic, etc.) of a particular treatment modality.

## HISTORY

This writer's (Herbert A. Otto) interest in the concept of a wholistic treatment program grew from private practice and particularly my work with nonpatient groups as a part of the Human Potentialities Research Project at the University of Utah (1960- 1967). Based on this work, initial concepts and methods were developed and subsequently published in a chapter entitled 'Toward a Holistic Treatment Program." This appeared in Harold Greenwald's volume *Active Psychotherapy*. A detailed article, "Toward Wholistic Psychotherapy, Counseling and Social Work Treatment Program" is in press.

## TECHNIQUE

The wholistic treatment program has seven basic components. They are 1) the health model perspective of the person seeking treatment, 2) combined group and individual treatment, 3) body work, 4) optimum utilization of the life space in the treatment process, 5) working with the belief system, 6) the self-concept, and self-image, and human sexuality as major factors in treatment, 7) emphasis is on a new eclecticism and the expanded therapeutic team. I will briefly describe each of the preceding components.

*1. The health model perspective of the person seeking treatment.* The basic thrust of the human organism is seen to be toward health. From this perspective symptom formation is understood to be an expression of need, as well as providing clues to the underlying need structure of the person. Symptom formation, essentially a signal for help, progressively pervades or permeates the process of personality and can become a dominant force. In short, intensification of the symptom (or signaling) system can lead to organism dysfunctioning and exhaustion (and even death). The main function of the symptom system, however, is to initiate movement toward health by seeking to elicit help and support from the total environment. Finally, it is a message of the individual to himself.

*2. Combined group and individual treatment.* In the wholistic treatment program, most of the treatment takes place in group therapy with individual sessions scheduled as needed. Group treatment has a number of distinct advantages. The most important are: a) manipulation of the therapist is minimized, b) the function of "authority attitudes," hostility toward authority, is more easily worked through and minimized, c) in a well-functioning group the resources of participants are brought to bear on the treatment process. The participants are thus exposed to multiple health vectors, d) ego-supportive-self-esteem and self-image-enhancing treatment modalities appear to be more effective in group settings, and, finally, e) group treatment offers significant economy.

*3. The use of body work as an integral part of treatment.* An important aspect of the wholistic treatment program is the emphasis on treatment of the psyche and soma simultaneously. Today there is some use of "supportive touching" during therapy. The next step is the full utilization of body work modalities as an integral part of treatment. Training in body work systems has become increasingly available. Nevertheless, few professionals have the time to take the training. One way out of this dilemma is to work out a referral arrangement, with a qualified bodywork practitioner, or to add such a person to the professional team.

*4. Optimum utilization of the life space in treatment.* This life space consists of the total interpersonal and physical environment of the person seeking help. In the vast majority of instances, aspects of this life space can be used to support and foster therapeutic aims and goals. The wholistic use of the life space, in addition to the utilization of the interpersonal and physical environment also includes use of an Action Program concept (Otto, 1975).

*5. Working with the belief system.* This involves assessing as well as working with specific components of the belief system of the person seeking help. Emphasis is on: a) assessment of the life-style and life goals, b) exploration of the meaning of existence to the person—including the spiritual resources, or religious belief system, as well as the area of values and attitudes toward death and dying.

*6. The self-concept, the self-image, and human sexuality as major factors in treatment.* Throughout treatment a clear focus is maintained on the enhancement of the self-concept and self-image. In this connection specific ego-supportive treatment methods are used, such as the Self-image Projection Experience, Strength Acknowledgment, and others (Otto, 1975). Finally, regardless of the type of problem, the wholistic treatment program always includes work in the area of human sexuality, particularly relating to sexual attitudes and the sexual self-image (Otto, 1973).

*7. The new eclecticism and the expanded therapeutic team.* The hallmark of the new eclecticism is the helping person's acquaintance with a considerable range of theory and treatment modalities drawn from various schools, coupled with a willingness to try out and use diverse treatment methods based on the individual needs of the person seeking help. The expanded therapeutic team also includes the bodywork practitioner and, if possible, a person with proven capacities as a psychic healer.

### APPLICATIONS

The wholistic treatment program has application to the broad range of therapeutic treatment modalities utilized by the helping professions. Finally, the wholistic treatment concept is designed to yield maximum treatment benefits through a total approach.

# Will Therapy of Otto Rank

*Abraham Schmitt*

### DEFINITION

For Otto Rank, Will Therapy meant that man was primarily directed by his own will and he was not the victim of either internal or external forces. Therapy then became the process of freeing the client to assume responsibility for his choices and for the direction that his life was evolving. The goal of therapy was to enable the person to accept himself as a separate, unique individual who could risk his newfound emotional freedom for creative self-expression and fulfillment.

## HISTORY

Otto Rank (1884–1939) was a member of the Freudian inner circle for the first twenty-four years of its existence. Then he severed his ties to pursue his own theoretical development of Will Therapy. He became one of the first psychologists to stress the self-directed nature of growth. On this foundation of psychoanalytic theory and practice, in opposition to Freudian theory, was built much of the humanistic, experiential, and existential theory that followed in the decades after his death. It would even be fair to say that Rank, having come out of such an intimate affiliation with Freud and the most productive era of the Freudian movement, is personally responsible for launching the anti-Freudian swing in the West out of which grew the whole human potential movement. Most of the leaders of this movement, including Carl R. Rogers, Abraham H. Maslow, Clark E. Moustakas, Rollo May, and Herbert Otto, actually participated in his seminars or were greatly influenced by his writings.

Rank should be credited with being the father of humanistic psychology and psychotherapy. This honor passed him by because he founded no school in his name, he asked for no disciples, and his voluminous writings are too difficult to read.

Unfortunately, much of Rank's writing is polemic. His personal conflict with Freud overshadowed his remarkable ideas so that much of what he said could not be integrated into the psychoanalytic movement until it was rediscovered in the 1960s and 1970s.

When Rank left the Freudian inner circle in 1924, he had arrived theoretically at the exact opposite pole from Freud. It could be said that Rank was individualistic, voluntaristic, and humanistic in contrast to Freud's universalistic, mechanistic, and deterministic orientation.

Rank was a brilliant, productive member of the committee who contributed actively to the basic psychoanalytic concepts. Freud said this when he arrived: "The little society acquired in him a zealous and dependable secretary and I gained in Otto Rank a faithful helper and co-worker."

Because Rank had a nonmedical education, but rather one of philosophy, history, and religion, he quickly attempted to broaden the view of man beyond the biological basis. This led him beyond psychoanalysis and finally resulted in severing his ties with the Vienna group and going on his own.

## TECHNIQUE

The basic orientation of Otto Rank can be stated very explicitly. Rank rejected the key concept of the Oedipal situation as the source of psychopathology and adopted the birth experience as the origin of the essential trauma. He conceptualized that during the intrauterine experience the child experienced total union, which forever continued as the key motivation in a person's search for total fulfillment. The union man has once known is longed for, even as he experiences partial union in each relationship, and it is longed for in the hoped-for ultimate union after death. The birth experience terminated the original state of bliss and thus became such a traumatic experience that it became the origin of all anxiety due to the fear of separation.

The emphasis that Rank placed on the will is what gives his therapy the title Will Therapy. He called the will "a positive guiding organization and integration of the self, which utilizes creativity as well as inhibits and controls the instinctual drives." By this he meant that man was not a victim of his id impulses, but rather he was capable of directing these forces, either negatively for his own destruction or else he could organize them positively for creative self-expression and growth.

This leads to Rank's concept of creativity. For him the essential struggle of man was not to achieve health or normalcy but rather to express himself creatively in an art form most appropriate to oneself so as to discover and express one's own uniqueness and distinctiveness. The therapeutic task therefore became one of enabling the patient to take responsibility for his own life and use it creatively in his life situation.

For Rank the Neurotic was *an artiste manque,* a frustrated artist, who has artistic temperament but fails to create. The essential skill in therapy, then, is to help the patient face his own guilt and fear that has resulted in negative will organization, and break loose from this pattern and risk the courage to create.

At this moment in therapy the patient returns to the initial birth trauma, since every act of creativity is a rebirth process, when a person faces his own longing to be like humanity, but he realizes that he must assert his difference at the possible price of being rejected by others. He must relive the separation experience in every creative act.

The goal of therapy then, according to Rank, means that "he must also believe ... in himself as a self-reliant individual, different and differentiated from others. He has to face in this separation process the guilt which he cannot deny nor pay off, but can only bear and expiate as best he may in actual living."

One of the most outstanding proclamations of Otto Rank was his absolute belief in the uniqueness of every human being. The most quoted statement of his says it precisely: "Will people ever learn ... that there is no other equality possible than the equal right of every individual to become and to be himself, which actually means to accept his own difference and have it accepted by others."

The core of Rankian therapeutic technique focused on the dynamic relationship between the patient and therapist, which the patient used to discover his creative self.

## APPLICATIONS

Rankian therapy has found its most direct use in "functional" social work practice, as it was taught at the universities of Pennsylvania and North Carolina schools of social work. The services of agencies were offered in such a way that each client was helped to discover his own will for independent functioning. In asking for and using the therapeutic experience, the client only temporarily yielded to the limits of his predicament until he could reorganize his "will energy" for self-directed living.

In a very limited way therapists practiced Will Therapy following the Rankian model. It was especially useful for crisis intervention and short-term treatment, when a client needed to quickly discover that he could become accountable for his life.

Its most universal application has been the use that the entire human potential movement has made of the major concepts of Rankian theory and now promotes under an infinite number of labels, all of which fall under the general heading of humanistic psychology.

# Writing Therapy
## Les Schwartz

### DEFINITION AND TECHNIQUE

Writing Therapy may serve 1) to develop writing skills, 2) for manual rehabilitation, 3) to improve impaired writing, 4) as compensation for speech impairment, 5) to develop self-awareness of dysfluent speech and associated symptoms, and 6) as a vehicle of transcribing emotions. It is therefore employed for deficient writing and/or as an alternate means of communication.

1. The development of acceptable writing is an integral part of the rehabilitation of the dyslexic and/or learning disabled child (Bryant, 1967). Tasks related to tracing, copying, and guideline writing are generally included.

2. Impaired motor ability is a frequent result of a neurological disorder. Various items are commercially available for enabling the neurologically impaired patient to gain a firmer grasp on writing instruments.

3. Writing serves as a compensatory means of communicating for apraxic and/or dysarthric patients. Beukelman and Yorkston (1977) successfully employed initial letter pointing as a speech aid for dysarthric patients. One might anticipate that initial letter *writing* would be similarly helpful for these patients.

4. The writing of emotionally laden messages is sometimes carried out, as a part of a psychotherapeutic program (Bastien and Jacobs, 1974). Anxiety-producing situations/persons are written about, and reviewed. The slower and more deliberate act of writing generally allows for a better organization of ideas.

5. Writing has also been incorporated into therapy for stutterers. The technique of talking and writing in stuttering therapy was discussed by Van Riper (1958). The author posited that the stutterer's experience with speaking and writing may accomplish several (somewhat controversial) goals. It may a) increase the basic margin of cerebral dominance, so that fewer "neuromuscular blockings" occur, b) help the maintenance of the speech mechanism in action, on a highly voluntary level, and c) encourage stutterers to make a sudden direct contact with words that were often feared. He noted that experiences with speaking and writing better enabled the stutterer to understand his basic reactions to his dysfluent behavior. Van Riper reported that writing a message before it was said seemed to produce a marked reduction in the frequency and severity of stuttering, and served to clarify verbalization of thought.

6. The language disorder referred to as aphasia is most often the result of left cerebral damage. The patient most often has difficulty both in the comprehension and expression of spoken and written verbal language and, for right-handed patients, a paresis of the dominant hand generally results. Therefore, these right-handed patients often experience motor as well as linguistic writing problems. In general, Writing Therapy for this patient progresses from letter to word to sentence production. Several other factors must be considered. The clinician should also consider the extent of concomitant linguistic, motor, *and* cognitive components. Although all are not mutually exclusive, these may

include frequency, syllable length, word and letter length, as well as sound structure, part of speech, degree of abstraction, etc., of the stimuli (Carroll, et al., 1971).

Haskins (1976) and a number of other researchers have discussed plans and procedures for aphasia writing rehabilitation. A sampling of tasks includes 1) tracing copying shapes, 2) tracing alphabet letters with, and without, auditory stimulation, 3) the use of guide arrows for forming the letters, 4) the fading out of guidelines, 5) writing letters in serial order, then progressing, to random order, 6) writing the names of pictured or actual objects, 7) writing words to dictation with and without an accompanying sentence frame, 8) writing the names of items in specified categories, 9) writing short sentences from dictation, and 10) the written formation of short sentences. Letters are written both in printed and in cursive style.

The results of Writing Therapy for the aphasia patient will depend on several factors. These include the patient's age, etiology, site and extent of brain damage, level of linguistic functioning, motivation, concomitant psychological and/or physical problems, etc.

## APPLICATIONS

In summary, Writing Therapy may be employed by various disciplines, for obviously different reasons. It is used both for developmental and for acquired disorders, of either physical and/or psychological origins, and generally as one component of a total therapy program.

# Zaraleya Psychoenergetic Technique

## *Zaraleya*

### DEFINITION

Used in the framework of a humanistic psychotherapy, the Zaraleya Psychoenergetic Technique is a theory, instrument, and method of gaining greater consciousness and fuller awareness of potential toward self-actualization through a conceptualization of the flow of psychic energy within and between people.

The technique includes keeping a journal record of the process of the psychotherapy and using a series of four charts with inkblots and protocol sheets.

### HISTORY

The Zaraleya Psychoenergetic Technique, consistent with the principles of humanistic psychology, values the concept of self-actualization described by Abraham Maslow as the "desire to become everything one is capable of becoming," and the concept that individuals can consciously control their own behavior and live creatively.

Work with psychic energy traces back to Freud's libidinal theory, dealing with cathexis and direction of sexual energy, and with Kundalini Yoga based on the mastery of energy toward its positive direction and a state of well-being.

The emphasis on the inner self has roots in the depth psychology of C. G. Jung. Jung's subject ot study is the psychic life of the person—the events that take place *within* the human being. He refers to the energy operating in the psyche as psychic energy—the energy of the processes of life. Particularly pertinent to this technique, Jung observed that whenever persons become too extreme in their self-interest or interest centered in the external world, they are also likely to become emotionally disturbed. Jung also speaks of harmony and disharmony within the energy balance.

For myself (Dr. Zaraleya), this technique began when I traced depression to the use of energy behaving out of harmony with one's own thoughts and feelings. Depression is mourning for the lost self (the self that is abandoned in the interest of safeguarding relationships). Especially since so many of life's problems presented in psychotherapy had to do with autonomy, independence, and integrity in juxtaposition to dependence, melding, and nurturance needs, I became interested in finding a model of psychic energy flow that would encompass ways of being independent, separate, and alone with ways of being closely involved with others; namely, the ability to move between yielding to the flow of one's separate existence and yielding to the flow of the Universe.

## TECHNIQUE

The Zaraleya Psychoenergetic Technique is used in the setting of humanistic psychotherapy, which is more flexible than traditional therapy and permits the therapist to use a variety of techniques. Other major issues in relation to other therapies include the tendency to emphasize and strengthen individual differences and uniqueness. Both positive and negative energy forces are respected. The people seen in therapy are viewed not as diseased patients in need of treatment, but rather as travelers through life's journey, struggling to make growth choices, integrate them, and experience themselves anew. Rather than having their "mental illnesses cured," individuals are helped to control and direct the flow of their own psychic energy toward growth, development, and fulfillment of potential. The focus in the therapy is the continuous creative process of free and full engagement with life, taking risks and meeting challenges. The therapist offers a much more personal self and his life becomes a model for how one person finds a way to live and in so doing helps others to find their way.

*Theory.* There is a natural human psychic energy flow and one can learn to yield to oneself and alternately to the Universe. One can learn to control the flow of one's psychic energy, make it work positively for oneself, and have a more balanced harmonious existence.

*Instrument.* A series of four charts graphically represent four consecutive phases of psychic energy flow. In the process of psychotherapy the participants use the series to locate the phase they are in and to focus their energy direction constructively. The Transitions are the important areas of struggle.

### The Phases and Transitions

*I. Transcendence.* Quiet Energy; period of quiet, peace and solitude.

*Transition I.* Readiness to exchange energy between the newly formed self and the world.

*II. Inter-Activity.* Exchange of energy between the person and the world.

*Transition II.* Readiness to pull away from exchange to private integration.

*III. Synergy.* Private integration of energy leads to decision making and creative acts.

*Transition III.* Readiness to accept change.

*IV. Transformation.* Actually experiencing oneself as having changed.

*Transition IV.* Readiness to move toward quiescence, solitude.

*Method.* The *Journal record* is kept in a large loose-leaf notebook that comes with a set of the charts, celluloid containers for the *inkblots* (with directions for making them), and a set of *protocol sheets*.

*Inkblots* are made in individual and group therapy sessions. Individuals who have learned the method and who keep a Zaraleya Psychoenergetic Technique journal record make inkblots at set intervals to keep check on the process and flow of their psychic energy. These inkblots are made by folding a page in half after dropping various colored inks on it.

An art form outside of the self, the the inner process of psychic energy flow. One may look at an inkblot and conceive of inkblots provide a vehicle to describe it as a representation of the present energy constellation or life space. In doing so, they look for the phases represented by the charts in the inkblots, marking them off with a thick pen and numbering the sections accordingly.

When this is done, there is a concrete representation of the process of our energy flow that makes clearer the individual's situation and the positive direction possible. The structure of the four energy phases and the inkblots provides a springboard for looking at and talking about the inner self.

For each inkblot there is a *protocol sheet*. On the protocol sheet there is room for a description of the inkblot in terms of the four phases of psychic energy flow in the present life experience of the individual.

The *discussion section* is used to indicate how energy is being used and what changes may be desirable for more constructive use of energy. It is equally important to notice how one thinks and feels and all the awareness without a plan for change. This is followed by a space where a commitment of intention to change is stated when desired. The commitment is made only when the individual who made the inkblot is seriously devoted to making a change. The initiative to make the commitment must come from the person making it. This is followed by a space for the name, address, and phone number of a contact person. The contact person is usually the therapist. However, depending on the context, the contact person could be a school psychologist, a teacher, or a counselor. People in group therapy often use a group member who agrees to be available and supportive during a difficult period when encouragement to reach a goal may be essential.

## APPLICATIONS

This form of psychotherapy is generally useful and effective with individuals and groups of all ages, including young children who have been found to understand it easily. It is particularly good with creative people who sometimes need help to pull away from further stimulation and to begin to put together and integrate their saturated energy. A minor variation in the format contributes also to classroom learning by offering a refreshing new perspective and means of communicating that helps the learners know just where they are in the learning process and see the next step in the progression. It provides a common language of communication to express energy states of inner self or to request help to stay longer in a phase or to move to the next one.

## THE ZARALEYA PSYCHOENERGETIC TECHNIQUE PROTOCOL SHEET

NAME _____ DATE _____

### DISCUSSION:

How am I using my energy?

How may I use it more constructively?

How do I feel now?

What do I think now?

What is a next possible step?

### COMMITMENT:

(if desired)
Contact person

Address and phone

### KEY TO INKBLOT

(use black marking pen to outline or indicate by numbers areas on Inkblot)

1. Transcendence—Quiet Energy

2. Inter-Activity—Energy Exchange

3. Synergy—Energy Integration

4. Transformation—Volitional Energy Change

5. Transcendence—Quiet Energy after Change

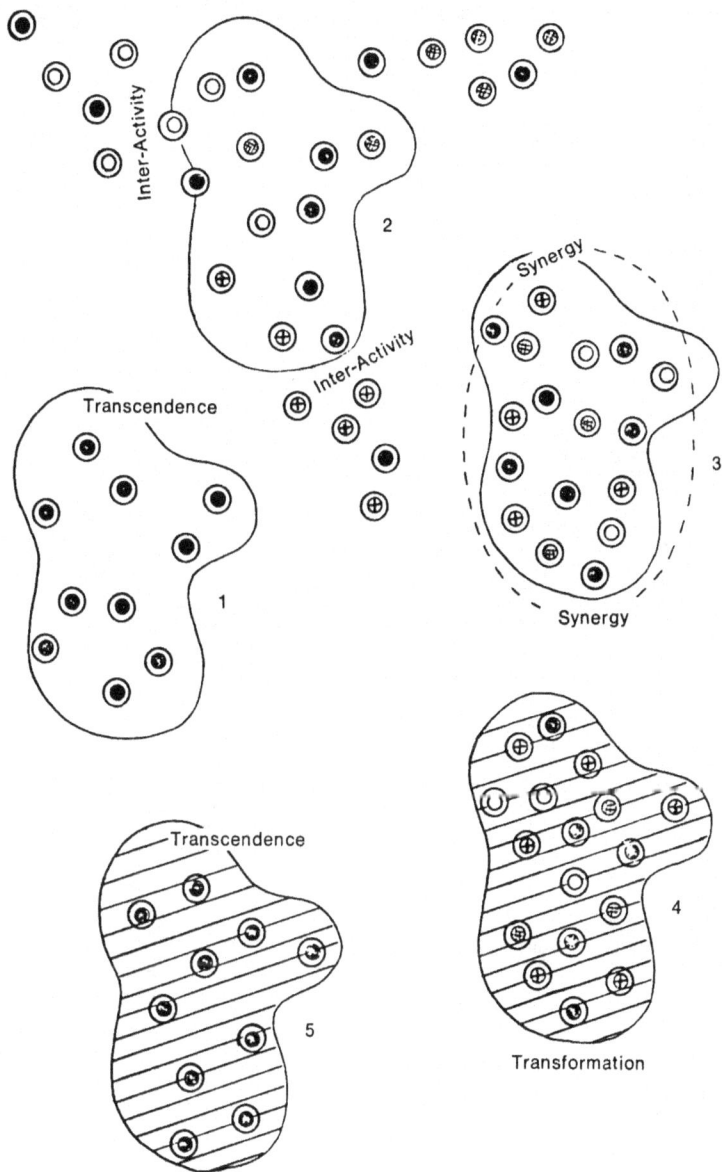

# Contributors

Winthrop R. Adkins, Ph.D.
Teachers College, Columbia University
New York, New York

Donna C. Aguilera, Ph.D.
California State University
Los Angeles, California

Akhter Ahsen, Ph.D.
Eidetic Analysis Institute
Yonkers, New York

Robert E. Alberti, Ph.D.
California Polytechnic State University
San Luis Obispo, California

Alcoholics Anonymous
General Service Staff
New York, New York

Jon G. Allen, Ph.D.
The Menninger Foundation
Topeka, Kansas

Robert D. Allen, M.A.
Association for Psychotheatrics
Sacramento, California

Robert E. Allen, M.D.
University of Southern California Medical
    School
Los Angeles, California

Nelita Ano, M.D.
Halifax Hospital
Daytona Beach, Florida

Marvin L. Aronson, Ph.D.
Postgraduate Center for Mental Health
New York, New York

George R. Bach, Ph.D.
The Bach Institute
Los Angeles, California

Elsworth F. Baker, M.D.
Private Practice
Fair Haven, New Jersey

H. Thomas Ballantine, Jr., M.D.
Harvard Medical School
Boston, Massachusetts

Chris Barker, M.A.
University of California, Los Angeles
Los Angeles, California

Thad J. Barringer, M.D.
Private Practice
Raleigh, North Carolina

Alexander Bassin, Ph.D.
Florida State University
Tallahassee, Florida

Irving Beiman, Ph.D.
University of Georgia
Athens, Georgia

John Elderkin Bell, Ed.D.
Stanford University
Stanford, California

Penny Lewis Bernstein, M.A.
Antioch-New England Graduate School
Keene, New Hampshire

Carl V. Binder, M.A.
W. E. Fernald State School
Belmont, Massachusetts

Virginia Binder, Ph.D.
California State University, Long Beach
Long Beach, California

Gail Bleach, Ph.D.
Private Practice
Columbia, Maryland

Douglas D. Blocksma, Ph.D.
Private Practice
Grand Rapids, Michigan

Harold H. Bloomfield, M.D.
Center for Holistic Health
San Diego, California

Melvin Boyce, M.A.
Private Practice
Corte Madera, California

Nathaniel Branden, Ph.D.
Private Practice
Los Angeles, California

Jeffrey M. Brandsma, Ph.D.
University of Kentucky
Lexington, Kentucky

I. Emery Breitner, M.D.
Private Practice
Roslyn, New York

James F. T. Bugental, Ph.D.
Humanistic Psychology Institute
San Francisco, California

George M. Burnell, M.D.
Kaiser-Permanen Medical Center
Santa Clara, California

Morton B. Cantor, M.D.
Postgraduate Center for Mental Health
New York, New York

Deborah Caplan, M.A.
Private Practice
New York, New York

Sheldon Cashdan, Ph.D.
University of Massachusetts
Amherst, Massachusetts

Daniel Casriel, M.D.
The Casriel Institute
New York, New York

Ven. Norbu L. Chan, Ph.D., Ed.D.
Buddhist Chaplain, San Francisco County Jail
San Francisco, California

Suk C. Chang, M.D.
Yale University School of Medicine
New Haven, Connecticut

Alan Shifman Charles, M.D.
Academy of Eastern Medicine
Walnut Creek, California

Theodore Chemodurow, M.D.
Private Practice
Billings, Montana

Richard D. Chessick, M.D., Ph.D.
Northwestern University
Evanston, Illinois

John A. Chiles, M.D.
University of Washington
Seattle, Washington

Richard Corriere, Ph.D.
Center for Feeling Therapy
Los Angeles, California

Raymond J. Corsini, Ph.D.
University of Hawaii
Honolulu, Hawaii

Aris W. Cox, M.D.
Charity Hospital at New Orleans
New Orleans, Louisiana

Norma Crockett, M.A.
Private Practice
Palo Alto, California

Robert S. Daniels, M.D.
University of Cincinnati
Cincinnati, Ohio

Carole Dilling, Ph.D.
Training Institute for Mental Health
    Practitioners
New York, New York

Julius Dintenfass, B.S., D.C.
Private Practice
New York, New York

William J. DiScipio, Ph.D.
Bronx Children's Psychiatric Center
Bronx, New York

Sarah Donahue, Ed.D.
Fairleigh Dickinson University
Teaneck, New Jersey

Edgar Draper, M.D.
University of Mississippi
Jackson, Mississippi

George L. Duerksen, Ph.D.
University of Kansas
Lawrence, Kansas

Albert Ellis, Ph.D.
Institute for Advanced Study in
    Rational Psychotherapy
New York, New York

Michael L. Emmons, Ph.D.
California Polytechnic State University
San Luis Obispo, California

Frieda England, M.S.W.
Private Practice
New York, New York

Ann O'Neil Enscoe, M.S.W.
Atlantis Institute
Galloway, New Jersey

Gerald Enscoe, Ph.D.
Stockton State College
Pomma, New Jersey

Joan Erdheim, Ph.D.
Private Practice
New York, New York

D.M. Eshbaugh, Ph.D.
The Ohio State University
Columbus, Ohio

Ian M. Evans, Ph.D.
University of Hawaii
Honolulu, Hawaii

James Fadiman, Ph.D.
California Institute for Transpersonal
    Psychology
Menlo Park, California

Frank Farrelly, A.C.S.W.
Family Social and Psychological Services
Madison, Wisconsin

Jean Ferson, Ph.D.
Philadelphia Child Guidance Clinic
Philadelphia, Pennsylvania

Ronald R. Fieve, M.D.
Columbia College of
    Physicians and Surgeons
New York, New York

Ben C. Finney, Ph.D.
San Jose State University
San Jose, California

Jefferson M. Fish, Ph.D.
Pontificia Universidade Catolica
Campinas, Sao Paulo, Brazil

Daniel B. Fishman, Ph.D.
Rutgers University
Piscataway, New Jersey

Edna B. Foa, Ph.D.
Temple University Medical School
Philadelphia, Pennsylvania

Elizabeth T. Foulkes
Group-Analytic Society
London, England

Robert Frager, Ph.D.
California Institute of Transpersonal
    Psychology
Menlo Park, California

Viktor E. Frankl, M.D., Ph.D.
University of Vienna Medical School
Vienna, Austria

Vincent Frein, M.S.W.
Training Institute for Mental Health
Practitioners
New York, New York

Richard E. Frenkel, M.D.
Albert Einstein College of Medicine
Bronx, New York

Maurice Friedman, Ph.D.
San Diego State University
San Diego, California

Philip H. Friedman, Ph.D.
Jefferson University
Philadelphia, Pennsylvania

Richard A. Gardner, M.D.
College of Physicians and Surgeons
New York, New York

Lester A. Gelb, M.D.
State University of New York,
Downstate Medical Center
Brooklyn, New York

Eugene T. Gendlin, Ph.D.
University of Chicago
Chicago, Illinois

Alvin I. Gerstein, Ph.D.
Philadelphia Psychiatric Center
Philadelphia, Pennsylvania

John S. Gillis, Ph.D.
Oregon State University
Corvallis, Oregon

Kenneth E. Godfrey, M.D.
Topeka Veterans Administration Hospital
Topeka, Kansas

George D. Goldman, Ph.D.
Private Practice
New York, New York

Robert Golembiewski, Ph.D.
University of Georgia
Athens, Georgia

Gerald Goodman, Ph.D.
University of California, Los Angeles
Los Angeles, California

Janet M. Goodrich, Ph.D.
Vital Health Center
Encino, California

F. William Gosciewski, Ph.D.
Edinboro State College
Edinboro, Pennsylvania

Roger P. Greenberg, Ph.D. S
tate University of New York,
    Upstate Medical Center
Syracuse, New York

Thayer A. Greene, B.D., S.T.M.
Private Practice
New York, New York

Eric Green leaf, Ph.D.
Private Practice
Berkeley, California

Harold Greenwald, Ph.D.
United States International University
San Diego, California

John H. Greist, M.D.
University of Wisconsin
Madison, Wisconsin

Gerald Groves, M.B.B.S.
Temple University
Philadelphia, Pennsylvania

Dominick E. Grundy, Ph.D.
Institute for Sociotherapy
New York, New York

Bernard Guerney, Jr., Ph.D.
Pennsylvania State University
University Park, Pennsylvania

Louise F. Guerney, Ph.D.
Pennsylvania State University
University Park, Pennsylvania

Alan S. Gurman, Ph.D.
University of Wisconsin Medical School
Madison, Wisconsin

Jay Haley, Ph.D.
Family Therapy Institute
Chevy Chase, Maryland

Seymour Halpern, Ph.D.
Private Practice
Huntington, New York

Thomas Hanna, Ph.D.
Novato Institute
Novato, California

Loretta Mason Haroian, M.A., Ph.D.
Institute for Advanced Study of
    Human Sexuality
San Francisco, California

I. H. Hart, Ph.D.
Camarillo State Hospital
Camarillo, California

Joseph Hart, Ph.D.
The Center for Feeling Therapy
Los Angeles, California

Renatus Hartogs, M.D., Ph.D.
American Institute for Psychotherapy and
    Psychoanalysis
New York, New York

Leston L. Havens, M.D.
Harvard Medical School
Boston, Massachusetts

Evelyn Phillips Heimlich, B.S.
New York State Psychiatric Institute
New York, New York

Karen Hellwig, R.N., M.N.
El Camino College
Torrance, California

Wendy Helms, M.A.
John F. Kennedy University
Orinda, California

Gay Hendricks, Ph.D.
University of Colorado
Colorado Springs, Colorado

A. Hoffer, M.D., Ph.D.
Private Practice
Victoria, British Columbia, Canada

E. Michael Holden, M.D.
The Primal Institute
Los Angeles, California

Monica Holmes, Ph.D.
Community Research Applications
New York, New York

John G. Howells, M.D.
Institute of Family Psychiatry
Ipswich, England

Thomas D. Hurwitz, M.D.
97th General Hospital
Frankfurt, West Germany

Eleanor C. Irwin, Ph.D.
Pittsburgh Child Guidance Center
Pittsburgh, Pennsylvania

Virginia B. Jacko, M.S.
Private Practice
West Lafayette, Indiana

Edgar N. Jackson
Private Practice
Corinth, Vermont

David R. Johnson, M.S.
Yale University
New Haven, Connecticut

Gurushabd Singh Josephs, Ed.D.
Kundalini Research Institute
Boston, Massachusetts

Jaques Kaswan, Ph.D.
Ohio State University
Columbus, Ohio

Yoram Kaufmann, Ph.D.
The C.G. Jung Training Center
New York, New York

Alan E. Kazdin, Ph.D.
Pennsylvania State University
University Park, Pennsylvania

Charles R. Kelley, Ph.D.
The Radix Institute
Santa Monica, California

Gary F. Kelly, M.Ed.
Clarkson College
Potsdam, New York

Gurucharan Singh Khalsa, Ed.M.
Kundalini Research Institute
Boston, Massachusetts

Dan Kiley, Ph.D.
Private Practice
Decatur, Illinois

Anne F. Kilguss, M.S.W.
The Faulkner Hospital
Boston, Massachusetts

Grace Kirsten, M.A.
Private Practice
Brooklyn, New York

Jack Kornfield, Ph.D.
Insight Meditation Society
Barre, Massachusetts

Nina Krebs, Ed.D.
Private Practice
Sacramento, California

Stanley Krippner, Ph.D.
Humanistic Psychology Institute
San Francisco, California

Klaus Kuch, M.D.
University of Toronto
Toronto, Ontario, Canada

Judith Kuppersmith, Ph.D.
The City University of New York
Brooklyn, New York

Jesse K. Lair, Ph.D.
Montana State University
Bozeman, Montana

Donald G. Langsley, M.D.
University of Cincinnati
Cincinnati, Ohio

H. Peter Laqueur, M.D.
University of Vermont
Burlington, Vermont

Lark
Theta Seminars
San Francisco, California

Arnold A. Lazarus, Ph.D.
Rutgers University
Piscataway, New Jersey

Carol J. Leavenworth, M.S.Ed.
Colorado College
Colorado Springs, Colorado

Jack J. Leedy, M.D.
Association for Poetry Therapy
New York, New York

John Ransom Lewis, Jr., M.D.
Institute of Aesthetic Plastic Surgery
Atlanta. Georgia

Julian Lieb, M.B., B.Ch.
Yale University School of Medicine
New Haven, Connecticut

Louis Linn, M.D.
Mount Sinai School of Medicine
New York, New York

Chalsa Loo, Ph.D.
University of California, Santa Cruz
Santa Cruz, California

Leonore R. Love, Ph.D.
University of California, Los Angeles
Los Angeles, California

Charles McArthur, Ph.D.
Career Ventures
Cambridge, Massachusetts

James P. McGee II, Ph.D.
Sheppard and Enoch Pratt Hospital
Baltimore, Maryland

Robert MacGregor, Ph.D.
Team-Family Methods Association
Lombard, Illinois

Michael T. McGuire, M.D.
University of California, Los Angeles
Los Angeles, California

Ted McIlvenna M. Dv., Ph.D.
Institute for Advanced Study of
   Human Sexuality
San Francisco, California

Shaun A. McNiff, Ph.D.
Lesley College
Cambridge, Massachusetts

Margaret MacRae, ATR
St. Joseph's and Barnert Hospitals
Paterson, New Jersey

Cloe Madanes
Family Therapy Institute
Chevy Chase, Maryland

Arthur Maglin, Ph.D.
Mount Sinai Hospital
New York, New York

Michael J. Mahoney, Ph.D.
Pennsylvania State University
University Park, Pennsylvania

D. H. Malan, M.D.
Tavistock Clinic
London, England

David G. Martin, Ph.D.
University of Manitoba
Winnipeg, Manitoba, Canada

Max Mastellone, Ph.D.
Intercommunity Action, Inc.
Philadelphia, Pennsylvania

Frederick Towne Melges, M.D.
Duke University Medical Center
Durham, North Carolina

Dan Miller, M.A.
Mountaintop Farm
Livingston Manor, New York

Gerald J. Miller, Ph.D.
University of Kansas
Lawrence, Kansas

George Mora, M.D.
Private Practice
Poughkeepsie, New York

Felix Morrow, B.S.
Dialogue House Associates
New York, New York

C. Scott Moss, Ph.D.
Federal Correction Institution
Lompoc, California

O. Hobart Mowrer, Ph.D.
University of Illinois
Champaign-Urbana, Illinois

Robert Mucchielli, Ph.D., M.D.
University of Nice
Nice, France

William F. Murphy, M.D.
McLean Hospital
Waverley, Massachusetts

Renee Nell, Ed.D.
The Country Place
Litchfield, Connecticut

Robert C. Ness, Ph.D.
University of Connecticut Health Center
Farmington, Connecticut

Morris Netherton
Private Practice
Los Angeles, California

Walter E. O'Connell, Ph.D.
V.A. Glass Ark Treatment Center
Houston, Texas

Earl J. Ogletree, Ed.D.
Chicago State University
Chicago. Illinois

Keigo Okonogi, M.D.
Keio University School of Medicine
Tokyo,Japan

Robert F. Ostermann, Ph.D.
Fairleigh Dickinson University
Teaneck, New Jersey

Herbert A. Otto, Ph.D.
National Center for the Exploration of
    Human Potential
La Jolla, California
Helen Papanek, M.D.
Private Practice
New York, New York

Rolland S. Parker, Ph.D.
Private Practice
New York, New York

Louis Parrish, M.D.
Private Practice
New York, New York

E. Mansell Pattison, M.D.
University of California,
Irvine Irvine, California

Albert Pesso, B.A.
Psychomotor Institute
Boston, Massachusetts

Diane Pesso
Psychomotor Institute
Boston, Massachusetts

Dorothy E. Peven, MSW
Private Practice
Chicago, Illinois

David G. Phillips, M.S.W.
Postgraduate Center for Mental Health
New York, New York

Donald E. Polkinghorne, Ph.D.
Humanistic Psychology Institute
San Francisco, California

Herbert Potash, Ph.D.
Fairleigh Dickinson University
Madison, New Jersey

Helen C. Potter, Ph.D.
Purdue University
Lafayette, Indiana

Hector A. Prestera, M.D.
Private Practice
Monterey, California

Magda Proskauer
Private Practice
San Francisco, California

Justin S. Psaila, M.D.
Private Practice
Pearl River, New York

Richard T. Rada, M.D.
University of New Mexico
Albuquerque, New Mexico

Benzion J. Rapoport, Ph.D.
Private Practice
Forest Hills, New York

Harold L. Raush, Ph.D.
University of Massachusetts
Amherst, Massachusetts

Joseph Rechetnick, Ph.D.
State University of New York,
    Downstate Medical Center
Brooklyn, New York

Sherry Reiter, M.A.
Association for Poetry Therapy
New York, New York

Paula Diane Relf, Ph.D.
Virginia Polytechnic Institute
Blacksburg, Virginia

Ruth Riesenberg-Malcolm
Private Practice
London, England

Paul Roazen, Ph.D.
York University
Toronto, Ontario, Canada

Richard C. Robertiello, M.D.
Private Practice
New York, New York

Mary Robertson, Ph.D.
University of Florida, Mental Health Center
Gainesville, Florida

Ida P. Rolf, Ph.D.
Rolf Institute
Boulder, Colorado

Ruth Ronall, M.S.
Workshop Institute for Living-Learning
New York, New York

Sidney Rose, M.D.
Private Practice
New York, New York

John N. Rosen, M.D.
Private Practice
Doylestown, Pennsylvania

Renée Royak-Schaler, M.Ed.
Lomi School East
Washington, D.C.

Ilana Rubenfeld, B.S.
Private and Group Practice
New York, New York

Alexander Runciman, Ph.D.
California State University
Northridge, California

A. John Rush, M.D.
University of Oklahoma
Oklahoma City, Oklahoma

William S. Sahakian, Ph.D.
Suffolk University
Boston, Massachusetts

Andrew Salter, D.Sc.
Private Practice
New York, New York

Nolan Saltzman, Ph.D.
New School for Social Research
New York, New York

Jacquelyn Sanders, Ph.D.
University of Chicago
Chicago, Illinois

Robert S. Schachter, Ed.D.
Schachter Schools of Social Education
Brookline, Massachusetts

Amy Schaffer, M.A.
Institute for Sociotherapy
New York, New York

Jeffrey A Schaler, B.A.
Lomi School East
Washington, D.C.

Muriel Schiffman
Private Practice
Menlo Park, California

Howard H. Schlossman, M.D.
Private Practice
Englewood, New Jersey

Abraham Schmitt, D.S.W.
Private Practice
Souderton, Pennsylvania

Will Schutz, Ph.D.
Private Practice
Muir Beach, California

Les Schwartz, Ph.D.
Northport V.A. Hospital
Northport, New York

Sharon Henderson Sclabassi, A.C.S.W.
Private Practice
Felton, California

Alfred L. Scopp, Ph.D.
Private Practice
Santa Clara, California

Johannah Segers, Ph.D.
Center for Modern Psychoanalytic Studies
New York, New York

Diane Shapiro, M.A.
American Occupational Therapy Association
Rockville, Maryland

Florence A. Sharp, Ph.D.
Private Practice
Los Angeles, California

Joan Shea, Ed.D.
Private Practice
New York, New York

Robert A. Shearer, Ph.D.
Sam Houston State University
Huntsville, Texas

John L. Shelton, Ph.D.
University of Washington
Seattle, Washington

Nancy Shiffrin, M.A.
Private Practice
Los Angeles, California

Joseph E. Shorr, Ph.D.
Institute of Psycho-Imagination Therapy
Los Angeles, California

Peter E. Sifneos, M.D.
Harvard University Medical School
Boston, Massachusetts

Phyllis R. Silverman, Ph.D.
Harvard Medical School
Boston, Massachusetts

Erwin Singer, Ph.D.
The City University of New York
New York, New York

Ellen K. Siroka, Ed.D.
Institute for Sociotherapy
New York, New York

Robert W. Siroka, Ph.D.
Institute for Sociotherapy
New York, New York

Andrew E. Slaby, M.D.
Yale-New Haven Hospital
New Haven, Connecticut

Charles W. Slack, Ph.D.
Social Welfare Department
Melbourne, Australia

Eileen N. Slack, Ed. D.
Social Welfare Department
Melbourne, Australia

S. R. Slavson
Private Practice
New York, New York

Stanley E. Slivkin, M.D.
Boston V.A. Hospital
Boston, Massachusetts

Burke M. Smith, Ph.D.
University of Virginia School of Medicine
Charlottesville, Virginia

Nina Smith, B.A.
Central Counseling Service
New York, New York

Ted Smith, D. Min.
Central Counseling Service
New York, New York

Bernard J. Somers, Ph.D.
California State University, Los Angeles
Los Angeles, California

Ross V. Speck, M.D.
Private Practice
Philadelphia, Pennsylvania

Kathleen Speeth, Ph.D.
The California Institute for
   Transpersonal Psychology
Menlo Park, California

David Stafford-Clark, M.D.
Consultant Emeritus Guys Hospital
London, England

Arthur Stein, Ph.D.
Private Practice
Brookville, New York

Albert Steinkirchner, M.D.
Private Practice
Venice, California

Richard M. Stephenson, Ph.D.
Douglass College
New Brunswick, New Jersey

John O. Stevens, M.A.
Box F
Moab, Utah

Lowell H. Storms, Ph.D.
Veterans Administration Hospital
San Diego, California

Peter Suedfeld, Ph.D.
University of British Columbia
Vancouver, British Columbia, Canada

Max Sugar, M.D.
Louisiana State University
   School of Medicine
New Orleans, Louisiana

Roberta Temes, Ph.D.
Grief Groups
Brooklyn, New York

Dorothy Tennov, Ph.D.
University of Bridgeport
Bridgeport, Connecticut

Frederick C. Thorne, M.D., Ph.D.
Private Practice
Brandon, Vermont

H. C. Tien, M.D.
Michigan Institute of Psychosynthesis
Lansing, Michigan

Donald W. Tiffany, Ph.D.
Psychological Growth Associates
Hays, Kansas

D. J. Tosi, Ph.D.
The Ohio State University
Columbus, Ohio

Jerry A. Treppa, Ph.D.
University of Illinois Medical Center
Chicago, Illinois

Elinor Ulman, ATR
George Washington University
Washington, D.C.

Gerard van den Aardweg, Ph.D.
Private Practice
Overveen, Holland

Edward Vogelsong, Ph.D.
Pennsylvania State University
University Park, Pennsylvania

Elaine Waldman, M.A.
City University of New York
New York, New York

Patricia Blevins Webster, M.S.N.
Durham County General Hospital
Durham, North Carolina

Sharon Wegscheider, M.A.
Johnson Institute
Minneapolis, Minnesota

Melvin L. Weiner, Ph.D.
Private Practice
Davis, California

Myron F. Weiner, M.D.
University of Texas Health Science Center
Dallas, Texas

Richard A. Wells, M.S.W.
University of Pittsburgh
Pittsburgh, Pennsylvania

Richard L. Wessler, Ph.D.
Pace University
Pleasantville, New York

Allen E. Wiesen, Ph.D.
Private Practice
Bellevue, Washington

Lee G. Wilkins, Ph.D.
Murray Hill Psychological Group, P.C.
New York, New York

Bradford Wilson, M.A.
Workshop Institute for Living-Learning
New York, New York

William P. Wilson, M.D.
Duke University Medical Center
Durham, North Carolina

Ronald M. Wintrob, M.D.
University of Connecticut Health Center
Farmington, Connecticut

William B. Woodson, Ph.D.
Center for the Healing Arts
New York, New York

Julie Wright, M.Ed.
The Radix Institute
Santa Monica, California

Lewis Yablonsky, Ph.D.
California State University
Northridge, California

Elaine Yudkovitz, Ph.D.
Henry Ittleson Center for Child Research
Riverdale, New York

Manuel D. Zane, M.D.
White Plains Hospital Medical Center
White Plains, New York

Zaraleya, Ed.D.
Rockland Children's Psychiatric Center
Orangeburg, New York

Joan Ellen Zweben, Ph.D.
Pacific Institute for Clinical Training,
   Education and Consultation
Berkeley, California

# Cross Reference Index

Many otherwise identical or very similar therapies have varying names. This index is provided to facilitate reference to a therapy which appears in *The Psychotherapy Handbook*.

Abhidhamma (see: Buddhish Insight Meditation)
Activities Therapy (see: Occupational Therapy)
Anaclitic Therapy (see: Restricted Environmental Stimulation Therapy)
Anti-Complaining Therapy (see: Exaggeration Therapy)
Arica (see: Holistic Counseling)
Assertiveness Training (see: Assertive Behavior Therapy)
Authoritarian Psychotherapy (see: Frommian Influence)
Aversive Conditioning (see: Aversion Therapy)
Behavior Therapy (see: Behavior Modification)
Character Analysis (see: Medical Orgonomy)
Chemopsychotherapy (see: Pharmacotherapy)
Clarification Counseling (see: Holistic Counseling)
Consciousness Raising (see: Feminist Therapy)
Cosmetic Surgery (see: Aesthetic Plastic Surgery)
Direct-Decision Therapy (see: Decision Therapy)
Ecological Therapy (see: Social System Psychotherapy)
ECT (see: Electroconvulsive Therapy)
Electrosleep Therapy (see: Neurotone Therapy)
Empathy-Based Therapy (see: Client-Centered Therapy)
Environmental Therapy (see: Psychoanalytically Oriented Milieu Therapy)
Eurythony (see: Bioplasmic Therapy)
Existential Analysis (see: Logotherapy)
Family Networks (see: Social Network Intervention)
Freudian Psychoanalysis (see: Psychoanalysis)
General Systems Theory (see: Social System Psychotherapy)
Homework (see: Instigation Therapy)
Id-Level Therapy (see: Psychoanalysis)
I.G. Process (see: Integrity Groups)
Individual Psychology (see: Adlerian Psychotherapy)
Insight Meditation (see: Buddhist Insight Meditation)
Integrity Therapy (see: Integrity Groups)
Intensive Experiential Interactive Therapy (see: Depth Therapy)
Interpersonal Psychotherapy (see: Sullivanism)
Life Coping Skills (see: Life Skills Counseling)
LSD Therapy (see: Psychedelic Therapy)
Movement Therapy (see: Dance Therapy)
Narcosynthesis (see: Narcoanalysis)
Network Intervention (see: Social Network Intervention)

www.ingramcontent.com/pod-product-compliance
Lightning Source LLC
Chambersburg PA
CBHW072037020426
42334CB00017B/1303